MMPI-A: Assessing Adolescent Psychopathology

Third Edition

MMPI-A: *Assessing Adolescent Psychopathology*

Third Edition

Robert P. Archer
Eastern Virginia Medical School

LAWRENCE ERLBAUM ASSOCIATES, PUBLISHERS
2005   Mahwah, New Jersey   London

Senior Consulting Editor:	Susan Milmoe
Editorial Assistant:	Victoria Forsythe
Cover Design:	Kathryn Houghtaling Lacey
Textbook Production Manager:	Paul Smolenski
Full-Service Compositor:	TechBooks
Text and Cover Printer:	Hamilton Printing Company

This book was typeset in 10/12 pt. Palatino, Italic, Bold, and Bold Italic. The heads were typeset in Palatino and Berling, Bold, Italics, and Bold Italics.

Lawrence Erlbaum Associates, Inc., Publishers
10 Industrial Avenue
Mahwah, New Jersey 07430
www.erlbaum.com

Library of Congress Cataloging-in-Publication Data

Archer, Robert P.
   MMPI-A : assessing adolescent psychopathology / Robert P. Archer.—3rd ed.
      p. cm.
    Includes bibliographical references (p.) and indexes.
    ISBN 0-8058-5187-9 (hardcover : alk. paper)
    1. Minnesota Multiphasic Personality Inventory for Adolescents.
   2. Adolescent psychopathology—Diagnosis. I. Title.

   RJ503.7.M56A73   2005
   616.89′00835—dc22   2005002244

Books published by Lawrence Erlbaum Associates are printed on acid-free paper, and their bindings are chosen for strength and durability.

Printed in the United States of America
10 9 8 7 6 5 4 3 2

To my good friends and colleagues,
Denise Holloway and David Elkins,
my gratitude for your efforts that have made possible this third edition.

To all of us there come days when the earth is stale, flat and tedious. . . . At that extremity of misanthropy some men start a revolution and others take to drink; but for my part I go to sea. Every man to his own recreation.

—Raymond B. Cattell
Under Sail Through Red Devon

Contents

Foreword

Yossef S. Ben-Porath
Kent State University

In the preface to this edition of his MMPI-A interpretive guide, Robert Archer observes that the empirical literature available to guide the test's interpretation has expanded considerably since the second edition's publication in 1997. As the individual who has played the leading role in generating this research and who has been recognized as *the* authority on adolescent applications of the MMPI since the publication of his first book on the topic in 1987, Dr. Archer is uniquely qualified to provide this updated text on the MMPI-A.

This edition retains all of the strengths of its predecessors. In the first chapter, use of the MMPI-A is placed in the broader context of current understanding of adolescent development in general and psychopathology in particular. This chapter provides vital background for interpreting the MMPI-A in adolescent assessment, and I would admonish readers not to give in to the temptation to skip it and head straight for the book's "interpretive meat." The second chapter, on the development of the MMPI and MMPI-A, similarly provides important background information that should not be overlooked.

The adolescent MMPI literature, although substantially expanded, remains manageable enough in size to allow Dr. Archer to follow in the tradition of Dahlstrom and Welsh's original *MMPI Handbook* by combining in one volume a scholarly review of the test's empirical literature and a practical guide to its interpretation. The book's users, especially students gaining their first introduction to the test, would do well to first read the entire text of each chapter before using the "Interpretation Guidelines" tables for the scales in routine MMPI-A interpretation. These tables provide a scale-by-scale user-friendly summary of Dr. Archer's review of the extensive empirical literature, supplemented by his broad clinical experience with the test. They remain the heart of this text, and many users will refer to them routinely in day-to-day practice.

Since the 1997 edition, several new scales and a critical item set have been introduced for the MMPI-A, and this edition provides much-needed guidance on their incorporation into MMPI-A interpretation. The most important innovation of this edition is the inclusion of a new, comprehensive chapter on forensic applications of the MMPI-A. This chapter will be of greatest interest to the increasing number of psychologists who use the test in forensic evaluations; however, it should be studied by all of the test's users. As the mental health field becomes increasingly litigious and psychologists play an expanding role in the forensic evaluation of adults and adolescents, anyone using the MMPI-A, even primarily for clinical assessments, would be well advised to become familiar with the background for and literature on forensic applications of the test. Chapter 7 provides this much-needed information.

The appendixes also continue in the tradition of the *MMPI Handbook* by providing a complete set of tables needed for scoring the MMPI-A. They incorporate in one volume scoring keys and (where appropriate) T-score lookup tables for all currently used and researched MMPI-A scales, including many that are not available in the test's manual, published in 1992. The eight appendixes therefore constitute the most current, comprehensive resource available for scoring the MMPI-A.

It's fair to say that this, the third edition of *MMPI-A: Assessing Adolescent Psychopathology*, is the most up-to-date, and authoritative MMPI-A interpretive guide. The text places at users' fingertips all the information needed to administer, score, and interpret the MMPI-A based on current knowledge about the test and experience with its use. Students of the MMPI-A will find in it a rich, integrative review of the instrument's history and empirical literature. Users of the test will find an unparalleled comprehensive yet highly practical guide for MMPI-A interpretation.

Preface to the Third Edition

The first edition of *MMPI-A: Assessing Adolescent Psychopathology* was published in August 1992 to coincide with the original release of the MMPI-A manual testing materials. The second edition was published in 1997 and incorporated nearly 100 new references, but most of these citations were related to MMPI-2 studies, and relatively limited work had been done on the MMPI-A to that point. This third edition, published nearly 12 years after the release of the MMPI-A, reflects the extensive body of literature that has now developed on the MMPI-A. It incorporates 165 new references, most of these based directly on research investigations with the MMPI-A. It also discusses new features of the MMPI-A that have been developed since the second edition, including the MMPI-A Psychopathology-Five (PSY-5) scales, the MMPI-A Content Component scales, and the critical item set developed by Forbey and Ben-Porath. In addition, this edition contains a new chapter that covers forensic applications of the MMPI-A in recognition of the rapid and dramatic expansion of the field of forensic psychology in the last few years.

In summary, the purpose of the current revision is to update the information provided and take into account the rapid expansion of the MMPI-A literature. Its basic structure, however, is essentially the same as that of its predecessors. For example, it continues to include a chapter on the critical issue of adolescent development and psychopathology as well as a comprehensive review of the development, administration, and scoring procedures of the MMPI-A. Likewise, separate chapters are devoted to the interpretation of validity scales, clinical scales, and content and supplementary scales, and a final chapter addresses the challenging task of integrating MMPI-A data into an overall interpretive report. As previously noted, an additional chapter gives an overview of the application of the MMPI-A in providing information to judges and juries involved in determining civil and criminal issues. It is my hope that this revised text keeps the best features of the earlier editions while expanding coverage to include the newest literature on this test instrument. My intention was to produce a text that provides useful and practical information to the clinician in utilizing the MMPI-A in clinical assessments while also providing sufficiently detailed information to stimulate future research efforts with this instrument.

In addition to the individuals mentioned in the prefaces to my original and second editions, I would also like to give recognition to several individuals who played an invaluable role in the creation of this third edition. David Elkins, Research Associate at the Eastern Virginia Medical School, has been a central resource and colleague in the development of this text and in all of our research efforts since 1992. Additionally, I wish to express my sincerest appreciation to Denise Holloway, who has handled the demands of the second and third edition of this text with much grace and competence while also recently completing her 10-year tenure as the Editorial Assistant for the journal *Assessment*. I would also like to express my thanks to Beverly Kaemmer of the University of Minnesota Press for all of her help and assistance in providing me with the materials necessary for this revision. It has been my privilege to work with a number of outstanding psychologists in pursuing my interest in the MMPI-A. Dr. Rebecca V. Stredny, EVMS post-doctoral fellow in forensic psychology, has been very kind in helping review and prepare the materials for this text. Dr. Richard Handel is a colleague and member of our faculty at the Eastern Virginia Medical School, and his energy, creativity, and enthusiasm for the MMPI-2 and MMPI-A have contributed to a very enjoyable and productive collaborative process. Dr. Yossef Ben-Porath of Kent State University has facilitated and collaborated on many of our research studies, and his support is deeply appreciated. Drs. Roger Greene, David Nichols, and Irving Gottesman have been friends and colleagues for many years and have been invaluable in their willingness to share their time, resources, and data sets to explore many MMPI-A and MMPI-2 issues. Further, the funding support from the University of Minnesota Press and from the Norfolk Foundation has played a crucial role in providing the resources necessary to conduct systematic investigations of the MMPI-A. Finally, I would like to express my deepest gratitude for the longstanding patience of my wife, Dr. Linda R. Archer, and my daughter, Elizabeth M. Archer, and for their critical support on all of my MMPI, MMPI-2, and MMPI-A projects. While the MMPI-A may never "love me back," I am very grateful that this is most assuredly not true of my wife and daughter.

I conclude this preface with the observation that the MMPI and MMPI-A have served as a splendid focus for my research career. When I began investigations in the mid-1970s on the use of the MMPI with adolescents, my initial research question involved the effects of using various normative sets with adolescents (e.g., adolescent versus adult norms) and the implications of these choices on profile characteristics and interpretation. Now, nearly 30 years later, I continue to pursue issues that directly follow from those original questions; for example, how effective are the MMPI-A adolescent norms in distinguishing between adolescents in various clinical and nonclinical settings, and what factors contribute to the relatively low mean T-score values often found among adolescents in clinical settings? It has been a rare privilege to be engaged with a psychological assessment instrument that exhibits the complexity, popularity, and clinical utility of the MMPI-A. It is my hope that this third edition will reflect my passion for this instrument as well as provide the necessary information to stimulate other clinicians and researchers in the pursuit of similar careers.

MMPI-A: Assessing Adolescent Psychopathology

Third Edition

Adolescent Development and Psychopathology

Much of the confusion and controversy traditionally surrounding the use of the MMPI with adolescent respondents has resulted from the application of this instrument without an adequate understanding of the unique characteristics of adolescent development. Unfortunately, many clinicians and researchers have attempted to interpret adolescents' MMPI profiles using procedures that have been established for the assessment of adults. There are areas of interpretation in which the approach developed for adults will work effectively in the understanding of adolescents' responses. There are also numerous areas, however, in which the use of practices or procedures derived for adults will result in substantial interpretive errors when applied to adolescents. Although development of the Minnesota Multiphasic Personality Inventory–Adolescent (MMPI-A) has substantially assisted in deriving interpretive comments of direct relevance to adolescents, using this specialized form of the MMPI does not substitute for an awareness of salient developmental issues. Thus, the purpose of this chapter is to provide a brief overview of adolescent development and psychopathology, with particular attention focused on ways in which developmentally related issues may affect MMPI/MMPI-A interpretation practices.

DEVELOPMENTAL TASKS DURING ADOLESCENCE

Achenbach (1978) suggested that an understanding of psychopathology in children and adolescents must be firmly grounded in the study of normal development. Human development is a continuous process, but there may be critical periods in our development during which adaptational success or failure heavily influences the course of later development in the life cycle. Adolescence clearly is one of these critical developmental transitions. Holmbeck and Updegrove (1995) observed that adolescence is "characterized by more biological, psychological, and social role changes than other life stages except infancy" (p. 16). As noted by Petersen and Hamburg (1986), the number and extent of changes that occur simultaneously during adolescence present major challenges to the development of mature and effective coping strategies. Ineffective coping strategies may contribute to a variety of problem behaviors during adolescent development. Further, failures in adolescent development may result in the manifestation of psychopathology during later life stages.

Three major areas of changes and challenges that face the individual during adolescence are here reviewed: physiological processes, cognitive processes, and psychological and emotional challenges.

Physiological/Sexual Maturation

Kimmel and Weiner (1985) defined puberty as "the process of becoming physically and sexually mature and developing the adult characteristics of one's sex" (p. 592). Petersen (1985) noted several characteristics of puberty that are important in understanding adolescent development. Puberty is a universal experience that may, however, be delayed, or in some cases even prevented, by the occurrence of physical disease or traumatic psychological events. Paikoff and Brooks-Gunn (1991) noted that the timing of puberty has been shown to vary as a function of the adolescent's health status, nutrition, ethnicity, genetic inheritance, exercise level, and stress experiences. They observed that the parent-child relationship is typically affected by pubertal development, with decreases in time spent with parents and submissiveness to parental decisions typically found during early adolescence. Further, Petersen stressed that puberty is a process rather than an isolated temporal event. This process involves physical changes that result in a sexually immature child achieving full reproductive potential. These changes are typically manifested in the growth of underarm and pubic hair, maturation of genitalia, and the first menstruation in girls. Often, the clearest signs of adolescent development are physical changes associated with the onset of puberty.

Fundamental physical changes, including changes in endocrinological, biochemical, and physiological processes, occur during adolescence. For example, Stone and Church (1957) noted that an individual is expected to increase 25% in height and 100% in weight during this developmental stage. Additionally, there is a marked increase in pituitary activity leading to increased production of hormones by the thyroid, adrenal, and other glands centrally involved in sexual maturation.

There are notable differences in the rate of physical maturation between boys and girls, and there are also very wide individual variations in sexual maturation within genders. Figures 1.1 and 1.2 show varying degrees of sexual maturation for $14\frac{3}{4}$-year-old boys and $12\frac{3}{4}$-year-old girls and the velocity of growth in height by year of life. The data in Fig. 1.1 for pubertal development illustrates both the earlier maturation of females in relation to males and the wide differences in pubertal development within genders at identical chronological ages. To the extent that pubertal development is precocious or significantly delayed, stress may occur that can be reflected in lower self-esteem or self-concept for the adolescent during this period. A recent monograph by the American Psychological Association (APA, 2002) provided data indicating that currently pubertal development among American adolescents is occurring substantially earlier than the guideposts originally provided by Tanner in the late 1960s for his British sample of adolescents. For example, the average age of menarche for girls in the United States is now around 12.5, and for boys the onset of puberty (as marked by the enlargement of the testes) occurs at around age 11.5, with the first ejaculation typically occurring between the ages of 12 and 14. A recent survey of 17,000 healthy girls between the ages of 3 and 12 who were participating in office visits with their pediatricians found that 6.7% of white girls and 27.2% of African American girls showed some signs of puberty as early as age 7, including pubic hair or breast development (Herman-Gliddens et al., 1997; Kaplowitz & Oberfield, 1999). A recent description of the adolescent growth spurt by Hofmann and Greydanus (1997) is generally consistent with the earlier data by Tanner in indicating that the rapid skeletal development that

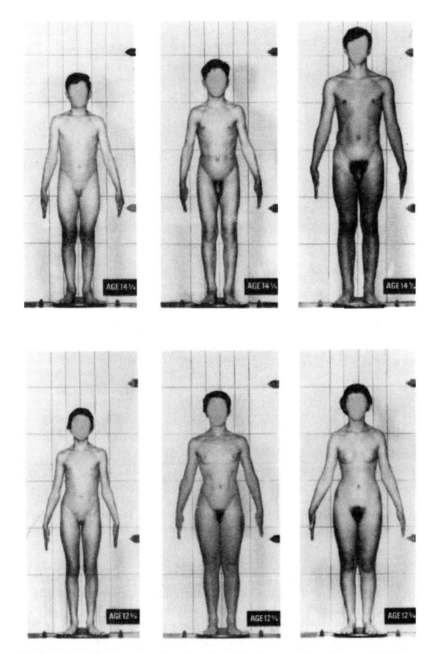

FIG. 1.1. Variations in male and female pubertal development. (From Tanner, 1969. Copyright © by W. B. Saunders Company. Reprinted by permission.)

marks the growth spurt usually begins at around ages 10 to 12 in girls and around ages 12 to 14 in boys. The most dramatic rate of physical growth tends to occur between the ages of 12 and 15, with the peak of the growth curve occurring approximately 2 years earlier for females than for males (Fig. 1.2).

An illustration of the influence of developmental forces on MMPI responses is provided by the abbreviated item "worried about sex." This item serves as a member of scales 3, 5, and 8. The *Minnesota Multiphasic Personality Inventory–2 (MMPI-2) Manual*

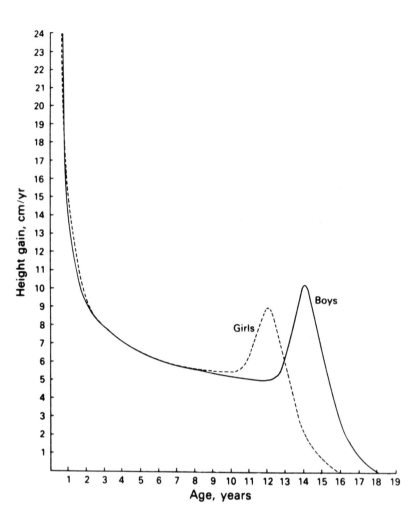

FIG. 1.2. Velocity of growth in height at various ages. (From Tanner, Whitehouse, and Takaishi, 1966. Copyright © by the Archives of Disease in Childhood. Reprinted by permission.)

(Butcher, Dahlstrom, Graham, Tellegen, & Kaemmer, 1989) indicates that this item is endorsed in the *true* direction by 13% of adult female respondents in the MMPI-2 normative sample and 15% of adult men. In contrast to adult samples, however, this item was endorsed as true by 37.2% of adolescent females and 30.2% of adolescent males in the MMPI-A normative sample (Butcher et al., 1992). The higher rate of endorsement of this item in the critical direction by the 14- to 18-year-old teenagers probably reflects the high level of stress for adolescents related to issues of sexual maturation as well as sexual identity.

Cognitive Maturation

Adolescence may also be defined in terms of changes that occur in cognitive processes. The work of Piaget and his colleagues offers an approach to understanding these cognitive changes, with the final stage of cognitive development in Piaget's (1975) paradigm unfolding during adolescence. Specifically, Piaget postulated that, during early adolescence, the individual typically makes the transition from the Concrete Operations stage to the Formal Operation stage, the latter characterized by the capacity to manipulate ideas and concepts. According to Piaget (1975), "The adolescent is an individual who is capable . . . of building and understanding ideas or abstract theories and concepts. The child does not build theories" (p. 105). Thus, the adolescent is able to discern the real from the ideal and to become passionately engaged by abstract concepts and notions. Adolescents begin to think of their world in new ways and to develop the ability to "think about thinking." Related to these changes in cognitive skills, Elkind (1978, 1980) argued that, as adolescents become capable of thinking about their thoughts, they may also become excessively concerned with how they are perceived by others. This preoccupation includes an exaggerated view of the uniqueness of their own experiences and the amount of time devoted by others to their appraisal. Elkind labeled the egocentric tendency of adolescents to believe that their behavior is intensely scrutinized by others as "the imaginary audience" (Elkind & Bowen, 1979).

Part of this self-absorption and belief in the uniqueness of one's own experiences may be reflected in the endorsement rate differences between adults and adolescents for the following abbreviated item, which is a member of scales *Pt* and *Sc*:

"Strange thoughts."
(Endorsed true by 15% of MMPI-2 adult males and 10% of adult females vs. 45% of boys in the MMPI-A normative sample and 46% of MMPI-A teenage girls.)

and to the following abbreviated item, a member of scales *Pd*, *Pa*, and *Sc*:

"Misunderstood."
(Endorsed true by 9% of adult men and 9% of adult women in the MMPI-2 normative sample vs. 25.6% of adolescent boys and 37.4% of adolescent girls in the MMPI-A normative sample.)

and to the following abbreviated item, a member of the *Mf* and *Si* scales:

"Unbothered by not being better looking."
(Endorsed true by 77% and 59% of the MMPI-2 male and female normative samples, respectively, vs. 49% of adolescent boys and 38% of adolescent girls in the MMPI-A normative sample.)

Psychological Development

Finally, a host of psychological and emotional tasks, including the processes of in-dividuation, the formation of ego identity, and ego maturation, are accomplished during adolescence. Blos (1967) discussed individuation as a process involved with the development of relative independence from family relationships, the weakening of infantile object ties, and an increased capacity to assume a functional role as a member of adult society. Blos defined and described this task as similar to the more primitive struggle for individuation in the attainment of object constancy that occurs toward the end of the third year of life. Thus, early adolescents have marked ambiva-lence concerning issues of independence versus dependence, particularly in terms of their relationships to their parents. This ambivalence is likely to be seen in rapid and marked attitudinal and behavioral changes (e.g., one moment protesting any parental involvement or supervision and the next moment regressing to marked dependency on mother or father).

Erikson (1956) described ego identity formation during adolescence as the assembly of converging identity elements that occur at the end of childhood—an assembly achieved through a process of *normative crises*. Ego identity was viewed by Erikson as including the conscious sense of individual identity as well as an unconscious striving for a continuity of personal character. In the process of ego formation, the ego integrates previous childhood identifications into a new totality, which lays the foundation of the adult personality. Positive resolution of this issue leads to a sense of *ego identity*, or continuity in one's self-definition. Negative resolution could result in *ego diffusion*, or uncertainty about who one is and what one will become in the future. The failure to achieve ego identity is related to the diagnostic category of identity problem (313.82) as described in the American Psychiatric Association's (1994) *Diagnostic and Statistical Manual of Mental Disorders (DSM–IV)*. Marcia (1966) further defined Erikson's concept of ego identity in terms of two variables: commitment (whether or not the individual has accepted a set of values) and crisis (whether or not the individual has experienced an inner struggle in arriving at personal acceptance of a set of values). These two variables combine to yield four identity statuses in Marcia's model: *diffusion* (no commitment, no crisis), *foreclosure* (commitment without crisis), *moratorium* (crisis without commitment), and *achievement* (commitment after crisis). Marcia argued that these categories, in the order given, represent developmental levels of increasingly advanced maturation.

The process of individuation is most clearly noted during early phases of adolescence, whereas the process of identity formation and consolidation is typically manifested during later stages of adolescence. As a result of these processes, adolescents will typically modify the way in which they interact with and relate to others. Specifically, adolescents begin to increase their involvement with peers and to decrease their immediate identification with family members. Further, the early stages of individuation may result in an increase in conflict with parents, as the adolescents attempt preliminary definitions of the self based on identifying the ways in which their feelings, thoughts, and attitudes may differ from those of their parents.

Loevinger (1976) articulated a concept of ego development in reference to the frameworks of meaning that individuals impose on their life experiences. In Loevinger's model, the concept of ego development is a dimension of individual differences as well as a developmental sequence of increasingly complex functioning in terms of impulse control, character development, interpersonal relationships, and cognitive complexity. At the three lowest levels of ego development, collectively grouped into the *preconformist* stage, the individual may be described as impulsive, motivated by personal gain and the avoidance of punishment, and oriented to the present rather than the past or future. Cognitive styles are stereotyped and concrete, and interpersonal relationships are opportunistic, exploitive, and demanding. During the second broad stage of development, referred to as the *conformist* stage, the individual begins to identify his or her welfare with that of the social group. The individual places emphasis on conformity with socially approved norms and standards and on issues of social acceptability in terms of attitudes and behaviors. As the individual enters the *postconformist* stages of development, self-awareness, cognitive complexity, and interpersonal style become increasingly complex, and a balance is achieved between autonomy and interdependence. The maturational stages described by Loevinger do not refer to specific age groups, but she noted that the higher stages of ego development would rarely be achieved by adolescents. Loevinger's view of development is very comprehensive and served as a basis for the development of the MMPI-A Immaturity (*IMM*) scale, which is described in chapter 6.

The following five MMPI abbreviated items illustrate substantial differences in endorsement frequency between adults in the MMPI-2 normative sample and adolescents in the MMPI-A normative sample:

"Rarely quarrel with family."

(Endorsed true by 78% of adult women and 79% of adult men vs. 38% of adolescent girls and 46% of adolescent males.)

"Habits of some family members very irritating."

(Endorsed true by 66% of adult women and 48% of adult men vs. 79% of adolescent girls and 67% of adolescent boys.)

"Most of family sympathetic."

(Endorsed true by 53% of adult women and 56% of adult men vs. 31% of adolescent girls and 37% of adolescent boys.)

"Occasionally hate family members I love."

(Endorsed true by 44% of adult women and 32% of adult men vs. 72% of adolescent girls and 59% of adolescent boys.)

"Judged unfairly by family."

(Endorsed true by 14% of adult women and 11% of adult men vs. 43% of adolescent females and 40% of adolescent males.)

These differences in item endorsement patterns between adults and adolescents may be meaningfully viewed in reference to the adolescents' struggles with individuation from the family and the tasks of identity formation and ego maturation. Tables 1.1 and 1.2 provide information on abbreviated items that show at least a 20% endorsement rate difference between adolescents and adults, separated by gender, as noted in the normative data for the MMPI-2 and MMPI-A.

TABLE 1.1

Items Showing the Largest Differences for Males in Percentage Endorsement as True Between the Adult (MMPI-2) Normative Sample and the Adolescent (MMPI-A) Normative Sample

| *MMPI-A* | | % *Endorsement as True* | |
Item No.	*Item Content*	*MMPI-2*	*MMPI-A*
3	Feel rested in morning.	68.0	34.5
79	Rarely quarrel with family.	79.0	46.2
82	Like loud parties.	45.0	75.3
128	Like to pick fights.	16.0	47.7
137	Been unjustly punished.	9.0	42.4
162	When bored, stir things up.	43.0	73.0
208	Often dream about things that shouldn't be talked about.	28.0	62.9
296	Strange thoughts.	15.0	45.3
307	Obsessed by terrible words.	9.0	39.4
371	Too unsure of future to make plans.	12.0	42.1

Note. MMPI-A abbreviated items reproduced by permission. MMPI-A test booklet copyright © 1992 by the Regents of the University of Minnesota; MMPI-A abbreviated item test booklet copyright © 2004 by the Regents of the University of Minnesota.

TABLE 1.2

Items Showing the Largest Differences for Females in Percentage Endorsement as True Between the Adult (MMPI-2) Normative Sample and the Adolescent (MMPI-A) Normative Sample

MMPI-A Item No.	Item Content	% Endorsement as True	
		MMPI-2	MMPI-A
3	Feel rested in morning.	66.0	29.3
21	Uncontrolled laughing and crying.	18.0	63.8
79	Rarely quarrel with family.	78.0	37.5
81	Want to do shocking things.	16.0	52.6
82	Like loud parties.	39.0	80.1
114	Like collecting plants.	79.0	43.2
123	Actions dictated by others.	26.0	62.3
162	When bored, stir things up.	43.0	80.1
205	Often very restless.	24.0	62.3
208	Often dream about things that shouldn't be talked about.	27.0	65.3
235	Often strangers look at me critically.	25.0	64.9
296	Strange thoughts.	10.0	46.1

Note. MMPI-A abbreviated items reproduced by permission. MMPI-A test booklet copyright © 1992 by the Regents of the University of Minnesota; MMPI-A abbreviated item test booklet copyright © 2004 by the Regents of the University of Minnesota.

The Effects of Maturation on MMPI Response Patterns

The preceding paragraphs discussed the implications of maturation for item-level response patterns. Maturational effects can also be demonstrated on the scale level, particularly in relation to scales F, Pd, Sc, and Ma. These latter scales have traditionally shown substantial differences in mean values obtained from adolescent and adult samples (Archer, 1984, 1987b). For example, Fig. 1.3 presents the mean raw score values for adolescent and adult males and females on the MMPI-2 60-item F scale, with findings presented separately by chronological age. As shown in this figure, mean raw score values on F continue to decrease as the chronological age of the groups increases. It is most reasonable to interpret these differences as a reflection of maturational processes rather than levels of psychopathology. Thus, MMPI scales are subject to maturational effects that may serve to obscure or confound the interpretation of psychopathology based on test scores. In this regard, Achenbach (1978) commented as follows:

> An often overlooked complication of the search for individual differences in children is that developmental differences account for significant variance in almost every measurable behavior. One consequence is that measurements repeated on the same subjects more than a few weeks apart are likely to differ as a function of development, even if the subjects show stability with respect to their rank ordering within their cohort. A second consequence is that unless all subjects in a sample are at the same developmental level with respect to the behavior in question, individual differences in the behavior may in fact reflect differences in developmental level rather than traitlike characteristics. A third consequence is that covariation among several measures may merely reflect the variance that they all share with development rather than an independent trait. (p. 765)

This phenomenon is certainly not limited to adolescent populations, and Colligan, Osborne, Swenson, and Offord (1983) and Colligan and Offord (1992) showed substantial age and maturational effects on standard MMPI scales studied across a broad range of age groups. Figures 1.4 and 1.5, for example, present cross-sectional changes

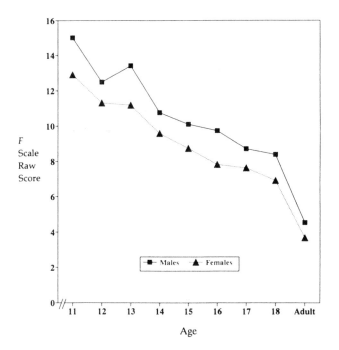

FIG. 1.3. Mean *F* scale raw score values for male and female adolescents and adults.

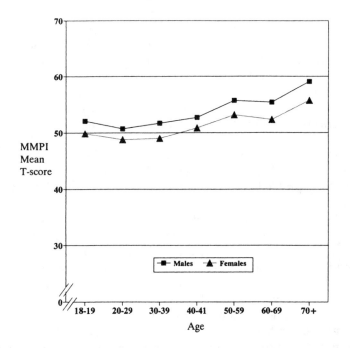

FIG. 1.4. Cross-sectional changes in mean T-score values for scale 1 by age group and gender. (From Colligan et al., 1983. Copyright © by the Mayo Foundation. Reprinted by permission.)

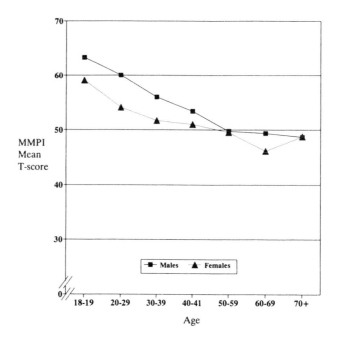

FIG. 1.5. Cross-sectional changes in mean T-score values for scale 9 by age group and gender. (From Colligan et al., 1983. Copyright © by the Mayo Foundation. Reprinted by permission.)

in mean values on the *Hs* scale and on the *Ma* scale, respectively, for males and females across age categories ranging from 18/19 to 70+. Similarly, Pancoast and Archer (1992) reported substantial differences in mean MMPI profiles for large samples of adolescents, college students, and adults when the mean values of all three groups are plotted on the standard reference point of adult norms, as shown in Fig. 1.6.

Thus far, maturational influences have been discussed in relation to chronological age, but, as will be seen later in the description of the development of the Immaturity scale for the MMPI-A, maturational effects can be clearly demonstrated on MMPI response patterns when chronological age is held constant and maturity is measured more directly.

Another method of examining maturational influences on MMPI scale-level data—a method that involves looking at patterns of adolescent responses on the Harris-Lingoes subscales profiled on standard adult norms—was used in research by Pancoast and Archer (1988). Harris and Lingoes (1955) rationally divided six of the MMPI clinical scales (2, 3, 4, 6, 8, and 9) into subscales based on items that appeared logically similar in content. As discussed later, the Harris-Lingoes subscales are frequently used in clinical practice to determine which content areas of a standard clinical scale were critically endorsed in producing an overall *T*-score elevation on the parent or standard scale. Adult norms for these subscales have been developed, and adolescent norms are available for the Harris-Lingoes subscales of the MMPI and the MMPI-A. In the Pancoast and Archer study, adolescent values were examined on adult norms in order to evaluate the ways in which adolescent response patterns might differ from those typically found for normal adults. These mean data are based on the adolescent normative data collected by Colligan and Offord (1989) at the Mayo Foundation and data from a smaller sample of adolescents collected in Virginia in

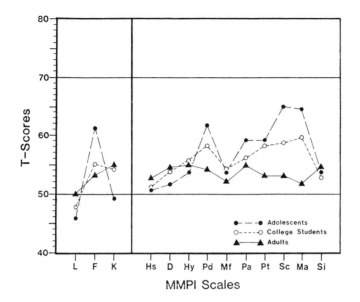

FIG. 1.6. Mean MMPI T-score values for adolescents, college students, and adults as shown on adult non-K-corrected norms. (From Pancoast & Archer, 1992. Copyright © by John Wiley & Sons, Inc. Reprinted by permission.)

1987. Figure 1.7 presents findings for the Harris-Lingoes MMPI subscales on adult norms for MMPI scales D, Hy, and Pd. Results show that subscales related to the Pd scale exhibit a general trend toward more extreme elevations than subscales related to scales D or Hy. Although most of the subscales for Pd are elevated, the highest elevation occurs for Pd_1 (Familial Discord), which deals with a struggle against familial controls and the perception of marked family conflict. In contrast, there is no elevation for Pd_3 (Social Imperturbability), which deals with denial of social anxiety and

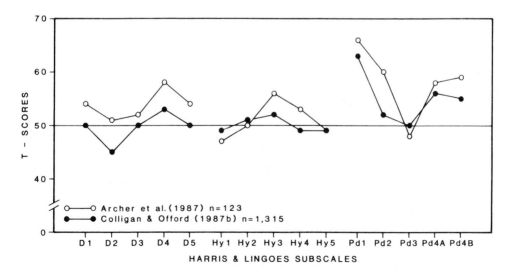

FIG. 1.7. Harris-Lingoes subscale T-score values for adolescents based on adult norms: Subscales for D, Hy, and Pd. (From Pancoast & Archer, 1988. Copyright © by Lawrence Erlbaum Associates. Reprinted by permission.)

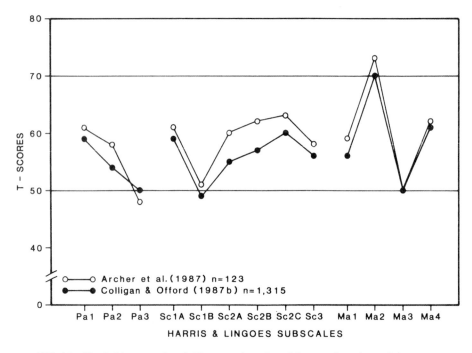

FIG. 1.8. Harris-Lingoes subscale T-score values for adolescents based on adult norms: Subscales for *Pa*, *Sc*, and *Ma*. (From Pancoast & Archer, 1988. Copyright © by Lawrence Erlbaum Associates. Reprinted by permission.)

the experience of discomfort in social situations. Thus, although normal adolescents' experiences typically involve substantial degrees of family conflict, such conflict appears to be restricted primarily to familial issues and does not include a generalized social discomfort (Pd_3), nor does it necessarily include general conflicts with authority as measured by Pd_2 (Authority Conflicts).

Figure 1.8 presents Harris-Lingoes findings for the remaining three MMPI scales (*Pa*, *Sc*, and *Ma*). Findings from these scales also reveal an interpretable subscale pattern. For *Pa*, the highest subscale is Pa_1 (Persecutory Ideas), which primarily deals with the externalization of responsibility for one's problems and the perception of being treated unfairly and punished by others. On the *Sc* scale, the highest subscale is Sc_2 (Lack of Ego Mastery, Defective Inhibition), which deals with feelings of restlessness, hyperactivity, and not being in control of one's impulses. On the *Ma* scale, the elevated Ma_2 (Psychomotor Acceleration) subscale relates to restlessness, excitement, and pressure for action. Overall, the Harris-Lingoes subscale pattern suggests that the normal adolescent, as evaluated by adult norms or standards, is typically preoccupied with the familial struggle for independence and is focused on the perception of family conflicts and that there is a driven, restless, and excited quality to this developmental experience that often involves a sense of being confined or misunderstood.

In summary, the use of the MMPI-A with adolescents requires a developmental perspective to understand and interpret test findings. This chapter briefly discussed the dramatic physiological/sexual maturational changes, the changes in cognitive processes, and some of the psychological challenges that occur during adolescence. These changes and challenges contribute to the observed differences between adults and adolescents in MMPI response patterns on the item, scale, and profile level. Recognition of the influence of such maturational and developmental factors played a major role in the decision to create a specialized form of the MMPI for the assessment of adolescents, the MMPI-A. One of the main goals of this book is to accurately discriminate and describe those administration, scoring, and interpretive situations that require a unique approach when performed in relation to adolescent clients.

ADOLESCENCE AND PSYCHOPATHOLOGY

Methodological Issues

In addition to an awareness of adolescent developmental issues, it is important for the MMPI-A user to develop an understanding of the nature and extent of psychopathology typically encountered during adolescence. Attempts to estimate the prevalence of psychiatric disturbance among adolescents, however, are directly affected by several methodological issues. These include the definition and measures employed to identify psychiatric disorders among adolescents as well as the methods and informants (parents, teachers, direct psychiatric interviews) on which such estimates are based. Weissman et al. (1987), for example, evaluated the results from independent interviews of 220 subjects between the ages of 6 and 23. The diagnostic data for this study were gathered by child interviews using the Schedule for Affective Disorders and Schizophrenia for School-Age Children and were also derived using *DSM–III–* related interviews with parents and other informants. The authors noted that considerable discrepancies were found between parents' and children's reports on the nature and degree of the children's psychopathology. They found that children's self-reports or self-descriptions produced evidence of considerably more psychopathology than did the descriptions of the children provided by their parents. Similar findings have also been reported by Reich and Earls (1987) when parental interview results are compared with the results of structured interview techniques used directly with children and adolescents, such as the Diagnostic Interview for Children and Adolescents (DICA). Further, an investigation by Rosenberg and Joshi (1986) found a significant relationship between the degree of marital discord and discrepancies within parental reports of child behavior problems. These researchers reported that the greater the marital difficulty, the greater the difference in adults' ratings of child behavior difficulties on the Achenbach and Edelbrock (1983) Child Behavior Checklist (CBCL). Williams, Hearn, Hostetler, and Ben-Porath (1990) compared structured interview findings on the Diagnostic Interview Schedule for Children (DISC) with self-report measures of psychopathology that included the MMPI. In addition, subjects' parents completed the Achenbach and Edelbrock CBCL, and teachers completed the teacher form of the CBCL. Findings indicated substantial levels of disagreement between these measures in the identification of psychologically disturbed subjects. More recently, Cantwell, Lewinsohn, Rohde, and Seeley (1997) evaluated the degree of agreement between parent and adolescent reports of major psychiatric disorders in adolescents from ages 14 through 18 inclusive. A total of 281 parent-adolescent pairs were interviewed separately regarding psychopathological symptoms using a version of the K-SADS structured interview. The kappa value for parent-adolescent agreement ranged widely by disorder, from .19 for alcohol abuse/dependence to .79 for conduct disorder, with an average kappa of .42 across all diagnostic categories. Parent-adolescent agreement was not found to be influenced by adolescent's gender, age, parental educational level, age of the onset of the disorder, or the severity of the disorder. Cantwell and his colleagues concluded, similar to earlier researchers, that adolescent self-reports tended to produce higher estimates of psychopathology than did parental reports, particularly for diagnoses that may be classified as internalizing disorders such as major depression or anxiety disorders. In contrast, externalizing disorders such as conduct disorders and oppositional defiant disorder produced relatively high rates of agreement, and it appeared viable to base estimates of these latter disorders on the concensual reports of adolescents and their parents. Thus, it is clear that our estimates of adolescent psychopathology relate not only to how diagnostic questions are asked but to whom such questions are addressed. Despite these methodological problems and limitations, it appears possible to offer some general conclusions concerning the overall prevalence of psychiatric disorders during adolescence as well as some meaningful observations concerning the form of these disorders.

Prevalence Findings

One of the most widely cited studies on the prevalence of child and adolescent psychiatric disorders is the "Isle of Wight" study reported by Rutter, Graham, Chadwick, and Yule (1976) and summarized by Graham and Rutter (1985). In the Isle of Wight study, a total population of over 2,000 British 14- and 15-year-olds were screened using questionnaires administered to parents and teachers to identify those adolescents with "deviant" adjustment patterns. Adolescents for whom deviant scores were produced on either questionnaire, along with a group of randomly selected control subjects, were then given individual psychiatric assessments involving direct interviews with parents, teachers, and the adolescents. Each assessment was conducted in a blind fashion in terms of interviewer's knowledge of the adolescent's membership in the deviant or control groups. The authors estimated that the 1-year period prevalence rate for psychiatric disorder in their sample was 21%. In general, psychiatric conditions appeared to occur with a slightly higher frequency during adolescence than during middle childhood (based on the available data for that age period). Certain psychiatric conditions, however, did show substantial increases during adolescence, including the occurrence of affective disorders and depressive conditions. Along with the increase in depression, there was also a dramatic increase in the frequency of attempted and completed suicide.

In the United States, Gould, Wunsch-Hitzig, and Dohrenwend (1981) reported that the median prevalence rate for clinical maladjustment among children and adolescents was 11.8%, based on a review of 25 prevalence studies conducted between 1928 and 1975. The majority of these studies employed teachers' reports as a means of identifying psychiatrically disturbed children. Brandenburg, Friedman, and Silver (1989) noted that more recent epidemiologic field studies of child and adolescent psychopathology have employed diverse methods of case definition and have more frequently used a multimethod, multistage approach to case identification. Based on a review of eight recent studies, these authors placed the prevalence estimate of psychiatric disorder in children and adolescents at 14% to 20%. More recently, Breton et al. (1999) used the DISC to evaluate 12- to 14-year-old adolescents and their parents in the Quebec Child Mental Health Survey (QCMHS). Similar to prior studies, these authors found that parents and adolescents had the highest rate of agreement for disruptive or externalizing disorders and the lowest rate of agreement for internalizing disorders. The overall 6-month prevalence rate of psychopathology reported for the 2,400 children and adolescents in this study was 15.8%. Romano, Tremblay, Vitaro, Zoccolillo, and Pagani (2001) examined psychological functioning in a community sample of 1,201 adolescents ages 14 through 17 inclusive. Each of the adolescents and their mothers were administered the DISC to obtain prevalence estimates of DSM–III–R disorders and the amount of perceived impairment associated with each of these disorders. Adolescent females were found to report the highest prevalence of psychiatric disorders (15.5%), in contrast to the prevalence rate of 8.5% reported by male adolescents. Compared to their male counterparts, female adolescents reported significantly higher rates of internalizing disorders, including anxiety and depressive disorders. In contrast, the 6-month prevalence of externalizing disorders among male adolescents was significantly higher. Roberts, Attkisson, and Rosenblatt (1998) reviewed 52 studies conducted between 1963 and 1996 that provided estimates of the overall prevalence of child and adolescent psychiatric disorders. They noted that, whereas the prevalence estimates for psychopathology among adolescents varied widely, the median prevalence estimate was 15%, with little evidence that the prevalence of psychopathology was significantly changing across time. Kazdin (2000) recently noted evidence of some gender differences in the rate and expression of psychopathology. For example, the prevalence of depression and eating disorders is much higher for females than males in the adolescent age grouping.

Beyond these prevalence studies of general psychopathology, several studies have attempted to identify the relative prevalence of specific types of psychiatric symptomatology or disorder within adolescent samples. Kashani et al. (1987) utilized both child and parent structured interviews to determine the prevalence of psychiatric disorder among 150 adolescents selected in a community sample. Roughly 41% were found to have at least one *DSM–III* diagnosis, and 19% were judged to have a diagnosis *and* to be functionally impaired to a degree indicating the need for psychiatric treatment. The three most common diagnoses found in this total sample were anxiety disorder (8.7%), conduct disorder (8.7%), and depression (8%; this category included major depression and dysthymic disorder).

Kashani and Orvaschel (1988) randomly selected 150 adolescents between the ages of 14 and 16 from a roster of 1,703 students in a Midwestern public school system. In this study of anxiety disorders during adolescence, both children and their parents were interviewed in their homes using the standard and parental interview forms of the DICA. Interview results were videotaped and scored by three trained raters with established interrater reliability. Additionally, participants received several objective personality assessment instruments related to self-concept, affect, and coping. Seventeen percent of this sample were found to meet the criteria for one or more forms of psychiatric disorder, and 8.7% were identified as positive cases of anxiety disorder. The most frequently occurring anxiety disorder in this sample was overanxious disorder. Results of this study tend to support the view that anxiety disorders are a major form of psychopathology in adolescent populations. In other research, Hillard, Slomowitz, and Levi (1987) studied 100 adult and 100 adolescent admissions to a university hospital psychiatric emergency service. The authors reported that adolescents were less likely to receive diagnoses of personality disorders or psychoses but were more likely to receive diagnoses involving conduct disorder and adjustment disorder. Further, self-destructive ideation or behavior was present in 40% of the adolescents seen in the emergency room visits.

Lewinsohn, Hops, Roberts, Seeley, and Andrews (1993) recently reported findings from the Oregon Adolescent Depression Project (OADP), a large-scale community-based investigation of the epidemiology of depression and other psychiatric disorders in a population of approximately 10,200 students in nine high schools in two urban communities in west central Oregon. The authors presented data on the prevalence of psychiatric disorders in the 14- to 18-year-old age range, which coincidentally corresponds to the age grouping employed in the MMPI-A normative sample. Additionally, an important characteristic of this study was that it relied exclusively on diagnostic information provided by adolescents in structured interviews and standardized questionnaires. Overall, this study indicated that 11.2% of girls and 7.8% of boys met the criteria for a current *DSM–III–R* psychiatric diagnosis based on interview findings. Among these psychiatric diagnoses, major depression, unipolar depression, anxiety disorders, and substance abuse disorders were particularly prevalent. In general, female students were more likely than male students to receive diagnoses of unipolar depression, anxiety disorders, eating disorders, and adjustment disorders, whereas boys were more likely to receive a diagnosis of disruptive behavior disorder. Lewinsohn, Klein, and Seeley (1995) followed up this research by evaluating the self-reports of 1,709 adolescents between the ages of 14 and 18 on the SADS to specifically focus on the prevalence and clinical characteristics of bipolar and manic disorder. The lifetime prevalence of bipolar disorder in this Oregon sample (primarily bipolar disorder and cyclothymia) was approximately 1%. Costello and colleagues (1996) found a 3-month prevalence rate for any *DSM–III–R* Axis I disorder of 20.3% in a sample of 9-, 11-, and 13-year-old boys and girls in the southeastern United States. The more common diagnoses were anxiety disorders (5.7%), enuresis (5.1%), tic disorders (4.2%), conduct disorders (3.3%), oppositional defiant disorders (2.7%), and hyperactivity (1.9%).

The issue of suicidal ideation and behavior has received special focus in recent studies of adolescence. Friedman, Asnis, Boeck, and DiFiore (1987), for example, investigated 300 high school students who were anonymously surveyed regarding their experiences with suicidal ideation and behaviors. Roughly 53% of this sample stated that they had thought about killing themselves but did not actually try, and 9% of the total sample stated that they had attempted suicide at least once. These findings indicated that suicidal ideation is relatively common among adolescents but also suggested that actual suicide attempts were disturbingly frequent. In this regard, Kimmel and Weiner (1985) noted that suicide is the third most common cause of death for adolescents aged 15 to 19, with the suicide rate particularly marked for White male adolescents. Further, the rate of adolescent suicide has nearly doubled from 1960 to 1975, and about 10% of adolescents seen in mental health clinics and more than 25% of those admitted to psychiatric units in general hospitals have threatened or attempted suicide (Kimmel & Weiner, 1985). Boys appear 4 times more likely than girls to actually kill themselves, whereas girls appear three times more likely to make a suicide attempt.

Within the MMPI-A normative sample, 21% of boys and 38% of girls responded true to abbreviated Item 177, "Think about killing self."

In 1996 the age-specific U.S. mortality rate for suicide was 1.6 per 100,000 for 10- to 14-year-olds, and 9.5 per 100,000 for adolescents in the 15- to 19-year-old age grouping. In this latter age grouping, boys were 4 times more likely than girls to commit suicide, while girls were twice as likely to attempt suicide (Center for Disease Control and Prevention [CDC], 1999). In addition, there have been some important demographic patterns recently emerging from national studies on mortality rates. For example, Hispanic high school students are more likely than students from other ethnic backgrounds to attempt suicide (CDC, 1999). The rate among White adolescent males appears to have reached a peak in the late 1980s (18 per 100,000 in 1996) and has since declined to approximately 16 per 100,000 in 1977 (CDC, 1999). In contrast, the suicide rate among Black male adolescents has increased substantially across the same period

(7.1 per 100,000 in 1966 versus 11.4 per 100,000 in 1997; CDC, 1999). Further, from 1979 through 1992, the Native American male adolescent and young adult suicide rate as reported by the Indian Health Service Areas was the highest in the United States, with a suicide rate of 62 per 100,000 (Wallace, Calhoun, Powell, O'Neil, & James, 1996).

Several general conclusions seem possible from these and other investigations of psychopathology during adolescence. First, the majority of adolescents do not show evidence of psychopathology that would result in psychiatric diagnosis. The rate of psychopathology during adolescence appears "only slightly higher than that found earlier in childhood or later in life" (Petersen & Hamburg, 1986, p. 491). There is evidence that the frequency and severity of depression does increase during adolescence, and there is a marked increase in both suicide attempts and suicide fatalities during this period of development. Several disorders tend to make their first appearance during adolescence, including anorexia nervosa, bipolar illness, bulimia, obsessive-compulsive disorder, schizophrenia, and substance abuse, although other disorders, such as enuresis and encopresis, become less frequent (Burke, Burke, Regier, & Rae, 1990; Graham & Rutter, 1985). Although the rate of anxiety disorders and conduct disorders may show little change during adolescence, the expression of symptoms related to these disorders does change. The rate of specific phobic disorders appears to decrease during adolescence, whereas conduct disorders more frequently involve violence (Graham & Rutter, 1985; Petersen & Hamburg, 1986).

The "Storm and Stress" Model and Psychopathology

G. Stanley Hall (1904), considered by many to be the father of child psychology in the United States, was the formulator of the *Sturm und Drang* (Storm and Stress) model of adolescent development. This model, consistent with the view of Anna Freud (1958), postulates that adolescence is typically accompanied by emotional upheavals and behavioral turbulence. Freud held that adolescents who did not demonstrate turbulent features of adjustment were at risk for the development of serious psychopathological symptoms in adulthood. Freud's formulation of this view is represented in her statement that "the upholding of a steady equilibrium during the process [of adolescence] is, in itself, abnormal" (p. 275). Freud's view of adolescent development may be best illustrated by the following quotation:

> I take it that it is normal for an adolescent to behave for a considerable length of time in an inconsistent and unpredictable manner; to fight his impulses and to accept them; to ward them off successfully and to be overrun by them; to love his parents and to hate them; to revolt against them and to be dependent on them; to be deeply ashamed to acknowledge his mother before others and, unexpectedly, to desire heart-to-heart talks with her; to thrive on imitation and identification with others while searching unceasingly for his own identity; to be more idealistic, artistic, generous, unselfish than he will ever be again, but also the opposite—self-centered, egoistic, calculating. Such fluctuations between extreme opposites would be deemed highly abnormal at any other time of life. At this time they may signify no more than that an adult structure of personality takes a long time to emerge, that the ego of the individual in question does not cease to experiment and is in no hurry to close down on possibilities. (p. 276)

Blos (1962) also felt that the psychiatric symptoms typically presented during adolescence were often ill-defined, unstable, and transitory in nature and did not signify stable markers of psychiatric illness. Similarly, Erikson (1956) proposed that the adolescent's struggles for self-definition frequently resulted in deviations from expected or normal behavior, which he termed *identity diffusion* or *identity confusion* and differentiated from stable psychopathology.

Many have objected to the Storm and Stress view of adolescent development, particularly the implication that normal adolescent development is characterized by substantial turbulence and lability. Bandura (1964), for example, argued that many adolescents establish more trusting and relaxed relations with their parents during adolescence while also increasing contact with peer groups. Thus, the shifting away from the nuclear family to the peer group is not necessarily and inevitably a source of family tension. Offer and Offer (1975) investigated suburban male adolescents and found that, although transient episodes of nondisabling depression and anxiety were common, only 20% of adolescents demonstrated moderate to severe symptomatology. This estimate, as we have seen, is generally consistent with reports of the prevalence of significant psychopathology in adolescent populations. Further, these investigators also found that 20% of their sample did not appear to experience any significant turmoil during their adolescent development and were able to successfully cope with the wide variety of challenges it presented.

Rutter et al. (1976) examined the concept of adolescent turmoil within the context of their findings in the Isle of Wight study of 14- and 15-year-olds. These authors concluded that parent-child alienation was not common among adolescents in general but rather appeared restricted to adolescents who already showed signs of psychiatric problems. On the other hand, "inner turmoil," which was defined by the researchers as feelings of misery and self-depreciation, appeared to be frequently associated with adolescence. The authors concluded that "adolescent turmoil is a fact, not a fiction, but its psychiatric importance has probably been overestimated in the past. Certainly it would be most unwise to assume that adolescents will grow out of their problems to a greater extent than do younger children" (p. 55).

In their review of the literature on adolescent psychopathology, Weiner and Del Gaudio (1976) offered the following three conclusions: First, psychiatric symptoms are not a normal feature of adolescence; second, boundaries between normal and abnormal adolescence may be drawn despite inherent difficulties; and third, rather than a passing phase, psychological disturbance during adolescence typically requires treatment for remission. This concept has also been expressed by Kimmel and Weiner (1985) in their statement that, "by and large, people remain basically the same in how they think, handle interpersonal relationships, and are perceived by others. For better or worse, adults tend to display many of the same personality characteristics and same relative level of adjustment they did as adolescents" (p. 449).

Viewed within the context of our data on the prevalence of psychiatric disorders during adolescence, the debate surrounding the stability of adolescent symptomatology appears to center on the distinction between psychopathology as defined by *DSM–IV* categories and terms such as *turbulence* and *Storm and Stress*. Prevalence estimates of psychopathology during adolescence appear to fall within a reasonably stable range of 12% to 22% (National Institute of Mental Health, 1990; Powers, Hauser, & Kilner, 1989). The adolescents identified in these studies do, in fact, appear to suffer from stable *DSM–IV*–related disorders that would not be expected to remit without active and effective treatment. For example, it is estimated that almost half of children or adolescents receiving conduct disorder diagnoses will become antisocial adults and that untreated depression and anxiety disorders during adolescence often persist into adulthood (National Institute of Mental Health, 1990). Further, a recent study by

Hofstra, Van der Ende, and Verhulst (2002) also demonstrated a continuity between child and adult psychopathology in a sample of 1,578 children and adolescents selected from the Dutch general population and followed up 14 years later. These authors found that childhood behavior and emotional problems were related to DSM–IV diagnoses in adulthood. The strongest associations between specific childhood problem areas and adult diagnoses were found for social problems in girls, which were generally predictive of the occurrence of DSM–IV disorders. Rule-breaking behavior in boys was also predictive of later mood disorder and/or disruptive disorders in adulthood. On the other hand, many more adolescents go through a period of turbulence and lability that would *not* qualify as a DSM–IV disorder but is commonly associated with accomplishing the mastery of the various adaptational challenges presented during adolescence. Although it is clear that the dividing line between these two groups is frequently blurred and difficult to discern, it serves little purpose to view these groups as homogeneous in terms of the severity of their symptoms or the implications for long-term adjustment. It might be expected that MMPI-A test results, based on contemporary adolescent norms for this instrument, should prove of substantial value to the clinician in rendering this important diagnostic distinction.

Stability of Adolescents' MMPI/MMPI-A Features

Whether adolescent symptomatology is stable or transitory, it appears relatively clear that those features and characteristics measured by the MMPI or MMPI-A in the assessment of adolescents serve to accurately describe the teenagers at the moment of testing. Adolescents' test scores often do not, however, provide the types of data necessary to make accurate long-term predictions concerning psychopathology or personality functioning. The MMPI/MMPI-A is best used as a means of deriving an overall estimate and current description of adolescent psychopathology rather than as a tool for making long-range predictions regarding future adjustment.

An illustration of the variability inherent in adolescent personality structure may be found in data reported by Hathaway and Monachesi (1963) in their classic study of adolescents' MMPI response patterns. These authors evaluated 15,300 Grade 9 children within Minnesota school systems between 1948 and 1954 and retested 3,856 students when they reached Grade 12 during the 1956–1957 school year. Examining adolescents who were tested in both the 9th and 12th grade, Hathaway and Monachesi found test-retest correlation coefficients ranging from the low to mid .30s on scales such as *Pd* and *Pa* to values in the high .50s and low .60s for scale *Si*. Hathaway and Monachesi concluded that these correlations underscored the degree of change that may occur within an adolescent's MMPI profile, reflecting the fluid nature of adolescents' overall personality organization. Hathaway and Monachesi noted, however, that the stability of an adolescent's profile tends to increase when *T*-score values are substantially elevated in the initial testing. Thus, clinically elevated profile characteristics may be subject to less change than marginally elevated profile features. Even in clinical or preclinical adolescent populations, however, substantial change often occurs in MMPI profile features. Similar to the study by Hathaway and Monachesi, Lowman, Galinsky, and Gray-Little (1980) reported that relatively pathological MMPI profiles of eighth graders in a rural county in North Carolina were generally not predictive of level of psychological disturbance or achievement for this sample at young adulthood.

Gottesman and Hanson (1990) reported pilot findings from a study that has continued to follow the Hathaway and Monachesi data set of adolescents administered

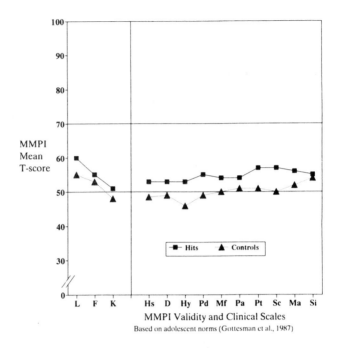

FIG. 1.9. MMPI mean profiles for boys who grew up to be schizophrenic ($N = 16$) and their normal matched controls. (From Gottesman & Hanson, 1990. Copyright © by I. I. Gottesman. Reprinted by permission.)

the MMPI in the late 1940s and early 1950s. These authors located individuals admitted to Minnesota psychiatric hospitals or correctional facilities more than 20 years following their initial ninth-grade MMPI assessment. The researchers identified 183 men and women admitted to these public institutions, of which 26 cases were identified as schizophrenics. Figure 1.9 shows the MMPI profiles of 16 boys who were evaluated in the ninth grade and later received a diagnosis of schizophrenia and a group of normal matched control subjects from the ninth-grade testing. Figure 1.10 shows similar findings for 10 girls who were evaluated in the ninth-grade sample and later manifested schizophrenia and their matched cohorts. These remarkable data illustrate the difficulties involved in attempting to make long-term predictions from MMPI profiles of adolescents. Differences did occur in these ninth-grade samples between groups of adolescents who did and did not develop schizophrenia. These differences, however, clearly would not permit specific diagnostic predictions. As noted by Hanson, Gottesman, and Heston (1990) in reference to these data, an effort to predict schizophrenia from ninth-grade test results would have been an exercise in futility.

Hathaway and Monachesi (1963) indicated that MMPI profiles produced by an adolescent often change across time because of the "transient organization of the personality" during adolescence. They noted that such psychometric changes, rather than indicating difficulties in test construction, indicate the sensitivity of instruments such as the MMPI to ongoing change during the maturational process. These phenomena do, however, limit the utility of tests such as the MMPI when such instruments are applied in a long-range predictive rather than descriptive manner.

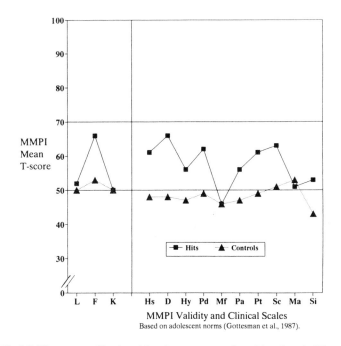

MMPI Validity and Clinical Scales
Based on adolescent norms (Gottesman et al., 1987).

FIG. 1.10. MMPI mean profiles for girls who grew up to be schizophrenic ($N = 10$) and their normal matched controls. (From Gottesman & Hanson, 1990. Copyright © by I. I. Gottesman. Reprinted by permission.)

SUMMARY

This chapter has provided a brief review of adolescent development and issues related to developmental psychopathology during this maturational stage. As is discussed in the following chapters in this text, the MMPI-A presents a variety of features that could potentially improve the identification and description of psychopathology among adolescents as compared with the original test instrument. For example, the development of the MMPI-A included extensive revisions of the original MMPI item pool to improve item clarity and relevance for adolescents. New items were also included in the MMPI-A that are related to forms of psychopathology of importance during adolescent development, including suicidal ideation, alcohol and drug abuse, and eating disorders. On the scale level, the MMPI-A has incorporated new measures of psychopathology of particular relevance to adolescents, including conduct disorder, school problems, depression, anxiety, and immaturity. Additionally, the MMPI-A development included the collection of an adolescent normative sample of 1,620 adolescents representing various geographic, socioeconomic, and ethnic groups. The release of an "official" set of adolescent norms for the MMPI-A by the University of Minnesota Press has substantially assisted in eliminating the inappropriate but widespread practice of applying adult norms in the interpretation of adolescent response patterns.

Finally, the MMPI-A profile sheet contains a "gray zone" area denoting a range of marginal or transitional elevations in place of the traditional use of a specific T-score designation as a cutoff between normal range scores and clinically elevated values. This use of a range of T-scores to mark the transition between normal range values and clinical values is particularly important in the assessment of adolescents, where the conceptual and psychometric dividing line between normalcy and pathology may be less clear than during adult development. Thus, the MMPI-A contains a number of features that may improve the assessment of adolescent psychopathology when employed by a clinician who is sensitive to developmental issues in this population.

Development of the MMPI and the MMPI-A

DEVELOPMENT OF THE MMPI

Work on the instrument that was to become the Minnesota Multiphasic Personality Inventory (MMPI) was begun in 1937 by Stark R. Hathaway, a psychologist, and J. C. McKinley, a neuropsychiatrist. The test authors were motivated to develop a "personality inventory" by their pursuit of several objectives. First, they had noticed that a large proportion of patients presenting for medical treatment manifested "one or more complaints that turn out to be psychoneurotic in nature" (McKinley & Hathaway, 1943, p. 161). The two test authors sought to develop an instrument that would be useful in identifying and describing these patients in a manner that was more efficient and effective than the psychiatric interview techniques traditionally used for psychological evaluations of medical patients. Apparently, Hathaway also believed that such an instrument might assist researchers in evaluating the efficacy of new treatment interventions by allowing for the systematic matching and evaluation of treatment groups. For example, Hathaway (1964), in reference to the use of insulin therapy, which was prevalent in the 1930s, noted:

> There was no way that our hospital staff could select a group of patients for the new treatment who would be surely comparable in diagnosis and severity of illness to those from some other setting. It became an obvious possibility that one might devise a personality test which, like intelligence tests, would somehow stabilize the identification of the illness and provide an estimate of its severity. Toward this problem the MMPI research was initiated. (p. 205)

Finally, Hathaway was also interested in the development of a personality assessment instrument that could assess changes in symptomatology across time. Further, when such a measure was administered at various stages of the treatment process, it would provide the clinician with an index of therapeutic change. In this regard, Hathaway (1965) stated that the MMPI was designed to serve as an "objective aid in the routine psychiatric case workup of adult patients and as a method of determining the severity of the condition. As a corollary to this, the inventory was expected to provide an objective estimate of psychotherapeutic effect and other changes in the severity of their conditions over time" (p. 463).

As noted by Colligan et al. (1983), the first published reference to the MMPI project was listed as a footnote to a 1939 paper (Hathaway, 1939). The MMPI was initially referred to as the "Medical and Psychiatric Inventory," later titled the "Multiphasic Personality Schedule" in a 1940 paper by Hathaway and McKinley, and finally designated the Minnesota Multiphasic Personality Inventory in the 1943 publication of the instrument by the University of Minnesota Press. Hathaway and McKinley had initial difficulty in finding a publisher for the MMPI, and Hathaway noted that "Dr. McKinley and I had faith sufficient to carry us through several rejections before the University of Minnesota Press finally undertook publication" (cited in Dahlstrom & Welsh, 1960, p. vii). Despite this humble beginning, the MMPI has become the most widely used objective personality assessment instrument across a wide variety of clinical settings (Lees-Haley, Smith, Williams, & Dunn, 1996; Lubin, Larsen, & Matarazzo, 1984; Lubin, Larsen, Matarazzo, & Seever, 1985; Lubin, Wallis, & Paine, 1971; Piotrowski & Keller, 1989, 1992). Butcher (1987a) estimated that over 10,000 books and articles have been produced on the MMPI, and Butcher and Owen (1978) reported that 84% of all research on personality inventory instruments has been focused on the MMPI. Butcher and Williams (2000) noted that by 1989 there were over 140 MMPI translations in 46 countries.

Historical Context

In their development of the MMPI, Hathaway and McKinley were sensitive to many of the problems that existed in the personality inventories of that era. For example, the Woodworth Personal Data Sheet (Woodworth, 1920) was a 169-item self-rating scale designed to detect neurotic maladjustment used in screening draftees during World War I. Respondents answered *yes* or *no* to the series of questions, and the total number of positive answers was used to determine whether the individual was referred for additional psychiatric interview. Following the development of the Woodworth Personal Data Sheet, several other rationally developed questionnaires were created, including the Bell Adjustment Inventory (Bell, 1934) and the Bernreuter Personality Inventory (Bernreuter, 1933). Rational scale construction involves the selection of items that logically or rationally appear to measure important areas. The selection of these items is based on the developer's theory, clinical experience, and intuition. A fundamental assumption inherent in this test construction method was that the items actually measured what the authors assumed they measured. Over time, however, it became clear that items selected exclusively on a rational basis were not always indicative of deviant behavior and that test subjects did not always respond accurately and honestly to test instruments. As noted by Greene (1980), critical studies and reviews by several authors, including Landis and Katz (1934) and Super (1942), strongly criticized the effectiveness of these rationally derived personality inventories. For example, test scores produced by normal subjects and subjects in clinical settings were often found to show little difference on these measures.

Hathaway and McKinley were also aware of the rudimentary efforts to develop validity scales as employed in the Humm-Wadsworth Temperament Scale (Humm & Wadsworth, 1935). This symptom checklist measure contained a "no count" score consisting of the number of items or symptoms denied (i.e., not endorsed by the subject) in responding to the instrument. Thus, a high no count score was seen as reflective of a subject who was excessively guarded or defensive, whereas a very low no count score might indicate a tendency to exaggerate or overreport symptoms. Additionally, Hathaway and McKinley began work on the MMPI following Strong's (1927, 1943) use of criterion groups in the development of a vocational or occupational-interest inventory (i.e., the Strong Vocational Interest Blank). Thus, Hathaway and McKinley had available a model of scale construction that stood in contrast to the rational development procedures that had typically been used for personality measures. They were also motivated by the need for an inventory that would be of practical use in clinical settings. By the late 1930s, much of personality assessment was seen as irrelevant by applied psychologists, as acknowledged by Hathaway (1965) in his comment that "it was so widely accepted that personality inventories were valueless that some program directors did not feel that any course work in their nature and interpretation was worth the effort" (p. 461).

Development Methods for the Original MMPI

Greene (2000) dramatically noted that "out of the psychiatric wilderness of the early 1930s appeared two men, Stark Hathaway and J. C. McKinley, who, under the banner of empiricism, waged a new battle for the scientific advancement of personality assessment" (p. 5). The developmental procedures used in the creation of the MMPI have been extensively documented by authors such as Colligan et al. (1983), Dahlstrom, Welsh, and Dahlstrom (1972, 1975), Friedman, Webb, and Lewak (1989), Friedman, Lewak, Webb, and Nichols (2001), Graham (2000), and Greene (2000). The procedures employed by Hathaway and McKinley are therefore only briefly summarized in this text.

A salient feature of Hathaway and McKinley's approach to the creation of the MMPI was their use of the *criterion keying* method, or the empirical method of inventory construction. Indeed, the MMPI is usually cited as the outstanding example of this test construction method (e.g., Anastasi, 1982). In the criterion keying approach, items are presented to two or more groups of subjects. One subject group serves as the criterion group, the group that manifests a defining diagnosis or characteristic that the test is meant to measure, and one or more others act as comparison groups, which do not manifest the trait or characteristic under study. Responses of the criterion and comparison groups are compared, and items are then selected for inventory membership that empirically demonstrate significant differences in response frequency. As noted by Friedman et al. (2001), scales constructed utilizing this methodology are usually named after the criterion group. For example, if the criterion group consisted of clinically depressed patients, the scale would probably be labeled a *Depression scale*. Further, scoring is usually accomplished by assigning one point to each item answered in the direction that is more frequently endorsed by criterion subjects. Additionally, the higher an individual scores on this type of measure, the more items he or she has answered in a direction consistent with that of the criterion group members.

Much as earlier researchers did, Hathaway and McKinley began their construction of the MMPI by generating an extensive pool of items from which various scales might be constructed. Specifically, they created nearly 1,000 self-referenced statements inspired from a wide variety of sources, including psychiatric examination forms, psychiatric textbooks, previously published scales of personality and social attitudes, and their own clinical experience (Hathaway & McKinley, 1940). They then reduced this list to 504 items by deleting items that duplicated content or that the authors subjectively felt had relatively little significance or value. Thus, the authors used a subjective and rational method to create the initial item pool. To simplify the task of identifying item duplication, Hathaway and McKinley constructed 25 content categories (Table 2.1) for the original MMPI item pool. In addition to the items shown in Table 2.1, 55 items

TABLE 2.1
Content Categories of the Original 504 MMPI Items as Determined
by Hathaway and McKinley

No.	Category	Number of Items
1.	General health	9
2.	General neurologic	19
3.	Cranial nerves	11
4.	Motility and coordination	6
5.	Sensibility	5
6.	Vasomotor, trophic, speech, secretory	10
7.	Cardiorespiratory	5
8.	Gastrointestinal	11
9.	Genitourinary	6
10.	Habits	20
11.	Family and marital	29
12.	Occupational	18
13.	Educational	12
14.	Sexual attitudes	19
15.	Religious attitudes	20
16.	Political attitudes—law and order	46
17.	Social attitudes	72
18.	Affect, depressive	32
19.	Affect, manic	24
20.	Obsessive, compulsive	15
21.	Delusions, hallucinations, illusions, ideas of reference	31
22.	Phobias	29
23.	Sadistic, masochistic	7
24.	Morale	33
25.	Items to "indicate whether the individual is trying to place himself in an improbably acceptable or unacceptable light"	15

Note. From Colligan et al. (1983). Copyright © 1983 by the Mayo Foundation. Adapted by permission of the Mayo Foundation.

were subsequently added "primarily related to masculinity-femininity" (McKinley & Hathaway, 1943, p. 162), and 9 items were apparently deleted (Colligan et al., 1983), resulting in the creation of a final pool of 550 items. These items were then employed to construct scales by comparing the item responses of normal individuals against those of psychiatric patients who held membership in relatively homogeneous clinical criterion groups.

Normative Groups

The normal criterion group primarily used in developing the MMPI consisted of individuals ($N = 724$) who were visiting friends or relatives receiving treatment at the University of Minnesota Hospital. These subjects, aged 16 years and older, were approached in the halls or waiting rooms of the hospital and invited to participate in the research project if preliminary screening indicated that they were not receiving treatment for any psychiatric or medical illness. The overall age, gender, and marital status of this University of Minnesota group were reported to be comparable to the 1930 U.S. Census findings (Hathaway & McKinley, 1940). Dahlstrom et al. (1972) described the Minnesota normative sample as follows: "In 1940, such a Minnesota normal adult was about thirty-five years old, was married, lived in a small town or rural area, had had eight years of general schooling, and worked at a skilled or semiskilled trade (or was married to a man with such an occupational level)" (p. 8).

In addition, Hathaway and McKinley collected data from two other samples of "normals." One of these samples consisted of 265 high school graduates who were coming to the University of Minnesota Testing Bureau for college counseling and guidance, and 265 individuals who were contacted through the local Works Progress Administration (WPA), a federally funded employment project. This latter group consisted of skilled workers who were "all white-collar workers and were used as controls for urban background and socioeconomic level" (Dahlstrom & Welsh, 1960, p. 46).

Colligan et al. (1983) noted that the original normative data collected by Hathaway and McKinley are no longer available. However, a subsample of these data, referred to as the Minnesota normal "purified" sample, was developed by Hathaway and Briggs (1957). The Hathaway and Briggs sample consists of 225 males and 315 females drawn from the general Minnesota normal sample. These data have been preserved and were the basis for the development of Appendix K in the *MMPI-2 Manual* (Butcher et al., 1989). Appendix K provides T-score values, based on the purified sample of the original Hathaway-McKinley norms, for MMPI-2 basic scales.

Clinical Scales

The clinical criterion groups utilized by Hathaway and McKinley defined the eight basic MMPI scales and consisted of carefully selected psychiatric patients in the following diagnostic categories: Hypochondriasis (scale 1), Depression (scale 2), Hysteria (scale 3), Psychopathic Deviant (scale 4), Paranoia (scale 6), Psychasthenia (scale 7), Schizophrenia (scale 8), and Hypomania (scale 9). Detailed descriptions of these clinical criterion groups were provided by Colligan et al. (1983), Dahlstrom and Dahlstrom (1980), Dahlstrom et al. (1972), and Greene (1980, 2000). In addition, a group consisting of "homosexual invert males" was employed by Hathaway and McKinley in the development of the Masculinity-Femininity scale (scale 5). Finally, the Social Introversion-Extroversion scale, developed by Drake (1946), was eventually added as the 10th basic scale of the MMPI (scale 0). The *Si* scale remains the only standard scale that was developed outside of the original Hathaway group and the only scale for which a psychiatric criterion group was not obtained (Colligan et al., 1983).

Validity Scales

In addition to the 10 standard clinical scales, Hathaway and McKinley also developed 4 validity scales for the MMPI, the purpose of which was to detect deviant test-taking attitudes or response sets. These measures included the Cannot Say or (?) scale, which was simply the total number of MMPI items that were either omitted or endorsed as both true and false, and the *L* or Lie scale, which consisted of 15 rationally derived items that present common human faults or foibles. The *L* scale was designed to detect crude attempts to present oneself in an unrealistically favorable manner. The *F* scale was composed of 64 items that were selected because they were endorsed in a particular direction by 10% or fewer of the Minnesota normal group. Hathaway and McKinley (1943) suggested that high scores on the *F* scale would imply that the clinical scale profile was invalid because the subject was careless or unable to comprehend the items or because extensive scoring errors had occurred. The T-score conversion values for *F*, like those for the Cannot Say scale and the *L* scale, were arbitrarily assigned by

McKinley and Hathaway rather than based on a linear transformation of raw score data from the Minnesota normal sample.

The final validity scale developed for the MMPI was the K scale. The K scale was developed by selecting 25 male and 25 female psychiatric patients who produced normal-range clinical scale values (i.e., T-score values $\leq$ 69 on all clinical scales). These subjects, therefore, could be considered to be false negatives (Meehl & Hathaway, 1946). The profiles of these false-negative patients were compared with the responses of the Minnesota normal cases, that is, true negatives. Item analysis revealed 22 items that discriminated the "true- and false-negative profiles in their item endorsements by at least 30%" (Dahlstrom et al., 1972, p. 124). Eight additional items were eventually added to the K scale to aid in accurately discriminating depressed and schizophrenic patients from subjects in the normative group. The main function of the K scale was to improve the discriminative power of the clinical scales in detecting psychopathology, and varying proportions of the K scale raw score total have traditionally been added to scales 1, 4, 7, 8, and 9 when using the K-correction procedure with adult respondents. The standard validity and clinical scales are discussed in more detail in later chapters dealing with validity assessment and clinical interpretation strategies.

Important Features

Before leaving the topic of the development of the original form of the MMPI, two general points should be made regarding characteristics of the instrument that have largely contributed to its popularity among clinical practitioners. First, as discussed by Graham (2000), it rapidly became apparent following the publication of the MMPI that its interpretation was considerably more complex than was initially anticipated. Rather than producing an elevated score on a single clinical scale, many psychiatric patients produced multiple elevations involving several scales. Thus, for example, depressed patients often produced elevations on the Depression scale but also obtained high scores on other standard clinical scales of this instrument. According to Graham, this phenomenon resulted from several factors, including a high degree of intercorrelation among the MMPI standard scales. Indeed, a variety of approaches have been used with MMPI data over the past 40 years in attempts to yield useful diagnostic information. No approach has produced more than modest correspondence between MMPI-derived diagnoses and psychiatric diagnoses based on clinical judgment or standard diagnostic interviews (e.g., Pancoast, Archer, & Gordon, 1988).

For these reasons, the MMPI has come to be used in a manner different from that originally envisioned by Hathaway and McKinley, particularly in terms of profile interpretation. Specifically, the usefulness of the particular scale labels or names has been deemphasized, a practice reflected in the tendency of MMPI interpreters to refer to MMPI scales by their numbers rather than criterion group labels (e.g., references to scale 7 rather than to the Psychasthenia scale). Accompanying this change, numerous researchers have set about to establish the meaning of clinical scales through extensive clinical correlate research. In this research approach, the actual extra test correlates of the MMPI scales are identified through empirical research efforts based on careful studies of individuals who produce certain patterns of MMPI scale elevations. The net impact of this shift in interpretive focus has been that the MMPI is standardly used as a *descriptive* instrument and that this descriptive capacity of the MMPI is based on the accumulation of numerous research studies concerning the test characteristics of specific MMPI configuration groups. As noted by Graham (2000):

Thus, even though the MMPI was not particularly successful in terms of its original purpose (differential diagnosis of clinical groups believed in the 1930s to be discrete psychiatric types), it has proven possible, subsequently, to use the test to generate descriptions of and inferences about individuals (normal persons and patients) on the basis of their own profiles. It is this behavioral description approach to the utilization of the test in everyday practice that has led to its great popularity among practicing clinicians. (p. 6)

It should also be noted that this approach to the interpretation of the MMPI has linked the usefulness of the test not to aspects of its original psychometric construction but rather to the massive accumulation of research literature that has been developed for this test instrument. Thus, the major clinical value of the MMPI lies in what we have come to know about what test results "mean."

A second important feature of the MMPI concerns the development of a broad variety of validity scales and indices through which to evaluate the consistency and accuracy of the clients' self-reports. The MMPI was among the first personality assessment instruments to strongly emphasize the use of validity scales to assist in determining the interpretability of clinical test findings. Thus, the MMPI interpreter can estimate the degree to which test findings are influenced by a number of factors related to the respondents' willingness and capacity to respond in a valid manner. This feature, in turn, has allowed the extension of the MMPI to assessment issues not originally envisioned by Hathaway and McKinley. These latter tasks have included the psychological screening of individuals in personnel and forensic settings, which differ substantially from the typical psychological treatment setting. Beyond the original four validity scales, numerous other MMPI measures have been subsequently developed to assess issues related to technical profile validity (e.g., the Carelessness scale and the Test-Retest Index). Many of these have been reviewed extensively by Greene (1989a, 2000).

MMPI-2

The MMPI was updated and restandardized, and a new version, the MMPI-2, was released in 1989 (Butcher et al., 1989), 46 years after the original publication of this instrument. The revision involved a modernization of the content and language of test items, the elimination of objectionable items, and the creation of new scales, including a series of 15 content scales (Archer, 1992c; Nichols, 1992). The development of the MMPI-2 also involved the collection of a nationally representative normative data sample of 2,600 adult men and women throughout the United States. The MMPI-2 contains 567 items that heavily overlap with items from both the original version of the MMPI and the adolescent version (MMPI-A). Several comprehensive guides to the MMPI-2 are now available (Butcher, 1990; Friedman et al., 2001; Graham, 2000; Greene, 2000; Nichols, 2001), and a text has been specifically devoted to a description of the MMPI-2 content scales (Butcher, Graham, Williams, & Ben-Porath, 1990). In addition, a research base is gradually developing for the interpretation of MMPI-2 profile codes (e.g., Archer, Griffin, & Aiduk, 1995; Graham, Ben-Porath, & McNulty, 1999). It should be specifically noted, however, that the MMPI-2 was designed and normed for individuals who are 18 years of age or older. Adolescent norms were *not* developed for the MMPI-2, nor was it intended for use in the assessment of adolescents.

USE OF THE MMPI WITH ADOLESCENTS

The application of the MMPI to adolescent populations for both clinical and research purposes occurred early in the development of this instrument. Although the MMPI was originally intended for administration to individuals who were 16 years of age or older, Dahlstrom et al. (1972) noted that the test could be used effectively with "bright children as young as 12" (p. 21). The delineation of age 12 as the lower limit for administration of the MMPI was probably related to the estimate that a sixth-grade reading level was a prerequisite for understanding the MMPI item pool (Archer, 1987b).

Early Applications

The first research application of the MMPI with adolescents appears to have occurred in 1941, 2 years prior to the formal publication of the MMPI in 1943. Using the instrument, Dora Capwell (1945a) demonstrated its ability to accurately discriminate between groups of delinquent and nondelinquent adolescent girls based on *Pd* scale elevation. Further, the MMPI *Pd* scale differences between these groups were maintained in a follow-up study that reevaluated MMPI profiles 4 to 15 months following the initial MMPI administration (Capwell, 1945b). Early studies by Monachesi (1948, 1950) also served to provide validity data concerning the *Pd* scale by demonstrating that delinquent boys scored significantly higher on this measure than normal male adolescents. In addition, the 1950 study by Monachesi included a sample of incarcerated female delinquents who produced findings that replicated the earlier reports of Capwell. Following these initial studies, the MMPI was used with adolescents in various attempts to predict, diagnose, and plan treatment programs for delinquent adolescents (e.g., Ball, 1962; Hathaway & Monachesi, 1951, 1952). Pursuing this research topic, Hathaway and Monachesi eventually collected the largest MMPI data set ever obtained on adolescents, in a longitudinal study of the relationship between MMPI findings and delinquent behaviors.

Hathaway and Monachesi administered the MMPI to 3,971 Minnesota ninth-graders during the 1947–1948 school year in a study that served as a prelude to the collection of a larger sample, termed the *statewide sample*. The statewide sample was collected during the spring of 1954, when Hathaway and Monachesi tested 11,329 ninth graders in 86 communities in Minnesota. Their combined samples involved approximately 15,000 adolescents, including a wide sample of Minnesota children from both urban and rural settings. In addition to the MMPI, the subjects' school records were obtained, and teachers were asked to indicate which students they felt were most likely either to have psychiatric or legal difficulties. Hathaway and Monachesi also gathered information concerning test scores on such instruments as intelligence tests and the Strong Vocational Interest Blank. The MMPI was then repeated on a sample of 3,976 of these children when they reached 12th grade during the 1956–1957 school year.

Follow-up data were obtained by field-workers in the children's community area, who searched files of public agencies, including police and court records. The authors continued to acquire biographical information on members of this sample until the mid-1960s (e.g., Hathaway, Reynolds, & Monachesi, 1969), and other researchers are currently performing follow-up studies on various subsections of the sample (e.g., Hanson et al., 1990). A summary of the early findings from this investigation was published in a 1963 book by Hathaway and Monachesi entitled *Adolescent*

Personality and Behavior: MMPI Patterns of Normal, Delinquent, Dropout, and Other Outcomes.

Hathaway and Monachesi (1953, 1961, 1963) undertook the collection of this massive data set in order to implement a longitudinal/prospective study that would identify personality variables related to the onset of delinquency. Rather than retroactively identifying a group of delinquent adolescents based on psychosocial histories, they chose to follow adolescents longitudinally to *predict* involvement in antisocial or delinquent behaviors. Thus, Hathaway and Monachesi hoped to identify MMPI predictors that could serve as indicators of risk factors associated with the later development of delinquent behaviors. Monachesi and Hathaway (1969) summarized their results as follows:

> Scales 4, 8, and 9, the excitatory scales, were found to be associated with high delinquency rates. When profiles were deviant on these scales, singly or in combination, delinquency rates were considerably larger than the overall rate. Thus, it was found that boys with the excitatory MMPI scale codes (where scales 4, 8, and 9 in combination were the most deviant scales in the profile) had a delinquency rate of 41.9% in contrast to the overall rate of 34.6%. Again, scales 0, 2, and 5 are the suppressor scales and were the dominant scales in the profiles of boys with low delinquency rates (27.1% as against 34.6%). The variable scales 1, 3, 6, and 7 were again found to have little relationship with delinquency. Of great interest is the fact that some of these relationships are even more marked for girls. In this case, the MMPI data are so closely related to delinquency that it was found that girls with the excitatory code profile had a delinquency rate twice as large as the overall rate. Again, the more deviant scores on scales 4, 8, and 9, the higher the delinquency rate. Girls with inhibitor or suppressor scale scores have lower delinquency rates than the overall rate. (p. 217)

Systematic follow-up and extensions of this work, usually based on further analyses of the Minnesota statewide sample, have provided relatively consistent support for the concept that elevations on scales *Pd*, *Sc*, and *Ma* serve an *excitatory* function. Higher scores on these scales are predictive of higher rates of "acting out" or delinquent behavior in adolescent samples (e.g., Briggs, Wirt, & Johnson, 1961; Rempel, 1958; Wirt & Briggs, 1959). Findings by Briggs et al. indicated that the accuracy of prediction of delinquent behaviors increased when MMPI data were combined with data regarding the family history of severe disease or death. Specifically, Briggs et al. found that when elevations on excitatory scales were combined with positive histories for family trauma, the frequency of delinquent behavior was twice that of the general population. Similarly, Rempel reported that he could accurately identify 69.5% of a delinquent sample based on analysis of MMPI scales. When MMPI data were combined with school record data in a linear regression procedure, the accurate identification rate for delinquent boys rose to 74.2%. More recently, Huesmann, Lefkowitz, and Eron (1978) found that a simple linear summation of the sums of scales *Pd*, *Ma*, and *F* served as the best predictor of delinquent and aggressive behavior in a sample of 426 nineteen-year-old adolescents. This procedure was effective in predicting concurrent incidents of aggression and delinquency as well as retroactively accounting for significant proportions of variance in the ratings of aggressiveness for subjects at age 9.

The research by Hathaway and Monachesi has proved to be very valuable in several ways. First, this research established that the MMPI could usefully predict at least one broad area of important behavior displayed by adolescents: delinquency. Second, their investigation provided a body of crucial information concerning differences in item endorsement for male versus female adolescents and for adolescents versus adults, and it also identified important longitudinal test-retest differences in item endorsement patterns occurring between middle and late adolescence. Third, the data collected by Hathaway and Monachesi provided a major component of the traditionally used adolescent norms later developed by Marks and Briggs (1972) and also served as the exclusive data source for another set of adolescent norms developed by Gottesman, Hanson, Kroeker, and Briggs (published in Archer, 1987b). Further, Hathaway and Monachesi empirically established the clinical correlates of high and low scores for each of the 10 standard clinical scales separately for each gender. Finally, this project has provided an extraordinarily rich source of data for follow-up investigations of the original Hathaway and Monachesi subjects, spanning topics from the prediction of juvenile delinquency to the personality precursors of schizophrenia (e.g., Hanson et al., 1990).

Development of Adolescent Norms and Codetype Correlates

The most frequently used adolescent norms for the original MMPI form were derived by Marks and Briggs in 1967 and first published in Dahlstrom et al. (1972, pp. 388–399). These norms have also been published in several other texts, including Marks, Seeman, and Haller (1974, pp. 155–162) and Archer (1987b, pp. 197–213; 1997a, pp. 343–360). The Marks and Briggs adolescent norms were based on the responses of approximately 1,800 normal adolescents, and were reported separately for males and females at ages 17, 16, and 15 and also at age 14 and below. The sample sizes used to create these norms ranged from 166 males and 139 females at age 17 to 271 males and 280 females at age 14 and below.

The Marks and Briggs adolescent norms were based on responses of 720 adolescents selected from the data collected by Hathaway and Monachesi (1963) in the Minnesota statewide sample combined with additional data from 1,046 adolescents collected during 1964 and 1965 in six states: Alabama, California, Kansas, Missouri, North Carolina, and Ohio. Marks et al. (1974) reported that this sample consisted of White adolescents who were not receiving treatment for emotional disturbance at the time of their MMPI evaluation. Much of the research performed on the use of the MMPI with adolescent populations has been based on the Marks and Briggs normative set.

Like the original Minnesota adult norms, the norms developed by Marks and Briggs converted raw scores to T-scores using the standard linear transformation procedure. T-scores were therefore determined by taking the nearest integer value of T through the use of the following formula:

$$T = 50 + \frac{10(X_i - M)}{SD}$$

In this formula, M and SD represent the mean and standard deviation of the raw scores for a particular scale based on the normative distribution of subjects in the appropriate age category and gender, and X_i is equal to the raw score value earned by a particular subject. Like the Minnesota adult sample norms, the adolescent norms were based on data from White respondents.

There were several distinguishing features of the adolescent norms developed by Marks and Briggs (1972). First, Marks and Briggs did not develop a K-correction procedure for use with their adolescent norms. Marks et al. (1974) listed several reasons for this decision. They noted that the original K weights were developed on a small sample of adults and that their applicability and generalizability to adolescents was questionable. Further, they cited research findings indicating that K-correction procedures with adolescents reduced rather than increased the relationships to external criteria. Second, the normative data reported by Marks and Briggs included the scores from all respondents, without screening out subjects based on validity criteria related to scores on L, F, or K. Thus, all profiles were utilized in this data set, regardless of validity scale values. The most extensive description of the adolescent norms developed by Marks and Briggs is provided in the Marks et al. (1974) text entitled *The Actuarial Use of the MMPI With Adolescents and Adults*.

In addition to adolescent norms, the Marks et al. (1974) text also contained actuarial-based personality descriptors for a series of 29 MMPI high-point codetypes. The main subject pool utilized by Marks and his colleagues to derive these codetype descriptors comprised 834 adolescents between the ages of 12 and 18. These adolescents were evaluated after receiving at least 10 hours of psychotherapy between 1965 and 1970. They were described as White teenagers who were not "mentally deficient or retarded" (p. 138). Marks et al. also reported that they later added an additional sample of 419 adolescents who received psychiatric services in the years 1970 to 1973. Adolescents in their samples completed the MMPI and a personal data form that included a self-description adjective checklist and questions covering such topics as attitudes toward self, attitudes toward others, motivational needs, and areas of conflict. The study also employed 172 therapists from 30 states, who provided descriptive ratings on the adolescents. According to Marks et al.:

> Of the 172 psychotherapists who provided patient ratings, 116 were either Board certified psychiatrists, Ph.D. level clinical psychologists, or M.S.W. level social workers with two additional years of therapy experience. These "experienced" therapists rated 746 patients or 90% of the cases; an additional 24 therapists who were either third- or fourth-year clinical psychology interns, third-year psychiatric residents, or recent M.S.W. graduates rated 83 patients or 10% of the cases. (p. 139)

Clinician ratings involved multiple instruments, including a case data schedule, an adjective checklist, and a Q-sort of personality descriptors. Therapists' ratings were based on available evidence, including case records, chart notes, and psychological test findings, excluding MMPI results.

Taken together, the preliminary codetype pool available to Marks et al. consisted of 2,302 descriptors that were potentially relevant to adolescents' experiences. The authors then selected from these potential correlates or descriptors 1,265 descriptors that were deemed to be relevant for both male and female respondents, that occurred with sufficient frequency to allow for statistical analyses, and that offered information that was clinically relevant in terms of patient description. Data from adolescents were then grouped into descriptive categories related to 29 high-point codetypes, with an average sample size of 13.4 respondents per codetype. Descriptors were developed that differentiated between *high* and *low* profiles (profiles above and below the median two-point codetype elevation for that grouping, respectively) as well as between two-point code reversals (e.g., 2-4 in contrast to 4-2 codes). A detailed discussion of the codetype procedures used in this correlate study is presented in Marks et al. (1974) and in Archer (1987b).

The Marks et al. (1974) clinical correlate study was crucial in providing clinicians with the first correlate information necessary to interpret adolescents' codetype patterns. Further, the information provided by Marks et al. was sufficiently comprehensive and sufficiently flexible in terms of application that their system was capable of classifying a large proportion of adolescent profiles typically obtained in clinical settings. The Marks et al. actuarial data descriptions for adolescents represented a substantial improvement over the Hathaway and Monachesi (1961) text, *An Atlas of Juvenile MMPI Profiles*, which was composed of 1,088 MMPI codes representing individual profile configurations from their sample of Minnesota ninth graders. Each profile was accompanied by a short case history and a brief description of that subject's most salient personality features. A clinician using this atlas identified the cases with profiles most similar to the one produced by his or her patient and then read the accompanying case descriptions. The clinician had to derive his or her own summary of personality features commonly found for the codetype without the assistance of statistical evaluations to identify the most relevant descriptors for the codetype in general.

More Recent Contributions (1975–1991)

Since the publication of the text by Marks et al. (1974), substantial work has been done in applying the MMPI to adolescents. This work was summarized by Archer (1984, 1987b), Butcher and Williams (2000), Archer and Krishnamurthy (2002), and Colligan and Offord (1989). Specifically, Archer reviewed the numerous studies indicating that adolescent response patterns should be evaluated exclusively with reference to adolescent norms and not with reference to the adult norms. Colligan and Offord (1989) noted research done with adolescent samples in the areas of medical evaluation, school adjustment, and juvenile delinquency. Of particular interest is the work subsequent to Marks et al. (1974) in the areas of adolescent norm development and clinical correlates.

In addition to the adolescent norms developed by Marks and Briggs (1972), adolescent MMPI norms for the traditional MMPI instrument were developed by Gottesman et al. 1987 (published in Archer, 1987b) and by Colligan and Offord (1989) at the Mayo Clinic. The norms developed by Gottesman and his colleagues represent a comprehensive analysis of the approximately 15,000 ninth-grade adolescents tested between 1948 and 1954 and the approximately 3,500 12th graders tested during 1956 and 1957 by Hathaway and Monachesi in their statewide sample. Sample size, validity criterion, raw score, and T-score data for this project are reported in Archer (1987b) in Appendix C. In addition to standard scale data, Gottesman et al. provided T-score conversions for a variety of MMPI special scales, including Barron's (1953) Ego Strength scale, MacAndrew's (1965) Alcoholism scale, Welsh's (1956) Anxiety and Repression scales, the Wiggins (1969) Content scales, and the special scales developed by Rosen (1962) for differential diagnosis of psychiatric patients.

Colligan and Offord (1989) also collected normative data for the original version of the MMPI based on the responses of 691 girls and 624 boys between the ages of 13 and 17, inclusive. In collecting these data during the mid-1980s, the authors randomly sampled from 11,930 households in Minnesota, Iowa, and Wisconsin that were within a 50-mile radius of the Mayo Clinic, which is located in Rochester, Minnesota. Telephone interviews established that slightly more than 10% of these households contained adolescents within the appropriate age groups, and after excluding adolescents with potentially handicapping disabilities, 1,412 adolescents were targeted for evaluation. MMPI materials were then mailed to these households, resulting in return rates of 83% for female adolescents and 72% for male adolescents. Colligan and Offord found little evidence of significant differences in mean raw score values across age groups, and therefore the final norms are based on normalized T-score conversions for 13-through 17-year-olds, with conversions presented separately by gender. Colligan and Offord (1991) also recently provided K-corrected T-score values for these norms.

Both the Gottesman, Hanson, Kroeker, and Briggs (1987) and the Colligan and Offord (1989) adolescent norm projects have substantial strengths. Although the Gottesman et al. data are based on MMPI responses of adolescents tested nearly 40 years ago, their current analyses are the first to comprehensively evaluate this very large and important data set. Additionally, the Marks and Briggs (1972) norms and the Gottesman et al. (1987) norms share common subjects and produce T-score conversion values for the standard MMPI scales that are similar. The Gottesman et al. MMPI special scale T-score values are, therefore, probably relatively close to those that would have been provided by Marks and Briggs had they attempted to derive normative data for MMPI special scales. The work of Colligan and Offord is based on a solid methodology employed with a contemporary sample of adolescents and therefore provides very useful data concerning how modern teenagers respond to the original version of the MMPI. A complete evaluation of both of these adolescent norm sets, however, would require several years of investigation.

Preliminary studies by Archer, Pancoast, and Klinefelter (1989) and Klinefelter, Pancoast, Archer, and Pruitt (1990) examined the degree to which the Gottesman et al. (1987) and Colligan and Offord (1989) norm sets produce profile elevations and configurations that differ from those produced by the traditional Marks and Briggs (1972) norms. These studies employed samples of normal, outpatient, and inpatient adolescents scored on all three normative sets. Results indicated significant differences in profile elevation by norm set, with the lowest T-score values typically produced by the Colligan and Offord norms. Using standardized criteria to judge profile congruence, the congruence rates ranged from 53% for profiles generated by Marks and Briggs versus Colligan and Offord to approximately 60% for profiles scored on the Marks and Briggs and Gottesman et al. norms. These data suggest that the more recent norms generate codetypes that may often differ from those generated by the traditional Marks and Briggs norms. Therefore, the existing codetype literature related to the traditional version of the MMPI may not apply to all profiles generated by these recently published adolescent norms. Given this observation, it seems most reasonable to apply Gottesman et al. or Colligan and Offord norms in conjunction with the traditional Marks and Briggs norms on the original version of the MMPI rather than employing either of these as a substitute for the Marks and Briggs norms.

In addition to the work that has been done on adolescent normative values, several investigations have examined the clinical correlates of single-scale and two-point codetypes based on the traditional Marks and Briggs adolescent norms. Archer, Gordon, Giannetti, and Singles (1988), for example, examined descriptive correlates of single-scale high-point elevations for scales 2, 3, 4, 8, and 9 in a sample of 112 adolescent inpatients. Clinical descriptors were collected for subjects based on their psychometric self-reports and patient ratings by parents, nursing staff, and individual psychotherapists. In general, findings from this study produced correlate patterns that were highly similar to those reported for basic MMPI scales in the adult literature. Using a similar methodology, Archer, Gordon, Anderson, and Giannetti (1989) investigated the clinical correlates of the MacAndrew Alcoholism scale, Welsh's Anxiety and Repression scales, and Barron's Ego Strength scale in a sample of 68 adolescent inpatients. Results from this study also indicated patterns of clinically relevant descriptors that were largely consistent with findings derived from studies of adult respondents. Ball,

Archer, Struve, Hunter, and Gordon (1987) found evidence of subtle but detectable neurological differences between adolescent psychiatric inpatients with and without elevated scale 1 values. Further, Archer and Gordon (1988) found that scale 8 elevation was an effective and sensitive indicator of the presence of schizophrenic diagnoses in a sample of adolescent inpatients.

Williams and Butcher (1989a) also examined single-scale correlates in a sample of 492 boys and 352 girls primarily evaluated in either substance abuse or psychiatric inpatient units. Standard scale values were investigated in relationship to data derived from psychiatric records and parental and treatment staff ratings and reports. Similar to Archer et al. (1988), the authors concluded that the single-scale descriptors found for these adolescents were consistent with those reported in adult studies. Additionally, Williams and Butcher (1989b) investigated codetype correlates for this sample of 844 adolescents and found that although some of the codetype descriptors reported by Marks et al. (1974) were replicated in this study, other descriptor patterns were not supported. Studies by Lachar and Wrobel (1990) and by Wrobel and Lachar (1992) examined the issue of gender differences in correlate patterns and found evidence of substantially different correlate patterns for male and female adolescents. Their findings underscore the need for more emphasis to be placed on the issue of potential gender differences in MMPI clinical correlate studies of adolescents.

Several researchers have also examined the effects of using both adolescent and adult norms in terms of profile elevation and configuration. Specifically, studies by Archer (1984), Ehrenworth and Archer (1985), Klinge, Lachar, Grissell, and Berman (1978), Klinge and Strauss (1976), and Lachar, Klinge, and Grissell (1976) examined the effects of using adolescent and adult norms in profiling responses of male and female adolescents admitted to inpatient psychiatric services. These studies have consistently shown that the degree of psychopathology displayed by adolescent respondents tends to be more pronounced when adult norms are employed, particularly on scales F, 4, and 8. Finally, factor analytic studies have been reported based on scale-level data (Archer, 1984) and on both item- and scale-level data (Archer & Klinefelter, 1991). In general, the results of these studies produced factor patterns that are reasonably consistent with those that have been typically derived from factor analytic findings in adult samples.

Frequency of Use of the MMPI in Adolescent Assessments

As we have seen, research attention has been increasingly focused on the use of the MMPI in adolescent populations. Until the early 1990s, however, no surveys of test usage were specifically targeted at practitioners working mainly with adolescents. Therefore, the relative popularity of instruments such as the MMPI among such practitioners remained unclear. In addressing this issue, Archer, Maruish, Imhof, and Piotrowski (1991) asked psychologists how frequently they used each of 67 instruments in their assessment of adolescent clients. The results for the these assessment instruments were evaluated based on total number of "mentions" as well as tabulated with adjustments for frequency of test usage. The MMPI was the third most frequently mentioned assessment instrument for evaluating adolescents (behind the Wechsler scales and the Rorschach) and the sixth most frequently employed instrument when scores were adjusted for frequency of use (following the Wechsler, Rorschach, Bender-Gestalt, TAT, and Sentence Completion instruments). The MMPI was the most frequently employed objective personality assessment instrument for evaluating teenagers when either total mentions or weighted scores were calculated.

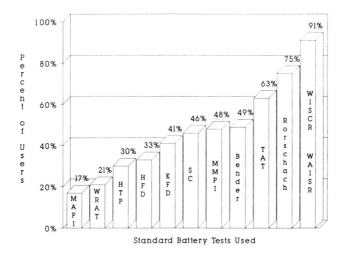

FIG. 2.1. Most frequently used psychological instruments in "standard batteries" with adolescents. (From Archer, Maruish, et al., 1991. Copyright © 1991 by the American Psychological Association. Reprinted by permission.)

Respondents were also asked to indicate those instruments used in their standard test batteries with adolescents. As shown in Fig. 2.1, the Wechsler IQ measures and the Rorschach were the most frequently reported tests included within standard batteries. The MMPI ranked fifth and was included by roughly half of the survey respondents. In contrast, the only other objective personality assessment instrument included in Fig. 2.1 is the Millon Adolescent Personality Inventory (Millon, Green, & Meagher, 1977), which was included in only 17% of the standard test batteries reported by the respondents. Overall, the results of the survey by Archer, Maruish, et al. (1991) indicated that the MMPI, consistent with surveys of test use in adult populations (e.g., Lubin et al., 1985), was the most frequently used objective personality assessment instrument in evaluations of adolescents.

DEVELOPMENT OF THE MMPI-A

Despite the popularity of the MMPI, researchers and clinicians have expressed concerns regarding several aspects of the use of the MMPI to assess teenagers. For example, Archer, Maruish, et al. (1991) asked survey respondents to indicate their perceptions of the major advantages and disadvantages of using the MMPI with adolescents. Major advantages reported included the comprehensive and accurate nature of clinically relevant descriptors, the relative ease of administration and scoring, and the extensive adolescent research database available for this instrument. Forty-nine percent of respondents, however, indicated that they felt the test was too long, 20% of respondents had concerns regarding inadequate or outdated adolescent norms, 18% felt that the reading level of the original MMPI was too high, and 17% objected to the use of inappropriate or outdated language in the item pool. Consistent with most of the survey respondents' views, Table 2.2 summarizes a variety of factors pointing to the need for revision of the original test instrument.

Serious concerns have been expressed regarding the nature of the adolescent norms available for the original MMPI. Specifically, the Marks and Briggs (1972) adolescent

TABLE 2.2
Factors Contributing to the Development of the MMPI-A

I.	Need for contemporary norms
	A. Current norms
	B. National sample
	C. Ethnic representation
II.	Need for revision of item pool
	A. Elimination of offensive items
	B. Elimination of items inappropriate for adolescents
	C. Rewritten items to simplify wording or sentence structure
	D. Inclusion of new items of specific relevance for adolescents
III.	Need for creation of scales to assess adolescent problem areas
	A. New supplementary scales, including the Immaturity scale
	B. Several new content scales, including the School Problems and Conduct Problems scales
IV.	Need to standardize MMPI assessment practices for adolescents
	A. Confusion regarding appropriate norms
	B. Confusion regarding interpretation practices
	C. Fostering interest in special scale use

Note. Reprinted from Archer (1992a). Copyright © 1992 by Lawrence Erlbaum Associates, Inc. Reprinted by permission.

norms were based on data samples collected in the late 1940s through mid-1960s on White adolescents. This adolescent data set is therefore substantially dated and dramatically limited in terms of ethnic representation. Pancoast and Archer (1988) examined the adequacy of the traditional adolescent norms in an analysis of normal adolescent samples collected between 1947 and 1965 and normal adolescent samples collected in the decade following 1975. Findings supported the adequacy of the traditional adolescent norms for evaluations of samples of normal adolescents collected between 1947 and 1965. This interval of time coincides with the data collection period for the adolescent samples used in the Marks and Briggs (1972) norms. MMPI patterns produced by more contemporary samples of adolescents, however, were elevated above the Marks and Briggs mean values on most clinical scales. These findings suggest that the traditional adolescent norms may not provide an accurate normative baseline, in terms of mean fit, for evaluations of contemporary adolescents.

Also, some of the item content of the original MMPI has been criticized as inappropriate for the assessment of teenagers. Most clinicians who have used the original version with teenagers have probably been aware that an item concerning "drop the handkerchief" has little meaning for today's adolescents and that questions concerning "deportment" are not readily understood by many adolescents. Similarly, statements such as "my sex life is satisfactory" may have a substantially different meaning when asked of a 13-year-old and a 30-year-old. Further, awkwardly worded items, a source of concern in administration of the MMPI to adults, was a major problem in the assessment of adolescents. Finally, the MMPI item pool, although quite extensive, has historically lacked items of specific relevance to adolescent experiences, including problem areas that typically emerge during the teenage years, such as drug use, eating disorders, and school-related problems. In addition to modifications at the item level, the creation of MMPI items related to adolescence provided an opportunity to develop scale measures of specific relevance to adolescent development and psychopathology. Although several special MMPI scales developed for adults had been applied to adolescents (e.g., the Welsh Anxiety and Repression scales and the MacAndrew Alcoholism scale), these scales were not specifically developed for this population.

On July 1, 1989, the MMPI Adolescent Project Committee, consisting of James N. Butcher, Auke Tellegen, and Robert P. Archer, was appointed by Beverly Kaemmer of the University of Minnesota Press to consider the advisability of creating an adolescent version of the MMPI and the features such a version should incorporate if development was undertaken.

Goals of the MMPI-A Project

A number of goals were envisioned in the creation of the MMPI-A. Some of these goals were in conflict and required varying degrees of compromise for work to move forward on the adolescent version. It was clear that adult norms would not be applicable to an adolescent version (Archer, 1984, 1987b, 1990; Williams, Graham, & Butcher, 1986) and that a national normative sample representative of the general population of U.S. teenagers would be required for the MMPI-A. An emphasis was also placed on shortening the length of the MMPI, to the extent that this could be achieved without loss of substantive clinical information. Maintaining continuity between the original MMPI and the MMPI-A was also stressed, including preservation of the standard or basic MMPI validity and clinical scales. Within this context, however, opportunities were taken to improve MMPI scales *F*, *Mf*, and *Si* based on observations concerning adolescent response characteristics on these measures in the MMPI-A normative sample. If a version of the MMPI was to be developed for adolescent assessment, it was also deemed desirable to include items and scales directly relevant to adolescent development and expression of psychopathology. Finally, it was anticipated that the release of an adolescent version would help to standardize assessment practices with adolescents. As noted by Archer (1984, 1987b), there has been considerable controversy and confusion regarding the optimal approach to interpreting adolescents' MMPI profiles. Questions concerning the most appropriate administration criteria, norm sets, special scales, and clinical correlates have been the subject of substantial debate, without clear and consistent resolution. The development and release of the MMPI-A and the extensive manual for this instrument (Butcher et al., 1992) served to standardize and improve assessment practices for both clinician and researcher.

The Experimental Booklet (Form TX)

The development of the MMPI-A was initiated with the creation of an experimental test booklet for adolescents, identified as MMPI Form TX. This experimental test booklet contained 704 items to be used in normative data collection efforts and in preliminary analyses to determine the feasibility of creating an adolescent form. The first section of this booklet contained 550 items from the traditional MMPI form; it was followed by a new experimental item pool for which scale membership and clinical correlates had not yet been established. The 154 items included in the second section involved content areas such as negative peer group influence, alcohol and drug abuse, family relationship difficulties, school and achievement problems, eating disorders, and identity problems (Archer, 1987b). Of the original 550 items, approximately 13% had been reworded to increase content clarity or quality. The 16 repeated items in the traditional MMPI version were eliminated from MMPI Form TX. In addition to MMPI Form TX, adolescents in the normative samples were administered a 16-item Biographical Information Form and a 74-item Life Events Form. The biographical questionnaire obtained data on a number of variables, including age, ethnic background, family structure, parental education and occupation, and academic

TABLE 2.3
Geographic Distribution of Adolescents in the MMPI-A Normative Sample

Location	Males (N = 805)		Females (N = 815)	
	Frequency	%	Frequency	%
California	99	12.3	127	15.6
Minnesota	201	25.0	300	36.8
New York	168	20.9	0	00.0
North Carolina	119	14.8	84	10.3
Ohio	101	12.5	109	13.4
Pennsylvania	34	4.2	55	6.7
Virginia	82	10.2	127	15.6
Washington State	1	0.1	13	1.6

Note. From Butcher et al. (1992). Copyright © 1992 by the Regents of the University of Minnesota. Reproduced by permission.

performance. The life events questionnaire requested information on the occurrence and effect of life events such as major illnesses, loss of family members, and parental separation or divorce.

The MMPI-A Normative Sample

The collection of adolescent normative data was undertaken in eight states, seven of which also served as primary sites for adult normative data collection for the MMPI-2. Adolescent normative subjects were generally solicited by mail from the rosters of junior and senior high schools in predetermined areas, and subjects were tested in group sessions generally conducted within school settings. Adolescents who participated in the MMPI-A normative data collection were paid for their voluntary participation. A total of approximately 2,500 adolescents were evaluated using the MMPI Form TX in data collection efforts in Minnesota, Ohio, California, Virginia, Pennsylvania, New York, North Carolina, and Washington. Various exclusion criteria were applied to these data, including the following: (a) subjects with incomplete data; (b) Carelessness scale values > 35; (c) original F scale value > 25; (d) subject age < 14 or > 18. Employing these exclusion criteria resulted in the creation of a final adolescent normative sample that included 805 males and 815 females. Table 2.3 shows the geographic distribution of this adolescent sample, and Table 2.4 provides

TABLE 2.4
Age Distribution of Adolescents in the MMPI-A
Normative Sample

Age	Males (N = 805)		Females (N = 815)	
	Frequency	%	Frequency	%
14	193	24.0	174	21.3
15	207	25.7	231	28.3
16	228	28.3	202	24.8
17	135	16.8	163	20.0
18	42	5.2	45	5.5

Note. From Butcher et al. (1992). Copyright © 1992 by the Regents of the University of Minnesota. Reproduced by permission.

TABLE 2.5
Ethnic Origin of Adolescents in the MMPI-A Normative Sample

	Males (N = 805)		Females (N = 815)	
Ethnicity	Frequency	%	Frequency	%
White	616	76.5	619	76.0
Black	100	12.4	100	12.3
Asian	23	2.9	23	2.8
Native American	21	2.6	26	3.2
Hispanic	18	2.2	16	2.0
Other	20	2.5	21	2.6
None reported	7	0.9	10	1.2

Note. From Butcher et al. (1992). Copyright © 1992 by the Regents of the University of Minnesota. Reproduced by permission.

age distribution data. The mean age of male adolescents in the MMPI-A normative sample was 15.5 years ($SD = 1.17$ years), and the mean age for females was 15.6 years ($SD = 1.18$ years).

Table 2.5 provides information concerning the ethnic origins of adolescents in the MMPI-A normative sample. The ethnic distribution of the MMPI-A normative sample represents a reasonable match against U.S. Census figures, with approximately 76% of the data derived from Whites, 12% from Blacks, and the remaining 12% from other ethnic groups.

Tables 2.6 and 2.7 provide data on fathers' and mothers' educational levels, respectively, for adolescents in the MMPI-A normative sample. In general, these data show that the parents of adolescents used in the MMPI-A normative sample are well educated and that higher educational levels are overrepresented in comparison to the 1980 U.S. Census data. Specifically, roughly 50% of the fathers and 40% of the mothers of children in the MMPI-A normative sample reported achieving a bachelor's degree or attaining a higher educational level, whereas only 20% of males and 13% of females in the 1980 U.S. Census data reported comparable educational achievement. This degree of overrepresentation of better educated individuals is very similar to that found in the MMPI-2 adult normative sample (Archer, 1997a). This phenomenon is probably related to the use of volunteer subjects in normative data collection procedures, in which better educated and higher socioeconomic status subjects are differentially more likely to participate. Black (1994) criticized specifically this aspect of the MMPI-A

TABLE 2.6
Fathers' Educational Level for Adolescents in the MMPI-A Normative Sample

	Males (N = 805)		Females (N = 815)	
Educational Level	Frequency	%	Frequency	%
Less than high school	17	2.1	15	1.8
Some high school	59	7.3	88	10.8
High school graduate	173	21.5	191	23.4
Some college	114	14.2	108	13.3
College graduate	272	33.8	262	32.1
Graduate school	152	18.9	122	15.0
None reported	18	2.2	29	3.6

Note. From Butcher et al. (1992). Copyright © 1992 by the Regents of the University of Minnesota. Reproduced by permission.

TABLE 2.7
Mothers' Educational Level for Adolescents in the MMPI-A Normative Sample

Educational Level	Males (N = 805)		Females (N = 815)	
	Frequency	%	Frequency	%
Less than high school	9	1.1	11	1.3
Some high school	38	4.7	54	6.6
High school graduate	250	31.1	230	28.2
Some college	145	18.0	183	22.5
College graduate	260	32.3	244	30.0
Graduate school	91	11.3	68	8.3
None reported	12	1.5	25	3.0

Note. From Butcher et al. (1992). Copyright © 1992 by the Regents of the University of Minnesota. Reproduced by permission.

normative sample and concluded that "the socioeconomic skewing of the normative sample brings into question the interpretation of protocols of respondents from low socioeconomic status levels" (p. 11).

Finally, Table 2.8 provides data concerning the living situation of the adolescents in the MMPI-A normative sample in terms of the family members with whom they resided. As shown in this table, approximately two thirds of the adolescents in the MMPI-A normative sample reported that they lived with both parents, approximately 24% reported living with their biological mother only, approximately 3.4% reported living with their biological father, approximately 2% reported living in other home settings, and 4.2% of the sample did not provide information on this variable.

Structure of the MMPI-A

After examining the preliminary data, a decision was reached by the MMPI Adolescent Project Committee during January 1990 to recommend the creation of the MMPI-A instrument. The final version of the MMPI-A contains 478 items. Administration of the first 350 items of the MMPI-A booklet are sufficient to score validity scales L, F_1, and K and the standard clinical scales. The remaining 128 items are necessary to score the remaining validity scales and the supplementary and content scales. The standard MMPI clinical scales were retained in the MMPI-A. Fifty-eight standard scale items were deleted from the original scales, however, with about 88% of these item deletions occurring on scales F, Mf, and Si. Items deleted from the MMPI-A standard

TABLE 2.8
Family Characteristics of Adolescents in the MMPI-A Normative Sample

In Home With	Males (N = 805)		Females (N = 815)	
	Frequency	%	Frequency	%
Mother and father	557	69.2	518	63.6
Father only	28	3.5	34	4.2
Mother only	191	23.7	229	28.0
Other	29	3.6	34	4.2
Total	805		815	

Note. From Butcher et al. (1992). Copyright © 1992 by the Regents of the University of Minnesota. Reproduced by permission.

TABLE 2.9
Item Changes in Original MMPI Basic Scales and Resulting
Effects on the MMPI-A Basic Scales

MMPI-A Scale	Items Retained	Number of Items Deleted
L	14	1
F	66[a]	27
K	30	0
1 (Hs)	32	1
2 (D)	57	3
3 (Hy)	60	0
4 (Pd)	49	1
5 (Mf)	44	16
6 (Pa)	40	0
7 (Pt)	48	0
8 (Sc)	77	1
9 (Ma)	46	0
0 (Si)	62	8

[a] Twelve items were deleted from the MMPI-A F scale but retained in the MMPI-A item pool, 12 items from original test not scored on the F scale were transferred to the MMPI-A F scale, and 17 new items were added to the MMPI-A F scale.

scales included the 13 items that were also deleted from the traditional MMPI in the creation of the MMPI-2. In general, items deleted from the MMPI-A dealt with religious attitudes and practices, sexual preferences, and bowel and bladder functioning or were deemed inappropriate given adolescents' life experiences. A variety of empirical criteria were used to delete items from scales F, Mf, and Si. Specifically, an item was deleted from the F scale if it was endorsed with a frequency of 21% or greater for either boys or girls in the MMPI-A normative sample. An item was deleted from Mf or Si if it loaded only on that particular scale (i.e., did not overlap on other standard measures) and either did not demonstrate significant gender differences (in the case of the Mf scale) or did not contribute to factor patterns established for the Si scale. Table 2.9 indicates the number of items deleted and retained for each of the standard MMPI-A validity and clinical scales, and Table 2.10 provides a listing of items deleted from the basic validity and clinical scales.

TABLE 2.10
Item Deletions From the Original MMPI Basic Validity and Clinical Scales

Scale	MMPI Item Numbers
L	255
F	14, 20, 31*, 40*, 53, 85, 112*, 115*, 139, 146, 156*, 164*, 169, 197, 199, 206, 211, 215*, 218, 227, 245*, 246, 247*, 256*, 258, 269*, 276*
1	63
2	58, 95, 98
4	20
5	4, 19, 25, 69, 70, 87, 126, 133, 198, 203, 204, 214, 229, 249, 261, 295
8	20
0	25, 126, 229, 371, 427, 440, 455, 462

Note. Adapted from Butcher et al. (1992). Copyright © 1992 by the Regents of the University of Minnesota. Reproduced by permission.
*Original MMPI F scale item not appearing on the MMPI-A F scale but appearing on other MMPI-A scales.

The final form of the MMPI-A includes the original 13 standard scales combined with 4 new validity scales, 15 content scales, 6 supplementary scales, and the 28 Harris-Lingoes and 3 Si subscales. Table 2.11 provides an overview of the scale structure of the MMPI-A. The new validity measures for the MMPI-A include the F_1 and F_2 subscales of the standard F scale as well as the True Response Inconsistency scale ($TRIN$) and the Variable Response Inconsistency scale ($VRIN$) developed by Auke Tellegen. The supplementary scales for the MMPI-A involve measures that were developed for the original MMPI, including the Anxiety (A) scale, the Repression (R) scale, and the MacAndrew Alcoholism scale (MAC). In addition, the supplementary scales include a variety of new measures developed for the MMPI-A, including the Immaturity (IMM) scale, the Alcohol/Drug Problem Acknowledgment (ACK) scale, and the Alcohol/Drug Problem Proneness (PRO) scale. Most of the 15 content scales developed for the MMPI-A overlap with similar measures developed for the MMPI-2, but several of these scales were created specifically and uniquely for the adolescent version. The Harris-Lingoes content subscales developed for the original MMPI version were carried over to the MMPI-A, with a few item deletions resulting from the deletion of items on the basic scales. The Si subscales were directly carried over from their counterparts in the MMPI-2. The MMPI-A manual by Butcher et al. (1992) contains a listing of MMPI-A items accompanied by data concerning endorsement frequencies and reading requirements. Appendix B provides the composition of each of the MMPI-A basic scales, content and supplementary scales, and Harris-Lingoes and Si subscales. Finally, Butcher et al. (1992) showed item number conversion information for the group form of the original MMPI and MMPI-A and for conversions between items in the MMPI-2 and MMPI-A.

MMPI-A Normative Sample: Comparisons With Earlier Normative Groups

Newsom, Archer, Trumbetta, and Gottesman (2003) examined the changes in adolescent self-presentation on the MMPI and MMPI-A over a 40-year period. The primary samples used by these researchers for comparison included 1,235 adolescents between the ages of 14 and 16 who were in the MMPI-A normative sample for which data was collected in 1989 and 10,514 adolescents between the ages of 14 and 16 for which data was collected between 1948 and 1954 in the Hathaway and Monachesi (1963) study of adolescent personality and behavior. MMPI basic scale and item-level data were also included for 817 adolescents, aged 14 through 16, used by Colligan and Offord (1992) in their 1985 study of the original form of the MMPI. Overall, the result of these evaluations revealed that adolescents from the MMPI-A normative sample scored significantly higher across the basic clinical scales and lower on validity scales L and K than did adolescents from the Hathaway and Monachesi (1963) sample. The MMPI basic scale mean data reported by Colligan and Offord typically fell in a midrange between these two. Results were interpreted as reflecting moderate to large changes in response frequencies between eras of data collection, with evidence of a relatively higher frequency of item endorsement by contemporary adolescents in the clinical direction on most MMPI basic clinical scales, particularly scales Ma, Sc, and Hs. Thus, contemporary normal adolescents not only endorse more psychopathological symptoms than do adults but also endorse more pathology than did adolescents evaluated 40 years ago in the Monachesi and Hathaway sample. As we will explore in more detail later, these response patterns may indicate that normal adolescents experience enough psychological turmoil and distress to render accurate discrimination between normal and abnormal functioning particularly difficult during this developmental age.

TABLE 2.11
Overview of the MMPI-A Scales and Subscales

Basic profile scales (17 scales)

Standard scales (13)

　　L through *Si*

Additional validity scales (4)

　　F_1/F_2　(subscales of *F* scale)

　　VRIN　(Variable Response Inconsistency)

　　TRIN　(True Response Inconsistency)

Content and supplementary scales (21 scales)

Content scales (15)

　　A-anx　(Anxiety)

　　A-obs　(Obsessiveness)

　　A-dep　(Depression)

　　A-hea　(Health Concerns)

　　A-aln　(Alienation)

　　A-biz　(Bizarre Mentation)

　　A-ang　(Anger)

　　A-cyn　(Cynicism)

　　A-con　(Conduct Problems)

　　A-lse　(Low Self-esteem)

　　A-las　(Low Aspirations)

　　A-sod　(Social Discomfort)

　　A-fam　(Family Problems)

　　A-sch　(School Problems)

　　A-trt　(Negative Treatment Indicators)

Supplementary scales (6)

　　MAC-R (MacAndrew Alcoholism–Revised)

　　ACK　(Alcohol/Drug Problem Acknowledgment)

　　PRO　(Alcohol/Drug Problem Proneness)

　　IMM　(Immaturity)

　　A　　(Anxiety)

　　R　　(Repression)

Harris-Lingoes and Si subscales (31 scales)

Harris-Lingoes subscales (28)

　　D_1　(Subjective Depression)

　　D_2　(Psychomotor Retardation)

　　D_3　(Physical Malfunctioning)

　　D_4　(Mental Dullness)

　　D_5　(Brooding)

　　Hy_1　(Denial of Social Anxiety)

　　Hy_2　(Need for Affection)

　　Hy_3　(Lassitude-Malaise)

　　Hy_4　(Somatic Complaints)

　　Hy_5　(Inhibition of Aggression)

　　Pd_1　(Familial Discord)

　　Pd_2　(Authority Problems)

　　Pd_3　(Social Imperturbability)

　　Pd_4　(Social Alienation)

　　Pd_5　(Self-Alienation)

　　Pa_1　(Persecutory)

　　Pa_2　(Poignancy)

　　Pa_3　(Naivete)

　　Sc_1　(Social Alienation)

　　Sc_2　(Emotional Alienation)

　　Sc_3　(Lack of Ego Mastery, Cognitive)

　　Sc_4　(Lack of Ego Mastery, Conative)

(Continued)

TABLE 2.11
(Continued)

	Sc_5	(Lack of Ego Mastery, Defective Inhibition)
	Sc_6	(Bizarre Sensory Experiences)
	Ma_1	(Amorality)
	Ma_2	(Psychomotor Acceleration)
	Ma_3	(Imperturbability)
	Ma_4	(Ego Inflation)
Si Subscales (3)		
	Si_1	(Shyness/Self-Consciousness)
	Si_2	(Social Avoidance)
	Si_3	(Alienation—Self and Others)

Further, Archer, Handel, and Lynch (2001) recently demonstrated that many MMPI-A items, perhaps approaching nearly 50% of the basic scale item pool, did not show significantly higher rates of endorsement frequency among adolescent inpatients than among adolescents from the normative sample. The implications of these findings for clinical applications of the MMPI-A are discussed in detail in Chapter 6.

Clinical Popularity of the MMPI-A

As previously noted, Archer, Maruish, et al. (1991) presented survey findings on the popularity of the MMPI among psychologists who perform psychological assessments with adolescent clients. Archer and Newsom (2000) designed an investigation to update these results by examining the test use practices reported by 346 psychologists who work with adolescents in a variety of clinical and academic settings. These respondents had an adjusted survey return rate of 36% and predominantly consisted of doctoral prepared psychologists (95%) in private practice settings (51%). The survey respondents had a mean of 13.6 years of postdegree clinical experience and spent an average of 45% of their clinical time working with adolescents. Table 2.12 presents the

TABLE 2.12
Test Usage Ratings for the Ten Most Widely Used Assessment Instruments With Adolescents

Instrument	Usage Rating Totals							
	a	*b*	*c*	*d*	*e*	*f*	TM	WS
Wechsler Intelligence Scales	82	23	37	27	63	101	251	935
Rorschach Inkblot Technique	108	46	48	22	38	71	225	715
Sentence Completion Tasks (any form)	109	31	57	32	49	55	224	712
Thematic Apperception Test	114	46	55	38	33	47	219	637
MMPI-A	128	45	55	25	39	41	205	591
Child Behavior Checklist,								
Parent Report Form	133	62	50	18	30	41	201	541
The House-Tree-Person Technique	139	52	63	18	23	38	194	514
Wide Range Achievement Test								
(any format)	154	44	50	26	31	28	179	486
Child Behavior Checklist,								
Teacher's Report Form	138	54	65	25	29	22	195	485
Conners' Rating Scales–Revised	135	46	82	27	31	12	198	475

Note. a = never; b = infrequently; c = occasionally; d = about 50% of the time; e = frequently; f = almost always; TM = total mentions; WS = weighted score (sum of $n \times$ numerical weight of ratings; a = 0, b = 1, c = 2, d = 3, e = 4, f = 5). From Archer and Newsom (2000). Copyright © 2000 by Sage Publications. Reproduced by permission.

usage rating totals, arranged in order of decreasing weighted scores, for the ten most frequently reported instruments in the Archer and Newsom survey. As shown in the table, these include the Wechsler Intelligence Scales, several projectives, one objective self-report measure (MMPI-A), and Parent and Teacher Behavioral Rating Forms. The MMPI-A was ranked fifth in both total mentions by respondents in the survey and by a score weighted by frequency of use. Further, the MMPI-A was the only self-report objective personality assessment instrument included in these top ten instruments. In general, there is a considerable degree of similarity between the findings of the 1991 survey by Archer et al. and the Archer and Newsom (2000) results. For example, the Wechsler Intelligence Scales, the Rorschach, the TAT, and the MMPI remain among the most widely used tests with adolescents. In addition to questions related to test utilization, Archer and Newsom requested respondents to indicate the primary strengths associated with the use of the MMPI-A. The responses were, in order, the MMPI-A's ability to provide a comprehensive clinical picture, the availability of contemporary adolescent norms, the instrument's ease of administration and psychometric soundness, and the comprehensiveness of the research base available for the instrument. The most frequently cited disadvantages reported by the respondents included (in order) the length of test instrument and associated demands for prolonged cooperation, a reading level that is too demanding or difficult for many adolescents, time requirements for scoring and interpretation, time requirements related to the administration of the test, and, finally, the expense associated with purchasing and using the test instrument in a managed care environment. Overall, Archer and Newsom observed that the MMPI-A has attained the status achieved by its predecessor, quickly becoming the objective personality assessment instrument most commonly used to evaluate adolescents.

Research Popularity of the MMPI-A

In 1987, Archer noted that there were roughly 100 studies reporting on the original version of the MMPI in adolescent populations from its release in 1943 to the mid-1980s. Forbey (2003) recently reviewed the literature on the MMPI-A and identified approximately 112 books, chapters, and research articles published on this instrument since its release in 1992. As a point of further comparison, Forbey noted that only 15 works on the Millon Adolescent Clinical Inventory (MACI) have been published in the same 10-year period, and 781 published articles on or descriptions of the MMPI-2. Forbey observed that the content areas addressed in the developing MMPI-A literature have been fairly broad, and he grouped these publications into several not mutually exclusive categories. The publications included 6 studies on the use of the MMPI-A as an external criterion in validation of other instruments; 2 studies in which the MMPI-A had been used to address forensic or child custody issues; 14 investigations in which the MMPI-A addressed cross-cultural or multicultural issues; 9 books and book chapters serving as instructional guides to the MMPI-A; 22 articles related to the use of the MMPI-A with specific populations, such as juvenile offenders, academically gifted adolescents, or eating disordered adolescents; 25 articles dealing with specific methodological issues, such as the factor structure of the test instrument, normative samples, or reliability issues; and 21 articles related to the development of specific scales or groups of scales, such as the Immaturity (*IMM*) supplementary scales or the MMPI-A content scales. Finally, Forbey reported an additional group of studies focused on methodological issues, the largest subcomponent of which comprises 10 studies specifically investigating the MMPI-A validity scales. Forbey concluded that research with the MMPI-A is progressing at a much faster pace than research on adolescence done with the original version of the MMPI.

SUMMARY

The MMPI-A is closely related to both the original version of the MMPI and the MMPI-2. The MMPI-A, however, also contains features that are unique to it. Much of the research on adolescence done with the original version of the MMPI appears generalizable to the MMPI-A. It also seems that much of the research currently being generated using the MMPI-2 (e.g., validation of MMPI-2 content scales and studies focused on codetype congruence) has relevance for the use of the MMPI-A. The development of the MMPI-A, however, represents the first time in the roughly 50-year history of this instrument that a specialized set of adolescent norms and a specific adolescent version have been released by the test publisher. The MMPI-A, therefore, has the potential to produce significant improvements in the assessment of psychopathology in adolescents by underscoring the unique aspects of MMPI interpretation necessary with this age group. The research by Archer and Newsom (2000) demonstrates that the MMPI-A rapidly replaced the MMPI as the most widely used objective personality assessment instrument for evaluating adolescents, and Forbey's 2003 survey indicates that research findings achieved with this new instrument are accumulating quickly.

3

Administration and Scoring Issues

QUALIFICATION AND BACKGROUND OF TEST USERS

The use of the MMPI-A with adolescents requires specific training and experience in several areas. First, the clinician should be adequately trained in the essential features of test theory and test construction as well as specifically in the development and uses of the MMPI-A. Therefore, the test user should have completed graduate-level courses in psychological testing and reviewed introductory or basic texts, such as the texts by Archer and Krishnamurthy (2002) and Butcher and Williams (2000). Those seeking greater familiarity with the development of the original MMPI or the MMPI-2, including the composition of the basic validity and clinical scales and the basic interpretive strategies, should refer to the general guides written by Friedman et al. (2001), Graham (1987, 2000), Greene (1980, 2000), and Nichols (2001). Reference works by Archer (1987b), Hathaway and Monachesi (1963), and Marks et al. (1974) concern the use of the original MMPI in the assessment of adolescents. Before administering the MMPI-A, the clinician should also thoroughly review the MMPI-A manual (Butcher et al., 1992), which provides a summary of the development, administration, scoring, and interpretation of this instrument.

In addition to an understanding of psychological assessment issues, individuals who use the MMPI/MMPI-A in the evaluation of adolescents should have training in adolescent development, personality, psychopathology, and psychodiagnosis.

Administration Personnel

Because the actual administration of the MMPI or MMPI-A appears deceptively simple, it is frequently entrusted to individuals operating under the supervision of a psychologist. If these individuals are carefully trained, closely supervised, and well informed concerning appropriate test procedures, their administration of the test should not negatively affect test validity. Unfortunately, there are many instances of invalid MMPI findings related to incorrect administration procedures used by untrained or unsupervised clerks or secretaries. Greene (2000) noted that although a clinician may delegate the task of MMPI administration to an assistant, a clinician

cannot delegate the responsibility for proper administration. This responsibility remains with the clinician utilizing and interpreting the test findings. Because testing
conditions, test instructions, and response to clients' questions about test materials
or purposes can all profoundly affect test results, the clinician must ensure that the
accepted standards for administration procedures are fully met.

Purposes of MMPI-A Administration

The MMPI-A is designed to assess psychopathology among adolescents aged 14
through 18 inclusive and may be selectively used with 12- and 13-year-old adolescents under certain circumstances, which are discussed later. As noted in the MMPI-A
manual (Butcher et al., 1992), 18-year-olds may be evaluated with this instrument if
they are living with their parents in a dependent environment but should be assessed
with the adult form of the revised MMPI (i.e., the MMPI-2) if living independently.
The MMPI-A is appropriate for evaluating adolescents who are experiencing, or may
be suspected of experiencing, some type of psychopathology. The MMPI-A has two
major functions in the assessment of adolescent psychopathology. First, the MMPI-
A provides the ability to objectively evaluate and describe an adolescent's level of
functioning in relation to selected standardized dimensions of psychopathology. A
clinician may examine MMPI-A test findings, for example, in order to assess the degree to which an adolescent's psychological functioning deviates from that typically
reported by normal adolescents. For such a purpose, the clinician compares the adolescent's test scores against those obtained from the MMPI-A normative sample. If
the adolescent exhibits clinical levels of psychopathology on the MMPI-A, the clinician may also consult the clinical literature on the MMPI and the MMPI-A to find the
most appropriate descriptors for that adolescent. These descriptors are established
based on research with adolescents who have produced similar MMPI-A patterns.
Second, the repeated administration of the MMPI-A can provide the clinician with
a means of assessing changes in psychopathology across time. The ability to assess
temporal changes is particularly important in dealing with adolescents because adolescence is defined by rapid changes in personality and psychopathology. When the
MMPI-A is administered at various stages in the treatment process, test results may
also provide the clinician with a sensitive index of therapeutic change. Because the
MMPI-A was developed as a means of describing psychopathology, it was not intended to serve as a primary measure for describing normal-range personality traits or
functioning.

ADMINISTRATION ISSUES

A number of administration guidelines or criteria may be offered for using the MMPI-
A with adolescents. Table 3.1 provides an overview of these criteria, with suggested
responses that may be utilized by the clinician in dealing with specific administration
issues and problems.

Age Criteria

General administration guidelines for the use of the original version of the MMPI
with adolescents were provided by Dahlstrom et al. (1972), Williams (1986), and
Archer (1987b, 1989). Guidelines for the administration of the MMPI-A have been

TABLE 3.1
Administration Guidelines for Adolescents Using the MMPI-A

Criteria	Possible Responses
1. Adolescent should be 14 to 18 years old.	A. Adolescents 12- to 13-years old may be evaluated with MMPI-A if they meet all other criteria. B. Above 18 administer MMPI-2. C. Under age 12 do not administer MMPI (any version).
2. Adolescent must be able to read and understand item pool.	A. Evaluate reading ability on standardized measure of reading comprehension. B. If below seventh-grade reading level, administer MMPI-A orally using audiotape. C. If IQ is below 70 or reading level below third grade, do not administer MMPI (any version).
3. Adolescent must have appropriate supervised environment to take MMPI-A.	A. Provide continuous supervision by trained personnel in appropriate setting. B. Do not attempt MMPI-A testing in nonsupervised environment.
4. Adolescent must be willing to tolerate testing with lengthy instrument.	A. Establish rapport with subject prior to testing. B. Discuss the importance of MMPI-A testing. C. Clearly explain to adolescents that they will receive test feedback. D. Consider administering only standard scale items, but do not administer "short forms." E. Consider dividing testing into two or more sessions.

provided more recently by Archer and Krishnamurthy (2002) and by Butcher and Williams (2000). The test manual observes that the MMPI-A can be administered to "bright immature adolescents" as young as age 12, and Archer and Krishnamurthy (2002) recommended that younger subjects (i.e., those aged 12 and 13) be carefully evaluated before MMPI-A administration is undertaken. In recognition of the difficulty that many 12- and 13-year-olds encounter in attempting to respond to the MMPI-A, the MMPI-A normative sample was restricted to 14- through 18-year-olds. If a 12- or 13-year-old meets all administration criteria, however, including adequate reading ability and cognitive and social maturity, it is possible to administer the MMPI-A to him or her. A set of MMPI-A adolescent norms for 13-year-old boys and girls, based on linear T-score conversions and using the same exclusion criteria employed for the 14- through 18-year-old MMPI norms (e.g., original F scale raw score >25), was included in the prior editions of this text (Archer, 1992a, 1997b).

A study by Janus, de Grott, and Toepfer (1998) examined two questions concerning the use of the MMPI-A with 13-year-old inpatients. These questions involved the extent to which the profiles of 13-year-old inpatients differed substantively from those produced by 14-year-olds and the effects of scoring 13-year-olds using the standard MMPI-A norms versus the MMPI-A norms for 13-year-olds reported by Archer (1992a, 1997b). Janus and his colleagues analyzed the protocols from fifty-six 13-year-old and eighty-five 14-year-old psychiatric inpatients. They reported no significant differences for age in mean T-scores and no clear pattern of differences in the percentage of elevated profiles. A strong multivariate effect was found, however, for the use of the Archer (1992a, 1997b) MMPI-A norms, which resulted in lower T-score values than the use of the standard MMPI-A adolescent norms. However, pervasive univariate differences based on the use of 13-year-old versus standard adolescent norms were not found, and statistically significant differences occurred for only 2 of 38 scales for boys and 7 of 38 scales for girls. In general, the results of this study suggest that 13- and 14-year-old adolescents respond in similar ways and that the use of a separate set of 13-year-old norms may not result in any tangible improvements in MMPI-A interpretation for this age group.

It is cautioned, however, that 13-year-old adolescents typically represent an age group difficult to evaluate with the MMPI-A. All criteria for administration must be carefully assessed to determine if these younger adolescents are capable of producing valid responses. Younger adolescents may not have a wide enough range of life experiences, including exposure to cultural and educational opportunities commonly encountered in U.S. society, to render the item content psychologically and semantically meaningful. Limitations in developmental opportunities as well as reading ability clearly contraindicate the administration of the MMPI or MMPI-A to younger adolescents.

At the other end of the adolescent age range, the MMPI-2 and MMPI-A normative samples overlap at age 18, and it is possible that an 18-year-old respondent could be evaluated with either instrument. The MMPI-A manual contains the following recommendation concerning the evaluation of 18-year-olds:

> The clinicians should make a case-by-case judgment about whether to use the MMPI-A or the MMPI-2 with 18-year-olds because the normative and clinical samples for both tests include 18-year-olds. A suggested guideline would be to use the MMPI-A for those 18-year-olds who are in high school and the MMPI-2 for those who are in college, working, or otherwise living an independent adult lifestyle. (Butcher et al., 1992, p. 23)

However, in the application of this guideline, it is possible to encounter an adolescent for whom selection of the most appropriate form would be difficult. For example, an 18-year-old single mother with a 6-month-old infant who is in her senior year in high school but living at home with her parents presents a considerable challenge in terms of identifying the most appropriate MMPI version for use with this individual. In such difficult cases, an important question arises concerning what effects, if any, the selection of the MMPI-A versus the MMPI-2 might have on the resulting profile in terms of T-score elevation and configuration. Shaevel and Archer (1996) examined the effects of scoring 18-year-old respondents on the MMPI-2 and MMPI-A and found that substantial differences can occur in T-score elevations as a function of this decision. Specifically, these authors reported that 18-year-olds scored on MMPI-2 norms generally produced lower validity scale values and higher clinical scale values than the same adolescents scored on MMPI-A norms. These differences ranged as high as 15 T-score points and resulted in different single-scale and two-point profile configurations in 34% of the cases examined. Shaevel and Archer concluded that for those relatively rare assessment cases in which selection of the proper instrument is difficult, a reasonable practice would be to score the individual on both MMPI-A and MMPI-2 norms in order to permit the clinician to assess the relative effects of instrument selection on profile characteristics.

Two other studies have examined the effects of scoring 18-year-olds on MMPI-A versus MMPI-2 norms. Gumbiner (1997) compared the MMPI-2 versus MMPI-A profiles of a group of 18-year-old male and female college students. In general, the resulting MMPI profiles were often dissimilar in terms of codetype classifications, with a marked tendency for MMPI-2 profiles to produce greater T-score elevations. Osberg and Poland (2002) also administered both the MMPI-2 and the MMPI-A to 18-year-old male and female college students. In addition, they used the Global Severity Index (GSI) of the SCL-90-R to classify participants as either psychopathology present or psychopathology absent to permit an assessment of the usefulness of MMPI-A and MMPI-2 scores in detecting the presence of psycopathology. Consistent with prior findings, the MMPI-A and MMPI-2 produced profiles in this study that were often inconsistent in terms of clinical elevation status (46% of respondents produced incongruent findings). All of the 70 participants in this study who produced incongruent MMPI-2 versus MMPI-A profiles had the same overall pattern: clinically elevated MMPI-2 T-scores and normal range MMPI-A T-scores. Further, analysis of incongruent profiles in comparison with subject classification as psychopathology present or absent based on SCL-90-R scores indicated that 18-year-olds were overpathologized by the MMPI-2 scores and underpathologized by the MMPI-A scores.

Reading Requirements

Reading level is obviously a crucial factor in determining whether an adolescent can complete the MMPI-A. Inadequate reading ability may serve as one of the major causes of invalid test protocols for adolescents. Ball and Carroll (1960) found that adolescents with lower IQs and below-average academic records tended to produce higher Cannot Say scores, suggesting that the failure to respond to MMPI items often reflects problems in item comprehension. An inverse relationship ($r = -.10$, $p < .05$) between reading grade level and raw score values on the Cannot Say scale was also found by Archer and Gordon (1991a). This study examined a sample of 495 normal adolescents who received the MMPI-A and the Ohio Literacy Test, a measure of reading comprehension. Thus, adolescents who have difficulty reading MMPI or MMPI-A items tend to omit items at a higher frequency than other adolescents. Unfortunately, many adolescents also attempt to respond to items that they cannot adequately read or comprehend, often resulting in invalid test protocols.

For many years, a sixth-grade reading level was generally accepted as a requirement for MMPI evaluation. Johnson and Bond (1950), for example, assessed the readability of MMPI items using the Flesch Reading Ease Formula (Flesch, 1948) and derived an overall estimate of sixth-grade reading difficulty for a sample of MMPI items. The sixth-grade reading level estimate was used in most standard texts on the MMPI. Ward and Ward (1980), however, reevaluated the MMPI items using the Flesch readability measure and reported that MMPI items on the basic scales have an average reading difficulty level of grade 6.7. Individual scale readability levels range from grade 6.4 (the *Mf* scale) to grade 7.2 (the *K* scale). Their findings resulted in the recommendation that individuals taking the MMPI have a seventh-grade reading level. Further increasing reading ability requirements, Butcher et al. (1989) recommended that clients have at least an eighth-grade reading level in order to ensure adequate comprehension of the MMPI-2 item pool. This recommendation was based on the analysis of MMPI-2 items using item difficulty ratings referred to as *Lexile ratings* in the MMPI-2 manual. Paolo, Ryan, and Smith (1991) also examined the Lexile values for the 567 items of the MMPI-2 and for each of the scales and subscales associated with this measure. Paolo and his colleagues reported that approximately 90% of MMPI-2 items require less than a ninth-grade reading level and that the mean for all items corresponded roughly to the fifth-grade reading level. In addition, the authors identified a number of scales or subscales in which at least 25% of the total number of scale items required more than an eighth-grade reading level. When the MMPI-2 item pool is evaluated using other standardized measures of reading difficulty such as the Flesch Reading Ease Formula (Flesch, 1948), however, there are some indications that the Lexile ratings may have produced an overestimate of reading requirements. In the highest estimate of reading difficulty, Blanchard (1981) reported that 9 years of education was necessary to meet the criterion of accurate comprehension of 90% of the MMPI items. As noted by Greene (2000), this reading level appears particularly restrictive in that most freshman-level college textbooks are written at a ninth-grade reading level.

Part of the difficulty of evaluating the reading requirements of the MMPI involves the differences in standardized methods of estimating the reading difficulty of individual items. Additionally, lack of agreement on the number or percentage of items that must be successfully read and comprehended before an individual is deemed suitable to take the inventory has added to the variation in estimates. Unfortunately, reading ability is frequently discussed in a dichotomous manner; that is, the subject either does or does not have the reading ability to take the MMPI. Many subjects, however, can successfully comprehend some but not all of the MMPI or MMPI-A items. The central question concerns the number of items that must be successfully read in order to ensure the overall validity of the test findings.

The MMPI-A manual (Butcher et al., 1992) provides an analysis of the reading difficulty for each of the MMPI-A items using several standard methods of measuring reading difficulty. The methods include the Flesch-Kincaid method, which has been used in previous studies of the MMPI and other assessment instruments. Based on the Flesch-Kincaid method, the MMPI-A item pool varies in reading difficulty from the 1st-grade to the 16th-grade level. Employing a criterion that at least 80% of the MMPI-A item pool should be accurately read and comprehended in order to ensure valid test findings, a seventh-grade reading level would be required for the MMPI-A, based on the Flesch-Kincaid reading comprehension standard. This seventh-grade reading level serves as the current recommendation for adolescents evaluated with the MMPI-A.

Dahlstrom, Archer, Hopkins, Jackson, and Dahlstrom (1994) evaluated the reading difficulty of the MMPI, MMPI-2, and MMPI-A using various indices of reading difficulty, including the Flesch Reading Ease index and the Lexile index. One important finding derived from this study was that the instructions provided in the MMPI test booklets tended to be somewhat more difficult to read than the typical item contained within the inventories. Therefore, clinicians should ensure that the instructions are fully understood by respondents, and it is often appropriate to ask the test taker to read the instructions aloud and explain their meaning in order to ensure adequate comprehension. The average difficulty level for all three forms of the MMPI was approximately the sixth-grade level. The MMPI-A test instructions and items were slightly easier to read than the MMPI-2 or the original version of the MMPI; however, the total differences tended to be relatively small. If the most difficult 10% of items were excluded, the remaining 90% of items on all three versions of the MMPI had an average difficulty level of grade 5. On average, the most difficult items appeared on scale 9, whereas the easiest items tended to be within the item pool of scale 5. The authors also reported, based on the Flesch Reading Ease index, that approximately 6% of the MMPI-A items required a 10th-grade reading level or better. Dahlstrom et al. noted that the number of years of education completed by a subject is often an unreliable index of the individual's reading competence.

Adolescents' reading abilities may be evaluated by the use of any of a number of reading comprehension instruments, including the Gray Oral Reading Tests (GORT;

Gray & Robinson, 1963; GORT-R; Wiederholt & Bryant, 1986), the Peabody Individual Achievement Test–Revised (PIAT-R; Markwardt, 1989), and the reading component of the Wide Range Achievement Test–Third Edition (WRAT-III; Wilkinson, 1993). Results of analyses by Dahlstrom et al. (1994) indicated that both the GORT and the Wechsler Individual Achievement Test (WIAT; Wechsler, 1992) showed a relatively smooth progression of scores in relation to student grade levels, and both measures were recommended if a reading test is to be employed for evaluating an individual's competence to deal with the item difficulty of any version of the MMPI. A reasonably accurate reading screen can be devised, however, by requesting the adolescent to read aloud and explain several MMPI-A items. The items that appear to be the most useful markers in this regard are items that have an eighth-grade reading level rating. Among the initial abbreviated MMPI-A test statements, eighth-grade level items include the following:

   5. Easily awakened by noise.
  17. Often nauseated.
  18. Seldom constipated.
  25. Upset stomach.
  29. Unusual experiences.

An adolescent may have difficulty in responding to the MMPI-A because of specific reading ability deficits, in contrast to limitations in overall intellectual cognitive functioning. Under these circumstances, administration may still be undertaken using the standardized audiotape versions of this instrument available through Pearson Assessments. Generally, procedures in which an examiner reads test items to the adolescent are not recommended because of the degree of intrusion into the response process associated with this method. Research by Newmark (1971), for example, indicated that MMPI profiles produced by adolescents for whom items were read aloud by an examiner had higher *K* scale scores than profiles obtained with traditional administration methods. In contrast, Brauer (1992) showed that there is no significant effect found for the signer when selected MMPI items were translated into American Sign Language and recorded on videotape for use with hearing-impaired or deaf individuals. If an adolescent scores below 70 on the standardized IQ assessment measure or has less than a fourth-grade reading level, administration of the MMPI-A should not be attempted through any format.

When questions are asked by adolescents concerning the specific meaning of an MMPI-A statement or word, the examiner should attempt to provide useful but neutral information. For example, dictionary definitions can be given for commonly misunderstood words (e.g., *constipation, nausea,* or *diarrhea*). However, the frequency with which adolescents encounter unfamiliar or awkwardly worded items should be reduced on the MMPI-A, in comparison with the original test instrument, because 69 of the original items have been reworded or modified in order to improve the readability of the MMPI-A and/or its relevance to contemporary adolescents' life experiences. Research by Archer and Gordon (1994) and Williams, Ben-Porath, and Hevern (1994) indicated that these revised items may be considered to be psychometrically equivalent to the original items in terms of response characteristics. When questions are raised by the adolescent concerning items that he or she clearly understands and comprehends, however, the examiner must always be careful to remind the adolescent to respond to the item as it applies to him or her and to base the answer on his or her own judgments and opinions.

Despite reasonable efforts to evaluate reading ability, the clinician is likely to encounter adolescents who have responded to the MMPI-A item pool without reading and/or understanding many items. Nonreading or noncomprehension may occur because of reading deficits, motivational issues, or a combination of these factors. A simple method of checking for most types of random response patterns involves recording the total MMPI-A administration time. Total administration time provides one useful index for aiding in the identification of random response sets among adolescents, particularly when the administration time is unusually brief (e.g., less than 40 minutes for the full-length MMPI-A). Unless the test administration time is recorded, however, this valuable information source is lost. Other methods of detecting potential problems in reading ability based on MMPI-A scales, including *TRIN* and *VRIN*, are discussed in chapter 4.

MMPI-A Translations

The original version of the MMPI was translated into a wide range of foreign languages and there was an impressive amount of research on the cross-cultural applications of this test instrument. The MMPI-2 is currently available in a wide array of languages, including Croatian, Czech, Dutch/Flemish, French, French-Canadian, German, Hebrew, Hmong, and Italian, and three Spanish language translations exist for use in the United States. Several other foreign language translations are currently underway, into Japanese, Korean, Chinese, Thai, Vietnamese, Chilean Spanish, Norwegian, Icelandic, Russian, Greek, Arabic, and Farsi (Butcher, 1996). The MMPI-A is following in the same tradition, and there is currently a Spanish version available for use in the United States, a Spanish version for use in Mexico, and Dutch/Flemish, French, and Italian translations. Cheung and Ho (1997) recently evaluated a Chinese language version of the MMPI-A in a sample of 565 boys and 664 girls aged 14–18 in Hong Kong schools settings. The authors concluded that moderate elevations shown on several scales using T-scores based on the U.S. adolescent norms indicate possible cultural differences in the reporting of psychopathology on the MMPI-A. In addition, several other MMPI-A translation projects are currently in progress.

Supervision Requirements

It is important that the adolescent be provided with an appropriate testing environment in which to complete the MMPI-A. This environment should include adequate privacy and supervision. The testing environment should be as comfortable as possible, with a minimum of extraneous noise or other distractions. It is inappropriate to allow an adolescent to complete the MMPI-A in any unsupervised setting or in a setting in which privacy cannot be assured, such as at home or in a clinic waiting room. Unsupervised test administration does not provide adequate data for valid test interpretation and is subject to successful legal challenge if the findings are presented in a courtroom. Adequate test supervision means that a proctor or examiner is available to continuously monitor the test-taking process and to provide appropriate assistance when necessary. Adequate proctoring does not require, however, that the proctor monitor each individual response by the subject or otherwise become overly intrusive.

Increasing Adolescents' Cooperation With Testing Procedures

A final criterion in the evaluation of adolescents involves their willingness to answer the lengthy item pool of the MMPI-A. For the angry and oppositional adolescent, the MMPI-A may present a welcome opportunity to exhibit hostility and resistance by refusing to respond to items or by responding in an inappropriate or random manner (Newmark & Thibodeau, 1979). Once the adolescent has entered into an "anal-retentive" struggle with the examiner over test completion, there is often little the examiner can do that will effectively decrease the conflict. Prior to the administration of the MMPI-A, however, several steps may be taken to increase the motivation of most adolescents. These include (a) establishing adequate rapport with the adolescent prior to testing, (b) providing clear and concise instructions concerning the purposes of testing, and (c) providing the adolescent with an opportunity to receive testing feedback.

Clear and concise instructions should be given to the adolescent so that he or she has a general understanding of the purposes of the MMPI-A administration. When clear instructions are not provided, many adolescents will project their own meaning onto the testing in a manner that may serve to render test results invalid. For example, an adolescent may erroneously believe that the test results will be used by the therapist to determine whether a psychiatric hospitalization is indicated or to mete out blame or punishment for family conflict or family dysfunction. Poorly worded instructions may also negatively influence a subject's test-taking attitude and cooperation with testing procedures. The instructions, therefore, should be carefully presented in the standardized manner. The adolescent should read the instructions provided in the MMPI-A test booklet and also receive a verbal summary, which might, for example, include the following: "Read each statement and decide whether it is true as applied to you or false as applied to you. Remember to give your own opinion of yourself. There are no right or wrong answers. Your test results will help us to understand you."

In addition to these introductory instructions, adolescents frequently ask questions concerning various aspects of testing, which often reflects their anxiety concerning the evaluation process. The following are frequently encountered questions, with suggested responses, as adapted from the Caldwell Report (Caldwell, 1977a) and from Friedman et al. (2001).

1. Q. How long will this take?
   A. About an hour to an hour and a half, usually. Some teenagers take longer, whereas other teenagers finish in less time.
2. Q. Will it make any difference if I skip some questions and come back to them?
   A. If you do it carefully, skipping some questions and returning to them probably will not make any difference. But it is easy to get mixed up in marking your answers, and that will make a difference, so it is better to do them in order, if possible.
3. Q. Suppose I cannot answer all the questions?
   A. Try to answer all of them. If you omit a few items, it will not matter, but try to do them all. When you are finished, take a few minutes to check your answer sheet for any missing answers, incomplete erasures, or double-answered questions.

4. Q. What is the MMPI-A?
   A. MMPI-A is short for the Minnesota Multiphasic Personality Inventory–Adolescent. It is a widely used test to help understand the kinds of problems that happen to teenagers.
5. Q. How do I try to answer these questions?
   A. Answer the questions as you currently feel. Work quickly, and do not spend time worrying over your answers.
6. Q. What if I don't agree with the results from the test or the test results are wrong?
   A. That is something that you and I will get a chance to discuss during the feedback process. Teenagers often learn some things about themselves that they did not know, and the therapist often learns which parts of the testing were more accurate than others. It is hoped we will *both* learn something from the feedback process.

It is important to present the MMPI-A to adolescents in a careful and serious manner that underscores the importance of the testing process. Attempts to assist the adolescent in feeling more comfortable by minimizing the importance of the MMPI-A evaluation are usually counterproductive. A "casual" presentation of the MMPI-A may actually result in a reduction in the adolescent's cooperation and motivation to complete testing because his or her doubts about the importance of the test findings will appear to have been validated.

Providing Test Result Feedback

In addition to establishing rapport with the adolescent prior to testing and providing clear and concise test instructions, it is very helpful to inform the adolescent that he or she will receive feedback on the test results. If an adolescent does not have the opportunity to learn from the testing experience, there is often little inherent motivation to cooperate with the demanding testing procedures. Finn and Tonsager (1992) reported data indicating that the provision of MMPI-2 feedback to college students awaiting psychotherapy was associated with a significant decline in subjects' psychological distress and a significant increase in their levels of self-esteem. The MMPI or MMPI-2 test feedback process is discussed in detail in three texts: *MMPI-2 in Psychological Treatment* (Butcher, 1990), *Therapist Guide to the MMPI and MMPI-2: Providing Feedback and Treatment* (Lewak, Marks, & Nelson, 1990), and *Manual for Using the MMPI-2 as a Therapeutic Intervention* (Finn, 1996). In addition, a computer software package was developed by Marks and Lewak (1991) to assist clinicians in providing meaningful MMPI test feedback to adolescent clients and was revised to include feedback for the MMPI-A. The interpretive information provided in this report includes statements designed to be provided directly to clients.

Archer and Krishnamurthy (2002) emphasized a method of providing feedback to the adolescent that enhances the adolescent's curiosity about the testing process and increases the personal relevance of the test findings. Adapting the general guidance given by Finn (1996), these authors recommend actively engaging the adolescent in constructing questions that can be answered from test findings prior to the administration of the MMPI. The ultimate goal is to encourage the adolescent to produce a manageable number of practical issues or questions that can be systematically addressed in test feedback. Archer and Krishnamurthy presented the following example of a typical discussion that might ensue in this collaborative process (pp. 24–25):

Examiner: I understand that you are not sure about how this testing may be useful to you. Often, this type of testing helps teenagers to learn things about themselves that they hadn't been fully aware of, or actively thought about.

Adolescent: What kinds of things?

Examiner: For example, most people don't really think about how they come across to other people, or whether their ways of thinking and feeling are very different from those of others. The MMPI-A can shed light on these issues. Does that make sense to you?

Adolescent: I guess.

Examiner: The testing could also help you to better understand things that adolescents might already suspect about themselves. For example, a teenager might be aware that she often feels unhappy or grouchy but not have a clear idea about what's going on. The MMPI-A results may help her to realize that she is depressed, which may include being very sensitive to other's reactions, having negative thoughts about herself, and feeling that no one really understands her. Does this give you an idea of how this works?

Adolescent: Yes.

Examiner: Okay. Now all of this can be best done if you take a few moments to think about some questions you have about yourself that you would like answered by the testing.

Adolescent: Uh . . . about feeling depressed?

Examiner: The type of question varies from person to person and is up to you. What are some things that you have wondered about regarding yourself?

Adolescent: I don't know. . . . Sometimes I feel that everyone in my class, and all my friends, are so sure of themselves and know what they want better than I do.

Examiner: That is a good place to start. It sounds like you feel uncertain about yourself and your goals and don't feel like you have as much confidence as other teenagers. Is that correct?

Adolescent: Yes. Seems like I'm the only one who doesn't have a clue.

Examiner: The question for testing, then, can be, "Am I low in self-confidence and self-esteem compared to other teenagers?" How does that sound?

Adolescent: That sounds right.

Examiner: Good. The MMPI-A can certainly give us an answer to this question and help us see what kinds of things contribute to this feeling. Let's make a note of that question and then try another one.

Adolescent: Well, I also get mad at people who show off or are in my face. My parents make me mad too. I can really pitch a fit and it comes out of nowhere. I guess I wonder why I blow up so easily.

Examiner: That is an excellent issue for which we should get useful information from the MMPI-A. It sounds like there are two related questions here, one being, "Do I get angry more quickly than other people?" and the other one being, "Why do I get easily angered?"

Adolescent: That's exactly it.

Archer and Krishnamurthy noted that this collaborative process involves the adolescent identifying issues of concern and the examiner helping to restate and clarify these issues. This preadministration dialogue should be conducted in an unhurried pace until a satisfactory list of queries has been produced. Archer and Krishnamurthy also noted that modified versions of this procedure may be used. For example, the adolescent's legal guardians might be included in the process, or, alternatively, another referring professional who is involved in the adolescent's care might act as the adult party in the collaborative process.

Butcher (1990) provided general guidelines for MMPI-2 feedback that are also applicable to the MMPI-A. For example, Butcher recommends that the therapist explain the test to the client, including giving a brief description of the meaning of the scales and T-scores, and that the therapist then review the client's scores in relation to test norms. Furthermore, responses are encouraged from the client during the feedback process in order to make it an interactive experience. Butcher also underscored the therapist's need to appraise the degree of acceptance of test feedback by asking the client to summarize his or her understanding of and reaction to major findings. Butcher cautioned that the therapist should present feedback as "provisional" information and should gauge how much feedback the client can realistically absorb or incorporate without becoming overwhelmed or excessively defensive.

The feedback approach favored by Lewak et al. (1990) and Marks and Lewak (1991) is described as an empirical-phenomenological approach based on the theoretical formulations of Alex Caldwell. Caldwell (1976, 1977b, 2001) postulated that MMPI scales measure dimensions of psychopathology that are related to fear-conditioned defensive responses. These defensive responses are acquired as a result of the interaction between individuals' predispositions and the occurrence of certain environmental stresses during their development. Table 3.2 lists each of the eight clinical scales for which Caldwell described an associated fear-conditioned defensive response.

TABLE 3.2
MMPI-2 Scales and Associated Fear-Conditioned Defensive Responses Postulated by Alex Caldwell

Scale	Fear	Response
1	Death, physical attack, illness, or pain	Maintaining physical integrity by overprotecting the body
2	Significant and irretrievable loss	Blocking of wanting or needing in order to avoid further loss
3	Emotional pain	Positivizing unpleasant experiences by selectively blocking inputs (e.g., blindness, numbness)
4	Rejection, being unwanted or abandoned	"Numbing out" emotional responding, not allowing oneself to get emotionally involved to avoid letdown
6	Being criticized, devalued, or humiliated	Maintaining constant vigilance against attack
7	Shock, unexpected and unpleasant events	Thinking ahead and worrying to anticipate onset of shock
8	Hostility, being disliked or despised by those on whom one depends	"Shutting down" cognitive processing to avoid unbearable reality
9	Deprivation or failure	Increasing activity level in an attempt to maintain reward schedule

Note. Adapted from Friedman et al. (2001). Copyright © 2001 by Lawrence Erlbaum Associates, Inc. Reprinted by permission.

The Caldwell model provides a basis for offering nonthreatening feedback to adolescent and adult clients. Much of the traditional descriptive literature regarding MMPI interpretation, however, contains psychological terms that may be viewed by clients as negative, pejorative, critical, or irrelevant. The Lewak et al. (1990) approach to providing feedback attempts to move beyond this problem. Their feedback strategy focuses on the client's phenomenological experience of the stressors that initially induced maladaptive response patterns rather than providing an objective clinical description of the defenses themselves. For example, Lewak et al. noted that high T-score values for MMPI scale 1 are typically related to descriptions that emphasize personality characteristics such as immaturity, dependency, psychological naiveté, and excessive preoccupation with somatic concerns. From the client's perspective, however, high scale 1 elevations may represent a reasonable response to the perception that his or her physical health is fragile and that their physical integrity may be threatened by pain, illness, or even death. Therefore, feedback statements for marked elevations on scale 1 include the following:

> Your body is a constant source of anxiety and fear for you, so right now your worries about health take up most of your time and energy. This constant fear and worry about your physical health may be taking its toll and leaving you feeling extremely defeated, pessimistic, and bitter. You may even find yourself resigned to living the rest of your life chronically ill and in pain. You probably have to rely on others to help you in your daily living; this is usually very frustrating for you. (Lewak et al., 1990, pp. 55–56)

Test Administration Procedures to Increase Cooperation

Several additional steps may be taken in order to increase adolescents' willingness to cooperate with testing procedures. For example, it is often preferable to divide the administration of the MMPI-A between several sessions in cases where the total test administration can be spread over a few days. If the administration is attempted in one session, it is advisable to provide a rest period whenever the adolescent becomes fatigued. Placement of the MMPI-A at the earlier stages of an extensive test battery decreases the probability that an adolescent will employ a random response set in order to finish the testing session as quickly as possible. Finally, a clinician may elect to administer only the first 350 items of the MMPI-A as an abbreviated administration of the test. This administration format utilizes only those items necessary to score the standard validity and clinical scales. If the motivation or cooperation of the adolescent would be increased significantly by using an abbreviated administration format, or if time restrictions necessitate this format, this option allows the clinician to fully score and interpret the standard clinical scales and the Harris-Lingoes and *Si* subscales. Abbreviated administration of the MMPI-A does not, however, provide information concerning the content scales, several of the supplementary scales, or validity scales *VRIN*, *TRIN*, F_1, and F_2.

Short Form Issues

Ball, Archer, and Imhof (1994) reported findings from a national survey of practitioners related to the time requirements associated with the administration, scoring, and interpretation of 24 commonly used psychological test instruments. Findings derived for the MMPI indicated a mean administration time of 66.16 minutes and a modal value of 90 minutes. This modal time estimate was exceeded only by the time require-ments associated with administration of the Halstead-Reitan neuropsychological test battery. In response to the problems created by the lengthy MMPI item pool, Newmark and Thibodeau (1979) recommended the development and use of short forms of the MMPI in the assessment of adolescents. As defined by Butcher and Hostetler (1990), the term *short form* is "used to describe sets of scales that have been decreased in length from the standard MMPI form. An MMPI short form is a group of items that is thought to be a valid substitute for the full scale score even though it might contain only 4 or 5 items from the original full scale" (p. 12).

The MMPI-168 was developed by utilizing the first 168 items to appear in the group booklet form of the MMPI (Overall & Gomez-Mont, 1974). The 71-item Mini-Mult was devised by Kincannon (1968) based on factor analyses used to identify item cluster groups. Investigations of MMPI-168 characteristics in adolescent samples were done by MacBeth and Cadow (1984) and Rathus (1978). In addition, Mlott (1973) reported Mini-Mult findings for adolescent inpatients. Vondell and Cyr (1991) evaluated the influence of gender on eight MMPI short forms, including the Mini-Mult and the MMPI-168, in a sample of 318 male and 248 female adolescent psychiatric inpatients. The authors concluded that gender differences occur on all of these short forms in adolescent populations, a result that parallels similar findings obtained in short form investigations of adult samples.

Butcher (1985) and Butcher and Hostetler (1990) noted a series of potential prob-lems with the use of MMPI short forms: The smaller number of items in MMPI scales in short form versions reduces the overall reliability of the measurement of scale constructs. The shortened versions of the MMPI have also not been sufficiently vali-dated against external criteria. Additionally, the short form profiles and codetypes are frequently different from the results that would have been achieved from the admin-istration of the full MMPI item pool. Research by Hoffmann and Butcher (1975), for example, showed that the Mini-Mult and the standard MMPI tend to produce the same MMPI codetypes in only 33% of cases and that the standard MMPI and the MMPI-168 produce the same codetypes in only 40% of adult cases. Consistent with these find-ings, Lueger (1983) reported that 2-point codetypes derived from the standard MMPI and the MMPI-168 were different in over 50% of a sample of male adolescents. Greene (1982) suggested that short forms of the MMPI may constitute new test mea-sures that require additional validation to identify external correlates. In addition to issues related to scale reliability and codetype congruence, Butcher and Hostetler (1990) questioned the ability of the MMPI short forms to accurately determine profile validity.

The problems with MMPI short forms identified in studies with adult popula-tions appear to have important implications for clinical and/or research uses of the MMPI-A. In particular, there is a significant loss of valuable clinical information when short forms are used in place of the full MMPI. The use of a short form procedure, although it saves administration time, appears likely to introduce more than an ac-ceptable range of confusion and "noise" into the interpretation process for adolescent profiles. In recognition of these problems, no efforts were made by the MMPI-2 or MMPI-A advisory committees to preserve any of the currently existing MMPI short forms. Consequently, as noted by Butcher and Hostetler (1990), "Some of the items constituting previously developed MMPI short forms may have been deleted from the MMPI in the revision process" (p. 18).

Archer, Tirrell, and Elkins (2001) recently reported psychometric properties related to a short form of the MMPI-A based on the administration of the first 150 items of this test instrument. Results were based on analysis of the MMPI-A normative sample of 1,620 adolescents as well as a clinical sample of 565 adolescents in a variety of treatment settings. Correlational analysis showed short-form to full administration basic scale score correlations in the range of .71 for the *Mf* scale to a high of .95 for the *L* scale when computed for all the MMPI-A basic validity and clinical scales. In addition to the correlational analyses, these authors also examined the degree of difference found in mean T-score values produced for the MMPI-A basic scales by the full administration of the test instrument and when T-score values were prorated from MMPI-A short form results. Although comparisons for several of the basic validity and clinical scales reached significance, at least partially because a relatively large sample size was utilized in these analyses, the mean T-score differences between the actual and prorated values exceeded 2 T-score points only for scales 4 and 9 in the clinical sample. Further, these analyses showed relatively high scale correlations and mean profile similarities but relatively lower rates of congruence in profile configural patterns. Specifically, only 30.6% of the normative sample and 32.2% of the clinical sample produced basic scale profiles that were congruent (i.e., identical 2-point elevations produced by short form and full-length administrations). The potential advantages of the MMPI-A 150 included a reduction of the total item pool of nearly 70% and a reduction in the typical administration time from 60 to 20 minutes. This item and time savings, however, appeared to be largely offset by the limitations in profile congruency illustrated in this study and in all prior research findings related to MMPI short forms.

The use of MMPI-A short forms, in contrast to an abbreviated administration, is not recommended in the assessment of adolescents. As previously noted, however, the abbreviated form of the MMPI may serve as a reasonable resource in coping with poorly motivated or resistant adolescents. Additionally, several approaches to abbreviating the administration of the MMPI-2 item pool by adapting MMPI-2 items to computer administration are currently being developed and evaluated (e.g., Ben-Porath, Slutske, & Butcher, 1989; Roper, Ben-Porath, & Butcher, 1991, 1995). Computer-adapted administration approaches present only those items that would add clinically relevant information about the client given the client's prior MMPI-2 responses. Several approaches have been developed for this purpose, including one based on item response theory (IRT) and another on the *countdown method*, the latter approach terminating item administration for a given scale once sufficient information for that scale has been obtained from the respondent. Butcher and Hostetler (1990) noted that although none of these approaches are currently practical, it is likely that effective, adaptive programs will eventually be developed for automated administration of the MMPI-2 and MMPI-A. In this regard, Forbey, Handel, and Ben-Porath (2000) recently evaluated a real data simulation of a computerized adaptive administration of the MMPI-A conducted using the item responses from three groups of participants. The first group included 196 adolescents (aged 14 through 18) tested at a midwestern residential treatment facility for adolescents, the second group consisted of the MMPI-A normative sample, and the third group was the clinical sample reported in the MMPI-A test manual (Butcher et al., 1992). The MMPI-A data for each group were run through a modified version of the MMPI-2 adaptive testing computer program to determine the amount of item savings produced by simulations based on three different orderings of MMPI-A items. These orderings included the presentation of items from least to most frequently endorsed in the critical or key direction, the presentation of items from least to most frequently endorsed in the critical or key direction with the qualification that the first 120 items are arranged in their usual booklet order, and the presentation of all items as presented in the test book-let. The mean number of items administered for each group was computed for each administration using T-score cutoffs of 60 and 65 to define clinical range elevations. Substantial item administration savings were achieved for the groups, and the mean number of items saved ranged from 50 items to 123 items (in contrast to the 478-item total item pool), depending on the T-score cutoff classification method. This study shows that the development of a computerized adaptive administration format for the MMPI-A holds the promise of reduced administration time.

TEST MATERIALS

Original MMPI Forms

Several forms of the original MMPI were developed, including the MMPI Group Form, which was a reusable group booklet, and MMPI Form R, which was a hardcover, spiral-bound test booklet. Of these two, the Group Form was more widely used. Furthermore, as Greene (1980) noted, most of the MMPI research literature has been based on data derived from the Group Form. The Form R booklet is particularly useful, however, when a subject does not have a hard surface on which to enter responses to the test items. The Form R answer sheet is inserted over two pegs in the back of the test booklet. Form R pages are arranged in a step-down format such that the turning of each consecutive page reveals another column of answer spaces matched with the booklet column of the corresponding questions. The step-down format allows only one column of questions and answers to be shown at a time, thereby reducing the possibility of misplacing a response to a specific question.

The numbering system for items in the Group Form booklet and Form R booklet of the original MMPI were identical for the first 366 items but diverged for the latter parts of the item pool. This discrepancy created substantial confusion for both researchers and clinicians. Dahlstrom et al. (1972), however, provided tables for converting be-tween the Group Form and Form R. An abbreviated administration of the first 399 items on Form R permitted the scoring of all basic standard and validity scales. Un-fortunately, there was not a straightforward method of performing an abbreviated administration of the Group Form booklet.

On September 1, 1999, the University of Minnesota Press and the test distributor (Pearson Assessments) discontinued publication of the original version of the MMPI. This version was discontinued because the material surrounding its use had become considerably dated and the MMPI-2 and MMPI-A had largely replaced it in clinical and research uses. The University of Minnesota Press also noted that the concurrent use of the original version and the revised versions had become a source of poten-tial confusion for many test users, particularly those in forensic settings. Further, the MMPI-2 and MMPI-A had the benefit of containing a more appropriate and con-temporary item pool as well as more contemporary and nationally representative normative samples.

MMPI-A Test Materials

Testing materials related to the use of the MMPI-A (and the MMPI-2) are available from Pearson Assessments. Fortunately, the order of the 478 items in the softcover, hardcover, and audiocassette versions of the MMPI-A is identical, and the items are arranged in such a way that the standard validity and clinical scales may be scored based on the administration of the first 350 items. It should again be noted, however, that the content scales and several of the supplementary scales of the MMPI-A cannot be scored when an abbreviated administration is utilized, resulting in the loss of valuable information. The audiocassette version of the MMPI-A is useful for the visually impaired as well as for adolescents with sufficient reading-related disabilities to make standard form administration impractical. Administration of the audiocassette version requires approximately 1 hour and 40 minutes (Archer & Krishnamurthy, 2002). Software for computerized administration of MMPI-A items can also be purchased from Pearson Assessments.

Different answer sheets are available for the MMPI-A, depending on whether the examiner intends to score the test using hand-scoring keys or by computer. Therefore, the examiner should consider the scoring mechanism that will be utilized before selecting the answer sheet. It should be noted that answer sheets designed for the original MMPI or the MMPI-2 are not applicable to the MMPI-A.

SCORING THE MMPI-A

The examiner should take substantial care to eliminate the common sources of error that occur in scoring and profiling MMPI-A responses. This process should start with a careful examination of the adolescent's answer sheet to ensure that items were not left unanswered or endorsed in both the true and false directions. Additionally, answer sheets should be examined for evidence of response patterns indicative of random markings or all true or all false response sets.

Obtaining the raw scores for all of the MMPI-A standard and supplementary scales may be accomplished by computer or hand scoring. If hand scoring is used, conversion of raw scores to T-score values should be done using MMPI-A profile sheets based on the gender-specific adolescent norms for this instrument. Adolescent profile sheets for the MMPI-A are available from Pearson Assessments; these use the normative values for the MMPI-A described and presented in the MMPI-A manual (Butcher et al., 1992) and in Appendix C of this text. It is important to realize that the raw score K-correction procedure is *not* used in deriving or profiling T-scores for adolescents with the MMPI-A. As previously noted, Marks et al. (1974) reported several reasons why the K-correction procedure was not developed for adolescent norms, including their preliminary evidence that adolescent MMPI profiles achieve greater discrimination between adolescent subgroups without the addition of a K-correction factor. As is presented in more detail later, an investigation by Alperin, Archer, and Coates (1996) examined the effectiveness of a K-correction factor for the MMPI-A and concluded that the adoption of a K-correction procedure would not result in systematic improvement in test accuracy for this instrument.

As reviewed by Archer (1989) and, more recently, by Archer and Krishnamurthy (2002), the procedures for scoring and profiling adolescent responses may be summarized as follows: First, carefully examine the answer sheet for evidence of deviant response sets, unanswered items, or double-marked items. Second, obtain the raw score value for each scale using the computer scoring reports available from Pearson Assessments or the hand-scoring keys. Third, convert the non-K-corrected raw scores to T-scores for each scale using the appropriate adolescent norm tables, with

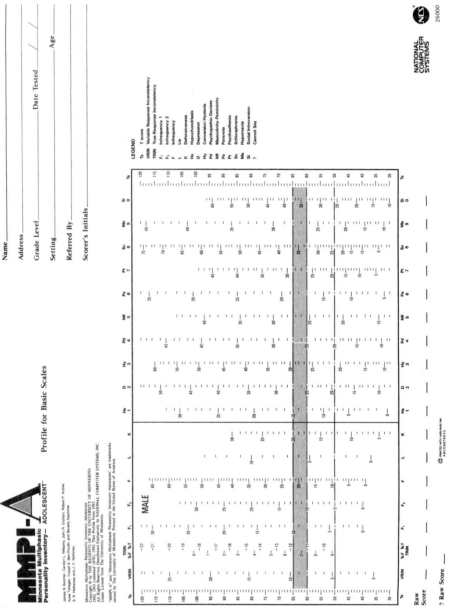

FIG. 3.1. MMPI-A Profile for Basic Scales (Male).

66

particular attention to the gender of the respondent. Fourth, plot T-score values on the MMPI-A profile sheet. The MMPI-A Profile for Basic Scales (male form) is shown in Fig. 3.1.

Scoring of the MMPI-A may be accomplished through several different methods. A computer software program is available from Pearson Assessments that permits test users to administer and score the standard validity and clinical scales as well as all other scales, including the content and supplementary scales, using their personal microcomputers. Specifically, the Basic Scale Profile Report provides raw scores and T-scores for 4 validity scales (L, F, F_1, K) and the 10 basic clinical scales and is suitable for scoring an abbreviated administration encompassing the first 350 MMPI-A items. The Extended Score Report includes raw scores and T-scores for all MMPI-A scales and subscales, including a list of items omitted by the adolescent. An example of the output from the MMPI-A Extended Score Report is included in Appendix 3.1. The test may also be administered via paper and pencil, with the responses hand scored or key entered into the scoring package later by trained support staff. High-volume test users might wish to consider the scanner option for their personal computer, in which answer sheets are scanned and responses tabulated by the scoring program. In addition, answer sheets may be mailed to Pearson Assessments (in Minnesota), which will score the test responses and return the results to the test user.

In addition to computerized scoring services, hand-scoring templates for use with specialized answer sheets are available for all MMPI-A standard, content, and supplementary scales and for all subscales. The template for a given scale is placed over the answer sheet, and the darkened spaces are counted; the total is the raw score for that scale. Special care should be taken when scoring scale 5 (Masculinity-Femininity) to use the scoring key designed for the adolescent's gender, and caution should also be used in scoring *TRIN* (True Response Inconsistency) and *VRIN* (Variable Response Inconsistency), given the complexity of the scoring for these scales. The *TRIN* and *VRIN* scales require separate recording grids for hand-scoring purposes, and the scoring formats for these validity scales are described in more detail in chapter 4. A recording grid for the *TRIN* scale is shown in Fig. 3.2.

Computer Administration and Scoring Issues

There are several special considerations that should be evaluated when using computer software for administering or scoring the MMPI/MMPI-A. With online administration of the inventory, clear instructions for entering and changing responses should be provided to the respondent. The examiner should ensure that the respondent is instructed in how to accurately enter or change responses. The respondent's entry of responses should be monitored to ensure that he or she understood the instructions. Computer administration programs often have summary or editing screens that permit the monitoring of item omissions.

Several studies have examined the possibility that computer-administered MMPI scores may differ from scores produced by administration of the instrument using the standard test booklet. Watson, Thomas, and Anderson (1992) undertook a meta-analysis that compared the MMPI scaled scores produced by standard test booklet and computer administration as reported in nine studies encompassing 967 respondents. The authors found that computer administration produced systematically lower scores than standard test booklet administration, although these differences were relatively small and typically accounted for less than 1.5 T-score points. They

Minnesota Multiphasic
Personality Inventory— ADOLESCENT

James N. Butcher, Carolyn L. Williams, John R. Graham, Robert P. Archer,
Auke Tellegen, Yossef S. Ben-Porath, and Beverly Kaemmer
S. R. Hathaway and J. C. McKinley

RECORDING GRID
TRIN Scale
(True Response Inconsistency)

The TRIN scale is made up of 21 items that are opposite in
content. If a subject responds inconsistently by answering True to both
items of certain pairs, one point is added to the TRIN score; if the
subject responds inconsistently by answering False to certain item pairs,
one point is subtracted. (Refer to the *MMPI-A Manual for Administration,
Scoring, and Interpretation* for directions on interpreting scores.)

Directions for scoring:

1. Transfer responses to the item pairs from the answer
   sheet to the recording grid on the right by blackening in the
   appropriate circle:
   Example: If response to item 14 was False: 14 Ⓣ ●

2. Place the scoring template TRIN-1 over the grid; in the blank
   provided in the third column, enter a "+" (plus sign) for each item
   pair in which both template boxes show a blackened response.
   Example: the response   14 ● Ⓕ   424 ● Ⓕ   would receive a "+"
   because both template boxes show a blackened response.

3. Count the number of "+"s and enter the TRIN-1 total.

4. Place the TRIN-2 scoring template over the grid; in the blank
   provided in the third column, enter a "−" (minus sign) for each item
   pair in which both template boxes show a blackened response.

5. Count the number of "−"s and enter the TRIN-2 total.

6. Subtract the TRIN-2 total from the TRIN-1 total and enter the result.

7. Add 9 points to obtain the TRIN total.
   Example: TRIN-1 total   2
            TRIN-2 total   −1
                          ───
                            1
                          +9
                          ───
            TRIN Total   10

14 Ⓣ Ⓕ	424 Ⓣ Ⓕ	____
37 Ⓣ Ⓕ	168 Ⓣ Ⓕ	____
46 Ⓣ Ⓕ	475 Ⓣ Ⓕ	____
53 Ⓣ Ⓕ	91 Ⓣ Ⓕ	____
60 Ⓣ Ⓕ	121 Ⓣ Ⓕ	____
62 Ⓣ Ⓕ	360 Ⓣ Ⓕ	____
63 Ⓣ Ⓕ	120 Ⓣ Ⓕ	____
70 Ⓣ Ⓕ	223 Ⓣ Ⓕ	____
71 Ⓣ Ⓕ	283 Ⓣ Ⓕ	____
82 Ⓣ Ⓕ	316 Ⓣ Ⓕ	____
95 Ⓣ Ⓕ	294 Ⓣ Ⓕ	____
119 Ⓣ Ⓕ	184 Ⓣ Ⓕ	____
128 Ⓣ Ⓕ	465 Ⓣ Ⓕ	____
146 Ⓣ Ⓕ	167 Ⓣ Ⓕ	____
158 Ⓣ Ⓕ	288 Ⓣ Ⓕ	____
242 Ⓣ Ⓕ	260 Ⓣ Ⓕ	____
245 Ⓣ Ⓕ	257 Ⓣ Ⓕ	____
264 Ⓣ Ⓕ	331 Ⓣ Ⓕ	____
304 Ⓣ Ⓕ	335 Ⓣ Ⓕ	____
355 Ⓣ Ⓕ	367 Ⓣ Ⓕ	____
463 Ⓣ Ⓕ	476 Ⓣ Ⓕ	____

TRIN-1   ____

− TRIN-2   ____

=   ____

+9

TRIN TOTAL   ____

FIG. 3.2. TRIN Scale Recording Grid.

concluded that the underestimates due to computer administration, although small, appeared consistent enough to suggest that the development of separate norms and profile sheets might be useful for computer-administered protocols, particularly for basic scales 3, 4, and 8.

As previously noted, a mail-in scoring service is available for the MMPI-A. When this option is used, the respondent enters his or her responses on the computer-scored MMPI-A answer sheet, which is sent to Pearson for scoring and reporting. As with the hand-scored version of the MMPI-A, the computer-scored answer sheet should be checked by the examiner for item omissions, double-marking, and deviant response sets before being sent for processing. The clinician should also eliminate any stray marks or incomplete erasures because these may be interpreted as valid responses in the computer-scoring process. These same cautions apply to examiners who use in-office scanning equipment for response entry. Although clinical lore has held that the degree of neatness or sloppiness displayed by the respondent in filling out an MMPI response sheet may be related to personality features, findings by Luty and Thackrey (1993) provided no evidence of a meaningful relationship between neatness and test scores. MMPI-A users who elect to employ a computer-scoring method should be aware that the profiles will be printed only if the age entered is within the 14–18 age range inclusive.

Selection of Appropriate Norms

The adolescent norms to be used with the MMPI-A are based on the MMPI-A normative sample described in chapter 2 and provided in Appendix C of this text. Because the MMPI-2 was specifically created for adult respondents, and adolescent norms have not been developed for this form, the MMPI-2 should *not* be used with respondents under the age of 18 (Butcher et al., 1989).

Archer (1984, 1987b) discussed in detail the statistical and interpretive problems related to the use of adult norms when applied to adolescent response patterns. In particular, the use of adult norms with adolescent clients tends to overestimate the occurrence and degree of symptomatology related to conduct disorder and antisocial personality features as well as psychotic and schizophrenic disorders.

Adolescent Norm Transformation Procedures

The adolescent norms developed by Marks and Briggs (1972) for the original form of the MMPI were based on linear transformation procedures that convert raw scores to T-score values. These are identical to the transformation procedures used in developing the adult norms for the original MMPI by Hathaway and McKinley (Dahlstrom et al., 1972). The MMPI-A retains the use of linear T-scores for the validity scales (i.e., VRIN, TRIN, F_1, F_2, F, L, and K), for scales 5 (Masculinity-Femininity) and 0 (Social Introversion), and for the supplementary scales, including the MacAndrew Alcoholism Scale–Revised (MAC-R) and the Alcohol/Drug Problem Acknowledgment (ACK), Alcohol/Drug Problem Proneness (PRO), Immaturity (IMM), Repression (R), and Anxiety (A) scales. Eight of the clinical scales on the MMPI-A (1, 2, 3, 4, 6, 7, 8, and 9) and all of the 15 content scales have T-score values derived from uniform T-score transformation procedures.

Uniform transformation procedures were developed to address a problem that has been associated with the use of linear T-score values for the MMPI. This problem is that identical T-score values do not represent the same percentile equivalents across the standard MMPI scales when derived using linear procedures. This phenomenon occurs because MMPI scale raw score distributions are not normally distributed, and the degree to which they vary from the normal distribution fluctuates from scale to scale. Thus, using linear T-score conversion procedures, a T-score value of 70 on one scale may not represent a percentile value equivalent to that represented by a T-score value of 70 on another MMPI clinical scale. This discrepancy resulted in difficulties when directly comparing T-score values across the MMPI scales. These difficulties were first discussed in detail by Colligan et al. (1983).

In the development of the MMPI-2, uniform T-score transformation procedures were used in order to provide equivalent T-score values across the clinical and content scales (Tellegen & Ben-Porath, 1992). This same approach was used in the development of the MMPI-A. Uniform T-score values were developed for the clinical scales by examining the distributions for scales 1, 2, 3, 4, 6, 7, 8, and 9 for males and females separately. MMPI-A scales 5 and 0 were not included in the uniform T-score procedures because these scales were derived differently than the other clinical scales, and the distribution of scores on scales 5 and 0 are less skewed (i.e., more normally distributed). A composite or averaged distribution of raw scores was then created across the eight basic scales for each gender, adjusting the distribution of each individual scale so that it would match the composite distribution. The purpose of developing a composite distribution was to allow for the assignment of T-score conversion values for each scale such that a given T-score value would convert to equivalent percentile values across each of these scales. Uniform T-score conversions were separately derived for the 15 content scales based on the distribution of scores for this group of measures.

Because uniform T-scores represent composite linear T-scores, this procedure serves to produce equivalent percentile values across scales for a given T-score. This procedure, however, also maintains the underlying positive skew in the distribution of scores from these measures. Thus, uniform T-scores are generally similar to values that would be obtained from linear T-scores (Edwards, Morrison, & Weissman, 1993b). Nevertheless, differences in T-score transformation procedures, combined with marked differences in mean raw score values produced by the Marks and Briggs (1972) and the MMPI-A (Butcher et al., 1992) normative sample, result in adolescent norms that will often produce differences in overall elevation and profile configuration for a particular response pattern. This topic is discussed in more detail in chapter 5 in the section on codetype congruence issues. At this point, it is important to stress that the clinician or researcher should not assume that the traditional MMPI and the MMPI-A will necessarily produce equivalent profiles, either in elevation or in codetype.

Honaker examined the issue of equivalence between the MMPI and MMPI-2 in the assessment of adults at a 1990 symposium. According to Honaker, the issue of psychometric equivalence is critically important because this factor determines, to a large extent, the degree to which the vast research literature on the original instrument may be generalized to the revised and restandardized version. Honaker noted that psychometric theory and standards require four conditions to be met before the two versions can be considered equivalent or parallel:

1. Both should yield identical scores (mean scores, high-point codes, etc.).
2. Both should yield the same distribution of scores.

3. The individual rank orderings produced by both should be identical (i.e., individuals should be ranked on a given dimension in the same order based on test scores from each version).
4. Scores generated from each version should correlate equally well with independent external criteria.

In evaluating this issue, Honaker examined a sample of 101 adult psychiatric patients who had received both the MMPI and the MMPI-2 in a counterbalanced, repeated-measures design. Findings indicated that the MMPI and the MMPI-2 did produce parallel score dispersion and rank ordering of respondents but did not yield equivalent mean scores. MMPI-2 scores were consistently lower for scales *F*, *2*, *4*, *8*, *9*, and *0*. Further, the congruence of high-point codes between the MMPI and MMPI-2 was lower than that found for repeated administrations of the MMPI or the MMPI-2. These findings indicate that the MMPI and MMPI-2 are highly interrelated but not equivalent test instruments. A similar conclusion was supported by research done by Archer and Gordon (1991a), who administered the MMPI-A and MMPI to a sample of normal high school students. Findings from this study indicate significant and pervasive elevation differences between T-scores produced by these two instruments, with MMPI-A scores significantly lower on most clinical scales.

Although it is quite clear that, using the criteria offered by Honaker (1990), the MMPI-A and MMPI are not psychometrically equivalent instruments, there is also a substantial body of research literature that indicates that a high degree of congruence is found between adolescent profiles generated from the original MMPI and from the MMPI-A. As we shall see in later chapters, this degree of congruence is taken to support the conclusion that much of the research literature developed for adolescents using the original test may be validly generalized to users of the MMPI-A.

Deriving the Welsh Code

Two major coding systems have been developed for MMPI profiles. The first, devised by Stark Hathaway (1947), was later modified and made more comprehensive by George Welsh (1948). Because the Welsh system is more widely used than the Hathaway system and allows for a more precise classification of profile features, this system is recommended for classification of adolescents' MMPI-A responses. A complete description of both the Hathaway and Welsh systems, however, is contained in such texts as Dahlstrom et al. (1972) and Friedman et al. (2001).

The general function of profile coding is to summarize the most salient features of the profile without the loss of substantial information. These features include the range of elevation of scales and the pattern of relationships between the scales when ordered from highest to lowest elevation.

The Welsh code requires that all standard clinical scales (designated by number) be arranged (left to right) in descending order of magnitude of T-score elevation. The traditional validity scales (*L*, *F*, and *K*) are then coded immediately to the right of the clinical scales, again arranged from most to least elevated. The relative degree of elevation for any scale within the code is denoted by the following system of symbols (as modified for the MMPI-A and described in the test manual for this instrument):

T-score Values	Symbol
120 and above	!
110–119	!!
100–109	**
90–99	*
80–89	"
70–79	'
65–69	+
60–64	−
50–59	/
40–49	:
30–39	#
29 and below	No symbol (scale is presented to the right of the # symbol)

In the Welsh coding system, the relevant symbol is placed to the immediate right of the scale or scales related to that range of elevation. For example, if scale 2 has a T-score value of 98 and scale 4 has a T-score value of 92, the expression 24* would symbolically represent this occurrence. Further, if two or more scales are within 1 T-score point of each other, this occurrence is denoted by underlining all affected scales. For example, if scale 2 was elevated at 53 and scale 3 was elevated at 52, they would be denoted as follows: 23/. The following example, adapted from Friedman et al. (2001), illustrates the Welsh coding system for the MMPI-A:

Scales:	L	F	K	1	2	3	4	5	6	7	8	9	0
T-scores:	44	60	49	49	99	62	50	67	62	79	63	38	70
Welsh Code:					2* " 70 ' 5+836-4/1:9## F-/KL:								

Several features of this illustration may be noted. For example, scales 3 and 6 both produced an identical T-score value of 62, and therefore by convention the scale identified by the lowest numerical value (i.e., scale 3) is presented first in the descending order. Additionally, scales 3, 6, and 8 vary by only one T-score value and therefore all three scales are underlined in the code. Finally, double quotation marks (") immediately follow the asteric (*) after scale 2. This indicates that no MMPI scale produced values in the T-score range of 80 to 89, illustrating the convention that although no value in this specific T-score range may occur, the appropriate symbol should nevertheless be recorded in the code. Typically, most clinicians apply the Welsh code first to the standard clinical scales and then to the validity scales. An example of the use of Welsh coding for the MMPI-A is provided in the manual for this test instrument (Butcher et al., 1992).

APPENDIX 3.1

Sample Output from the MMPI-A Extended Score Report

Extended Score Report

MMPI-A™

Minnesota Multiphasic Personality Inventory-Adolescent™

ID Number 12345

Doe John

Male

Age 15

Date Assessed 1/01/2004

MMPI-A VALIDITY AND CLINICAL SCALES PROFILE

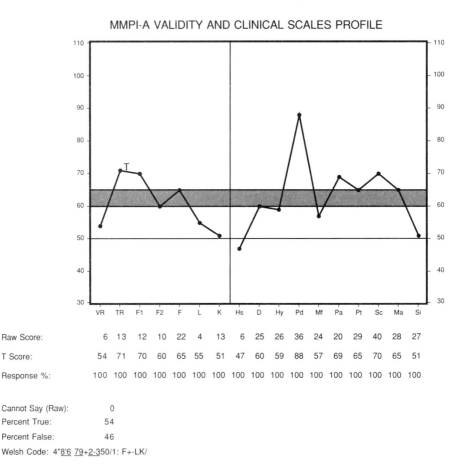

	VR	TR	F1	F2	F	L	K	Hs	D	Hy	Pd	Mf	Pa	Pt	Sc	Ma	Si
Raw Score:	6	13	12	10	22	4	13	6	25	26	36	24	20	29	40	28	27
T Score:	54	71	70	60	65	55	51	47	60	59	88	57	69	65	70	65	51
Response %:	100	100	100	100	100	100	100	100	100	100	100	100	100	100	100	100	100

Cannot Say (Raw):　　　0
Percent True:　　　54
Percent False:　　　46
Welsh Code:　4"8'6 79+2-350/1: F+-LK/

MMPI-A ™
ID 12345

Extended score Report
Page 3

MMPI-A CONTENT SCALES PROFILE

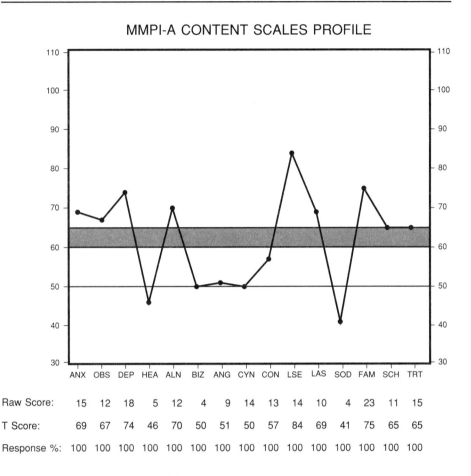

	ANX	OBS	DEP	HEA	ALN	BIZ	ANG	CYN	CON	LSE	LAS	SOD	FAM	SCH	TRT
Raw Score:	15	12	18	5	12	4	9	14	13	14	10	4	23	11	15
T Score:	69	67	74	46	70	50	51	50	57	84	69	41	75	65	65
Response %:	100	100	100	100	100	100	100	100	100	100	100	100	100	100	100

SUPPLEMENTARY SCORE REPORT

	Raw Score	T Score	Resp %
MacAndrew Alcoholism-Revised (MAC-R)	23	54	100
Alcohol/Drug Problem Acknowledgement (ACK)	1	38	100
Alcohol/Drug Problem Proneness (PRO)	24	67	100
Immaturity Scale (IMM)	27	72	100
Anxiety (A)	28	69	100
Repression (R)	13	49	100
Depression Subscales (Harris-Lingoes)			
Subjective Depression (D1)	18	72	100
Psychomotor Retardation (D2)	4	46	100
Physical Malfunctioning (D3)	2	42	100
Mental Dullness (D4)	10	76	100
Brooding (D5)	7	71	100
Hysteria Subscales (Harris-Lingoes)			
Denial of Social Anxiety (Hy1)	5	61	100
Need for Affection (Hy2)	5	50	100
Lassitude-Malaise (Hy3)	8	66	100
Somatic Complaints (Hy4)	3	46	100
Inhibition of Aggression (Hy5)	3	51	100
Psychopathic Deviate Subscales (Harris-Lingoes)			
Familial Discord (Pd1)	7	69	100
Authority Problems (Pd2)	5	60	100
Social Imperturbability (Pd3)	6	67	100
Social Alienation (Pd4)	12	83	100
Self-Alienation (Pd5)	9	69	100
Paranoia Subscales (Harris-Lingoes)			
Persecutory Ideas (Pa1)	12	78	100
Poignancy (Pa2)	5	61	100
Naivete (Pa3)	3	45	100

	Raw Score	T Score	Resp %
Schizophrenia Subscales (Harris-Lingoes)			
Social Alienation (Sc1)	17	83	100
Emotional Alienation (Sc2)	7	76	100
Lack of Ego Mastery, Cognitive (Sc3)	7	68	100
Lack of Ego Mastery, Conative (Sc4)	11	77	100
Lack of Ego Mastery, Defective Inhibition (Sc5)	3	48	100
Bizarre Sensory Experiences (Sc6)	4	47	100
Hypomania Subscales (Harris-Lingoes)			
Amorality (Ma1)	3	52	100
Psychomotor Acceleration (Ma2)	8	57	100
Imperturbability (Ma3)	5	62	100
Ego Inflation (Ma4)	6	58	100
Social Introversion Subscales (Ben-Porath, Hostetler, Butcher, & Graham)			
Shyness / Self-Consciousness (Si1)	3	40	100
Social Avoidance (Si2)	1	43	100
Alienation--Self and Others (Si3)	12	63	100

Uniform T scores are used for Hs, D, Hy, Pd, Pa, Pt, Sc, Ma, and the content scales; all other MMPI-A scales use linear T scores.

ITEM RESPONSES

1: 2	2: 1	3: 2	4: 2	5: 2	6: 1	7: 1	8: 2	9: 2	10: 1
11: 2	12: 1	13: 2	14: 1	15: 1	16: 1	17: 2	18: 1	19: 1	20: 1
21: 2	22: 2	23: 2	24: 1	25: 2	26: 1	27: 2	28: 1	29: 2	30: 2
31: 1	32: 1	33: 1	34: 1	35: 2	36: 2	37: 2	38: 1	39: 1	40: 2
41: 2	42: 1	43: 2	44: 1	45: 2	46: 1	47: 2	48: 1	49: 1	50: 1
51: 2	52: 1	53: 1	54: 1	55: 1	56: 2	57: 1	58: 2	59: 1	60: 2
61: 2	62: 1	63: 1	64: 2	65: 1	66: 2	67: 2	68: 2	69: 1	70: 1
71: 1	72: 1	73: 1	74: 1	75: 1	76: 2	77: 1	78: 1	79: 1	80: 2
81: 2	82: 1	83: 1	84: 1	85: 1	86: 1	87: 1	88: 1	89: 2	90: 1
91: 2	92: 2	93: 2	94: 1	95: 1	96: 2	97: 2	98: 1	99: 2	100: 1
101: 2	102: 1	103: 2	104: 1	105: 2	106: 2	107: 1	108: 2	109: 1	110: 1
111: 2	112: 1	113: 2	114: 2	115: 1	116: 1	117: 2	118: 1	119: 2	120: 2
121: 1	122: 2	123: 2	124: 1	125: 1	126: 1	127: 2	128: 2	129: 1	130: 2
131: 2	132: 1	133: 1	134: 1	135: 1	136: 1	137: 1	138: 1	139: 2	140: 1
141: 1	142: 2	143: 2	144: 2	145: 2	146: 1	147: 1	148: 2	149: 2	150: 2
151: 2	152: 1	153: 2	154: 2	155: 2	156: 1	157: 1	158: 1	159: 2	160: 2
161: 2	162: 1	163: 1	164: 1	165: 2	166: 1	167: 2	168: 1	169: 1	170: 2
171: 2	172: 1	173: 1	174: 1	175: 2	176: 2	177: 2	178: 2	179: 1	180: 1
181: 1	182: 1	183: 2	184: 1	185: 1	186: 2	187: 2	188: 2	189: 2	190: 2
191: 1	192: 1	193: 1	194: 1	195: 1	196: 2	197: 1	198: 1	199: 2	200: 1
201: 2	202: 2	203: 1	204: 2	205: 1	206: 1	207: 2	208: 1	209: 1	210: 1
211: 1	212: 2	213: 2	214: 1	215: 1	216: 1	217: 1	218: 1	219: 1	220: 1
221: 1	222: 2	223: 2	224: 2	225: 1	226: 2	227: 2	228: 1	229: 1	230: 2
231: 2	232: 2	233: 2	234: 2	235: 1	236: 2	237: 2	238: 2	239: 1	240: 1
241: 2	242: 2	243: 1	244: 2	245: 1	246: 2	247: 2	248: 1	249: 1	250: 2
251: 2	252: 1	253: 1	254: 1	255: 1	256: 1	257: 2	258: 1	259: 1	260: 1
261: 1	262: 2	263: 2	264: 1	265: 2	266: 1	267: 1	268: 2	269: 1	270: 2
271: 2	272: 2	273: 2	274: 1	275: 2	276: 1	277: 1	278: 2	279: 1	280: 1
281: 2	282: 1	283: 1	284: 2	285: 1	286: 1	287: 2	288: 2	289: 2	290: 2
291: 1	292: 1	293: 2	294: 1	295: 1	296: 2	297: 2	298: 2	299: 2	300: 1
301: 2	302: 1	303: 2	304: 1	305: 1	306: 1	307: 1	308: 2	309: 2	310: 1
311: 1	312: 1	313: 1	314: 1	315: 2	316: 2	317: 1	318: 1	319: 1	320: 1
321: 2	322: 2	323: 2	324: 1	325: 1	326: 1	327: 1	328: 2	329: 2	330: 1
331: 1	332: 2	333: 1	334: 2	335: 1	336: 1	337: 2	338: 2	339: 1	340: 1
341: 1	342: 2	343: 2	344: 1	345: 1	346: 1	347: 1	348: 1	349: 2	350: 2
351: 2	352: 2	353: 2	354: 1	355: 2	356: 1	357: 2	358: 2	359: 1	360: 2
361: 2	362: 1	363: 1	364: 1	365: 2	366: 2	367: 2	368: 1	369: 1	370: 1
371: 1	372: 1	373: 1	374: 1	375: 2	376: 2	377: 1	378: 2	379: 1	380: 2
381: 1	382: 1	383: 2	384: 1	385: 1	386: 1	387: 1	388: 1	389: 1	390: 2
391: 1	392: 1	393: 2	394: 1	395: 2	396: 1	397: 2	398: 1	399: 2	400: 2
401: 1	402: 1	403: 1	404: 1	405: 1	406: 2	407: 1	408: 2	409: 2	410: 2

411: 2 412: 2 413: 1 414: 1 415: 1 416: 1 417: 2 418: 2 419: 1 420: 2
421: 1 422: 2 423: 2 424: 2 425: 1 426: 1 427: 1 428: 2 429: 2 430: 1
431: 1 432: 1 433: 2 434: 1 435: 2 436: 1 437: 1 438: 1 439: 2 440: 2
441: 1 442: 1 443: 2 444: 1 445: 2 446: 2 447: 2 448: 2 449: 2 450: 1
451: 2 452: 1 453: 2 454: 1 455: 1 456: 1 457: 1 458: 2 459: 2 460: 1
461: 1 462: 2 463: 1 464: 2 465: 2 466: 1 467: 2 468: 1 469: 1 470: 1
471: 2 472: 1 473: 2 474: 2 475: 2 476: 1 477: 2 478: 1

End of Report

Validity Scales and Validity Assessment Interpretation

There are several methods of assessing the technical validity of adolescents' MMPI-A profiles. These methods have traditionally involved the individual and configural interpretation of standard validity scale findings and have often been extended to include an analysis of the overall MMPI basic scale profile configuration for evidence of atypical response set features. Additional methods of evaluating profile validity have also been developed. These methods include the Test-Retest (*TR*) Index and the Carelessness (*CLS*) scale for the original form of the MMPI. For the MMPI-A, new validity measures were developed: the Variable Response Inconsistency (*VRIN*) and True Response Inconsistency (*TRIN*) scales and the F_1 and F_2 subscales. The inclusion of these four new validity scales at the beginning of the MMPI-A basic scale profile (in conjunction with reordering *L*, *F*, and *K* to *F*, *L*, and *K*) is among the most readily apparent changes associated with the revised instrument. In addition to discussing these validity assessment tools, this chapter reviews a conceptual model developed by Roger Greene (1989a, 2000) for interpreting technical validity patterns. This model emphasizes the distinction between response consistency and response accuracy as components of technical validity.

MMPI-A VALIDITY SCALES

Traditional Validity Scales and Derivative Subscales

The traditional validity scales (*F*, *L*, and *K*) originally developed by Hathaway and McKinley were created to detect deviant test-taking attitudes and responses. Determining the technical validity of the adolescents' MMPI-A profiles is particularly important because invalid profiles probably occur with a higher frequency in adolescent samples (these profiles result from problems related to response consistency as well as response accuracy). Pogge, Stokes, Frank, Wong, and Harvey (1997), for example, observed that although the MMPI-A has scales specifically designed to evaluate the effects of response styles on the disclosure of psychopathology, many of the self-report instruments commonly used with adolescents (e.g., the Symptom Checklist–90–Revised and the Beck Depression Inventory) do not contain validity scales. Further, these researchers noted that some clinicians prefer to use observer ratings of adolescents, rather than self-report data, as a means of attempting to minimize the possible effects of response styles. Pogge and his colleagues examined these issues in a study of self-report and therapist ratings of psychopathology for 235 adolescent psychiatric inpatients. All the participants in this study completed three self-report rating scales, the MMPI, the SCL-90-R, and the BDI. The results from this study demonstrated that the best prediction of self-report and therapist ratings of adolescent symptomatology was based on a prediction model incorporating individual scores from clinical scales and from the validity scales L, F, and K. In fact, one third of the adolescent patients used in this study manifested clinical range elevations on at least one of these three MMPI validity scales, underscoring the relatively high prevalence of validity scale issues for this population. Pogge et al. concluded that their findings strongly indicate that the use of validity scales is central to the assessment of psychopathology among adolescents and that the use of clinician ratings does not eliminate self-presentation biases and does not serve as an adequate substitute for the evaluation of self-reported psychopathology. As research has accumulated on the standard validity measures, however, Graham (2000) noted that we have come to view the traditional validity scales as additional sources of inferences about the respondents' extratest behaviors. Thus, these validity scales provide information not only about the technical validity of the MMPI response pattern but also about concerning behavioral correlates or descriptors that are likely to apply to the respondent.

The Cannot Say (?) Scale

The Cannot Say scale consists of the total number of items that a respondent fails to answer or answers in both the true and false directions. The Cannot Say scale is not a formal MMPI scale because it does not have a consistent or fixed item pool. Profile sheets for the traditional MMPI have shown the Cannot Say scale as the first in the series of standard validity scales on the profile grid. The MMPI-2 and MMPI-A profile sheets, although still providing a space to record the raw score for the Cannot Say scale, have deemphasized its role as a "scale" by placing it in the lower left portion of the profile sheet.

   Although several studies have examined the characteristics of Cannot Say values in adult populations (as reviewed in Greene, 1980, 1989a, 1991, 2000), very little research has been focused on this issue among adolescent respondents. Ball and Carroll (1960) examined correlates of the Cannot Say scores among 262 ninth-grade public school students in Kentucky. They reported that male respondents had a higher mean number of Cannot Say responses than females. The items omitted by these adolescents tended to fall into broad categories, including statements not applicable to adolescents, religious items, items related to sexuality and bodily functions, and items that required adolescents to make a decision concerning personal characteristics about which they were ambivalent. Similarly, Hathaway and Monachesi (1963) found 23 items that were left unanswered by at least 2% of the male or female respondents in their statewide Minnesota sample of normal adolescents. They reported that items with content related to religion and sex appeared to be the most frequently omitted items for both boys and girls. Additionally, girls tended to leave a significantly larger number of sex-related items unanswered.

   In general, findings on the original MMPI by Ball and Carroll (1960) and on the MMPI-A by Archer and Gordon (1991a) indicated a relationship between intellectual functioning/reading ability and Cannot Say scale scores. Ball and Carroll found no evidence of a relationship between Cannot Say scores and delinquent behaviors in

TABLE 4.1
Frequency of Omitted Items on the MMPI in Adult and Adolescent Psychiatric Samples by Gender

Number of Omitted Items	Psychiatric Patients (Hedlund & Won Cho, 1979)			
	Adults		Adolescents	
	Male ($N = 8,646$)	Female ($N = 3,743$)	Male ($N = 693$)	Female ($N = 290$)
0	29.8%	28.4%	28.0%	27.9%
1–5	32.3%	30.4%	31.0%	30.8%
Cumulative (0–5)	62.1%	58.8%	59.0%	58.7%
6–10	16.8%	17.2%	21.1%	21.7%
Cumulative (0–10)	78.9%	76.0%	80.1%	80.4%
11–30	14.7%	17.4%	14.6%	13.1%
Cumulative (0–30)	93.6%	93.4%	94.7%	93.5%
31+	6.4%	6.6%	5.3%	6.5%
M	8.7	9.3	7.7	8.4
SD	18.1	19.2	13.1	15.1

Note. From Roger L. Greene *The MMPI-2/MMPI: An Interpretive Manual*, © 1991. Published by Allyn & Bacon, Boston, MA. Copyright © 1991 by Pearson Education. Adapted by permission of the publisher.

their sample, but did find higher Cannot Say scores to be inversely related to adolescents' scores on intelligence measures and their academic grades. Archer and Gordon (1991a) found a significant relationship ($r = -.10$, $p < .05$) between the number of unanswered MMPI-A items and adolescents' reading abilities in a sample of 495 junior high and high school students. These findings suggest that adolescents' failure to complete items may often be related to intellectual and reading limitations rather than oppositional and defiant characteristics.

Table 4.1 provides information from Greene (1991) concerning the frequency of omitted items for the original MMPI in psychiatric samples of adults and adolescents. This table shows approximately equivalent rates of item omission between these two age groups.

Gottesman et al. (1987) reported that the mean Cannot Say scale value for normal adolescents in the Hathaway and Monachesi (1963) data set was roughly 3. Further, a raw score value of 5 to 6 converts to a T-score range of 70 to 80 in the Gottesman et al. adolescent norms. It should be noted, however, that the Marks and Briggs (1972) adolescent norms for the traditional MMPI indicate that a Cannot Say raw score value of 30 converts to a T-score value of 50 for both male and female adolescents. This T-score conversion appears to be a continuation of the arbitrary assignment of T-score values to Cannot Say raw score values of 30 used by Hathaway and McKinley (1967) in the original adult MMPI norms. In both adolescent and adult samples, however, a raw score value of 30 on the Cannot Say scale occurs *much* less frequently than is implied by the T = 50 value. The data from the MMPI-A normative sample indicate that the mean raw score value for the Cannot Say scale is 1.01 for males ($SD = 3.70$) and .80 for females ($SD = 2.50$).

Greene (1991) identified traditional MMPI items most frequently omitted in a sample of 983 adolescent psychiatric patients. Of these 17 items, 10 were deleted in the formation of the MMPI-A, and 3 additional items underwent revision. The very low Cannot Say scale mean raw score values found for the MMPI-A normative sample suggest that the MMPI-A item revision process may have been successful in creating

TABLE 4.2
Most Frequently Omitted Items for 805 Male Adolescents in the MMPI-A Normative Sample

MMPI Item No.	Item Content	Freq. of Omission	% of Sample
203	Ruminate a lot.	25	3.1
441	Not thought attractive.	13	1.6
16	Life unfair.	10	1.2
199	Lead life based on duty.	8	1.0
395	Worked with people who take credit for good work but blame others for bad.	8	1.0
404	Feel I'm going to "lose it."	8	1.0
177	Think about killing self.	7	.9
406	May misbehave sexually.	7	.9
448	Thought to be dependable.	7	.9
467	Like marijuana.	7	.9

Note. MMPI-A abbreviated items reproduced by permission. MMPI-A test booklet copyright © 1992 by the Regents of the University of Minnesota; MMPI-A abbreviated item test booklet copyright © 2004 by the Regents of the University of Minnesota.

a test booklet of increased relevance to adolescents when contrasted with the original test form. It should be noted, however, that MMPI-A Cannot Say scale mean values were affected by the elimination of adolescents from the normative sample with Cannot Say scale raw score values of 35 and above. Tables 4.2 and 4.3 show the abbreviated items most frequently omitted by 805 boys and 815 girls, respectively, in the MMPI-A normative sample.

Table 4.4 provides interpretive guidelines for the MMPI-A Cannot Say scale based on raw score values. As noted in this table, adolescents who omit more than 30 items should be requested to complete the unanswered items or retake the entire test. Research findings relating omissions to intelligence and reading ability, however, strongly indicate that the examiner should assess an adolescent's capacity to comprehend items before instructing him or her to respond to unanswered MMPI-A

TABLE 4.3
Most Frequently Omitted Items for 815 Female Adolescents in the MMPI-A Normative Sample

Item No.	Item Content	Freq. of Omission	% of Sample
203	Ruminate a lot.	24	2.9
199	Lead life based on duty.	12	1.5
93	Head feels "full."	10	1.2
16	Life unfair.	8	1.0
31	No trouble because of sexual activities.	7	.9
213	Fine for people to take all they can get.	7	.9
431	Talking about problems often more helpful than taking medications.	7	.9
196	Seldom does heart pound or is breath short.	6	.7
244	Very few fears.	6	.7
251	Bothered by sexual thoughts.	6	.7
429	Harmful habits.	6	.7
432	Have faults I can't change.	6	.7
442	Follow beliefs no matter what.	6	.7

Note. MMPI-A abbreviated items reproduced by permission. MMPI-A test booklet copyright © 1992 by the Regents of the University of Minnesota; MMPI-A abbreviated item test booklet copyright © 2004 by the Regents of the University of Minnesota.

TABLE 4.4
Interpretation Guidelines for the Cannot Say (?) Scale

Raw Score	Interpretation
0–3	*Low*. These adolescents are willing and able to respond to the item pool and were not evasive of item content.
4–10	*Moderate*. These adolescents have omitted a few items in a selective manner. Their omissions may be the result of limitations in life experiences that rendered some items unanswerable. There is little probability of profile distortions unless all omissions were from a single scale.
11–30	*Marked*. These adolescents are omitting more items than expected and may be very indecisive. Their omissions may have distorted their profile elevations. Check the scale membership of missing items to evaluate profile validity.
31 and above	*Invalid*. Adolescents in this range have left many items unanswered, possibly as a result of a defiant or uncooperative stance or serious reading difficulties. The profile is invalid. If possible, the adolescent should complete unanswered items or retake the entire test.

Note. Adapted from Archer (1987b). Copyright © 1987 by Lawrence Erlbaum Associates, Inc. Reprinted by permission.

statements. Clopton and Neuringer (1977) demonstrated that random omissions of 30 items or fewer from the traditional MMPI do not seriously distort MMPI profile features when scored on adult norms. As previously noted, a substantial majority of adolescents would be expected to omit fewer than 10 items on either the traditional MMPI or the MMPI-A. Raw score values of 11 to 30 on the Cannot Say scale represent substantially more omissions than is typical. This degree of item omission may be produced by adolescents who have impaired reading ability or have life experience limitations that render some items meaningless or unanswerable. It is unlikely, however, that this range of Cannot Say scale values will result in profile elevation or configuration distortions unless the omitted items are concentrated within a few scales.

The Frequency (F) Scale and the F_1 and F_2 Subscales

The original MMPI F scale consisted of 64 items selected using the criterion that no more than 10% of the Minnesota normative adult sample answered these items in the deviant direction. As a result of this development procedure, the F scale was often referred to as the Frequency or Infrequency scale. The F scale includes a variety of items related to strange or unusual experiences, thoughts, and sensations; paranoid ideation; and antisocial attitudes and behaviors. The F scale on the original MMPI was also one of the most problematic scales when applied to adolescent populations, because adolescents typically produced much higher F scale raw scores than adults. Significant F scale mean raw score differences between adolescent and adult respondents were consistently reported in both normal and clinical samples (e.g., Archer, 1984, 1987b). Because of the high F scale values typical of adolescents, the use of F scale validity criteria to assess the technical validity of teenagers' MMPI profiles was very complex and often ineffective. Interestingly, elevated F scale values have also been found in other populations or groups, when their responses are placed on standard norms developed in the United States, including Chinese subjects from the People's Republic of China and Hong Kong (Cheung, Song, & Butcher, 1991). Cheung et al.

TABLE 4.5

MMPI-2 F Scale Items Producing Endorsement Frequencies Exceeding 20% in the MMPI-TX Normative Data Collection Sample

MMPI-2 Item No.	Item Content	Endorsement Frequency[a]
48	Like to daydream.	42.0%
288	Judged unfairly by family.	41.7%
12	Satisfactory sex life.	32.8%
174	Like to study what I'm working on.	32.3%
132	Believe in eternity.	31.2%
168	Sometimes do things and don't remember doing them.	29.8%
324	Like making people afraid of me.	28.2%
300	Jealous of some family members.	26.3%
150	Feel need to injure self or others.	26.3%
312	Like only comic strips in newspaper.	25.8%
264	Used alcohol a lot.	22.6%

Note. MMPI-2 abbreviated items reproduced by permission. MMPI-2 test booklet copyright © 1989 by the Regents of the University of Minnesota; MMPI-2 abbreviated item test booklet copyright © 2004 by the Regents of the University of Minnesota.
[a] Analyses based on 1,435 adolescents sampled as part of the MMPI-A normative data collection.

(1991) attributed the *F* scale elevations produced by Chinese respondents to cultural differences in attitudes, practices, and beliefs. Thus, *F* scale item endorsement patterns have been shown to be affected by both developmental and cultural factors.

In the development of the MMPI-A, it was apparent that adolescents produced marked elevations on the *F* scale because many of the *F* scale items had high rates of endorsement in this age group. Specifically, 11 of the 60 *F* items that appear on the MMPI-2 form for adults had item endorsement frequencies exceeding 20% in the MMPI-A normative sample. For example, roughly 26% of both male and female adolescents in the MMPI-A normative sample responded *true* to the traditional *F* scale abbreviated item "Feel need to injure self or others," and roughly 36% of males and 45% of females answered *true* to the abbreviated item "Like to daydream." Table 4.5 provides the abbreviated item content and endorsement frequencies for the 11 *F* scale items most frequently endorsed by adolescents in the MMPI-A normative sample using the MMPI-TX experimental test form.

The traditional *F* scale also contains several items that might be deemed offensive because statement content was related to religious beliefs (e.g., "Believe in God") or sexual attitudes and functioning (e.g., "Children should be taught about sex"). Based on these observations, the *F* scale underwent a major revision in the development of the MMPI-A, leading to the creation of a new 66-item *F* scale, which is subdivided into the F_1 and F_2 subscales.

The MMPI-A *F* scale was created by selecting items endorsed in a deviant direction by no more than 20% of the 805 boys and 815 girls in the MMPI-A normative sample. In creating the MMPI-A *F* scale, 27 items were deleted from the original *F* scale because adolescents' endorsement of these items exceeded the 20% criterion for selection or because the items contained content deemed inappropriate for inclusion in the MMPI-A. In addition, 12 items that appeared in the original version of the MMPI but were not traditionally scored on *F* were included in the MMPI-A *F* scale because these items met the 20% criterion rule. Finally, the MMPI-A *F* scale includes 17 new items that appear only on the MMPI-A.

TABLE 4.6
Interpretation Guidelines for the MMPI-A F Scale

T-Score	Interpretation
45 and below	*Low.* Scores in this range may reflect very conventional life experiences among normal adolescents and possible "fake good" attempts among disturbed adolescents.
46–59	*Normal.* Adolescents in this range have endorsed unusual experiences to a degree that is common during adolescence.
60–65	*Moderate.* These adolescents have F scores in the range typically found among teenagers exhibiting some evidence of psychopathology.
66–89	*Marked.* Validity indicators should be checked carefully for adolescents in this range. Valid profiles most likely reflect significant psychopathology, including symptoms typically exhibited by adolescents in inpatient settings.
90 and above	*Extreme.* Protocols with F scores in this range are likely to be invalid. If "fake-bad" and other response set issues are ruled out, may reflect severely disorganized or psychotic adolescents.

Note. Adapted from Archer (1987b). Copyright © 1987 by Lawrence Erlbaum Associates, Inc. Reprinted by permission.

Table 4.6 provides five levels of interpretive suggestions for the MMPI-A F scale. Adolescents who produce marked or extreme elevations on the MMPI-A F scale may be suffering from severe psychiatric illnesses, may be attempting to "fake-bad" or overreport symptomatology, or may be engaging in a random response pattern either through conscious intent or as a result of inadequate reading ability. For example, Krakauer (1991) investigated the relationship between MMPI-A F scale elevation and reading ability in a sample of 495 adolescents. She found that 11% of adolescents scored below a sixth-grade reading level in the total sample. In a subsample of 231 adolescents who produced F scale T-score values equal to or greater than 65, however, the percentage of adolescents reading below the sixth-grade level increased to 18%. Similarly, a subsample of 120 adolescents who produced F scale T-score values of 80 or greater yielded a poor-reader base rate of 24%. This increased to 29% in the subsample of 68 adolescents who produced F scale T-score values of 90 or greater.

The F_1 scale is a direct descendant of the original F scale and consists of 33 items, of which 24 appeared in the original. The remaining nine F_1 items are new items that did not appear in the original instrument. All of the F_1 items occur among the first 350 items of the MMPI-A booklet and therefore may be used even when the MMPI-A is given in the abbreviated format. The F_2 scale also consists of 33 items, all of which occur after item 242 and 16 of which occur after item 350. The F_2 scale consists predominantly of items that appeared in the original MMPI (28 of the 33 F_2 items), but only 12 of these items were scored on the F scale in the original instrument. Eight of the F_2 items are new items that did not appear in the original MMPI. Table 4.7 provides examples of MMPI-A F scale abbreviated items, with the F_1 and F_2 membership indicated within parentheses. Each F_1 or F_2 item, as part of the MMPI-A F scale, was selected based on the criterion that fewer than 20% of normal adolescent subjects in the MMPI-A normative sample endorsed the item in the scored or critical direction.

The F_1 and F_2 scales for the MMPI-A may be used in an interpretive strategy similar to that employed for the F and F_b scales found in the MMPI-2 (Butcher et al., 1989). Specifically, the F_1 scale provides information concerning the validity of the adolescent's responses to the basic MMPI-A scales, whereas F_2 provides information

TABLE 4.7
Sample Items From the MMPI-A F Scale With F_1 or F_2
Subscale Membership

Examples of items scored if true
22. Possessed by spirits. (F_1)
250. Spirit leaves body. (F_2)

Examples of items scored if false
74. Liked by most. (F_1)
258. Love(d) mother. (F_2)

Note. MMPI-A abbreviated items reproduced by permission. MMPI-A test booklet copyright © 1992 by the Regents of the University of Minnesota; MMPI-A abbreviated item test booklet copyright © 2004 by the Regents of the University of Minnesota.

concerning the adolescent's responses to the latter part of the MMPI-A test booklet and data necessary to score the MMPI-A content scales and supplementary scales. If an adolescent's F_1 score is within the acceptable range, but the F_2 score is extremely elevated (T ≥ 90), use of a random response strategy during the latter half of the MMPI-A test is indicated. Under these conditions, it may be possible to interpret the data from the standard scales while treating the content scale and supplementary scale findings as invalid. If the F_1 score exceeds the acceptable range, however, the entire protocol should be treated as invalid, and further interpretation should not be undertaken.

Because the F_1 and F_2 scales are newly developed for the MMPI-A, research data are currently fairly limited concerning the optimal cutoff score for identifying invalid records. Berry et al. (1991) demonstrated the usefulness of the MMPI-2 F and F_b scales in detecting random responding in a college student sample. However, Archer and Elkins (1999) reported that F, F_1, and F_2 were each useful when employed individually to identify random MMPI-A profiles, but the T-score difference between F_1 and F_2 did not appear to be of practical assistance in this task. Further, Archer, Handel, Lynch, and Elkins (2002) found these F scales and subscales individually useful in detecting profiles with varying levels of random responding but noted that the F_1-F_2 T-score difference was ineffective in this regard because "when the T-score difference cutoffs became large enough to generate acceptable levels of positive predictive power (probability an elevated score reflects a random protocol), so few random protocols were found above that criterion score that test sensitivity was markedly low" (p. 429). Archer et al. (2002) noted that a partial explanation of the failure of the F_1-F_2 index to produce useful results may lie in the tendency of the F_1 subscale to produce higher T-score values than the F_2 subscale under standard administration conditions as well as in most random response conditions. Table 4.6 provides some T-score interpretation guidelines for the MMPI-A F scale, and these T-score recommendations also appear to be applicable to the F_1 and F_2 subscales when interpreted as individual measures. Clinicians should be particularly cautious concerning validity inferences based on the observed T-score differences that occur between the F_1 and F_2 subscales, however, given the limited usefulness of this index found in the research conducted thus far on this issue.

Two other frequency-related scales or indices have shown promise as means of identifying the overreporting of symptomatology among adolescents. Rogers, Hinds, and Sewell (1996) evaluated the clinical usefulness of three measures in assessing the overreporting of symptomatology: the MMPI-A, the Structured Interview of Reported Symptoms (SIRS), and the Screening Index of Malingered Symptoms (SIMS). Employing a within-subjects analog study of 53 dually diagnosed adolescents in residential treatment, Rogers and his colleagues found that the MMPI-A scales F, F_1, and F_2 were not useful in identifying adolescents' responses under honest versus feigning conditions, but they did observe that the raw score difference between the F and K scale (the F-K index) did appear promising using values equal to or greater than 20 in this classification task. Further, the authors reported that the optimal combination of data from the SIRS and MMPI-A F-K index showed evidence of incremental validity in this classification task. Although the results for the F-K index were promising in this investigation, cross-validation of these findings is clearly required before conclusions can be reached regarding their generalizability. McGrath et al. (2000) described the development and initial validation of the Infrequency-Psychopathology scale (Fp-A) for the MMPI-A, which paralleled the development of a similar scale for the MMPI-2. Their findings demonstrated that the 40-item Fp-A scale appeared somewhat more effective than the F scale at discriminating between fake-bad and accurate reports of psychopathology for samples of normal adolescents and adolescents in an inpatient treatment program and a sample of 140 high school students who were instructed to respond to the MMPI-A in a manner that simulated serious psychopathology. Although the authors conclude that there is tentative evidence that the Fp-A scale may serve as a useful adjunct to the MMPI F scale as an indicator of overreporting, the evidence that the Fp-A scale provided incremental validity beyond the F scale in this study was relatively limited, and future research is needed before this scale is utilized in standard clinical practice with the MMPI-A.

The Lie (*L*) Scale

The L scale in the traditional MMPI consists of 15 items that were originally selected to identify individuals deliberately attempting to lie or to avoid answering the item pool in an open and honest manner. The L scale is keyed in the false direction for all items and was created using a rational/intuitive identification of items. The MMPI-A L scale retains all but one item from the original measure and thus is a 14-item scale. The traditional L scale item "Sometimes in elections I vote for men about whom I know very little" was deleted because of its limited relevance for many adolescents. Table 4.8 presents examples of the abbreviated items contained in the MMPI-A L scale.

The MMPI-A L scale covers a variety of content areas, including aggressive or hostile impulses, representing common human failings for the majority of individuals. Higher L scale values have been related to longer treatment duration for hospitalized

TABLE 4.8
Sample Items From the *L* Scale

Items scored if true
None
Examples of items scored if false
26.   Want to swear.
38.   Sometimes don't tell truth.

Note. MMPI-A abbreviated items reproduced by permission. MMPI-A test booklet copyright © 1992 by the Regents of the University of Minnesota; MMPI-A abbreviated item test booklet copyright © 2004 by the Regents of the University of Minnesota.

TABLE 4.9
Interpretation Guidelines for the MMPI-A L Scale

T-Score	Interpretation
45 and below	*Low.* May reflect an open, confident stance among normal adolescents. "All-true" or "fake-bad" response sets are possible in this range.
46–55	*Normal.* Scores in this range reflect an appropriate balance between the admission and denial of common social faults. These adolescents tend to be flexible and nonrigid.
56–65	*Moderate.* May reflect an emphasis on conformity and conventional behaviors among adolescents. Scores in this range for adolescents in psychiatric settings may reflect the use of denial as a central defense mechanism.
66 and above	*Marked.* Scores in this range reflect extreme use of denial, poor insight, and lack of sophistication. Treatment efforts are likely to be longer and associated with guarded prognosis. An "all-false" or "fake-good" response set may have occurred.

Note. Adapted from Archer (1987b). Copyright © 1987 by Lawrence Erlbaum Associates, Inc. Reprinted by permission.

adolescents (Archer, White, & Orvin, 1979). In general, the clinical correlates of L scale elevations for adolescents appear to be similar to those in adult populations. Thus, moderate elevations, in the range of T-score values of 60 to 65, are related to an emphasis on conformity and the use of denial among adolescent respondents. Marked elevations in excess of a T-score value of 65 raise the possibility of a "nay-saying" response set or an unsophisticated attempt by a respondent to present personal characteristics in a favorable light and in a "saintly" manner. Because all L scale items are keyed in the false direction, this measure (in conjunction with the *TRIN* scale discussed later in this chapter) serves as a valuable index in detecting all-true and all-false response patterns. Table 4.9 presents a variety of interpretive suggestions for four levels of L scale elevations on the MMPI-A.

The Defensiveness (K) Scale

In contrast to the F scale, the K scale did not undergo any item deletions in the development of the MMPI-A, and the wording of only two items was modified. Thus, the MMPI-A K scale consists of 30 items that were empirically selected to identify individuals who display significant degrees of psychopathology but produce profiles that are within normal limits (Meehl & Hathaway, 1946). Only one of these items is scored in the true direction. Table 4.10 provides examples of abbreviated items from the MMPI-A K scale.

K scale item content is quite diverse and covers issues ranging from self-control to family and interpersonal relationships (Greene, 1980, 2000). Although the K-correction procedure for basic scales 1, 4, 7, 8, and 9 has become standard practice with adult respondents, K-correction *was not* used with adolescent profiles on the original MMPI and *is not* used with the MMPI-A. Marks et al. (1974) presented three reasons why K-correction procedures should not be employed with adolescents. First, they noted that K-correction was originally developed on a small sample of adult patients and "hence its applicability to adolescents is at best questionable" (p. 134). Second, they noted that Dahlstrom et al. (1972), as well as other authorities, have repeatedly cautioned against the use of K-weights with samples that differ significantly from those employed by

TABLE 4.10
Sample Items From the MMPI-A *K* Scale

Item scored if true (one only)
79.   Rarely quarrel with family.
Items scored if false
34.   Would like to destroy things.
72.   Hard to convince people of truth.

Note. MMPI-A abbreviated items reproduced by permission. MMPI-A test booklet copyright © 1992 by the Regents of the University of Minnesota; MMPI-A abbreviated item test booklet copyright © 2004 by the Regents of the University of Minnesota.

Meehl in the development of the original *K*-correction weights. Finally, they cited previous research using adolescent samples that indicated that adolescents' MMPI scores produced a stronger relationship to external criteria without use of the *K*-correction procedure. This latter pattern was also reported by Weed, Ben-Porath, and Butcher (1990) in MMPI data collected in adult samples and by Archer, Fontaine, and McCrae (1998) in MMPI-2 results for adult psychiatric inpatients. These latter findings raise questions concerning the usefulness of *K*-correction even in the interpretation of adult profiles.

Alperin et al. (1996) derived experimental *K*-weights for the MMPI-A to determine the degree to which the use of this correction procedure could improve test accuracy when weighting was based on results obtained in adolescent samples. Empirically determined *K*-weights were systematically added to raw score values from the eight basic scales (excluding *Mf* and *Si*) to optimally predict adolescents' membership in the MMPI-A normative sample of 1,620 adolescents versus a clinical sample of 122 adolescent psychiatric inpatients. Hit rate analyses were utilized to assess the degree to which the *K*-corrected uniform T-scores resulted in improved classification accuracy in contrast to the standard MMPI-A non-*K*-corrected adolescent norms. Results indicated that the use of a *K*-correction procedure for the MMPI-A did not result in any systematic improvement in test accuracy in the classification task used in this study. The authors concluded that their findings did not support the clinical application of a *K*-correction procedure with the MMPI-A.

In general, the *K* scale is unique (relative to the basic clinical scales) in that *K* scale mean raw score values for adolescents tend to be *lower* than that found for adult samples. For example, the *K* scale mean raw score values for males and females in the MMPI-2 adult normative sample were 15.30 and 15.03, respectively (Butcher et al., 1989), whereas the normative values for males and females in the MMPI-A normative sample were 12.7 and 11.5, respectively (Butcher et al., 1992). Although little research has been devoted to this issue, the available data indicate that *K* scale elevations in adolescents may be related to the same clinical correlate patterns that have been established for adult respondents. Thus, markedly low elevations on the *K* scale tend to be produced by adolescents who may be consciously or unconsciously exaggerating their degree of symptomatology in an attempt to fake-bad or as a "cry for help" in response to acute distress. Conversely, elevations on the *K* scale are often produced by adolescents who are defensive and who underreport psychological problems and symptoms. Further, this latter group of adolescents often fail to perceive a need for psychological treatment and attempt to deny psychological problems. They often hide behind a facade of adequate coping and adjustment. In both the adolescent and

TABLE 4.11
Interpretation Guidelines for the MMPI-A K Scale

T-Score	Interpretation
40 and below	*Low.* These adolescents may have poor self-concepts and limited resources for coping with stress. Scores in this range may be related to "fake-bad" attempts among normals or acute distress for adolescents in psychiatric settings.
41–55	*Normal.* Scores in this range reflect an appropriate balance between self-disclosure and guardedness. Prognosis for psychotherapy is often good.
56–65	*Moderate.* Scores in this range among normal adolescents may reflect a self-reliant stance and reluctance to seek help from others. For adolescents in psychiatric settings, this level of K is related to an unwillingness to admit psychological problems and a denial of the need for treatment or psychiatric help.
66 and above	*Marked.* Scores in this range reflect extreme defensiveness often related to poor treatment prognosis and longer treatment duration. The possibility of a "fake-good" response set should be considered.

Note. Adapted from Archer (1987b). Copyright © 1987 by Lawrence Erlbaum Associates, Inc. Reprinted by permission.

adult MMPI literatures, high K scale profiles have been linked to a poor prognosis for positive response to psychological intervention because of the respondents' inability or refusal to cooperate with treatment efforts (Archer et al., 1979). Table 4.11 offers interpretive guides for four elevation levels on the MMPI-A K scale.

Traditional Validity Scale Configurations

A configural approach to validity scale interpretation may be applied to adolescents' MMPI-A profiles in a manner analogous to the interpretive suggestions for adults by Friedman et al. (2001), Graham (1987, 2000), Greene (1980, 2000), and Nichols (2001). The reordering of the traditional validity scales, however, in the MMPI-A (i.e., F, L, and K) requires us not to expect the validity scale configural patterns obtained with the original MMPI. Figure 4.1 provides a dimension along which to evaluate possible MMPI-A validity scale configurations. The "most closed" validity configuration occurs when scales L and K are markedly elevated and scale F (including F_1 and F_2) is below a T-score of 50. The greater the degree of elevation manifested in scales L and K relative to the F scale and its subscales, the more the adolescent is attempting to present an extremely favorable self-report that minimizes or denies the occurrence of any psychological problems. This type of validity configuration would most likely be encountered among adolescents who were involuntarily placed in treatment by parents or court officials. The utility of the MMPI-A validity scales of defensiveness (L and K) in detecting underreporting of symptoms on the MMPI-A was recently investigated in clinical and community samples of adolescents by Baer, Ballenger, and Kroll (1998). Half of the subjects in each of the samples were instructed to complete the MMPI-A in such a manner as to create an impression of excellent psychological adjustment and functioning. The remaining respondents completed the MMPI-A under standard instructions. The traditional L and K scales were found to be moderately effective in discriminating standard from underreported profiles, with correct classification rates ranging from 68% to 84%. Both the community and clinical samples of adolescents instructed to underreport symptomatology produced significantly higher

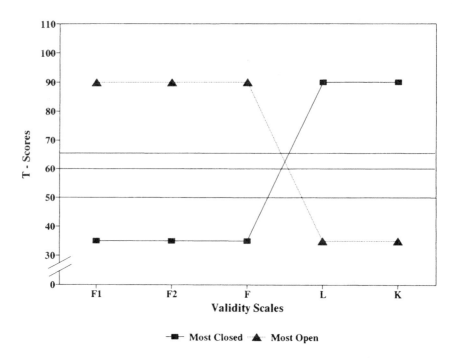

FIG. 4.1. Validity scale configurations: Most open to most closed.

means on these scales than those given the standard instructions. At the opposite extreme is the "most open" profile configuration characterized by elevated F scale and
subscale values and L and K scale T-score values below 50. As the elevation difference
between the F scale and the L and K scales becomes more pronounced or extreme, it
is increasingly likely that the adolescent is exaggerating symptomatology or psychological problems as a cry for help. This pattern may reflect a conscious or unconscious
effort to overreport symptomatology.

On the original form of the MMPI, configural approaches to validity scale interpretation were rendered complex because adolescents' F scale values were typically
higher than those found for adults, and thus interpretive inferences needed to be adjusted accordingly. The "most open" profile type was very frequently encountered
for adolescents on the original instrument, whereas the "most closed" profile type
occurred infrequently. Additionally, related to the issue of high F scale elevations,
the F-K index was not useful when employed with adolescents (Archer, 1987b). Because of the major revision that occurred in creating the MMPI-A F scale, validity
scale configuration patterns have become correspondingly more useful for this instrument. For example, Stein, Graham, and Williams (1995) found the F-K index as
successful as the F scale in detecting faked profiles on the MMPI-A, and, as noted
earlier, Rogers et al. (1996) reported that the F-K index was more effective than the
MMPI-A F scale and subscales in detecting overreported profiles. However, until
more research has been conducted using the F-K index with adolescent samples, the
standard clinical use of this index is not advised. This is consistent with the recommendation by Rothke et al. (1994) that separate F-K guidelines should be established
for male and female subjects in specific populations or diagnostic groups. In addition,
Baer, Wetter, and Berry (1992) and Bagby, Rogers, Buis, and Kalemba (1994) noted that

TABLE 4.12
Examples of Variable Response Inconsistency (*VRIN*) Scale Items

---

Sample VRIN pairs that add one point when both marked true
70. Not self-confident.
223. Wholly self-confident.
Sample VRIN pairs that add one point when both marked false
304. Try to avoid crowds.
335. Like excitement of a crowd.
Sample VRIN pairs scored when marked differently (T-F or F-T)
6. Father a good man.
86. Love(d) father.

Note. MMPI-A abbreviated items reproduced by permission. MMPI-A test booklet copyright © 1992 by the Regents of the University of Minnesota; MMPI-A abbreviated item test booklet copyright © 2004 by the Regents of the University of Minnesota.

generally accepted cutoff values for the *F-K* index have not been established, and a wide variety of cutting scores have been employed in different studies.

ADDITIONAL VALIDITY SCALES FOR THE MMPI-A

The Variable Response Inconsistency (*VRIN*) and True Response Inconsistency (TRIN) Scales

A *VRIN* scale and a *TRIN* scale were originally developed for the MMPI-2 and served as models for their counterparts in the MMPI-A. Both the *VRIN* and *TRIN* scales provide data concerning an individual's tendency to respond to MMPI-A items in a consistent manner. The *VRIN* scale consists of 50 pairs of items with either similar or opposite content. Each time an adolescent answers an item pair inconsistently, one raw score point is added to the *VRIN* scale score. Table 4.12 provides illustrations of *VRIN* scale items. As shown in this table, the content of the item pairs determines the response combination that would result in a point added to the *VRIN* total. For some item pairs, two true responses are scored; for other combinations, two false responses are scored; and for others, a combination of true and false responses produces an inconsistent response pattern, resulting in a point added to the raw score value. The *VRIN* findings can serve as a warning that an adolescent has responded to the MMPI-A in an indiscriminate and random manner. For example, Berry et al. (1992) and Berry et al. (1991) demonstrated the sensitivity of the MMPI-2 *VRIN* scale to the presence of random responding in college student samples. Elevated *VRIN* scale values can also be used to support the inference that an elevation on the *F* scale is likely to reflect carelessness or a random response pattern. Illustrating this point, Wetter, Baer, Berry, Smith, and Larsen (1992) found that both random responses and malingered responses produced elevations on the MMPI-2 *F* scale in a college student sample but that elevated *VRIN* scale scores resulted solely from random response patterns. Thus, a high *VRIN* score combined with a high *F* scale score strongly suggests the possibility of a random response pattern. It should be noted, however, that *VRIN* T-score values within the acceptable range do not necessarily imply that an MMPI-A profile is subject to valid interpretation. Although *VRIN* scale values are related to inferences concerning the consistency of an adolescent's response pattern, findings from this scale do not permit judgments concerning the accuracy of the subject's responses. The distinction between accuracy and consistency as subcomponents of validity assessment is discussed later in this chapter.

The effectiveness of the MMPI-A *VRIN* scale in adolescent populations has been the focus of several relatively recent studies. Baer, Ballenger, Berry, and Wetter (1997), for example, examined random responding on the MMPI-A in a sample of 106 normal adolescents. Participants were asked to report on the frequency, location, and reason for any random responses that occurred during the standard administration of the MMPI-A, and relationships between self-reported random responding and validity scales scores were examined, including the F, F_1, F_2, and *VRIN* scales. In addition, participants were assigned to groups that varied in the extent of random responding (0%, 25%, 50%, 75%, or 100% random). Findings indicated that most adolescents acknowledged one or more random responses during the standard administration process, and the number of self-reported random responses was significantly corre-lated with the F scale. Further, scores on the F and *VRIN* scales were effective in discriminating standard protocols from protocols with various levels of randomness. The authors concluded that their study provided strong support for the utility of the *VRIN* scale because this scale is designed to be sensitive to random responding but unlike the F scale does not typically elevate under conditions of symptom over-reporting. Archer and Elkins (1999) followed up this line of research by evaluating the utility of MMPI-A validity scales in detecting differences in response patterns between protocols produced by 354 adolescents in clinical settings and a group of 354 randomly produced MMPI-A protocols. Results indicated that the MMPI-A va-lidity scales F, F_1, F_2, and *VRIN* all appeared to be useful in correctly identifying protocols from actual clinical participants versus randomly generated response pat-terns. Further, it was noted that the optimal MMPI-A scale cutoffs for these validity scales were largely consistent with the interpretive recommendations provided in the MMPI-A test manual (Butcher et al., 1992), that is, T ≥ 80 on *VRIN* and T ≥ 90 on F, F_1, F_2. Archer et al. (2002) extended this methodology by examining the ability of the MMPI-A validity scales to detect varying degrees of protocol randomness. They compared MMPI-A protocols resulting from the administration of the instrument to 100 adolescent inpatients under standard conditions and 100 protocols containing varying degrees of computer-generated random responses. In general, the overall classification accuracy reported by Archer et al. (2002) was highly consistent with the overall classification accuracy reported by Archer and Elkins (1999) and by Baer et al. (1997). T-score values for the *VRIN* scale consistently climbed as increasing levels of randomness were introduced into the protocols, with a T-score value ≥80 on the *VRIN* scale generally functioning as a useful cutoff across varying levels of random responding. However, the *VRIN* scale was more effective in distinguishing standardly administered protocols from protocols that contained larger proportions of random responding. No MMPI-A validity scale was particularly effective in detecting par-tially random responding that involves less than half of the items in the second half of the test booklet. In general, the MMPI-A *VRIN* scale has demonstrated sufficient effectiveness to serve as a model for similar attempts to detect random responding on other test instruments. For example, a variable response inconsistency scale has been developed for the Jesness Inventory, a self-report instrument designed for use with delinquent boys and girls aged 8 through 18 (Pinsoneault, 1997, 1999).

The *TRIN* scale for the MMPI-A, like its counterpart in the MMPI-2, was devel-oped to detect an individual's tendency to indiscriminately respond to items as either *true* (acquiescence response set) or *false* (nay-saying) regardless of item content. This

TABLE 4.13

Examples of True Response Inconsistency (*TRIN*) Scale Items

Sample TRIN pairs that add one point when both marked true
   14. Work atmosphere tense.
 424. Not much stress.

Sample TRIN pairs that subtract one point when both marked false

   46. Friendly.
 475. Quiet around others.

Note. MMPI-A abbreviated items reproduced by permission. MMPI-A test booklet copyright © 1992 by the Regents of the University of Minnesota; MMPI-A abbreviated item test booklet copyright © 2004 by the Regents of the University of Minnesota.

MMPI-A scale consists of 24 pairs of items that are negatively correlated and semantically opposite in content. The *TRIN* scale was developed in such a manner that raw score values must convert to T-scores of 50 or greater (i.e., raw scores cannot convert to T-score values below 50). *TRIN* T-scores greater than 50 may represent deviations from the mean in either the acquiescent or nay-saying direction. In the computer scoring of the MMPI-A provided by Pearson Assessments, the direction of deviation is indicated by a "T" or "F" following the T-score assigned to the *TRIN* scale. For example, 80 T would indicate inconsistency in the true-response direction, whereas 80 F would represent an equal magnitude of inconsistency in the direction of false responding. Table 4.13 provides examples of *TRIN* items. As shown in Table 4.13, *true* responses to some item pairs and *false* responses to other item pairs result in scores on the *TRIN* scale. *TRIN* scores provide information on the degree to which an adolescent has tended to employ an acquiescent or nay-saying response style. As noted by Greene (2000), however, these scores should not be used to determine whether an adolescent has endorsed MMPI-A items in a random manner. As shown later in this chapter in the example of a random profile, the *TRIN* scale may often produce acceptable T-score values under a random response set condition. The specific formula for *TRIN* scoring, as provided in the MMPI-A manual (Butcher et al., 1992, 2001), is as follows:

1. For each of the following response pairs *add* one point:

   14 T–424 T   119 T–184 T
   37 T–168 T   146 T–167 T
   60 T–121 T   242 T–260 T
   62 T–360 T   264 T–331 T
   63 T–120 T   304 T–335 T
   70 T–223 T   355 T–367 T
   71 T–283 T   463 T–476 T
   95 T–294 T

2. For each of the following response patterns *subtract* one point:

   46 F–475 F   128 F–465 F
   53 F–91 F   158 F–288 F
   63 F–120 F   245 F–257 F
   71 F–283 F   304 F–335 F
   82 F–316 F

3. Then add 9 points to the total raw score.

Both *TRIN* and *VRIN* are new MMPI-A scales, and limited information is currently available concerning the characteristics of these measures in adolescent samples. Because both scales include items beyond item 350, the full MMPI-A must be administered to score *TRIN* or *VRIN*. The following rough guidelines in interpreting these scales are tentatively recommended:

VRIN T-scores of 70–79 indicate marginal levels of response inconsistency.

VRIN T-scores ≥ 80 indicate unacceptable levels of response inconsistency.

TRIN T-scores of 70–79 indicate marginal levels of response inconsistency.

TRIN T-scores ≥ 80 indicate unacceptable levels of response inconsistency.

Inconsistent item endorsement patterns for adolescents may be related to inadequate reading ability, limited intellectual ability, active noncompliance or test resistance, or thought disorganization related to substance abuse–induced toxicity or active psychosis.

The Items-Easy (*Ie*) and Items-Difficult (*Id*) Scales

The evaluation of response consistency among adolescents administered the MMPI-A may include the use of the Items-Easy (*Ie*) and Items-Difficult (*Id*) scales developed by Krakauer, Archer, and Gordon (1993). These scales were designed to assess or estimate the degree to which reading comprehension deficiencies may be responsible for inconsistent item endorsement patterns on the MMPI-A. Using a combination of two criteria, two 13-item scales were empirically created for this purpose. The 13 items selected for the *Ie* scale were evaluated objectively on three standardized reading measures and were shown to be among those MMPI-A items exhibiting relatively low levels of reading difficulty. In addition, these items did not produce significant correlations with subjects' scores on a measure of reading ability. In contrast, the 13 items selected for the *Id* scale were shown to be among those with a higher level of reading difficulty, and each exhibited a significant inverse correlation with reading level scores. Items on both scales were additionally subjected to the requirement that all items must have a critical-direction endorsement frequency of 35% or less in the MMPI-A normative sample of 1,620 adolescents. Based on these procedures, items were selected in such a way that the two scales had the same number of items and the same percentage of items keyed true and false. Additionally, the two scales were roughly equivalent in terms of mean item endorsement frequency and the percentage of items loading on each of the basic clinical scales. Preliminary research supported the hypothesis that adequate readers would endorse the items in the *Ie* and *Id* scales with approximately equal frequency whereas deficient readers would endorse more *Id* scale items than *Ie* scale items. Krakauer et al. (1993) concluded that these scales held the potential to assist clinicians in detecting possible reading limitations, particularly for those subjects who produced significant elevations on the *VRIN* scale and the *F* scale. For example, high *VRIN* scale scores in combination with a small *Id-Ie* difference score could be illustrative of a random response pattern produced by a noncooperative teenager. In contrast, a high *VRIN* scale score in combination with a higher endorsement rate for *Id* items than *Ie* items might be reflective of a response pattern produced by a cooperative subject who simply did not have adequate reading ability to understand many of the MMPI-A items. Krakauer et al. (1993) cautioned that the *Ie* and *Id* scales had not undergone clinical research evaluation, however, and suggested that these measures be employed only in research investigations. Unfortunately, no published studies have appeared on these scales over the past decade, and their use remains restricted to research investigations at this time. The item composition of the MMPI-A *Ie* scale is as follows:

Scored true: 28, 66, 88, 93, 159, 344, 345, 347, 348

Scored false: 77, 122, 324, 346

The item composition of the *Id* scale is as follows:

Scored true: 30, 101, 183, 219, 250, 273, 276, 349, 350

Scored false: 48, 89, 98, 120

EFFECTS OF RESPONSE SETS ON STANDARD SCALES

Graham (2000) described the characteristics of MMPI-2 profiles that are generated by adults based on systematic response sets such as all-true, all-false, and random patterns, and Graham, Watts, and Timbrook (1991) described MMPI-2 fake-good and fake-bad profiles. Similar response set data for adolescents on the original test instrument were presented by Archer, Gordon, and Kirchner (1987) and summarized for the MMPI-A by Archer and Krishnamurthy (2002) and Butcher and Williams (2000). Archer and Krishnamurthy (2002) noted that adolescents employing all-true and all-false response sets on the MMPI-A are easily detected and that the extreme validity scale profile features are similar to those produced by their adult counterparts. Additionally, the fake-bad or overreporting response set found for adolescents is relatively easy to identify based on the occurrence of an extremely elevated F scale combined with clinical-range elevations on all clinical scales (excluding *Mf* and *Si*). In contrast, adolescents' production of random response sets and particularly on fake-good or underreporting response sets were more difficult to detect on the MMPI-A. The following section provides a summary of the effects of a variety of response sets on the MMPI-A.

All-True

The all-true response pattern is indicated by extremely low scores on scales L and K and markedly elevated scores (T > 90) on scales F, F_1, and F_2. The male and female all-true profiles on MMPI-A norms are presented in Fig. 4.2. The raw score value for *TRIN* (raw score = 24) clearly indicates response inconsistency (in particular, an extreme yea-saying response style), whereas the *VRIN* value (raw score = 5) is within acceptable limits. In addition to the extreme "most open" validity scale pattern formed by scales F_1, F_2, F, L, and K, there is a very noticeable positive or psychotic slope to the profile, with elevations on scales 6, 7, 8, and 9. These characteristics are similar to those found for all-true response patterns among adolescents on the original form of the MMPI (Archer, 1989).

   Figure 4.3 shows the content scale and supplementary scale profiles for the all-true response pattern for males and females. Because the majority of items in the content scales are keyed in the true direction, these profiles exhibit very elevated T-score values for most content scales.

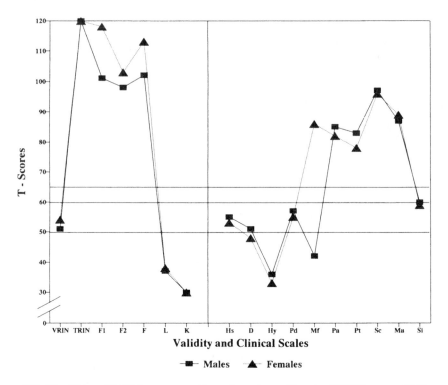

FIG. 4.2. All-true MMPI-A response patterns for males and females (*TRIN* T-score = 120T for males and females).

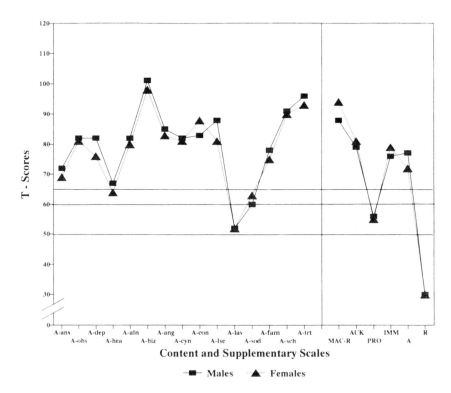

FIG. 4.3. All-true MMPI-A content and supplementary scale patterns for males and females.

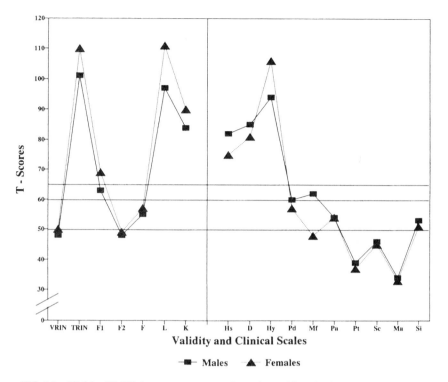

FIG. 4.4. All-false MMPI-A response patterns for males and females (*TRIN* T-score = 101F for males and 110F for females).

All-False

The profiles shown in Fig. 4.4 will be produced if adolescents respond *false* to all MMPI-A items. The *TRIN* raw score value is zero (T > 100) and the *VRIN* raw score value is 4. The *TRIN* value indicates response inconsistency (in particular, an extreme nay-saying response style). In addition, the F_1 values produce marginally elevated T-scores, whereas the F_2 and F T-scores fall within normal limits. The all-false profiles are characterized by extreme elevations on validity scales *L* and *K* and on the first three clinical scales of the MMPI, which are frequently referred to as the *neurotic triad*. The clinical scale profiles have a distinctive negative slope; that is, scale values decrease as the numerical scale designations increase. Further, these profiles are similar to the all-false profiles for adolescents on the original MMPI reported by Archer et al. (1987) and for adults on the MMPI-2 reported by Graham (2000). The characteristic profile features of both the all-true and the all-false patterns clearly indicate profile invalidity. It should be clearly noted, however, that these deviant response sets should typically be detected by the inspection of the completed answer form prior to the profiling of response features.

Figure 4.5 shows the content and supplementary scale profiles associated with an all-false pattern. Because all content scales except Health Concerns (*A-hea*) and Low Aspirations (*A-las*) are composed of items predominantly keyed in the *true* direction, an all-false response set produces low T-scores for these scales. In contrast, the Repression (*R*) scale is composed of items exclusively keyed in the *false* direction and therefore produces a very elevated T-score value under this response set.

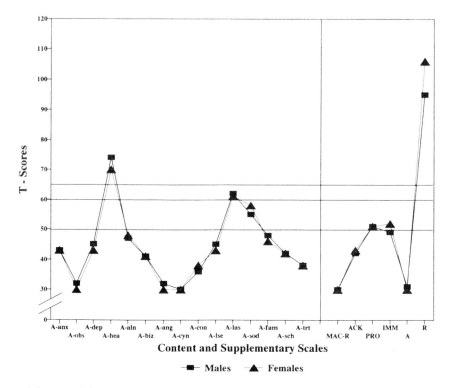

FIG. 4.5. All-false MMPI-A content and supplementary scale patterns for males and females.

Random Response Sets

An adolescent may also respond to MMPI-A items randomly. The profiles resulting from equal numbers of true and false item endorsements on each MMPI-A basic scale (i.e., the effect of an infinite number of random sorts) are presented in Fig. 4.6.

Consistent with the findings for adolescents on the original test instrument (Archer et al., 1987), random MMPI-A profiles are more difficult to detect than other response sets. The MMPI-A validity scale *VRIN* is a useful indicator of random response sets in adolescents. The *TRIN* scale, however, may often produce acceptable T-score values under a random response set condition. The random profile is also characterized by a highly unusual validity scale configuration in which clinical-range elevations on scales F, F_1, and F_2 are accompanied by a clinical-range L scale elevation. The actual profile characteristics of a random response set will vary substantially depending on the particular approach used to randomize the response pattern. The profile characteristics will also vary quite markedly depending on the degree of randomness in the profile, and Archer et al. (2002) demonstrated that "partially random" protocols may be difficult or impossible to detect through the examination of validity scale results. Random response patterns should always be considered when an adolescent completes the MMPI-A too quickly (i.e., in less than 40 minutes).

Figure 4.7 shows the effects of a totally random response pattern on the MMPI-A content and supplementary scales. Similar to the corresponding basic scale profiles, even these profiles are relatively difficult to detect based on shape and elevation features.

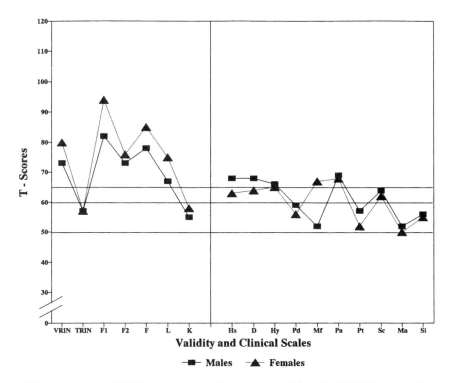

FIG. 4.6. Random MMPI-A response profiles for males and females. (*TRIN* T-score = 60T for males and females).

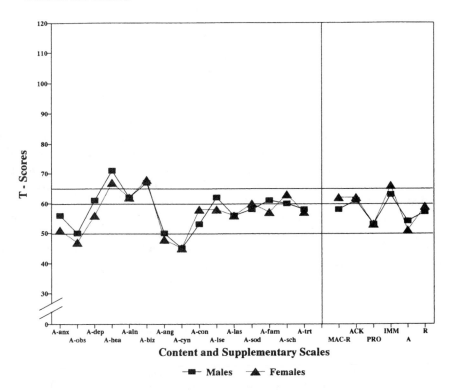

FIG. 4.7. Random MMPI-A content and supplementary scale patterns for males and females.

(Fake-Good) Underreporting

Another response set issue concerns the characteristics of MMPI-A profiles produced by adolescents who distort the accuracy of their responses. Adolescents may
fake-good, or underreport problems on the MMPI-A, or they may fake-bad, completing the MMPI-A in a manner that overreports symptomatology. Because these types
of profiles may be produced by individuals who consciously or unconsciously distort
their responses, Greene (2000) and Archer and Krishnamurthy (2002) emphasized
the use of the terms *underreporting* and *overreporting* to describe these response sets.
Graham (2000) used the terms *positive self-presentation* and *negative self-presentation* to
describe these distortions in a subject's test responses, and Friedman et al. (2001) used
the terms *self-favorable* and *self-unfavorable*.

Studies with adult psychiatric patients have found that the ability to simulate
a normal profile is significantly related to a favorable treatment outcome among
schizophrenics (Newmark, Gentry, Whitt, McKee, & Wicker, 1983) and across psychiatric diagnoses (Grayson & Olinger, 1957). Additionally, Bonfilio and Lyman (1981)
investigated the ability of college students to simulate the profile of "well-adjusted"
peers. Results from this study indicated that simulations produced by college students
classified as *neurotic*, *normal*, and *psychopathic* based on actual MMPIs administered
under normal instructions were essentially within normal limits. Simulated profiles
produced by psychotic or hypomanic college students, however, contained clearly
pathological or clinical-range features. Graham, Watts, et al. (1991) presented MMPI-2
fake-good response features generated by college students who were administered
the MMPI with instructions to respond as they would if they were applying for a
highly valued job. The clearest indication of a fake-good profile in these data was
the occurrence of the "most closed" validity scale configuration, in which scales L
and K show marked elevations (in this study, the elevations in L were especially
high). Baer, Wetter, and Berry (1995) examined the effects of two levels of information
about the MMPI-2 validity scales on the ability of college students to underreport
symptomatology. Findings indicated that the MMPI-2 standard validity scales, including L and K, were effective in accurately identifying uncoached fakers. However,
these scales were far less effective in discriminating standard subjects from coached
subjects given either detailed or general information concerning the operation of the
MMPI-2 validity scales. These findings suggest that providing information about the
presence and functions of validity scales may enable some subjects to distort their
responses on the MMPI-2 (and potentially the MMPI-A) in a way that effectively
evades detection. Finally, Bagby, Rogers, and Buis (1994) examined the effectiveness
of various MMPI-2 validity scales and indices in the detection of malingering and
faking-good in samples consisting of 165 college students and 173 forensic inpatients.
Although several validity indicators appear to be moderately effective at detecting
fake-bad profiles, only the F-K index and the Subtle-Obvious index appeared to have
utility in the detection of efforts to underreport symptomatology.

To investigate fake-good profiles in an adolescent sample, Archer et al. (1987) administered the original form of the MMPI to a group of 22 adolescents (mean age =
14.76 years) in an inpatient psychiatric setting. Ten of these adolescents were female
and 12 were male. These adolescents were individually administered the MMPI with
the following instructions:

> We would like you to respond to the MMPI as you believe a well-adjusted teenager
> would who is not experiencing emotional or psychological problems. By well-adjusted,
> we mean an adolescent who is doing well and is comfortable in school, at home, and with
> their peers. As you read the items in the MMPI, please respond to them as you believe a

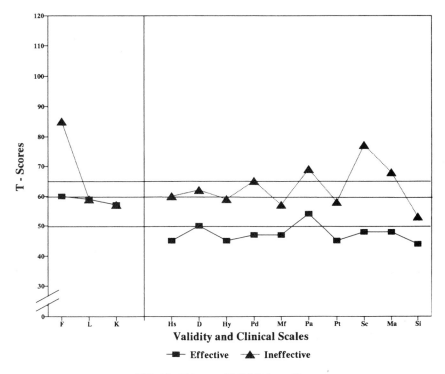

FIG. 4.8. Fake-good MMPI-A profiles.

well-adjusted adolescent would who is not in need of psychiatric counseling, and who is relatively happy and comfortable. (pp. 508–509)

As noted by Archer et al. (1987), two distinct profile groups emerged in response to this fake-good instructional set. Eight adolescents produced profiles termed *ineffective*, because they were very poor simulations of a normal profile (i.e., one or more clinical scales were elevated above a T-score value of 70). In contrast, a group of 14 adolescents were able to produce normal (effective) profiles in that none of the clinical scale values were elevated within clinical ranges. In general, adolescents in the effective group tended to be older, have less severe diagnoses, and produce less elevated profiles under the standard administration conditions.

These data were reanalyzed using information that allows for T-score conversions between the MMPI and the MMPI-A (this information is contained in the MMPI-A manual and reproduced in Appendix D). Figure 4.8 presents the corresponding MMPI-A T-score profiles for the effective and ineffective groups under fake-good instructions.

The data indicate a validity scale configuration for the effective group characterized by elevations on scales *L*, *F*, and *K*, that are generally within the acceptable ranges. Clinical scale values present a "hypernormal" configuration, with T-scores at or below 50 on most clinical scales. Therefore, the mean fake-good profile for the effective group would be difficult to distinguish from the responses of a somewhat guarded and defensive normal adolescent without significant psychiatric problems. The following guidelines, however, should serve to improve screening for adolescents who attempt to fake-good on the MMPI-A:

1. Elevations on validity scales L and K are equal to or greater than 65.
2. All clinical scale T-score values are less than or equal to 60 but are produced by an adolescent with known or established psychopathology.

Overreporting (Fake-Bad)

The ability of normal adults to simulate psychopathology, or to fake-bad, has been investigated by numerous researchers, including Anthony (1976), Exner, McDowell, Pabst, Stackman, and Kirk (1963), Gough (1947, 1954), Lanyon (1967), and Meehl and Hathaway (1946). Results have consistently shown that adults fail to accurately simulate the types of symptomatology typically reported by psychiatric patients. In general, normals tend to overreport psychopathology on the MMPI in an exaggerated and nonspecific manner that is easily detected as a fake-bad attempt (Dahlstrom et al., 1975; Greene, 1980, 2000). Graham, Watts, et al. (1991) requested male and female college students to take the MMPI-2 with instructions to present themselves as if they had "serious psychological or emotional problems" (p. 267). The fake-bad profiles for both men and women were characterized by highly elevated F scale values and clinical-range elevations on all standard clinical scales except Mf and Si. Rogers, Sewell, and Ustad (1995) investigated the MMPI-2 characteristics of 42 chronic psychiatric outpatients who were administered the MMPI-2 under standard (honest) and fake-bad instructional sets. Whereas subjects under both conditions produced relatively elevated scores on the F and F_b scales, the use of an F raw score greater than 29 was found to accurately discriminate between protocols derived under the two administration conditions. Rogers, Sewell, and Salekin (1994) recently provided a meta-analysis of several MMPI-2 validity scales or indices potentially useful in the evaluation of faking-bad or overreporting psychopathology. Of these measures, the authors reported that scale F, the F-K index, and the Obvious-Subtle subscales showed particularly strong effects and demonstrated effectiveness across a variety of samples. Rogers et al. (1996) specifically evaluated the MMPI-A validity scales in terms of the capacity of these scales to detect adolescents' efforts to overreport symptomatology and concluded that the F-K index appeared most effective and promising with this population.

A number of investigations have examined the effects of providing symptom or diagnostic information on subjects' ability to effectively fake-bad or overreport symptomatology on the MMPI-2. Rogers, Bagby, and Chakraborty (1993) compared the MMPI-2 profiles of subjects who had been provided information or coached on the symptoms of schizophrenia, coached on strategies used to detect faking-bad efforts on the MMPI-2, coached on both symptoms and detection strategies, or were uncoached. These authors reported that knowledge concerning the operation and use of MMPI-2 scales and indices used to detect malingering was sufficient to allow approximately one third of their sample to elude detection. In contrast, knowledge concerning schizophrenia appeared to be less useful to simulators attempting to feign a schizophrenic disorder "of sufficient severity as to warrant hospitalization" (p. 218). Wetter, Baer, Berry, Robison, and Sumpter (1993) provided two groups of normal adults with information concerning the symptoms of posttraumatic stress disorder and paranoid schizophrenia and instructed these subjects to simulate these disorders on the MMPI-2, with monetary rewards offered for successful simulation. Wetter and her colleagues concluded that providing symptom information about a psychological disorder did not enable fakers to avoid detection. Their fake-bad groups produced lower scores on K and higher scores on F and the 10 clinical scales than actual patient groups. A variety of other investigations have examined the effects of providing symptom information on borderline personality disorder (Wetter, Baer, Berry, & Reynolds,

1994), somatoform disorder and paranoid psychosis (Sivec, Lynn, & Garske, 1994), and closed head injury (Lamb, Berry, Wetter, & Baer, 1994). In general, the results of these investigations indicate that the effects of symptom coaching are relatively limited and that the MMPI-2 validity scales are generally capable of accurately identifying malingered profiles. Illustrating this latter point, Bagby et al. (1997) reported that psychiatric residents and clinical psychology graduate students, who presumably have considerable information about psychopathology and psychological testing, were easily detected when they attempted to feign schizophrenia on the MMPI-2. Further, Storm and Graham (1998) evaluated the scores of students who were instructed to simulate general psychopathology on the MMPI-2 after being provided with information concerning the validity scales in contrast to patients who took the MMPI-2 under standard instructions. Scores on the MMPI-2 F and $F(p)$ scales were effective in discriminating students simulating psychopathology from actual patients, and the $F(p)$ scale was found to be particularly effective in this regard.

Given the plethora of studies recently emerging in this area, Ben-Porath (1994) focused on the ethical issues surrounding research in which investigators attempt to evaluate the effectiveness of various coping strategies for eluding the MMPI-2 validity scales. Ben-Porath noted that the specific coping strategies detailed in these publications could be used in forensic settings to help individuals fake MMPI profiles in a manner that successfully avoids detection. Thus, this body of literature could be misused in a manner that compromises the integrity of the instrument. Underscoring this area of concern, Wetter and Corrigan (1995) recently conducted a survey of 70 attorneys and 150 law students that indicated that almost 50% of the attorneys and over 33% of the law students believed that their clients should typically or always be informed of validity scales on psychological tests.

Research by Archer et al. (1987) investigated the characteristics of fake-bad profiles among normal adolescents. The original form of the MMPI was administered to a group of 94 public high school students in four psychology classes, with the subjects ranging in age from 14 to 18 years and roughly equally divided in terms of gender and ethnic background (Black-White). Subjects were administered the MMPI with the following instructions:

> We would like you to respond to the MMPI as you believe you would if you were experiencing serious emotional or psychological problems. By serious problems, we mean problems that were severe enough that hospitalization for treatment would be necessary. As you read the items in the MMPI, please respond to them as if you were seriously disturbed and in need of hospital treatment for psychiatric care. (p. 508)

The mean profile produced by this group showed a grossly exaggerated picture of symptomatology, including a very elevated mean F scale value of $T = 130$ and clinical-range elevations on all MMPI clinical scales except Mf and Si. Data from the fake-bad administration were reprofiled using the values provided in Appendix D of this text to derive MMPI-A norm-based T-score values. Figure 4.9, plotted on these MMPI-A norms, presents this fake-bad profile (the $TRIN$ and $VRIN$ scales cannot be derived from these data). Consistent with the findings by Archer et al. (1987) for the original MMPI and the MMPI-2 results reported by Graham, Watts, et al. (1991) for college students, the fake-bad profile on the MMPI-A is characterized by extremely elevated F scale T-score values and multiple clinical-range elevations on the standard clinical scales. These data indicate that adolescents will probably encounter substantial difficulty in successfully simulating psychiatric illness on the MMPI-A. The $TRIN$ and $VRIN$ raw score values for fake-bad and fake-good profiles, although not shown in

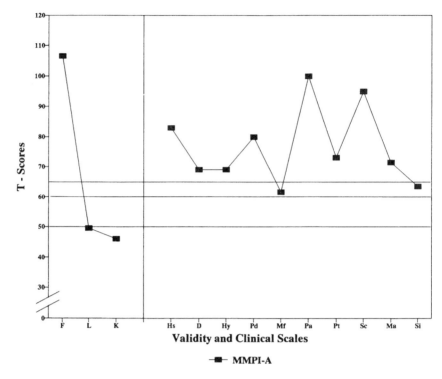

FIG. 4.9. Fake-bad MMPI-A profile.

Figs. 4.8 and 4.9, would typically be within acceptable limits for response consistency, underscoring the difference between response inconsistency and response accuracy. Greene (1989a, 2000) noted that individuals who attempt to underreport or overreport on the MMPI often produce highly consistent (although inaccurate and invalid) response patterns.

The F scale and clinical scale criteria summarized here should serve to effectively screen for most adolescents who attempt to fake-bad on the MMPI-A:

1. F scale raw score value ≥ 90.
2. Presence of a floating profile characterized by clinical scale elevations within the clinical ranges (shaded zone or higher), with the exception of *Mf* and *Si* scale values.

A CONCEPTUAL MODEL FOR VALIDITY ASSESSMENT

Greene (1989a, 2000) presented a conceptual approach or model for understanding validity assessment issues, as well as a number of empirical criteria through which to assess the validity of MMPI profiles. Figure 4.10 provides an overview of Greene's model.

Greene emphasized the use of sequential steps or stages in the validity assessment process. The first stage involves determining the number of omitted items (i.e., the Cannot Say scale raw score value), with the omission of more than 25 items related to invalid profiles potentially requiring test readministration. Greene noted that excessive item omissions not only may reflect characteristics of the respondent but can also serve as a signal of problems in the MMPI administration process.

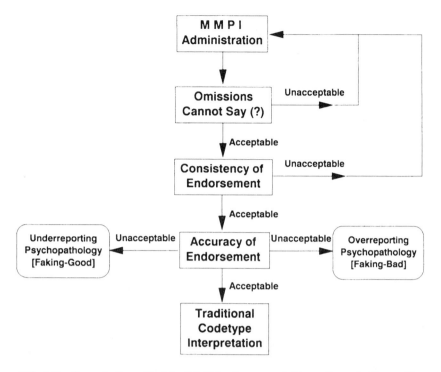

FIG. 4.10. Greene's Stage Model of Validity Assessment. (From Roger L. Greene *The MMPI-2/MMPI: An Interpretive Manual (2nd Ed.)*. Published by Allyn & Bacon, Boston, MA. Copyright © 2000 by Pearson Education. Adapted by permission of the publisher.)

Consistency of Item Endorsement

The next step in evaluating the validity of the responses involves assessing the consistency of item endorsement. As noted by Greene (2000):

> Consistency of item endorsement verifies that the client has endorsed the items in a reliable manner for this specific administration of the MMPI-2. It is necessary to ensure that the patient has endorsed the items consistently before it is appropriate to determine the accuracy with which the client has endorsed the items.... The consistency of item endorsement (may be conceptualized) as being independent of or irrelevant to item content, whereas the accuracy of item endorsement is dependent on or relevant to item content. (p. 51)

On the original version of the MMPI, item endorsement consistency has been measured by the use of the Test-Retest (*TR*) Index (Buechley & Ball, 1952) and the Carelessness (*CLS*) scale developed by Greene (1978).

The *TR* Index and the *CLS* scale are not applicable to the MMPI-A because of the changes in item content in the creation of this instrument. In particular, the repeated presentation of 16 items in the original MMPI has been eliminated in the MMPI-A. Nevertheless, as previously noted, there are new scales available on the MMPI-A to evaluate response consistency. The *TRIN* and *VRIN* scales are descendants of Greene's *CLS* scale and provide substantial information concerning the adolescent's response consistency. Further, the comparison of F_1 and F_2 values *may* allow for the detection of inconsistent response patterns that occur during the latter stages of the MMPI-A test booklet, although the effectiveness of this comparison does not appear supported by the research findings of Archer et al. (2002).

Regardless of the cause, substantial inconsistency renders the MMPI-A profile invalid, in which case further profile interpretation should not be undertaken. Greene's model of validity assessment indicates that unacceptably high levels of response inconsistency require readministration of the MMPI in order to obtain interpretable clinical data.

Accuracy of Item Endorsement

The next step in the process of assessing MMPI or MMPI-A validity is to derive an estimate of item endorsement accuracy. Greene (2000) noted several assumptions relevant to this stage of validity assessment. First, overreporting and underreporting represent a continuum, and any particular respondent may be placed at some point along this dimension. Second, attempts to overreport and underreport symptomatology tend to be generalized rather than specific. For example, adults who underreport tend to deny the presence of any type or dimension of psychopathology, and individuals engaged in overreporting tend to endorse psychopathology related to a wide variety of mental disorders. Third, Greene pointed out that the occurrence of overreporting or underreporting is relatively independent of the client's actual psychopathology. It would be inappropriate to assume that evidence of underreporting or overreporting can be used to conclude that the client does or does not have actual psychopathology. A client may overreport *and* manifest actual and severe symptomatology or may substantially underreport and also be relatively free from actual symptomatology. Finally, Greene observes that the MMPI-2 (and MMPI-A) scales used to assess consistency of item endorsement (*VRIN* and *TRIN*) are not appropriate or useful for evaluating the accuracy of item endorsement.

Greene cited several indices that may be used in determining response accuracy with the MMPI-2, including the Wiener-Harmon Subtle-Obvious subscales (Wiener, 1948), the Lachar-Wrobel (1979) Critical Item List, and, most recently, the $F(p)$ scale devised by Arbisi and Ben-Porath (1995). Because of the empirical method of scale construction used by Hathaway and McKinley in the development of the original version of the MMPI, the clinical scales contain numerous subtle items that seem unrelated to the construct that is the focus of measurement. Wiener and Harmon rationally developed Subtle and Obvious subscales for five of the MMPI clinical scales: *D*, *Hy*, *Pd*, *Pa*, and *Ma*. Greene (2000) noted that when individuals overreport symptomatology, scores on the Obvious subscales would be expected to increase relative to Subtle scale values. Conversely, when individuals attempt to underreport symptomatology, Subtle subscale values will become elevated in relation to Obvious subscale values.

Research on the Subtle-Obvious subscales in adult samples has been marked by controversial and mixed findings. Boone (1994, 1995) observed that the internal reliability estimates for the Subtle subscales are unacceptably low and that the inclusion of the Subtle subscale items attenuates the reliability estimates for the basic clinical scales. Brems and Johnson (1991) explored the utility of the Subtle-Obvious subscales as profile validity indicators in a sample of 291 psychiatric inpatients. The researchers found these scales useful in identifying individuals who tend to overreport symptomatology on the MMPI and other self-report measures. Dannenbaum and Lanyon (1993) requested groups of college undergraduates to take the MMPI under one of three instructional sets involving standard administration, faking-good, and faking-bad. As expected, faking-bad subjects scored significantly lower than subjects in the standard administration condition on the 100 most subtle items, a result interpreted as consistent with the presence of multiple items whose content relevance or face validity is opposite to the keyed direction of scoring on the Subtle subscales. These authors cautioned that although the subtle items have generally been shown to lack predictive ability, these items may prove useful in the detection of deception. Timbrook, Graham, Keiller, and Watts (1993) examined the MMPI-2 profiles of 49 psychiatric patients and 105 college students under various instructional sets to evaluate the degree to which the Subtle-Obvious subscales correctly classified faked versus accurate profiles. Although the authors found that the Subtle-Obvious subscales correctly classified a relatively high proportion of profiles, they also reported that information from the Subtle-Obvious subscales provided no incremental gain above that achieved through the use of the L and F scales in accurately classifying profiles. Bagby, Buis, and Nicholson (1995) compared the MMPI-2 responses of participants asked to fake-bad with protocols from general psychiatric and forensic inpatient samples. In addition, these investigators examined the MMPI-2 responses of subjects asked to fake-good in comparison with the MMPI-2 protocols of college students responding accurately to the instrument. These investigators also found that the F scale was superior to the Subtle-Obvious subscales in detecting fake-bad attempts but reported that the Subtle-Obvious index and the L scale were equally effective in detecting efforts to fake-good. Finally, Hollrah, Schlottmann, Scott, and Brunetti (1995) reviewed the literature on the MMPI subtle items and concluded that the degree of support for the subtle items varies depending on the type of methodology employed by the investigators and the specific Subtle subscale evaluated. These authors called for a clearer and more consistent research methodology to be employed by future studies investigating this important issue. They also concluded that the strongest current support for the Subtle-Obvious subscale items lies in their apparent ability to detect fake-good profiles in psychiatric settings.

Graham (2000) reached several conclusions critical of the use of the Subtle-Obvious subscales with the MMPI-2. First, he suggested that the subtle items were originally included in the MMPI basic scales because the item analyses and the selection process did not employ a cross-validation procedure. Second, he observed that obvious rather than subtle items are consistently related to extratest behaviors. Third, he acknowledged that although individuals attempting to under- or overreport on the MMPI and MMPI-2 may correctly endorse subtle versus obvious items, the Subtle-Obvious subscales do not permit accurate and consistent differentiation of valid profiles and under- or overreported profiles. Fourth, Graham noted that the standard validity scales of the MMPI-2 appear to be as effective as or more effective than the Subtle-Obvious subscales in detecting deviant response sets. Graham concluded that these and other problems with the Subtle-Obvious subscales led to the recent University of Minnesota Press decision to no longer include the Subtle-Obvious subscales in MMPI-2 test materials, interpretive reports, or scoring services.

Very little is known about the usefulness of the Wiener-Harmon Subtle-Obvious subscales in the assessment of adolescents. Herkov, Archer, and Gordon (1991) provided the only study of the Wiener-Harmon subscales in an adolescent sample. These investigators compared the use of the standard validity scales in relation to the Wiener-Harmon subscales in terms of ability to accurately identify adolescents in four groups: normal adolescents, psychiatric inpatients, normal adolescents instructed to fake-bad, and psychiatric inpatients instructed to fake-good. Table 4.14 compares the classification accuracy achieved by using of the sum of the difference in T-score values between

TABLE 4.14
Response Set Prediction Accuracy Based on the Wiener-Harmon Subtle-Obvious Subscales
and Traditional Validity Indices of the Original MMPI

Accuracy Measure	Fake-Bad Versus Inpatient			Fake-Good Versus Normal	
	Predictors			Predictors	
	Obv. − Sub. ≥ +140	F + K + Pa-Obv.	F ≥ T = 100	Obv. − Sub. ≤ 0	L ≥ T = 55
Hit rate	84.7%	94.1%	93.5%	77.7%	89.3%
Sensitivity	71.9%	92.2%	92.2%	50.0%	71.4%
Specificity	92.5%	95.3%	94.3%	79.5%	90.4%
PPP	85.2%	92.2%	90.1%	13.5%	32.3%
NPP	84.5%	95.3%	95.2%	96.1%	98.0%

Note. Adapted from Herkov, Archer, and Gordon (1991). Copyright © 1991 by the American Psychological Association. Reproduced by permission. Obv. − Sub. = Obvious minus Subtle difference score; Pa-Obv. = Obvious subscale for the Paranoia basic scale; PPP = positive predictive power; NPP = negative predictive power.

the Wiener-Harmon subscales (Obvious minus Subtle) and by using the traditional validity scales. Several points may be made in relation to these findings. First, the optimal Obvious minus Subtle subscale difference values used in identifying overreporting ($\geq$140) and underreporting ($\leq$0) differ substantially from those recommended by Greene (1989a) and others for adult respondents. Additionally, the Subtle-Obvious subscales were of use in identifying various response sets but were not as helpful as simple prediction rules applied to the standard validity scales. Specifically, identifying adolescents who produced F scale T-score values of 100 or above as overreporters and adolescents who produced L scale T-score values of 55 or above as underreporters proved more accurate than predictions based on the Subtle-Obvious subscales. Because of these findings, combined with the observations offered by Graham (2000) concerning limitations of the Subtle-Obvious subscales, the use of these subscales is not recommended in clinical practice with the MMPI-A.

The Lachar and Wrobel (1979) critical items consist of 111 empirically selected MMPI items related to symptoms that may motivate individuals to seek psychological treatment or related to symptomatology crucial in the clinician's diagnostic decision making. Greene (1991, 2000) recommended that the total number of Lachar-Wrobel critical items endorsed be used as an index of accuracy of item endorsement. A patient who is attempting to overreport symptomatology, for example, might be expected to endorse a large number of these items, whereas a patient underreporting psychopathology would be expected to endorse relatively few critical items.

Data on adolescent response patterns for the Lachar-Wrobel (1979) critical items on the original MMPI were provided by Greene (1991). This author reported the frequencies of the critical item endorsement produced by adolescents and adults receiving services in the Missouri public mental health system. These data, shown in Table 4.15, indicate roughly comparable levels of critical item endorsement for these two groups. Archer and Jacobson (1993) examined the frequency of endorsement of the Koss-Butcher (1973) and the Lachar-Wrobel (1979) critical items in normative and clinical samples administered the MMPI-A or the MMPI-2. Adolescents in both the normal and clinical samples endorsed clinical items with a higher frequency than did normal adults. Further, whereas adult clinical subjects consistently endorsed more critical

TABLE 4.15
Distribution of the Total Number of Lachar and Wrobel (1979) Critical Items Endorsed on the Original
MMPI in Psychiatric Samples Grouped by Age and Gender

| | Psychiatric Patients (Hedlund & Won Cho, 1979) | | | |
| | Adults | | Adolescents | |
Total Critical Items	Male (N = 8,646)	Female (N = 3,743)	Male (N = 693)	Female (N = 290)
91+	0.3%	0.3%	0.7%	0.0%
81–90	1.8	1.4	2.6	1.7
71–80	3.9	3.2	4.8	4.2
61–70	6.9	7.3	6.6	11.7
51–60	10.7	12.7	13.0	13.8
41–50	14.3	18.0	16.2	19.3
31–40	18.6	18.7	16.7	15.2
21–30	20.3	19.3	21.7	14.4
11–20	17.3	14.1	13.9	16.9
0–10	5.9	5.0	3.8	2.8
Raw Score				
M	36.5	38.0	39.2	40.5
SD	19.3	18.3	19.5	19.3

Note. From Roger L. Greene *The MMPI-2/MMPI: An Interpretive Manual,* © 1991. Published by Allyn & Bacon, Boston, MA. Copyright © 1991 by Pearson Education. Adapted by permission of the publisher.

items than adults in the normative sample, similar comparisons between adolescents in the clinical and normative samples typically showed that adolescents in clinical settings did not endorse more critical items than did normal adolescents. Tables 4.16 and 4.17 provide the MMPI-2 and MMPI-A mean item endorsement percentages for male and female subjects for the Lachar-Wrobel critical categories as reported in Archer and Jacobson (1993). These findings underscore the difficulties inherent in creating a critical item list specifically for adolescents using the type of empirical methodology that has been employed with adults (i.e., selection of items based on item endorsement frequency differences found between comparison groups). Beyond the technical difficulty of creating a critical item list for the MMPI-A, several conceptual issues were raised related to the application of critical items to the MMPI-A. Specifically, Archer and Jacobson noted that the concept of critical items has not been defined consistently throughout the history of the MMPI. Further, both the reliability and validity of critical items may be inherently limited in adolescent populations. The authors concluded that the commonly used MMPI/MMPI-2 critical item lists that have been developed based on adult samples may not be useful in the assessment of adolescents with the MMPI-A.

Forbey and Ben-Porath (1998) recently developed a set of critical items specifically for the MMPI-A. Their research attempted to address the inadequacies inherent in previous attempts to extend critical item lists generated for adults to use with adolescents. Item endorsement frequencies for boys and girls in the MMPI-A normative sample were examined, and any item that was endorsed in the scored direction by more than 30% of the normal sample was removed from the pool of potential critical items. Items that were endorsed 30% of the time or less in the keyed direction were then subjected to further analysis utilizing the response frequencies of adolescents in a clinical sample. Items differing in response frequency by more than 10 percentage

TABLE 4.16
MMPI-2 and MMPI-A Mean Item Endorsement Percentages for Males for the Lachar-Wrobel
Critical Item Categories

Number of Items			MMPI-2			MMPI-A		
MMPI-2	MMPI-A	MMPI	Normal	Clinical	X^2	Normal	Clinical	X^2
Anxiety and Tension								
11	11	11	18.36	45.18	15.66***	35.25	34.01	0.00
Sleep Disturbance								
6	5	6	18.50	42.67	12.67***	29.26	29.26	0.02
Deviant Thinking and Experience								
10	10	10	17.50	35.20	6.78**	33.45	28.72	0.21
Antisocial Attitude								
9	9	9	28.11	49.67	9.27**	38.21	63.16	11.52**
Depression and Worry								
16	15	16	15.06	45.94	21.23***	27.92	30.42	0.02
Deviant Beliefs								
15	13	15	7.53	27.33	11.22***	19.67	19.25	0.00
Substance Abuse								
3	2	3	27.67	49.00	8.45**	26.00	43.85	6.35*
Family Conflict								
4	4	4	18.75	53.25	23.63***	42.85	60.45	5.12*
Problematic Anger								
4	4	4	23.25	37.75	4.62*	44.58	52.67	0.98
Somatic Symptoms								
23	22	23	12.74	32.91	10.19**	22.60	19.15	0.27
Sexual Concern and Deviation								
6	4	6	20.67	35.00	4.19*	23.80	14.90	2.04

Note. The item endorsement frequencies for the MMPI-2 normative and clinical samples are reported in
Butcher et al. (1989) and for the MMPI-A samples are reported in Butcher et al. (1992). Adapted from Archer
and Jacobson (1993). Copyright © 1993 by Lawrence Erlbaum Associates, Inc. Reprinted by permission.
  *p < .05.   **p < .01.   ***p < .001.

points between the normative and clinical samples were then subjected to additional
statistical and subjective item selection processes. Finally, all of the 82 items identified
as having "critical" content in the previous steps were rationally examined by Forbey
and Ben-Porath and placed into 15 item content groups: Aggression, Anxiety, Cognitive Problems, Conduct Problems, Depression/Suicidal Ideation, Eating Problems,
Family Problems, Hallucinatory Experiences, Paranoid Ideation, School Problems,
Self-Denigration, Sexual Concerns, Somatic Complaints, Substance Use/Abuse, and
Unusual Thinking. Appendix E gives the item numbers in the Forbey–Ben-Porath
MMPI-A critical item list. The authors recommend a number of ways in which the
MMPI-A critical item list may facilitate test interpretation and feedback but also caution that adolescents' responses to individual test items should never be taken as
psychometrically sound indicators of psychopathology or maladjustment. With this
caution in mind, the authors note that the MMPI-A critical items may be incorporated
into the interpretive process to provide the clinician with a sense of the specific nature
and severity of the adolescent's problems as revealed in self-report. For example, an
inspection of the Depression/Suicidal Ideation content area may aid in determinat-
ing whether a depressed adolescent has endorsed items suggestive of an increased
risk for suicide. Further, the authors note that the MMPI-A critical items may be very
usefully employed in feedback to the adolescent. For example, the test interpretor

TABLE 4.17

MMPI-2 and MMPI-A Mean Item Endorsement Percentages for Females for the Lachar-Wrobel
Critical Item Categories

Number of Items			MMPI-2			MMPI-A		
MMPI-2	MMPI-A	MMPI	Normal	Clinical	X^2	Normal	Clinical	X^2
Anxiety and Tension								
11	11	11	20.00	39.22	16.24***	39.22	40.09	0.02
Sleep Disturbance								
6	5	6	24.83	38.52	11.35***	38.52	40.04	0.00
Deviant Thinking and Experience								
10	10	10	16.80	36.04	9.16**	36.04	27.53	1.13
Antisocial Attitude								
9	9	9	17.11	29.48	10.03**	29.48	48.37	6.84**
Depression and Worry								
16	15	16	16.94	33.09	20.51***	33.09	40.37	0.78
Deviant Beliefs								
15	13	15	6.53	17.05	16.05***	17.05	18.87	0.03
Substance Abuse								
3	2	3	18.67	38.33	7.95**	25.45	42.00	5.75*
Family Conflict								
4	4	4	22.50	53.75	19.43***	52.25	70.68	6.84**
Problematic Anger								
4	4	4	20.25	39.75	8.60**	45.88	48.30	0.04
Somatic Symptoms								
23	22	23	16.13	36.61	10.27**	27.30	25.31	0.03
Sexual Concern and Deviation								
6	4	6	20.17	41.83	10.31**	34.65	30.48	0.36

Note. The item endorsement frequencies for the MMPI-2 normative and clinical samples are reported in
Butcher et al. (1989) and for the MMPI-A samples are reported in Butcher et al. (1992). Adapted from Archer
and Jacobson (1993). Copyright © 1993 by Lawrence Erlbaum Associates, Inc. Reprinted by permission.
  *$p < .05$.   **$p < .01$.   ***$p < .001$.

may identify critical items that have been endorsed in a manner that is seemingly
inconsistent with the adolescent's history of current functioning and may invite the
adolescent to provide further information that might explain these responses.

The Forbey–Ben-Porath critical item set for the MMPI-A can generally be recommended as a means of understanding the nature and severity of the adolescent's
responses. This critical item list was not designed, however, and is not recommended
as a means of evaluating profile validity. Although it certainly warrants substantially
more research and empirical evaluation, its development is well documented, and
the clinical uses recommended by Forbey and Ben-Porath appear both prudent and
appropriate. As noted by Forbey and Ben-Porath, the alternative to using an MMPI-A
critical item set, from a practical standpoint, is for each clinician to select his or her
own critical items and check the responses in the MMPI-A test booklet to ensure
these items are useful for interpretive or feedback purposes. Forbey and Ben-Porath
observed that searching through item responses to determine whether a client responded in the keyed direction to particular items is both inefficient and ineffective.
Clearly, the use of a standard list of critical items identified through a series of empirical procedures such as those employed by Forbey and Ben-Porath is much preferable
to individual clinicians' reliance on nonstandard critical item selection.

SUMMARY

This chapter has provided an overview of the traditional MMPI validity scales in the assessment of MMPI-A technical validity and has reviewed a number of MMPI-A profile features produced by various response sets. In addition, it has discussed several sets of validity-related measures developed for the MMPI-A, including *TRIN* and *VRIN* scales and the F_1 and F_2 subscales. Finally, it has presented the validity assessment model developed by Greene (1989a, 2000). This model encompasses a sequential approach to MMPI and MMPI-A validity assessment and takes into account the distinction between item endorsement consistency and accuracy. Within the Greene model, item endorsement consistency may be viewed as a necessary but not sufficient component of valid response patterns.

Adolescents are most likely to overreport psychopathology as a conscious or unconscious plea for help in order to communicate their desire for attention and support. Conversely, adolescents are most likely to underreport symptomatology when they have been involuntarily placed in treatment by their parents or court officials and wish to underscore their perception that they do not have any significant problems. Additionally, adolescents will often underreport or overreport on the MMPI-A as a result of inappropriate test instructions or testing procedures that influence them, either consciously or unconsciously, to distort their responses.

Overall, there are currently insufficient data to support the use of the Wiener-Harmon Subtle-Obvious subscales. The MMPI-A Advisory Committee did not recommend the creation of MMPI-A Subtle-Obvious subscale profile sheets because of the lack of empirical evidence supporting the use of these measures in adolescent populations. The use of the traditional validity scales, individually and configurally, is recommended for the evaluation of response accuracy on the MMPI-A. As previously noted, elevations of *L* and *K*, singly or in combination, in relation to the *F* scale and subscales are related to conscious and unconscious efforts to underreport symptomatology. Further, the most open validity configuration (elevated *F*, low *L* and *K*) is related to conscious or unconscious efforts to overreport symptomatology on the MMPI-A.

Basic Clinical Scale and Codetype Correlates for Adolescents

PROFILE ELEVATION ISSUES AND THE MMPI-A
PROFILE "SHADED" ZONE

As noted in previous chapters, adolescent MMPI-A responses should be interpreted exclusively through the use of age-appropriate adolescent norms. The conclusion that adolescent norm conversion is the most appropriate means of interpreting adolescent responses does not imply that such a procedure renders the evaluation of MMPI-A profiles either simple or straightforward. The most important difficulties that occur when interpreting adolescent responses scored on adolescent norms is that the resulting profiles typically produce subclinical elevations, even for adolescents in inpatient psychiatric settings if a T-score value of 65 or above is employed as the criterion for determining clinical-range elevation. The inherent contradiction in interpreting a normal-range profile for an adolescent who exhibited evidence of serious psychopathology probably contributed to the inappropriate but widespread practice of using adult norms for adolescents on the original version of the MMPI. Thus, just as the application of adult norms to adolescent patterns tends to produce profiles that grossly overemphasize or exaggerate psychiatric symptomatology, so the application of adolescent norms, either on the original version of the MMPI or the MMPI-A, produces profiles that often appear to underestimate an adolescent's psychopathology.

Normal-range mean profiles (e.g., mean T-score values < 70) for inpatient adolescent populations on the original version of the MMPI have been reported by Archer (1987b), Archer, Ball, and Hunter (1985), Archer, Stolberg, Gordon, and Goldman (1986), Ehrenworth and Archer (1985), and Klinge and Strauss (1976). The result of this phenomenon for adolescent MMPI profile interpretation on the original MMPI instrument was that the application of a T-score criterion of 70 or above, traditionally found useful in defining clinical symptomatology for adult respondents, had substantially less utility with adolescents. Based on these observations, Ehrenworth and Archer (1985) recommended the use of a T-score value of 65 for defining clinical-range elevations for adolescents on the original instrument. Employment of this criterion in inpatient and outpatient adolescent samples served to substantially reduce the frequency of normal-range profiles obtained for adolescents (Archer, 1987b). For example, Archer, Pancoast, and Klinefelter (1989) found that the use of clinical scale T-score values of 65 or above (rather than 70 or above) to detect the presence of

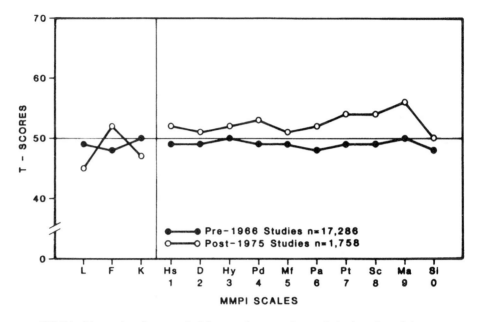

FIG. 5.1. Mean values for normal adolescents from two time periods plotted on adolescent norms by Marks and Briggs (1972). From Pancoast and Archer (1988). Copyright © by Lawrence Erlbaum Associates. Reprinted by permission.

psychopathology resulted in increased sensitivity in accurately identifying profiles produced by normal adolescents versus adolescents from outpatient and inpatient samples. Archer (1987b) speculated that the "within normal limits" T-score elevations typically found for adolescents on the original instrument were partially related to the absence of K-correction procedures as well as the high base rate of endorsement of clinical symptoms typically found in samples of normal adolescents. Alperin, Archer, and Coates (1996) more recently showed, however, that an MMPI-A K-correction procedure was not effective in significantly reducing the number of false negatives produced by this instrument.

Figure 5.1 presents the profile of normal adolescents, scored on the Marks and Briggs (1972) traditional adolescent norms, from eight studies conducted between 1947 and 1965 and compares it with the mean profile produced by normal adolescents in four studies conducted between 1975 and 1987 (Pancoast & Archer, 1988). These profiles (which present the validity scales in the traditional order) suggest that detectable changes have occurred in adolescent MMPI response patterns over the past 40 years, thus lending support to the view that a contemporary adolescent MMPI norm set needs to be created.

Figures 5.2 and 5.3 compare the post-1975 mean profile from the Pancoast and Archer (1988) review with the MMPI-A normative response patterns, separately by gender, as profiled on the Marks and Briggs (1972) adolescent norms using the conversion table in Appendix D. These data show that mean values from the MMPI-A normative sample are relatively consistent with other samples of normal adolescents that have been collected since 1975. Because the MMPI-A normative set is based on adolescent response patterns that have higher mean scale raw score values than do the original Marks and Briggs adolescent norms, a major effect of the MMPI-A norms is to reduce profile elevation for a given set of raw score values in comparison with

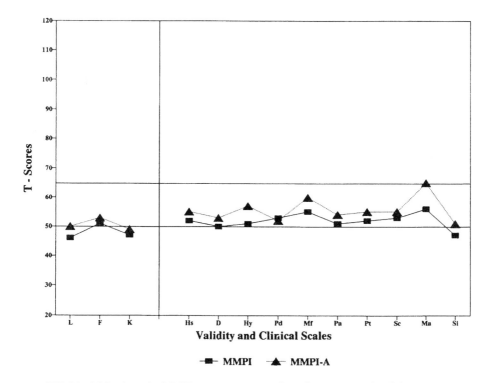

FIG. 5.2. Males from the MMPI-A normative sample and post-1975 male adolescents on the original MMPI: Profiles on Marks and Briggs (1972) adolescent norms.

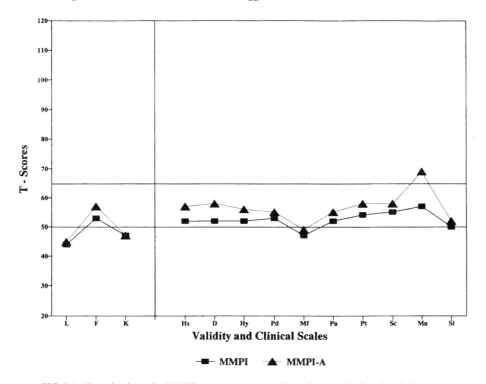

FIG. 5.3. Females from the MMPI-A normative sample and post-1975 female adolescents on the original MMPI: Profiles on Marks and Briggs (1972) adolescent norms.

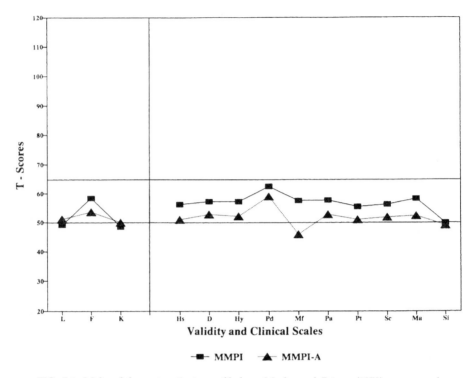

FIG. 5.4. Male adolescent patients profiled on Marks and Briggs (1972) norms and MMPI-A adolescent norms.

the original Marks and Briggs norms. This is illustrated in Figs. 5.4 and 5.5, which provide a comparison of the MMPI profile elevations produced for a group of female ($n = 1,032$) and male ($n = 730$) adolescent psychiatric patients as profiled on the traditional Marks and Briggs (1972) norms and on the MMPI-A adolescent norms (using the conversion tables in Appendix D). A comparison of profile elevations in these figures clearly demonstrates a reduction in MMPI scale T-score elevations related to the use of the more recent adolescent norm set.

In response to the profile elevation issues related to the use of the MMPI with adolescents and the further reduction in profile elevations produced by the MMPI-A adolescent norms, an innovative strategy for determining clinical-range elevations was developed for the MMPI-A. Specifically, rather than a "black line" value, that is, a single T-score value that denotes the beginning of clinical-range elevations, a range of values was created that serves as a transitional zone between normal-range and clinical-range elevations. The use of this zone concept explicitly recognizes that T-score values between 60 and 65 constitute a marginal range of elevations in which the adolescent may be expected to show some but not necessarily all of the clinical correlate patterns or traits associated with higher range elevations for a specific MMPI-A scale. Conceptually, the use of a "shaded" zone recognizes that the demarcation point or dividing line between normalcy and psychopathology during adolescence may be less clear than during adulthood. Adolescents who are not deviant in a statistical sense (i.e., who do not produce clinical-range elevations in excess of a particular T-score value) may still display behaviors or report experiences disturbing enough to be labeled as clinically significant and to require psychological intervention. As noted by Archer (1987b), the "typical" adolescent may experience sufficient psychological

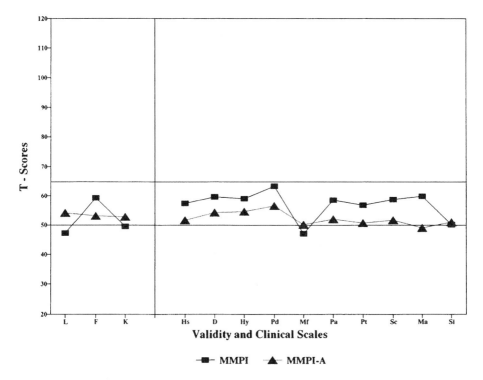

FIG. 5.5. Female adolescent patients profiled on Marks and Briggs (1972) norms and MMPI-A adolescent norms.

turbulence and distress during adolescent development that relatively minor deviations in the course of normal development may warrant psychiatric intervention and response. Thus, in addition to the traditional categories of *within-normal-limits* and *clinical-range* elevations that have been typically associated with MMPI responses, the MMPI-A has included a new category consisting of *marginally elevated* T-score values.

Recent Studies on MMPI-A Profile Elevation Issues

Newsom et al. (2003) sought to explore changes in adolescent self-presentation on the MMPI and MMPI-A over a 40-year period. The primary data used for comparison included data collected in 1989 from 1,235 adolescents aged 12 to 16 inclusive who were part of the MMPI-A normative sample and data collected in 1948–1954 from 10,514 adolescents in the same age grouping as part of Hathaway and Monachesi's (1963) study of adolescent personality and behavior. Results showed a pattern of moderate to large changes in response frequencies between the eras of data collection, with a substantially higher rate of endorsement of items in the pathological direction by adolescents in the contemporary MMPI-A normative sample. This study provided evidence of changes in mean raw score values for many of the MMPI basic scales and Harris-Lingoes subscales and reported significantly higher rates of item endorsement for contemporary adolescents on the 393 items shared in common by the MMPI and MMPI-A. Overall, the results showed that contemporary normal adolescents not only endorse more psychopathological symptoms than do adults but also endorse more pathology than did adolescents 40 years previously.

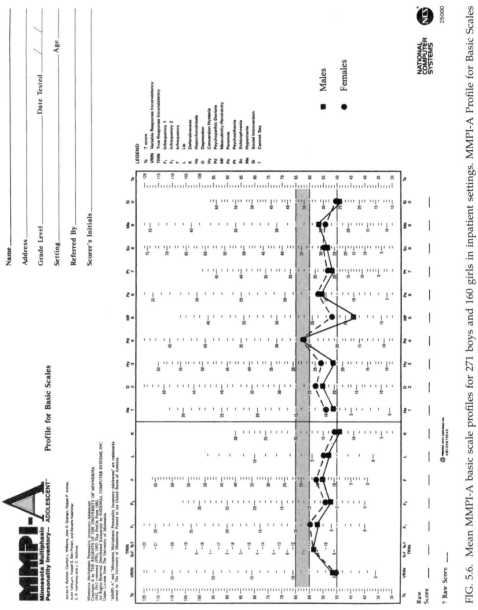

FIG. 5.6. Mean MMPI-A basic scale profiles for 271 boys and 160 girls in inpatient settings. MMPI-A Profile for Basic Scales reproduced by permission. Copyright © 1992 by the Regents of the University of Minnesota.

Research by Archer, Handel, and Lynch (2001) compared the item endorsement frequencies for the MMPI-A normative sample with results from two adolescent clinical samples, and these results were also compared with the item endorsement frequencies reported for the MMPI-2 normative sample and a clinical sample of adult psychiatric inpatients. Figure 5.6 shows the mean MMPI-A basic scale profiles for 271 boys and 160 girls in inpatient settings reported in the MMPI-A manual. Results of this study demonstrated that the MMPI-A contained a substantial number of items that do not show a significant difference in item endorsement frequency between normal and clinical samples. Furthermore, MMPI-A basic and content scales generally showed a much lower percentage of effective items than do corresponding scales of the MMPI-2. Archer et al. (2001) discussed these results as a possible factor in the relatively low range MMPI-A profiles found for clinical samples.

Following up on the research by Archer and his colleagues (2001), Lynch, Archer, and Handel (2004) examined the item endorsement frequencies found for the MMPI-A supplementary scales, Harris-Lingoes scales, and Subtle-Obvious items in criterion groups of adolescents in clinical settings grouped by gross diagnostic category. Additionally, these authors revised the basic scales by eliminating ineffective items, defined as items that failed to show a significant item endorsement frequency difference between normative and clinical populations. The results demonstrated that item effectiveness did not appear to be significantly related to the homogeneity of diagnostic grouping, nor to factors such as the obviousness or subtlety of item content. These findings are shown in Table 5.1 for items classified as effective based on the discrimination performance between the normative sample and two adolescent clinical samples (the sample reported in the MMPI-A manual and an independent clinical sample) as well as for items classified as ineffective in similar comparisons for the MMPI-2. Further, these results demonstrated that the overall effectiveness of the MMPI-A basic scales could be increased, in terms of sensitivity, specificity, positive and negative predictive

TABLE 5.1

MMPI-A Basic Scale Items Classified Based on Discrimination Performance Between the Normative Sample and Two Adolescent Clinical Samples, With Similar Item Comparisons for the MMPI-2 Normative Sample and an Adult Clinical Sample

	MMPI-A Percent Effective Items Normative/Clinical Samples		MMPI-A Percent Effective Items Normative/Independent Samples		MMPI-2 Percent Effective Items	
	Boys	Girls	Boys	Girls	Men	Women
Hs (1)	3% (1/32)	13% (4/32)	28% (9/32)	50% (16/32)	84% (27/32)	91% (29/32)
D (2)	28% (16/57)	40% (23/57)	40% (23/57)	54% (31/57)	70% (40/57)	66% (38/57)
Hy (3)	25% (15/60)	28% (17/60)	28% (17/60)	38% (23/60)	60% (36/60)	55% (33/60)
Pd (4)	63% (31/49)	71% (35/49)	69% (34/49)	67% (33/49)	72% (36/50)	72% (36/50)
Mf (5)	16% (7/44)	25% (11/44)	14% (6/44)	16% (7/44)	45% (25/56)	14% (8/56)
Pa (6)	30% (12/40)	33% (13/40)	48% (19/40)	23% (16/40)	73% (29/40)	70% (28/40)
Pt (7)	23% (11/48)	29% (14/48)	35% (17/48)	40% (19/48)	94% (45/48)	94% (45/48)
Sc (8)	18% (14/77)	30% (23/77)	45% (35/77)	44% (34/77)	92% (72/78)	97% (76/78)
Ma (9)	35% (16/46)	17% (8/46)	48% (22/46)	29% (14/46)	57% (26/46)	65% (30/46)
Si (0)	11% (7/62)	19% (12/62)	24% (15/62)	19% (12/62)	70% (48/69)	64% (44/69)

Note. Percent figures reflect the total percentage of items within each scale that showed significant differences in item endorsement frequencies between the normative and clinical sample (i.e., items classified as "effective" in terms of discrimination between samples). The first number within each parentheses indicates the number of "effective" items within the scale, and the second number indicates the total number of items in the scale. Reprinted by permission of the authors.

power, and overall hit rate, when the basic clinical scales were revised to remove the presence of ineffective items. In general, the results of these recent studies clearly show that adolescents in the MMPI-A normative sample endorsed psychopathological symptoms at a relatively high frequency and that this overall endorsement pattern for the normative sample may be a significant factor in the tendency of adolescents in clinical samples to produce within-normal-limits profiles.

Hilts and Moore (2003) examined the frequency base rates of normal range MMPI-A profiles in an inpatient sample of 388 adolescents. Further, these researchers examined the differences between adolescents with normal-range profiles (defined as profiles with clinical scale T-scores all below 60) and adolescents with elevated profiles in terms of psychotherapy history, reported internalizing and externalizing symptoms, and MMPI-A validity scale scores. Hilts and Moore reported that 30% of male and 25% of female adolescents produced MMPI-A profiles in which none of the clinical scales were elevated and that normal-range profiles could not be adequately explained by a less pathological history prior to hospitalization. Both male and female adolescents with normal-range profiles were generally less likely to report internalizing symptoms than adolescents with elevated profiles, but both groups reported comparable levels of externalizing symptoms. Hilts and Moore (2003) concluded:

> The present study has implications for both clinicians and researchers. Clinicians encountering MMPI-A profiles with no significant elevations should consider the hypotheses that the adolescents may not be experiencing feelings of distress or may not see themselves as having problems; a profile with no elevations may not mean that the adolescent is not having problems in some area of his or her life. Future research should address the issue of lack of apparent or acknowledged internal distress in some adolescents who present with externalizing symptoms. (p. 271)

Two studies have examined the usefulness of reducing the standard T-score cutoff employed to define clinical-range elevation on the MMPI-A from the standard $T \geq 65$ to the $T \geq 60$ criterion used by Hilts and Moore. Janus, Toepfer, Calestero, and Tolbert (1996) used a sample of 300 adolescents in a psychiatric inpatient setting and reported that no significant gender differences in frequency of elevations on the MMPI-A when either the traditional or modified cutoff scores were used. These authors did report, however, that using T-scores < 60 on all basic scales as the within-normal-limits criterion produced a substantial reduction in the number of false negative classifications for this clinical population in comparison with the traditional $T < 64$ criterion. In the absence of a sample of normal adolescents, however, Janus, Toepfer, et al. were not able to evaluate the overall impact of reducing the T-score standard used to define clinical-range elevations on the occurrence of false positives (i.e., the misclassification of adolescents functioning normally produced by elevations on the MMPI-A basic scales). Fontaine, Archer, Elkins, and Johansen (2001) were able to address this latter issue by comparing MMPI-A profiles from a sample of 203 adolescent inpatients with subsamples from the MMPI-A normative group. Fontaine and her colleagues compared the T-score elevation criteria $T \geq 60$ and $T \geq 65$ in defining clinical-range elevations when the clinical base rate for actual psychopathology was 20% and when it was 50%. Classification accuracy analyses indicated that $T \geq 65$ resulted in higher levels of accurate identification while minimizing misclassifications of both clinical and normal cases. The results clearly suggest that using the $T \geq 60$ criterion to reduce the frequency of false-negative misclassifications of adolescents in clinical samples is problematic and may result in an unacceptably high rate of false-positive misclassifications for normal adolescents.

In summary, the current literature indicates that the MMPI-A tends to produce relatively low scores for adolescents in clinical settings. The evidence also suggests that this issue is not effectively resolved by developing a K-correction procedure for the MMPI-A or by reducing the T-score elevation criterion from 65 to 60 in defining clinical-range elevations. Recent findings appear to indicate that the relatively high rate of endorsement of items in the pathological direction by adolescents in the MMPI-A normative sample may be one of the primary causes for the frequent within-normal-limit profiles found for adolescents in clinical settings. In this regard, Lynch et al. (2004) have noted that adolescents in the MMPI-A normative sample were not excluded based on history of psychotherapy. Approximately 200 of the adolescents in the normative sample responded yes to an item on a life events form asking if they had "been referred to a therapist or a counselor" within 6 months of the administration of the MMPI-A. This referral frequency is generally consistent with the 10% to 15% estimates of the national incidence of adolescent psychopathology (as reported in chapter 1), and subsequent analyses by Lynch et al. found that basic scale T-scores were significantly higher for this referral group than for their counterparts in the MMPI-A normative sample who did not report being referred for therapy or counseling. While the current evidence suggests that refinement of the MMPI-A normative sample to exclude adolescents receiving psychotherapy services or "improvement" of the MMPI-A item pool by deleting ineffective items may serve to reduce the disturbingly high frequency of within-normal-range profiles for adolescents in clinical settings, more research on this complex issue is clearly indicated.

UNIFORM T-SCORE TRANSFORMATION PROCEDURES FOR THE MMPI-A

As previously stated, the traditional adolescent norms developed by Marks and Briggs (1972), as well as the original MMPI norms for adults, used linear T-score transformations to convert raw score values to T-scores. Colligan, Osborne, and Offord (1980, 1984) and Tellegen and Ben-Porath (1992), in their presentation of uniform T-scores, noted that linear T-score values have presented problems in the interpretation of MMPI profiles because a given linear T-score value typically converts to differing percentile equivalents across the various MMPI scales. Thus, a given T-score value on the original Marks and Briggs (1972) norms may convert to percentile equivalent values that range as much as 10 to 15 percentile points across the 10 MMPI basic scales. This occurs because the raw score distribution for different MMPI scales varies in shape (e.g., in skewness), whereas a linear T-score transformation procedure will produce equivalent percentile values for a given T-score only if the raw score distributions for the basic scales were each normally distributed. Because the basic scales display varying degrees of skewness, the same linear T-score value will have different percentile equivalency scores across the different scales. Uniform T-scores represent composite or averaged linear T-scores and serve to promote percentile equivalence across MMPI-A clinical scales (excluding 5 and 0) and content scales. Uniform T-scores do not, however, have major effects on the underlying distribution of raw scores and do not serve to "normalize" the underlying raw score distributions. This is important in that the "true" distribution of scores on the MMPI scales may in fact *not* be normal, and therefore a normalizing procedure may actually serve to distort T-score values by artificially lowering those in the higher range (Tellegen & Ben-Porath, 1992). Table 5.2 shows the percentile values of uniform T-scores as derived for the basic scales on the

TABLE 5.2
Percentile Values of Uniform T-scores for the
MMPI-A and MMPI-2

T-Score	MMPI-A Percentile	MMPI-2[a] Percentile
30	0.6	0.2
35	4.2	3.7
40	15.1	15.1
45	36.5	34.2
50	59.1	54.9
55	76.0	72.3
60	85.7	84.7
65	92.2	92.1
70	95.8	96.0
75	98.3	98.1
80	99.4	99.3
85	99.9	99.8

[a] MMPI-2 values reported by Ben-Porath (1990).
Copyright © 1992 by the Regents of the University
of Minnesota. Reprinted by permission.

MMPI-A and for the MMPI-2 as reported by Ben-Porath (1990). As shown in this table, uniform T-scores do not correct or normalize the underlying raw score distributions in such a way that a T-score value of 50 equals a percentile value of 50. Rather, the uniform T-score procedure makes relatively small adjustments in individual scale raw score distributions achieved by creating a composite or overall distribution across the affected scales. These adjustments permit comparable percentile equivalents to be assigned to T-score values so that a given T-score will yield equivalent percentile ranks across the eight clinical scales and the content scales. Edwards et al. (1993b) compared the effects of MMPI-2 linear versus uniform T-score transformations for a sample of 200 psychiatric outpatients. These authors reported that the differences created by the uniform technique were relatively slight and that observed differences between MMPI and MMPI-2 T-scores were mainly attributable to differences in response patterns in the normative sample rather than the use of uniform T-score transformation procedures. Appendix C of this text contains uniform T-score transformations for the MMPI-A basic scales (with linear T-scores for the validity scales and basic scales 5 and 0) and the content scales. Appendix C also contains linear T-score transformations for the MMPI-A supplementary scales and for the Harris-Lingoes and *Si* subscales.

CODETYPE CONGRUENCE ISSUES

A major area of controversy concerning the development of the MMPI-2 centered on the degree to which adult profiles produced by the revised instrument were comparable to or congruent with adult profiles produced by the original MMPI (Archer, 1992c). For example, a series of articles by Dahlstrom (1992) and Humphrey and Dahlstrom (1995) suggested that the MMPI and MMPI-2 often produce substantially different profiles, whereas Tellegen and Ben-Porath (1993) and Ben-Porath and Tellegen (1995) responded with perspectives that stressed the comparability of profiles produced by these two instruments. This issue has received substantial attention because it relates to the degree to which the research literature available on the interpretation of the traditional MMPI may be generalized to the MMPI-2.

Empirical research has slowly been accumulating on the congruence between the MMPI and MMPI-2. The MMPI-2 manual (Butcher et al., 1989) provides congruence data for 2-point codes using MMPI-2 norms and the original test instrument norms in a sample of 232 male and 191 female psychiatric patients. These data indicate a congruence rate of approximately 70% for males and 65% for females when high points were defined as the most elevated clinical scale regardless of the magnitude of the elevation. Graham, Timbrook, Ben-Porath, and Butcher (1991) reexamined these data and reported that when 2-point codetype elevations were "well defined"—that is, there was at least a 5-point T-score difference between the second and third most elevated scales in the clinical scale codetype—the congruence rate increased to 81.6% for males and 94.3% for females. Edwards, Morrison, and Weissman (1993a), Husband and Iguchi (1995), and Morrison, Edwards, Weissman, Allen, and DeLaCruz (1995) reported congruence rates ranging from 60% to 94% for well-defined code-types derived in clinical samples, with findings varying as a function of the definition of congruence employed in these studies. In general, it is possible to conclude that although the MMPI and MMPI-2 are not psychometrically equivalent, the two instruments are likely to produce similar profiles, particularly when a 2-point codetype represents a well-defined configural pattern. For example, Clavelle (1992) asked experienced MMPI users to review pairs of MMPI and MMPI-2 profiles derived from the same test responses and to determine if these data yielded comparable clinical results. The 35 clinical psychologists in this study estimated that 92% to 96% of their diagnoses and 89% to 93% of their narrative interpretations would be essentially the same or only slightly different between the two instruments. Harrell, Honaker, and Parnell (1992) administered the MMPI, the MMPI-2, or both in a counterbalanced repeated-measures study with adult psychiatric patients. Although MMPI-2 T-scores were generally lower than MMPI T-scores on several of the clinical scales, the rank ordering of T-scores and the dispersion of basic scale scores were essentially equivalent.

Table 5.3 provides data from the MMPI-A manual (Butcher et al., 1992) on the congruence rate between profiles generated by normal adolescents based on the Marks and Briggs (1972) original norms and on the MMPI-A adolescent norm set. It also provides similar data comparing MMPI and MMPI-A profile characteristics for a group of adolescents in psychiatric treatment settings. As shown, the overall congruence rate for profiles generated from the original test instrument and from the MMPI-A is 67.8% for boys and 55.8% for girls, with the congruence rate increasing to 95.2% for boys and 81.8% for girls when the criterion for 2-point codetype definition requires at least a 5-point T-score difference between the second and third most elevated scale. In the clinical sample of adolescents, the overall congruence rate is 69.5% for boys and 67.2% for girls, and it reaches 95% for boys and 91% for girls when well-defined codetype classification procedures are employed. Table 5.3 also shows the very dramatic reductions that occur in the number of profiles classified into 2-point codetypes when the 5-point level of definition is required. These estimates for MMPI and MMPI-A congruence for adolescent samples are comparable to the congruence agreement rates reported for adults on the MMPI and MMPI-2 (Butcher et al., 1989; Graham, Timbrook, et al., 1991). Thus, it seems reasonable to assume that much of the MMPI clinical research literature for adolescent samples is generalizable to the MMPI-A, but it is erroneous to assume that all adolescent patients will produce equivalent or congruent profiles across the two test instruments.

TABLE 5.3

Two-Point Codetype Congruence Rates as a Function of Codetype
Definition for Profiles Scored on the MMPI-A Norms and the Marks,
Seeman, and Haller (1972) Adolescent Norms

Definition[a]	Boys		Girls	
	N	%	N	%
Normal Sample				
0	805	67.8	815	55.8
1	692	71.7	703	57.8
2	518	81.1	521	64.1
3	384	87.8	379	70.4
4	288	92.4	277	76.9
5	208	95.2	203	81.8
6	152	94.7	125	88.0
7	116	95.7	89	88.8
8	81	97.5	63	90.5
9	63	96.8	41	90.2
10	43	100.0	23	95.7
Psychiatric Sample				
0	420	69.5	293	67.2
1	368	72.6	266	70.7
2	294	82.0	213	75.6
3	223	89.2	169	81.1
4	175	93.7	134	87.3
5	141	95.0	100	91.0
6	105	94.3	80	93.8
7	85	96.5	56	92.9
8	65	96.9	41	95.1
9	45	100.0	27	92.6
10	32	100.0	22	95.5

Note. From Butcher et al. (1992). Copyright © 1992 by the Regents
of the University of Minnesota. Reprinted by permission.
[a] T-score difference between the second and third most elevated clinical scales in the MMPI codetype (using the Marks et al. norms).

In the only study to explore the important issue of the relative accuracy of
adolescents' MMPI versus MMPI-A profiles, Janus, Tolbert, Calestro, and Toepfer
(1996) requested that clinicians blindly rate the accuracy of interpretive statements
based on MMPI-A responses scored on (1) MMPI-A norms, (2) the Marks and Briggs
adolescent norms for the original MMPI, and (3) adult *K*-corrected norms for the original MMPI. Both sets of adolescent norms (original and MMPI-A) produced higher
accuracy ratings than did the adult norms, but the adolescent norms did not produce
ratings that differed between them. Janus, Tolbert, et al. (1996) concluded that MMPI-
A profiles based on standard MMPI-A norms produced clinical utility (accuracy) that
was equivalent to profiles based on the Marks and Briggs adolescent norms for the
original instrument. Table 5.4 provides data on the frequency of profile assignments to
2-point codes as reported in the MMPI-A manual (Butcher et al., 1992) for samples of
normal adolescents and psychiatric patients scored on the MMPI-A adolescent norms.

Table 5.5 provides data from Archer, Gordon, and Klinefelter (1991) on 1,762 adolescent inpatients and outpatients scored on the Marks and Briggs norms and rescored
on MMPI-A norms presented separately by gender. The adolescents used in these

TABLE 5.4
Frequency Distribution of MMPI-A Codetypes With No Definition

Codetype	Normative Boys N = 805	Normative Girls N = 815	Clinical Boys N = 420	Clinical Girls N = 293
1-2/2-1	21	26	3	4
1-3/3-1	51	60	4	8
1-4/4-1	16	6	7	2
1-6/6-1	16	12	0	2
1-7/7-1	23	12	3	3
1-8/8-1	6	11	2	3
1-9/9-1	23	24	3	4
2-3/3-2	69	43	18	20
2-4/4-2	21	36	50	44
2-6/6-2	16	25	6	7
2-7/7-2	35	39	9	14
2-8/8-2	7	13	0	1
2-9/9-2	16	12	4	0
3-4/4-3	27	27	35	43
3-6/6-3	27	47	6	4
3-7/7-3	6	3	1	2
3-8/8-3	5	4	1	3
3-9/9-3	32	30	13	2
4-6/6-4	25	19	35	25
4-7/7-4	11	18	27	9
4-8/8-4	13	14	9	8
4-9/9-4	48	42	87	37
6-7/7-6	14	21	10	2
6-8/8-6	23	17	4	4
6-9/9-6	29	37	9	3
7-8/8-7	36	30	14	3
7-9/9-7	45	23	6	3
8-9/9-8	24	36	7	3

Note. From Butcher et al. (1992). Copyright © 1992 by the Regents of the University of Minnesota. Reprinted by permission.

analyses were 12 to 18 years old ($M = 16.19$ years; $SD = 1.51$) and completed the group booklet form of the MMPI, produced F scores of T < 100 on the Marks and Briggs norms, and omitted less than 30 responses. The data sources, which include psychiatric settings in Missouri, Minnesota, and Texas, are described in Archer and Klinefelter (1991). Table 5.5 shows codetype frequency data for 45 codetype combinations and for no-code profiles. A no-code profile was defined as a profile containing no clinical scale T-score value equal to or greater than 65 for the Marks and Briggs norms and no clinical scale T-score value equal to or greater than 60 for MMPI-A norms.

Basic Scale Reliability

The MMPI-A manual (Butcher et al., 1992) provides information concerning the internal consistency, test-retest reliability, and factor structure of the MMPI-A scales. The test-retest correlations for the MMPI-A basic scales range from $r = .49$ for F_1 to $r = .84$ for Si, and in general these values are very similar to the test-retest correlations

TABLE 5.5

A Comparison of MMPI-A and MMPI Codetype Frequencies for 1,762 Adolescents Receiving Mental Health Services

| | MMPI-A | | | | MMPI | | | |
| | Males | | Females | | Males | | Females | |
Codetype	N	%	N	%	N	%	N	%
1-2/2-1	9	0.9%	16	2.2%	14	1.4%	25	3.4%
1-3/3-1	23	2.2%	44	6.0%	33	3.2%	38	5.2%
1-4/4-1	16	1.5%	2	0.3%	21	2.0%	7	1.0%
1-5/5-1	4	0.4%	5	0.7%	12	1.2%	2	0.3%
1-6/6-1	12	1.2%	3	0.4%	14	1.4%	2	0.3%
1-7/7-1	7	0.7%	2	0.3%	13	1.3%	4	0.5%
1-8/8-1	9	0.9%	6	0.8%	19	1.8%	24	3.3%
1-9/9-1	6	0.6%	6	0.8%	13	1.3%	12	1.6%
1-0/0-1	7	0.7%	2	0.3%	4	0.4%	1	0.1%
2-3/3-2	25	2.4%	30	4.1%	25	2.4%	22	3.0%
2-4/4-2	52	5.0%	24	3.3%	38	3.7%	50	6.9%
2-5/5-2	12	1.2%	9	1.2%	25	2.4%	3	0.4%
2-6/6-2	8	0.8%	5	0.7%	4	0.4%	7	1.0%
2-7/7-2	11	1.1%	6	0.8%	9	0.9%	16	2.2%
2-8/8-2	1	0.1%	2	0.3%	5	0.5%	7	1.0%
2-9/9-2	0	0.0%	0	0.0%	2	0.2%	5	0.7%
2-0/0-2	19	1.8%	28	3.8%	9	0.9%	13	1.8%
3-4/4-3	51	4.9%	26	3.6%	41	4.0%	20	2.7%
3-5/5-3	10	1.0%	22	3.0%	34	3.3%	5	0.7%
3-6/6-3	6	0.6%	10	1.4%	4	0.4%	5	0.7%
3-7/7-3	0	0.0%	4	0.5%	2	0.2%	3	0.4%
3-8/8-3	1	0.1%	5	0.7%	0	0.0%	4	0.5%
3-9/9-3	7	0.7%	6	0.8%	6	0.6%	15	2.1%
3-0/0-3	1	0.1%	3	0.4%	0	0.0%	1	0.1%
4-5/5-4	17	1.6%	28	3.8%	37	3.6%	8	1.1%
4-6/6-4	64	6.2%	29	4.0%	58	5.6%	33	4.5%
4-7/7-4	25	2.4%	9	1.2%	18	1.7%	12	1.6%
4-8/8-4	29	2.8%	15	2.1%	21	2.0%	31	4.3%
4-9/9-4	104	10.1%	29	4.0%	82	7.9%	63	8.6%
4-0/0-4	24	2.3%	15	2.1%	7	0.7%	5	0.7%
5-6/6-5	5	0.5%	8	1.1%	20	1.9%	0	0.0%
5-7/7-5	1	0.1%	1	0.1%	5	0.5%	1	0.1%
5-8/8-5	1	0.1%	5	0.7%	7	0.7%	3	0.4%
5-9/9-5	3	0.3%	19	2.6%	29	2.8%	9	1.2%
5-0/0-5	3	0.3%	8	1.1%	4	0.4%	0	0.0%
6-7/7-6	14	1.4%	4	0.5%	16	1.5%	1	0.1%
6-8/8-6	33	3.2%	25	3.4%	25	2.4%	21	2.9%
6-9/9-6	22	2.1%	12	1.6%	22	2.1%	17	2.3%
6-0/0-6	3	0.3%	2	0.3%	1	0.1%	1	0.1%
7-8/8-7	19	1.8%	14	1.9%	21	2.0%	17	2.3%
7-9/9-7	18	1.7%	5	0.7%	16	1.5%	10	1.4%
7-0/0-7	13	1.3%	9	1.2%	4	0.4%	2	0.3%
8-9/9-8	16	1.5%	7	1.0%	12	1.2%	18	2.5%
8-0/0-8	2	0.2%	7	1.0%	1	0.1%	0	0.0%
9-0/0-9	6	0.6%	0	0.0%	4	0.4%	0	0.0%
No Code	314	30.4%	212	29.1%	276	26.7%	186	25.5%
Total	1,033		729		1,033		729	

Note. From Archer (1992a). Copyright © 1992 by Lawrence Erlbaum Associates. Reprinted by permission.

reported for the MMPI-2 basic scales. Stein, McClinton, and Graham (1998) evaluated the long-term (one-year) test-retest reliability of MMPI-A scales and reported basic clinical scale values ranging from $r = .51$ for *Pa* to $r = .75$ for *Si*. Test-retest correlations for the content scales, in contrast, ranged from $r = .40$ for *A-trt* to $r = .73$ for *A-sch*. The typical standard error of measurement for the MMPI-A basic scales is estimated to be 2 to 3 raw score points (Butcher et al., 1992), which generally converts to 5 T-score points. Thus, it is possible to state, as noted by Archer and Krishnamurthy (2002), that if an adolescent is readministered the MMPI-A within a relatively short time interval and without significant change in psychological functioning, his or her basic scale T-scores would fall in a range of roughly ±5 T-score points of the original scores approximately 50% of the time. The standard error of measurement is very important when attempting to evaluate changes shown on the MMPI-A in terms of separating significant clinical changes from changes attributable to the standard error of measurement. In general, changes in T-score values of 5 T-score points or less are more likely to reflect measurement error rather than reliable change.

The internal consistency of the MMPI-A basic scales, as represented in coefficient alpha values, ranges from relatively low values on such scales as *Mf* and *Pa* ($r = .60$) to substantially higher values for other basic scales such as *Hs* ($r = .78$) and *Sc* ($r = .89$). In contrast, internal consistency scores tend to be higher for other MMPI-A scales, such as content scales, because alpha coefficient estimates were utilized in the construction of these more recent MMPI-A scales. In addition to test-retest and internal consistency measures of reliability, the MMPI-A manual (Butcher et al., 1992) also provides information concerning the item endorsement frequencies and reading levels required by each of the MMPI-A items and the principal components analysis (PCA) structure of the MMPI-A basic scales using a varimax rotation procedure. Butcher et al. (1992) reported that a PCA of the MMPI-A basic scales resulted in a four-factor solution, appropriate for both boys and girls, with a large first factor labeled General Maladjustment. The second factor was labeled Over Control and is marked by high loadings on *L* and *K*, and the third and fourth factors appear to be best described as nonclinical dimensions related to *Si* and *Mf*, respectively.

THE CODETYPE INTERPRETATION APPROACH

As noted by Graham (2000), configural approaches to the interpretation of the MMPI have been viewed as potentially the richest source of diagnostic and descriptive information derivable from this test instrument. The early writings on the MMPI (Meehl, 1951, 1956; Meehl & Dahlstrom, 1960) emphasized the interpretation of codetype information, and several of the early MMPI validity studies were focused on identifying reliable clinical correlates of MMPI 2-point codetypes (e.g., Meehl, 1951).

A 2-point codetype is usually referred to by the numerical designation of the two basic clinical scales that are most elevated in that profile, with convention dictating that the most elevated scale be designated first in the codetype sequence. Thus, if an adolescent produces his or her highest T-score elevations on scales *Pd* and *Ma* (in that order), the profile would be classified as a 4-9 codetype. Throughout this text, individual MMPI-A scales have often been referred to by their names or alphabetic abbreviations rather than numerical designations. This procedure has been followed to minimize confusion for the novice MMPI-A user. In discussing codetype classifications, however, MMPI-A scales are referred to in this chapter by their numerical designation, as in the codetype literature. In addition to MMPI tradition, numerical designation of scales is the generally preferred practice among experienced MMPI-2 and MMPI-A users for a very important reason: The names that were originally given to clinical scales may be misleading and may serve as inadequate labels of what that scale is currently believed to measure. For example, the Psychasthenia scale was originally developed to measure symptomatology related to what was later referred to as obsessive-compulsive neurosis and now is termed obsessive-compulsive disorder. Psychasthenia is not a psychiatric label in common use today, and Graham (2000) noted that the *Pt* scale is currently thought of as a reliable index of psychological distress, turmoil, and discomfort, particularly as these relate to symptoms of anxiety, tension, and apprehension.

Several codetype "cookbook" systems have been developed, such as those provided by Gilberstadt and Duker (1965) and Marks and Seeman (1963), and these have employed very complex rules for classifying multiscale elevations. However, the more recent efforts regarding codetype descriptors have tended to employ much simpler 2-point approaches to classifying MMPI profiles. These systems, such as those exemplified in Friedman et al., (2001), Graham (2000), and Greene (2000), have typically interpreted codetypes based on the two scales with the highest clinical-range elevations. Several investigations, such as that by Lewandowski and Graham (1972), demonstrated that reliable clinical correlates can be established for profiles that are classified based on the simpler 2-point code systems. Data reported by Pancoast et al. (1988) also indicate that assignments to simple codetype systems can be made with acceptable levels of reliability by independent raters. Additionally, diagnoses derived by the simpler MMPI classification systems provide levels of agreement with clinicians' diagnoses comparable to those achieved with more complex methods of MMPI profile classification. The obvious advantage of using the 2-point code system is that a much larger percentage of profiles can be classified in a typical clinical setting when numerous stringent criteria are not required for codetype assignment (Graham, 2000).

Of primary importance in employing codetype descriptors with any population is a clear understanding that the attribution of correlate descriptors to a particular client entails probability estimates. These estimates of accuracy may vary greatly based on the source of the descriptor statement (adequacy of research methodology, characteristics of the population sampled, statistical strength of findings) and the individual characteristics of the client being assessed (the base rate for similar symptoms/diagnoses in the general psychiatric population). Additionally, it is likely that the accuracy of descriptor statements will vary based on the degree of elevation and definition exhibited by a codetype (i.e., the degree to which the 2-point code is clinically elevated and whether it is elevated substantially above the remainder of the clinical scale profile). Even under optimal conditions, such as where cross-validated research has led to the derivation of clinical correlates from MMPI profiles highly similar to that of the individual being evaluated, a specific clinical correlate may be found not to apply to a specific individual. Thus, as Greene (2000) noted, MMPI cookbooks, even in adult populations, "have not been the panacea that was originally thought: Increasing the specificity of a particular codetype helps by enhancing the homogeneity of the group and increasing the probability of finding reliable empirical correlates; however, it also substantially reduces the number of profiles that could be classified within a codetype" (pp. 289–290). Nevertheless, codetypes continue to serve as a valuable source of hypotheses concerning client characteristics when such cautions are borne in mind by the interpreter.

DERIVING A CODETYPE CLASSIFICATION FOR ADOLESCENTS

In the adult codetype information provided by such sources as Graham (2000), Greene (2000), and Friedman et al. (2001), profiles are typically classified as 2-point codetypes based on the two clinical scales that show the greatest degree of clinical-range elevation. In these and most other systems, few high-point codetypes involve the scales 5 and 0 because these scales have often been excluded from designation as clinical scales. These scales were also frequently excluded in codetype research in early MMPI investigations (Graham, 2000).

In general, 2-point codes are used interchangeably; for example, 2-7 codetypes are seen as equivalent to 7-2 codetypes, unless differences are specifically noted. Furthermore, the absolute elevation of two high-point scales within the profile is typically not considered beyond the assumption that such elevations occur within clinical ranges. The relative elevation of the two highest scales in relation to the remaining profile is also not typically considered or discussed in codetype narratives. As previously noted, however, the degree to which the 2-point codetype is well defined appears to be related to the short-term stability of the codetype (i.e., the degree to which profile characteristics are subject to change over relatively brief periods of time) and the degree to which clinical correlate patterns will be applicable for a codetype configuration. In standard codetype interpretation practice, if a profile does not fit any of the two-point codetypes presented, the clinician is generally advised to employ an interpretation strategy based on clinical correlates found for the individual MMPI scales that are elevated.

Marks et al. (1974) developed a classification system for adolescent MMPI profiles designed to increase the clinician's flexibility in rendering codetype assignments. Once an adolescent's MMPI profile had been plotted, Marks et al. recommended that the resulting configuration be compared to the codetype profiles they provided in terms of the two highest elevations occurring within that particular profile. If the codetype for the individual adolescent corresponded to one of the 2-point codetypes presented by Marks et al., the clinician was referred to the codetype descriptors appropriate for that configuration. If the respondent's codetype was not classifiable, however, the authors recommended dropping the second high-point scale and substituting the third-highest scale to produce a new 2-point code. If this procedure then resulted in a classifiable codetype, the clinician was encouraged to interpret the profile based on the clinical correlate information provided for that code. If the profile remained unclassifiable following this "substitution and reclassification" procedure, Marks et al. suggested that their actuarial interpretation system not be applied for that respondent. As commonly recommended in the interpretation of MMPI-2 profiles, these authors encouraged clinicians with unclassifiable profiles to employ a single-scale correlate interpretive strategy.

Alex Caldwell (as reported in Friedman et al., 2001) developed a system for classifying and interpreting profiles that, because of multiple-scale clinical-range elevations, do not fit cleanly into simple two-point codetypes. This system, which is referred to as the *A-B-C-D Paradigm*, divides the multiply elevated clinical-scale profile into discrete two-point codetype entities and builds the interpretive narrative based on clinical correlate descriptors that are commonly found across these 2-point codes. Figure 5.7 provides an illustration of the Caldwell A-B-C-D Paradigm applied to an adolescent MMPI-A profile characterized by elevations on scales 4, 8, 2, and 6. This profile is used to demonstrate Caldwell's method of breaking down a multiply elevated profile into more easily interpretable 2-point codes.

132

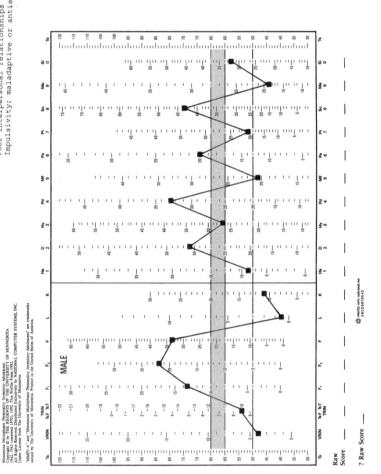

FIG. 5.7. Illustration of the Caldwell A-B-C-D Paradigm.

As shown in this figure, the four most elevated clinical scales (elevated within clinical ranges) are assigned a corresponding letter of the alphabet in order of elevation magnitude. The profile is then divided into high-point pairs using the combinations A-B, A-C, A-D, B-C, B-D, and C-D. Descriptors commonly shared by these 2-point codetype classifications apply to an adolescent who might be described as impulsive, maladaptive, and antisocial and whose interpersonal relationships are characterized by conflict. The interpretation would place more emphasis on codetype correlates for *4-8* and *4-2* given the relative prominence of these features within this MMPI-A profile and place less emphasis on codetypes such as *8-6* and *2-6* because of the relatively weaker elevations for these latter configural features. When contradictory descriptors are derived, emphasis will be placed on the primary codetype descriptors (e.g., A-B) rather than the secondary scale pairs (e.g., C-D).

As for recommendations for the clinician deriving codetype assignments, it appears most appropriate to employ a simple codetype strategy that seeks to place an individual profile into a codetype classification based on the highest 2-point characteristics occurring within clinical ranges for that profile. The clinician should be mindful, however, that less elevated and less well defined codetypes (the degree of elevation of the 2-point code relative to the remainder of the profile) are likely to manifest fewer of the correlate features associated with that particular codetype. When classification does not result in an appropriate two-point codetype placement for which clinical correlate information is available from standard sources, it is suggested that the clinician interpret the profile based on single-scale correlates. The substitution and reclassification procedure suggested by Marks et al. (1974) is *not* recommended. For clinical profiles with more than two scales elevated within clinical ranges, the experienced interpreter may wish to consider use of the Caldwell A-B-C-D Paradigm as an interpretive strategy.

SINGLE-SCALE AND TWO-POINT CODETYPES

A substantial research literature has developed on the clinical correlate patterns exhibited by adolescents on the basic MMPI scales. Hathaway and Monachesi (1963), for example, investigated high-point and low-point correlate patterns for approximately 15,000 ninth graders who were administered the MMPI in the Minnesota public school system in 1948 and 1954. Lachar and Wrobel (1990) and Wrobel and Lachar (1992) more recently examined single-scale correlate patterns in a sample of adolescents predominantly from outpatient settings, with analyses conducted separately by gender. Information concerning the correlates of basic MMPI scales for inpatient adolescents was examined in research studies by Archer et al. (1985), Archer and Gordon (1988), Archer et al. (1988), Ball et al. (1987), and Williams and Butcher (1989a). Single-scale correlates for the MMPI-A basic clinical scales were reported in the manual for this instrument by Butcher et al. (1992). Additionally, information concerning correlate patterns for various codetype configurations was presented by Archer (1987b), Archer and Klinefelter (1992), Archer and Krishnamurthy (2002), Marks et al. (1974), and Williams and Butcher (1989b). These research investigations and summaries serve as the primary sources of single-scale and codetype correlate data presented in this chapter.

In deriving the following codetype descriptors for adolescents, the 29 codetypes reported by Archer (1987b) were selected for presentation. In general, the core of this clinical correlate information is based on the Marks et al. (1974) data reported for high-point codetypes occurring within clinical ranges. This information was then supplemented with adult correlate information for these 29 high-point pairs from Friedman et al. (2001), Graham (2000), Greene (2000), and Lachar (1974). The typical narrative created by this method begins with statements found to be common across both the adolescent and adult descriptors for a particular MMPI configuration, based on the observations by Archer (1987b) and Archer et al. (1988) that MMPI scale descriptors found in studies of adolescents have typically been consistent with those found in adult studies. Further, when sources of adult correlate data were not available for a particular codetype, a relatively rare occurrence, this is noted in the first few sentences of the narrative. When marked or important differences occur between descriptors derived from adolescent and adult clinical populations, the interpretive implications of these discrepancies are presented. Finally, codetype frequency data for adolescents are based on our analyses of the codetype classification data for 1,762 adolescent patients (Table 5.5), as scored on MMPI-A norms.

In addition to the 29 codetype narratives, the following sections also contain information on the characteristics of each of the 10 MMPI-A basic clinical scales. High and low single-scale correlates are suggested based on findings reported in studies of adolescent samples in normal and/or psychiatric settings. In the case of single-scale high-point correlates, the descriptions are enriched by the MMPI-A correlate research reported in the test manual (Butcher et al., 1992). Much of the codetype correlate information provided in the following sections is based on research conducted with the original form of the MMPI utilizing the traditional adolescent norms as derived by Marks and Briggs (1972). This approach is similar to that taken by Butcher (1990), Friedman et al. (2001), Graham (2000), and Greene (2000) in the generation of codetype findings for the MMPI-2. The generalization of MMPI findings to the MMPI-A appears supported in that the MMPI-A clinical scales (except *Mf* and *Si*) have retained basically the same items as their counterparts in the original instrument. Further, as previously discussed in this chapter, the codetype congruence data for the MMPI and MMPI-A indicate that these instruments will produce similar or equivalent profiles in a majority of cases. Empirical research findings are still needed, however, concerning the degree to which codetype correlates found for adolescents on the original test instrument may be validly generalized to the MMPI-A. Examinations of MMPI-2 codetype correlates for adult psychiatric patients have found a striking degree of similarity in the descriptors identified for MMPI-2–based codetypes in inpatient settings (Archer et al., 1995) and outpatient settings (Graham et al., 1999) in relation to corresponding codes derived from the original MMPI. The issue of generalizability of findings from the original MMPI will become less important, however, as research projects generate a new correlate literature based directly on studies conducted with the MMPI-A.

Scale 1 (*Hs*: Hypochondriasis) Codetypes

Scale 1 originally consisted of 33 items developed to identify respondents who manifested a history of symptomatology associated with hypochondriasis. These symptoms include vague physical complaints and ailments and a preoccupation with bodily functioning, illness, and disease. One item was dropped from the original scale in the creation of the MMPI-A due to objectionable content, resulting in a revised scale length of 32 items. Graham (2000) reported that scale 1 appears to be the most unidimensional and homogeneous MMPI clinical basic scale in terms of item composition and content. All of the items on scale 1 relate to somatic concerns and complaints.

Research using adult samples has established that individuals who score high on scale 1 typically report many somatic symptoms and exaggerated complaints regarding physical functioning. Additionally, Graham (2000) noted that adults who produce elevated scale 1 MMPI profiles are not psychologically minded and often use physical complaints as a means of controlling or manipulating significant others in their environment.

Reports concerning physical functioning on scale 1 would also be expected to be influenced by the individual's actual physical condition—respondents with physical illness typically produce moderate subclinical elevations on this measure. For example, Ball et al. (1987) found subtle but detectable neurological differences between adolescent psychiatric inpatients with and without marked scale 1 elevations. MMPI profiles with scale 1 elevations have also been reported for adolescents with medical problems, including epilepsy (Dodrill & Clemmons, 1984), muscular dystrophy (Harper, 1983), nonprogressive physical impairments (Harper & Richman, 1978), Gilles de la Tourette's syndrome (Grossman, Mostofsky, & Harrison, 1986), sleep disorders (Monroe & Marks, 1977), surreptitious insulin administration among insulin-dependent diabetics (Orr, Eccles, Lawlor, & Golden, 1986), and rheumatic fever (Stehbens, Ehmke, & Wilson, 1982). Colligan and Osborne (1977) investigated the MMPI response features of 659 female and 534 male adolescents (aged 15–19) who presented at the Mayo Clinic for medical evaluation, and they found that these adolescents produced higher scores on the neurotic triad (scales 1, 2, and 3). Profiles with elevations on scale 1 were unusual in the normal adolescent data collected by Hathaway and Monachesi (1963), although a larger number of these adolescents were classified as producing their lowest value on this scale.

High Scores on Scale 1

The following is a summary of descriptors for high scale 1 scores (T ≥ 60):

- Excessive somatic and bodily concerns that are likely to be vague in nature.
- Likely to display somatic responses to stress, which may include eating problems.
- Increased likelihood of problems related to neurotic diagnoses.
- Likely to be seen by others as self-centered, pessimistic, dissatisfied, and cynical.
- Demanding, critical, selfish, and whining in interpersonal relationships.
- Likely to display little insight in psychotherapy.
- Less likely to engage in delinquent behaviors.
- Likely to report school problems, including academic and adjustment difficulties.

Low Scores on Scale 1

Low scale 1 scores have been associated with the following characteristics (T ≤ 40):

- Few physical symptoms and freedom from somatic preoccupation.
- Higher scores on tests of intelligence.
- More likely to come from urban than rural settings.
- Greater psychological sophistication and insight.

1-2/2-1 Codetype. Adolescent and adult clients with this codetype frequently complain of physical symptoms, including weakness, fatigue, and tiredness. These individuals often show a consistent pattern of somatic preoccupation and overreaction to minor physical dysfunction. Marked affective distress appears to be associated with the *1-2/2-1* codetype, and these individuals are often described as ruminative, tense, anxious, and insecure. There are also frequent reports of depression, social withdrawal, and isolation.

In both the adult and adolescent literatures, the *1-2/2-1* codetype has been associated with a very low probability of acting out being used as a primary defense mechanism. There are often marked interpersonal concerns and unmet needs for attention and approval by others. Thus, individuals who produce this codetype have been described as fearful and hypersensitive in their interactions with others and often as dependent and indecisive.

The *1-2/2-1* codetype occurred with a frequency of 0.9% for males and 2.2% for females in our sample of adolescent psychiatric patients scored on MMPI-A norms. Marks et al. (1974) reported that obsession and compulsion are the primary mechanisms of defense employed by adolescents with the *1-2/2-1* codetype. Adolescents with this codetype in the Marks et al. sample often complained of being teased by others during their childhood and indicated that they were afraid of making mistakes. They appeared to be quiet, depressed teenagers who established very few friendships and often manifested obsessional defenses. Although Graham (2000) reported that adults with the *1-2/2-1* profile often displayed excessive use of alcohol, the adolescents in the Marks et al. study with this codetype did not manifest significant drug or alcohol involvement. Finally, Marks and his colleagues noted that adolescents with this codetype often had histories that included parental separation and divorce, academic problems (in several cases, school phobias), and delayed academic progress.

1-3/3-1 Codetype. Sources of adult and adolescent clinical correlate data indicate that individuals with the *1-3/3-1* codetype typically present themselves as physically or organically ill. Indeed, when the T-score values for scales *1* and *3* are each above 65 and also each exceed the T-score value for scale *2* by at least 10 points, this profile may be described as a classic *conversion V*. The types of physical complaints that have been noted in the general literature for the *1-3/3-1* codetype include headaches, dizziness, chest pain, abdominal pain, insomnia, blurred vision, nausea, and anorexia. It would be expected that these physical symptoms would increase in times of psychological stress, and the clinician might be advised to attempt to identify secondary gain characteristics associated with this symptomatology.

In the literature on adults and adolescents, the *1-3/3-1* codetype is associated more with neurotic and psychophysiological symptomatology than with diagnoses related to psychoses. These respondents are frequently perceived as insecure and attention seeking. Behaving in socially acceptable ways appears important to the *1-3/3-1* person. The adult or adolescent *1-3/3-1* has problems establishing relationships with members of the opposite sex. Often, these problems are related to the lack of development of appropriate skills in these interpersonal areas. Primary defense mechanisms for this codetype consist of somatization, denial, and externalization.

As shown in Table 5.5, 2.2% of male and 6.0% of female adolescents in psychiatric settings produce the *1-3/3-1* codetype. Data unique to adolescent clinical sources for this profile indicate that *1-3/3-1* teenagers are more frequently referred for treatment because of problems or concerns in their academic settings. The majority of adolescents in the Marks et al. (1974) sample indicated that they had a fear of receiving poor grades, a concern that appeared realistic in view of the fact that 44% of this sample were a year behind their age-appropriate academic placement. In general, Marks et al. noted that adolescents with this codetype often displayed "diagnostic insight" into the descriptive features of their psychological problems. They were able to talk superficially about conflicts and were not evasive in psychotherapy. These features are in contrast to the descriptors in the adult literature indicating that *1-3/3-1* individuals typically display little willingness to acknowledge psychological factors in their life problems and little insight into their problems. Of the 20 patients in the Marks et al. 1970–1973 sample who produced a *1-3/3-1* codetype, over two thirds had no history of drug abuse or drug involvement.

1-4/4-1 Codetype. The *1-4/4-1* codetype is relatively rare among adults, and it is found in approximately 1.5% of male and 0.3% of female adolescents in psychiatric settings. In the sources of adult and adolescent clinical correlate information, the *1-4/4-1* individual appears to be defensive, negativistic, resentful, pessimistic, and cynical. Furthermore, research findings suggest these individuals may be described as self-centered and immature. The use of somatic complaints is a primary defense mechanism for both adolescents and adults, although this feature is more prevalent among adolescents with higher elevation on scale *1* than on scale *4*.

In addition to these features, derived from the combined literature, a number of characteristics appear to be uniquely related to the adolescents' *1-4/4-1* codetypes. Specifically, more scale *4* features are reported as descriptive of adolescents with this codetype, including defiance, disobedience, and provocative behaviors. These problem areas are most likely manifested in the relationship between the adolescent and his or her parents. In the psychotherapy relationship, adolescents with this codetype have been described as superficial, cognitively disorganized, and moderately impaired in judgment. Therapists in the Marks et al. (1974) study rated most adolescents with a *1-4/4-1* profile as manifesting a mild to moderate degree of psychiatric disturbance overall. In addition to the somatization, adolescents with this codetype often employ acting out as their primary defense mechanism. Therapists describe adolescent patients with this codetype as aggressive, outspoken, resentful, headstrong, and egocentric. Despite the use of acting out as a primary defense mechanism, adolescents with the *1-4/4-1* codetype in the Marks et al. sample were typically not found to be substance abusers.

1-5/5-1 Codetype. The *1-5/5-1* is a relatively infrequent codetype among adults and is found in less than 1% of male and female adolescents in psychiatric treatment. In both the adult and adolescent literatures, the *1-5/5-1* is often accompanied by somatic complaints of a hypochondriacal nature, and patients with this codetype often present as physically ill. Additionally, these individuals are often seen as passive, and the adolescent data indicate that teenagers with this codetype are unlikely to enter into open conflict or disagreement with their parents.

Teenagers with this codetype are often referred for treatment by parents and by school officials. Primary therapists view these adolescents as displaying mildly inappropriate affect, and compulsion appeared to be a primary defense mechanism of this codetype. Interestingly, many of the *1-5/5-1* teenagers in the Marks et al. (1974) sample actually had experienced serious physical illnesses as children. Therapists described *1-5/5-1* adolescent patients as having difficulty in discussing their problems and conflict areas, and these teenagers were seen as unreliable in terms of the information they provided to their therapists. They were not generally liked by others and had difficulty in forming close relationships. Finally, teenage males with this codetype were described as effeminate.

1-6/6-1 Codetype. Of the adult sources reviewed, only Greene (1980, 2000) and Friedman et al. (2001) provide descriptive summaries for the *1-6/6-1* profile. Greene's brief description of this codetype emphasizes the occurrence of hypochondriacal symptomatology combined with hostile and suspicious traits related to elevations on scale 6. Additionally, he noted that the personality structure of the adult *1-6/6-1* appeared resistant to change resulting from psychotherapy. In contrast, the investigation of adolescent *1-6/6-1* codetypes by Marks et al. (1974) produced a quite different picture. Confidence in any codetype descriptors for this configuration must be tempered, however, by awareness that little research has been done in adult settings and that the *1-6/6-1* codetype reported by Marks et al. was based on a very small sample size ($N = 11$). Among adolescent psychiatric patients, only 1.2% of males and 0.4% of females produced *1-6/6-1* codetypes (see Table 5.5).

Hypochondriacal tendencies and somatic complaints do not appear to be characteristics of adolescents with the *1-6/6-1* codetype. Rather, these adolescents were primarily referred for psychotherapy because of excessive emotional control. Therapists viewed these teenagers as evasive, defensive, and fearful of emotional involvement with others. More than half of these adolescents lived with their mothers in father-absent homes. When fathers were present in the family of these teenagers, their attitude toward the adolescents was reported to be rejecting. The *1-6/6-1* adolescent was viewed as egocentric and prone to rationalization as a defense mechanism. Data from the Marks et al. (1974) sample indicated some drug abuse for this codetype, but it was not widespread or characteristic of this code. Intense anger directed at parents was frequently displayed by this group, including occasional violent outbursts. Suicidal attempts, perhaps representing an internalization of rage and anger, were also characteristic of the *1-6/6-1* adolescent in the 1970–1973 sample.

1-8/8-1 Codetype. The adolescent and adult literatures emphasize that those with a *1-8/8-1* codetype exhibit correlates commonly associated with both scales 1 and 8. Individuals with this profile type frequently present somatic concerns such as headaches and insomnia and often perceive themselves as physically ill. There are additional data from adolescent sources to suggest that teenagers with this codetype in fact often had serious health problems during childhood. These adolescents also frequently reported histories of poor social adjustment and social inadequacy. Further, individuals with the *1-8/8-1* profile appear to have difficulty in forming and maintaining interpersonal relationships. There is evidence in both the adolescent and adult literatures that the *1-8/8-1* codetype is often associated with delusional or disordered thinking, including symptoms related to difficulty in concentration and thought processes. Adolescents with the *1-8/8-1* codetype often described themselves as distractible and forgetful.

Approximately 0.9% of male and 0.8% of female adolescents in psychiatric settings produce the *1-8/8-1* codetype. Several clinical descriptors are uniquely available for this codetype classification from the Marks et al. (1974) study. The *1-8/8-1* adolescents frequently reported problems during childhood involving being teased and harassed by peers and often had difficulty with academics, including reading. Overall, their adjustment appeared to be problematic both in and outside of school settings, and they experienced substantial difficulty in making friends. Nearly one half of the *1-8/8-1* teenagers in the Marks et al. sample were a grade behind their expected academic placement.

Unique among the groups with 2-point codetypes involving scale 1, the *1-8/8-1* adolescents in the Marks et al. sample were likely to be involved in drug abuse, and over 50% reported a drug use history. Data from Archer and Klinefelter (1992) also indicate that adolescents with this codetype frequently exhibit elevated values on the MacAndrew Alcoholism scale. Additionally, attempted suicides frequently occurred among these adolescents; indeed, 65% had attempted to take their own lives. Finally, intense family conflict was present for a very high percentage of the 1-8/8-1 teenagers, often involving fighting or overt conflict with their parents. Two thirds of these adolescents were from families in which the parents were divorced.

Scale 2 (D: Depression) Codetypes

Scale 2 originally consisted of 60 items, of which 57 were retained in the MMPI-A scale 2. The essential characteristics of this MMPI-A dimension include poor morale, lack of hope for the future, and general dissatisfaction with one's life status and situation (Hathaway & McKinley, 1942). The major content areas involved in this scale include lack of interest in activities or general apathy, physical symptoms such as sleep disturbances and gastrointestinal complaints, and excessive social sensitivity and social withdrawal. Graham (2000) described scale 2 as a sensitive measure of the respondent's life discomfort and dissatisfaction. He noted that although very elevated values on this scale are suggestive of clinical depression, more moderate scores have generally been seen as reflective of a life attitude or lifestyle characterized by apathy and poor morale. The content subscales derived by Harris and Lingoes (1955) for scale 2 include Subjective Depression (D_1), Psychomotor Retardation (D_2), Physical Malfunctioning (D_3), Mental Dullness (D_4), and Brooding (D_5).

Scale 2 high points were very infrequent among adolescents in the Hathaway and Monachesi (1963) Minnesota sample. Profiles whose lowest values were on scale 2, however, were relatively more common among these adolescents. Greene (2000) reported that adult psychiatric patients who produce elevations on scale 2 generally have characteristics of clinically depressed individuals, including feelings of inadequacy, lack of self-confidence, guilt and pessimism, and self-depreciation. Greene also noted that individuals who produce spike 2 profiles tend to be good psychotherapy candidates and often show significant improvement as a result of relatively brief psychiatric interventions. Consistent with this finding, Archer et al. (1988) found that high scale 2 inpatient adolescents were perceived by clinicians and psychiatric staff as more motivated to engage in psychotherapy and openly discuss their feelings and perceptions. They were also less likely than other adolescents to engage in rebellious, deceitful, manipulative, or hostile behaviors. In addition, Archer and his colleagues found that high scale 2 adolescents were described as more introspective, self-critical, guilty, and ashamed and more likely to have problems involving suicidal thoughts or ideation. Butcher et al. (1992), based on analyses of MMPI-A data, found that adolescent inpatients with scale 2 elevations were more likely to be characterized as depressed and more likely to have problems related to suicidal ideation and/or gestures. Archer and Gordon (1988), however, found no evidence of a significant relationship between scale 2 elevations among adolescent inpatients and clinicians' use of depression-related diagnoses, including dysthymia and major depression. Research by Nelson (1987) suggested that scale 2 may more accurately identify clinically depressed individuals when only face-valid or obvious Depression scale items are employed. Nelson and Cicchetti (1991) replicated and expanded these findings in an outpatient adult sample composed of individuals suffering from milder forms of maladjustment.

Although clinical lore holds that scale 2 results may be predictive of suicide attempts, the empirical literature does not appear to support this assumption. Marks and Haller (1977) compared groups of male and female adolescents who made sui-cide attempts and other emotionally disturbed adolescents without suicidal histories. The authors reported that MMPI scales 3 and 5 were significantly higher for male attempters, whereas scale 9 elevations were associated with suicide attempts among females. In contrast, Archer and Slesinger (1999) found single-scale elevations on scale 2 or 8 and coelevations on the 4-8 and 4-9 codetypes to be related to higher levels of sui-cidal ideation among adolescents. Spirito, Faust, Myers, and Bechtel (1988), however, found no significant differences in scale 2 mean elevations between female adolescent suicide attempters and a control group of female adolescents initially hospitalized for medical problems and referred for psychiatric consultation. Based on very simi-lar profiles produced by these two groups, in conjunction with the largely negative findings in the adult literature, Spirito et al. concluded that "primary reliance on the MMPI alone to determine suicidal risk seems non-judicious" (p. 210).

High Scores on Scale 2

The following is a summary of descriptors for high scale 2 scores ($T \geq 60$):

- Feelings of dissatisfaction, hopelessness, and unhappiness.
- General apathy and lack of interest in activities.
- Presence of guilt feelings, shame, and self-criticism.
- Lack of self-confidence and a sense of inadequacy and pessimism.
- Social withdrawal and social isolation.
- A degree of emotional distress that may serve as a positive motivator for psy-chotherapy efforts.

Low Scores on Scale 2

The following are characteristics that have been associated with low scale 2 scores ($T \leq 40$):

- Higher levels of intelligence and academic performance.
- Freedom from depression, anxiety, and guilt.
- Self-confidence and emotional stability.
- The ability to function effectively across a variety of situations.
- Alertness, activity, and competitiveness.
- Rebelliousness, argumentativeness, irresponsibility, and manipulativeness (among adolescent psychiatric patients with low scale 2 scores).

2-3/3-2 Codetype. There is substantial overlap in the correlates of the 2-3/3-2 code-type for adolescent and adult psychiatric patients. They are characteristically de-scribed as emotionally overcontrolled and unlikely to employ acting out as a primary defense mechanism. They typically have histories that reflect a lack of involvement or interest in relationships with others, and when relationships are established, they tend to have dependent characteristics. Adjectives such as *passive, docile,* and *dependent* are frequently applied to individuals with the 2-3/3-2 profile, and they are often described as unassertive, inhibited, insecure, and self-doubting. Both adolescents and adults with the 2-3/3-2 code are very achievement oriented and set high goals for their own performance. These goals are often unrealistic and appear to be a contributor to their sense of inferiority and depression. Antisocial personality or psychopathic diagnoses are markedly rare for adolescents and adults who produce the 2-3/3-2 codetype. There is also little evidence of thought disorder or the presence of schizophrenic or psychotic diagnoses among these individuals. Defense mechanisms involving somatization and hypochondriasis appear to be central to the 2-3/3-2 codetype. In particular, weakness, fatigue, and dizziness appear to be common physical symptoms.

Among adolescent patients, the 2-3/3-2 codetype is relatively common and found in 2.4% of males and 4.1% of females (see Table 5.5). Data on 2-3/3-2 adolescents indicate that the majority of these adolescents were referred for treatment because of poor peer relationships. These adolescents were seen as socially isolated and lonely. They have few friends inside the school environment and are loners outside of academic settings. The 2-3/3-2 adolescent reported a relatively passive, compliant, and obedient childhood that often involved an underinvolved father in a professional occupation and a mother who may have been overinvolved with these children. Sexual acting out and drug abuse do not appear to be high-frequency problem areas for these adolescents, and 76% of the teenagers in the Marks et al. (1974) sample reported no history of drug abuse. In research by Archer and Klinefelter (1992), the *MAC* scale raw scores for these adolescents were typically quite low. In the adult literature, the 2-3/3-2 codetype is more prevalent among women, and the majority of patients with this codetype are seen as psychoneurotic or reactive depressive. The 2-3 codetype was the modal pattern found for bulimia and anorexic adolescent patients in a study by Cumella, Wall, and Kerr-Almeida (1999).

2-4/4-2 Codetype. Among teenagers and adults, 2-4/4-2 profiles are typically produced by individuals who have difficulty with impulsive control and often act without sufficient deliberation. They exhibit a marked disregard for accepted social standards, and problems with authority figures are manifested by inappropriate or antisocial behaviors and actions. Hypochondriacal and somatic defense mechanisms are not typically displayed by these individuals. Acting out, displacement, and externalization appear to be primary defense mechanisms. There is often a history of legal violations, including incidents of arrest, legal convictions, and court actions. Indeed, one half of the adolescents in the Marks et al. (1974) sample had been placed on probation or held in detention.

In the adult and adolescent literatures, there are also frequent references to substance abuse and alcohol problems associated with this codetype. In the adult literature, the 2-4/4-2 profile is often the mean profile produced by samples of alcoholics (Greene & Garvin, 1988; Sutker & Archer, 1979). Marks et al. (1974) also noted that adolescents with the 2-4/4-2 codetype reported a wide variety of drug use that included all pharmacological categories except narcotics. Indeed, Marks et al. found patterns indicating drug addiction as well as drug abuse among their 2-4/4-2 sample of adolescents. The 2-4/4-2 codetype occurred with high frequency in the findings shown in Table 5.5, reported for 5.0% of males and 3.3% of females in this sample. In hospital settings, adolescents with the 2-4/4-2 profile were often found to be elopement risks. They also had frequent histories of promiscuous sexual behavior, truancy, and running away from home. In general, the 2-4/4-2 adolescents indicated that much of their antisocial behaviors were attempts to escape or run away from what they perceived to be intolerable or highly conflicted home situations. In the adult literature, the 2-4/4-2 codetype has been associated with a relatively poor prognosis for change. The major difficulty in treating adult psychiatric patients with this codetype is their tendency to terminate psychotherapy prematurely when situational stress has been reduced but before actual attitudinal or behavioral change has occurred. Adolescents with this codetype are frequently referred for treatment because of difficulty with concentration. Further, these adolescents often perceive their parents as unaffectionate and inconsistent. The majority of adolescents in the Marks et al. sample stated that they had no one in their family with whom to discuss their personal concerns, feelings, and thoughts. Williams and Butcher (1989b) found that 2-4/4-2 adolescents were frequently described as depressed.

2-5/5-2 Codetype. The 2-5/5-2 codetype is quite rare among adults and is produced by 1.2% of male and female adolescents in psychiatric settings. Among the commonly used MMPI-2 sources, Greene (2000) and Friedman et al. (2001) reported information concerning this codetype. Greene noted, based on findings from King and Kelley (1977), that male college students in outpatient psychotherapy who produced a 2-5/5-2 codetype were anxious, disoriented, and withdrawn and often had a history of somatic complaints. Further, 2-5/5-2 college students displayed relatively poor heterosexual adjustment and dated infrequently.

Adolescents with this codetype were typically referred for treatment because of poor sibling relationships, indecisiveness, shyness, extreme negativism, hypersensitivity, and suspiciousness (Marks et al., 1974). As a group, these adolescents were seen to be quite vulnerable to stress, anxious, guilt-ridden, self-condemning, and self-accusatory. Similar to findings in the adult literature, these adolescents appeared to be quite anxious and indecisive and to have substantial difficulty committing themselves to a definite course of action. The 2-5/5-2 adolescents typically displayed defense mechanisms involving obsession (manifested in perfectionistic and meticulous concerns) and intellectualization. They were described as depressed and socially awkward and showed evidence of poor heterosexual adjustment. Individuals with a 2-5/5-2 profile were described as unathletic, and they performed poorly in sports. Males with this codetype were described as not masculine.

In general, teenagers with this codetype were interpersonally shy, passive, and unassertive. Unsurprisingly, drug use and abuse was not found to be associated with adolescents who produced this codetype. MacAndrew Alcoholism scale (*MAC*) raw scores for males with this codetype are typically below critical elevation levels (Archer & Klinefelter, 1992). Although many of these adolescents were seen to be intellectually and academically achieving at high levels, one third of them were teased by their peers in school settings (Marks et al., 1974).

2-7/7-2 Codetype. The 2-7/7-2 codetype occurs with a relatively high frequency in adult psychiatric patients and appears to be less prevalent among adolescents in psychiatric settings, where it is produced by only 1.1% of males and 0.8% of females. The adjectives and description for the 2-7/7-2 codetype, however, are quite consistent across both populations. Individuals with this profile are anxious, tense, depressed, and highly intropunitive. They are often self-preoccupied and rigidly focused on their personal deficiencies and inadequacies. The 2-7/7-2 adolescents in the Marks et al. (1974) sample consistently employed negative adjectives in their self-descriptions.

Individuals with the 2-7/7-2 codetype tend to employ obsessive-compulsive defenses. They typically do not come into conflict with others, and when interpersonal conflicts or difficulties do arise, they are handled by the 2-7/7-2 individuals in a self-punitive and self-accusatory manner. These individuals are rigid in their thinking and tend to be meticulous and perfectionistic in their everyday lives. They are seen by psychotherapists as self-defeating and behaviorally passive. Strong feelings of depression and anxiety frequently co-occur, and there is often a history of overreaction or over-response to minor life stress events. These individuals are commonly described as overcontrolled and unable to deal with or express their feelings in an open manner. In interpersonal relationships, they often exhibit a pattern of dependency, passivity, and lack of assertiveness. Adolescents with a 2-7/7-2 codetype appear to have the capacity to form deep emotional ties with others and typically report close relationships with family members. The primary reasons for referral among these adolescents include tearfulness, restlessness, anxiety, excessive worry, and nervousness. Acting out behaviors such as drug use or school truancy were markedly infrequent among these teenagers. Roughly 40% of the 2-7/7-2 adolescents in the Marks et al. (1974) sample admitted to or expressed suicidal thoughts. Roughly one out of four was characterized as exhibiting severe depression.

2-8/8-2 Codetype. Both teenagers and adults with the 2-8/8-2 codetype are characterized by fearfulness, timidity, anxiety, and social awkwardness. This codetype appears with a frequency of less than 1% for both males and females in the clinical sample of adolescents reported by Butcher et al. (1992). These teenagers appear to prefer a large degree of emotional distance from others and are fearful and anxious concerning interpersonal relationships. Isolation and repression have been reported as primary defense mechanisms. Impaired self-concept and poor self-esteem are also associated with the 2-8/8-2 codetype. Kelley and King (1979) found that 2-8/8-2 female college outpatients were described as having characteristics related to affective distress and schizophrenic symptomatology, whereas 2-8/8-2 males were withdrawn and displayed flat or blunted affect. In the adult literature, individuals with a 2-8/8-2 codetype are often described as fearful of losing control, whereas the adolescent literature describes these individuals as highly emotional and characterized by deficits in the ability to moderate or modulate emotional expression. Further, adolescents with this codetype describe themselves as awkward and fearful of making mistakes. A high percentage of 2-8/8-2 adolescents in the Marks et al. (1974) study (44%) presented histories involving active suicide attempts. In the adult literature, the 2-8/8-2 codetype is associated with suicidal preoccupation, and Graham (2000) noted that adults with this codetype frequently have suicidal thoughts accompanied by specific plans for suicidal actions.

In adolescents and adults, the 2-8/8-2 codetype is also frequently associated with more profound psychiatric symptomatology, particularly when marked elevations occur on these two scales. Schizophrenic, schizoaffective, and manic depressive diagnoses are often attributed to adults with this codetype, and adolescents with these profile features have been found to display a higher than average frequency of such symptoms as hallucinations, preoccupation with bizarre or unusual concerns, and unusual sexual beliefs and practices. In the Marks et al. (1974) sample, over 25% of the 2-8/8-2 codetype adolescents were found to have vague and nonlocalized organic deficits such as minimal brain damage or a history of seizure disorders, including epilepsy.

2-0/0-2 Codetype. Among both teenagers and adults, the 2-0/0-2 codetype has been associated with symptomatology that includes depression, feelings of inferiority, anxiety, social introversion, and withdrawal. These individuals are typically described as conforming, passive persons who are highly unlikely to engage in antisocial or delinquent behavior. Many 2-0/0-2 individuals have areas of social ineptitude and a general lack of social skills. Greene (2000) noted that social skills and assertiveness training may be beneficial in helping individuals with this codetype, along with cognitive-behavioral approaches that focus on decreasing depressive cognitions.

The 2-0/0-2 codetype is produced by 1.8% of male and 3.8% of female adolescents in psychiatric treatment settings (see Table 5.5). It is also produced more frequently by adolescents on the MMPI-A than on the original test instrument. Adolescents with this codetype were typically referred for psychiatric treatment with presenting problems such as tension and anxiety, apathy, shyness, lethargy, and excessive interpersonal sensitivity. As both children and adolescents, teenagers with the 2-0/0-2 codetype appear to be meek, socially isolated loners who conform to parental demands and who do not engage in alcohol or drug abuse. They typically express concerns to their therapists regarding feelings of inferiority, social rejection, and a self-perception of unattractiveness. They describe themselves as awkward, dull, gloomy, cowardly, shy, silent, and meek. Primary defense mechanisms include social withdrawal, denial, and obsessive-compulsive mechanisms. Psychotherapists in the Marks et al. (1974) study tended to view adolescents with a 2-0/0-2 codetype as schizoid, and individuals with this profile had a very low frequency of drug or alcohol abuse. In the Marks et al., 1970–1973 sample, teenage girls with this profile reported that they wished to appear younger and less mature than their actual chronological age. Both boys and girls were seen as socially awkward, unpopular, and maintaining few significant friendships. Cumella et al. (1999) reported that the 2-0/0-2 codetype was associated with an increased frequency of eating disorders, including bulimia and anorexia.

Scale 3 (Hy: Hysteria) Codetypes

The MMPI-A scale 3 consists of 60 items originally selected to identify individuals who react hysterically to stressful situations. No items were deleted from this scale in the creation of the MMPI-A. The item pool for scale 3 includes items on specific somatic concerns and items related to the presentation of self as well socialized and well adjusted. Greene (2000) noted that although these two areas of item content are often unrelated or even negatively correlated in well-adjusted individuals, they tend to be positively correlated and closely associated in individuals with hysterical features. Graham (2000) noted that individuals who obtain a clinically elevated T-score value on scale 3 typically endorse a substantial number of items in both content areas.

The subscales derived by Harris and Lingoes (1955) for scale 3 include Denial of Social Anxiety (Hy_1), Need for Affection (Hy_2), Lassitude Malaise (Hy_3), Somatic Complaints (Hy_4), and Inhibition of Aggression (Hy_5). In the adult literature, marked elevations on scale 3 are typically associated with pathological conditions of hysteria. More moderate elevations have been found to be associated with a number of characteristics, including social extroversion, superficial relationships, exhibitionistic behaviors, and self-centeredness, but do not necessarily involve the classic hysterical syndrome.

Hathaway and Monachesi (1963) found that a scale 3 profile high point (i.e., the highest elevation among the clinical scales) tended to occur with a greater frequency among Minnesota normal adolescents than scale 1 or scale 2 high points. They speculated that children who employ somatic complaints or "play sick" as a way of avoiding school and manipulating their parents would be expected to show elevations on scale 3. Further, these authors noted that moderate elevations on this scale might be expected among well-behaved and intelligent children who expressed what the authors referred to as "middle-class social conformity." In fact, Hathaway and Monachesi found that high scale 3 profiles were related to higher levels of intelligence and achievement and that these children often had parents in the professions. In contrast, a scale 3 low point (i.e., the lowest clinical scale value) among normal adolescents was associated with lower academic achievement and a lower socioeconomic background.

Among adolescent psychiatric inpatients, Archer et al. (1988) found that those with a high scale 3 were perceived by psychiatric staff as dependent, nonassertive, and prone to quickly modify their behaviors in order to meet social expectations and demands. Additionally, high scale 3 adolescents were described by treatment staff as more likely to express anxiety or stress through somatization and physical symptoms. Butcher et al. (1992) found that female adolescent patients with elevations on MMPI-A scale 3 manifested more somatic complaints and concerns than other adolescents, and Cumella et al. (1999) found a relationship between scale 3 elevations and various forms of eating disorders.

High Scores on Scale 3

The following is a summary of characteristics associated with high scale 3 profiles (T ≥ 60):

- Somatic concerns and preoccupations.
- Achievement oriented, socially involved, friendly.
- Patterns of overreaction to stress often involving development of physical symptoms.
- Self-centered, egocentric, and immature.
- Higher levels of educational achievement.
- Strong needs for affection, attention, and approval.
- Often from families of higher socioeconomic status.
- Psychologically naive, with little insight into problem areas.

Low Scores on Scale 3

The following are characteristics of individuals who produce low scores on scale 3 (T ≤ 40):

- Narrow range of interests.
- Limited social involvement and avoidance of leadership roles.
- Unfriendly, tough minded, realistic.
- School underachievement and lower socioeconomic status.
- Unadventurous and unindustrious.

3-4/4-3 Codetype. There appear to be at least three common features of adolescents and adults with the 3-4/4-3 codetype. First, these individuals often present with hypochondriacal or somatic complaints, including symptoms of weakness, fatigue, loss of appetite, and headaches. Second, both teenagers and adults with this codetype tend not to perceive themselves as emotionally distressed, although they are often perceived as such by their therapists. Finally, individuals in both age groups tend to exhibit problems with impulse control and often report histories that include both antisocial behaviors and suicide attempts.

Their problems with impulse control are often manifested in several ways. Sexual promiscuity appears to be relatively common among females with this codetype during adolescence and adulthood, and problems with substance abuse and dependence also appear prevalent. Adolescents with this codetype frequently have a history of theft, school truancy, and running away from home. Psychiatric inpatients with a 3-4/4-3 codetype often pose an elopement risk for the hospital unit. Drug use is also associated with this codetype, particularly among the adolescent sample. In the Marks et al. (1974) study, 63% of adolescents with this codetype reported a drug use history. Further, roughly one third of these adolescents had made suicide attempts, a finding also characteristic of adults with a 3-4/4-3 codetype.

In the adult literature, the 3-4/4-3 individual is typically described as chronically angry and as harboring hostile and aggressive impulses. Particularly when scale 4 is higher than scale 3, overcontrolled hostility may be expressed by episodic outbursts that could take the form of aggressive or violent behavior. Graham (2000) noted that prisoners with the 4-3 codetype frequently have histories of assaultive and violent crimes.

The 3-4/4-3 codetype is relatively common among adolescents and was found in 4.9% of male and 3.6% of female adolescent patients (see Table 5.5). Teenagers with this codetype are typically referred to treatment for sleep difficulties and for suicidal thoughts. They are often known as "roughnecks" in school, and their main problems and concerns relate to conflicts with their parents. Therapists of these teenagers frequently describe them as depressed, although they also find adequate ego strength among these teenagers. As Marks et al. (1974) noted, however, several of the descriptors that apply to adults with the 3-4/4-3 codetype may not apply to adolescents. The overcontrolled hostility syndrome that has been associated with the 3-4/4-3 codetype among adults, for example, does not appear to be thus associated among teenagers. In support of this observation, Truscott (1990) also reported that among teenagers elevations on the Overcontrolled Hostility (O-H) MMPI special scale do not appear to be associated with the overcontrolled hostility syndrome because teenagers do not typically employ repression or overcontrol as a defense mechanism.

3-5/5-3 Codetype. This profile is extremely rare in the adult literature, and Greene (2000) reported that it occurs with a frequency well below 1%. He noted that adults with this codetype are difficult to treat because they typically experience little emotional distress. No discussion of this codetype is available in either Graham (2000) or Lachar (1974), although Friedman et al. (2001) did briefly review it and stated that "this is generally a male profile about which there is limited empirical information" (p. 288).

This codetype was produced by 1.0% of male and 3.0% of female adolescents in psychiatric treatment (Archer, Gordon, et al., 1991). Marks et al. (1974) were able to identify only 13 individuals who produced this codetype, all of whom were male. Among adolescents, those with the 3-5/5-3 codetype have many features that would be associated with individual scale high points for scales 3 and 5. None of the 3-5/5-3 adolescents in the Marks et al. sample were referred to treatment by court agencies or authorities, an unusual finding in adolescent psychiatric populations. Many of the teenagers with this codetype came from homes in which moral and religious values were firmly and perhaps rigidly enforced, and the teenagers in this sample viewed the moral and ethical judgments of their parents as highly predictable. Adolescents with this codetype were seen by their therapists as moderately depressed. However, perhaps because of the utilization of denial associated with elevations on scale 3, several of these adolescents described themselves as "elated." A major symptom pattern connected with this codetype was one of withdrawal and inhibition.

Although these adolescents were perceived as basically insecure and as having a strong need for attention, they were also perceived as shy, anxious, inhibited, and socially uncomfortable. They were often found to be affectively shallow, and their rate of speech was described as rapid. They did not employ acting out as a primary defense mechanism and in fact tended to overcontrol their impulses. When adolescents with this codetype were involved with drug abuse, the substances employed were alcohol, marijuana, amphetamines, and sopors. Interestingly, 43% of the teenagers in the Marks et al. sample were found to have weight problems, including obesity and anorexia.

3-6/6-3 Codetype. There are a variety of characteristics commonly displayed by adolescents and adults who produce a 3-6/6-3 profile type. They tend to be generally suspicious and distrustful individuals who manifest poor interpersonal relationships and have substantial difficulty in acknowledging the presence of psychological problems and conflicts. In general, both teenagers and adults with this codetype utilize rationalization and projection as defenses and often have difficulty in understanding why others are concerned about their behavior. Among adolescents, descriptors associated with suspicion and paranoia were often used to characterize those with this codetype. In general, individuals with this codetype appear difficult to get along with, self-centered, and distrustful and resentful of others. They maintain an egocentric and guarded stance toward the world around them.

The 3-6/6-3 codetype was found among 0.6% of male and 1.4% of female adolescents receiving psychiatric services. Among adolescents, the most distinctive characteristic of the 3-6/6-3 group was a relatively high incidence of attempted suicide, and one third of adolescents in the Marks et al. (1974) study were seen for psychotherapy following such behaviors. In the Marks et al. 1970–1973 sample, this profile was associated with substance abuse but not as extensively as other adolescent codetypes. In this sample, roughly 50% of 3-6/6-3 adolescents acknowledged drug involvement. Interestingly, 40% were academically superior students.

Scale 4 (*Pd*: Psychopathic Deviate) Codetypes

This MMPI-A scale consists of 49 items, with one item deleted from the original *Pd* scale due to inappropriate content. Scale 4 was originally designed to identify or diagnose psychopathic personality, referred to in the *DSM–IV–TR* as *antisocial personality disorder*. As described by Dahlstrom et al. (1972), the criterion group for scale 4 consisted largely of individuals who were court referred for psychiatric evaluation because of delinquent actions such as lying, stealing, truancy, sexual promiscuity, alcohol abuse, and forgery. The 49 items in the MMPI-A *Pd* scale cover a diverse array of content areas, including family conflicts, problems with authority figures, social isolation, delinquency, and absence of satisfaction in everyday life. Scale 4 has a substantial degree of item overlap with many of the validity and clinical scales, and it contains an almost equal number of true and false responses that are keyed in the critical direction.

In the adult literature, individuals who score high on scale 4 are typically described in pejorative or unfavorable terms; for example, they are said to exhibit anger, impulsivity, interpersonal and emotional shallowness, interpersonal manipulativeness, and unpredictability. Thus, a marked elevation on scale 4 often indicates the presence of antisocial beliefs and attitudes, although Greene (2000) noted that such elevations do not necessarily imply that these traits will be expressed overtly. The degree to which antisocial behaviors are manifested is typically seen as related to the individual's standing on additional MMPI scales, including scales 9 and 0. Higher scale 9 and lower scale 0 values, in combination with an elevated scale 4, increase the likelihood of overt behavioral expression of antisocial attitudes, beliefs, and cognitions. Harris and Lingoes (1955) identified five content subscales within scale 4: Familial Discord (Pd_1), Authority Problems (Pd_2), Social Imperturbability (Pd_3), Social Alienation (Pd_4), and Self-Alienation (Pd_5).

Scores on scale 4 have been determined to vary with the respondent's age and race. Colligan et al. (1983) provided data from cross-sectional studies of 18- to 70-year-old adults that indicated that scale 4 values tend to decrease with age among both men and women. There is quite clear evidence that scale 4 values differ as a function of stage of life (adolescence versus adulthood) in both normal and clinical populations (Archer, 1984). It has also been reported that African American, Native American, and Hispanic subjects may score somewhat higher on scale 4 than Caucasians and Asian Americans (Graham, 2000), based on findings from the MMPI-2 normative samples.

In normal samples, adolescents tend to endorse more scale 4 items in the critical direction than do adult respondents, and the mean scale 4 value for the MMPI-A sample would produce a T-score value of approximately 55 if scored using MMPI-2 norms. Research by Pancoast and Archer (1988) indicated that adolescents, in contrast to adults, are particularly likely to endorse items in the scale 4 content area labeled by Harris and Lingoes (1955) as Familial Discord (Pd_1). Hathaway and Monachesi (1963) found that a scale 4 high point was more common than other high points among normal adolescents in the Minnesota statewide sample, with the highest frequency of scale 4 elevations found for girls and for adolescents from urban settings. The Minnesota data also indicate that scale 4 elevations increased as a function of severity of delinquent behavior. Further, high scale 4 profiles for both boys and girls were associated with higher rates of broken homes.

Within clinical samples, although codetypes involving scale 4 are frequent in adult populations, they could be described as virtually ubiquitous among adolescents. Nine of the 29 codetypes reported for adolescents by Marks et al. (1974) involved a scale 4 2-point code (i.e., scale 4 was one of the two scales most elevated in the profile), and nearly one half of their clinical cases involved a high-point code that included scale 4. Similarly, in the analysis by Archer, Gordon, et al. (1991) of MMPI profiles produced by adolescents in clinical settings, roughly 48% involved 2-point codetypes that included scale 4.

Archer et al. (1988) found that adolescent inpatients who produced elevations on scale 4 were described by psychiatric staff members as evasive and unmotivated in psychotherapy. These adolescents were also found to be rebellious, hostile, and incapable of profiting from prior mistakes. Additionally, these adolescents had a high frequency of presenting problems involving drug and alcohol abuse, and nearly half received conduct disorder diagnoses. In the research by Archer and Klinefelter (1992), adolescent codetypes that involved scale 4 often produced substantially elevated mean raw score values on the MacAndrew Alcoholism scale. More recent research by Gallucci (1997a, 1997b) also found the MMPI-A profiles of adolescent substance abusers often produced clinical range elevations on scale 4 and the *MAC-R* scale. Butcher et al. (1992) found that, in their clinical sample, adolescent boys and girls with elevations on MMPI-A scale 4 were more likely to be described as delinquent and were prone to acting out or externalizing behaviors. In addition, girls in this group were more likely to engage in sexual activity, and boys in this group were more likely to run away.

High Scores on Scale 4

The following is a summary of characteristics for high scale 4 profiles (T ≥ 60):

- Poor school adjustment and problems in school conduct.
- Increased probability of delinquent, externalizing, and aggressive behaviors.
- Increased probability of a family history involving parental separation and divorce.
- Increased probability of an urban background.
- Difficulty incorporating or internalizing the values and standards of society.
- Rebelliousness and hostility toward authority figures.
- Increased likelihood of diagnoses involving conduct disorder.
- Inability to delay gratification.
- Poor planning ability and impulsivity.
- Low tolerance for frustration and boredom.
- Reliance on acting out as a primary defense mechanism.
- Increased probability of parent-adolescent conflicts and familial discord.
- Risk-taking and sensation-seeking behaviors, including use of drugs and alcohol.
- Selfishness, self-centeredness, and egocentricity.
- Ability to create a favorable first impression.
- Extroverted, outgoing interpersonal style.
- Relative freedom from guilt and remorse.
- Relatively little evidence of emotional/affective distress.

Low Scores on Scale 4

The following features have been associated with individuals who score low on scale 4 (T ≤ 40):

- Conventional, conforming, and compliant with authority.
- Lower probability of delinquency.
- Concerns involving status and security rather than competition and dominance.
- Accepting, passive, and trusting interpersonal style.
- Lower likelihood of delinquent behaviors.

4-5/5-4 Codetype.   The adult and adolescent literatures for the 4-5/5-4 profile codetype are substantially discrepant. Adults with these profile characteristics are typically discussed in terms of immaturity, emotional passivity, and conflicts centered around dependency. Friedman et al. (2001) noted that this codetype among adults is almost exclusively produced by male respondents because scale 5 is rarely clinically elevated among women. Adults with this codetype are frequently rebellious in relation to social conventions and norms, and their nonconformity is often passively expressed through selection of dress, speech, and social behavior. Although these individuals appear to have strong dependency needs, there are also conflicts created by their fear of domination by others. This latter pattern appears most marked in the relationships of males, with 4-5/5-4 men often entering into heavily conflicted relationships with females.

Although adults with these codetypes typically display adequate control, there are also indications that these individuals are subject to brief periods of aggressive or antisocial acting out. Sutker, Allain, and Geyer (1980) reported that the 4-5/5-4 codetype is found in 23% of women convicted of murder. Among male college students, King and Kelley (1977) related this codetype to passivity, heterosexual adjustment problems, and both transient and chronic interpersonal difficulties. This sample did not display significant evidence of personality disorders, nor was homosexuality apparently characteristic of this group. Friedman et al. (2001) noted that detection of homosexual drive or behavior in adults with this codetype is difficult, and "should the individuals want to conceal their homosexuality, they could do so readily without flagging any of the validity scales" (p. 299).

As shown in Table 5.5, the 4-5/5-4 codetype is found in 1.6% of male and 3.8% of female adolescents in psychiatric treatment settings. Marks et al. (1974) indicated that teenagers with this codetype appear to get along well with their peer group and are gregarious and extroverted in their social interactions. In contrast to teenagers with other codetypes, 4-5/5-4 adolescents were described by their therapists as better adjusted, as easier to establish rapport with, and as demonstrating greater ego strength. Further, therapists felt that teenagers with this codetype typically displayed relatively effective defenses in terms of protection of the adolescent from conscious awareness of depression or anxiety. The typical defense mechanisms utilized by these adolescents included acting out and rationalization. In contrast to 5-4s, 4-5 adolescents appeared to have greater difficulty in controlling their tempers, and they described themselves as argumentative, opinionated, and defensive. Over half of the adolescents in the 4-5 codetype were rated by their therapists as having a good prognosis. In contrast to adults with this codetype, over 80% of the 4-5/5-4 adolescents in the Marks et al. study were engaged in heterosexual dating, a figure substantially higher than the base rate for other adolescent codetype groups.

Respondents with the 4-5/5-4 configuration in the Marks et al. 1970–1973 sample reported a high frequency (72%) of drug abuse history. The drug use patterns found for these teenagers appeared to involve a broad variety of substances. In addition, adolescents in this sample had a high rate of antisocial behaviors, including shoplifting, auto theft, breaking and entering, and drug dealing. As a group, they were described as emotionally reactive and prone to temper tantrums and violent outbursts. Finally, teenagers in this sample also evidenced significant problems in school adjustment, including histories of truancy, school suspension, and failing academic grades.

4-6/6-4 Codetype. A relatively consistent picture emerges from the adolescent and adult literatures for individuals with the 4-6/6-4 codetype. They are uniformly described as angry, resentful, and argumentative. Adolescents with this codetype who are referred for treatment typically present symptomatology involving defiance, disobedience, and negativism. Treatment referrals for 4-6/6-4 adolescents are often made from court agencies, and Archer and Krishnamurthy (2002) noted that recent studies have associated elevations on these scales with delinquency.

Individuals with this codetype typically make excessive demands on others for attention and sympathy but are resentful of even mild demands that may be placed on them in interpersonal relationships. They are generally suspicious of the motives of others and characteristically avoid deep emotional attachments. Adolescents with this codetype appear to be aware of deficits in their interpersonal relationships and often report that they are disliked by others. For both adults and teenagers, however, there is very little insight displayed into the origins or nature of their psychological problems. They tend to deny serious psychological problems, and they rationalize and transfer the blame for their life problems onto others. In short, they characteristically do not accept responsibility for their behavior and are not receptive to psychotherapy efforts. Although adolescents with this codetype are rated by others as aggressive, bitter, deceitful, hostile, and quarrelsome, they often appear to view themselves as attractive, confident, and jolly.

The *4-6/6-4* codetype is relatively common among adolescents and is found in 6.2% of male and 4.0% of female adolescents in psychiatric treatment settings (Table 5.5). Among adolescents, the *4-6/6-4* codetype is almost inevitably associated with child-parent conflicts, which often take the form of chronic, intense struggles. These adolescents typically undercontrol their impulses and act without thought or deliberation. Williams and Butcher (1989b) found that adolescents with this codetype were more likely to engage in acting out behaviors, including sexual acting out. Marks et al. (1974) reported that the *4-6/6-4* adolescent typically encountered problems with authority figures. Narcissistic and self-indulgent features appear prevalent among both adolescents and adults with the codetype. Therapists in the Marks et al. study described the *4-6/6-4* adolescent as provocative and indicated that major defense mechanisms included acting out and projection. About half of the adolescents with this codetype in the Marks et al. sample reported a history of drug abuse, most frequently involving the use of alcohol.

4-7/7-4 Codetype. The *4-7/7-4* codetype appears to be characteristic of adolescents and adults who employ acting out as their primary defense mechanism but experience substantial feelings of guilt, shame, and remorse over the consequences of their behavior. Thus, they tend to alternate between behaviors that show a disregard for social norms and standards and excessive and neurotic concern regarding the effects of their actions. Possessing underlying impulse control problems and tendencies to behave in a provocative and antisocial manner, these individuals appear to be insecure and dependent. They have strong needs for reassurance and attention.

The *4-7/7-4* codetype occurs in 2.4% of male and 1.2% of female adolescents in psychiatric treatment settings. In the Marks et al. (1974) research, *4-7/7-4* teenagers were described by therapists as impulsive, provocative, flippant, and resentful. At the same time, they demonstrated evidence of substantial conflicts concerning emotional dependency and sexuality. The majority of these adolescents exhibited substantial feelings of guilt and shame and were viewed by their therapists as guilt-ridden and self-condemning. Williams and Butcher (1989b) found that adolescents with the *4-7/7-4* codetype presented a mixed picture of internalizing and externalizing behaviors and concluded that tension/nervousness, substance abuse, and acting out behaviors were associated with this profile.

4-8/8-4 Codetype. The *4-8/8-4* codetype is associated with marginal social adjustments for both adolescents and adults. Marks et al. (1974) described the *4-8/8-4* adolescents as "one of the most miserable groups of adolescents we studied" (p. 218). They were frequently perceived as angry, odd, peculiar, and immature individuals who displayed impulse control problems and often had a history of chronic interpersonal conflict. Only 16% of teenagers with this codetype were rated as showing a definite improvement as a result of psychotherapy, and only 9% were rated as showing a good prognosis for future adjustment. Adolescents with this codetype were often evasive in psychotherapy and frequently attempted to handle their problems by denying the presence of any difficulties.

The *4-8/8-4* codetype is found with a frequency of 2.8% among male and 2.1% among female adolescent psychiatric patients. Teenagers with this profile typically display patterns of very poor academic achievement and were often seen in psychotherapy as frequently as three times a week. Their family lives were described as chaotic, and unusual symptomatology, such as anorexia, encopresis, enuresis, or hyperkinesis, was often noted. Although excessive drinking and drug abuse are common among adults with this codetype, 4-8/8-4 teenagers do not appear to be among the heavy drug abuse groups. Although the 8-4 adolescents were described as more regressed than the 4-8s, the latter were also noted to display thought patterns that were unusual and sometimes delusional. Thus, individuals with this codetype display antisocial features related to elevations on scale 4 in combination with schizoid or schizophrenic symptomatology characteristic of elevations on scale 8. Williams and Butcher (1989b) reported that the 4-8/8-4 adolescents were more likely than other teenagers to have a history of sexual abuse, and Losada-Paisey (1998) reported that this codetype was associated with adolescent sex offenders. Archer and Slesinger (1999) found that adolescents with this codetype frequently endorsed MMPI-A items related to suicidal ideation.

4-9/9-4 Codetype. A striking degree of similarity exists in the description of teenagers and adults who produce a 4-9/9-4 codetype. These individuals almost always display a disregard for social standards and are likely to have difficulties in terms of acting out and impulsivity. They are characteristically described as egocentric, narcissistic, selfish, and self-indulgent and are often unwilling to accept responsibility for their own behavior. They are seen as high sensation seekers who have a markedly low frustration tolerance and are easily bored. In social situations, the 4-9/9-4s are often extroverted and make a positive first impression. They also, however, appear to manifest chronic difficulties in establishing close and enduring interpersonal relationships and are highly manipulative and shallow in dealing with others. Classic features of the antisocial personality type are usual among adults with this codetype, and adolescents with the codetype often receive conduct disorder diagnoses.

The 4-9/9-4 is a very frequently occurring codetype among adolescent psychiatric patients, although there is a substantial gender difference. Specifically, 10.1% of male and 4.0% of female patients produce this codetype when scored on MMPI-A norms (Table 5.5). Huesmann et al. (1978) reported findings indicating that the summation of T-score values on scales F, 4, and 9 serves as a viable predictor of aggression in older adolescents. In the Marks et al. (1974) research, the 4-9/9-4 adolescents were invariably referred for treatment because of defiance, disobedience, impulsivity, provocative behaviors, and truancy from school. In most cases, there were constant conflicts between the adolescents and their parents resulting from their history of misbehaviors. Intriguingly, fewer 4-9/9-4 adolescents in the Marks et al. sample were raised in their natural homes than youngsters from any other codetype grouping. Specifically, 17% of adolescents with this codetype grew up in foster or adoptive homes, and 20% did not reside with their parents at the time of their evaluation in this study. As a group, these adolescents appeared to be socially extroverted and reported an earlier age of dating than other teenagers. Williams and Butcher (1989b) reported 4-9/9-4 teenagers were more sexually active than other adolescents. Nearly 50% of the subjects with this codetype in the Marks et al. study had a history of illegal behaviors resulting in placement in detention or on probation. Ninety-three percent of these teenagers employed acting out as their primary defense mechanism, and problems with affective distress such as anxiety or feelings of inadequacy were not found for these teenagers. Archer and Krishnamurthy (2002) reported that this codetype is frequent among adolescents with drug and alcohol abuse problems as well as male juvenile delinquents.

Therapists described adolescents with this codetype as resentful of authority figures, socially extroverted, narcissistic, egocentric, selfish, self-centered, and demanding. Further, these adolescents were noted to be impatient, impulsive, pleasure-seeking, restless, and emotionally and behaviorally undercontrolled. Sixty-one percent of the adolescents with this codetype in the Marks et al. 1970–1973 sample reported a history of drug abuse. These teenagers, however, appeared to be selective in regard to the substances they used and tended to avoid drugs such as hallucinogens or opiates. Archer and Klinefelter (1992) found that the *4-9/9-4* adolescents produced higher mean *MAC* scores than any other codetype group. This finding probably re-flects the influence of a variety of factors, including the degree of item overlap between scales *4* and *9* and the *MAC* scale and the degree to which both the *4-9/9-4* code-type and the *MAC* scale commonly measure an extroverted, high sensation–seeking, risk-taking lifestyle. In the Marks et al. (1974) study, 83% of the *4-9/9-4*s were either chronically truant from school, had run away from home, or had run away from treat-ment settings. Many of these adolescents had engaged in all three of these activities. Marks et al. described these adolescents as provocative and seductive problem chil-dren with histories of lying, stealing, and other antisocial behaviors. These authors used the phrase "disobedient beauties" in reference to the *4-9/9-4* codetype. In the adult literature, typical features of the *4-9/9-4* individual have been repeatedly related to a poor prognosis for personality or behavioral change as a result of psychotherapy. It should be remembered, however, that adolescents who produce this codetype are likely to show substantially greater capacity for change and benefit from treatment than adults. The *4-9/9-4* personality structure is not as firmly entrenched and solidified during adolescence as it later can become during adulthood.

4-0/0-4 Codetype.   As noted by Greene (2000), the *4-0/0-4* codetype is quite rare in adults (less than 1% frequency), and there is little empirical data on which to base a de-scription of these individuals. Conceptually, there is an inherent conflict presented by high-point elevations on both scales *4* and *0*. Whereas individuals who score high on scale *4* tend to be relatively comfortable around others, often show extroverted, traits and are impulsive, high scale *0* respondents are often socially uncomfortable, intro-verted, and cautious. Thus, codetype elevations involving both scales are infrequent. Among adolescents in psychiatric settings, 2.3% of males and 2.1% of females pro-duced the *4-0/0-4* codetype based on MMPI-A norms (Archer, Gordon, et al., 1991). Marks et al. (1974) were able to identify 22 adolescents who produced the *4-0/0-4* codetype, evenly divided between high- and low-point codes.

Surprisingly, *4-0/0-4* adolescents appeared to display more features related to ele-vations on scale *6* than those related to elevations on either scale *4* or scale *0*. They were described as suspicious and distrustful by their therapists. Additionally, they frequently expressed grandiose ideas, and their main defense mechanism consisted of projection. They were often resentful and argumentative and perceived themselves as shy and socially uncomfortable. Therapists described the *4-0/0-4* adolescents as quiet, passively resistant, and relatively underinvolved in activities around them. They had few close friends, and establishing friendships tended to be one of their primary prob-lem areas. Furthermore, they were judged to display moderate ego strength and to demonstrate a pattern of overreaction to minor stressors.

Scale 5 (*Mf*: Masculinity-Femininity) Codetypes

Sixteen items were eliminated from the original MMPI *Mf* scale in the creation of the 44-item MMPI-A *Mf* scale. The content areas of scale *5* are heterogeneous and include work and recreational interests, family relationships, and items related to fears and sensitivity. This scale was originally developed by Hathaway and McKinley to identify homosexual males, but the authors encountered difficulty in identifying or defining a clear diagnostic grouping to create a single criterion group. The primary criterion group eventually selected consisted of 13 homosexual males who were relatively free from neurotic, psychotic, or psychopathic tendencies. Items were assigned to the *Mf* scale, however, if they differentiated between high- and low-scoring men on an attitude interest test or if they showed a significant difference in endorsement between males and females. Dahlstrom et al. (1972) noted that an unsuccessful attempt was made by Hathaway and McKinley to develop a corresponding scale to identify female "sexual inversion," that is, an *Fm* scale.

Forty-one of the 44 items in scale 5 are keyed in the same direction for both sexes. The three remaining items, which deal with overt sexual material, are keyed in opposite directions for males and females. T-score conversions are reversed for males and females so that a high raw score value for boys results in a high T-score placement, whereas a high raw score value for girls is converted to a low T-score value. Thus, the *Mf* scale represents a bipolar measure of gender role identification. The *Mf* scale and scale 0 are the two basic scales for which linear T-score conversions were retained in the MMPI-A, in contrast to the remaining eight standard clinical scales, for which uniform T-score procedures are used. Linear T-scores were employed for *Mf* and *Si* because the distributions for these scales were different than those for the remaining basic scales and more closely approximated a normal distribution.

Serkownek used item-factor loading patterns to construct six subscales for the *Mf* scale (Schuerger, Foerstner, Serkownek, & Ritz, 1987). The Serkownek subscales for *Mf* are Mf_1 (Narcissism-Hypersensitivity), Mf_2 (Stereotypic Feminine Interest), Mf_3 (Denial of Stereotypic Masculine Interests), Mf_4 (Heterosexual Discomfort-Passivity), Mf_5 (Introspective-Critical), and Mf_6 (Socially Retiring). Attempts to create a factor-analytically derived set of subscales for *Mf* were unsuccessful in the MMPI-2 Restandardization Project, and no similar attempt was undertaken in the development of the MMPI-A.

Substantial controversy and debate has surrounded the meaning and interpretation of scale 5, particularly in recent years. Graham (2000) noted that scores on scale 5 have been related to level of formal education, although this relationship appears more limited on the MMPI-2 than the original test instrument. As suggested by Greene (2000) and Friedman et al. (2001), the usefulness of scale 5 in identifying homosexuality appears to be substantially limited because elevations on this scale may reflect the influence of a variety of factors in addition to sexual identification and orientation. Further, in the creation of both the MMPI-A and the MMPI-2, items directly related to sexual preferences were deleted, thereby essentially eliminating the usefulness of this scale as a measure of homosexuality. Finlay and Kapes (2000) compared scale 5 of the MMPI and the MMPI-A in a repeated measures study with 60 emotionally disturbed adolescents. Test-retest results (with administration order balanced for the two test versions) showed generally higher scores for the original version of scale 5 and surprising low correlations between the two versions. The authors concluded that the deletion of 16 items and the rewording of 6 additional in the creation of the MMPI-A scale 5 may have significantly altered the measurement of the underlying construct. Greene (2000) and Friedman et al. (2001) noted that when scale 5 shows the only clinical-range elevation in an MMPI profile, the individual is unlikely to be diagnosed as manifesting a psychiatric disorder. Midrange elevations (T ≥ 40 and T ≤ 60) on the *Mf* scale have been difficult to interpret due to the variety of item endorsement patterns that may create this range of scores (e.g., a balance between masculine and feminine characteristics versus low endorsement of both content areas may result in midrange values).

Markedly low T-scores on the *Mf* scale for women appear to indicate a substantial identification with traditional feminine roles, which may include passivity, submissiveness, and the adaptation of many aspects of traditional femininity. Todd and Gynther (1988) found that low *Mf* females described themselves as tender and emotional. Low-scoring males have been described by Greene (2000) as displaying an "almost compulsive masculinity" in an inflexible and rigid manner (p. 153). Todd and Gynther found that low-scoring males described themselves as domineering and impersonal. Among women, T-scores of 60 or more on the *Mf* scale appear to be associated with a lack of interest in a traditional feminine role, and moderate elevations for men have been related to aesthetic interests. Todd and Gynther found that high *Mf* females describe themselves as self-confident and exploitive and were rated by their peers as unsympathetic and bold. High *Mf* scores for males in this study were related to the perception of self as undemanding and shy, and clinical-range elevations on scale 5 have also been related to passivity for males. More recently, Blais (1995) found elevated *Mf* scores among adult female psychiatric inpatients to be related to higher levels of anger, aggression, and suspiciousness and a tendency to be manipulative and egocentric in interpersonal relationships. Long and Graham (1991) provided findings that do not support the usefulness of scale 5 in describing behaviors or personality characteristics for normal men.

With the original version of the MMPI, there was relatively little difference in the mean *Mf* raw score values found between normal male adolescents and adults, but there was a tendency for female adolescents to produce raw score values 2 to 3 points lower than female adults (Archer, 1987b). Data from Hathaway and Monachesi (1963) indicated that the boys in their Minnesota normal sample who produced their highest values on scale 5 tended to be of higher socioeconomic status, with parents from professional and semiprofessional occupations. These adolescents tended to have higher intelligence scores and academic grades. They also exhibited a lower frequency of delinquent and antisocial behaviors. In contrast, boys with low scale 5 scores tended to display patterns of school underachievement and delinquency and produced lower intelligence test scores than high scale 5 boys. Similarly, female adolescents from the Minnesota normal sample who scored low on scale 5 had higher intelligence scores and displayed evidence of higher levels of academic achievement. Female adolescents scoring high on scale 5 were less clearly defined but appeared to come from rural environments and did less well in school. Wrobel and Lachar (1992) found that male adolescents who scored high on scale 5 were more frequently described by their parents as fearful, and high scale 5 females were more frequently rated as aggressive. Williams and Butcher (1989a) reported that they were unable to find clinically relevant descriptors for scale 5 in their study of adolescent inpatients. In a reanalysis of these data for MMPI-A scales, however, Butcher et al. (1992) found high scores to be related to the occurrence of behavior problems for girls and fewer legal actions for boys.

High Scores on Scale 5

The following is a summary of descriptors for high scale 5 males (T ≥ 60):

- Intelligent, aesthetic interests, higher levels of academic achievement.
- Possible areas of insecurity or conflict regarding sexual identity.
- Emotional and comfortable in expressing feelings and emotions with others.
- Passive and submissive in interpersonal relationships.
- Lower likelihood of antisocial or delinquent behaviors.

The following is a summary of descriptors for high scale 5 females (T ≤ 60):

- Vigorous and assertive.
- Competitive, aggressive, tough minded.
- Greater problems in terms of school conduct.
- Increased frequency of behavioral problems.
- Possibility of "masculine" interests in academic areas and sports.

Low Scores on Scale 5

The following is a summary of descriptors for low scale 5 males (T ≥ 40):

- Presentation of self with extremely masculine emphasis.
- Higher frequency of delinquency and school conduct problems.
- Overemphasis on strength, often accompanied by crude and coarse behaviors.
- Lower intellectual ability and academic achievement.
- Relatively narrow range of interests defined by traditional masculine role.

The following is a summary of descriptors for low scale 5 females (T ≤ 40):

- Presentation of self in stereotyped female role.
- Passive, yielding, and submissive in interpersonal relationships.
- Lower socioeconomic background.
- Higher levels of academic performance.
- Lower incidence of learning disabilities.

5-6/6-5 Codetype Friedman et al. (2001) and Greene (2000) have provided the only available information about the 5-6/6-5 codetype among the commonly used guides to interpretation of adult profiles. Both sources indicate that little is known about this codetype among adults. The 5-6/6-5 codetype is found with a frequency of only 0.5% for male and 1.1% for female adolescents in treatment settings (Table 5.5). Marks et al. (1974) presented the 5-6/6-5 codetype based on findings from 11 adolescents. Thus, the 5-6/6-5 is a relatively rare codetype, and very limited data are available concerning the characteristics of individuals who produce this MMPI configuration.

Most of the descriptors identified by Marks et al. (1974) for adolescents with the 5-6/6-5 profile appear to be related to the scale 6 elevation. Although teenagers with this codetype were able to acknowledge psychological problems with their therapists, they were often hesitant to establish deep or frequent contacts with them. In general, they were seen as fearful of emotional involvement with others. Of this group, 30.6% were given a good prognosis by their therapists, a percentage that is roughly three times higher than that found by Marks et al. for therapists' ratings for other codetypes. The 5-6/6-5 adolescents were described as resentful and insecure, and acting out was their primary defense mechanism.

The majority of teenagers in this small codetype grouping had a history of drug abuse involving a variety of psychoactive drug classes. Additionally, a history of violent actions appeared to be associated with the 5-6/6-5 codetype. Legal actions and arrests were reported for such offenses as assault and battery and assault with a deadly weapon. Marks et al. (1974) described this group as preoccupied with themes of death, murder, and brutality.

5-9/9-5 Codetype. Like the previous codetype, the *5-9/9-5* profile has received little research attention in the adult literature. A summary of the literature on this configuration may be found in Friedman et al. (2001) and in Greene (2000). This codetype is found with a frequency of only 0.3% for male and 2.6% for female adolescent psychiatric patients (Archer, Gordon, et al., 1991). Marks et al. (1974) identified 10 teenagers with the *5-9* code and 10 teenagers with the *9-5* code in the clinical samples they used to develop codetype descriptors.

In general, teenagers with the *5-9/9-5* codetype appeared to display substantially less psychopathology than adolescents from other codetype groups. Their overall degree of disturbance was typically judged to be mild to moderate. Primary defense mechanisms for these teenagers appear to be rationalization (for the *5-9* group) and denial (for the *9-5* group). Psychotherapists found that conflicts regarding emotional dependency and assertiveness were primary problems among these adolescents. One third of the adolescents in the Marks et al. (1974) sample reported that they were raised by their mothers in a single-parent household.

A slight majority of *5-9/9-5* adolescents (56%) were found to have a history of drug abuse in the Marks et al. 1970–1973 sample. In contrast to adolescents from other codetype groups, members of the *5-9/9-5* group typically did well in school. None of these teenagers had been suspended or expelled from school, and in general they appeared to value academic achievement and possess aesthetic interests. Nevertheless, the parents of the teenagers with this codetype reported that they were unmanageable and rebellious. Family conflicts rather than peer conflicts appear to be most characteristic of this group.

5-0/0-5 Codetype. As with the other high-point codes involving scale 5, little information is available on adults with the *5-0/0-5* codetype, and the data that exist are summarized in Friedman et al. (2001) and in Greene (2000). This codetype is found in 0.3% of male and 1.1% of female adolescents evaluated in clinical settings. The Marks et al. (1974) *5-0/0-5* codetype was created based on a sample of only 11 adolescents.

Consistent with the elevations on scales 5 and 0, adolescents with the *5-0/0-5* codetype in the Marks et al. study were seen as cautious, anxious, and inhibited teenagers who were fearful of emotional involvement with others. They did not employ acting out as a defense mechanism, generally exhibited few problems in impulse control, and did not report histories of antisocial behaviors. In fact, teenagers with this codetype typically exhibited overcontrol and were ruminative and overideational. Slightly more than one third of the teenagers in the *5-0/0-5* codetype group were involved in special education classroom settings, including classes for emotionally disturbed children.

The majority of adolescents with the *5-0/0-5* codetype perceive their major problems as social awkwardness and difficulty in forming friendships. In general, they describe themselves as awkward, shy, timid, inhibited, cautious, and submissive. Therapists tend to view these adolescents as manifesting severe anxiety. Major conflicts for these adolescents typically involve sexuality and difficulties in assertive behavior. The general picture that emerges for this codetype group is that of adolescents who retreat into personal isolation rather than reaching out to others in interpersonal relationships.

Scale 6 (*Pa*: Paranoia) Codetypes

Scale 6, in both the MMPI and the MMPI-A, consists of 40 items that were created to assess an individual's standing in relation to symptomatology involving ideas of reference, suspiciousness, feelings of persecution, moral self-righteousness, and rigidity. Although many of the items in scale 6 deal with overt psychotic symptoms such as ideas of reference and delusions of persecution, there are also large groups of items dealing with interpersonal sensitivity, cynicism, and rigidity, which are not necessarily psychotic markers or symptoms. Further, Graham (2000) noted that it is possible to achieve an elevated T-score value on scale 6 without endorsing overtly or blatantly psychotic symptomatology. Harris and Lingoes (1955) identified three subscales for scale 6: Persecutory Ideas (Pa_1), Poignancy (Pa_2), and Naivete (Pa_3).

Although individuals who produce marked clinical elevations on scale 6 usually present paranoid symptomatology, some paranoid patients are able to achieve within-normal-limits values on this scale. Greene (2000), for example, noted that normal-range T-score values on scale 6 are typically produced by individuals in two categories: first, respondents without paranoid symptomatology, and, second, individuals who have well-established paranoid symptomatology but maintain sufficient reality contact to avoid critically endorsing obvious items on this dimension. Unfortunately, little research has been focused on this latter group, and most of the information concerning these individuals is based on MMPI clinical lore.

Extreme elevations on MMPI-A scale 6 (T-score values above 70) typically identify persons with a psychotic degree of paranoid symptomatology such as paranoid schizophrenics and individuals manifesting paranoid states (Graham, 2000). Moderate elevations (T-scores of 60 to 70) are often produced by individuals who are relatively free of psychotic symptomatology. They may be characterized, however, by excessive sensitivity to the opinions and actions of others, a suspicious or guarded approach to interpersonal exchanges, and the use of rationalization and projection as primary defense mechanisms. They frequently present as suspicious, resentful, hostile, and argumentative as well as rigid and inflexible. A mild elevation on scale 6 (a T-score of 55 to 59) is often seen as a positive sign when the respondent is not in a psychiatric setting. Individuals within this elevation range are frequently described as sensitive to the needs of others and trusting and frank in their interpersonal relationships. They may also be submissive and dependent in their interpersonal relationships and describe themselves as prone to worry and anxiety. Greene (2000) noted that mental health workers frequently score within the moderate range of T-score values (55–64) on scale 6, perhaps reflective of interpersonal sensitivity.

Adolescents have traditionally scored somewhat higher on scale 6 than adults on the original version of the MMPI (Archer, 1987b). Pancoast and Archer (1988) found that normal adolescents endorsed more scale 6 items contained in the Harris-Lingoes Pa_1 (Persecutory Ideas) subscale than adults, suggesting they often believed themselves misunderstood and unjustly punished or blamed by others. Data from Hathaway and Monachesi (1963), based on Minnesota normal adolescents, indicated that boys who scored high on scale 6 are more likely to drop out of school, perhaps as a function of their interpersonal sensitivity in the school environment. In contrast, girls who scored high on scale 6 in this sample tended to have higher IQ scores and better academic grade averages and were considered well-adjusted by others. Hathaway and Monachesi observed that moderate elevations on scale 6 appear to be an academic and social asset for girls, whereas boys with elevations on scale 6 tended to get into more academic and social difficulties, perhaps reflecting greater aggressiveness among the boys. Hathaway, Monachesi, and Salasin (1970) reported, in a follow-up study of the Hathaway and Monachesi (1963) sample, that elevations on scales 6 and 8 were associated with poor academic and social outcomes primarily among adolescents with average or lower levels of intelligence. Lachar and Wrobel (1990) found that outpatient adolescent males who produced high scale 6 scores were more likely to be described as distrustful and suspicious and more likely to manifest delusions of persecution or paranoia. Butcher et al. (1992) found scale 6 elevations related to neurotic/dependent and hostile/withdrawn behaviors among male adolescent inpatients. Overall, it appears that clinically relevant scale 6 descriptor patterns for female adolescents have been difficult to identify in these research investigations and that more is known about the correlate patterns for teenage boys.

High Scores on Scale 6

The following is a summary of the characteristics of individuals who produce marked elevations on scale 6 (T ≥ 70):

- Anger, resentment, hostility.
- Use of projection as primary defense mechanism.
- Disturbances in reality testing.
- Delusions of persecution or grandeur.
- Ideas of reference.
- Diagnoses often associated with the manifestation of thought disorder as exhibited in psychosis or schizophrenia.
- Social withdrawal.

The following are features usually associated with moderate elevations on scale 6 (T = 60 to 69):

- Marked interpersonal sensitivity.
- Suspicion and distrust in interpersonal relationships.
- Tendencies toward hostility, suspiciousness, resentfulness, and argumentativeness.
- Problems in school adjustment.
- Increased disagreements with parents.
- Difficulty in establishing therapeutic relationships due to interpersonal guardedness.

Low Scores on Scale 6

The following are associated with low scale 6 scores (T ≤ 40):

- Lower levels of intelligence and academic achievement.
- Presentation of self as cheerful and balanced.
- Cautiousness and conventionality.
- Interpersonal insensitivity, unawareness of the feelings and motives of others.
- If psychiatric patient, possibility of overcompensation for paranoid symptoms.

6-8/8-6 Codetype. The 6-8/8-6 codetype is indicative of serious psychopathology for both teenagers and adults. This codetype has clearly been associated with paranoid symptomatology, including delusions of grandeur, feelings of persecution, hallucinations, and outbursts of hostility. Individuals with this codetype appear to be socially isolated and withdrawn, and their behavior is frequently unpredictable and inappropriate. Difficulties in thought processes are often apparent, ranging from deficits in concentration to bizarre and schizophrenic ideation. It would appear that the 6-8/8-6 individual frequently has difficulty in differentiating between fantasy and reality and will often withdraw into autistic fantasy in response to stressful events.

The 6-8/8-6 codetype occurs with a frequency of 3.2% for male and 3.4% for female adolescents in psychiatric settings (Table 5.5). Adolescents with this codetype are typically referred for treatment in response to the occurrence of bizarre behaviors or excessive fantasy. They also appear generally to have been subjected to physical punishment during childhood as a primary form of discipline. Nearly half of the adolescents with this codetype in the Marks et al. (1974) sample had received beatings as punishment for misbehavior. Additionally, the majority of these adolescents had fathers who had committed either minor or major legal offenses, and 30% of these teenagers had attended five or more schools within their elementary education years.

Adolescents with the 6-8/8-6 codetype often have a violent temper and, when angry, may express their feelings directly (e.g., hitting others or throwing objects). They are not liked by their peers, and they often perceive their peers as "picking on" them or teasing them. In general, these adolescents are preoccupied with their physical appearance, and ratings by their psychotherapists indicate that they are indeed below average in appearance. The predominant types of affective distress for these teenagers include moderate depression and feelings of guilt and shame. Adolescents with this codetype were frequently delusional and displayed grandiose ideas. In the Marks et al. (1974) sample, slightly over half of these teenagers had used drugs, although much of their drug use was connected with suicide attempts. As might be expected for a group of adolescents who produced this codetype, these teenagers typically displayed little or no insight into their psychological problems.

Scale 7 (*Pt*: Psychasthenia) Codetypes

Scale 7 in both the MMPI and MMPI-A consists of 48 items designed to measure psychasthenia, a neurotic syndrome that was later conceptualized as obsessive-compulsive neurosis and was most recently labeled *obsessive-compulsive disorder*. Individuals with obsessive-compulsive disorder are characterized by excessive doubts, compulsions, and obsessions and high levels of tension and anxiety. Because this symptom pattern is more typically found among outpatients, the original criterion group employed by McKinley and Hathaway in the development of this scale was restricted to a relatively small group of 20 inpatients with this condition. McKinley and Hathaway were reluctant to use outpatients in their criterion groups because of their inability to confirm diagnoses for such patients (Greene, 2000). The content areas of scale 7 cover a wide array of symptoms, including unhappiness, physical complaints, deficits in concentration, obsessive thoughts, anxiety, and feelings of inferiority and inadequacy. Harris and Lingoes (1955) did not identify subscales for scale 7, perhaps because of the relatively high degree of internal consistency (as reflected in Cronbach coefficient alpha) typically found for this MMPI basic scale.

In general, those who score high on scale 7 have been described as anxious, tense, and indecisive as well as very self-critical and perfectionistic. At extreme elevations, there are often patterns of intense ruminations and obsessions constituting disabling symptomatology. Low scores on this scale are frequently indicative of self-confident, secure, and emotionally stable individuals who are achievement and success oriented. Greene (1980) noted that women typically endorse more scale 7 items than men. Data from normal adolescents as reported by Hathaway and Monachesi (1963) showed that scale 7 high-point elevations were more common in adult than adolescent profiles, although scale 7 was the most frequently elevated neurotic scale in adolescent MMPI profiles. Scale 7 has also been reported to be a relatively rare high point in adolescent profiles in clinical settings (Archer, 1989). Data for adolescent outpatients, reported by Lachar and Wrobel (1990), indicated that high scale 7 males and females were described as overly self-critical, anxious, tense, nervous, and restless. Wrobel and Lachar (1992) reported that high scale 7 scores for male and female adolescents were related to an increased frequency of nightmares. Butcher et al. (1992) found that a clinical sample of girls who produced elevations on MMPI-A scale 7 were more likely to be described as depressed and to report more disagreements with their parents.

High Scores on Scale 7

The following is a summary of descriptors associated with high scale 7 scores (T ≥ 60):

- Anxious, tense, and apprehensive.
- Self-critical, perfectionistic approach to life.
- Feelings of insecurity, inadequacy, and inferiority.
- Emotionally overcontrolled and uncomfortable with feelings.
- Introspective and ruminative.
- Lacking in self-confidence and ambivalent in decision-making situations.
- Rigid, moralistic, and conscientious.
- At marked elevations, obsessive thought patterns and compulsive behaviors.

Low Scores on Scale 7

The following are descriptors associated with low scale 7 scores (T ≤ 40):

- Lack of emotional distress and freedom from anxiety and tension.
- Capable and self-confident in approach to problems.
- Perceived as warm, cheerful, and relaxed.
- Flexible, efficient, and adaptable.

7-8/8-7 Codetype. The 7-8/8-7 profile appears to be related to the occurrence of inadequate defenses and poor stress tolerance for both adults and adolescents. These individuals are frequently described as socially isolated, withdrawn, anxious, and depressed. There is also evidence that individuals with the *7-8/8-7* codetype feel insecure and inadequate. They have substantial difficulty in modulating their feelings and expressing their emotions in appropriate ways.

The *7-8/8-7* codetype is found among 1.8% of male and 1.9% of female adolescents in psychiatric settings (Table 5.5). Among adolescents, this profile configuration appears to be related to the presence of substantial tension resulting from failing defenses. Adolescents with this codetype are typically described as anxious and depressed. They are also inhibited and conflicted in terms of their interpersonal relationships, particularly those involving aspects of emotional dependency. Many of these teenagers express fears of failure in school, and Marks et al. (1974) reported that roughly one half of the *7-8/8-7* adolescents in their sample had failed at least one academic grade.

In the adult literature, the relationship in elevation between scales 7 and 8 is frequently cited as a highly significant factor in the interpretation of this profile. Scale 7 characteristics are thought to suppress scale 8 symptomatology, and individuals with higher elevations on scale 7 (relative to scale 8) are seen as more neurotic, whereas profiles containing higher elevations on scale *8* (relative to scale *7*) are frequently seen as indicative of more schizophrenic symptomatology. Marks et al. (1974) noted that there is no evidence of this phenomenon among the adolescents with the *7-8/8-7* codetype. Specifically, based on their data from the 1970–1973 sample, they observed that *7-8*s and *8-7*s were both quite deviant in thought and behavior, and nearly one half of these adolescents had experienced either auditory or visual hallucinations.

7-9/9-7 Codetype. Across both adult and adolescent respondents, the *7-9/9-7* codetype appears to be associated with tension, anxiety, and rumination. Over three fourths of the adolescents with this codetype were characterized by their therapists as worriers who were vulnerable to both realistic and unrealistic fears. For adults with this codetype, Greene (2000) recommended that the possibility of manic features be investigated and that psychopharmacological medications be considered for the reduction of the very high levels of anxiety, agitation, and excitement.

In clinical settings, the *7-9/9-7* codetype occurs with a frequency of 1.7% for male and 0.7% for female adolescents (Table 5.5). Adolescents with this codetype were described by Marks et al. (1974) as insecure. These adolescents also tended to have strong needs for attention, conflicts involving emotional dependency issues, and fears of losing control. They were tense and had difficulty "letting go" but did not show evidence of scale *9* manic characteristics such as elation. In general, these teenagers appeared to be defensive when discussing their psychological problems and to be very sensitive to demands placed on them by others. Within the adolescent sample, scale *7* correlates were more predominant for this codetype than scale *9* characteristics.

7-0/0-7 Codetype. The *7-0/0-7* codetype appears to be rare among adults and is found with a frequency of 1.3% for male and 1.2% for female adolescents in clinical settings (Table 5.5). Marks et al. (1974) were able to identify only 11 adolescents with this codetype in their research sample. For both adolescents and adults, this codetype appears related to the presence of neurotic symptomatology, including excessive anxiety, tension, social introversion, and shyness.

The predominant presenting problems for the *7-0/0-7* adolescents were shyness and extreme sensitivity. Although defiant and disobedient behaviors were relatively common for this group, these characteristics tended to occur with a base rate frequency that was lower than that of many other adolescent codetype groups. Interestingly, almost one half of these adolescents had family members with a history of psychiatric disorder. Psychotherapists responded positively to adolescents with the *7-0/0-7* codetype and indicated that they displayed moderate motivation for treatment, good treatment prognosis, and good cognitive-verbal insight. These teenagers performed well in academic settings and maintained a high need for achievement. Reaction formation and isolation appear to be the predominant defense mechanisms for the *7-0/0-7* adolescents. These individuals become intropunitive in response to stress or frustration and have a decided tendency toward emotional overcontrol. Marks et al. (1974) noted that these adolescents are basically insecure and tend to have conflicts regarding emotional dependency and assertion.

Scale *8* (*Sc*: Schizophrenia) Codetypes

Scale *8*, which consists of 77 items, is the largest scale in the MMPI-A. One item, related to sexuality, was deleted from the original scale *8* in modifying this measure for the MMPI-A. Scale *8* was developed to identify patients with schizophrenia, and it deals with content areas involving bizarre thought processes, peculiar thoughts, social isolation, difficulties in concentration and impulse control, and disturbances in mood and behavior. Harris and Lingoes (1955) identified six subscales within the schizophrenia scale: Social Alienation (Sc_1); Emotional Alienation (Sc_2); Lack of Ego Mastery, Cognitive (Sc_3); Lack of Ego Mastery, Conative (Sc_4); Lack of Ego Mastery, Defective Inhibition (Sc_5); and Bizarre Sensory Experiences (Sc_6).

Individuals who score high on scale *8* are typically described as alienated, confused, and delusional. They often display psychotic features and are socially isolated, withdrawn, shy, and apathetic. Extreme elevations on scale *8*, particularly T-score values in excess of 100 for adults and 90 for adolescents, are typically produced by clients who are not schizophrenic but are experiencing intense, acute situational distress. Greene (1980) noted that an adolescent undergoing a severe identity crisis may frequently score in this extreme range. Individuals who score markedly low in scale *8* have typically been described as conventional, cautious, compliant persons who may be overly accepting of authority and who place a premium on practical and concrete thinking. Comprehensive reviews of the MMPI literature on schizophrenia in adult populations were provided by Walters (1983, 1988).

Research on scale *8* has shown a large degree of difference in the mean raw score endorsement patterns between adolescent and adult normals, with adolescents typically endorsing substantially more scale *8* items than their adult counterparts (Archer, 1984, 1987b; Pancoast & Archer, 1988). Hathaway and Monachesi (1963) found that boys were more likely than girls to have a profile with the scale *8* elevation as the highest point. Further, both male and female adolescents who produced high scale *8* scores were likely to be lower in intelligence and in academic achievement than other adolescents. High scale *8* girls were also more likely to drop out of school. Archer et al. (1988) found that high scale *8* adolescent inpatients were described as mistrustful, vulnerable to stress, interpersonally isolated, and socially withdrawn. Often, these adolescents had presenting problems that included impaired reality testing. Archer and Gordon (1988) found that scale *8* scores were significantly associated with schizophrenic diagnoses in an adolescent inpatient sample. Employing a criterion of a T-score value of 75 or above to identify schizophrenia, an overall hit rate of 76% was obtained. This result is comparable to Hathaway's (1956) original finding for this scale in adult samples. Butcher et al. (1992) found MMPI-A scale *8* elevations to be associated with higher levels of acting out, schizoid, and psychotic behaviors among adolescent male inpatients. They also reported an association between scale *8* elevations and histories of sexual abuse for both male and female inpatients. In addition to schizophrenia, an adolescent's scale *8* elevation may reflect his or her drug use history, particularly previous experiences with hallucinatory drugs (Archer, 1989). Interpretation of elevated scale *8* values, therefore, require the clinician's awareness of the adolescent's drug-taking history and behaviors (Archer & Krishnamurthy, 2002). Review of critical item endorsements and Harris-Lingoes subscales may often be used as a vehicle for determining whether an adolescent's scale *8* elevation is a result of drug-taking experiences or represents actual schizophrenic symptomatology. Finally, Lachar and Wrobel (1990) found high scale *8* scores among adolescent inpatients to be related to frequent experiences of frustration, and Wrobel and Lachar (1992) found high scale *8* adolescents were often rejected and teased by other children.

High Scores on Scale 8

The following are descriptors associated with high scale *8* scores (T ≥ 60):

- Withdrawn, seclusive, and socially isolated.
- Confused and disorganized.
- Presence of schizoid features.
- Feelings of inferiority, incompetence, low self-esteem, and dissatisfaction.
- Feelings of frustration and unhappiness.
- Rejection and teasing by peers.
- Poor school adjustment and performance.
- Vulnerable and easily upset.
- Reluctance to engage in interpersonal relationships, including psychotherapy relationships.
- Nonconforming, unconventional, and socially deviant.
- Poor reality testing.
- At marked elevations (T ≥ 70), associated with delusions, hallucinations, and other schizophrenic symptoms.

Low Scores on Scale 8

The following are descriptors associated with low scale *8* scores (T ≤ 40):

- Conforming, conventional, and conservative.
- Logical, practical, and achievement oriented.
- Unimaginative and cautious in approaches to problem solving.
- Responsible, cooperative, and dependable.

8-9/9-8 Codetype. The occurrence of an *8-9/9-8* codetype in either adolescence or adulthood appears to be related to the presence of serious psychopathology. Individuals who produce this MMPI configuration have been referred to as immature, self-centered, argumentative, and demanding. Although they seek a great deal of attention, they are resentful and hostile in interpersonal relationships and display little capacity to form close relationships with others. Acting out, often of an unpredictable nature, is a salient defense mechanism for individuals with this codetype.

As shown in Table 5.5, the *8-9/9-8* codetype is found in 1.5% of male and 1.0% of female adolescents in psychiatric settings. Many of the respondents with this codetype display evidence of thought disorder, including grandiose ideas, as well as evidence of hyperactivity and a very rapid personal tempo. Marks et al. (1974) noted that adolescents with a *9-8* codetype appear to "think, talk, and move, at an unusually fast pace" (p. 239). For both adolescents and adults, this codetype has been associated with the presence of both schizophrenic and paranoid symptomatology. In the Marks et al. 1970–1973 sample, this codetype was not particularly associated with substance abuse or addiction. In the Archer and Klinefelter (1992) study, however, the *8-9/9-8* code was related to significantly higher *MAC* scale elevations for female adolescent psychiatric patients. In a recent study by Archer and Slesinger (1999), this codetype was associated with a higher frequency of report of suicidal ideation on the suicide-related MMPI-A items (177, 283, and 399).

Scale 9 (*Ma*: Hypomania) Codetypes

Scale 9, in both the original MMPI and the MMPI-A, consists of 46 items developed to identify patients manifesting hypomanic symptomatology. The content areas covered in this scale are relatively broad and include grandiosity, egocentricity, irritability, elevated mood, and cognitive and behavioral overactivity. Harris and Lingoes (1955) identified four content subscales contained in the hypomania scale: Amorality (Ma_1), Psychomotor Acceleration (Ma_2), Imperturbability (Ma_3), and Ego Inflation (Ma_4).

Greene (2000) noted that scale 9 elevations are often difficult to interpret in isolation. In fact, characteristics associated with elevations on scale 9 are often seen as facilitating or moderating the expression of characteristics associated with elevations on other clinical scales, particularly scales *D* and *Pd*. High scores on scale 9 have been related to impulsivity, excessive activity, narcissism, social extroversion, and a preference for action in contrast to thought and reflection. In addition, individuals who score high on this scale may display manic features such as flight of ideas, delusions of grandeur, and hyperactivity. Lumry, Gottesman, and Tuason (1982), however, demonstrated that individuals with bipolar manic-depressive disorder provide very different MMPI profiles depending on the phase of the disorder during which the patient is assessed. For example, patients in the depressed phase produced a profile characterized by elevations on scales 2 and 7, whereas patients assessed during the manic phase produced spike 9 profiles. These findings indicate that the accurate diagnosis of bipolar disorder may require a longitudinal series of MMPI administrations because of the state dependency nature of MMPI assessment. Markedly low scores on scale 9 (T-score values below 40) have been related to lethargy, apathy, listlessness, and decreased motivational states. Low scale 9 scores have also been associated with the presence of serious depressive symptomatology, including vegetative signs (Greene, 2000).

Normal adolescents typically endorse substantially more scale 9 items than do adults (Archer, 1984, 1987b). Pancoast and Archer (1988) showed that adolescents are particularly likely to endorse scale 9 items contained in the Harris-Lingoes Psychomotor Acceleration subscale, which measures feelings of restlessness and the need to engage in activity. Hathaway and Monachesi (1963) found low scores on scale 9 in their sample of normal adolescents to be associated with lower rates of delinquency. In general, the teenagers who scored low on this scale in the Minnesota sample were well behaved and conforming and demonstrated high levels of achievement in the academic setting.

In adolescent psychiatric outpatient samples, Lachar and Wrobel (1990) reported that elevations on scale 9 are related to the occurrence of temper tantrums. Boys who scored high on scale 9 were described as hostile or argumentative, and girls with high scores were found to display rapid mood shifts and a tendency not to complete tasks that they undertook. Archer et al. (1988) reported that high scale 9 adolescent inpatients were described as impulsive, insensitive to criticism, and unrealistically optimistic in terms of their goal setting and aspirations. Archer and Klinefelter (1992) found that elevations on scale 9 were associated with higher scores on the *MAC* scale. Butcher et al. (1992) found high MMPI-A scale 9 scores among adolescents in inpatient settings to be associated with amphetamine abuse for boys and more frequent school suspensions for girls.

High Scores on Scale 9

The following descriptors are associated with high-point elevations on scale 9 (T ≥ 60):

- Accelerated personal tempo and excessive activity.
- Preference for action rather than thought and reflection.
- Impulsivity, restlessness, and distractibility.
- Lack of realism, and grandiosity in goal setting and aspirations.
- Outgoing, socially extroverted, and gregarious.
- Talkative and energetic.
- Egocentric, self-centered, insensitive, and self-indulgent.
- Greater likelihood of school conduct problems and delinquent behaviors.
- Emotionally labile.
- Flight of ideas, euphoric mood, and grandiose self-perceptions.

Low Scores on Scale 9

The following are descriptors associated with low scale 9 scores (T ≤ 40):

- Low energy level.
- Quiet, seclusive, withdrawn, and depressed.
- Overcontrolled, inhibited, and overly responsible.
- Decreased probability of acting out or delinquent behaviors.
- Depressed, lethargic, and apathetic.

Scale *0* (*Si*: Social Introversion) Codetypes

The MMPI-A *Si* scale consists of 62 items, reflecting the deletion of 8 items from the original *Si* scale. Additionally, 2 items retained on the MMPI-A *Si* scale are keyed in the opposite direction from traditional scoring for this scale. These abbreviated items are as follows:

No. 308   Bothered by trivial thoughts. (Scored in *true* direction on MMPI-A, *false* direction on original MMPI.)

No. 334   People often jealous of my ideas. (Scored in *true* direction on MMPI-A, *false* direction on original MMPI.)

The scoring direction of these items was modified for the MMPI-A because of the belief that the original scoring was counterintuitive and incorrect. The *Si* scale was originally developed by Drake (1946) based on the responses of college students who produced extreme scores on a social introversion/extroversion measure. Elevated T-scores on the *Si* scale reflect greater degrees of social introversion. Although Harris and Lingoes did not attempt to create specific subscales for the social introversion scale, three *Si* subscales were created for the MMPI-2 and the MMPI-A based on a factor analytic approach. The MMPI-A *Si* subscales are discussed in the next chapter. Graham (2000) indicated that the *Si* scale contains two broad clusters of items, namely, items related to social participation and items related to neurotic maladjustment and self-depreciation. Graham noted that high scores on scale *0* can occur by the endorsement of either or both of these content areas.

Individuals who produce elevated scores on scale *0* are likely to be socially introverted, insecure, and markedly uncomfortable in social situations. They tend to be shy, timid, submissive, and lacking in self-confidence. When high scores occur for scale *0*, the potential for impulsive behaviors and acting out is decreased, and the likelihood of neurotic rumination and introspection is increased. Individuals who produce low scores on the *Si* scale are described as socially extroverted, gregarious, friendly, and outgoing. These individuals appear to have strong affiliation needs and are interested in social status, acceptance, and recognition. Low scorers may be subject to impulse control problems, and their relations with others may be more superficial than sincere and long enduring.

Greene (2000) noted that adolescents and college students typically score toward the extroverted pole of the *Si* scale and that *Si* scores tend to decrease somewhat with increasing years of education. Hathaway and Monachesi (1963) found an interesting pattern of correlates for scale *0* scores in their sample of Minnesota normal adolescents. Social introversion was a relatively frequent finding among boys and girls from rural farm settings, whereas social extroversion was characteristic of adolescents from families with parents in professional occupations. Intriguingly, low scale *0* profiles were found among children with higher intelligence levels but with spotty records of academic achievement. Hathaway and Monachesi interpreted these findings as indicating that there was a potential conflict between an adolescent's social interest and success and his or her academic achievement.

Among psychiatrically disturbed adolescents, Lachar and Wrobel (1990) found that outpatients who produce high values on scale *0* are described as having few or no friends and as being very shy. These teenagers often avoided calling attention to themselves and did not initiate relationships with other adolescents. Butcher et al. (1992) found that adolescent inpatients with elevations on scale *0* were described as socially withdrawn and manifesting low self-esteem. In addition, female adolescents with elevated scale *0* scores had lower levels of delinquency, acting out, and drug or alcohol use.

High Scores on Scale 0

The following are descriptors associated with adolescents who score high on scale *0* (T ≥ 60):

- Social introversion and social discomfort.
- Low self-esteem.
- Reserved, timid, and socially retiring.
- Decreased probability of delinquent or acting out behaviors.
- Submissive, compliant, and accepting of authority.
- Insecure and lacking in self-confidence.
- Overcontrolled, difficult to get to know, and interpersonally hypersensitive.
- Reliable, dependable, and cautious.
- Lacking in social skills.

Low Scores on Scale 0

The following are descriptors associated with adolescents who score low on scale *0* (T ≤ 40):

- Sociable, extroverted, and gregarious.
- Intelligent, with a possible history of academic underachievement.
- Active, energetic, and talkative.
- Interested in social influence, power, and recognition.
- Socially confident and competent.

FACTORS POTENTIALLY AFFECTING CODETYPE INTERPRETATION

A substantial amount of research literature has established that demographic variables such as race, gender, and age *may* significantly influence the MMPI profiles of adult respondents (Dahlstrom et al., 1975). To investigate this issue among adolescents, Schinka, Elkins, and Archer (1998) used multiple regression analyses to examine the effects of age, gender, and ethnic background on variance in MMPI-A raw scores for adolescents in normal and clinical settings. The analyses were designed to measure the incremental contribution of demographic variables to scale variance beyond that explained by the presence of psychopathology. In all of the MMPI-A validity and clinical scales small amounts of variance (<10%) in MMPI-A scores were accounted for by demographic variables. Similarly, the MMPI-A content and supplementary scales did not appear to be meaningfully influenced by an adolescent's age, gender, or ethnic background. Nonetheless, each of these areas is now examined in more detail in terms of the probable effects of these variables on codetype interpretation practices for the MMPI-A.

Race/Ethnic Factors

Gynther (1972) reviewed the literature on the influence of race on adults' MMPI scores and concluded that distinctive racial differences reliably occur that reflect differences in the cultural and environmental backgrounds of Black and White respondents. In particular, Gynther interpreted findings from the analyses of item differences as indicating that the high scores for Blacks on scales *F*, *Sc*, and *Ma* reflected differences in perceptions, expectations, and values rather than differential levels of psychological adjustment. He called for the development of MMPI norms for Black respondents in order to allow for more accurate assessment of psychopathology in Black populations. More recently, Gynther (1989) reevaluated the literature on comparisons of MMPI profiles from Blacks and Whites and concluded that, in the absence of studies employing unbiased criterion measures to evaluate potential racial differences, "definite conclusions to the racial bias question may be exceptionally difficult to reach" (p. 878).

The early studies that investigated the variable of subject race within adolescent populations appeared to support Gynther's 1972 position regarding the presence of racial differences in MMPI scale values. Ball (1960) examined MMPI scale elevations for a group of 31 Black and 161 White ninth graders and found that Black males tended to score higher on scale *Hs* than White male students and that Black female students produced significantly higher elevations on scales *F*, *Sc*, and *Si* than White female students. Similarly, McDonald and Gynther (1962) examined the MMPI response patterns of Black and White students within segregated high school settings. These findings indicated that Black students produced higher scores than their White counterparts on scales *L*, *F*, *K*, *Hs*, *D*, and *Ma*. Further, Black female students had significantly higher scores on all MMPI scales, with the exception of *K* and *Sc*, than did White female students.

More recently, research results have suggested that when Blacks and Whites have experienced common cultural influences and socioeconomic backgrounds, racial differences are less likely to be found in MMPI profile elevations. Klinge, and Strauss (1976) and Lachar, Klinge, and Grissell (1976) reported no significant MMPI differences between samples of Black and White adolescents. These results were attributable to the observation that the Black and White respondents in these investigations had been raised and educated in similar or equivalent environments. Bertelson, Marks, and May (1982) matched 462 psychiatric inpatients (of whom 144 were adolescents) on variables such as gender, age, residence, education, employment, and socioeconomic status. No significant MMPI differences were found for the matched racial samples in this study. Archer (1987b) reported evidence of minimal racial differences between groups of Black and White male and female adolescents from a predominantly middle-class public high school setting.

Marks et al. (1974) included 61 Black subjects in the clinical population they used to derive correlate descriptors of adolescent codetype profiles. These subjects were part of their Ohio State University Health Center sample. The authors found few Black-White differences among the descriptors generated for their adolescent codetypes, and statements regarding race of subject are seldom made in the Marks et al. text. Green and Kelley (1988) investigated the relationship between MMPI scores and external behavioral and interview criteria in 333 White and 107 Black male juvenile delinquents. They reported that as the apparent objectivity of the criteria increased, evidence of racial bias decreased (i.e., the predictability of the criteria did not differ as a function of race).

Figures 5.8 and 5.9 show the MMPI-A profile findings for Black, White, and other male respondents in the normative sample for this instrument, and Figs. 5.10 and 5.11 show comparable data for females. These profiles show racial or ethnic differences of about 3 to 5 T-score points across MMPI clinical scales *L, F, 4, 6, 7, 8,* and *9*. Demographic data for this sample, however, indicate a significant socioeconomic difference between these three ethnic groupings as reflected in adolescents' reports of parental occupation and socioeconomic status. Thus, the relatively limited profile differences found between these groups reflect both ethnic and socioeconomic differences.

Greene (1980, 1987) surveyed the literature on the issue of racial differences in MMPI response patterns. His review of studies examining Black-White differences within normal samples failed to reveal any MMPI scale that consistently demonstrated racial differences across 10 independent investigations. A similar conclusion was also reached in a review by Pritchard and Rosenblatt (1980). Greene noted that scales *F* and *Ma* were most frequently affected by race but that significant differences were not found for scale *Sc*, which had been reported by Gynther (1972) as one of the scales typically elevated among Black populations. Further, Greene noted that the actual mean differences in studies reporting significant differences between Black and White respondents typically were equal to or less than 5 T-score points, a range comparable to the largest racial differences found for the MMPI-A normative sample. Greene (2000) recently updated his review in this area and observed that moderator variables, including socioeconomic status (SES), education, and intelligence, are critical for evaluating any research on MMPI-2 or MMPI-A ethnic group differences. He concluded that, based on the existing literature on Black-White, Hispanic-White, Black-Hispanic, Native American–White, and Asian American–White, no reliable or consistent pattern of ethnic differences has been established for any group. Dahlstrom, Lachar, and Dahlstrom (1986) provided a comprehensive review of the relationship between ethnic status and MMPI response patterns that included data from both adolescent and adult samples. These authors concluded that this literature supports the use of the MMPI in the assessment of psychological functioning for Black clients, "since the relative accuracy of these scores were as good or better for this ethnic minority as it was for white clients" (p. 205). Goldman, Cooke, and Dahlstrom (1995) reported on the MMPI and MMPI-2 profiles of undergraduate college students who varied in ethnic background, gender, and socioeconomic status. The findings from this

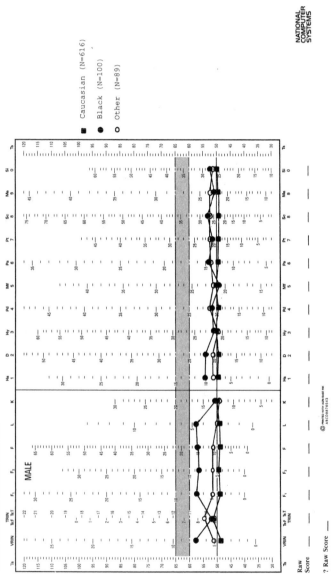

FIG. 5.8. MMPI-A basic scale profiles produced by males from various ethnic groups in the MMPI-A normative sample. *Note.* TRIN T-score values were calculated based on conversions from the mean raw score value for each sample.

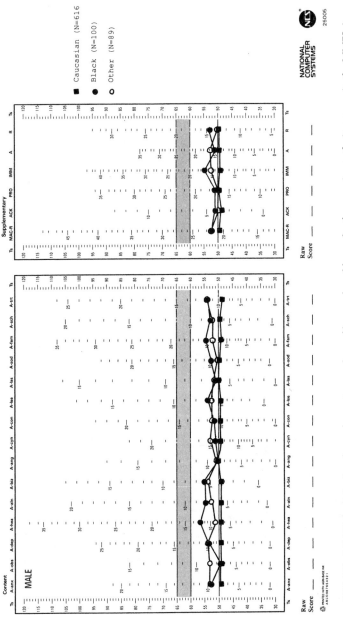

FIG. 5.9. MMPI-A content and supplementary scale profiles produced by males from various ethnic groups in the MMPI-A normative sample.

171

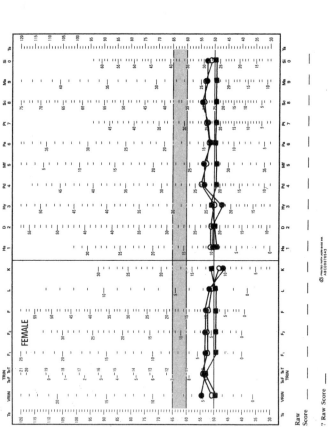

FIG. 5.10. MMPI-A basic scale profiles produced by females from various ethnic groups in the MMPI-A normative sample.
Note. TRIN T-score values were calculated based on conversions from the mean raw score value for each sample.

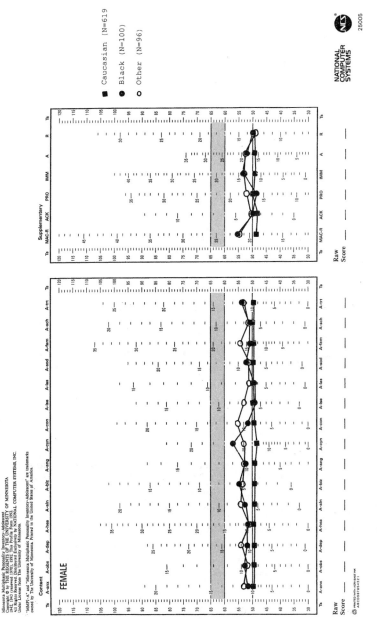

FIG. 5.11. MMPI-A content and supplementary scale profiles produced by females from various ethnic groups in the MMPI-A normative sample.

173

investigation indicated that the MMPI-2 showed patterns of fewer racial or ethnic differences than the original MMPI, a result attributable to the inclusion of a significant number of Black subjects in the MMPI-2 normative sample. Timbrook and Graham (1994) examined racial or ethnic differences by analyzing the responses of 75 Black and 725 White men and 65 Black and 742 White women who were part of the MMPI-2 normative sample. The authors reported that mean differences on the MMPI-2 basic scales between ethnic groups were small for both genders and that when subjects were matched for age, education, and income, fewer MMPI-2 mean scale differences were observed. In a crucial component of this study, MMPI-2 basic scale T-score values were correlated with personality ratings derived for these subjects. Findings did not indicate a systematic difference in the accuracy of these correlates for Black versus White subjects. The authors cautioned that the degree to which these findings may be generalized to other ethnic minorities, including American Indians, Hispanics, or Asian Americans, is currently unknown.

Archer and Krishnamurthy (2002) briefly reviewed the literature on MMPI-A responses of ethnic minorities and concluded that the MMPI-A may be used in assessing individuals from various ethnic minority groups using the standard adolescent norms available for this instrument. They also noted that given the relatively limited literature in this area, clinicians should be "appropriately conservative in interpreting the MMPI-A profiles of ethnic minority adolescents" (p. 148). They offered several further cautions, including the observation that the bulk of MMPI research studies involving ethnicity have dealt with comparisons of profiles from Black and White groups and that relatively little is known about other minority group profile patterns.

A number of studies, however, have recently been conducted examining MMPI-A profiles of Hispanic adolescents. Corrales et al. (1998), for example, provided a comprehensive listing of research studies conducted with the MMPI-2 and the MMPI-A using U.S. Latino samples, including samples consisting of Puerto Ricans. This bibliography includes a total of 52 studies completed since 1989, and six additional resources. Gumbiner (2000) provided a critique of the limitations in ethnic research studies on the MMPI-A, noting that most investigators have simply compared the mean scale scores from two or more ethnic groups. Gumbiner recommended that greater research attention be focused on the external correlates found for MMPI-A scales among various ethic minorities and that data analyses present separate findings for male and female adolescents. Illustrating this latter approach, Gumbiner (1998) compared validity, clinical, content, and supplementary MMPI-A scores of male and female Hispanic adolescents as profiled on the MMPI-A normative data. Analysis indicated moderately elevated T-score values for boys on the L, F, F_1, and F_2 validity scales, basic scales 1, 2 and 8, content scales A-hea, A-biz, A-lse, A-las, and A-sch, and the IMM supplementary scale. For girls, T-score values were not elevated on any MMPI-A scales. Gumbiner speculated that Hispanic boys' discomfort with school and lower aspirations were related to the lower educational and employment levels of their fathers and that their scores on the IMM scale may prove useful in identifying boys "at risk" for dropping out of school.

Negy, Leal-Puente, Trainor, and Carlson (1997) investigated the MMPI-A responses of 120 Mexican-American adolescents based on the observation that Hispanic adolescents were underrepresented in the MMPI-A normative sample. Adolescents in this study completed the MMPI-A, a short demographic questionnaire, and a measure of acculturation designed for Mexican Americans. Results indicated that the MMPI-A responses of these adolescents differed minimally from those of the MMPI-A normative group and that their performance varied as a function of socioeconomic status and level of acculturation. Additionally, two studies have examined the performance of Hispanic adolescents in cross-national research studies. Scott, Butcher, Young, and Gomez (2002) administered the MMPI-A translation developed for use with Spanish-speaking adolescents in the United States to 385 Spanish-speaking adolescents in Columbia, Mexico, Peru, Spain, and the United States. The results of this study showed a high degree of similarity across the five countries on the MMPI-A basic, content, and supplementary scales. Most scales were within 5 T-score points of the U.S. Hispanic mean scores, and no group produced scale elevations greater than $T = 65$. Scott et al. concluded that the Hispanic MMPI-A, with its established norms, is appropriate for adoption in Spanish-speaking countries. Scott, Knoth, Beltran-Quiones, and Gomez (2003) recently reported on their use of the Hispanic MMPI-A to compare potential psychopathology in a group of 59 adolescent earthquake victims in Columbia and a control group of 62 Columbian adolescents with similar socioeconomic, educational, and ethnic backgrounds. The results of this study demonstrate the utility of the Hispanic MMPI-A in evaluating psychopathology, including evidence of posttraumatic stress disorder, in an Hispanic adolescent sample outside of the United States. Scott and his colleagues noted:

> The strength of this study is the use of the MMPI-A as the measure of psychological damage. Internationally, the MMPI-2 and the MMPI-A are the most widely recognized and most valid and clinically useful instruments to assess psychopathology. The Spanish versions of these tests are now being adapted for use throughout Latin America, including Columbia. This is the first study to use the recently released Hispanic MMPI-A to investigate the psychological effects of a natural disaster. Additional research is needed to further refine the instrument's appropriateness with disaster victims as well as other cross national populations. (p. 55)

In summary, the studies done on ethnic or racial effects on the MMPI-A have provided mixed findings and do not permit firm conclusions. If ethnic differences independent of socioeconomic factors do occur on MMPI-A profiles, however, it appears likely that the interpretive significance of such differences is relatively limited. (Note that, as discussed in chapter 6, there *is* evidence that the *MAC* scale [MacAndrew, 1965] and the *MAC-R* scale may be less useful with Black populations [i.e., may produce more false-positive errors] than with White respondents.)

Gender

Hathaway and Monachesi (1963), in their Minnesota statewide sample, identified gender differences in item endorsement patterns and in the frequency of occurrence of high-point codetypes. The authors identified the presence of 63 items for which the difference between the *true* endorsement rates for boys and girls was 25% or more. Regarding this pattern of item endorsement differences, Hathaway and Monachesi stated, "It is informative to imply generalized adjectives like 'sensitive' or 'fearful' or 'candid.' Such adjectives organize the pattern of correlated items expressing the feminine role, while 'inquisitive' or 'desirous of active outdoor activities' or 'aggressive' may better characterize the male role" (p. 41). Table 5.6 provides the MMPI-A abbreviated items that show the largest percentage differences in *true* responses by boys and girls in the normative sample. In general, this pattern of gender-related item differences is consistent with those found by Hathaway and Monachesi for the original version of the MMPI. In total, roughly 100 items showed an endorsement rate difference of at least 10% in the MMPI-A normative sample when data were analyzed

TABLE 5.6
Fifteen MMPI-A Items Showing the Greatest Gender Differences in Percentage of Endorsement as True

MMPI-A Item No.	Content	% True	
		Male	Female
61	Like romances.	19.0	77.8
131	Keep a diary.	19.3	73.5
59	Wish was a girl or happy that am.	9.3	60.5
139	Cry readily.	16.9	55.5
254	Never liked to play with dolls.	53.5	16.0
21	Uncontrolled laughing and crying.	30.2	63.8
64	Like poetry.	37.6	70.1
1	Like mechanics magazines.	34.5	4.0
114	Like collecting plants.	15.2	43.2
121	Very sensitive to criticism.	34.5	61.3
60	Feelings not hurt easily.	49.6	23.4
190	Like hunting.	32.0	7.1
241	Would like to be a sports reporter.	55.2	31.4
319	Love going to dances.	47.5	69.9
19	Wanted to leave home.	47.3	69.6

Note. MMPI-A abbreviated items reproduced by permission. MMPI-A test booklet copyright © 1992 by the Regents of the University of Minnesota; MMPI-A abbreviated item test booklet copyright © 2004 by the Regents of the University of Minnesota.

separately by gender. The issue of gender differences in item endorsement frequency on the item level, along with the interpretation of such differences, has been the subject of considerable controversy. Lindsay and Widiger (1995), for example, noted the presence of several MMPI items that appear to be systematically related to the gender of the respondent but not to personality dysfunction or psychopathology. The authors concluded that items producing such correlate patterns displayed evidence of gender bias. Additionally, significant gender differences have traditionally been found in the number of items omitted on the original version of the MMPI by adolescent respondents. Although religion and sex were the content areas of the items most frequently omitted by both boys and girls, items related to sex were more often left unanswered by female than male respondents (Archer, 1987b).

In terms of codetype profiles on the original version of the MMPI, girls more frequently displayed peak elevations on scale *Si* whereas boys were more likely to have a high score on scale *Sc*. Hathaway and Monachesi (1963) noted that these gender differences were likely to be more marked when adolescents were viewed against the backdrop of adolescent norms rather than adult norms. Interactional effects between gender of respondent and type of norms utilized to score the profile (adolescent versus adult) on the original version of the MMPI were also reported by Ehrenworth (1984), Klinge and Strauss (1976), and Lachar et al. (1976). The direction and meaning of these interactional findings, however, have been difficult to determine. In the study by Ehrenworth, for example, T-score values for male adolescent inpatients on scales *F*, *Pt*, and *Sc* were significantly higher than female values when adult norms were employed but nonsignificant when adolescent norms were used. In contrast, females had appreciably higher *Si* T-scores than males when adolescent norms were used, but the difference was less marked when adult norms were used.

Moore and Handal (1980) examined the MMPI profile elevations of 16- and 17-year-old male and female volunteers from school settings in the St. Louis area. These data were analyzed by gender of respondent for adult K-corrected T-scores. The authors reported substantial evidence that males tend to score significantly higher than females on scales F, Pd, Mf, Pt, Sc, and Ma. MMPI gender differences were more prevalent in this sample than racial differences, with males producing MMPI profiles more suggestive of impulsivity, problems with authority, identity confusion, and rebelliousness than their female counterparts. Similarly, Ehrenworth and Archer (1985) examined the MMPI profiles of adolescents in psychiatric treatment and found that males produced higher T-score elevations than females on several scales when adult norms were employed. Differences in profile elevations by gender were minimal, however, when adolescent norms were used. Equivalent profiles for males and females were also reported by Archer (1984) for inpatient samples employing adolescent norms. When the data on MMPI-A codetype frequencies presented in Table 5.5 were analyzed separately by gender, the *4-9/9-4* and the *4-6/6-4* codetypes were found to be the most frequent for males, whereas the *1-3/3-1* and *2-3/3-2* codetypes were most frequent for females.

On the 2-point codetype level, Marks et al. (1974) stated that they found no significant differences between males and females relative to clinical correlates of codetype descriptors. The Marks et al. text, therefore, provided codetype narratives that were not differentiated by gender. Williams and Butcher (1989a) analyzed correlate data for individual scales separately by gender and concluded that "our results, in most respects, show a rather limited impact of gender on MMPI descriptors for adolescents from clinical settings when using established procedures for determining MMPI behavioral correlates. Further research, especially studies using T-scores, could combine male and female subjects when sample size is a critical issue and when studying adolescents in treatment settings" (p. 259). In contrast, Wrobel and Lachar (1992) and Lachar and Wrobel (1990), in their studies of adolescent outpatients, found substantial evidence of gender-related differences in single-scale correlates. Their findings indicate that the majority of significant correlates are gender specific and that gender may play an important role as a moderator variable in the interpretation of MMPI findings from adolescents. As previously noted in the discussion of ethnicity, Gumbiner (2000) has recently called for analyzing data from boys and girls separately in investigations of ethnic influences on the MMPI-A.

In summary, it is clear that significant gender differences occur in item endorsement patterns for adolescent respondents and that these differences are reflected in the perceived need for the development of separate T-score conversions for male and female respondents in both adolescent and adult MMPI norms. Significant gender differences in mean raw score values can also be shown for MMPI-A special scales. For example, boys produce higher mean values than girls on the *MAC-R* and *IMM* scales. The degree to which gender differences occur following T-score conversions, however, is currently unclear. Most importantly, the research by Lachar and Wrobel (1990) and Wrobel and Lachar (1992) suggest that significant gender-related differences in correlate patterns for MMPI scales may exist, underscoring that this issue is in crucial need of systematic research. Until such research is completed, however, firm conclusions cannot be drawn concerning the degree to which reliable gender differences occur in the correlate patterns of adolescents.

Age

Differences between adult and adolescent MMPI response patterns were briefly discussed in the first chapter of this book. It is evident that numerous items show dramatic differences in endorsement frequency depending on whether the respondents are adolescents or adults. Further, on the item level, Hathaway and Monachesi (1963) identified 24 items that showed more than a 39% change in item endorsement frequency from the time of assessment in the 9th grade to reevaluation during the senior year of high school. Additionally, 29 items for boys and 30 items for girls were identified as showing more than a 17% change in endorsement frequency between the 9th- and 12th-grade assessments. The authors noted that these item endorsement shifts may be the result of item instability as well as true changes in personality occurring across this 3-year period of adolescent development. Finally, these changes in item endorsement frequency were found to be specifically related to the gender of the respondent; that is, no common items appeared on the lists for both males and females. In general, those items that were most likely to shift in endorsement frequency tended to involve personal attitudes or perceptions rather than biographical information.

Herkov, Gordon, Gynther, and Greer (1994) examined the influence of age and ethnicity on perceived item subtlety in the MMPI. Sixty-seven White and 54 Black subjects were asked to rank items from scales F and 9 to indicate how strongly the items indicated the presence of a psychological problem. Results indicated that adolescents often perceived MMPI item subtlety in a manner that differed significantly from that of adults and reflected discernable developmental influences. Although differences in subtlety ratings were also found between Black and White adolescents on scale F, these differences were relatively small and substantially less than those accounted for by age. Based on these findings, the authors recommended that the Wiener-Harmon Subtle-Obvious subscales not be used with adolescents and be used cautiously with minorities.

A central question concerns the degree to which MMPI scale values are related to the age of the adolescent respondent. McFarland and Sparks (1985), for example, showed that the internal consistency of a variety of personality measures is related to age and educational level in a sample of adolescents and young adults ranging in age from 13 to 25. The traditional adolescent norms created by Marks et al. (1974) provided separate adolescent T-score conversions for 17-year-olds, 16-year-olds, 15-year-olds, and those 14 years old and younger, suggesting that age-related raw score differences might affect adolescents' response patterns. In contrast, Colligan and Offord (1989) found little evidence of age-related effects on MMPI raw score values in their sample of 1,315 adolescents between the ages of 13 and 17, inclusive. Based on this observation, these authors produced a contemporary set of adolescent norms for the original version of the MMPI that collapsed across age groupings. In the development of the MMPI-A, there was evidence that adolescents under the age of 14 produced response patterns that differed significantly from adolescents 14 to 18 years old. Based on this observed pattern of differences, the MMPI-A norms were collapsed across ages 14 to 18 and excluded 12- and 13-year-olds from the normative sample. Thus, the age differences that occurred in MMPI-A basic scale raw score values were primarily manifested in the comparison of younger adolescents (ages 12 and 13) versus adolescents 14 years of age and older. Janus et al. (1998), however, examined the profiles of fifty-six 13-year-old and eighty-five 14-year-old psychiatric inpatients. They report no significant differences by age in mean T-scores, nor did they find evidence of age effects in frequency of occurrence of elevated profiles.

A final question concerns the degree to which MMPI profiles of adolescents in different age groups yield differences in interpretive accuracy and validity. Three studies have produced findings relevant to this issue. Findings by Lachar et al. (1976), Ehrenworth and Archer (1985), and Wimbish (1984) contained no evidence of significant age effects for clinical accuracy ratings of narrative MMPI reports for adolescents. Lachar et al. (1976) did find, however, significant age differences when comparing accuracy ratings produced from MMPI profiles using adolescent norms versus adult K-corrected norms. Specifically, the authors found that interpretations of profiles using adolescent norms produced more accurate ratings than interpretations using adult norms for adolescents in the 12- to 13-year-old age group. These norm-related differences were not significant for adolescents in the midadolescent and later adolescent groups. Examination of mean values show that although accuracy ratings remain relatively constant for adolescent norms across the three age groups (12–13, 14–15, and 16–17), ratings for profiles based on adult norms were substantially more inaccurate for the 12- to 13-year-old group than for the other two age groups.

In summary, there are known substantial differences in item endorsement patterns as a function of age when the responses of adults are contrasted with those of adolescents on the MMPI. As for differences between adolescent age groups, however, the developers of adolescent norms have dealt with possible age-related differences in a variety of ways. In the case of the MMPI-A, a major factor in excluding normative data from 12- and 13-year-old adolescents involved the degree to which the responses from this age group appeared to be substantially different than those produced by adolescents in the 14- to 18-year-old age group. Thus far, findings suggest that the accuracy of MMPI correlate statements based on profiles using adolescent norms tend to be relatively unaffected by the age of the adolescent.

Beyond the Basic Scales: Interpreting Additional MMPI-A Scales and Subscales

In addition to the standard or basic validity and clinical scales, many supplementary or special scales were created for the MMPI. Dahlstrom et al. (1972, 1975), for example, noted that more than 450 supplementary scales had been developed for the test instrument. Butcher and Tellegen (1978) observed that there may be more MMPI special scales than there are statements in the MMPI item pool! Clopton (1978, 1979, 1982), Butcher and Tellegen (1978), and Butcher, Graham, and Ben-Porath (1995) provided critical reviews of the methodological problems encountered in the construction of MMPI special scales. Several texts have been published specifically in the area of MMPI special scale use with the original instrument. Caldwell (1988) provided interpretive information on 104 supplementary scales based on his extensive clinical experience with these measures. Levitt (1989) and Levitt and Gotts (1995) provided an overview of special scale interpretation that includes discussions of the Wiggins (1966) content scales and the Harris and Lingoes (1955) subscales.

The MMPI-A special scales appear on two separate profile sheets. Fifteen content scales and six supplementary scales are placed on the Profile for Content and Supplementary Scales, as shown for females in Fig. 6.1. In addition, 28 Harris-Lingoes subscales and three *Si* subscales appear on the Profile for Harris-Lingoes and *Si* Subscales, shown for males in Fig. 6.2. The purpose of this chapter is to review these MMPI-A special scales, beginning with the supplementary scales.

CONTENT SCALES

As noted by Butcher et al. (1990), several approaches have been taken to the analysis of the content of MMPI responses. On the individual item level, a variety of "critical item" lists have been constructed that are composed of items believed to have a special significance in the task of clinical assessment. Grayson (1951), for example, employed a rational construction strategy to identify 38 items believed to serve as markers of significant symptomatology. Other critical item lists have also been constructed to analyze individual item responses, including those by Caldwell (1969), Koss and Butcher (1973), and Lachar and Wrobel (1979). Forbey and Ben-Porath (1998) recently developed a set of 82 critical items for the MMPI-A organized into a series of 15 content areas (see Appendix E).

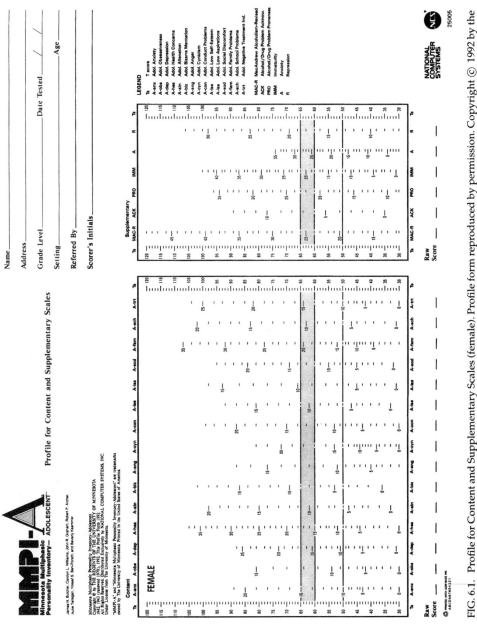

FIG. 6.1. Profile for Content and Supplementary Scales (female). Profile form reproduced by permission. Copyright © 1992 by the Regents of the University of Minnesota.

181

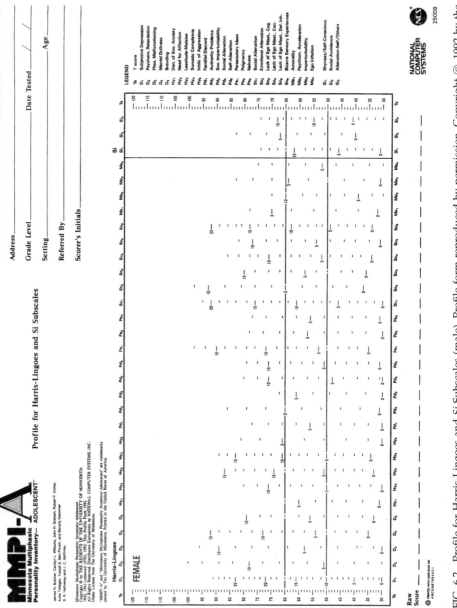

FIG. 6.2. Profile for Harris-Lingoes and *Si* Subscales (male). Profile form reproduced by permission. Copyright © 1992 by the Regents of the University of Minnesota.

A second approach to content analysis is exemplified by the work of Harris and Lingoes (1955). Because most of the MMPI basic scales contain a variety of content areas (i.e., the scales are heterogeneous), it is often difficult to infer what area of scale content was actually endorsed by a respondent in the production of a particular T-score elevation. This issue is particularly pronounced for T-scores representing marginal clinical-range elevations. To deal with this problem, Harris and Lingoes developed subscales for basic scales 2, 3, 4, 6, 8, and 9 by rationally grouping similar items into homogeneous content areas for each of these scales. The resulting 28 subscales have been carried over into the MMPI-2 and the MMPI-A. In addition, three subscales for the *Si* scale are available for the MMPI-A, based on the work of Ben-Porath, Hostetler, Butcher, and Graham (1989).

On a separate and third level of content analysis, the MMPI may be discussed and interpreted in relation to a number of content dimensions represented by the total item pool. Because Hathaway and McKinley utilized external criterion groups to create the original MMPI basic scales, these clinical groups served to define the measurement focus of the inventory. Such a development method, however, made no effort to use the full item pool in deriving the maximum number of meaningful dimensions of psychopathology in construction of clinical scales. Indeed, the basic MMPI scales utilized only about half of the total item pool (Nichols, 1987). Wiggins (1966) offered an approach to MMPI scale construction and measurement that was based on a more complete utilization of this item pool. Beginning with the 26 content categories described by Hathaway and McKinley (see chapter 1 for a description) to classify the total content array of all MMPI items, Wiggins derived 13 homogeneous content scales using a combination of rational and statistical scale construction methods. Nichols provided a 1987 monograph on the use of the Wiggins content scales in the clinical interpretation of the original MMPI, and Kohutek (1992a, 1992b) and Levitt, Browning, and Freeland (1992) identified the Wiggins content scale items that were retained in the MMPI-2. Correlate patterns for the Wiggins content scales in adolescent samples were reported by Archer and Gordon (1991b), Wrobel (1991), Wrobel and Gdowski (1989), and Wrobel and Lachar (1995). Based on a recognition of the usefulness of the Wiggins scales, content scales were developed for the MMPI-2 by Butcher et al. (1990) and for the MMPI-A by Williams, Butcher, Ben-Porath, and Graham (1992). Sherwood, Ben-Porath, and Williams (1997) noted that although the content scales were developed to measure homogeneous constructs, it was useful to identify different dimensions or salient components for most of these scales. Using a series of principal component analyses, these authors produced a total of 31 subscales for the 15 MMPI-A content scales shown in Table 6.1. Sherwood et al. (1997) were not able to identify meaningful item clusters for the Anxiety and the Obsessiveness content scales. Appendix F provides the item composition of the MMPI-A content component scales. The following section examines the analysis of content in the MMPI-A as represented by the MMPI-A content and content component scales and by the Harris-Lingoes and *Si* subscales.

Several investigations have focused on the degree to which the MMPI-2 content scales provide incremental gains in information beyond that provided by the basic clinical scales. Ben-Porath, McCully, and Almagor (1993), for example, evaluated the incremental contributions of MMPI-2 content scales to the prediction of scores on self-report measures of personality and psychopathology in a sample of 596 college undergraduates. Results indicated that the inclusion of content scales did add incrementally to the prediction of SCL–90–R score variance beyond prediction levels achieved

TABLE 6.1
MMPI-A Content Component Scales

Depression	**School Problems**
A-dep1: Dysphoria (5 items)	A-sch1: School Conduct Problems (4 items)
A-dep2: Self-Depreciation (5 items)	A-sch2: Negative Attitudes (8 items)
A-dep3: Lack of Drive (7 items)	**Cynicism**
A-dep4: Suicidal Ideation (4 items)	A-cyn1: Misanthropic Beliefs (13 items)
Health Concerns	A-cyn2: Interpersonal Suspiciousness (9 items)
A-hea1: Gastrointestinal Complaints (4 items)	**Conduct Problems**
A-hea2: Neurological Symptoms (18 items)	A-con1: Acting-out Behaviors (10 items)
A-hea3: General Health Concerns (8 items)	A-con2: Antisocial Attitudes (8 items)
Alienation	A-con3: Negative Peer Group Influences (3 items)
A-aln1: Misunderstood (5 items)	**Low Self-Esteem**
A-aln2: Social Isolation (5 items)	A-lse1: Self-Doubt (13 items)
A-aln3: Interpersonal Skepticism (5 items)	A-lse2: Interpersonal Submissiveness (5 items)
Bizarre Mentation	**Low Aspirations**
A-biz1: Psychotic Symptomatology (11 items)	A-las1: Low Achievement Orientation (8 items)
A-biz2: Paranoid Ideation (5 items)	A-las2: Lack of Initiative (7 items)
Anger	**Social Discomfort**
A-ang1: Explosive Behavior (8 items)	A-sod1: Introversion (14 items)
A-ang2: Irritability (8 items)	A-sod2: Shyness (10 items)
Family Problems	**Negative Treatment Indicators**
A-fam1: Familial Discord (21 items)	A-trt1: Low Motivation (11 items)
A-fam2: Familial Alienation (11 items)	A-trt2: Inability to Disclose (8 items)

Note: From Sherwood et al. (1997). Copyright © 1997 by the University of Minnesota. Reproduced by permission.

solely by the basic clinical scales. Ben-Porath, Butcher, and Graham (1991) examined the contribution of MMPI-2 content scales to differential diagnosis of schizophrenia and major depression in an inpatient psychiatric sample. Results from this study indicated that both content scales and clinical scales provided information that was useful in the differential diagnosis of these psychiatric categories. Specifically, findings from a stepwise hierarchical regression analysis indicated that the *DEP* and *BIZ* content scales contributed significantly to the differential diagnosis for males and that the *BIZ* content scale added to diagnostic discrimination for female patients. Archer, Aiduk, Griffin, and Elkins (1996) examined the MMPI-2 basic and content scales in relation to the ability of these measures to predict SCL–90–R scores and clinician ratings of psychopathology in a sample of 597 adult psychiatric patients. The findings from this study also demonstrated that the MMPI-2 content scales added incrementally, although modestly, to the prediction of variance in outcome measures of psychopathology.

Several studies have specifically focused on the potential incremental utility of the MMPI-A content scales. Forbey and Ben-Porath (2003) examined the MMPI-A content scales in an evaluation of 335 adolescents receiving mental health services at a residential treatment facility. Regression analyses were utilized to identify the additional or incremental amount of variance accounted for by the content scales (in contrast with the clinical scales) in predicting clinicians' ratings of psychological symptomatology. Several of the MMPI-A content scales demonstrated significant, although relatively limited, incremental validity beyond the clinical scales in predicting clinicians' ratings of adolescent behavior and personality characteristics. The clinical scales also demonstrated incremental validity in reference to the content scales, indicating that both content and basic scales provide useful and complementary information in assessing adolescent personality and psychopathology. McGrath, Pogge, and Stokes (2002) evaluated the incremental validity of the MMPI-A content scales in a sample of 629 adolescent psychiatric inpatients using criteria based on clinicians' ratings, admission and discharge diagnoses, and chart review data. Results from hierarchical multiple and logistic regression analyses indicated that content scales provided incremental information beyond that obtained through the clinical scales. McGrath and his colleagues concluded that the use of the content scales as an adjunct to the traditional basic scales appeared to be supported by their findings. Finally, Rinaldo and Baer (2003) also evaluated the incremental contributions of the MMPI-A content scales to the prediction of scores on other self-report measures of psychopathology in a sample of 62 adolescents receiving inpatient treatment and a nonclinical sample of 59 community adolescents. A series of hierarchical regression analyses indicated that the content scales held incremental validity beyond the clinical scales in predicting variance in the criterion measures used in this study. Similar to the research done by Forbey and Ben-Porath, the study also found that the clinical scales demonstrated incremental validity in relationship to the content scales when the order of entry of variables was reversed in the hierarchical design. Rinaldo and Baer concluded that their findings suggested that both clinical and content scales from the MMPI-A provide significant contributions to the assessment of adolescent psychological functioning. In summary, the results from these three recent MMPI-A studies are strikingly consistent in suggesting that both basic and content scales provide important information and that the content scales are capable of providing a modest incremental gain when contrasted with data restricted solely to the basic clinical scales.

MMPI-A Content Scales

The 15 MMPI-A content scales exhibit a substantial degree of overlap with many of the MMPI-2 content scales as well as several of the Wiggins content scales. As described in the MMPI-A manual (Butcher et al., 1992), the MMPI-A content scales were created in a series of five stages. The first stage involved an initial identification of those MMPI-2 content scales (and items within MMPI-2 content scales) that were appropriate for adaptation to the MMPI-A. Stage 2 of the development process involved the refinement of MMPI-A content scales by the addition or deletion of specific items designed to improve the psychometric properties, including reliability and validity coefficients, of these scales. The third stage included a rational review and examination of scale content in order to evaluate item relevance in terms of the target construct. Stage 4 involved further statistical refinement of the scales, including the elimination of items that showed higher correlations with content scales other than the content scale on which the item was scored. The final stage involved the selection of narrative descriptors for each content scale utilizing a combination of empirical findings and logical inferences based on the item content of the scale. In addition to the MMPI-A normative sample, Williams et al. (1992) utilized a clinical sample of 420 boys and 293 girls from Minneapolis treatment facilities to refine the MMPI-A content scales and to identify correlate patterns for these measures.

Several general statements may be made concerning the MMPI-A content scales:

1. The interpretation of MMPI-A content scales requires the administration of all 478 items in the MMPI-A booklet. The administration of the first stage of the MMPI-A booklet (i.e., the first 350 items) will not be sufficient to score the content scales.

2. Most of the MMPI-A content scales are predominantly composed of items from the original MMPI instrument. The School Problems (*A-sch*) scale and the Negative Treatment Indicators (*A-trt*) scale, however, consist primarily of items that do not appear on the original test instrument. In contrast, the Cynicism (*A-cyn*) scale consists entirely of items derived version the original version of the MMPI.

3. Eleven of the 15 MMPI-A content scales heavily overlap MMPI-2 content scales in terms of item membership and the constructs that are the focus of measurement. The content scales unique to the MMPI-A are Alienation (*A-aln*), Low Aspiration (*A-las*), School Problems (*A-sch*), and Conduct Problems (*A-con*).

4. Uniform T-score transformation procedures are consistently used in converting MMPI-A content scale raw score totals to T-score values. Thus, the content scales and eight basic clinical scales (*1, 2, 3, 4, 6, 7, 8,* and *9*) were the only MMPI-A scales to receive uniform T-scores.

5. The *true* response is typically the deviant endorsement direction for MMPI-A content scales, with the exception of Health Concerns (*A-hea*) and Low Aspirations (*A-las*). The MMPI-A Obsessiveness (*A-obs*) and Cynicism (*A-cyn*) content scales, for example, consist entirely of items scored in the *true* direction, and the Bizarre Mentation (*A-biz*) and Anger (*A-ang*) scales each contain only one item scored in the *false* direction. Most MMPI-A content scales, therefore, involve the affirmation of the occurrence or presence of various psychiatric symptoms.

6. MMPI-A content scales, similar to the MMPI-2 and the Wiggins content scales, are composed of items that are face-valid and obvious in terms of their relevancy to psychopathology. The MMPI-A content scales, therefore, are easily influenced by an adolescent's tendency to underreport or overreport symptomatology. The MMPI-A interpreter should carefully evaluate the validity of the adolescent's responses, particularly the accuracy component of technical validity, prior to interpreting MMPI-A content scales.

7. The MMPI-A content scales, like their counterparts on the MMPI-2, exhibit relatively high internal reliability as reflected in alpha coefficient values (range .55 to .83). This characteristic might be expected given the scale construction method employed to develop these measures. Nevertheless, most of the MMPI-A content scales contain two or more content subcomponents. Sherwood et al. (1997) provided content component subscales for 13 of the MMPI-A content scales in a manner similar to that used by Ben-Porath and Sherwood (1993) in developing component subscales for the content scales of the MMPI-2.

8. MMPI-A content scale results may be used by interpreters to supplement or refine the interpretation of the MMPI-A basic clinical scales. The content scales are most useful when interpreted within the context of the full array of data provided by the test instrument rather than interpreted independently.

Relatively limited information is available on the interpretation of the MMPI-A content scales. Empirically derived content scale descriptors are reported by Williams et al. (1992) for a clinical sample of 420 male and 293 female adolescents and by Archer and Gordon (1991b) in an independent sample of 64 male and 58 female adolescent psychiatric inpatients. In addition, the examination of content component scores within the MMPI-A content scales can offer some inferences concerning the characteristics of individuals who produce elevated scores on these measures. As with most other MMPI-A scales, T-scores greater than 65 on MMPI-A content scales may be regarded as clinical range scores, and T-scores of 60 to 65 inclusive may be described as marginally elevated. As additional research is conducted with the content scales, it should become possible to provide fuller descriptions of the clinical correlate patterns for these measures. Principal factor analyses by McCarthy and Archer (1998) show that the 15 MMPI-A content scales are generally accounted for by two broad factors labeled General Maladjustment and Externalizing Tendencies. The former factor was quite robust and identified by strong relationsips to *A-trt, A-dep, A-aln, A-anx, A-lse,* and *A-hea*. The second factor accounted for much less total variance and was marked by loadings on *A-cyn, A-con,* and *A-ang*. Table 6. 2 provides the intercorrelations for MMPI-A content scales in the normative sample. Tables 6.3, 6.4, 6.5, and 6.6 provide the correlations of these measures with the MMPI-A basic scales and the Wiggins content scales by gender. As shown in Tables 6.5 and 6.6, there is a very high degree of interrelationship between eight of the Wiggins content scales and seven counterparts on the MMPI-A. Specifically, the following Wiggins scale–MMPI-A content scale pairs produced correlations of $r = .79$ or greater for both genders: Depression and *A-dep*; Poor Health and *A-hea*; Organic Symptoms and *A-hea*; Family Problems and *A-fam*; Authority Conflict and *A-cyn*; Hostility and *A-ang*; Psychoticism and *A-biz*; and Social Maladjustment and *A-sod*. However, two of the Wiggins content scales (Feminine Interests and Religious Fundamentalism) produced consistently low correlations with MMPI-A content scales, and three other Wiggins scales (Poor Morale, Phobias, and Hypomania) produced moderate to high correlations with several MMPI-A scales. With the exception of the Religious Fundamentalism scale, the Wiggins content scales have retained a majority of scale items in the MMPI-A, with seven scales maintaining over 80% of their items. Table 6.7 provides an overview of the status of the Wiggins content scales within the structure of the MMPI-A.

Adolescent-Anxiety (A-anx) Scale. The MMPI-A Anxiety content scale consists of 21 items, 20 of which also appear on the MMPI-2 Anxiety scale. Adolescents who score high on this measure report symptoms of anxiety, including tension, apprehension, rumination, and the self-perception of being overwhelmed by stress. Most *A-anx* scale items involve cognitions and attitudes related to the experience of anxiety, with relatively few items related to physiological expression of anxiety symptoms. Table 6.8 provides examples of abbreviated items from the *A-anx* scale. As shown in Tables 6.3 through 6.6, the *A-anx* scale is highly correlated with scale 7 of the basic profile and is also highly correlated with the Wiggins Depression (*DEP*) content scale.

Butcher et al. (1992) reported that the *A-anx* scale appears to measure general maladjustment as well as symptoms relating to depression and somatic complaints. Clinical correlates in the Archer and Gordon (1991b) study were derived from staff ratings on the Devereux Adolescent Behavior (DAB) Rating Scale, parental reports on the Child Behavior Checklist (CBCL), and presenting problems as indicated in the adolescent's psychiatric records. These authors found that high *A-anx* scores for adolescent girls were related to low endurance and fatigue, domination by peers, obsessional thought processes, anxiety, and timidity, whereas high scores for males were related to problems in concentration, the occurrence of suicidal thoughts, and sadness and

TABLE 6.2
Raw Score Intercorrelations of MMPI-A Content Scales for 815 Females and 805 Males in the MMPI-A Normative Sample

									Females							
	Scale	A-anx	A-obs	A-dep	A-hea	A-aln	A-biz	A-ang	A-cyn	A-con	A-lse	A-las	A-sod	A-fam	A-sch	A-trt
	A-anx		.69	.74	.56	.61	.56	.51	.54	.41	.62	.32	.31	.53	.41	.62
	A-obs	.66		.61	.42	.48	.51	.54	.60	.44	.57	.31	.24	.44	.39	.64
	A-dep	.73	.55		.53	.70	.56	.43	.50	.47	.74	.42	.42	.57	.50	.71
	A-hea	.50	.27	.48		.50	.56	.33	.34	.37	.46	.26	.29	.41	.45	.48
	A-aln	.62	.46	.69	.47		.55	.38	.42	.50	.63	.37	.54	.61	.52	.74
M	**A-biz**	.54	.45	.56	.53	.53		.44	.49	.52	.48	.24	.26	.45	.44	.53
a	**A-ang**	.50	.52	.41	.23	.40	.36		.52	.54	.38	.27	.15	.47	.43	.49
l	**A-cyn**	.43	.57	.37	.07	.54	.37	.51		.52	.45	.22	.23	.46	.40	.61
e	**A-con**	.36	.44	.40	.22	.38	.41	.50	.47		.45	.37	.17	.53	.58	.56
s	**A-lse**	.60	.55	.68	.47	.62	.53	.36	.35	.37		.49	.48	.48	.51	.69
	A-las	.36	.22	.39	.39	.39	.32	.16	.10	.30	.45		.31	.35	.53	.48
	A-sod	.43	.26	.47	.35	.55	.33	.14	.14	.03	.49	.33		.28	.30	.47
	A-fam	.53	.43	.59	.48	.61	.51	.44	.35	.50	.51	.41	.28		.52	.58
	A-sch	.46	.40	.53	.48	.53	.50	.40	.31	.56	.52	.48	.29	.60		.57
	A-trt	.60	.58	.64	.42	.67	.56	.43	.49	.48	.67	.48	.45	.56	.58	

Note: From Butcher et al. (1992). Copyright © 1992 by the Regents of the University of Minnesota. Reproduced by permission.

TABLE 6.3
Raw Score Intercorrelations of the Content and Basic Scales for Female Adolescents in the MMPI-A Normative Sample

		Contents Scales														
		A-anx	A-obs	A-dep	A-hea	A-aln	A-biz	A-ang	A-cyn	A-con	A-lse	A-las	A-sod	A-fam	A-sch	A-trt
	F_1	.36	.27	.50	.54	.59	.60	.29	.30	.54	.47	.37	.35	.55	.61	.54
B	F_2	.41	.32	.54	.55	.60	.63	.34	.31	.49	.54	.38	.46	.51	.56	.60
a	**F**	.42	.32	.55	.58	.64	.65	.34	.32	.54	.54	.40	.44	.56	.61	.61
s	**L**	−.19	−.30	−.14	.06	.01	−.02	−.31	−.19	−.25	−.12	−.10	.14	−.11	−.10	−.08
i	**K**	−.62	−.68	−.53	−.31	−.50	−.41	−.62	−.70	−.40	−.48	−.23	−.29	−.46	−.35	−.55
c	**Hs**	.62	.44	.59	.91	.48	.50	.33	.36	.33	.49	.29	.29	.40	.42	.46
	D	.60	.33	.68	.51	.53	.34	.13	.22	.17	.57	.35	.47	.37	.31	.47
S	**Hy**	.33	.03	.34	.56	.15	.20	−.03	−.12	.03	.19	.14	−.02	.17	.16	.08
c	**Pd**	.59	.41	.68	.49	.59	.51	.39	.40	.50	.49	.31	.19	.68	.46	.51
a	**Mf**	.07	.05	.04	−.13	−.11	−.20	−.07	−.16	−.28	−.06	−.10	−.06	−.09	−.21	−.16
l	**Pa**	.56	.41	.63	.54	.55	.60	.28	.15	.38	.49	.23	.27	.42	.38	.47
e	**Pt**	.84	.78	.81	.58	.63	.62	.58	.57	.49	.73	.42	.39	.53	.50	.69
s	**Sc**	.76	.67	.79	.68	.71	.78	.54	.56	.60	.69	.44	.41	.66	.56	.74
	Ma	.43	.48	.36	.36	.33	.52	.46	.51	.57	.26	.11	−.11	.47	.36	.36
	Si	.54	.51	.59	.38	.60	.34	.31	.44	.24	.67	.47	.77	.37	.38	.62

Note: From Butcher et al. (1992). Copyright © 1992 by the Regents of the University of Minnesota. Reproduced by permission.

TABLE 6.4
Raw Score Intercorrelations of the Content and Basic Scales for Male Adolescents in the MMPI-A Normative Sample

Contents Scales

	A-anx	A-obs	A-dep	A-hea	A-aln	A-biz	A-ang	A-cyn	A-con	A-lse	A-las	A-sod	A-fam	A-sch	A-trt
F_1	.39	.21	.52	.63	.55	.64	.25	.11	.39	.47	.42	.34	.59	.64	.50
F_2	.42	.26	.53	.61	.56	.68	.24	.14	.35	.55	.45	.40	.56	.60	.58
F	.43	.25	.55	.65	.59	.70	.26	.13	.38	.54	.46	.40	.61	.65	.58
L	−.15	−.35	−.08	.28	.02	.06	−.33	−.39	−.29	−.02	.12	.14	−.01	.02	−.06
K	−.56	−.66	−.44	−.06	−.40	−.33	−.61	−.72	−.37	−.39	−.07	.22	−.33	−.26	−.44
Hs	.54	.27	.50	.90	.46	.47	.23	.09	.18	.44	.37	.35	.45	.40	.37
D	.50	.14	.54	.55	.43	.27	−.02	−.10	−.05	.45	.36	.46	.29	.24	.29
Hy	.21	−.15	.26	.63	.15	.16	−.14	−.39	−.09	.12	.24	.11	.20	.15	−.01
Pd	.54	.33	.64	.49	.57	.46	.33	.23	.43	.42	.38	.21	.67	.51	.43
Mf	.27	.14	.20	.11	.11	.04	.00	−.13	−.14	.16	.02	.20	.09	−.11	−.01
Pa	.53	.34	.62	.58	.56	.64	.24	.05	.25	.47	.35	.35	.50	.44	.45
Pt	.83	.76	.79	.48	.64	.60	.54	.50	.43	.69	.38	.46	.56	.52	.63
Sc	.74	.58	.79	.64	.73	.77	.49	.43	.50	.66	.46	.47	.72	.63	.69
Ma	.37	.50	.32	.18	.29	.44	.50	.54	.59	.25	−.09	.07	.46	.38	.37
Si	.58	.48	.58	.40	.61	.38	.26	.31	.13	.63	.42	.81	.39	.34	.57

Note: From Butcher et al. (1992). Copyright © 1992 by the Regents of the University of Minnesota. Reproduced by permission.

TABLE 6.5

Raw Score Intercorrelations of the MMPI-A Content Scales and the MMPI Wiggins Content Scales for 58 Females in an Adolescent Inpatient Sample

MMPI-A Content Scales

	A-anx	A-obs	A-dep	A-hea	A-aln	A-biz	A-ang	A-cyn	A-con	A-lse	A-las	A-sod	A-fam	A-sch	A-trt
HEA	.54	.38	.44	.84	.42	.39	.15	.26	.33	.51	.23	.51	.17	.21	.44
DEP	.87	.81	.92	.61	.69	.43	.42	.53	.37	.85	.64	.54	.50	.47	.72
ORG	.77	.64	.60	.90	.50	.57	.38	.41	.44	.62	.35	.50	.29	.54	.53
FAM	.35	.44	.46	.22	.61	.28	.43	.46	.54	.44	.42	.11	.94	.35	.56
AUT	.42	.49	.38	.32	.45	.43	.50	.86	.70	.47	.39	.15	.47	.50	.57
FEM	-.10	-.11	-.11	.05	-.11	-.12	-.14	-.33	-.35	-.20	-.13	-.05	-.12	-.17	-.26
REL	.02	-.14	-.04	.18	-.08	.00	-.25	-.18	-.24	.02	-.18	.01	-.44	-.28	-.15
HOS	.54	.71	.45	.45	.44	.55	.83	.63	.72	.43	.41	.14	.52	.72	.58
MOR	.80	.74	.85	.53	.64	.35	.33	.54	.29	.88	.53	.58	.38	.36	.65
PHO	.57	.52	.38	.54	.35	.41	.32	.21	.29	.42	.15	.45	.23	.36	.32
PSY	.65	.58	.57	.62	.62	.86	.54	.53	.62	.56	.35	.34	.47	.59	.58
HYP	.34	.44	.16	.24	.15	.42	.65	.58	.58	.15	.14	-.13	.31	.50	.28
SOC	.50	.39	.55	.45	.46	.07	-.09	.22	-.02	.62	.36	.93	.08	.12	.46

Note: From Archer (1997b). Copyright © 1997 by Lawrence Erlbaum Associates, Inc. Reprinted by permission.

TABLE 6.6

Raw Score Intercorrelations of the MMPI-A Content Scales and the MMPI Wiggins Content Scales for 64 Males in an Adolescent Inpatient Sample

	A-anx	A-obs	A-dep	A-hea	A-aln	A-biz	A-ang	A-cyn	A-con	A-lse	A-las	A-sod	A-fam	A-sch	A-trt
							MMPI-A Content Scales								
HEA	.46	.39	.56	.86	.46	.42	.02	−.11	−.14	.42	.09	.41	−.09	.14	.30
DEP	.78	.73	.90	.68	.66	.55	.16	.19	−.03	.66	.23	.50	.05	.30	.59
ORG	.57	.53	.65	.90	.54	.51	.01	−.10	−.06	.54	.11	.55	−.09	.23	.42
FAM	.19	.25	.08	.02	.18	.13	.47	.31	.26	.10	.21	−.06	.82	.27	.19
AUT	.03	.24	−.06	−.28	.15	.09	.61	.88	.65	.12	.29	−.05	.38	.39	.31
FEM	.24	.12	.12	.24	.03	.22	−.04	−.19	−.01	.05	−.02	.15	−.00	.03	−.08
REL	−.03	.19	−.00	.12	.11	.11	.08	−.07	.06	.08	−.24	.10	−.01	.06	.08
HOS	.34	.54	.18	.15	.27	.30	.79	.73	.59	.18	.27	.08	.45	.56	.42
MOR	.78	.83	.73	.55	.56	.47	.29	.39	−.02	.76	.20	.49	.02	.32	.59
PHO	.33	.33	.37	.62	.46	.55	.13	.00	.08	.32	.06	.47	−.12	.26	.36
PSY	.49	.61	.67	.63	.70	.89	.32	.29	.30	.64	.28	.59	.22	.47	.66
HYP	.38	.57	.04	.05	.14	.09	.72	.68	.40	.16	.06	−.04	.23	.34	.36
SOC	.39	.31	.41	.55	.47	.43	−.11	−.06	−.19	.46	.11	.86	−.04	.13	.43

Note: From Archer (1997b). Copyright © 1997 by Lawrence Erlbaum Associates, Inc. Reprinted by permission.

TABLE 6.7
Wiggins Content Scale Items Retained in the MMPI-A

Wiggins Content Scale	Items on MMPI	Number (and Percent) of Items Retained on MMPI-A
Social Maladjustment (SOC)	27	22 (81.5%)
Depression (DEP)	33	31 (93.9%)
Feminine Interests (FEM)	30	16 (53.3%)
Poor Morale (MOR)	23	20 (87.0%)
Religious Fundamentalism (REL)	12	1 (8.3%)
Authority Conflict (AUT)	20	20 (100.0%)
Psychoticism (PSY)	48	40 (83.3%)
Organic Symptoms (ORG)	36	31 (86.1%)
Family Problems (FAM)	16	16 (100.0%)
Manifest Hostility (HOS)	27	18 (66.7%)
Phobias (PHO)	27	15 (55.5%)
Hypomania (HYP)	25	18 (72.0%)
Poor Health (HEA)	28	17 (60.7%)

Note: From Archer (1997b). Copyright © 1997 by Lawrence Erlbaum Associates, Inc. Reprinted by permission.

depression. Arita and Baer (1998) explored the correlates of several MMPI-A content scales in a sample of 62 adolescent inpatients and reported that the *A-anx* and *A-dep* tended to share similar correlates reflective of emotional distress, tension, and nervousness. Kopper, Osman, Osman, and Hoffman (1998) found scores from the *A-anx* scale associated with results from a self-report suicide probability scale in a sample of 143 adolescent inpatients. The *A-anx* is one of only two content scales for which Sherwood and her colleagues (1997) were unable to derive meaningful subscale components.

The following descriptors are applicable to adolescents who produce high scores on the *A-anx* scale:

- Anxious, tense, nervous, and ruminative.
- Problems in concentration.
- Low endurance and fatigability.
- Sadness and depression.
- Higher probability of suicidal thoughts and ideation.

TABLE 6.8
Items From the Anxiety (*A-anx*) Scale

Examples of A-anx items scored if true
14. Work atmosphere tense.
28. Hard staying focused.
Examples of A-anx items scored if false
134. Sleep not bothered by thoughts.
196. Seldom does heart pound or is breath short.

Note: MMPI-A abbreviated items reproduced by permission. MMPI-A test booklet copyright © 1992 by the Regents of the University of Minnesota; MMPI-A abbreviated item test booklet copyright © 2004 by the Regents of the University of Minnesota.

TABLE 6.9
Items From the Obsessiveness (*A-obs*) Scale

Examples of A-obs items scored if true
52.   Persistence makes others impatient.
83.   Unable to make up mind.

Note: This content scale contains no items scored in the false direction. MMPI-A abbreviated items reproduced by permission. MMPI-A test booklet copyright © 1992 by the Regents of the University of Minnesota; MMPI-A abbreviated item test booklet copyright © 2004 by the Regents of the University of Minnesota.

Adolescent-Obsessiveness (A-obs) Scale. The *A-obs* scale consists of 15 items, 12 of which also appear on the MMPI-2 obsessiveness *(OBS)* scale and 13 of which appear on the original version of the MMPI. All of the items in the *A-obs* scale are scored in the *true* direction. The MMPI-A Obsessiveness scale contains items concerning ambivalence and difficulty in making decisions, excessive worry and rumination, and the occurrence of intrusive thoughts. Sherwood et al. (1997) did not report subscale components for the *A-obs* content scale. Adolescents who score high on the *A-obs* may also exhibit some compulsive behaviors. The *A-obs* scale is highly correlated with scale 7 of the basic profile and negatively correlated with scale K. Table 6.9 contains examples of some of the abbreviated items used in the *A-obs* scale.

Butcher et al. (1992) report that high *A-obs* scores in a clinical sample were related to anxious and dependent behaviors in boys and to suicidal ideations or gestures in girls. A clear correlate pattern was not identified in the Archer and Gordon (1991b) study.

The following are characteristics or correlates associated with high *A-obs* scores:

• Excessive worry and rumination.
• Difficulty in making decisions.
• The occurrence of intrusive thoughts and problems in concentration.

Adolescent-Depression (A-dep) Scale. The *A-dep* scale consists of 26 items, of which 25 also appear on the MMPI-2 Depression content scale. Further, 24 of the 26 items on the *A-dep* scale were derived from the original version of the MMPI. *A-dep* scale items appear to be related to depression and sadness, apathy, low energy, and poor morale. In the Archer and Gordon (1991b) inpatient sample, *A-dep* scores were highly correlated with scores from the Wiggins Depression *(DEP)* content scale ($r = .92$ for females and $r = .90$ for males). *A-dep* scores were not highly correlated with scale 2 but were strongly associated with scores from basic scales 7 and 8 (see Tables 6.3 and 6.4). Despite the relatively low correlation between scale 2 and the *DEP* content scale, research by Bence, Sabourin, Luty, and Thackrey (1995) showed that both scales have approximately equal effectiveness in accurately identifying depressed patients in a sample of adult psychiatric inpatients. Archer et al. (1996) found that the MMPI-2 *DEP* content scale added incrementally to information provided from basic scale 2 in the prediction of scores on both self-report and clinician ratings of depression. Cashel, Rogers, Sewell, and Holliman (1998) examined MMPI-A content scale correlates in clinical and non-clinical adolescent samples and reported that *A-dep* scores were positively correlated with several items from the Schedule of Affective Disorders and Schizophrenia for School Aged Children (K–SADS–III–R) reflective of depressive symptoms, including

TABLE 6.10
Items From the Depression (*A-dep*) Scale

Examples of A-dep items scored if true
49. Haven't led a good life.
53. Would like to be as happy as others.
Examples of A-dep items scored if false
 3. Feel rested in morning.
 9. Daily activities interesting.

Note: MMPI-A abbreviated items reproduced by permission. MMPI-A test booklet copyright © 1992 by the Regents of the University of Minnesota; MMPI-A abbreviated item test booklet copyright © 2004 by the Regents of the University of Minnesota.

depressed mood, guilt, and suicidal acts. Arita and Baer (1998) found the *A-dep* scale produced a correlation of $r = .58$ with the Reynolds Adolescent Depression Inventory (RADS) in their investigation of adolescent inpatients. Table 6.10 presents examples of abbreviated items from the *A-dep* scale. As shown in this table, several of the items on the *A-dep* scale involve feelings of pessimism and hopelessness. Two *A-dep* scale items (177 and 283) directly relate to the occurrence of suicidal ideation.

Butcher et al. (1992) reported that high *A-dep* scores for adolescents in clinical settings were associated with a variety of behaviors and symptoms related to depression and the occurrence of suicidal ideation and gestures. Archer and Gordon (1991b) also found suicidal thoughts to be related to high *A-dep* scores for girls, whereas suicidal attempts were related to high *A-dep* scores for boys. Sherwood et al. (1997) identified four component scales for *A-dep*: Dysphoria (*A-dep1*), Self-Depreciation (*A-dep2*), Lack of Drive (*A-dep3*), and Suicidal Ideation (*A-dep4*).

The following characteristics are associated with high *A-dep* scores:

- Sadness, depression, and despondency.
- Fatigue and apathy.
- A pervasive sense of hopelessness that may include suicidal ideation.

Adolescent-Health Concerns (A-hea) Scale. The MMPI-A Health Concerns scale includes 37 items, of which 34 also appear on the MMPI-2 Health Concerns (*HEA*) scale. Thirty-four of the 37 items on the *A-hea* scale appeared on the original version of the MMPI. Twenty-three items on the *A-hea* scale also appear on scale 1 of the standard or basic MMPI-A clinical scales, and scores from these two scales are highly correlated. The *A-hea* scale is one of only two MMPI-A content scales that contain a majority of items keyed in the *false* direction. Adolescents who produce elevated scores on the *A-hea* content scale are endorsing physical symptoms across a wide variety of areas, including gastrointestinal, neurological, sensory, cardiovascular, and respiratory systems. These adolescents feel physically ill and are worried about their health. Table 6.11 provides examples of abbreviated items contained in the *A-hea* scale. In the Archer and Gordon (1991b) inpatient sample, *A-hea* scale scores were also highly correlated ($r = .90$ for males and females) with scores from the Wiggins Organic Symptoms (*ORG*) content scale.

Williams et al. (1992) found high *A-hea* scores to be related to somatic complaints for adolescents in their clinical sample and to misbehavior, school problems, and poor academic performance for normal adolescents. Archer and Gordon (1991b) found high

TABLE 6.11
Items From the Health Concerns (*A-hea*) Scale

Examples of A-hea items scored if true
  11. Lump in throat.
  17. Often nauseated.
Examples of A-hea items scored if false
  87. Muscles don't twitch.
 113. Never vomited blood.

Note: MMPI-A abbreviated items reproduced by permission. MMPI-A test booklet copyright © 1992 by the Regents of the University of Minnesota; MMPI-A abbreviated item test booklet copyright © 2004 by the Regents of the University of Minnesota.

scores for females to be associated with the occurrence of suicidal thoughts, tiredness, and fatigue, whereas high-scoring boys were described as exhibiting poor reality testing, concentration difficulties, and somatic concerns. Future research should examine the extent to which poor physical health, including chronic medical conditions, affects *A-hea* scores. Sherwood et al. (1997) developed three component subscales for *A-hea*: Gastrointestinal Complaints (*A-hea1*), Neurological Symptoms (*A-hea2*), and General Health Concerns (*A-hea3*).

The following descriptors are associated with elevated scores on *A-hea*:

- General physical concerns and complaints and possibly more specific gastrointestinal or neurological symptoms.
- Tiredness, weakness, and fatigue.

Adolescent-Alienation (A-aln) Scale. The MMPI-A Alienation scale is 20 items in length and does not directly correspond to any of the MMPI-2 content scales. The *A-aln* scale is designed to identify adolescents who are interpersonally isolated and alienated and feel pessimistic about social interactions. They tend not to believe that others understand or are sympathetic to them and perceive their lives as being unfair or harsh. They may feel that they are unable to turn to, or depend on, anyone. These adolescents would be expected to have few or no close friends. Table 6.12 provides examples of *A-aln* scale abbreviated items. The *A-aln* scale is most highly correlated with MMPI basic scale *8* ($r = .71$ for females and $r = .73$ for males). Data from Archer and Gordon (1991b) indicate that this MMPI-A content scale is most highly correlated

TABLE 6.12
Items From the Alienation (*A-aln*) Scale

Examples of A-aln items scored if true
  16. Life unfair.
  20. Misunderstood.
Examples of A-aln items scored if false
  74. Liked by most.
 104. Hard workers usually succeed.

Note: MMPI-A abbreviated items reproduced by permission. MMPI-A test booklet copyright © 1992 by the Regents of the University of Minnesota; MMPI-A abbreviated item test booklet copyright © 2004 by the Regents of the University of Minnesota.

with the Wiggins Depression (*DEP*) content scale for females ($r = .69$) and with the Wiggins Psychoticism (*PSY*) scale for males ($r = .70$).

Williams et al. (1992) reported that in both the normative and clinical samples the *A-aln* scale was correlated with feeling emotionally distant from others. In the Archer and Gordon (1991b) clinical sample, high scores among girls were related to withdrawal, lying, and irritability, whereas high scores for boys were related to provocativeness, excessive use of fantasy, and the occurrence of hallucinations and suicidal thoughts. Kopper et al. (1998) reported that *A-aln* scale scores contributed significantly to adolescent inpatients' self-reports on a measure of suicide probability. Sherwood et al. (1997) provided three component subscales for the *A-aln* scale: Misunderstood (*A-aln1*), Social Isolation (*A-aln2*), and Interpersonal Skepticism (*A-aln3*).

The following are characteristics associated with high *A-aln* scores:

- Sense of interpersonal alienation and frustration.
- Social withdrawal and isolation.

Adolescent-Bizarre Mentation (A-biz) Scale. The *A-biz* scale consists of 19 items, of which 17 also appear on the MMPI-2 Bizarre Mentation (*BIZ*) scale. Eleven of the 19 items on the *A-biz* scale also appear on the MMPI-A *F* scale. All but one of the *A-biz* scale items can be found in the original MMPI item pool. Adolescents who produce elevated scores on the *A-biz* scale are characterized by the occurrence of psychotic thought processes. They report strange and unusual experiences, which may include auditory, visual, or olfactory hallucinations. They may also have paranoid symptoms and delusions, including beliefs that they are being plotted against or controlled by others. *A-biz* scores are highly correlated with scales *F* and 8 from the basic MMPI-A profile in the normative sample (see Tables 6.3 and 6.4) and with the Wiggins Psychoticism (*PSY*) scale in the Archer and Gordon (1991b) inpatient sample (see Tables 6.5 and 6.6). Table 6.13 provides examples of abbreviated items from the *A-biz* scale.

Williams et al. (1992) reported that the *A-biz* scale appeared to measure general maladjustment among normal adolescents and was associated in their clinical sample with the occurrence of bizarre sensory experiences and psychotic symptoms. Archer and Gordon (1991b) found that high *A-biz* scores among female inpatients were related to hallucinations, poor emotional control, and poor reality testing, whereas high scores for males were associated with fighting, legal difficulties, the perpetration of sexual abuse, hallucinations, and poor reality testing. Sherwood and her colleagues identified Psychotic Symptomatology (*A-biz1*) and Paranoid Ideation (*A-biz2*) components for the *A-biz* content scale.

TABLE 6.13
Items From the Bizarre Mentation (*A-biz*) Scale

Examples of A-biz items scored if true
22. Possessed by spirits.
29. Unusual experiences.
Single A-biz item scored if false
387. Never had a vision.

Note: MMPI-A abbreviated items reproduced by permission. MMPI-A test booklet copyright © 1992 by the Regents of the University of Minnesota; MMPI-A abbreviated item test booklet copyright © 2004 by the Regents of the University of Minnesota.

The following characteristics are associated with elevated *A-biz* scale scores:

- Poor reality testing.
- Deficits in impulse control.
- Strange and unusual beliefs or thoughts.
- Presence of paranoid symptomatology, including hallucinations and delusions, and possible thought disorder or psychosis.

Adolescent-Anger (A-ang) Scale. The MMPI-A Anger scale consists of 17 items, of which 11 also appear on the MMPI-2 Anger (*Ang*) scale. Twelve of the *A-ang* items appeared on the original form of the MMPI. Clark (1994) examined the relationship between the MMPI-2 *ANG* scale and concurrent measures of anger and subjective distress in a sample of 97 men admitted to an inpatient chronic pain program. Results of this study indicated that the MMPI-2 *ANG* scale is a reliable index of the predisposition to external expression of anger, and this scale was found to be correlated $r = .71$ with the Spielberger (1988) trait measure of anger. Additionally, individuals who produced elevated scores (T ≥ 65) on the MMPI-2 anger scale could be described as displaying frequent and intense anger, feeling frustrated, being quick-tempered, and being impulsive and prone to interpersonal problems. Although the MMPI-2 *ANG* scale was found to be an effective measure of anger externalization, scores on this content scale were not related to state experiences of anger or to patterns of inwardly directed anger.

Adolescents who score high on the MMPI-A *A-ang* scale may be described as irritable, grouchy, and impatient. Problems with anger may include the potential of physical assaultiveness, and four of the items on the *A-ang* scale (items 34, 128, 445, and 458) specifically relate to the issue of physical aggression. Williams et al. (1992) found that high *A-ang* scores among adolescents in clinical settings were related to histories of assaultive behavior. Table 6.14 provides examples of *A-ang* scale abbreviated items. As in the case of other MMPI-A scales related to externalizing behaviors, *A-ang* scores are negatively and highly correlated with scale *K* in the normative sample. In addition, *A-ang* scale scores were highly correlated ($r = .79$ for boys and $r = .83$ for girls) with scores from the Wiggins Hostility (*HOS*) scale in the Archer and Gordon (1991b) inpatient sample. Additionally, these authors found high *A-ang* scores were associated with truancy, poor parental relationships, defiance and disobedience, anger, and assaultiveness for girls and high heterosexual interest, drug abuse, hyperactivity, and threatened assaultiveness for boys. Toyer and Weed (1998) found *A-ang* scores positively correlated with counselor's ratings of anger in a sample of 50 court-adjudicated adolescents in outpatient treatment. Arita and Baer (1998) reported an

TABLE 6.14
Items From the Anger (*A-ang*) Scale

Examples of A-ang items scored if true
26. Want to swear.
34. Would like to destroy things.
Single A-ang item scored if false
355. Not easily angered.

Note: MMPI-A abbreviated items reproduced by permission. MMPI-A test booklet copyright © 1992 by the Regents of the University of Minnesota; MMPI-A abbreviated item test booklet copyright © 2004 by the Regents of the University of Minnesota.

intercorrelation of $r = 59$ between *A-ang* scale scores and scores from the Externalizing Youth Self-Report version of the Child Behavior Checklist (YSR–CBCL) and an $r = 59$ intercorrelation between *A-ang* scale scores and scores on the Trait form of the State-Trait Anger Expression Inventory (*STAXI–T*). Sherwood et al. (1997) developed two component subscales for *A-ang*, Explosive Behavior (*A-ang1*) and Irritability (*A-ang2*). The following features are associated with high *A-ang* scores:

- Anger and interpersonal hostility.
- Irritability, grouchiness, and impatience.
- Poor anger control and potential physical aggressiveness.

Adolescent-Cynicism (A-cyn) Scale. The *A-cyn* scale includes 22 items, 21 of which also appear on the MMPI-2 Cynicism (*Cyn*) scale. All of the *A-cyn* items are scored in the *true* direction and appeared on the original version of the MMPI. Adolescents who produce elevations on this MMPI-A content scale may be described as distrustful, cynical, and suspicious of the motives of others. They tend to believe that all individuals manipulate and use each other selfishly for personal gain. They assume that others behave in a manner that appears ethical or honest only because of the fear of being caught and punished for misbehavior. They expect others to lie, cheat, and steal in order to gain advantage. Table 6.15 provides examples of *A-cyn* scale abbreviated items. The *A-cyn* scale correlates highly and negatively with scale *K* of the MMPI-A basic scale profile. Data from the Archer and Gordon (1991b) adolescent inpatient sample indicate that the *A-cyn* scale correlates highly ($r = .86$ for females and $r = .88$ for males) with the Wiggins Authority Problems (*AUT*) content scale.

Williams et al. (1992) reported few meaningful external correlates for this scale in their investigation of MMPI-A normative and clinical samples. Archer and Gordon (1991b) found that high *A-cyn* scores among female adolescents were related to the occurrence of sexual abuse and poor parental relationships as primary presenting problems and to staff ratings of these adolescents as resistant and displaying a negative attitude. The *A-cyn* scale produced few correlates for male inpatient adolescents. Those correlates that were obtained involved the increased occurrence of hallucinations and the excessive use of fantasy. Clark (1994) examined correlates of the MMPI-2 *CYN* content scale in a sample of 97 male chronic pain patients. Results of this investigation provided few consistent descriptors associated with *CYN* scale elevations, and the authors concluded that caution should be employed in using the MMPI-2 *CYN* scale in clinical settings. The lack of consistency in clinical descriptors derived for the MMPI-A *CYN* scale also suggests caution in the use of this MMPI-A measure. The Sherwood

TABLE 6.15
Items From the Cynicism (*A-cyn*) Scale

Examples of A-cyn items scored if true
47. Those in authority often knew less than I.
72. Hard to convince people of truth.

Note: This content scale contains no items scored in the false direction. MMPI-A abbreviated items reproduced by permission. MMPI-A test booklet copyright © 1992 by the Regents of the University of Minnesota; MMPI-A abbreviated item test booklet copyright © 2004 by the Regents of the University of Minnesota.

TABLE 6.16

Items From the Conduct Problems (*A-con*) Scale

Examples of A-con items scored if true
32.   Stolen things.
99.   Betting enhances a race.
Examples of A-con items scored if false
96.   Not thrill-seeking.
249.   Never in trouble with law.

Note: MMPI-A abbreviated items reproduced by permission. MMPI-A test booklet copyright © 1992 by the Regents of the University of Minnesota; MMPI-A abbreviated item test booklet copyright © 2004 by the Regents of the University of Minnesota.

et al. (1997) components for the *A-cyn* content scale are Misanthropic Beliefs (*A-cyn1*) and Interpersonal Suspiciousness (*A-cyn2*).

Based on the item content of the *A-cyn* scale, the following descriptors may be associated with high scores on this measure:

- Guarded and suspicious of the motives of others.
- Unfriendly, manipulative, and hostile in relationships.

Adolescent-Conduct Problems (A-con) Scale.   The MMPI-A Conduct Problems scale is composed of 23 items, of which 7 appear on the MMPI-2 Antisocial Practices (*ASP*) scale. Twelve of the 23 items on the *A-con* scale were derived from the item pool of the original MMPI. The *A-con* scale was developed to identify adolescents who report problem behaviors, including impulsivity, risk-taking behaviors, and antisocial behaviors. Sherwood and her colleagues have developed three discrete components for this content scale: Acting-out Behaviors (*A-con1*), Antisocial Attitudes (*A-con2*), and Negative Peer Group Influences (*A-con3*). Adolescents who produce elevations on this scale are likely to exhibit behaviors that may result in school suspensions and legal violations, and they are more likely to receive conduct disorder diagnoses. In addition to behaviors and actions related to conduct problems, however, the *A-con* scale also measures attitudes and beliefs likely to be in conflict with societal norms and standards. Table 6.16 provides examples of abbreviated items from the *A-con* scale. In the MMPI-A normative sample, the *A-con* scale produced substantial correlations ($r > .50$) with scales 8 and 9 of the basic scale profile for both genders and was correlated ($r = .65$ for males and $r = .70$ for females) with the Wiggins Authority Problems (*AUT*) content scale in the inpatient sample.

Williams et al. (1992) reported that high scores on *A-con* were associated with the occurrence of significant behavior problems. Archer and Gordon (1991b) found high *A-con* scores among males to be associated with presenting problems such as theft, truancy, drug abuse, legal difficulties, alcohol abuse, and assaultive behaviors. Among females, high *A-con* scores were related to truancy, defiance and disobedience, anger, and running away from home. Arita and Baer (1998) reported *A-con* scores were correlated $r = .57$, $r = .56$ and $r = .48$ with the externalizing, delinquency, and aggressive scores, respectively, from the Youth Self-Report version of the Child Behavior Checklist (*CBCL*).

The following characteristics or correlates are associated with high *A-con* scores:

- Likelihood of being in trouble because of one's behavior.
- Poor impulse control and antisocial behaviors.

TABLE 6.17
Items From the Low Self-Esteem (*A-lse*) Scale

Examples of A-lse items scored if true
67. Easily defeated in argument.
70. Not self-confident.
Examples of A-lse items scored if false
58. Am important.
74. Liked by most.

Note: MMPI-A abbreviated items reproduced by permission. MMPI-A test booklet copyright © 1992 by the Regents of the University of Minnesota; MMPI-A abbreviated item test booklet copyright © 2004 by the Regents of the University of Minnesota.

- Attitudes and beliefs that conflict with societal norms and standards.
- Problems with authority figures.
- Increased likelihood of conduct disorder diagnoses.

Adolescent-Low Self-Esteem (A-lse) Scale. The *A-lse* scale consists of 18 items, all of which also appear on the MMPI-2 *LSE* content scale. The *A-lse* scale attempts to identify adolescents who have low self-esteem and little self-confidence. Adolescents who score high on this content scale often feel inadequate and useless and not as capable and competent as others. They recognize many faults and flaws in themselves, both real and imagined, and feel unrespected or rejected by others. Table 6.17 presents examples of *A-lse* scale abbreviated items. Among the basic scales, *A-lse* produces the highest correlations with scales 7, 8, and 0 (see Tables 6.3 and 6.4). In addition, *A-lse* scores are highly correlated with scores from the Wiggins Poor Morale (*MOR*) scale ($r = .76$ for males and $r = .88$ for females). The Sherwood et al. (1997) component subscales for this content scale are Self-Doubt (*A-lse1*) and Interpersonal Submissiveness (*A-lse2*).

Williams et al. (1992) reported that high scores on the *A-lse* scale were associated with negative self-view and poor school performance. Among girls in their clinical sample, high scores on this scale were also associated with the occurrence of depression. In the Archer and Gordon (1991b) inpatient sample, high *A-lse* scores among girls were related to the occurrence of obsessive thoughts, social withdrawal, tiredness and fatigue, and suicidal thoughts. High scores among boys were related to suicidal thoughts, passivity, and self-blame or condemnation.

The following descriptors or correlates are associated with elevated scores on *A-lse*:

- Poor self-esteem or self-confidence.
- Feelings of inadequacy and incompetency.
- Interpersonal passivity, discomfort, and withdrawal.

Adolescent-Low Aspirations (A-las) Scale. The MMPI-A Low Aspirations scale is composed of 16 items and does not have a direct counterpart among the MMPI-2 content scales. The Sherwood et al. (1997) components for this content scale are Low Achievement Orientation (*A-las1*) and Lack of Initiative (*A-las2*). As with the *A-hea* scale, the majority of items on the *A-las* content scale are scored in the *false* direction. Adolescents who score high on the *A-las* scale have few educational or life goals and view themselves as unsuccessful. They do not apply themselves, tend to procrastinate, and give up quickly when faced with a frustrating or difficult challenge. Table 6.18

TABLE 6.18
Items From the Low Aspirations (A-las) Scale

Examples of A-las items scored if true
  27.   Avoid facing difficulties.
  39.   More successful if people hadn't interfered.
Examples of A-las items scored if false
  170.   Like to study what I'm working on.
  324.   With opportunity, could greatly benefit the world.

Note: MMPI-A abbreviated items reproduced by permission. MMPI-A test booklet copyright © 1992 by the Regents of the University of Minnesota; MMPI-A abbreviated item test booklet copyright © 2004 by the Regents of the University of Minnesota.

provides examples of *A-las* scale abbreviated items. The *A-las* scale does not produce any correlations with the MMPI-A basic scales or the Wiggins content scales exceeding .50 (see Tables 6.3 through 6.6). Among supplementary scales, the *A-las* scale was most highly associated with the Immaturity (*IMM*) scale, reflected in a correlational value of $r = .59$ for the normative sample.

Williams et al. (1992) found *A-las* scores were related to poor achievement in school activities and to conduct-disordered behaviors, including running away and truancy. In the Archer and Gordon (1991b) inpatient sample, high *A-las* scores among boys were related to the occurrence of arrests, legal difficulties, and suicidal threats. High scores for females were related to an inability to delay gratification, a defiant and resistant attitude, and frustration and anger in response to difficulties in learning or mastering new concepts and materials.

The following correlates are associated with elevated scores on the *A-las* scale:

• Poor academic achievement.
• Low frustration tolerance.
• Lack of initiative and direction.
• Persistent pattern of underachievement.

Adolescent-Social Discomfort (A-sod) Scale. The MMPI-A Social Discomfort scale consists of 24 items, of which 21 also appear on the MMPI-2 Social Discomfort scale. Sixteen of the items on the *A-sod* scale also appear on the MMPI-A *Si* basic profile scale. Adolescents who produce elevated scores on the *A-sod* scale tend to be uncomfortable in social situations. They avoid social events and find it difficult to interact with others. Sherwood et al. (1997) labeled the component dimensions of this content scale Introversion (*A-sod1*) and Shyness (*A-sod2*). Table 6.19 provides examples of *A-sod* scale abbreviated items. Among the basic MMPI-A scales, the *A-sod* is most highly correlated ($r > .75$) with the *Si* scale for both males and females (see Tables 6.3 and 6.4). The *A-sod* scale is also very highly correlated ($r > .85$) with the Wiggins Social Maladjustment (*SOC*) scale, as shown in Tables 6.5 and 6.6.

Williams et al. (1992) found high *A-sod* scores to be associated with social withdrawal and discomfort for both boys and girls and with depression and eating disorder problems for females. Archer and Gordon (1991b) found high *A-sod* scores among inpatient girls to be related to social withdrawal, apathy, fatigue, shyness, and the avoidance of competition with peers. High *A-sod* scores among boys were related to an increased frequency of provocative behaviors, anxiety and nervousness, and

TABLE 6.19
Items From the Social Discomfort (*A-sod*) Scale

Examples of A-sod items scored if true
160. Hard to make conversation with strangers.
178. Dislike being shy.
Examples of A-sod items scored if false
 46. Friendly.
450. Get along with most.

Note: MMPI-A abbreviated items reproduced by permission. MMPI-A test booklet copyright © 1992 by the Regents of the University of Minnesota; MMPI-A abbreviated item test booklet copyright © 2004 by the Regents of the University of Minnesota.

suicidal thoughts. Arita and Baer (1998) reported the *A-sod* was correlated $r = .63$ with scores from the Social Introversion dimension of the Multiscore Depression Inventory (*MDI*) among adolescent inpatients.

The following characteristics are associated with high *A-sod* scores:

- Social discomfort and withdrawal.
- Shyness and social introversion.

Adolescent-Family Problems (A-fam) Scale. The MMPI-A Family Problems scale includes 35 items, of which 15 also appear on the MMPI-2 Family Problems content scale. Twenty-one of the items on the *A-fam* scale were derived from the original version of the MMPI. Adolescents producing elevations on the *A-fam* scale report the presence of substantial family conflict and discord. They are likely to have frequent quarrels with family members and report little love or understanding within their families. They feel misunderstood and unjustly punished by family members and may report being physically or emotionally abused. They may wish to run away or escape from their homes and families. Sherwood et al. (1997) divided the content of *A-fam* into two components, Familial Discord (*A-fam1*) and Familial Alienation (*A-fam2*). Table 6.20 provides examples of abbreviated items from the *A-fam* scale. Among the MMPI-A basic scales, *A-fam* is most highly correlated ($r > .65$) with scales *Pd* and *Sc* (see Tables 6.3 and 6.4). Among the Wiggins content scales, *A-fam* is most highly correlated ($r > .80$) with the Wiggins Family Problems (*FAM*) scale (see Tables 6.5 and 6.6).

TABLE 6.20
Items From the Family Problems (*A-fam*) Scale

Examples of A-fam items scored if true
 19. Wanted to leave home.
 57. Parents dislike friends.
Examples of A-fam items scored if false
  6. Father a good man.
 79. Rarely quarrel with family.

Note: MMPI-A abbreviated items reproduced by permission. MMPI-A test booklet copyright © 1992 by the Regents of the University of Minnesota; MMPI-A abbreviated item test booklet copyright © 2004 by the Regents of the University of Minnesota.

Williams et al. (1992) reported that high scores on the *A-fam* scale were associated with a variety of delinquent and neurotic symptoms and behaviors. Girls who produced high *A-fam* scores in the Archer and Gordon (1991b) inpatient sample were found to have more problems with anger, to be loud and boisterous, and to have a higher frequency of running away from home. Boys who scored high on this content scale were more likely to engage in drug and/or alcohol abuse, to have anger control problems, and to have a history of physical abuse.

The following characteristics are associated with high *A-fam* scores:

- Perception of family environment as unsupportive, hostile, unloving, or punitive.
- Increased probability of acting out, including running away from home.
- Resentment, anger, and hostility toward family members.

Adolescent-School Problems (A-sch) Scale. The MMPI-A School Problems scale consists of 20 items. This scale was created especially for the MMPI-A and does not have a counterpart among the MMPI-2 scales. Only nine of the items that appear on the *A-sch* scale were derived from items in the original instrument. Adolescents who score high on the *A-sch* scale do not like school and are likely to encounter many behavioral and academic problems within the school setting. They may have developmental delays or learning disabilities or may exhibit behavioral problems that have significantly interfered with academic achievement and their acquisition of academic skills. The Sherwood et al. (1997) components for this content scale are School Conduct Problems (*A-sch1*) and Negative Attitudes (*A-sch2*). Table 6.21 provides examples of *A-sch* scale abbreviated items. Among the MMPI-A basic scales, *A-sch* is most highly correlated with scales *F* ($r > .60$) and *Sc* ($r > .55$). The *A-sch* scale is also correlated with the Wiggins Hostility (*HOS*) scale ($r > .50$) and with the Immaturity (*IMM*) supplementary scale ($r > .70$).

Williams et al. (1992) reported that high *A-sch* scores were related to the occurrence of academic and behavioral problems in the school environment and may also serve as a measure of general maladjustment. Archer and Gordon (1991b) found that high scores on this MMPI-A content scale were related to the occurrence of academic decline and failure, truancy, and defiance among adolescent female inpatients. Among boys, high scores were associated with legal difficulties, drug abuse, fighting, and intense interest in the opposite sex. Toyer and Weed (1998) reported scores from the *A-sch* content scales correlated with juvenile offender status as well as counselors' ratings of court-adjudicated adolescents' extent of difficulty in academic settings. Milne and Greenway (1999) investigated a sample of 170 adolescents and found elevations on

TABLE 6.21
Items From the School Problems (*A-sch*) Scale

Examples of A-sch items scored if true
12.   Teachers don't like me.
69.   School useless.
Examples of A-sch items scored if false
153.   Like school.
459.   Grades average or more.

Note: MMPI-A abbreviated items reproduced by permission. MMPI-A test booklet copyright © 1992 by the Regents of the University of Minnesota; MMPI-A abbreviated item test booklet copyright © 2004 by the Regents of the University of Minnesota.

TABLE 6.22
Items From the Negative Treatment Indicators (*A-trt*) Scale

Examples of A-trt items scored if true
20. Misunderstood.
88. Don't care what happens to me.
Examples of A-trt items scored if false
419. Will attain main goals.
431. Talking about problems often more helpful than taking medicine.

Note: MMPI-A abbreviated items reproduced by permission. MMPI-A test booklet copyright © 1992 by the Regents of the University of Minnesota; MMPI-A abbreviated item test booklet copyright © 2004 by the Regents of the University of Minnesota.

A-sch related to lower scores on the Wechsler Intelligence Scale for Children–III (WISC–III) full scale and verbal IQ scores for boys, but this association was weaker for girls.

The following correlates or characteristics are associated with high *A-sch* scores:

- Negative attitude toward academic activities and achievement.
- Poor school performance, including behavioral and academic problems and deficits.
- Possibility of learning disabilities or significant developmental delays and learning problems.

Adolescent-Negative Treatment Indicators (A-trt) Scale. The MMPI-A Negative Treatment Indicator scale consists of 26 items, of which 21 also appear on the MMPI-2 *TRT* scale. Only 9 of the items on the *A-trt* scale are derived from the original MMPI instrument. Adolescents who produce elevations on the *A-trt* scale may present barriers to treatment stemming from apathy or despondency concerning their ability to change or from suspiciousness and distrust of help offered by others (including mental health professionals). These adolescents may feel that they are incapable of making significant changes in their lives or that working with others in the change process is ineffective or a sign of weakness. The Sherwood et al. (1997) components for this content scale are Low Motivation (*A-trt1*) and Inability to Disclose (*A-trt2*). Table 6.22 provides examples of *A-trt* scale abbreviated items. The *A-trt* scale is most highly correlated ($r > .60$) with scales *Pt* and *Sc* among the MMPI-A basic scales (see Tables 6.3 and 6.4). The *A-trt* scale is also highly correlated ($r > .60$) with the Immaturity (*IMM*) supplementary scale and the Wiggins Depression (*DEP*) and Psychoticism (*PSY*) content scales.

In the Archer and Gordon (1991b) inpatient sample, high *A-trt* scores among boys were associated with interest in the opposite sex, poor sibling relationships, the excessive use of fantasy, and a tendency to physically threaten peers. Elevated *A-trt* scores for girls were associated with poor physical coordination and odd physical movements. Williams et al. (1992) failed to find a clear pattern of clinical correlates for the *A-trt* scale.

Based on the content of the *A-trt* scale, the following are correlates likely to be associated with high scores:

- Presence of negative attitudes or expectations concerning mental health treatment.
- Pessimism concerning one's ability to change.
- The belief that talking about problems with others is not helpful or useful or is a sign of weakness.

SUPPLEMENTARY SCALES

The MMPI-A supplementary scales consist of a set of six measures created by a variety of researchers. Three of the supplementary scales were adopted from the original MMPI with relatively limited modification and were also included in the MMPI-2 (Butcher et al., 1989). These measures include Welsh's (1956) Anxiety and Repression scales and the MacAndrew Alcoholism scale (MacAndrew, 1965), denoted the *MAC–R* in the MMPI-A. In addition, the Immaturity (*IMM*) scale, the Alcohol-Drug Problem Acknowledgment (*ACK*) scale, and the Alcohol-Drug Problem Proneness (*PRO*) scale are measures created especially for the MMPI-A.

Three general statements may be offered concerning the MMPI-A supplementary scales:

1. The raw score totals for all supplementary scales are converted to T-score values based on linear T-score transformation procedures. As with the MMPI-A basic scales and content scales, however, a gray or shaded zone denoting marginal-range elevations for supplementary scales occurs from T-score 60 through 65 inclusive.

2. None of the supplementary scales may be scored within Stage 1, or the first 350 items of the MMPI-A booklet. Each of the supplementary scales requires the administration of the full test booklet.

3. Supplementary scale results should be used to refine but not replace the interpretation of the MMPI-A basic scales.

The following section provides a brief overview of each of the MMPI-A supplementary scales. Table 6.23 provides the intercorrelations of the supplementary scales, and Tables 6.24 and 6.25 show the correlations of these measures with the MMPI-A basic scales.

MacAndrew Alcoholism Scale–Revised (*MAC–R*)

The MacAndrew Alcoholism scale (*MAC*) was originally created by MacAndrew in 1965 by contrasting the item responses of 300 male alcoholics with those of 300 male psychiatric patients. Items selected for the *MAC* scale showed the greatest

TABLE 6.23
Raw Score Intercorrelations of the MMPI-A Supplementary Scales for Male and Female
Adolescents in the MMPI-A Normative Sample

	Scales	MAC-R	ACK	PRO	IMM	A	R
				Females			
	MAC-R		.56	.45	.43	.22	−.38
M	ACK	.57		.57	.64	.38	−.12
a	PRO	.45	.60		.54	.30	−.07
l	IMM	.40	.62	.54		.53	.05
e	A	.23	.41	.33	.58		−.22
s	R	−.26	−.09	−.05	.05	−.24	

Note: From Archer (1997b). Copyright © 1997 by Lawrence Erlbaum Associates, Inc. Reprinted by permission.

TABLE 6.24

Raw Score Intercorrelations of the MMPI-A Supplementary and Basic Scales for Female Adolescents in the MMPI-A Normative Sample

Scale	MAC-R	ACK	PRO	IMM	A	R
F_1	.49	.59	.45	.68	.34	.17
F_2	.46	.56	.35	.72	.40	.19
F	.50	.61	.41	.75	.40	.19
L	−.01	−.15	−.25	−.03	−.27	.39
K	−.22	−.30	−.22	−.43	−.73	.37
Hs	.26	.36	.29	.48	.54	.07
D	.02	.24	.22	.43	.54	.32
Hy	.05	.14	.20	.13	.16	.21
Pd	.43	.54	.53	.57	.55	−.02
Mf	−.32	−.23	−.13	−.35	.07	−.32
Pa	.35	.42	.30	.48	.54	.06
Pt	.26	.46	.36	.62	.90	−.17
Sc	.42	.58	.44	.73	.79	−.09
Ma	.52	.48	.41	.40	.43	−.39
Si	−.06	.20	.12	.52	.68	.18

Note: From Archer (1997b). Copyright © 1997 by Lawrence Erlbaum Associates, Inc. Reprinted by permission.

endorsement differences between these two groups (excluding two items directly related to alcohol consumption). The final 49 items selected by these procedures correctly classified 81.5% of subjects in the cross-validation sample of male alcoholic and nonalcoholic psychiatric outpatients (MacAndrew, 1965). Based on their review of the MMPI literature in the substance abuse area, Sutker and Archer (1979) concluded that research findings on the *MAC* scale supported the view that it was "the most promising of current MMPI-derived alcoholism scales" (p. 127).

TABLE 6.25

Raw Score Intercorrelations of the MMPI-A Supplementary and Basic Scales for Male Adolescents in the MMPI-A Normative Sample

Scale	MAC-R	ACK	PRO	IMM	A	R
F_1	.35	.61	.47	.70	.29	.22
F_2	.33	.57	.40	.70	.34	.20
F	.36	.62	.45	.74	.34	.22
L	−.06	−.04	−.11	.07	−.30	.47
K	−.24	−.20	−.13	−.30	−.70	.52
Hs	.12	.33	.29	.48	.40	.23
D	−.17	.13	.14	.32	.36	.48
Hy	−.12	.14	.19	.15	−.02	.46
Pd	.33	.54	.55	.58	.46	.05
Mf	−.29	−.08	−.03	−.12	.23	.13
Pa	.27	.48	.33	.54	.46	.17
Pt	.22	.41	.35	.58	.88	−.16
Sc	.30	.58	.46	.74	.74	−.06
Ma	.54	.50	.42	.40	.43	−.47
Si	−.09	.14	.06	.47	.67	.20

Note: From Archer (1997b). Copyright © 1997 by Lawrence Erlbaum Associates, Inc. Reprinted by permission.

The *MAC* scale is the only MMPI special scale that has received substantial empirical investigation with adolescents (Archer, 1987b). This literature has shown *MAC* scale scores to be related to substance abuse among adolescents in public school settings as well as in hospital and residential psychiatric and drug treatment programs. Recommended adolescent *MAC* raw score cutoff values across assessment settings have ranged from Wolfson and Erbaugh's (1984) cutoff of 24 for females and 26 for males to Archer's (1987b) recommended cutoff of 28 for both male and female adolescents. Findings by Gantner, Graham, and Archer (1992) indicated that a raw score cutoff value of 28 for males and 27 for females provided maximum accurate classification of substance abusers from psychiatric inpatients, whereas a value of 26 for males and 25 for females provided optimal discrimination of substance abusers from a sample of normal high school students. Further, as shown in Tables 6.26 and 6.27, findings

TABLE 6.26

MMPI Codetype Classification and MAC Scale Elevations at Two Criterion Levels for Male
Adolescent Psychiatric Patients

Codetype	MAC Cutoff Scores				MAC	MAC SD
	<24	>24	<28	>28		
3	8 (47%)	9 (53%)	15 (88%)	2 (12%)	23.7	4.7
4	4 (8%)	44 (92%)	17 (35%)	31 (65%)	28.8	4.0
5	10 (36%)	18 (64%)	20 (71%)	8 (29%)	24.7	4.0
9	3 (11%)	24 (89%)	8 (30%)	19 (70%)	29.3	4.6
13–31	10 (43%)	13 (57%)	15 (65%)	8 (35%)	24.3	5.9
14–41	1 (6%)	15 (94%)	5 (31%)	11 (69%)	29.3	4.2
15–51	1 (9%)	10 (91%)	6 (55%)	5 (45%)	27.7	4.9
17–71	0 (0%)	12 (100%)	9 (75%)	3 (25%)	26.4	2.4
18–81	0 (0%)	15 (100%)	6 (40%)	9 (60%)	29.4	3.7
23–32	9 (64%)	5 (36%)*[a]	13 (93%)	1 (7%)	20.6	5.4
24–42	7 (25%)	21 (75%)	20 (71%)	8 (29%)	25.3	4.0
25–52	11 (79%)	3 (21%)*[a]	12 (86%)	2 (14%)	21.6	4.5
34–43	3 (14%)	18 (86%)	9 (43%)	12 (57%)	26.9	4.3
35–53	2 (20%)	8 (80%)	5 (50%)	5 (50%)	27.4	3.6
45–54	9 (38%)	15 (62%)	15 (63%)	9 (37%)	25.3	5.0
46–64	1 (2%)	42 (98%)*[a]	9 (21%)	34 (79%)*[b]	30.1	3.6
47–74	0 (0%)	11 (100%)	2 (18%)	9 (82%)	30.1	3.0
48–84	3 (19%)	13 (81%)	9 (56%)	7 (44%)	27.4	4.3
49–94	1 (3%)	38 (97%)*[a]	8 (21%)	31 (79%)*[b]	31.5	4.2
56–65	3 (25%)	9 (75%)	7 (58%)	5 (42%)	25.6	5.1
67–76	2 (20%)	8 (80%)	5 (50%)	5 (50%)	27.4	4.9
68–86	5 (36%)	9 (64%)	8 (57%)	6 (43%)	26.3	5.4
69–96	1 (7%)	14 (93%)	3 (20%)	12 (80%)	31.5	5.9
78–87	3 (17%)	15 (83%)	6 (33%)	12 (67%)	28.8	5.0
No Code	70 (31%)	153 (69%)	141 (63%)	82 (37%)*[b]	26.1	4.5
Other Codes	32 (27%)	88 (73%)	64 (53%)	56 (47%)	26.8	5.4
Total	199 (24%)	630 (76%)	437 (53%)	392 (47%)	27.0	5.0

Note: From Archer and Klinefelter (1992). Copyright ©1992 by Lawrence Erlbaum Associates, Inc. Reprinted by permission. Values within parentheses indicate percent age of cases occurring at varying *MAC* scale values within specific codetypes.

[a] Significant *MAC* elevation frequency difference found for codetype comparisons using $MAC \geq 24$ criterion.

[b] Significant *MAC* elevation frequency difference found for codetype comparisons using $MAC \geq 28$ criterion.

*$p < .002$.

TABLE 6.27

MMPI Codetype Classification and *MAC* Scale Elevations at Two Criterion Levels for Female
Adolescent Psychiatric Patients

| Codetype | MAC Cutoff Scores | | | | MAC | MAC SD |
	<24	>24	<28	>28		
4	8 (31%)	18 (69%)	17 (65%)	9 (35%)	25.5	4.4
9	6 (29%)	15 (71%)	18 (86%)	3 (14%)	24.6	3.5
12–21	14 (74%)	5 (26%)	15 (79%)	4 (21%)	22.9	4.5
13–31	7 (41%)	10 (59%)	12 (71%)	5 (19%)	24.1	4.2
18–81	7 (41%)	10 (59%)	11 (65%)	6 (35%)	24.9	5.1
23–32	12 (86%)	2 (14%)*[a]	14 (100%)	0 (0%)	19.3	3.6
24–42	15 (44%)	19 (56%)	28 (82%)	6 (18%)	23.3	4.6
46–64	11 (50%)	11 (50%)	14 (64%)	8 (36%)	25.3	4.8
48–84	8 (36%)	14 (64%)	15 (68%)	7 (32%)	25.0	4.7
49–94	3 (10%)	27 (90%)*[a]	11 (37%)	19 (63%)*[b]	8.3	3.5
69–96	0 (0%)	10 (100%)	3 (30%)	7 (70%)*[b]	30.2	4.0
78–87	3 (25%)	9 (75%)	9 (75%)	3 (25%)	24.8	3.3
89–98	0 (0%)	11 (100%)	2 (18%)	9 (82%)*[b]	30.1	2.8
No Code	65 (48%)	70 (52%)	13 (84%)	22 (16%)	23.1	4.4
Other Codes	69 (54%)	59 (46%)	105 (82%)	23 (18%)	23.2	4.7
Total	228 (44%)	290 (56%)	387 (75%)	131 (25%)	24.1	4.8

Note: From Archer and Klinefelter (1992). Copyright © 1992 by Lawrence Erlbaum Associates,
Inc. Reprinted by permission. Values within parentheses indicate percent age of cases occurring at
varying *MAC* scale values within specific codetypes.
[a] Significant *MAC* elevation frequency difference found for codetype comparisons using $MAC \geq$
24 criterion.
[b] Significant *MAC* elevation frequency difference found for codetype comparisons using $MAC \geq$
28 criterion.
*$p < .004$.

by Archer and Klinefelter (1992) indicate that the probability of obtaining an elevated
MAC scale score is associated with the type of basic scale MMPI codetype produced
by an adolescent. Adolescents producing the 4-9/9-4 code, for example, were much
more likely to produce elevated *MAC* scores, whereas adolescents producing the
2-3/3-2 code were more likely to produce lower range *MAC* scale scores. Greene (1994)
also showed a strong relationship between adults, *MAC* scale elevations and MMPI
codetype, subject gender, and treatment setting.

Similar to findings in adult populations, high *MAC* scores among adolescents appear to be related to the abuse of a variety of drugs in addition to alcohol. Andrucci,
Archer, Pancoast, and Gordon (1989), for example, found high *MAC* scores related to
abuse of amphetamines, barbiturates, cocaine, hallucinogens, and marijuana. In addition to indicating the possibility of substance abuse problems, elevated *MAC* scale
scores have also been associated with a variety of personality characteristics. For example, Archer, Gordon, Anderson, and Giannetti (1989) found high *MAC* adolescents
to be described as assertive, independent, self-indulgent, undercontrolled, and much
more likely to have an arrest record and to receive conduct disorder diagnoses. These
findings are consistent with earlier reports by Rathus, Fox, and Ortins (1980), who
found that *MAC* scale scores were related to delinquent behaviors, as well as results
by Wisniewski, Glenwick, and Graham (1985), who found that high *MAC* scores in
a high school sample were related to a higher number of disciplinary incidents and
lower grade point averages. Basham (1992) examined a wide variety of MMPI scales

as measures of acting out in a sample of 327 adolescent inpatients. He concluded that the MAC scale appears to measure a broad antisocial personality dimension rather than the presence of a specific alcohol or drug abuse problem. Svanum and Ehrmann (1992) found that adult alcoholics with high *MAC* scores were characterized by gregariousness, social drinking, belligerence and aggression while drinking, and a high incidence of alcohol-related legal problems. MacAndrew (1981) described individuals who produce elevations on *MAC* as pursuing a bold, impulsive lifestyle, with little concern for the consequences of behaviors.

The *MAC* scale has probably received extensive attention in the adolescent MMPI literature because of the importance many clinicians and researchers have placed on drug and alcohol problems within this age group. Although the *MAC* scale holds substantial potential as a useful screening device for substance abuse among adolescents, several cautions appear appropriate regarding its use. Archer (1987b), for example, observed that the findings in adult samples suggest that the *MAC* scale may have little diagnostic utility among Black respondents and that substantial caution should be used when interpreting the *MAC* in non-White populations. According to Greene (1991), accuracy hit rates are probably too low to justify the use of the *MAC* as a screening device to detect substance abuse problems among patients in medical treatment settings. Wasyliw, Haywood, Grossman, and Cavanaugh (1993) reported findings that indicate that clinicians should be particularly cautious in interpreting the *MAC* scale when they suspect that respondents have attempted to minimize the report of psychopathology on the MMPI. Additionally, Gottesman and Prescott (1989) observed that lower range cutting scores, such as a value of 24 or above, which has frequently been employed for adults, would misclassify a very high percentage of normal adolescents as a result of false positive errors. For example, the *MAC–R* scale mean value for adolescents in the MMPI-A sample was 21.07 for males and 19.73 for females (Butcher et al., 1992). Both Gottesman and Prescott (1989) and Greene (1988) noted the critical effects of substance abuse base rates on the clinical usefulness of the *MAC* scale. Many studies have examined the validity of the *MAC* scale based on equal or nearly equal samples of substance abuse and nonsubstance abuse groups. These studies have often yielded impressive rates of accurate classification of approximately 80% (e.g., MacAndrew, 1979). However, when hit rates are recalculated using more realistic estimates of the base rate of substance abuse, substantially less impressive accuracy is often obtained (e.g., Gantner et al., 1992; Gottesman & Prescott, 1989).

In the creation of the MMPI-A, a revised form of the *MAC* scale (i.e., the *MAC–R* scale) was developed. The MMPI-A *MAC–R* scale contains 49 items and is identical in length to the original *MAC* scale. Forty-five of the original *MAC* items were retained in the *MAC–R* scale, with 4 *MAC–R* items added. These latter items were used to replace the 4 items deleted from the original *MAC* scale in the formation of the MMPI-A. Table 6.28 provides examples of *MAC–R* abbreviated items. Thus far, there have been no studies on the comparability of the *MAC* and *MAC–R* scales for the MMPI-A. Research by Greene, Arredondo, and Davis (1990), however, indicates that the original *MAC* scale and the *MAC–R* scale of the MMPI-2 appear to produce comparable scores and may be used in a similar manner by clinicians. Gallucci (1997b) examined the contributions of the *MAC–R* to the identification of substance abuse patterns among 88 male and 92 female adolescents receiving substance abuse treatment. He reported that the *MAC–R* scale made the largest contribution to the correct classification of adolescents into varying categories of substance abusers (e.g., undercontrolled versus overcontrolled), although all three MMPI-A substance abuse supplementary scales make significant contributions to this classification task. Gallucci (1997a) apparently

TABLE 6.28
Items From the MMPI-A MacAndrew Alcoholism
Scale–Revised (*MAC–R*)

Examples of items scored if true
7.   Like articles on crime.
46.   Friendly.
Examples of items scored if false
70.   Not self-confident.
153.   Like school.

Note: MMPI-A abbreviated items reproduced by permission. MMPI-A test booklet copyright © 1992 by the Regents of the University of Minnesota; MMPI-A abbreviated item test booklet copyright © 2004 by the Regents of the University of Minnesota.

employed the same sample to evaluate scale correlates and reported that the MMPI-A *MAC–R* and Alcohol/Drug Problem Proneness (*PRO*) scales produced similar patterns of correlates, with identical correlations of $r = .31$ with clinicians' ratings of substance abuse. In general, it is expected that the following correlates would be related to raw score values of 28 or greater on the *MAC–R* scale of the MMPI-A:

- Increased likelihood of alcohol or drug abuse problems.
- Interpersonally assertive and dominant.
- Self-indulgent and egocentric.
- Unconventional and impulsive.
- Greater likelihood of conduct disorder diagnoses.
- Greater likelihood of legal involvement and violation of social norms.

In addition, individuals who produce low-range scores on the *MAC-R* might be expected to be dependent, conservative, indecisive, overcontrolled, and sensation-avoidant. As noted by MacAndrew (1981), individuals who abuse alcohol but produce low *MAC* scores (false negatives) are likely to be neurotic individuals who may use alcohol to self-medicate their affective distress.

The Alcohol/Drug Problem Acknowledgment (*ACK*) Scale

The Alcohol/Drug Problem Acknowledgment (*ACK*) scale was developed for the MMPI-A to assess an adolescent's willingness to acknowledge alcohol or drug use–related symptoms, attitudes, or beliefs (Butcher et al., 1992). The *ACK* scale consists of 13 items initially selected based on the rational judgment that item content was relevant to drug use and were further refined based on statistical criteria, including item correlations. The *ACK* scale is quite similar to the Addiction Acknowledgment Scale (*AAS*) created for the MMPI-2 (Weed, Butcher, McKenna, & Ben-Porath, 1992). Svanum, McGrew, and Ehrmann (1994) demonstrated the relative usefulness of the *AAS* as a direct measure of substance abuse, in contrast to more subtle measures such as the *MAC-R* scale, in detecting substance dependence in a sample of 308 college students. Table 6.29 provides examples of abbreviated items found on the Alcohol/Drug Problem Acknowledgment scale. Elevations on the *ACK* scale indicate the extent to which an adolescent acknowledges or admits alcohol and/or drug problems in his or her MMPI-A self-description. It should be noted, however, that not all items on

TABLE 6.29
Items From the Alcohol/Drug Problem Acknowledgment (ACK) Scale

---

Examples of items scored if true
  81. Want to do shocking things.
 144. Problem with alcohol/drugs.
Example of items scored if false
 249. Never in trouble with law.
 431. Talking about problems often more helpful than taking medicine.

Note: MMPI-A abbreviated items reproduced by permission. MMPI-A test booklet copyright © 1992 by the Regents of the University of Minnesota; MMPI-A abbreviated item test booklet copyright © 2004 by the Regents of the University of Minnesota.

the *ACK* scale directly involve an acknowledgment of drug use. Some items, such as 81 and 249, deal with attitudes, beliefs, or behaviors that may be associated with drug use but do not directly indicate the presence or absence of alcohol or drug use behaviors. For both boys and girls in the MMPI-A sample, the mean raw score for *ACK* was approximately 4, and a raw score total of 9 or greater converts to T-score values that exceed 70.

Several studies have recently evaluated the performance of the MMPI-A *ACK* scale. Gallucci (1997a) compared the correlates of the *ACK* scale with patterns for the MMPI-A *MAC-R* and *PRO* scales in a sample of adolescents receiving substance abuse treatment. This researcher found that the *ACK* scale produced a correlation value that was very similar to the *MAC-R* and *PRO* scales correlations with clinicians' ratings of substance abuse but appeared to be a somewhat more specific measure in the sense of generally producing lower correlations with non-substance-abuse-related criteria. Gallucci concluded, "These results were consistent with interpretation of the *ACK* scale as a somewhat specific measure of a young person's willingness to acknowledge problematic substance abuse" (p. 91). Toyer and Weed (1998) examined the MMPI-A substance abuse scales, as well as other selected scales, in their investigation of 50 court-adjudicated youths participating in outpatient counseling. The results of their study indicated that the *ACK* scale produced a higher correlation with counselor ratings of drug and alcohol use ($r = .36$) than the other two MMPI-A substance abuse scales. Micucci (2002) investigated the accuracy of the MMPI-A substance abuse scales in identifying substance abuse problems in a sample of 79 adolescent psychiatric inpatients. In this study, 89.9% of substance abuse cases were accurately identified by at least one of the three scales, with the overall accuracy of classification similar across genders and ethnicity, although there was a tendency for more false positive misclassifications to occur for males. *ACK*, *MAC-R*, and *PRO* were better at screening out cases of substance abuse (identifying true negatives) than at accurately identifying adolescents who were using substances (identifying true negatives). The highest level of correct classification was achieved by identifying substance abuse using the criterion of T ≥ 60 or T ≥ 65 on the *ACK* scale. The former cutoff score achieved greater sensitivity whereas the latter achieved the highest degree of specificity. Most recently, Tirrell, Archer, and Mason (2004) examined the concurrent validity of the MMPI-A substance abuse scales *MAC-R*, *ACK*, and *PRO* in distinguishing adolescents in groups of 100 substance abusers, 100 non-substance-abusing psychiatric patients, and 100 adolescents selected from the MMPI-A normative sample. The overall findings clearly indicated that the *MAC-R*, *ACK*, and *PRO* scales generated the most impressive findings in the less challenging discrimination task of separating adolescent substance abusers

TABLE 6.30
Items From the Alcohol/Drug Problem Proneness (*PRO*) Scale

Examples of items scored if true
32. Stolen things.
57. Parents dislike friends.
Examples of items scored if false
40. Better judgment than before.
153. Like school.

Note: MMPI-A abbreviated items reproduced by permission. MMPI-A test booklet copyright © 1992 by the Regents of the University of Minnesota; MMPI-A abbreviated item test booklet copyright © 2004 by the Regents of the University of Minnesota.

from adolescents in the normative sample. Further, the *ACK* scale demonstrated the highest level of effectiveness in differentiating adolescent substance abusers from adolescent psychiatric patients and was the single best predictor for this classification task.

The Alcohol/Drug Problem Proneness (*PRO*) Scale

The Alcohol/Drug Problem Proneness (*PRO*) scale consists of 36 items. These items were empirically selected based on item endorsement differences found between adolescents in alcohol and drug treatment programs and adolescents receiving inpatient psychiatric services (Butcher et al., 1992). Thus, the scale construction method used for *PRO* is similar to that employed in the development of the *MAC* scale. Based on cross-validated research findings noted in the MMPI-A manual (Butcher et al., 1992), T-score values of 65 and greater are associated with an increased potential for the development of alcohol and drug problems. The 36 items on the *PRO* scale cover a wide variety of content, including familial characteristics, peer group features, antisocial behaviors and beliefs, and academic interests and behaviors. Table 6.30 provides illustrations of *PRO* scale abbreviated items.

The Immaturity (*IMM*) Scale

The Immaturity (*IMM*) scale was developed by Archer, Pancoast, and Gordon (1994) as a supplementary scale for the MMPI-A. The *IMM* scale assesses psychological maturation during adolescence using Loevinger's (1976) concept of ego development as a conceptual focus. Items for the *IMM* scale were selected based on a multistage procedure involving both rational and statistical criteria. The initial stage involved computing MMPI-TX item correlations with scores derived from the Holt (1980) Short-Form adaptation of the Loevinger and Wessler (1970) Sentence Completion Test of ego development in a sample of 222 normal adolescents. Preliminary items were selected for the *IMM* scale based on the occurrence of correlation coefficients achieving a significance level of $p \leq .01$. In the second stage of scale construction, raters independently evaluated the degree to which preliminary items were related to Loevinger's concept of ego development. Items were retained in the preliminary *IMM* scale if at least four of the six raters were in agreement on the appropriateness of the item to the ego development construct. In the third stage, preliminary *IMM* scale items were eliminated if the removal of the item increased the scale's internal reliability (alpha coefficient value) in either the normal sample of 222 adolescents or in a sample of 122

TABLE 6.31
Items From the MMPI-A Immaturity (*IMM*) Scale

Examples of items scored if true
16.   Life unfair.
20.   Misunderstood.
Examples of items scored if false
153.   Like school.
322.   Like children.

Note: MMPI-A abbreviated items reproduced by permission. MMPI-A test booklet copyright © 1992 by the Regents of the University of Minnesota; MMPI-A abbreviated item test booklet copyright © 2004 by the Regents of the University of Minnesota.

adolescent inpatients who had completed the MMPI-TX. Finally, each of the 704 items in the experimental MMPI-TX form was examined in terms of its' correlation with the *IMM* scale. New items were added to the *IMM* scale if items demonstrated both a conceptual and statistical relationship to the ego development construct. The final version of the *IMM* scale consists of 43 items. Examples of these abbreviated items are shown in Table 6.31. The alpha coefficient value for the *IMM* scale in the MMPI-A normative sample was .83 for females and .80 for males. As expected, *IMM* mean raw score values were significantly higher for males than for females in both the clinical sample (18.69 vs. 14.88) and the MMPI-A normative sample (13.47 vs. 11.75). This gender-related difference in *IMM* mean scores is consistent with conclusions from a recent review (Cohn, 1991) of results from 63 studies using the Sentence Completion Test. Cohn reported that females consistently showed higher developmental levels than males during adolescence.

The 43 items in the *IMM* scale concern aspects of personality including lack of self-confidence, externalization of blame, lack of insight and introspection, interpersonal and social discomfort and alienation, "living for the present" without concern for future consequences, the occurrence of hostile and antisocial attitudes, and egocentricity and self-centeredness. High scores on the *IMM* scale would be expected to be associated with impulsive adolescents who have a limited capacity for self-awareness. Their egocentricity is likely to impair their ability to engage in reciprocal and mutually satisfying interpersonal relationships, and their cognitive processes could be characterized as concrete and simplistic. In Loevinger's model of ego development, individuals producing elevated *IMM* scores are likely to reflect a *preconformist* stage of development. Interpersonal relationships during the preconformist stage have been described as opportunistic, demanding, and exploitive (Loevinger, 1976).

Preliminary data on the *IMM* scale (Archer, Pancoast, et al., 1994) from both normal and clinical samples indicated that adolescents who produced high scores on this measure had a higher incidence of school difficulties and problems. Research by Imhof and Archer (1997) examined the concurrent validity of the *IMM* scale in a residential treatment sample of 66 adolescents aged 13 through 18 inclusive. In addition to the MMPI-A, participants were administered measures of intelligence, reading ability, and maturation. The results of this study provided support for the construct validity of the MMPI-A as a measure of maturational development. As predicted, individuals who scored higher on the *IMM* scale tended to produce lower full scale and verbal IQ scores and to exhibit lower levels of moral and ego development. Results from a multiple regression analysis indicated that a linear combination of three variables—identity development, reading ability, and moral development—accounted for nearly half (46%) of the total variance in *IMM* scale raw scores. Zinn, McCumber, and Dahlstrom (1999) used 75 female and 76 male college undergraduates to cross-validate the MMPI-A *IMM* scale. In addition to the 43 items from the *IMM* scale, all these participants completed the Washington University Sentence Completion Test (WUSCT) developed by Loevinger and Wessler (1970) as a projective method of assessing ego development and also completed a brief biographical questionnaire. High interrater reliability (.80) was established for scoring the WUSCT. The distribution of *IMM* scale scores was used to partition adolescents into groups of low, medium, and high scores, and WUSCT scores were found to vary significantly between these categories. Zinn and her colleagues concluded that the MMPI-A *IMM* scale could be used as a reliable objective measure of Loevinger's concept of ego maturity. Based on the current literature, the following correlates appear applicable to adolescents who produce high *IMM* scores:

- Easily frustrated and quick to anger.
- Impatient, loud, and boisterous.
- Tend to tease or bully others.
- Not trustworthy or dependable.
- Defiant and resistant.
- Likely to have a history of academic and social difficulties.
- Likely to have lower verbal IQs and lower language ability.

Additionally, adolescents who produce low scores on the *IMM* scale are likely to be described as controlled, stable, patient, cooperative, and predictable.

Welsh's Anxiety (A) and Repression (R) Scales

As noted by Graham (2000), a large volume of factor analytic literature on the MMPI scale data has typically found two basic MMPI dimensions or factors accounting for a majority of basic scale score variance. The first factor has been assigned a variety of labels, including *general maladjustment* and *lack of ego resiliency*, and the second factor has been referred to as *ego control* or *inhibition*. Welsh (1956) developed the Anxiety (A) and Repression (R) scales to assess the respondent's standing along these first and second dimensions, respectively.

The Anxiety scale was originally created as a 39-item scale keyed in such a manner that higher scores on the *A* scale were associated with a greater degree of psychopathology. High scores have been described as reflective of individuals who are maladjusted, anxious, depressed, pessimistic, inhibited, and uncomfortable (Graham, 2000). Although these adjectives are largely negative in tone, it has also been noted that high scores on the *A* scale are associated with substantial emotional distress, which may serve as a motivator for positive change in the psychotherapeutic process. In contrast, low scores on the *A* scale have been related to a preference for activity, freedom from anxiety and discomfort, sociability, manipulativeness, and impulsivity (Graham, 2000). Archer, Gordon, et al. (1989) examined special scale correlates in a sample of 68 adolescent inpatients. These authors reported that the high *A* adolescent could be described as fearful, anxious, guilt-prone, overwhelmed, and self-critical. High *A* adolescents also tended to be viewed by both self (on other self-report instruments) and others, including family members and treatment staff, as significantly more maladjusted than other adolescent inpatients. MMPI scale *A* and basic scale *Pt*

TABLE 6.32
Items From the MMPI-A Anxiety (A) Scale

Examples of items scored if true
   28. Hard staying focused.
   35. Can't get going for long periods.
All items scored if false
   360. Seldom sad.

Note: MMPI-A abbreviated items reproduced by permission. MMPI-A test booklet copyright © 1992 by the Regents of the University of Minnesota; MMPI-A abbreviated item test booklet copyright © 2004 by the Regents of the University of Minnesota.

were highly correlated ($r = .90$) in this sample, and a higher incidence of presenting problems related to suicide attempts, thoughts, and ideations were related to elevations on the *A* scale.

In the MMPI-A, Welsh's *A* scale has been reduced to 35 items. Table 6.32 provides examples of these abbreviated items, including two examples of items deleted from the *A* scale.

In general, the following correlates are associated with elevations on scale *A*:

- Tense and anxious.
- Fearful and ruminative.
- Maladjusted and ineffective.
- Self-critical and guilty.
- Overwhelmed.

The Repression scale originally consisted of 40 items developed by Welsh (1956) to assess the second dimension that emerges when the standard MMPI scales are subjected to factor analysis. Like the *A* scale, the *R* scale appears in the original version of the MMPI, the MMPI-2, and the MMPI-A. In the MMPI-A, the *R* scale has been reduced to 33 items, all of which are scored in the *false* direction. Table 6.33 provides examples of abbreviated items retained and deleted in the MMPI-A *R* scale. In research by Archer, Gordon, et al. (1989), *R* scale scores were found to be negatively correlated with scale *9* and *MAC* scale values and positively correlated with several scales, including *L*, *K*, and the neurotic triad (scales *Hs*, *D*, and *Hy*). This finding is consistent with expectations based on the loading patterns reported for the second

TABLE 6.33
Items From the MMPI-A Repression (R) Scale

Examples of items scored if true
   None
Examples of items scored if false
   1. Like mechanics magazines.
   10. Able to work as always.

Note: MMPI-A abbreviated items reproduced by permission. MMPI-A test booklet copyright © 1992 by the Regents of the University of Minnesota; MMPI-A abbreviated item test booklet copyright © 2004 by the Regents of the University of Minnesota.

factor of the MMPI. This factor typically shows positive loadings on the neurotic triad and a negative loading on scale 9 (Graham, 2000; Greene, 2000). Significant correlates for the high R scale adolescent in the Archer, Gordon, et al. study included the following:

- Overcontrolled.
- Shows little feeling.
- Inhibited and constricted.
- Pessimistic and defeated.

In contrast, adolescents who produced low scores on R were described as talkative, spontaneous, and optimistic. Archer (1987b) also noted, however, that low R scores among adolescent psychiatric patients are related to aggressiveness, impulsivity, argumentativeness, and a tendency to employ acting-out defense mechanisms.

THE HARRIS-LINGOES AND S_i SUBSCALES

As noted, the empirical keying method employed by Hathaway and McKinley resulted in the creation of basic scales that were heterogeneous in terms of content areas. In order to help clinicians in determining the content endorsement associated with MMPI basic scale elevations, Harris and Lingoes (1955) constructed subscales for six of the basic scales, using the following process:

> The items scored in each scale were examined, and those which seemed similar in content, or to reflect a single attitude or trait, were grouped into a subscale. In effect, the item correlations were estimated, purely subjectively. The items were grouped on the basis of these estimates, and then given a name which was thought to be descriptive of the inferred attitude underlying the sorting of the items in the scored direction. (p. 1)

Harris and Lingoes used this method to develop 27 content subscales for six of the basic MMPI clinical scales, namely, 2, 3, 4, 6, 8, and 9. They did not attempt to restrict items to placement on only one subscale, and consequently there is substantial item overlap among the subscales and a high degree of subscale correlation. The authors did not develop content subscales for scales 1 or 7 because they considered these measures to be homogeneous (Graham, 2000), and they did not create subscales for 5 or 0 because these scales are often viewed as "nonclinical" scales or involving dimensions separate from the standard "clinical" scales. Caldwell (1988), Levitt (1989), and Levitt and Gotts (1995) reviewed the Harris-Lingoes subscales in their discussions of MMPI special scales, and a symposium was focused on these subscales (Colligan, 1988).

Relatively little research has been conducted on the Harris-Lingoes subscales in terms of the construct validity of these measures (Greene, 2000). Harris and Christiansen (1946) found significant differences on eight Harris-Lingoes subscales between patients judged successful versus unsuccessful in psychotherapy. Gocka and Holloway (1963) found few significant correlations between demographic variables and scores on the Harris-Lingoes subscales. Calvin (1975), however, empirically identified behavioral correlates for many of the Harris-Lingoes subscales, and these have been incorporated into the standard descriptions provided for these subscales in guides such as Graham's (2000) text. Wrobel (1992) investigated the concurrent validity of the MMPI Harris-Lingoes subscales in terms of the ability of these measures to predict clinicians' ratings of 85 adult outpatients. Results supported the validity of the majority of Harris-Lingoes subscales, but caution was urged in the interpretive use of subscales Hy_1(Denial of Social Anxiety), Hy_2 (Need for Affection), Pd_3 (Social Imperturbability), Pa_3(Naivete), *and* Ma_2 (Psychomotor Acceleration). In relation to this latter caution, Krishnamurthy, Archer, and Huddleston (1995) recently noted that a special problem arises for the Hy_1 and Pd_3 subscales because these measures cannot produce clinical-range elevations ($T \geq 65$) on the MMPI-2. Further, MMPI-A T-score values cannot exceed 66 for Hy_1 and 67 for Pd_3 for adolescents of either gender. These limitations occur because these subscales are markedly short (six items), and each mean raw score value equals approximately 4, with a standard deviation of approximately 2. Thus, it can be readily seen that the linear T-score transformation procedure cannot produce elevated T-scores for these subscales for any obtained raw score. Krishnamurthy et al. concluded that these two Harris-Lingoes subscales should be deleted from standard use on both the MMPI-2 and MMPI-A because they cannot provide useful information and the results are easily susceptible to misinterpretation.

Gallucci (1994) evaluated the validity of the Harris-Lingoes subscales in a sample of 177 adolescent inpatients using standardized criterion measures, including therapist ratings of symptomatology. The findings indicated that the Harris-Lingoes subscales Hy_2 (Need for Affection), Hy_5 (Inhibition of Aggression), and Pa_3 (Naivete) functioned as inhibitory scales and that Ma_1 (Amorality) and Ma_3 (Imperturbability) served as excitatory scales in this sample of adolescents. Pancoast and Archer (1988) showed that the standard adult norms produce marked elevations for normal adolescents on the Harris-Lingoes subscales, particularly for Pd_1 (Familial Discord), Pa_1 (Persecutory Ideas), several of the subscales related to scale 8, and Ma_2 (Psychomotor Acceleration). These findings support the belief that adult norms would tend to produce very substantial distortions in the interpretation of adolescents' MMPI profiles. Colligan and Offord (1989) provided a set of adolescent norms for the Harris-Lingoes subscales derived from their contemporary adolescent sample collected with the original MMPI instrument. The *MMPI Adolescent Interpretive System*, developed by Archer (1987a) and published by Psychological Assessment Resources, uses these Harris-Lingoes subscale T-score values in providing computer-based test interpretation for the *original* version of the MMPI , and these subscales are also included in the MMPI-A versions of this computer program (Archer, 1995, 2003).

The Harris-Lingoes subscales have been carried over into testing materials and scoring programs for the MMPI-2 and the MMPI-A. This was possible because very few standard scale items from scales 2, 3, 4, 6, 8, and 9 were deleted in the development of these instruments. A few Harris-Lingoes subscales have been slightly shortened in the revised instruments, however, because of item deletions. Further, because Harris and Lingoes apparently included some subscale items not scored on the corresponding basic scale (e.g., some items appear on *Pd* subscales that are not scored on the *Pd* scale), these items were deleted from the MMPI-A and MMPI-2 Harris-Lingoes subscales. Finally, the Harris-Lingoes subscales were renumbered in the MMPI-A and in the MMPI-2 to eliminate the lettered subscripts employed by Harris and Lingoes to delineate several of their subscales. The revised numbering system is designed to simplify the method used to denote specific subscales. Adolescent norms for the MMPI-A Harris-Lingoes subscales, based on the 1,620 boys and girls in the normative sample, are available in the test manual for this instrument (Butcher et al., 1992) and in Appendix C of this text.

Unlike the MMPI-A scales previously reviewed, the Harris-Lingoes subscales are not recommended for routine use if hand-scoring procedures are used. This is because hand scoring of the Harris-Lingoes subscales is quite time consuming, and these data are primarily useful in supplementing basic scale profiles under certain conditions (i.e., in selective cases). For example, Graham (2000) recommended the use of the Harris-Lingoes subscales if, first, "a subject receives an elevated score on a clinical scale when that elevation was not expected from the history and other information available to the clinician" (p. 118), or, second, the clinician is interpreting basic scale elevations that occur within a marginally elevated range (corresponding to a T-score range of 60–65 on the MMPI-A). This latter recommendation implicitly recognizes that when basic scale elevations are within normal limits or markedly elevated, Harris-Lingoes values are relatively less important. Additionally, Friedman et al. (2001) raised several apparently well founded concerns and cautions regarding the use of the Harris-Lingoes subscales. First, they noted that Harris and Lingoes made no attempts to cross-validate their subscales, and the external validity data concerning these measures are quite limited. In this regard, Friedman et al. cited the results of the investigation by Miller and Streiner (1985), in which independent judges were unable to accurately group items into the rational categories employed by Harris and Lingoes for the majority of these subscales. Friedman et al. also reviewed the factor analytic results of Foerstner (1986), which showed that several of the Harris-Lingoes subscales contained items that did not load on factors in a manner that might be expected given the names attributed to these subscales. Further, Friedman et al. noted that most of the Harris-Lingoes subscale items are obvious in nature and therefore susceptible to the effects of response set. Finally, the authors expressed normative concerns about the Harris-Lingoes subscales, an issue that has certainly been evident in terms of the absence of adolescent norms for these measures on the original MMPI.

The descriptions that follow for elevations on the Harris-Lingoes subscales are based on the original descriptions provided by Harris and Lingoes (1955), a rational inspection of the item content within each subscale, and a review of the descriptors provided for the scales in standard guides (e.g., Graham, 2000; Greene, 2000) to the use of the MMPI with adults. In addition, Harris-Lingoes correlates identified by Gallucci (1994) in his study of adolescent inpatients have been selectively included in the data provided here. It is emphasized, however, that the Harris-Lingoes subscales should only be used to supplement and refine interpretations derived from the standard validity and clinical scales. Further, given the lack of validity data on these measures, substantial caution should be employed in using the MMPI-A Harris-Lingoes subscales. In particular, the findings by Krishnamurthy et al. (1995) concerning the inability of the Hy_1 (Denial of Social Anxiety) and Pd_3 (Social Imperturbability) subscales to produce clinically elevated T-scores, combined with the report by Wrobel (1992) concerning the absence of concurrent validity for these two subscales, indicate that test users should strongly consider omitting data from the subscales in their standard interpretation procedures with the MMPI-A. The following are suggested interpretations for the MMPI-A Harris-Lingoes subscales grouped by parent scale.

Scale 2 (Depression) Subscales

Subjective Depression (D_1). High scores on the D_1 subscale may be associated with the following characteristics:

- Feelings of depression, unhappiness, and guilt.
- Lack of energy and interest in everyday activities.

- Deficits in concentration and attention.
- Self-critical tendencies.

Psychomotor Retardation (D_2). High scores on the D_2 subscale may be associated with the following characteristics:

- Lack of energy or inability to mobilize resources.
- Social withdrawal and social avoidance.
- Denial of hostile or aggressive impulses.

Physical Malfunctioning (D_3). High scores on the D_3 subscale may be associated with the following characteristics:

- Concern about and preoccupation with physical health.
- Reporting of a wide array of physical symptoms.

Mental Dullness (D_4). High scores on the D_4 subscale may be associated with the following characteristics:

- Complaints of difficulties with memory, concentration, or judgment.
- Lack of energy.
- Poor self-concept and feelings of inferiority.
- Difficulty in making decisions.

Brooding (D_5). High scores on the D_5 subscale may be associated with the following characteristics:

- Lack of energy, apathy, and lethargy.
- Excessive sensitivity to criticism.
- Feelings of despondency and sadness.

Scale 3 (Hysteria) Subscales

Denial of Social Anxiety (Hy_1). Higher scores on the Hy_1 subscale may be associated with the following characteristics:

- Social extroversion.
- Ease in talking to and dealing with others.

Need for Affection (Hy_2). High scores on the Hy_2 subscale may be associated with the following characteristics:

- Strong need for attention and affection.
- Optimistic and trusting in relationships.
- Denial of cynical, hostile, or negative feelings about others.

Lassitude-Malaise (Hy_3). High scores on the Hy_3 subscale may be associated with the following characteristics:

- Unhappiness and discomfort.
- Fatigue, physical problems, and the perception of poor physical health.

- Sadness and despondency.
- Poor appetite and sleep disturbance.

Somatic Complaints (Hy₄). High scores on the Hy_4 subscale may be associated with the following characteristics:

- Multiple somatic complaints and concerns.
- Head or chest pains.
- Fainting, dizziness, and problems with balance.
- Nausea, vomiting, and gastrointestinal disturbances.

Inhibition of Aggression (Hy₅). High scores on the Hy_5 subscale may be associated with the following characteristics:

- Denial of hostile or aggressive impulses.
- Perfectionistic tendencies.
- Self-perception as decisive.
- Self-perception as socially sensitive.

Scale 4 (Psychopathic Deviate) Subscales

Familial Discord (Pd₁). High scores on the Pd_1 subscale may be associated with the following characteristics:

- View of home and family as unpleasant, hostile, or rejecting.
- View of home situation as lacking in love, critical, and controlling.
- The occurrence of frequent quarrels and conflict within the family.

Authority Problems (Pd₂). High scores on the Pd_2 subscale may be associated with the following characteristics:

- History of legal violations and antisocial behaviors.
- History of conflicts with individuals in authority.
- Resentful of societal standards, customs, or norms.

Social Imperturbability (Pd₃). Higher scores on the Pd_3 subscale may be associated with the following characteristics:

- Denial of social anxiety and dependency needs.
- Social extroversion and social confidence.
- Tendency to hold strong opinions that are vigorously defended.

Social Alienation (Pd₄). High scores on the Pd_4 subscale may be associated with the following characteristics:

- Feeling misunderstood, alienated, and isolated.
- Feelings of loneliness, unhappiness, and estrangement from others.
- Tendency to blame others for problems or conflicts.
- Feelings of despondency and sadness.

Self-Alienation (Pd5). High scores on the Pd_5 subscale may be associated with the following characteristics:

- Emotional discomfort and unhappiness.
- Problems with concentration and attention.
- Feelings of guilt, regret, and remorse.
- Possibility of excessive alcohol use.

Scale 6 (Paranoia) Subscales

Persecutory Ideas (Pa1). High scores on the Pa_1 subscale may be associated with the following characteristics:

- A sense of being treated unfairly by others.
- Externalization of blame for problems and frustrations.
- Use of projection.
- Possible presence of persecutory ideas and delusions of persecution.

Poignancy (Pa2). High scores on the Pa_2 subscale may be associated with the following characteristics:

- View of self as sensitive, high-strung, and easily hurt.
- Belief that one feels emotions more intensely than do others.
- Loneliness, sadness, and a sense of being misunderstood.
- Self-perception of uniqueness or specialness.

Naivete (Pa3). High scores on the Pa_3 subscale may be associated with the following characteristics:

- Naively trusting and optimistic.
- Denial of hostile or cynical feelings or attitudes.
- Presentation of high moral or ethical standards.
- Unlikely to act impulsively.

Scale 8 (Schizophrenia) Subscales

Social Alienation (Sc1). High scores on the Sc_1 subscale may be associated with the following characteristics:

- Lack of rapport with others.
- Avoidance of social situations and withdrawal from relationships.
- Sense of being misunderstood, unfairly criticized, or unjustly punished by others.
- Hostility or anger toward family members.

Emotional Alienation (Sc2). High scores on the Sc_2 subscale may be associated with the following characteristics:

- Feelings of self-criticalness, despondency, depression, and despair.
- Possibility of suicidal ideation.

- View of life as difficult or hopeless.
- Possibility of sadistic or masochistic experiences.

Lack of Ego Mastery–Cognitive (Sc₃). High scores on the Sc_3 subscale may be associated with the following characteristics:

- Admission of strange thought processes.
- Feelings of unreality.
- Problems in concentration and attention.

Lack of Ego Mastery–Conative (Sc₄). High scores on the Sc_4 subscale may be associated with the following characteristics:

- Feelings of psychological weakness and vulnerability.
- Problems with concentration and attention.
- Lack of energy and psychological inertia.
- Guilt, despondency, depression, and possible suicidal ideation.

Lack of Ego Mastery–Defective Inhibition (Sc₅). High scores on the Sc_5 subscale may be associated with the following characteristics:

- Loss of control over emotions and impulses.
- Restlessness, irritability, and hyperactivity.
- Episodes of uncontrollable laughing or crying.
- Possible dissociative experiences or symptoms.

Bizarre Sensory Experiences (Sc₆). High scores on the Sc_6 subscale may be associated with the following characteristics:

- Strange or unusual sensory experiences.
- Loss of emotional control.
- The occurrence of a variety of neurological symptoms, including paralysis, loss of balance, or involuntary muscular movements.

Scale 9 (Hypomania) Subscales

Amorality (Ma₁). High scores on the Ma_1 subscale may be associated with the following characteristics:

- A tendency to perceive others as motivated by selfishness and self-gain.
- Endorsement of antisocial or asocial attitudes, beliefs, or behaviors.
- Drug abuse.

Psychomotor Acceleration (Ma₂). High scores on the Ma_2 subscale may be associated with the following characteristics:

- Acceleration of thought or speech.
- Tension, restlessness, and hyperactivity.
- Need to seek out excitement and stimulation.
- Attraction to sensation-seeking and risk-taking behaviors.

Imperturbability (Ma₃). High scores on the Ma_3 subscale may be associated with the following characteristics:

- Denial of social anxiety.
- Comfort and confidence in social situations.
- Freedom or independence from the influence of the opinions of others.
- Tendency to seek out excitement.

Ego Inflation (Ma₄). High scores on the Ma_4 subscale may be associated with the following characteristics:

- Feelings of self-importance, possibly including grandiosity.
- Resentfulness of perceived demands from or interference by others.

Si Subscales

As previously noted, Harris and Lingoes did not attempt to develop subscales for the MMPI basic scales *1, 5, 7,* and *0*. Graham, Schroeder, and Lilly (1971) performed factor analyses of scales *5* and *0* based on the item-level responses of adults in normal and psychiatric settings. Serkownek (1975) utilized the findings from the Graham et al. factor analyses to develop subscales for scales *5* and *0*. The Serkownek subscales received relatively limited clinical attention as applied to adolescents tested using the original version of the MMPI and may not be applicable to the MMPI-A because of the extensive item deletions that occurred for scales *5* and *0*.

Ben-Porath, Hostetler, et al. (1989) developed *Si* scale subscales for the MMPI-2 based on their analyses of the responses of normal college men and women. After creating preliminary scales based on item-level factor analysis, three subscales were developed using procedures to maximize internal consistency (alpha coefficient values) while producing scales that were composed of nonoverlapping or mutually exclusive items. Sieber and Meyer (1992) examined the relationship of the *Si* subscales to a variety of self-report measures believed to be differentially related to these three subscales in a sample of 410 college students. The results of this study provided evidence of the concurrent validity of the *Si* subscales and supported the use of these scales with the MMPI-2. The *Si* subscales developed by Ben-Porath et al. for the MMPI-2 were carried over to the MMPI-A without modification and are grouped with the Harris-Lingoes subscales on a single profile sheet.

TABLE 6.34
Items From the Shyness/Self-Consciousness (Si_1)
Subscale

Examples of items scored if true
160.   Hard to make conversation with strangers.
178.   Dislike being shy.
Example of items scored if false
  46.   Friendly.

Note: MMPI-A abbreviated items reproduced by permission. MMPI-A test booklet copyright © 1992 by the Regents of the University of Minnesota; MMPI-A abbreviated item test booklet copyright © 2004 by the Regents of the University of Minnesota.

TABLE 6.35
Items From the Social Avoidance (Si_2) Subscale

Example of items scored if true
304. Try to avoid crowds.
Examples of items scored if false
82. Like loud parties.
319. Love going to dances.

Note: MMPI-A abbreviated items reproduced by permission. MMPI-A test booklet copyright © 1992 by the Regents of the University of Minnesota; MMPI-A abbreviated item test booklet copyright © 2004 by the Regents of the University of Minnesota.

Si_1 has been labeled *Shyness/Self-Consciousness*, and Table 6.34 provides examples of the abbreviated item content from this subscale. The following characteristics may be associated with elevations on the Si_1 subscale:

- Shy around others and easily embarrassed.
- Ill at ease in social situations.
- Uncomfortable in new situations.

Ben-Porath, Hostetler, et al. (1989) labeled the Si_2 subscale *Social Avoidance*. Table 6.35 shows examples of abbreviated items from this subscale. The following characteristics or features are associated with elevations on this subscale:

- Dislike or avoidance of social activities.
- Avoidance of contact or involvement with others.

The Si_3 subscale was labeled *Alienation–Self and Others*. Table 6.36 provides examples of abbreviated items from this subscale. This Si subscale appears to involve psychiatric symptomatology that interferes with the ability to adaptively engage with or relate to others. The following are characteristics or features that may be associated with elevations on Si_3:

- Low self-esteem and poor self-concept.
- Self-critical and lack of confidence in judgment.
- Nervous, fearful, and indecisive.
- Suspicious or fearful of others.

TABLE 6.36
Items From the Alienation–Self and Others (Si_3) Subscale

Examples of items scored if true
53. Would like to be as happy as others.
107. Most cheat to get ahead.
Examples of items scored if false
None

Note: MMPI-A abbreviated items reproduced by permission. MMPI-A test booklet copyright © 1992 by the Regents of the University of Minnesota; MMPI-A abbreviated item test booklet copyright © 2004 by the Regents of the University of Minnesota.

Thus far in this chapter we have dealt with a variety of scales and subscales designed to augment the interpretation of the MMPI-A basic scales (e.g., the content and supplementary scales) or developed as a means of refining or "breaking out" components of other scales (e.g., content component scales and the Harris-Lingoes and *Si* subscales). We now turn our attention to MMPI-A special scales created to provide a broader or macro view of the individual's psychological functioning, namely, the Personality Psychopathology Five (PSY-5) scales and the MMPI-A Structural Summary.

The Personality Psychopathology Five (PSY-5) Scales

The Personality Psychopathology Five (PSY-5; Harkness & McNulty, 1994) is a descriptive, dimensional model of personality initially designed to complement categorical personality disorder diagnosis. It is one of a number of personality models based on a five-factor conceptual system of hierarchical personality traits. The PSY-5 model was originally applied to the MMPI-2 by Harkness, McNulty, and Ben-Porath (1995) in their development of the PSY-5 scales for this instrument, and the findings on the MMPI-2 PSY-5 scale have recently been summarized by Harkness, McNulty, Ben-Porath, and Graham (2002).

McNulty, Harkness, Ben-Porath, and Williams (1997) examined the MMPI-2 PSY-5 scales and selected 104 items that also appeared in the MMPI-A test booklet. Rational item selection was used to identify additional items from questions uniquely found on the MMPI-A, and preliminary scales were refined using statistical methods designed to increase internal consistency based on the MMPI-A normative sample and the clinical sample reported in the MMPI-A manual (Butcher et al., 1992). The resulting MMPI-A PSY-5 scales were identified as Aggressiveness (*AGGR*), Psychoticism (*PSYC*), Constraint (*CONS*), Negative Emotionality/Neuroticism (*NEGE*), and Positive Emotionality/Extroversion (*EXTR*). The Constraint and Positive Emotionality/Extroversion scales were later reversed and changed to Disconstraint (*DISC*) and Introversion/Low Positive Emotionality (*INTR*), respectively, to facilitate scoring and interpretation. The medium coefficient alpha for the five scales was .76 in both the clinical and normative sample. In addition, data collected from a record review form, the Child Behavior Checklist (CBCL), and the Devereux Adolescent Behavior Rating Scale (DAB) were utilized to explore the correlate patterns for each of these five dimensions. The item composition of the MMPI-A–based PSY-5 scales is shown in Table 6.37. Harkness et al. (1995) note that the PSY-5 scales differ from other MMPI scales in their emphasis on specific personality traits or dispositional differences rather than on major psychopathological dimensions. The data from McNulty and his colleagues (1997), as well as the descriptors provided by Butcher and Williams (2000), suggest the following correlate patterns for each of the PSY-5 scales.

The following characteristics may be associated with elevations on the Aggressiveness (*AGGR*) scale:

- Poor temper control.
- Assaultive or aggressive.
- More likely to exhibit externalizing and acting-out behaviors.

The following characteristics may be associated with elevations on the Psychoticism (*PSYC*) scale:

- More likely to exhibit psychotic-like behaviors.
- More likely to appear anxious and obsessive.

TABLE 6.37
Item Composition of the MMPI-A–based PSY-5 Scales

Scale	Items
Aggressiveness (AGGR)	24, 34, 47, **81**, **128**, 200, 201, 282, **303**, **325**, **334**, **354**, (355), 367, 378, **382**, 453, 458, 461, (465)
Psychoticism (PSYC)	12, **22**, 29, **39**, **45**, **92**, **95**, **132**, **136**, **225**, **250**, **286**, **295**, 296, **299**, **315**, **332**, **337**, (387), **417**, 439
Disconstraint (DISC) (originally named Constraint)	**32**, 69, **80**, (96), **99**, **101**, **117**, (120), 144, 197, 234, (246), (249), **323**, **338**, **361**, **380**, **389**, 440, 456, (457), (460), 462,
Negative Emotionality/ Neuroticism (NEGE)	**49**, (60), **78**, **89**, **111**, (134), **139**, **159**, **185**, (209), **271**, **281**, **285**, **357**, 364, **368**, (375), **383**, **392**, **394**, 412, (424)
Introversion/Low Positive Emotionality (INTR) (originally named Positive Emotionality/Extraversion)	(9), (46), (58), (71), (74), (82), (91), (105), (125), (170), (179), (180), (228), (262), (289), (292), (298), (319), (322), (329), (331), (335), (436), (447), (450), 463, 473, (476)

Note: Items in parentheses are scored if false; all others are scored if true. Items in boldface type also appear on the corresponding MMPI-2–based PSY-5 scale (see Table E-1 in Butcher et al., 1992, for item number conversions). Copyright © 1992 by the Regents of the University of Minnesota. Reproduced by permission.

The following characteristics or features may be associated with elevations on the Disconstraint (*DISC*) scale (originally named the *Constraint scale*):

- More likely to exhibit externalizing behaviors.
- More likely to engage in acting out and drug use.
- More likely to exhibit delinquent behavior.

The following characteristics or features may be associated with elevations on the Negative Emotionality/Neuroticism (*NEGE*) scale:

- Anxious, tense, worried.
- Guilt and remorse.
- Excessive reliance or dependency on adults.

The following characteristics may be associated with elevations on the Introversion (*INTR*) scale (originally named the *Positive Emotionality/Extroversion scale*):

- Social isolation.
- Interpersonally uncommunicative and withdrawn.

Bolinskey, Arnau, Archer, and Handel (2004) recently examined the MMPI-A PSY-5 scales in a sample of 545 adolescents receiving inpatient psychiatric treatment. These researchers employed item-level principal component analyses (PCA) to determine the internal structure of each of the PSY-5 scales and to aid in the creation of facet subscales for each of the PSY-5 scales. Results indicated that the MMPI-A PSY-5 scales, with the exception of the Negative Emotionality/Neuroticism scale, could be meaningfully subdivided into two components, and Table 6.38 shows the item composition and reliability of the PSY-5 domain and facet scores from this study. Overall, results supported the construct validity of the MMPI-A PSY-5 scales and provided a promising set of facet subscales. The authors noted that future research will be needed to establish the external correlate patterns found for the facet subscales as well as to

TABLE 6.38
Item Composition and Reliability of MMPI-A PSY-5 Domain and Facet Scores

Facet	Items	Alpha
AGGR		**.79**
Hostility	24, 34, 81, 128, 201, 282, 303, 354, (355), 367, 453, 458, 461, 465	.76
Grandiosity/Indignation	47, 200, 325, 334, 378, 382	.57
DISC		**.80**
Delinquent Behaviors and Attitudes	32, 80, (96), 101, 144, 197, 234, (246), (249), 323, 338, 361, 380, 440, (460), 467	.77
Norm Violation	69, 99, 117, (120), 389, 456, (457), 462	.57
INTR		**.83**
Low Drive/Expectations	(9), (58), (71), (74), (91), (105), (170), (179), (228), (329), (436), (447), (450), 473	.77
Low Sociability	(46), (82), (125), (180), (262), (289), (292), (298), (319), (322), (331), (335), 463, (476)	.72
PSYC		**.81**
Psychotic Beliefs/Experiences	12, 22, 39, 95, 132, 136, 250, 299, 315, 332, 337, (387), 439	.78
Odd Mentation	29, 45, 92, 296, 417	.59
NEGE[a]		**.78**

Note: Items in parentheses are scored in the false direction. AGGR = Aggressiveness; DISC = Disconstraint; INTR = Introversion/Low Positive Emotionality; PSYC = Psychoticism; NEGE = Negative Emotionality/Neuroticism. From Bolinskey et al. (2004). Copyright © Sage Publications. Reprinted with permission.

[a] Analyses indicated a single factor for NEGE; thus, no facet scales were constructed for this PSY-5 scale.

demonstrate the overall applicability of the PSY-5 constructs to the assessment of adolescents in light of the emphasis by Harkness and McNulty (1994) on personality disorder symptomatology in the original development of these scales.

THE MMPI-A STRUCTURAL SUMMARY

When clinicians used the original form of the MMPI with adolescents, interpretation was typically restricted to the basic clinical scales. In contrast, the MMPI-A presents a much larger number of standardly used scales and subscales that require careful integration in the course of test interpretation. This interpretive process is complicated by the observation that there is a substantial degree of intercorrelation between the MMPI-A basic scales and content scales and also between the MMPI-A content scales themselves (Williams et al., 1992). As a result, several scales provide redundant information concerning an adolescent's personality functioning or psychopathology. For example, the correlation derived from the normative sample between basic scale *1* and the Health Concerns *(A-hea)* content scale is .91 for girls and .90 for boys. Similarly, MMPI-A basic scale *8* and the Bizarre Mentation *(A-biz)* content scale produce a correlation of .78 for girls and .77 for boys, and MMPI-A basic scale *7* and the Anxiety *(A-anx)* content scale show a correlation of .84 for girls and .83 for boys. These patterns of intercorrelation suggest that it would be erroneous to interpret certain pairs of MMPI-A scales (e.g., scale *1* and *A-hea*) as yielding independent information. Given the degree of item overlap and intercorrelation found among various MMPI-A scales, an alternative approach to organizing the extensive information derived from this instrument might prove useful in organizing the test interpretation process. A promising approach to this type of simplification is based on the identification of common factorial dimensions that underlie the complex network of MMPI-A scales and subscales. This approach was inspired by Nichols and Greene (1995) in their work with the MMPI-2 and is directly based on the results of a factor analysis performed with the MMPI-A by Archer, Belevich, and Elkins (1994). The approach taken by Nichols and Greene involved the development of a clinical tool that emphasized the content validity of items, patterns of item overlap, and scale intercorrelations found in adult psychiatric samples. In contrast, the work of Archer, Belevich, et al. (1994) was based exclusively on the use of a factor analytic approach to identifying underlying dimensions within the total of 69 scales and subscales of this instrument. Specifically, these latter authors applied a principal factor analytic procedure to scale raw score values derived for the 1,620 adolescents in the MMPI-A normative sample and identified eight primary dimensions that accounted for 94% of the total variance in these values. The factor structure for these dimensions is presented in Appendix G of this text.

The MMPI-A Dimensions

The first factor of the MMPI-A was labeled *General Maladjustment*. This factor had received substantial attention in prior research investigations of the MMPI. Welsh (1956) found that the first factor of the MMPI was marked by high positive loadings on basic scales 7 and 8 and by a negative loading on scale K. This factor was originally termed *General Maladjustment* by Tyler (1951) and subsequently labeled *Anxiety* by Welsh (1956). The first factor has also been identified in factor analyses of adolescents' item and scale-level responses to the MMPI (Archer, 1984; Archer & Klinefelter, 1991) and the MMPI-A (Archer, Belevich, et al., 1994; Butcher et al., 1992). Thus, the MMPI-A first factor serves to account for the largest component of variance in the test instrument and is popularly identified as *Generalized Distress* or *General Maladjustment*. As shown in Appendix G, in addition to basic scales 2, 4, 7, and 8, this dimension is also related to higher scores on a variety of content scales, including *A-anx*, *A-obs*, *A-dep*, *A-aln*, *A-lse*, and *A-trt*. General Maladjustment is also reflected in elevations in a variety of subscales, including D_1, D_4, and D_5 of the Depression scale; Hy_3 of scale 3; Pd_4 and Pd_5 of scale 4; Pa_2 of scale 6; Sc_1 through Sc_4 of scale 8; and the Si_3 subscale. Adolescents who score high on these dimensions are self-critical, anxious, guilty, depressed, and overwhelmed. Among the best single markers for this dimension in both the MMPI and MMPI-A is Welsh's (1956) Anxiety scale. Adolescents who produce elevations on the General Maladjustment dimension might be expected to show the following characteristics:

- Substantial adjustment problems at school and at home.
- Socially withdrawn, timid, dependent, and self-conscious.
- Depressed, ruminative, and sad.
- Lack of competence and confidence in social activities.
- Avoidance of competitive situations.
- Self-reports of fatigue, tiredness, and sleep difficulty.

The second MMPI-A dimension found by Archer, Belevich, et al. (1994) was labeled *Immaturity* but might also have been referred to as *Unconventional Attitudes and Cognitions*. This dimension included basic scales F, F_1, F_2, 6, and 8; content scales *A-biz*, *A-con*, *A-trt*, *A-aln*, *A-fam*, and *A-sch*; and the supplementary scales *IMM*, *ACK*, and *MAC–R*. Among the Harris-Lingoes subscales, this factor was identified by elevations on the Persecutory Ideas (Pa_1) subscale of the Paranoia (6) scale and on the Emotional Alienation (Sc_2) and Bizarre Sensory Experiences (Sc_6) subscales of the Schizophrenia (8) scale. Among the best markers of this factor are the *IMM* supplementary scale and basic scale *F*. Adolescents who produce elevations on the scales and subscales of the Immaturity factor might be expected to show the following characteristics:

- Limited self-awareness and psychological insight.
- Self-centerdness and egocentricity.
- Poor impulse control and judgment.
- Repeated suspensions and poor academic grades.
- Poor peer relationships marked by bullying, physical aggression, and the use of threats.
- Increased likelihood of delinquent, aggressive, and hyperactive behaviors.

The third dimension identified by Archer, Belevich, et al. (1994) was related to Disinhibition and Excitatory Potential. The characteristics of this dimension appear to reflect adolescents' propensity to engage in impulsive and poorly controlled actions. Among the best markers for this dimension are basic scale 9 and the Harris-Lingoes subscale Psychomotor Acceleration (Ma_2). This dimension was also defined by higher scores on the content scales *A-ang*, *A-cyn*, and *A-con*; the *MAC–R* supplementary scale; and the Harris-Lingoes subscales Lack of Ego Mastery–Defective Inhibition (Sc_5) and Ego Inflation (Ma_4). This factor was also associated with the occurrence of lower scores on validity scales *L* and *K*, supplementary scale *R*, and the Harris-Lingoes Psychomotor Retardation (D_2) subscale. Adolescents who produce critical T-score values on the majority of scales and subscales of this factor are likely to display the following characteristics:

- Impulsivity leading to disciplinary problems.
- Boastful, talkative, loud, and attention-seeking.
- History of poor school achievement and failing grades.
- Greater likelihood of alcohol or drug abuse.
- Dominant or aggressive in interpersonal relationships.
- Conflicts with authority figures and peers.

The fourth dimension derived from factor analysis was initially labeled *Social Comfort* but might also have been labeled *Social Imperturbability*. The qualities of interpersonal relationships reflected in this factor involve low scores on basic scales 0 and 7, the Shyness/Self-Consciousness (Si_1) subscale, and the Social Discomfort (*A-sod*) and Low Self-Esteem (*A-lse*) content scales. This factor was also marked by elevated scores on the Harris-Lingoes subscales of Denial of Social Anxiety (Hy_1), Social Imperturbability (Pd_3), and Imperturbability (Ma_3). Among the best markers for this factor were the Harris-Lingoes subscales Hy_1 and Pd_3. In incorporating this factor dimension into the MMPI-A Structural Summary, the scoring direction of the scales defined by this factor were reversed, and the factor was labeled *Social Discomfort*. This modification was undertaken in order to create a cluster of factors that uniformly measure dimensions of psychopathology. Adolescents who produce critical T-score values on the majority of scales or subscales of this dimension are likely to display the following characteristics:

- Social self-consciousness and withdrawal.
- Fearful, timid, and docile in peer interactions.

- Lower likelihood of acting-out behaviors.
- Increased probability of internalizing behaviors.

The fifth factor derived by Archer, Belevich, et al. (1994) was labeled *Health Concerns* but might also have been entitled *Somatization*. MMPI-A basic scale *1* and the Harris-Lingoes subscale Somatic Complaints (Hy_4) are the best measures of this factor. In addition, basic scale *3*, the Health Concerns (*A-hea*) content scale, and the Harris-Lingoes subscales Physical Malfunctioning (D_3) and Lassitude-Malaise (Hy_3) serve to define this symptom dimension. Adolescents who produce critical-range elevations on the majority of scales and subscales related to this factor are likely to display the following characteristics:

- Fatigability and limited endurance.
- Likelihood of sleeping difficulties, histories of weight loss, and academic problems.
- Dependent and shy.
- Preoccupied with health functioning.
- Social isolation and lower levels of social competence.

The sixth factor yielded in the Archer, Belevich, et al. (1994) study was labeled *Naivete* because the best marker for this factor consisted of the Harris-Lingoes subscale Naivete (Pa_3). This dimension also included elevated scores on basic scale *K* and the Harris-Lingoes subscale Need for Affection (Hy_2) and lower scores on the Cynicism (*A-cyn*) content scale and the Alienation–Self and Others (Si_3) subscale of scale *0*. Adolescents who produce critical-range T-scores on the majority of scales and subscales of this factor are likely to display the following characteristics:

- Emphasis on conventionality and the avoidance of conflict
- Tendency to deny the presence of hostile or negative feelings and impulses.
- Presentation of self as socially conforming, optimistic, and trusting.

The seventh MMPI-A dimension was identified as *Family Alienation* but might also have been labeled *Family Conflict*. The best markers of this dimension are the Harris-Lingoes subscale Familial Discord (Pd_1) and the Family Problems (*A-fam*) content scale. Scores on basic scale *4* and on the Alcohol/Drug Problem Proneness (*PRO*) scale also serve to define this factor. The inclusion of the *PRO* scale in this dimension is probably related to the extensive number of items in this scale dealing with familial discord or family such as abbreviated item 451 ("Family does not have trouble talking to each other") and abbreviated item 57 ("Parents dislike friends"). Adolescents who produce elevations on a majority of the scales of this factor are likely to display the following characteristics:

- Likely to be seen by parents as delinquent, hostile, disobedient, or aggressive.
- Frequent familial conflicts.
- Loud, verbally abusive, or threatening.
- Increased likelihood of disciplinary problems in school resulting in suspensions or probations.

The eighth and last dimension of the MMPI-A scale analysis was labeled *Psychoticism* by Archer, Belevich, et al. (1994). This dimension is best defined by elevations on the Harris-Lingoes subscales Persecutory Ideas (Pa_1) and Bizarre Sensory Experiences

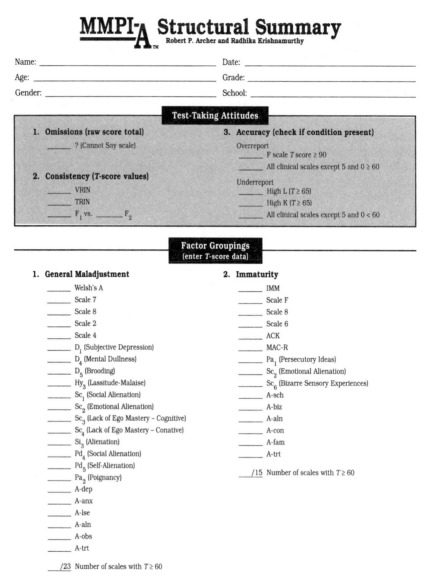

FIG. 6.3. MMPI-A Structural Summary Form. Reprinted by permission. Copyright ©
1994 by Psychological Assessment Resources, Inc.

(Sc_6), basic scale 6, and the Bizarre Mentation (*A-biz*) content scale. Adolescents who
produce elevations on the majority of scales and subscales of this dimension are likely
to show the following characteristics:

- Socially disengaged.
- Higher likelihood of being teased or rejected by peers.
- Poorly controlled expressions of mood, including sudden outbursts of anger.

As previously noted, the eight dimensions or factors described already were based
on factor analyses conducted with the MMPI-A normative sample. This factor structure, organized around the factor groupings presented above has also been adapted

3. Disinhibition/Excitatory Potential

_____ Scale 9

_____ Ma_2 (Psychomotor Acceleration)

_____ Ma_4 (Ego Inflation)

_____ Sc_5 (Lack of Ego Mastery, Defective Inhibition)

_____ D_2 (Psychomotor Retardation) (low score)*

_____ Welsh's R (low score)*

_____ Scale K (low score)*

_____ Scale L (low score)*

_____ A-ang

_____ A-cyn

_____ A-con

_____ MAC-R

___/12 Number of scales with $T \geq 60$ or ≤ 40 for scales with asterisk

4. Social Discomfort

_____ Scale 0

_____ Si_1 (Shyness/Self-Consciousness)

_____ Hy_1 (Denial of Social Anxiety) (low score)*

_____ Pd_3 (Social Imperturbability) (low score)*

_____ Ma_3 (Imperturbability) (low scores)*

_____ A-sod

_____ A-lse

_____ Scale 7

___/8 Number of scales with $T \geq 60$ or $T \leq 40$ for scales with asterisk

5. Health Concerns

_____ Scale 1

_____ Scale 3

_____ A-hea

_____ Hy_4 (Somatic Complaints)

_____ Hy_3 (Lassitude-Malaise)

_____ D_3 (Physical Malfunctioning)

___/6 Number of scales with $T \geq 60$

6. Naivete

_____ A-cyn (low score)*

_____ Pa_3 (Naivete)

_____ Hy_2 (Need for Affection)

_____ Si_3 (Alienation–Self and Others) (low score)*

_____ Scale K

___/5 Number of scales with $T \geq 60$ or $T \leq 40$ for scales with asterisk

7. Familial Alienation

_____ Pd_1 (Familial Discord)

_____ A-fam

_____ Scale 4

_____ PRO

___/4 Number of scales with $T \geq 60$

8. Psychoticism

_____ Pa_1 (Persecutory Ideas)

_____ Scale 6

_____ A-biz

_____ Sc_6 (Bizarre Sensory Experiences)

___/4 Number of scales with $T \geq 60$

Note. The presentation of scales under each factor label is generally organized in a descending order from the best to the least effective marker. Within this overall approach, scales are grouped logically in terms of basic clinical scales, Harris-Lingoes and Si subscales, and content scales. The majority of scales included in this summary sheet were correlated $\geq .60$ or $\leq -.60$ with the relevant factor for the MMPI-A normative sample.

PAR **Psychological Assessment Resources, Inc.**
P.O. Box 998/Odessa, Florida 33556/Toll-Free 1-800-331-TEST

FIG. 6.3. (Continued)

to form the basis of the MMPI-A Structural Summary developed by Archer and Krishnamurthy (1994a). Figure 6.3 presents the Structural Summary of the MMPI-A.

The first section of the Structural Summary organizes information relevant to the evaluation of the validity of the MMPI-A along three dimensions, including the number of item omissions, indices related to response consistency, and indices of response accuracy. The remainder of the Structural Summary presents groupings of MMPI-A scales and subscales organized around the eight factors identified by Archer, Belevich, et al. (1994). Within each factor, scales and subscales are grouped logically within the traditional categories of basic scales, content scales, and supplementary scales. Within each of these groupings, scales are presented in descending order from those measures that have the highest correlation with a particular factor (i.e., those scales and sub-scales serving as the most effective markers) to those scales that show progressively lower correlations with the total factor. With very few exceptions, all of the scales and subscales presented in the Structural Summary produce correlations $\geq .60$ or $\leq -.60$ with their assigned factor. The Structural Summary also presents spaces at the bottom of each factor grouping to derive the total number or percentage of scales that show critical values for a specific factor.

Studies on the MMPI-A Structural Summary

A number of studies have evaluated the replicability and utility of the MMPI-A Structural Summary in varied settings. Archer and Krishnamurthy (1997), for example, examined the scale-level factor structure of the MMPI-A in a clinical sample of 358 adolescents receiving outpatient or inpatient psychiatric services. A principal factor analysis (PFA) was performed using the raw score intercorrelation matrix generated from the 69 scales and subscales of the MMPI-A. The procedure yielded nine factors that accounted for a total of 75.6% of the variance found in scale and subscale raw scores. Results from this clinical sample also replicated 7 of the 8 dimensions of the MMPI-A Structural Summary in terms of producing highly similar factor structures defined by scale and subscale correlation coefficient patterns. Thus, this study demonstrated that the Structural Summary dimensions derived from the MMPI-A normative sample could be replicated among adolescents assessed in clinical settings.

Archer, Bolinksey, Morton, and Farris (2002) also examined the scale-level factor structure of the MMPI-A in a sample of 1610 male juvenile delinquents and reported a seven-factor solution that was largely consistent with the dimensions of the MMPI-A Structural Summary. Specifically, the seven primary factors found in this study accounted for a cumulative total of 79.9% of scale raw score variance, a result quite similar to the total variance accounted for by the nine factors in the clinical investigation by Archer and Krishnamurthy (1997). The seven factors also closely corresponded to the major dimensions represented in the MMPI-A Structural Summary, supporting the generalizability of this model to adolescents assessed in detention and other forensic settings. Morton and Farris (2002) also investigated the MMPI-A Structural Summary factor scores of 655 male delinquents. These scores were compared to the Structural Summary scores produced by the 805 boys in the MMPI-A normative sample. The Structural Summary results for the group of delinquent males was characterized by elevations on Factor 2 (Immaturity), with half of delinquent scores showing elevations on this dimension of at least one standard deviation. Discriminant function analyses suggested that linear combinations of structural summary scores were capable of distinguishing between normative and delinquent adolescents at a level comparable to that achieved by a linear combination of the MMPI-A basic clinical scales. Furthermore, the Structural Summary scores of these adolescents provided incremental validity in distinguishing between the two samples, increasing the positive predictive power by 20% to 40%, in contrast to predictions based solely on combinations of clinical, content, and supplementary scales.

Pogge, Stokes, McGrath, Bilginer, and DeLuca (2002) evaluated the prevalence and correlates of MMPI-A Structural Summary dimensions in a sample of 632 adolescent psychiatric inpatients. These analyses focused on the relationship between factor dimension elevations and scores on external criterion measures derived from chart review data, therapist ratings, chart diagnoses, and cognitive test performance. This examination of the pattern of correlations between the Structural Summary dimensions and external criteria revealed the presence of small to moderate relationships between these constructs and conceptually related criteria. For example, adolescents with elevated General Maladjustment scores had chart ratings suggestive of more severe problems. Additionally, *IMM* scale scores were found to be negatively correlated with full scale IQ scores, and Disinhibition/Excitatory dimension scores were related to a range of impulsive behaviors, including angry outbursts, temper tantrums, and running away in females and cannabis dependence in males. Correlates produced by the health concerns dimension included somatic complaints, lethargy, sleep disturbance, and a higher frequency of eating disorder diagnoses in females. Pogge and his colleagues concluded that Structural Summary dimensions "generally correlate as expected with external criteria in an adolescent psychiatric inpatient sample.... Although perhaps not replacing the traditional scale and codetype analyses, these data suggest that the SS approach may provide valuable assistance in reducing the large and sometimes confusing array of variables provided by the MMPI-A" (p. 341). Further, the Structural Summary dimensions were shown in this study to provide additional interpretive yield for adolescents producing within-normal-limits (WNL) profiles. Specifically, while 25% of this inpatient sample produced WNL basic scale profiles, 29% of this (WNL) group also produced Structural Summary dimensions that yielded interpretable factor scores.

Finally, Krishnamurthy and Archer (1999) undertook a study to empirically evaluate the best method of recording and utilizing the results of the Structural Summary in applied clinical settings. These researchers examined the frequency of single-factor, two-factor, and multifactor elevations in a clinical sample of 363 adolescents receiving inpatient, outpatient, or residential treatment. Two methods of determining factor elevation were compared in this study. One method was based on defining a dimension as elevated simply by verifying that a majority of scales and subscales within a specific factor produced T-score elevations reaching or exceeding a critical T-score level. The alternate approach involved a more complex method of calculating the mean T-score value generated for all the scales and subscales within each factor. The results of this research yielded comparable findings concerning the frequency and pattern of factor elevations, permitting reliance on the former, easier-to-use method to define elevation. Thus the results of this study led to the recommendation that clinicians interpret the MMPI-A Structural Summary based on a practical, common-sense approach in which a factor is defined as important in the comprehensive description of the adolescent simply if the majority of scales and subscales on that dimension show critical-range values. Krishnamurthy and Archer (1999) noted some significant differences in the frequency and pattern of single-factor, two-factor, and multifactor elevations and by gender and diagnosis. For example, boys were more likely than girls to show elevations on Disinhibition. Further, depressed adolescents were more likely to obtain factor elevations on Factor 4 (Social Discomfort) and Factor 5 (Health Concerns) than adolescents with conduct disorder and other diagnoses.

Summary of the Structural Summary Approach

The basic concept underlying the development of the MMPI-A Structural Summary involves the use of this form as a means of parsimoniously organizing the myriad data provided by the MMPI-A to assist the clinician in identifying the most salient dimensions to be utilized in describing an adolescent's personality functioning. Archer and Krishnamurthy (1994b) and Archer and Krishnamurthy (2002) provided a description

TABLE 6.39
Description of the MMPI-A Structural Summary Factors

Factor	Description
General Maladjustment (23 Scales or Subscales)	This factor is associated with substantial emotional distress and maladjustment. Adolescents who score high on this dimension experience significant problems in adjustment at home and school and feel different from other teenagers. They are likely to be self-conscious, socially withdrawn, timid, unpopular, dependent on adults, ruminative, subject to sudden mood changes, and to feel sad or depressed. They are viewed as less competent in social activities and as avoiding competitive situations with peers. Academic problems including low marks and course failures are common. These adolescents are more likely than other teenagers to report symptoms of tiredness or fatigue, sleep difficulties, and suicidal thoughts, and to be referred for counseling and/or psychotherapy.
Immaturity (15 Scales or Subscales)	The Immaturity dimension reflects attitudes and behaviors involving egocentricity and self-centeredness, limited self-awareness and insight, poor judgment and impulse control, and disturbed interpersonal relationships. Adolescents who obtain high scores on this factor often have problems in the school setting involving disobedience, suspensions, and histories of poor school performance. Their interpersonal relationships are marked by cruelty, bullying, and threats, and they often associate with peers who get in trouble. These adolescents act without thinking and display little remorse for their actions. Familial relationships are frequently strained, with an increased occurrence of arguments with parents. Their family lives are also often marked by instability that may include parental separation or divorce. High-scoring boys are more likely to exhibit hyperactive and immature behaviors, whereas girls are prone to display aggressive and delinquent conduct.
Disinhibition Excitatory Potential (12 Scales or Subscales)	High scores in this dimension involve attitudes and excitatory behaviors related to disinhibition and poor impulse control. Adolescents who score high on this factor display significant impulsivity, disciplinary problems, and conflicts with parents and peers. They are perceived as boastful, excessively talkative, unusually loud, and attention-seeking. They display increased levels of heterosexual interest and require frequent supervision in peer contacts. High-scoring adolescents typically have histories of poor school work and failing grades, truancy, disciplinary actions including suspensions, school drop-out, and violations of social norms in the home, school, and social environment. Their interpersonal relationships tend to be dominant and aggressive, and they quickly become negative or resistant with authority figures. These adolescents are likely to engage in alcohol/drug use or abuse. Their behavioral problems include stealing, lying, cheating, obscene language, verbal abuse, fighting, serious disagreements with parents, and running away from home. In general, they may be expected to use externalization as a primary defense mechanism.
Social Discomfort (8 Scales or Subscales)	Adolescents who elevate the scales involved in this dimension are likely to feel withdrawn, self-conscious, and uncertain in social situations, and display a variety of internalizing behaviors. They are frequently bossed or dominated by peers and tend to be fringe participants in social activities. These adolescents are typically perfectionistic and avoid competition with peers. They are viewed by others as fearful, timid, passive or docile, and acting young for their age. They may present complaints of tiredness, apathy, loneliness, suicidal ideation, and somatic complaints. These adolescents have a low probability of acting-out behaviors including disobedience, alcohol or drug use, stealing, or behavioral problems in school.

(Continued)

TABLE 6.39
(Continued)

Factor	Description
Health Concerns (6 Scales or Subscales)	Adolescents who obtain high scores on the Health Concerns dimension are seen by others as dependent, socially isolated, shy, sad, and unhappy. They are prone to tire quickly and have relatively low levels of endurance. They may display a history of weight loss and report sleep difficulties, crying spells, suicidal ideation, and academic problems. A history of sexual abuse may be present. High-scoring boys are likely to be viewed as exhibiting schizoid withdrawal whereas high-scoring girls are primarily seen as somatizers. These adolescents typically display lower levels of social competence in the school setting. They are unlikely to be involved in antisocial behaviors or have histories of arrests.
Naivete (5 Scales or Subscales)	High scores on the Naivete factor are produced by adolescents who tend to deny the presence of hostile or negative impulses and present themselves in a trusting, optimistic, and socially conforming manner. They may be described as less likely to be involved in impulsive, argumentative, or socially inappropriate behaviors, and are more often seen as presenting in an age-appropriate manner. They have a low probability of experiencing internalizing symptoms such as nervousness, fearfulness, nightmares, and feelings of worthlessness, or of acting-out and provocative behaviors including lying or cheating, disobedience, and obscene language.
Familial Alienation (4 Scales or Subscales)	Adolescents who score high on scales or subscales related to this dimension are more likely to be seen by their parents as hostile, delinquent, or aggressive, and as utilizing externalizing defenses. They are also viewed as being loud, verbally abusive, threatening, and disobedient at home. These adolescents tend to have poor parental relationships involving frequent and serious conflicts with their parents. Presenting problems in psychiatric settings may include histories of running away from home, sexual abuse, and alcohol/drug use. In addition to family conflicts, high-scoring adolescents are also more likely to have disciplinary problems at school resulting in suspensions and probationary actions.
Psychoticism (4 Scales or Subscales)	Adolescents who produce elevations on the Psychoticism factor are more likely to be seen by others as obsessive, socially disengaged, and disliked by peers. They may feel that others are out to get them, and are more likely to be teased and rejected by their peer group. Sudden mood changes and poorly modulated expressions of anger are likely. They may also exhibit disordered behaviors including cruelty to animals, property destruction, and fighting, and are likely to have histories of poor academic achievement.

Note: Reprinted from Archer, Krishnamurthy, and Jacobson (1994), *MMPI-A Casebook*, pp. 17–18. Copyright © 1994 by Psychological Assessment Resources, Inc. Reprinted by permission.

of the empirical correlates of the MMPI-A Structural Summary factors based on an investigation of the 1,620 adolescents in the MMPI-A normative sample and an inpatient sample of 122 adolescent respondents. A comprehensive presentation of all external correlates of the Structural Summary factors is provided in the *MMPI-A Casebook* by Archer, Krishnamurthy, and Jacobson (1994), and a narrative summary of these correlates is provided in Table 6.39. The research on the MMPI-A Structural Summary to date has generally been encouraging in terms of the ability to replicate this factor structure across diverse settings involving normal, clinical, and delinquent groups of adolescents and the capacity of the Structural Summary variables to generate correlate patterns that support the construct validity of these factors.

At this time, the MMPI-A Structural Summary is best used as a means of most effectively focusing the clinician's attention on the basic dimensions of overall importance in describing the adolescent's functioning. Archer and Krishnamurthy (1994b, 2002) recommended that more than half of the scales and subscales associated with a particular factor should reach critical values before an interpreter emphasizes that MMPI-A dimension as salient in describing the adolescent's functioning. Further, it seems reasonable to assume that the higher the percentage of scales or subscales within a factor that produce critical values, the greater the role of that particular factor in providing a comprehensive description of the adolescent. These two guidelines (i.e., a majority of scales within a factor must reach critical values in order to emphasize that factor, and the more scales endorsed, the greater the relative salience of the dimension) currently serve as the best practical advice for clinicians utilizing this approach. The findings of Krishnamurthy and Archer (1999) also indicate that a simple "check mark" system of identifying critically elevated scales serves as an effective mechanism for deriving the percentage of markers that show critical values. Archer and Krishnamurthy (2002) have recently suggested that it is possible to examine the specific pattern of elevated scales or subscales within a factor grouping to usefully refine the MMPI-A interpretation for an adolescent. For example, an adolescent may produce a pattern of scale or subscale elevations on the General Maladjustment factor (Factor 1) that highlight depression as the primary form of emotional distress, in contrast to anxiety, alienation, or other components of the first factor. Further, as noted by Archer and Krishnamurthy (2002), it may eventually be feasible to develop a configural pattern approach to the interpretation of the Structural Summary dimensions that is analogous to configural interpretation approaches utilized with basic scales. For example, it is possible that conduct disorder symptomatology might be best identified by co-occurring elevations on the dimensions of Immaturity, Disinhibition/Excitatory Potential, and Familial Alienation, whereas neurotic or internalizing symptomatology might be most effectively identified by elevations on the General Maladjustment and Social Discomfort dimensions. Future research is clearly needed, however, to support the use of this configural approach in clinical applications.

Use of the MMPI-A in Forensic Evaluations

The description of the MMPI-A scales and subscales presented thus far underscores that this instrument was intended for use in psychodiagnostic evaluations of adolescents in clinical treatment settings rather than for the description of normal adolescents' personality functioning. In addition to evaluating psychopathology in inpatient, outpatient, and residential treatment facilities, the MMPI-A can also be utilized in evaluating adolescents in specialized settings. For example, the MMPI-A has been widely used in the assessment of adolescent substance abusers, eating disordered adolescents, and sexually abused adolescents (Archer & Krishnamurthy, 2002). Indeed, there is a substantive research literature supporting the applicability of the test instrument in these and numerous other settings (Butcher et al., 1992).

This chapter focuses on the rapidly growing use of the MMPI-A as an important component of the forensic evaluation of adolescents. As shown in Fig. 7.1, the number of children and adolescents handled by juvenile courts has increased by more than fourfold since 1960 (Snyder & Sickmund, 1999). This increase in the number of adolescents processed in the juvenile justice system, combined with changes in this system as a result of Supreme Court decisions and modifications in state statutes, has created a greatly expanded role for psychological and forensic assessments in this setting. The chapter begins with a general overview of the juvenile justice system, then reviews the applications of the MMPI-A in juvenile justice settings as well as other forensic settings such as personal injury litigation and child custody hearings. It concludes with a discussion of the various components typically found in juvenile forensic assessments and the relative advantages of using the MMPI-A as one component of the forensic evaluation process.

OVERVIEW OF JUVENILE CRIME STATISTICS

Drawing on a number of important statistical summaries periodically released by the US Department of Justice and the Federal Bureau of Investigation (FBI), Godwin and Helms (2002) recently provided a comprehensive overview of the perceptions and the realities of crime committed by adolescents in the United States. These authors note that the popular media have often overemphasized the involvement of adolescents in criminal activities, in contrast to empirical data showing an actual reduction in

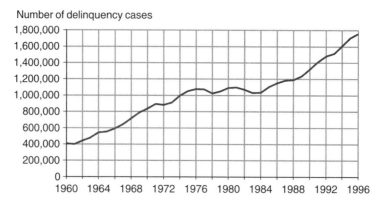

FIG. 7.1. Number of delinquency cases processed by juvenile courts 1960–1996. From Snyder and Sickmund (1999). *Juvenile Offenders and Victims: 1999 National Report.* Office of Juvenile Justice and Delinquency Prevention, U.S. Department of Justice. Reprinted by permission.

juvenile crime rates since the mid-1990s. For example, even in the mid-1990s, before juvenile crime rates began to ebb, 94% of the approximately 69,000,000 youths under the age of 18 in the United States had no history of arrest, and less than 10% of all youthful offenders had been arrested for violent crime. Further, Godwin and Helms reported that data from the FBI's Uniform Crime Reports for the period 1994 through 1999 showed a 31% decline in rape, a 53% decline in robbery, and a 39% decline in juvenile arrests for weapon violations. Additionally, the same five-year period saw a 24% decrease in the arrest rate for aggravated assault. Further, data shown in Table 7.1 from the National Center for Juvenile Justice (Snyder, 2003) showed a 62% decrease in juvenile arrest rates for murder and manslaughter for the period 1992 through 2001, a 40% decrease in burglary, and a 51% decrease in auto theft. Nevertheless, as shown in Fig. 7.2, juveniles accounted for 17% of all arrests in 2001 (Snyder, 2003).

As shown in Fig. 7.3, a higher percentage of juveniles aged 14 through 17 tend to be detained after arrest than children and adolescents 13 years old and younger. Figure 7.4, based on data from 1999 presented by Snyder (2003), shows that crime increases with the age of the juvenile across four broad offense categories.

Statistical data reviewed by Godwin and Helms (2002) also reflect several other notable trends in the relationship between demographic variables and adolescent crime. For example, children who begin offending before age 12 are 2 to 3 times more likely to eventually commit violent, serious crimes than adolescents whose offense history begins later in their adolescence. While juvenile crime traditionally has been viewed as involving males, the number of juvenile court cases involving females increased 83% in the period 1990 through 1999 (U.S. Department of Justice, Office of Juvenile Justice and Delinquency Prevention, 2000). Table 7.2 illustrates this point and shows that 26% of all juvenile arrests in the United States in 1997 involved females, including the majority of arrests for offenses involving running away from home and prostitution (Snyder & Sickmund, 1999).

There is also substantial research indicating that adolescents from minority ethnic and/or racial groups represent increasingly larger proportions of the juvenile offender population in the United States. For example, African-American juveniles are held in custody at a markedly higher rate than other ethnic and racial groups, and the proportion of African-American juveniles in the juvenile justice system is expected to

TABLE 7.1
The Number of Juvenile Arrests in 2001—2.3 Million—Was 4% Below the 2000 Level and 20% Below the 1997 Level

Most Serious Offense	2001 Estimated Number of Juvenile Arrests	Percent of Total Juvenile Arrests		Percent Change		
		Female	Under Age 15	1992–2001	1997–2001	2000–2001
Total	**2,273,500**	28%	32%	−3%	−20%	−4%
Crime Index total	587,900	29	73	−31	−28	−5
Violent Crime Index	96,500	18	33	−21	−21	−2
Murder and nonnegligent manslaughter	1,400	10	12	−62	−47	−2
Forcible rape	4,600	1	38	−24	−14	−1
Robbery	25,600	9	24	−32	−35	−4
Aggravated assault	64,900	23	37	−14	−13	−1
Property Crime Index	491,400	31	38	−32	−29	−6
Burglary	90,300	12	38	−40	−30	−6
Larceny-theft	343,600	39	39	−27	−30	−6
Motor vehicle theft	48,200	17	25	−51	−26	−2
Arson	9,300	12	64	−7	−9	8
Nonindex						
Other assaults	239,000	32	43	30	−2	2
Forgery and counterfeiting	5,800	36	11	−27	−26	−8
Fraud	8,900	33	16	−5	−18	−9
Embezzlement	1,800	44	7	152	24	−10
Stolen property (buying, receiving, possessing)	26,800	17	27	−45	−37	−6
Vandalism	105,300	13	44	−29	−22	−7
Weapons (carrying, possessing, etc.)	37,500	11	34	−35	−26	0
Prostitution and commercialized vice	1,400	69	15	−8	−5	15
Sex offenses (except forcible rape and prostitution)	18,000	8	54	−10	6	1
Drug abuse violations	202,500	15	17	121	−7	0
Gambling	1,400	3	13	−53	−47	−17
Offenses against the family and children	9,600	37	37	109	−11	6
Driving under the influence	20,300	18	5	35	5	−3
Liquor law violations	138,100	32	10	21	−9	−11
Drunkenness	20,400	21	13	4	−21	−10
Disorderly conduct	171,700	30	40	34	−21	1
Vagrancy	2,300	19	25	−37	−24	−10
All other offenses (except traffic)	397,200	26	28	27	−13	−3
Suspicion	1,300	36	33	−53	−42	9
Curfew and loitering	142,900	31	28	34	−29	−13
Runaways	133,300	59	38	−25	−30	−6

- In 2001, there were an estimated 1,400 juvenile arrests for murder. Between 1997 and 2001, juvenile arrests for murder fell 47%.
- Females accounted for 23% of juvenile arrests for aggravated assault and 32% of juvenile arrests for other assaults (i.e., simple assaults and intimidations) in 2001. Females were involved in 59% of all arrests for running away from home and 31% of arrests for curfew and loitering law violations.
- Between 1992 and 2001, there were substantial declines in juvenile arrests for murder (62%), motor vehicle theft (51%), and burglary (40%) and major increases in juvenile arrests for drug abuse violations (121%).

Note: Detail may not add to totals because of rounding.

Data Source: Crime in the United States 2001 (Washington, DC: U.S. government Printing Office, 2002), tables 29, 32, 34, 36, 38, and 40. Arrest estimates were developed by the National Center for Juvenile Justice. From Snyder (2003). Juvenile Justice Bulletin. Office of Juvenile Justice and Delinquency Prevention, U.S. Department of Justice. Reprinted by permission.

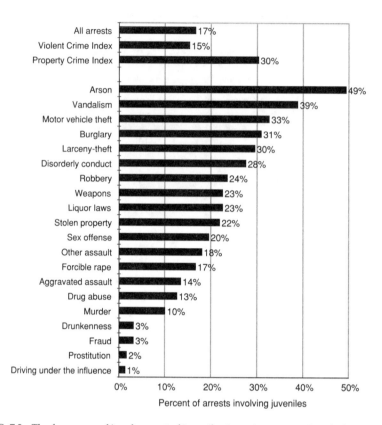

FIG. 7.2. The frequency of involvement of juveniles in various categories of crime given as an overall percent of total arrests for that category in the year 2001. From Snyder (2003). *Juvenile Justice Bulletin*. Office of Juvenile Justice and Delinquency Prevention, U.S. Department of Justice. Reprinted by permission.

Profile of detainees by age

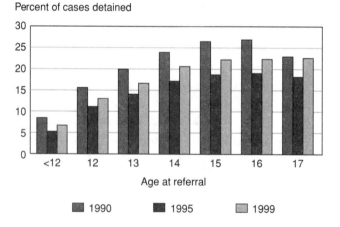

FIG. 7.3. Percentage of juveniles detained during the years 1990, 1995, and 1999 by chronological age. From Harms (2003). *Detention in Delinquency Cases, 1990–1999*. Office of Juvenile Justice and Delinquency Prevention, U.S. Department of Justice. Reprinted by permission.

Case rates increased continuously with age for all offenses in 1999

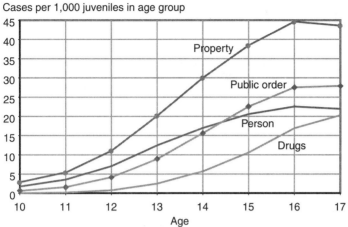

FIG. 7.4. Case rates for various categories of offenses in 1999 by age of adolescent at time of offense. From Puzzanchera, Stahl, Finnegan, Tierney, and Snyder (2003). *Juvenile Court Statistics 1999*. Office of Juvenile Justice and Delinquency Prevention, U.S. Department of Justice. Reprinted by permission.

increase in the future substantially faster than their White juvenile counterparts (Snyder & Sickmund, 1999). The data in Table 7.2 also show the percentage of African-American juveniles arrested for various types of offenses in 1997. Further, for the period 1992 through 1996, more than 75% of all youths newly admitted to state prison facilities were racial or ethnic minorities, and 6 out of 10 youths held in public facilities and 7 out of 10 held in custody for violent offenses were minorities. As noted by Snyder and Sickmund (1999), these data may not solely reflect the influence of ethnic differences in offense rates but may be confounded with the effects of socioeconomic status. Adolescents from more disadvantaged socioeconomic classes are more likely to be placed in the juvenile justice system, whereas adolescents from more privileged backgrounds are likely to be dealt with through alternative methods, including placement in mental health systems and private residential treatment facilities.

Types of Juvenile Offenses

In order to understand criminal behavior among adolescents, it is useful to briefly review the types of crimes committed by juveniles and the ways in which the justice system responds to these norm violations by juveniles. In 1646, Massachusetts passed the "Stubborn Child Law," which created the first status offense, defined as an act viewed as illegal because of the individual's age and status as a minor (Drowns & Hess, 2000). Status offenses, therefore, are offenses viewed as inappropriate solely because of the individual's age, and in most states the age limit for a status offense is set at 18, although some acts (e.g., alcohol consumption) are more typically deemed illegal until the individual reaches age 21. Other status offenses include truancy, violating curfew, running away, and engaging in conduct or behavior that is beyond parental control. Godwin and Helms (2002) observed that running away from home is the status offense most typically committed by female offenders. Further, for juveniles over the age of 16, the most likely status offense is alcohol violation, whereas for juveniles

TABLE 7.2

Law Enforcement Agencies in the U.S. Made 2.8 Million Arrests of Persons Under Age 18 in 1997

The most serious charge in over 40% of all juvenile arrests in 1997 was larceny-theft, simple assault, drug abuse violation, or disorderly conduct.

Most Serious Offense Charged	1997 Juvenile Arrest Estimates	Percent of Total Juvenile Arrests					
		Female	Ages 16–17	White	Black	American Indian	Asian
Total	2,838,300	26%	48%	71%	26%	1%	2%
Violent Crime Index	123,400	16	51	53	44	1	2
Murder and nonnegligent manslaughter	2,500	6	74	40	58	0	2
Forcible rape	5,500	2	45	56	42	1	1
Robbery	39,500	9	54	42	55	1	2
Aggravated assault	75,900	21	49	60	38	1	1
Property Crime Index	701,500	28	41	70	27	1	2
Burglary	131,000	10	43	73	24	1	2
Larceny-theft	493,900	34	40	70	26	1	2
Motor vehicle theft	66,600	16	51	59	37	2	2
Arson	10,000	11	20	79	19	1	1
Nonindex							
Other assaults	241,800	29	41	63	34	1	1
Forgery and counterfeiting	8,500	39	75	77	20	1	2
Fraud	11,300	35	71	69	29	1	1
Embezzlement	1,400	45	88	63	34	1	2
Stolen property (buying, receiving, possessing)	39,500	13	54	60	37	1	2
Vandalism	136,500	12	38	80	17	1	1
Weapons (carrying, possessing, etc.)	52,200	9	51	64	33	1	2
Prostitution and commercialized vice	1,400	56	70	60	39	1	1
Sex offenses (except forcible rape and prostitution)	18,500	9	33	70	28	1	1
Drug abuse violations	220,700	13	66	64	34	1	1
Gambling	2,600	3	69	10	89	0	1
Offenses against family and children	10,200	37	45	76	20	1	2
Driving under the influence	19,600	17	93	91	6	2	1
Liquor laws	158,500	30	74	90	5	3	1
Drunkenness	24,100	17	72	89	9	2	1
Disorderly conduct	215,100	26	46	64	34	1	1
Vagrancy	3,100	15	56	68	31	1	0
All other offenses (except traffic)	468,000	24	53	72	25	1	2
Suspicion	1,600	23	60	60	39	0	1
Curfew and loitering law violations	182,700	31	48	75	23	1	1
Runaways	196,100	58	33	77	18	1	4
U.S. population ages 10–17	30,640,000	49	25	79	15	1	4

- Five percent of juvenile arrests in 1997 were for the violent crimes of aggravated assault, robbery, forcible rape, or murder.
- While black youth accounted for 15% of the juvenile population in 1997, they were involved in more than half of the arrests for gambling (89%), murder (58%), and robbery (55%).
- Females accounted for the majority of juvenile arrests for running away from home (58%) and prostitution (56%).

Note: UCR data do not distinguish the ethnic group Hispanic; Hispanics may be of any race. In 1997, 91% of Hispanics ages 10–17 were classified racially as white. Detail may not add to totals because of rounding.

Source: Authors' analyses of data presented in the FBI's *Crime in the United States 1997*. National estimates of juvenile arrests were developed using FBI estimates of total arrests and juvenile arrest proportions in reporting sample. From Snyder and Sickmund (1999). *Juvenile Offenders and Victims: 1999 National Report*. Office of Juvenile Justice and Delinquency Prevention, U.S. Department of Justice. Reprinted with permission.

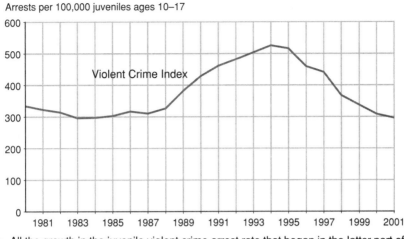

Arrests per 100,000 juveniles ages 10–17

♦ All the growth in the juvenile violent crime arrest rate that began in the latter part of the 1980s was erased by 2001.

FIG. 7.5. Juvenile violent crime rate for the years 1981 through 2001. From Snyder (2003). *Juvenile Justice Bulletin.* Office of Juvenile Justice and Delinquency Prevention, U.S. Department of Justice. Reprinted by permission.

under the age of 15, the most likely offense is truancy. In general, girls are more likely than boys to be arrested for status offenses. For example, 23% of juvenile female arrests in 1966 were for status offenses, whereas only 10% of male arrests in the same year were related to status offenses (Regoli & Hewitt, 2000).

The Uniform Crime Reports from the FBI present data within broad crime categories to allow useful trending across time. The two major indices included in the reports are the Violent Crime Index and the Property Crime Index. The Violent Crime Index includes the offenses of murder, manslaughter, robbery, aggravated assault, and forcible rape. As shown in Fig. 7.5, arrest rates for juveniles in 2001 were slightly below the rate of arrests for violent crimes in 1980, but serious crime saw a substantial decline from the peak recorded for juveniles in 1994 (Snyder, 2003). Between 1987 and 1994, for example, the Violent Crime Index more than doubled among female juveniles and increased by 64% among male juveniles. The decrease in violent crimes shown since the mid-1990s has predominantly reflected a decrease for male juveniles (Snyder, 2000). According to data released by the U.S. Department of Justice, Office of Juvenile Justice and Delinquency Prevention (2000), juveniles were arrested more frequently in 1999 for robbery than for any other crime included in the Violent Crime Index. Twenty-five percent of all persons arrested for robbery in 1999 were under the age of 18, and juveniles represented 17% of all arrests for rape, 14% of all arrests for aggravated assault, and 9% of all murder arrests (Snyder, 2000).

The Property Crime Index includes offenses such as larceny, burglary, arson, and auto theft and other crimes in which no threat of force against the victims occurred during the commission of the crime. Juveniles were involved in 32% of all arrests for property crimes in 1999, and approximately one in three juvenile arrests was related to property crimes (Godwin & Helms, 2002). Figure 7.6 shows that the rate of juvenile arrests for property crimes remained fairly constant from 1981 through 1994 and underwent an overall decline from 1995 to 2001 (Snyder, 2003).

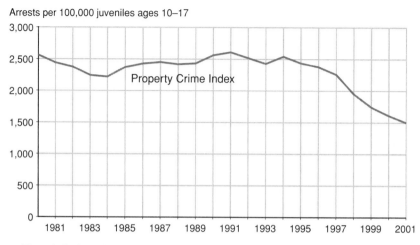

Arrests per 100,000 juveniles ages 10–17

◆ The relatively stable juvenile arrest rate trend between 1980 and the mid-1990s for Property Crime Index offenses stands in stark contrast to the Violent Crime Index arrest rate trend.

FIG. 7.6. Juvenile arrest rate for property crimes for the years 1981 through 2001. From Snyder (2003). *Juvenile Justice Bulletin*. Office of Juvenile Justice and Delinquency Prevention, U.S. Department of Justice. Reprinted by permission.

Societal Responses to Juvenile Crime

Any discussion of societal responses to juvenile offenses must include the phenomenon of *waiver* of jurisdiction of juveniles to an adult criminal court. Since the 1920s, some states have allowed juveniles to be transferred to an adult criminal court in cases that meet certain specific offense criteria. Transfer to an adult criminal court based on the waiver of adjudication from a juvenile court is typically reserved for those juveniles who commit habitual violent offenses and/or are viewed as a serious threat to the safety of the community. Grisso (1997), however, noted that recent trends in the United States have placed an increasingly wider subset of adolescents at jeopardy for transfer to adult criminal courts. Data for the period 1990 through 1996, for example, indicate that at least 40 states had passed legislation to expand the range of juvenile cases that may be transferred to adult courts. Table 7.3 shows the minimum age specified in state statutes for the transfer of juveniles to adult criminal courts (Snyder & Sickmund, 1999).

Godwin and Helms (2002) observed that there are a variety of procedures for transfers or waivers, and criminal courts may obtain jurisdiction in a juvenile case through any one of several procedures. Discretionary juvenile waiver is a process in which the juvenile court judge, on the basis of his or her review of the individual youth and the seriousness of the offense, renders a discretionary decision to waive jurisdiction over the youth and transfer him or her to an adult criminal court. Dawson (2000) noted that, as of 1998, 45 states and the District of Columbia have some form of discretionary judicial waiver. Statutory exclusion is a mechanism that requires youths to be charged automatically and exclusively in a criminal court if arrested for certain classes of serious crime, typically offenses such as murder, assault with a firearm, or aggravated sexual assault. Additionally, there is the process of reverse judicial waiver, which was available in 23 states as of 1997. This procedure is used by a criminal court judge to

TABLE 7.3
Minimum Age for Transfer of Juveniles to Criminal Court by State

In most states, no minimum age is specified in at least one judicial waiver, concurrent jurisdiction, or statutory exclusion provision for transferring juveniles to criminal court.

Minimum Transfer Age Indicated in Section(s) of Juvenile Code Specifying Transfer Provisions, 1997

No Minimum Age		10	12	13	14	15
Alaska	Nevada*	Kansas	Colorado	Illinois	Alabama	New Mexico
Arizona	Oklahoma*	Vermont	Missouri	Mississippi	Arkansas	
Delaware	Oregon*		Montana	New Hampshire	California	
Dist. of	Pennsylvania			New York	Connecticut	
Columbia	Rhode Island			North Carolina	Iowa	
Florida	South Carolina			Wyoming	Kentucky	
Georgia*	South Dakota				Louisiana	
Hawaii	Tennessee				Massachusetts	
Idaho*	Washington*				Michigan	
Indiana	West Virginia				Minnesota	
Maine	Wisconsin				New Jersey	
Maryland					North Dakota	
Nebraska					Ohio	
					Texas	
					Utah	
					Virginia	

*Other sections of state statute specify an age below which children cannot be tried in criminal court. This minimum age for criminal responsibility is 14 in Idaho, 12 in Georgia, 8 in Nevada and Washington, and 7 in Oklahoma. In Washington, 8- to 12-year-olds are presumed to be incapable of committing a crime. In Oklahoma, in cases involving 7- to 14-year-olds, the state must prove that at the time of the act, the child knew it was wrong.

Source: Authors' adaptation of Griffin et al.'s *Trying Juveniles as Adults in Criminal Court: An Analysis of State Transfer Provisions.*

Note: From Snyder and Sickmund (1999). *Juvenile Offenders and Victims: 1999 National Report.* Office of Juvenile Justice and Delinquency Prevention, U.S. Department of Justice. Reprinted with permission.

reverse the placement of the case back to juvenile court. This process is available in nearly half of the states that use statutory exclusion procedures to allow for placing a defendant back in the juvenile court system if the defendant appears to warrant this treatment. Godwin and Helms (2002) noted that a number of states have a blended system that combines elements of the juvenile and adult criminal justice systems. In some states, for example, a juvenile who commits a serious offense may be sentenced to placement in an adult correctional facility, but implementation of that sentence may be suspended based on the adolescent's subsequent behavior in a juvenile justice rehabilitation program.

OVERVIEW OF THE JUVENILE JUSTICE SYSTEM

Comprehensive overviews of the juvenile justice system in the United States typically begin with the establishment of the first juvenile courts in Cook County, Illinois, in 1899. Grisso (1998) noted that within 30 years almost all states had followed Chicago's model of enacting special laws in a system of rehabilitative services developed specifically for youthful offenders. The purpose of this early juvenile justice system was primarily rehabilitation rather than punishment and retribution. The objective of a juvenile court was to act as a *prens patriae*, or wise and benevolent father, in providing direction and correction for wayward youths. Consistent with this overall policy, juvenile courts essentially functioned as social service agencies. Juveniles were typically exempted from criminal court adjudication based on the presumption that they were unable to engage in behaviors involving criminal intent because of their age and development. As a corollary of this, juvenile courts were allowed to make decisions about youths without the usual legal constraints associated with due process that applied to criminal court proceedings for adults. Due process protections were largely considered irrelevant because youths in juvenile courts were not convicted of crimes, nor were they punished for their wrong doings. Rather, the purpose of these juvenile courts was to "correct" and rehabilitate juveniles so that their antisocial behaviors did not inevitably lead to adult criminality.

Grisso (1998) noted that two major areas of reform have led to profound changes in laws and procedures for juveniles, creating a modern system that is quite different from the juvenile justice system that existed in the United States in the early half of the 20th century. First, there was a set of reforms brought about by several U.S. Supreme Court decisions beginning in the 1960s. Second, a series of changes in juvenile laws occurred in almost all states during the 1990s in response to the popular perception of an increasing wave of violent offenses committed by juveniles.

Figure 7.7 presents a summary of U.S. Supreme Court decisions that shaped juvenile justice procedures and processes. In the mid-1960s, the U.S. Supreme Court rendered two important decisions, in *Kent v. U.S.* (1966) and *In re Gault* (1967), that signaled that the juvenile justice system could not continue to function in the informal

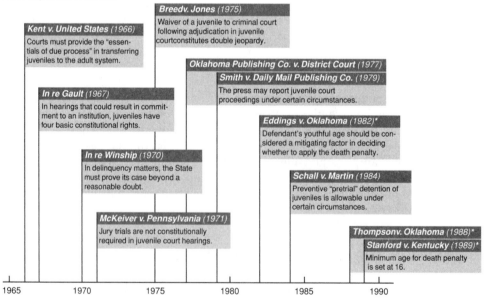

A series of U.S. Supreme Court decisions made juvenile courts more like criminal courts but maintained some important differences

Breed v. Jones (1975)
Waiver of a juvenile to criminal court following adjudication in juvenile court constitutes double jeopardy.

Kent v. United States (1966)
Courts must provide the "essentials of due process" in transferring juveniles to the adult system.

Oklahoma Publishing Co. v. District Court (1977)
Smith v. Daily Mail Publishing Co. (1979)
The press may report juvenile court proceedings under certain circumstances.

In re Gault (1967)
In hearings that could result in commitment to an institution, juveniles have four basic constitutional rights.

Eddings v. Oklahoma (1982)*
Defendant's youthful age should be considered a mitigating factor in deciding whether to apply the death penalty.

In re Winship (1970)
In delinquency matters, the State must prove its case beyond a reasonable doubt.

Schall v. Martin (1984)
Preventive "pretrial" detention of juveniles is allowable under certain circumstances.

McKeiver v. Pennsylvania (1971)
Jury trials are not constitutionally required in juvenile court hearings.

Thompson v. Oklahoma (1988)*
Stanford v. Kentucky (1989)*
Minimum age for death penalty is set at 16.

1965   1970   1975   1980   1985   1990
*Death penalty case decisions are discussed in chapter 7.

FIG. 7.7. U.S. Supreme Court decisions from 1965 through 1990 affecting juvenile courts and the juvenile justice system. From Snyder and Sickmund (1999). *Juvenile Offenders and Victims: 1999 National Report.* Office of Juvenile Justice and Delinquency Prevention, U.S. Department of Justice. Reprinted by permission.

TABLE 7.4
Themes and Trends in New Laws Targeting Violent or Other Serious Crime by Juveniles

Themes	Trends
Jurisdictional authority	More serious and violent juvenile offenders are being removed from the juvenile justice system in favor of criminal court prosecution.
Judicial Disposition/ sentencing authority	More state legislatures are experimenting with new disposition/ sentencing options.
Correctional programming	Correctional administrators are under pressure to develop programs as a result of new transfer and sentencing laws.
Confidentiality of juvenile court records and proceedings	Traditional confidentiality provisions are being revised in favor of more open proceedings and records.
Victims of juvenile crime	Victims of juvenile crime are being included as "active participants" in the juvenile justice process.

Note: Reprinted from Torbet et al. (1996). *State Responses to Serious and Violent Juvenile Crime.* Office of Juvenile Justice and Delinquency Prevention, U.S. Department of Justice. Reprinted with permission.

manner established during the first half of the century. *Kent* involved the claim that youths should have several of the same procedural due process rights associated with adult criminal proceedings when faced with hearings that could potentially lead to their transfer to adult criminal courts for trial. The question addressed in *Gault* was whether juveniles should have several basic rights, including the right to avoid self-incrimination and to consult legal counsel when questioned by police, in a manner similar to that affirmed by the Court for adults in the *Miranda v. Arizona* (1966) decision. As a consequence of both these cases, along with a series of subsequent decisions in the 1970s and 1980s, the constitutional rights of juveniles were clarified, and an increased burden was placed on states to prove their allegations in delinquency cases. Grisso (1998) summarized this latter issue by observing that "the juvenile court could not continue to take custody of delinquent youths without providing them the rights that would protect them against unlawful deprivation of freedom by the state" (p. 4).

The second set of changes in the objectives and processes of the juvenile justice system occurred in response to the increase in violent juvenile crimes that began in the latter part of the 1980s and extended to the mid-1990s. Societal concern arising from the perception of increasing numbers of potentially violent and undercontrolled adolescents led to changes in state criminal statutes, primarily changes allowing greater punitive actions in juvenile cases involving serious violent offenses. A summary of these changes is presented in Table 7.4. These statutory changes included modifications to make it easier to waive juveniles to criminal court for trial as adults and the creation of extended sentences for youths retained for adjudication in the juvenile court system.

The Typical State Juvenile Justice System

Every state has a juvenile justice system that is designed to respond to juvenile offenders in a manner consistent with the state statutes. As noted by Grisso (1998), clinical psychologists working in forensic systems (adolescent or adult) must be aware of the statutory requirements and code variations in their own state. However, state juvenile justice systems across the United States typically include the basic features shown in Fig. 7.8. For example, all states have secured detention centers where youths may be temporarily held prior to their adjudication. Further, most states have criteria to

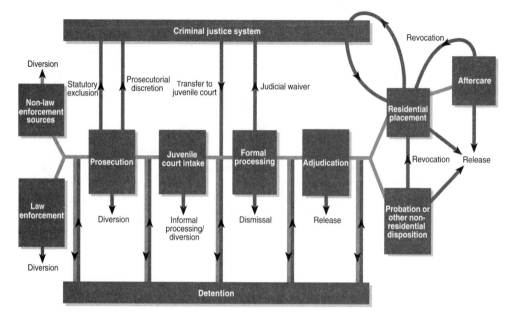

FIG. 7.8. Case flow diagram for typical juvenile justice systems. From Snyder and Sickmund (1999). *Juvenile Offenders and Victims: 1999 National Report*. Office of Juvenile Justice and Delinquency Prevention, U.S. Department of Justice. Reprinted by permission.

determine which youths should be detained prior to trial, based on such factors as the seriousness of the offense or the probability of reoffense should the juvenile be returned to the community. Many juveniles are retained in a detention center for only a few days, during which an evaluation is conducted; they are then returned to the community to await trial. Another smaller group of juveniles, particularly those facing serious offenses, may be retained for periods of 6 to 12 months, or even longer, while awaiting adjudication. Juvenile detention facilities often have agreements or arrangements with mental health service providers (typically through the state's department of mental health) to evaluate adolescents to determine their need for detention or to illuminate other issues relevant to eventual adjudication and placement.

In addition to detention facilities, each state has an administrative agency to operate and control its courts, typically with a separate division for the administration of juvenile courts. Many urban areas have a system of "juvenile and family courts" that have jurisdiction over a wide array of issues involving children and adolescents, including allegations of abuse, foster care placement, custody and visitation, and adoption. Juvenile courts typically have jurisdiction over detention centers and probation services. Further, most states have a system of juvenile corrections for those juveniles who are committed to state custody by the juvenile court following adjudication. As noted by Grisso (1998), the juvenile correction system is the counterpart of the criminal justice system's department of corrections, prisons and parole for adult offenders. The secure facilities for the incarceration and rehabilitation of juveniles are known by various names, including *training schools, youth correctional facilities*, and *reform schools*. Many states also operate a special initial screening or "front end" assessment center in the correctional facility system in order to determine the proper placement for each juvenile given the needs of that youth and the availability of placement options within the state system.

The juvenile courts in almost all states, as previously noted, may grant a waiver of jurisdiction and transfer the adjudication of a juvenile to an adult criminal court. When this referral is not automatic due to statutory exclusion, a hearing is usually conducted by the juvenile court to review evidence presented by the prosecutor to convince the judge that certain criteria have been met to justify the waiver. Typically, these criteria include a judgment that the youth represents a danger to society and/or is not amenable to rehabilitation in the juvenile justice system. When juvenile courts conduct a waiver hearing to review this evidence, the youth is typically represented by legal counsel to defend against the assertions offered by the prosecution. Some states also recognize a juvenile's right to be competent to stand trial, meaning that the youth must be able to understand the nature of the proceedings and to assist his or her legal counsel in preparing a defense. If a question concerning competency to stand trial is raised, it is typically decided by the juvenile court judge at a competency hearing prior to the waiver or adjudication hearing. Figure 7.9 provides an overview of the number and percentage of juveniles who entered the various stages and experienced the various outcomes in the juvenile justice system in 1999.

Figure 7.9 shows that approximately 57% of all delinquency cases were formally processed in 1999. Formal processing of a case involves the filing of a petition that requests an adjudication hearing. In contrast, nonpetitioned cases (43% of cases in 1999) are more informal and are handled without legal procedures such as a petition

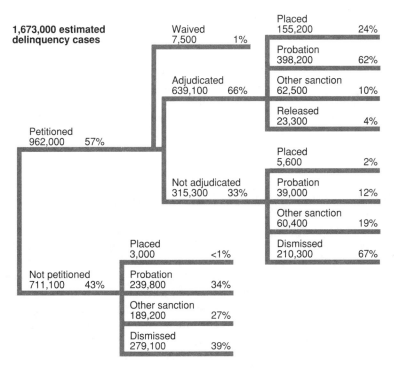

Note: Cases are categorized by their most severe or restrictive sanction. Detail may not add to totals because of rounding.

FIG. 7.9. Overview of case processing for juveniles in the United States in 1999. Reprinted from Puzzanchera, Stahl, Finnegan, Tierney, and Snyder (2003). *Juvenile Court Statistics 1999.* Office of Juvenile Justice and Delinquency Prevention, U.S. Department of Justice. Reprinted by permission.

or an adjudicatory hearing. Compared with nonpetitioned cases, petitioned cases in 1999 involved higher proportions of crimes against persons, drug crimes, and public order offenses and a lower proportion of property offenses. Regardless of the offense, juvenile courts are more likely to petition cases involving males than females, and delinquency cases involving Black juveniles were more likely to be petitioned than cases involving White youths (Puzzancera, Stahl, Finnegan, Tierney, & Snyder, 2003). Figure 7.9 also shows that the mechanism of transfer of adjudication to criminal court occurs in approximately 1% of all petitioned cases, but youths were adjudicated delinquent in approximately two thirds of all petitioned delinquency cases. The likelihood of adjudication in petitioned cases also appears to be related to demographic characteristics. For example, petitioned cases involving male juveniles were more likely to be adjudicated than those involving females, while petitioned cases involving Black juveniles were less likely to be adjudicated than cases involving White juveniles or juveniles from other races.

Following the adjudication process, dispositional hearings determine the most appropriate sanctions for delinquent youths. The range of dispositional options typically includes placement in a juvenile correction institution or other residential facility, probation supervision, and a variety of other less restrictive sanctions such as community service, restitution or the payment of fines, and referral to outside agencies or treatment programs. Probation was the most common restrictive disposition in 1999, used in nearly 400,000 adjudicated delinquency cases. For all offenses, females were more likely than males to be placed on probation following adjudication, and 67% of all adjudicated delinquency cases in 1999 involved females. Finally, it should be noted that in a relatively small percentage of cases (4%) adjudicated juveniles were released without further sanction or consequence and that 33% of all petitioned delinquency cases in 1999 were not subsequently adjudicated, with the most common outcome in these latter cases involving dismissal (67%). Although juvenile courts handle a little more than 4 in 10 delinquency cases without the filing of a formal petition, more than half of these latter cases receive some form of court sanction, such as probation, restitution, community service, or referral to another agency.

Components Typically Found in an Adolescent Forensic Evaluation

The forensic evaluation of a juvenile differs from the typical clinical assessment of an adolescent in a mental health treatment setting in a number of important ways. Heilbrun et al. (2003), for example, noted that the primary goal of a typical forensic assessment is not necessarily to improve the mental health functioning of the individual but to provide objective information to decision makers in the courtroom setting. In contrast, a therapeutic evaluation is usually conducted to assess the mental health needs of an individual and to assist in treatment planning. In a forensic assessment, the evaluator typically assumes an objective and neutral role with the examinee, whereas in a therapeutic setting the evaluator typically strives to provide the optimal services for the patient. In a forensic assessment, the evaluator typically does not represent the individual being assessed but rather serves as an agent of the court and attempts to provide accurate information for litigation purposes.

Heilbrun et al. (2003) noted that, as a consequence of differences in objectives, the types of information typically included in forensic assessments are substantially broader than those included in standard psychological examinations. Forensic mental health assessments, for example, usually incorporate collateral information obtained from family members, friends, or other sources. Forensic evaluation also places a substantially greater emphasis on record reviews, potentially including reports from schools, hospitals, police, and other sources of data that might shed light on the individual's psychological functioning, motivations, and/or intentions. Thus, it is not reasonable to assume that an individual with the skills necessary to perform a competent therapeutic evaluation would be able to generalize this expertise to the extent needed to conduct a competent forensic evaluation. One of the most dreaded questions for expert witnesses during cross-examination is the famous hypothetical, "Doctor, would it change your opinion of Mr. Jones if I told you that Mr. Jones was/had ———?" Usually this hypothetical question concludes with a particularly devastating piece of information concerning Mr. Jones's background that should have been uncovered by the expert witness in his or her evaluation. The best way of protecting against this cross-examination danger is for the expert to do a comprehensive and thorough evaluation employing data from multiple sources. However, as Sageman (2003) recently observed, in addition to gathering comprehensive and complete information, the expert must be knowledgeable about the relevant legal issues to be addressed and able to effectively summarize the evaluation findings in a manner appropriate to the audience (i.e., a judge or jury).

Grisso (1998) provided a set of guidelines for the types of information and data generally useful in the evaluation of adolescents for the juvenile justice system. As noted by Grisso, not all of these types will necessarily be relevant in any particular juvenile assessment, and different cases will usually require different data-gathering and interview approaches. Nevertheless, the following are important categories to consider in the assessment of most adolescents in the juvenile justice setting:

- *Health and medical history*. The juvenile justice system is responsible for meeting the medical and health needs of adolescents placed in this setting. Therefore, the examiner should be familiar with the medical records of the juvenile, including past and present illnesses, current medications, and the presence of chronic medical problems such as diabetes, epilepsy, or other disorders. It is also often important to gather any information on prior injuries, especially head injuries, that could potentially be related to impulsive or disinhibited behavior.
- *Family and social background*. Most clinical psychologists acquire information about family history as it might influence the adolescent's current treatment needs. The evaluation of an adolescent in a forensic setting, however, typically requires an assessment of the ability of the family to provide realistic limits and guidance for the adolescent. In addition to clinical interview data, there are a number of objective instruments available to gather information on such variables as the extent of parental stress and the nature and quality of the parent-child relationship.
- *Academic and intellectual functioning*. In addition to the evaluation of the adolescent with standardized measures of intellectual functioning, data gathering in forensic assessments often involves review of school records and interviews or evaluations with teachers. Grisso noted that a comprehensive history of the adolescent's academic performance often provides important information not only about the adolescent's capacities and abilities but also about achievement motivation.
- *Personality description*. The comprehensive evaluation of adolescent personality and psychopathology typically includes personality assessment measures, including the MMPI-A or the Millon Adolescent Clinical Inventory (Millon, 1993). Grisso observed that some clinicians have utilized Megargee's MMPI-based

classification method for offenders with adolescents but cautioned that no systematic attempt has been undertaken to adapt this system to classify adolescents and that this application has been subject to criticism (e.g., Zager, 1988).

- *Clinical diagnostic description.* The data from numerous research studies indicate that a large proportion of adolescents in the juvenile justice system meet the criteria for psychiatric diagnoses, particularly conduct disorder– and substance abuse–related diagnoses. In addition, many of these adolescents will also receive diagnoses related to mood disorders (especially depression and anxiety disorders), posttraumatic stress disorders, and a variety of attention deficit and hyperactivity disorders. In addition to psychological testing, reviewing the records of any past contacts with outpatient mental health centers or psychiatric hospitals as well as conducting interviews with parents and other collateral sources can aid in identifying an adolescent's mental and emotional disorders.
- *Delinquent behaviors and legal history.* In order to understand the context of an adolescent's current legal issues, it is important that the examiner also gain information about the juvenile's legal history. This type of information is typically obtained from school documents, law enforcement records, juvenile court records, and the juvenile's history of prior adjudications and commitments to state youth authority facilities, if such exists.
- *Response to past rehabilitation efforts.* Adolescents in the juvenile justice system often have an extended history of contact with individuals and agencies involved in attempting to change their behavior. Parents may have tried various forms of discipline, school systems may have placed an adolescent in one or more special programs, and the adolescent may have been placed by juvenile courts in a variety of rehabilitation programs in the past. Grisso recommended that the examiner describe the nature of these behavior modification attempts as well as their results.
- *Risk of harm.* Included in most evaluations in juvenile justice settings should be the clinician's summary of factors related to the likelihood of harm to self or others. This type of evaluation is often crucial to the decision whether to retain a youth in detention or release him or her back to the community prior to adjudication. A broad variety of factors have been shown to be related to homicide and suicide risk, including past behavior, substance abuse, exposure to family conflict and aggression, the presence of psychiatric disorders, the accessibility of weapons, and the presence of situational triggers provoking violent acts.
- *Description of rehabilitation objectives.* Many forensic evaluations include recommendations on what characteristics need to be changed to reduce the likelihood of an adolescent reoffending in the future. Such rehabilitation objectives may involve changes in the adolescent's personality functioning or psychiatric condition but may also involve changes in the situational context, including the adolescent's placement in the family or community.
- *Potential rehabilitation plan.* The rehabilitation plan recommended by the evaluator should be realistic given available community resources and should usually include a variety of placement options and services. In most cases, the evaluator will wish to comment on a range of possible placement options (typically varying in degree of restrictiveness), delineating the relative benefits and limitations involved in placement in each of these settings. The evaluator may also wish to note what service components should be present, such as mental or physical rehabilitation services, psychopharmacological services, educational programs, individual or group psychotherapy programs, and family support services.

- *Description of the probability of successful rehabilitation.* Successful rehabilitation should be defined in terms of salient criteria, including reduction in risk to the community, likelihood of reoffense, or successful adaptation to demands of the family or school environment. Typically, the likelihood of rehabilitation is also framed within the context of the adolescent's participation in a particular rehabilitation program, including the critical or essential service features that must be present in order to facilitate successful rehabilitation.

ROLE OF THE PSYCHOLOGIST IN FORENSIC ADOLESCENT EVALUATIONS

The previous discussion of juvenile crime and the juvenile justice system was intended to illuminate the role of the clinical psychologist in forensic adolescent assessments. Although a full discussion of the complexity of this role exceeds the limitations of a single chapter, some useful guidelines have been offered by Grisso (1998) on this topic, based on the types of requests a psychologist may receive in this system.

Grisso noted that juvenile courts, prosecutors, and defense attorneys may request clinical evaluations at any of a number of points in the processing of juvenile cases. At the point of entry into the system (i.e., the pretrial detention facility), psychologists are typically requested to evaluate adolescents for several reasons. They may be asked, for example, to evaluate the emergency mental health needs of a juvenile held in detention because the juvenile is exhibiting depressed or disorganized behavior. The evaluation may encompass suicide risk or include the assessment of psychotic-like behaviors possibly resulting from mental illness or substance intoxication or withdrawal and requiring immediate hospitalization. Second, a forensic evaluation may be requested at the pretrial stage to determine whether there is a continuing need for placement in a secure detention facility based on the probability that the youth may reoffend or engage in behaviors inconsistent with community placement. Additionally, evaluations are sometimes requested by courts, prosecutors, or defense attorneys in preparation for hearings on waiver to criminal court. In these latter cases, the evaluation can be quite comprehensive and include such issues as the short- and long-range risk of harm posed by the juvenile as well as his or her likely amenability to rehabilitation in the juvenile justice system.

Competency to stand trial is another pretrial issue for which an evaluation may be requested by the court, the prosecutor, or the defense attorney. Such an evaluation typically focuses on the juvenile's ability to understand key aspects of the charges against him or her, including the consequences of various pleas, and the juvenile's ability to meaningfully assist the attorney in preparation of the defense. Grisso (1998) observed that competency to stand trial is only one of several legal competency questions that may be raised in a criminal justice process. Further, he noted that virtually every state employs a legal statute or definition of competency to stand trial that is roughly patterned on the definition provided in the U.S. Supreme Court decision in *Dusky v. United States* (1960). That decision states, "The test must be whether he (the defendant) has sufficient present ability to consult with his attorney with a reasonable degree of rational understanding and a rational as well as factual understanding of the proceedings against him" (p. 402).

In a case proceeding to juvenile court adjudication, a psychologist may also be requested to perform an evaluation of the youth's ability to understand and make decisions regarding Miranda warnings, in particular, the youth's capacity to waive Miranda rights "knowingly, intelligently, and voluntarily." This type of evaluation involves an assessment of the juvenile's understanding of the key rights provided by the Miranda decision. Grisso (1998) observed that an examination of a juvenile's competency to waiver Miranda rights also entails an evaluation of his or her ability to comprehend the Miranda rights, to grasp the significance of those rights in the context of the legal process, and to process information accurately and meaningfully in arriving at a decision about the waiver.

Grisso has developed four standardized tools to measure an individual's understanding of the Miranda warnings and appreciation of the warnings within the context of the legal proceedings against him or her. These four measures include the Comprehension of Miranda Rights (CMR), which requires the examiner to present each of the four main Miranda warnings and statements to the youth and then to request the youth to explain what the statement means "in your own words." The youth's responses are scored as adequate, questionable, or inadequate based on standardized scoring criteria. A second measure of understanding, the Comprehension of Miranda Rights–Recognition (CMR–R), is intended as an adjunct. For each warning statement, the youth is told that the examiner will offer several statements that mean either the same thing as or something different from the Miranda warning. The youth is provided with a total of 12 statements (3 statements for each of the four Miranda warnings) and need only indicate which are the same and which are different. The third measure of understanding, the Comprehension of Miranda Vocabulary (CMV), is a vocabulary test that uses six words taken from the original Miranda warning in order to evaluate the adolescent's understanding of key vocabulary. The final instrument is the Function of Rights in Interrogation (FRI), which is designed to assess the youth's appreciation of the relevance of Miranda warnings within the context of the legal process. The FRI provides four situations described by brief vignettes and accompanied by drawings portraying each situation. For each of these situations, questions are asked that focus on the youth's appreciation of such aspects as the adversarial nature of the youth's initial encounters with police, the protective nature of the "right to remain silent," and the effect that such actions as asserting one's right to silence or offering a confession may ultimately have on the subsequent court hearing. An evaluation of a juvenile's capacity to waive Miranda rights typically results from a decision by the defense attorney to raise the juvenile's capacity to waive Miranda as an issue, and the prosecutor will sometimes request a similar type of evaluation be conducted by another independent clinician.

Grisso (1998) noted, however, that clinical psychologists typically do *not* play a role in the majority of juvenile court adjudications. Most adjudications focus narrowly on legal issues such as whether the youth committed the offense as charged and do not extend to the psychological or psychiatric functioning of the adolescent. Although an insanity defense (e.g., not guilty by reason of insanity) in delinquency proceedings is possible, it is quite rare, and many clinicians working in the juvenile forensic system have never been asked to perform an insanity evaluation for the court.

Most evaluations in the juvenile court system are requested by the court to aid in dispositional decisions. They typically involve providing the court with a recommendation concerning the optimal rehabilitation plan after a youth has been placed in the juvenile rehabilitation or correctional system. Following the youth's adjudication and placement, a clinician may also be requested to provide an evaluation of his or her rehabilitation progress. Grisso (1998) noted that these latter types of evaluation typically involve recommendations concerning potential changes in the youth's placement, such as a transition from a secure facility to a less secure community-based program.

Assessment of Emotional Damages in Personal Injury Litigation

Although in forensic settings the MMPI-A is mostly used to evaluate adolescents who have entered the juvenile justice system, it is sometimes employed in the evaluation of potential emotional damage in personal injury litigation. Greenberg, Otto, and Long (2003) recently provided an overview of this use to assist psychologists in preparing evaluations that are of maximum benefit to the court or trier of fact. Grisso (2003) stressed that psychologists conducting evaluations in personal injury litigation must understand the pertinent law(s) in order to provide evaluations and expert opinions relevant to the salient issues before the court. The legal framework for personal injury cases differs from that of the juvenile justice system in that the former is largely defined by the accumulation of relevant case law rather than by the network of state statutes that form the state's criminal law. Further, the general category of case law relevant to personal injury litigation is the law of torts. A tort is defined by Greenberg et al. (2003) as "a civil wrong that gives rise to a remedy in the form of a claim for compensation that is commenced with the filing of a complaint or petition" (p. 412). Tort laws recognize that a claim for monetary damages may arise when one person breaches a duty of care owed to another and that breach of responsibility proximately causes injury or harm.

In order to establish the viability of a personal injury claim, a plaintiff in the litigation must prove (a) that the defendant owed the plaintiff a duty, (b) that that duty was breached, (c) that as a result of this breach the plaintiff experienced a significant damage, and (d) that this damage was a proximate result of the breach of duty. In determining whether significant psychological or neuropsychological damage resulted from a breach of duty, courts may request that a psychologist provide objective information concerning the extent and nature of the psychological injury, and this information may in turn be useful in the court's subsequent determination of damages.

A survey by Boccaccini and Brodsky (1999) determined that the MMPI (in its original or revised form) was the most widely used psychological assessment instrument among psychologists who conduct personal injury litigation. These researchers found that the MMPI or MMPI-2 was used by 94% of the respondents in this survey, followed by the Wechsler scales (54%). Although comparable data are not available for personal injury examinations solely involving adolescents, it seems likely that the MMPI-A is the most commonly used objective personality assessment instrument with litigants in this age group.

The MMPI-A possesses particular utility in the evaluation of emotional or psychological damage in personal injury cases because of its ability to provide a comprehensive picture of the psychological functioning of an adolescent across multiple dimensions of personality and psychopathology. Further, MMPI-A results may be used to quantify the nature and extent of the adolescent's psychopathology or emotional distress in reference to well-established national norms for adolescents. In addition, as will be discussed in greater detail, the MMPI-A provides an opportunity to evaluate and quantify the adolescent's response style along a number of dimensions particularly relevant to personal injury cases, including the tendency to overreport or exaggerate symptomatology. As noted by Greenberg et al. (2003), other measures of general psychopathology typically include indices of response style that have not been well researched. Further, measures of more specific forms of adolescent psychopathology, such as measures of anxiety or depression, do not usually include any measurement of response style variables.

The Use of the MMPI-A in the Evaluation of Sexually Abused Adolescents

Psychologists may be called on to evaluate children and adolescents who have been sexually abused, and such evaluations typically occur within a forensic context. The literature on the use of the MMPI and MMPI-A in the evaluation of sexually abused adolescents was briefly reviewed by Archer and Krishnamurthy (2002). As noted by these authors, the MMPI profiles of sexually abused adolescents typically contain multiple scale elevations reflective of general emotional distress. In addition, sexually abused adolescents are likely to produce scale elevations indicative of feelings of alienation, interpersonal sensitivity, and social withdrawal. Further, sexually abused adolescents display overall levels of psychological disorganization and distress similar to those found among a broad range of adolescents in psychiatric treatment settings.

In looking at studies involving the original version of the MMPI, Hillary and Schare (1993) found that sexually abused adolescents typically produced elevations on scales measuring anxiety and depression, although elevations on scales *8* and *9* were also common for this group. Scott and Stone (1986) compared the MMPI profiles of adolescents and adults receiving psychotherapy who had been molested by their fathers or stepfathers. They found that both adolescents and adults produced elevations on scale *8* and that the adolescent sample also tended to produce elevations on scale *9*. Williams et al. (1992) reported the clinical correlates of several MMPI-A content scales for adolescents with histories of abuse. These authors reported that scales *A-dep*, *A-ang*, *A-lse*, and *A-sch* were frequently elevated for boys with a history of sexual abuse and that *A-fam* scale scores were correlated with a history of sexual abuse for girls and a history of physical abuse for boys. Additionally, sexually abused boys were likely to produce elevations on basic scales *7* and *8*, and sexually abused girls were more likely to obtain high scores on scales *4* and *8* (Butcher & Williams, 2000).

Forbey and Ben-Porath (2000) evaluated the MMPI-A profiles of 107 adolescents receiving residential treatment and found that a history of sexual abuse was related to higher scores on basic scales *2, 4, 6, 8*, and *0* and content scales *A-dep, A-lse, A-sod*, *A-fam*, and *A-aln*. These authors concluded that sexually abused adolescents report depression, feelings of hopelessness and worthlessness, low interest and lack of initiative, interpersonal distrust, and social withdrawal from others. Forbey and Ben-Porath also noted that these adolescents are more likely to have thoughts about self-injury and to have a history of running away from home.

Archer and Krishnamurthy (2002) summarized this literature by concluding that sexually abused adolescents are likely to produce multiple scale elevations on MMPI-A profiles and that no single profile pattern could be used effectively to identify or diagnose sexual abuse. However, the MMPI-A does provide important information about the extent and nature of the psychological dysfunction and associated treatment needs of adolescents subjected to sexual abuse.

The Use of the MMPI-A in Child Custody Evaluations

Otto and Collins (1995) observed that there is a "relative paucity of research related to the MMPI/MMPI-2/MMPI-A and its specific application in child custody proceedings" (p. 228). Nevertheless, the MMPI-2 has been used extensively in parental evaluations to assist the court in determining child custody or visitation arrangements. Graham (2000), for example, noted that while MMPI-2 scores do not permit direct inferences concerning how effective an individual might be in his or her parental role, many of the correlates associated with MMPI-2 scales provide important informa- tion about an individual's impulsivity, stability, and ability to appropriately handle frustration and anger. Keilin and Bloom (1986) surveyed psychologists who conduct child custody evaluations and reported that approximately 75% of these clinicians used psychological tests. Further, these authors found that the MMPI was the most frequently used test and was employed in 89% of these custody evaluations Ackerman and Ackerman (1997) more recently found that 98% of psychologists use psycholog- ical tests in child custody evaluations and that the MMPI-2 was the most commonly used instrument for this purpose.

Most domestic relations courts rendering decisions concerning child custody and visitation arrangements have considerable flexibility and generally attempt to arrive at decisions that are "in the best interest of the child." Graham (2000), however, noted that "parental characteristics that might be in the best interests of one child may not necessarily be in the best interest of another child who has different needs" (p. 376). This important point underscores the usefulness of the MMPI-A in assessing the unique emotional and psychological functioning of each adolescent involved in child custody proceedings and providing substantial assistance to domestic relations courts in rendering appropriate and meaningful individualized decisions. Otto and Collins (1995) stated, for example, that the MMPI-A provides a well-researched basis for identifying and describing the emotional adjustment of adolescents involved in the divorce and custody decision process. They cautioned, however, that much less is currently known about the optimal combination of parental MMPI-2 characteristics and adolescent MMPI-A features, making it difficult to predict the specific outcome of custody placement decisions.

Other Useful Instruments in Adolescent Forensic Assessments

We have just reviewed a variety of circumstances in which clinical psychologists may evaluate adolescents for forensic purposes. Psychologists, for example, may be asked to determine whether a juvenile is in need of mental health services while held in secure detention prior to trial, to determine whether the adolescent is competent to waive Miranda rights or to stand trial, and to advise the court about postadjudication placement options that might meet the needs of the juvenile. We have also briefly re- viewed the potential uses of the MMPI-A in other forensic contexts, including personal injury litigation, sexual abuse cases, and child custody proceedings. It is important to stress that traditional psychological testing provides important information in all of these contexts but cannot fully address any of the pertinent issues.

In addition to traditional testing instruments, almost all forensic assessments of ju- veniles should include a comprehensive record review that encompasses such items as law enforcement investigation and arrest reports, prior court records, school academic and disciplinary records, and admission and discharge records from mental health treatment episodes. Parental and teacher interviews are also typically very important and may involve the use of standardized tests such as the parent or teacher form of the Child Behavior Checklist (Achenbach, 1991a, 1991b). There are also a variety of specialized instruments in forensic adolescent assessment that provide critically use- ful information for addressing specific issues in this setting. For example, as will be discussed next, a self-report instrument has been developed to identify mental health needs among juveniles in detention settings, and a rating checklist has been designed to identify psychopathic characteristics among youthful offenders.

TABLE 7.5
Definitions of MAYSI-2 Scales With Sample Items as Provided by Grisso et al. (2001)

Scale Label and No. of Items	Definition and Sample Item
Alcohol/Drug Use (8)	Frequent use of alcohol or drugs; risk of substance abuse. "Have you used alcohol or drugs to make you feel better?"
Angry-Irritable (9)	Experiences frustration, lasting anger, and moodiness. "When you have been mad, have you stayed mad for a long time?"
Depressed-Anxious (9)	Experiences depressed and anxious feelings. "Have nervous or worried feelings kept you from doing things you want to do?"
Somatic Complaints (6)	Experiences bodily discomforts associated with distress. "Have you had bad headaches?"
Suicide Ideation (5)	Experiences thoughts and intentions to harm oneself. "Have you felt like hurting yourself?"
Thought Disturbance (5)	Experiences unusual beliefs/perceptions, possible thought disorder (boys only). "Have you heard voices other people can't hear?"
Traumatic Experiences (5)	Lifetime exposure to events the youth considers traumatic (separate versions for boys and girls). "Have you ever seen someone severely injured or killed (in person, not in movies or on TV)?"

Note: MAYSI-2 = Massachusetts Youth Screening Instrument–Second Version. From Grisso, Barnum, Fletcher, Cauffman, and Peuschold (2001). Massachusetts Youth Screening Instrument for Mental Health Needs for Juvenile Justice Youths. *Journal of the American Academy of Child and Adolescent Psychiatry, 40,* 541–548. Published by Lippincott, Williams and Wilkins. Reprinted by permission of the publisher.

Epidemiological studies of psychiatric disorders among youths within the juvenile justice system indicate that 40% to 60% of this population meet the criteria for a psychiatric diagnosis, even when conduct and substance abuse disorders are excluded (e.g., Teplin, Abram, McClelland, Dulcan, & Mericle, 2002). The need to develop a simple and effective screening tool to identify juveniles with significant mental health problems in detention settings has led to the development of the Massachusetts Youth Screening Instrument (MAYSI) by Grisso and Barnum (1998) and its successor, the MAYSI-2, by Grisso, Barnum, Fletcher, Cauffman, and Peuschold (2001) and Grisso and Barnum (2003). The MAYSI-2 is a 52-item self-report questionnaire that has a yes/no format and contains questions assessing symptoms across a range of psychopathology and behavior problems commonly seen in adolescents. Table 7.5 presents definitions of each of the seven dimensions or scales of the MAYSI-2.

Archer, Stredny, Mason, and Arnau (2004) independently evaluated the MAYSI-2 in a sample of 704 juveniles in Virginia detention facilities and reported findings strongly supportive of the psychometric utility of this instrument as a screening tool in this setting. These authors found the item-level factor structure of the MAYSI-2 was quite consistent with results reported by Grisso et al. (2001). Further, the scale alpha coefficients and test-retest reliabilities were also strikingly similar between these two studies. Evidence of concurrent validity was also found for the Suicidal Ideation and Alcohol/Drug scales in terms of meaningful patterns of correlation with adolescents' independent self-reports. Espelage et al. (2003) compared the mental health symptoms reported by male and female adolescents on the original version of the MMPI with MAYSI-2 scores. A sample of 141 juvenile offenders in California completed both instruments, and the data were subjected to cluster analysis, which identified four distinct profile types, two types for males and two for females. For example, the cluster pattern for boys labeled *Disorganized* by Epelage and her colleagues involved elevations on MMPI scales *F, 4, 6, 8,* and *9* and elevations on the MAYSI-2 Depressed-Anxious, Alcohol/Drug Use, and Thought Disturbance scales. The Impulse-Antisocial cluster for girls was marked by elevations on MMPI basic scales *4* and *9* and lower scores on the MAYSI-2 Depressed-Anxious and Suicide Ideation scales. This study provides a provocative demonstration of the manner in which data from the MMPI-A and MAYSI-2 might be combined to provide a fuller description of the psychological functioning of juvenile offenders.

In addition to the MAYSI-2, the Psychopathy Checklist: Youth Version (PCL:YV) by Forth, Kosson, and Hare (1996) has been used with adolescents in forensic settings (Frick, O'Brien, Wootton, & McBurnett, 1994). The PCL:YV is an adaptation of the Psychopathy Checklist Revised (PCL–R; Hare, 1991) for adolescents developed to assess factors related to such outcomes as recidivism and potential for interpersonal violence. The PCL–R is a 20-item expert rating scale designed for use with adult male forensic populations. Each of the items is scored on a 3-point scale ranging from 0 (does not apply) to 2 (item definitely applies). The 20 items included in the PCL–R include such dimensions as grandiose sense of self-worth, pathological lying, shallow affect, poor behavioral controls, impulsivity, and irresponsibility. The expert ratings on each of the 20 dimensions of the PCL–R rely heavily on record review and collateral information, and it is sometimes possible to score the PCL–R despite a lack of cooperativeness on the part of the respondent. The PCL:YV is psychometrically quite similar to the PCL–R but includes some modification of the scoring criteria for selected items to render them more suitable for use in adolescent populations. Grisso (1998) has suggested that the PCL:YV is useful in differentiating youths who are developing psychopathic characteristics from youths who may engage in antisocial behaviors but do not show the typical deficiencies in social attachment or emotional arousal associated with antisocial personality disorder in adults.

A growing body of research supports the potential usefulness of the PCL:YV in predicting to juvenile reoffense and violent offending in the community. Studies with adolescents using the PCL:YV, for example, have established a link between violent criminal behavior, earlier onset of antisocial behavior, increased symptoms of conduct disorder, and a higher incidence of substance abuse (e.g., Edens, Skeem, Cruise, & Cauffman, 2001; Forth & Burke, 1998; Kosson, Cyterski, Steuerwald, Neumann, & Walker-Matthews, 2002; Mailloux, Forth, & Kroner, 1997). Some criticisms have been offered, however, related to the psychometric limitations of the PCL:YV as well as the controversial nature of the construct of psychopathy in its application to adolescents (e.g., Hart, Watt, & Vincent, 2002; Kosson et al., 2002; Seagrave & Grisso, 2002). Although certain psychological features may tend to be relatively more stable than others during adolescence, the overall fluidity in personality structure typically associated with adolescent development serves as the major reason why the *Diagnostic and Statistical Manual of Mental Disorders* (*DSM–IV–TR*; 2000) of the American Psychiatric Association strongly discourages the application of personality disorder diagnoses to adolescents and specifically prohibits use of the antisocial personality disorder diagnosis for individuals under the age of 18.

Hicks, Rogers, and Cashel (2000) evaluated the usefulness of a 12-item screening version of the PCL (i.e., the PCL:SV) and the MMPI-A in a group of 120 male juvenile offenders with extensive delinquency histories. Scores from these instruments were used to predict occurrence of violent infractions (assaults and attempted assaults), self-injurious infractions (suicidal gestures or attempts and self-mutilations), and nonviolent infractions (e.g., possession of contraband). The authors reported that the MMPI-A appeared to be more useful in these prediction tasks than the PCL:SV. For example, MMPI-A scales 6 and 9 entered into a discriminant function in predicting violent infractions, but scores from the PCL:SV were essentially uncorrelated with this outcome measure. Similarly, MMPI-A basic scale 6 was the only significant predictor of self-injurious behaviors (scores from this single MMPI-A scale correctly identified 75% of self-injurious cases and 88.7% of non-self-injurious cases). Further, the authors noted ethnic differences in the correlate patterns for the PCL:SV that suggested it had limited usefulness for Anglo-American and Hispanic-American offenders. Although the results from this study suggest that the PCL:SV may add little to the data typically derived from the MMPI-A in terms of predicting to various classes of problematic detention behaviors, further investigations in this area are clearly warranted before reaching firm conclusions regarding the utility of the various versions of the PCL with juvenile offenders.

USE OF THE MMPI-A IN FORENSIC ADOLESCENT EVALUATIONS

Although the MMPI-A has typically been used and investigated as a measure of psychopathology among adolescents in traditional clinical settings, it also has a long and extensive history in the assessment of juvenile delinquents. Indeed, the MMPI appears to have been first applied to adolescents by Dora Capwell in 1941, prior to the publication of the MMPI. Capwell (1945a) demonstrated the ability of the MMPI to accurately discriminate between groups of delinquent and nondelinquent adolescents based primarily on elevations on scale *Pd*. Further, scale 4 differences between these groups were maintained in an MMPI follow-up study that reevaluated these adolescents 4 to 15 months following the initial MMPI administration (Capwell, 1945b).

An early MMPI study by Monachesi (1948) also provided construct validity data for scale 4 by demonstrating that normal male adolescents produced mean scores on scale 4 that were significantly lower than those produced by delinquent boys. In a 1950 study by Monachesi, the finding of higher scale 4 scores for delinquents, in comparison with normal adolescents, was also replicated in a sample of girls. Hathaway and Monachesi (1953, 1961, 1963) subsequently undertook the collection of a large data set based on the responses of 3,971 Minnesota ninth graders collected during the 1947–48 school year and 11,329 ninth graders in 86 Minnesota communities collected in the spring of 1954. In addition to MMPI data, extensive follow-up and correlate data were also collected by Hathaway and Monachesi, with the primary intent of identifying MMPI characteristics among adolescents who would later display delinquent or antisocial behaviors. Hathaway and Monachesi (1963) summarized their major findings from these investigations by noting that scales 4, 8, and 9 were associated with high delinquency rates, and these scales were labeled *Excitatory scales*. In contrast, Hathaway and Monachesi noted that scales 0, 2, and 5 appear to act as Suppressor scales, and these scales were elevated in the profiles of boys with lower delinquency rates.

Extensive follow-up research based on data collected by Hathaway and Monachesi has provided mixed support for the claim that elevations on scales 4, 8, and 9 serve an excitatory role predictive of higher rates of delinquency in adolescent samples. The research by Briggs et al. (1961), Huesmann et al. (1978), Rempel (1958), and Wirt and Briggs (1959) provide some of the stronger findings in support of the excitatory scales. Collectively, the early studies convincingly demonstrated the usefulness of the MMPI in identifying adolescents concurrently displaying delinquent behaviors as well as the potential applicability of the instrument in predicting the later onset of delinquency.

More recently, the MMPI-A has been effectively used to identify or describe juvenile delinquents. For example, Cashel, Rogers, Sewell, and Holliman (1998) examined the clinical correlates for the MMPI-A in a male delinquent sample consisting of 99 adolescents at a North Texas juvenile correction facility. Their clinical correlates were based on the Schedule of Affective Disorders and Schizophrenia for School Age Children (K–SADS–3–R; Ambrosini, Metz, Prabucki, & Lee, 1989), a structured diagnostic interview procedure for children with relatively high reliability. Many of the correlates identified in this study were consistent with expectations based on the underlying constructs measured by MMPI-A scales. For example, strong associations were identified between MMPI-A scale 2 elevations and the K–SADS–3–R symptoms of depressed mood, appetite disturbance, and need for reassurance. Further, correlates for scale 9 involved symptom correlates of hyperactivity and disturbances in mood and conduct. In contrast, other correlates identified in this study were surprising and underscore the potential for the existence of unique correlate patterns for adolescents in forensic settings. For example, cruelty toward others and suicidal ideation were among the unexpected correlates found for elevations on MMPI-A scale 3.

Hicks et al. (2000), as previously noted, used a residential male adolescent offender population to increase the usefulness of the MMPI-A and the screening version of the psychopathy checklist (PCL:SV) for predicting violent, self-injurious, nonviolent, and total infractions. In predicting the overall number of infractions, the MMPI-A proved superior to the PCL:SV. For example, the combination of scores from MMPI-A basic scales 6 and 9 resulted in correct classification of 60% of residents with violent infractions and 66% of residents without violent infractions. These authors suggested that clinicians may wish to routinely evaluate elevations on scale 6 with adolescent offenders in assessing risk factors for violent infractions. Interestingly, however, elevations on scale 4 in this study were not correlated with scores from the psychopathy measure, the number of infractions, or the number of conduct disordered symptoms. Thus, this study provided support for the predictive utility of some of Hathaway and Monachesi's (1963) excitatory scales (scale 9) but not others (scales 4 and 8). Cashel, Ovaert, and Holliman (2000) also used the MMPI-A to evaluate posttraumatic stress disorder (PTSD) in incarcerated adolescents. Scores from the MMPI-A were compared with diagnostic classifications derived from the Posttraumatic Stress Disorder Reaction Index (PTSD–RI; Frederick, 1985) in a sample of 60 male juvenile delinquents. Results indicated significant higher mean T-scores on MMPI-A validity scale F and basic scales 4, 8, and 9 for adolescents in the PTSD group than for non-PTSD adolescents. Cashel and her colleagues concluded that the MMPI-A may serve as a useful screening measure "indicating the need for further evaluation of traumatic experience in juveniles" (p. 1535).

In addition to the work of Cashel and her colleagues, a number of other researchers have examined the MMPI-A characteristics of male juvenile offenders. Hume, Kennedy, Patrick, and Partyka (1996) evaluated the usefulness of the MMPI-A for identifying adolescent offenders based on psychopathy classifications in a sample of 101 male juvenile delinquents committed to a state training school. These researchers hypothesized that MMPI-A scales could indicate psychopathy as measured by Hare's Psychopathy Checklist–Revised (PCL–R). Five MMPI-A validity scales and 10 basic clinical scales proved unsuccessful in predicting psychopathy scores at statistically useful levels, however, and these authors noted that the MMPI-A scores of their delinquent group were fairly similar to those typically found among normal adolescents.

Pena, Megargee, and Brody (1996) evaluated the MMPI-A in a sample of 162 delinquent boys in a state training school. The configural patterns for all MMPI-A scales and subscales were determined and compared with those of the 805 nondelinquent male adolescents in the MMPI-A normative sample and with the patterns produced on the original MMPI for 7,783 adolescents identified in their literature review. Pena et al. reported that the most prominent clinical elevations for their delinquent group involved scales 4, 6, and 9 and that the 4-9/9-4 codetype was the most frequent 2-point classification. Further, significantly different mean T-score values were found between the delinquent and nondelinquent adolescents on 17 of the 38 MMPI-A basic, supplementary, and content scales evaluated in this study. Overall, the authors concluded that their findings supported the concurrent and construct validity of the MMPI-A scales in assessing adolescents in forensic settings and observed that the MMPI-A patterns and configurations found in their study were largely consistent with the prior literature on male juvenile delinquents. They also reported that, by using a split session oral administration format, it had been possible to obtain valid MMPI-A profiles from 94% of the boys who completed the testing.

Glaser, Calhoun, and Petrocelli (2002) evaluated the ability of MMPI-A scales to successfully discriminate between three general types of criminal offenses among male juvenile offenders. Seventy-two male juvenile offenders were classified in this study according to the type of offense: crime against person, crime against property, or drug/alcohol offense. Results showed that these adolescents could be correctly identified in 79.2% of cases by the use of scores on selected MMPI-A scales. For example, adolescents who scored higher on basic scales 1 and 0 were less likely to develop alcohol and drug problems and more likely to be classified correctly as engaging in property crime. Adolescents who are more likely to engage in drug offenses produced lower scores on scale 9 and higher scores on the A-sch content scale. Overall, 12 MMPI-A scales significantly contributed to accurate discrimination between these three offense categories.

Morton, Farris, and Brenowitz (2002) recently examined the ability of the MMPI-A to discriminate between 855 male delinquents in a South Carolina detention center and 805 male adolescents from the MMPI-A normative sample. MMPI-A basic scale 5 was found to be the most effective scale in accurately identifying normal and delinquent adolescents, with lower, or more masculine, scale 5 scores characteristic of the delinquent sample. In addition, elevations on MMPI-A basic scales 4 and 6 were more common among male delinquents. These researchers concluded that their findings were generally consistent with earlier reports but observed that the relative importance of scale 5 had not been widely emphasized in prior research. Discriminant analysis based on the optimal combination of various groupings of MMPI-A scales effectively identified adolescents in the delinquent and normative samples, with the sensitivity ranging from 90% to 95% and the specificity ranging from 80% to 85%. Further, this level of accurate discrimination was maintained in replication with an independent sample.

Archer et al. (2003) followed up the Morton et al. (2002) study to evaluate the extent to which the MMPI-A profiles of 196 males from juvenile detention facilities could be successfully discriminated from the protocols of 200 male adolescent psychiatric patients and 151 dually diagnosed male adolescents receiving treatment for substance abuse and psychiatric symptomatology. Findings showed significant differences in mean T-score values among these three groups of adolescents across a variety of MMPI-A scales and subscales. Results from discriminant function analyses indicated that the treatment setting could be identified effectively from scores from six MMPI-A scales (F_2, ACK, IMM, R, Hy_3, and Si_2). Collectively, these findings suggested that delinquent boys could be characterized by emotional and psychological immaturity, accompanied by superficial attempts to appear emotionally controlled and well-adjusted. Further, these authors noted that although the MMPI-A profiles of adolescents in detention, psychiatric, and dual diagnosis facilities showed some distinctive features, they also shared many features across these settings.

Katz and Marquette (1996) attempted to identify the personality characteristics of juveniles who commit murder by examining the MMPI-A profiles of a group of 29 males, aged 16 through 23, convicted of first and second degree murder. This group was contrasted with a cohort of nonviolent offenders as well as a group of normal high school students. Contrary to their expectations, these researchers found that the MMPI-A profiles for the murderers in this study were relative free of serious psychopathology and did not differ significantly from the nonviolent offenders or even the high school students. They concluded that adolescents and young men who commit violent crimes may do so for many reasons beyond the issues of traditionally defined psychopathology. These researchers postulated, for example, that history of gang membership and prior involvement in violent behaviors may serve as more significant predictors of violent offenses. In this regard, Kaser-Boyd (2002) recently suggested that although a history of abuse and exposure to family violence commonly appear among children who commit murder, there is no single personality style or dynamic found in juveniles who commit homicide.

Stein and Graham (1999) examined the extent to which the MMPI-A validity scales could differentiate between male and female adolescents in correctional settings instructed to fake-good and adolescents in both correctional and noncorrectional settings who took the MMPI-A under standard instructions. Their results indicate that the MMPI-A validity scales can successfully identify fake-good profiles generated by adolescents. Adolescents attempting to fake-good (or underreport symptomatology) produced significantly higher mean scores on validity scales L and K and lower scores on all of the basic clinical scales, with the exception of *scale 5*. For scales L and K, the optimal cutoff score for identifying adolescents attempting to fake-good was 60, somewhat lower than the T-score of 65 recommended in the MMPI-A manual (Butcher et al., 1992).

Stein and Graham (2001) also evaluated the ability of the MMPI-A to detect substance abuse problems in a juvenile correctional setting. Specifically, these researchers evaluated the contributions of *MAC–R*, *ACK*, and *PRO* in relation to interviewers' ratings of substance abuse in a sample of 123 boys and girls in an Ohio juvenile correctional facility. Results indicated that scores from the *ACK* and *PRO* scales, but not from *MAC–R*, were related to interviewers' ratings of substance abuse. The authors concluded that the MMPI-A substance abuse scales could play an important role in screening for substance abuse problems in juvenile correctional settings. More recently, Tirrell et al. (2004) evaluated the ability of the MMPI-A substance abuse scales to effectively discriminate between juvenile offenders with a history of substance abuse, psychiatric patients without a history of substance abuse, and normal adolescents. The study found that scores from the *ACK* scale were most effective in differentiating juvenile offender substance abusers from nonabusing psychiatric patients and that *MAC–R* scale scores were most effective in differentiating juvenile offender substance abusers from their normal counterparts. Similar to the findings reported by Stein and Graham (2001), the optimal T-score cutoffs for the *ACK* and *PRO* scales generally fell in the 55–60 range, below the recommended levels found in the MMPI-A manual (Butcher et al., 1992).

Finally, Gomez, Johnson, Davis, and Velasquez (2000) evaluated potential ethnic differences in the MMPI-A profiles of 54 African-American and Mexican-American adolescent first-time offenders. The authors noted that both African Americans and Mexican Americans are overrepresented in juvenile justice settings, rendering the potential of ethnicity to affect MMPI-A responses particularly relevant for these adolescents. Their results, however, indicated relatively minimal ethnic differences in MMPI-A validity, content, and supplementary scores, with 50% of the African-American adolescents producing within-normal-limits profiles and 25% of the Mexican-American adolescents producing within-normal-limits profiles. The authors concluded that although their research did not show evidence of significant T-score differences between these two ethnic groups, further MMPI-A research is needed to evaluate the degree to which clinical correlates may differ at comparable T-score elevations for adolescents from various ethnic backgrounds.

In summary, the available literature on the use of the MMPI-A with adolescents in forensic settings is largely based on studies typically utilizing male adolescents in detention or correctional facilities. Given the dramatic increase in the number of juvenile court cases involving females, who accounted for 26% of all juvenile arrests in 1997 (Snyder, 2000), more MMPI-A investigations are clearly warranted with girls in forensic settings. The literature to date also indicates that adolescents in juvenile justice settings may be meaningfully distinguished from their counterparts in normal or psychiatric settings based on a variety of MMPI-A features, but the evidence from the more recent literature is mixed on the issue of whether Hathaway and Monachesi's excitatory scales (4, 8, and 9) or inhibitory scales (2, 5, and 0) are more effective than other basic scales in these discriminations.

Finally, it is notable that the MMPI-2 classification rules developed by Megargee for male (1994) and female (1997) adult offenders have not been extended to the MMPI-A. Megargee (1979) originally developed a configural system for classifying offenders into 10 MMPI profile types. He subsequently established a rich empirical correlate base for each of these 10 profile types that was specific to offender populations. A summary of the adult offender MMPI classification system is shown in Table 7.6. Among the impressive strengths of Megargee's classification system is the ability of these categories to encompass most profiles produced by adult offenders. For example, in Megargee's (1997) extension of this MMPI-2 base classification system to female offenders, he reported that the system had the ability to classify more than 98% of these women into these profile categories. Megargee's system has also proven very valuable in forensic applications because of its ability to generate accurate extratest descriptions relevant to forensic settings. These correlates for male and female offenders have included variables such as the need for close supervision in the correctional facility, probable response to rehabilitation programs, and reoffense risk following release. The extent to which the Megargee classification system could be successfully adapted for use with the MMPI-A is an important topic for future researchers.

The Value of Using the MMPI-A in Forensic Evaluations

As noted repeatedly in this chapter, the MMPI-A may be useful in forensic evaluations as a component of an overall comprehensive forensic assessment. Archer and Baker (in press) recently discussed the role of the MMPI-A in juvenile justice settings in relation to a number of the characteristics of the test instrument. These authors noted that the MMPI-A has a variety of validity scales, including reliable measures of defensiveness and overreporting, that can illuminate the adolescent's test-taking

TABLE 7.6
Summary of Megargee Types

Type	MMPI Characteristics	Behavioral Characteristics
Item	Scales generally unelevated	Stable, well adjusted, with minimal problems and lacking conflicts with authorities
Easy	Moderate elevations; scales 4 and 3 often elevated	Bright, stable; good adjustment, personal resources and interpersonal relationships; underachievers
Baker	Moderate elevations; scales 4 and 2 often elevated	Inadequate, anxious, constricted, dogmatic; tendency to abuse alcohol
Able	Moderate elevations; scales 4 and 9 typically elevated	Charming, impulsive, manipulative; achievement-oriented; adjust well to incarceration
George	Moderate elevations; scales 1, 2, and 3 elevated	Hardworking, submissive, anxious; have learned criminal values; often take advantage of educational and vocational programs
Delta	Moderate to high elevation on scale 4; other scales lower	Amoral, hedonistic, egocentric, manipulative, and bright; impulsive sensation seekers; poor relations with peers and authorities
Jupiter	Moderate to high elevations typically on scales 8, 9, and 7	Often overcome deprived backgrounds to do better than expected in prison and on release
Foxtrot	High elevations; scales 8, 9, and 4 often highest	Tough, streetwise, cynical, antisocial; deficits in most areas; extensive criminal histories; poor prison adjustment
Charlie	High elevations; peaks typically on scales 8, 6, and 4	Hostile, manipulative, alienated, aggressive, antisocial; extensive histories of poor adjustment, criminal convictions, and mixed substance abuse
How	Many very high scores	Unstable, agitated, disturbed mental health cases; extensive needs; function ineffectively in major areas

Note: Zager, L. D. (1988). The MMPI-based Criminal Classification System: A Review, Current Status, and Future Directions, by L. D. Zager, 1988, *Criminal Justice and Behavior, 15*, 39–57. Copyright 1988 American Association for Correctional Psychology. Reprinted by permission of Sage Publications, Inc.

attitude and evaluate the degree to which the adolescent's self-report has been influenced by conscious or unconscious attempts to distort his or her self-presentation. Further, the MMPI-A clinical scales possess relatively high levels of reliability and provide sensitive measures capable of evaluating possible changes in psychological functioning over time.

The MMPI-A also has a considerable research base, and Forbey (2003), for example, recently estimated that 112 books, chapters, and research articles have been published on the MMPI-A since its release in 1992. In contrast, Forbey noted that the Millon Adolescent Clinical Inventory (MACI) has been the subject of only 15 published works during the same time period. Further, the MMPI-A has a research literature specific to its use with juvenile delinquents that covers a span of 6 decades, beginning with the work of Dora Capwell in the early 1940s. Thus, the MMPI-A is the most widely researched objective measure of personality functioning among adolescents, including adolescents evaluated in forensic settings. As part of the forensic database available for the instrument, there are currently two MMPI-A interpretive software programs that include specific guidance in interpreting MMPI-A profiles for adolescents in forensic settings. These programs are the Minnesota Report: Adolescent System Interpretive Report, developed by Butcher and Williams (1992) and distributed through Pearson Assessments, and the MMPI-A Interpretive System (Version 3) developed by Archer (2003) and distributed through Psychological Assessment Resources (PAR).

In addition to the ability to detect numerous and broad dimensions of clinical psychopathology and to evaluate efforts to under- or overreport psychopathological symptoms, the MMPI-A also provides three supplementary scales focused on substance abuse, an issue of particular importance for adolescents in the juvenile justice system. Archer and Baker (in press) also observe that the MMPI-A provides critical data on important dimensions, including emotional distress, the quality and perception of family relationships, and impulsivity and behavioral disinhibition, and contains a variety of other scales and subscales potentially related to a juvenile's likelihood to behave in a predatory or victimlike manner in a detention or correctional environment. Thus, the MMPI-A offers a reliable and comprehensive method of describing the adolescent's current behavioral and psychological functioning and yields data on dimensions potentially relevant to the prediction of future behavior. It is also feasible to present and explain the MMPI-A in a court environment in a manner that is relatively accessible for most lay individuals. The development methods used in the creation of the instrument can be presented in a straightforward way, and the methods of interpretation may be concisely explained, including the development of the MMPI-A normative sample and the research-based correlates used for interpretation purposes.

Archer and Baker (in press) also discuss a number of potential limitations of the MMPI-A as this instrument is applied for forensic purposes. For example, the MMPI-A is a 478-item test that requires a seventh-grade reading level and a 60- to 75-minute administration period. The reading requirement means that many MMPI-A items may be too difficult for some adolescents in juvenile detention or juvenile justice settings, particularly adolescents in the younger portion of the adolescent age spectrum. Thus, adequate cognitive capacity and reading level are central to the effective use of this instrument in delinquent populations. It is important, however, not to overemphasize this issue in a manner that prevents psychologists from considering the administration of the MMPI-A for forensic evaluations. The data from Pena et al. (1996) indicate that the vast majority of adolescents in detention and correctional settings are capable of producing valid and useful MMPI-A profiles, particularly if testing is divided into two or more sessions and audiotape administration is utilized for adolescents with reading disabilities. This writer's experience in collecting MMPI-A data in detention and correctional facilities in several states also strongly indicates that a substantial majority of adolescents in these settings can produce valid and useful profiles.

Archer and Baker (in press) also emphasize that the MMPI-A is best viewed as an assessment instrument that provides a description of the adolescent's psychological functioning at "a moment in time." Although there is some evidence that certain psychological features tend to be more stable than others in the description of both adolescents and adults, it is particularly important to remember that the MMPI-A is quite limited in its ability to make long-term behavioral or diagnostic predictions. This is a limitation, however, not only of the MMPI-A but of *all* psychological assessment instruments standardly used with adolescents. In addition to issues related to the standard error of measurement inherent in any psychological assessment, adolescent development also includes important components of affective and behavioral instability that are characteristic of this stage of development. One consequence of these sources of temporal instability is that the MMPI-A is much more effective at describing how an adolescent is functioning at the current time and of less utility and reliability in rendering longer term predictions concerning future behaviors.

Suggested Points for Presenting Results From the MMPI-A in Court

Pope, Butcher, and Seelen (2000) provided an extensive overview of the use of the MMPI-2 and MMPI-A in forensic settings. These authors noted that the MMPI-2 not only is the most widely used objective personality assessment measure but is also "likely the most widely cited personality assessment instrument in litigation" (p. 61). Although the MMPI-A is probably used less extensively in court than the MMPI-2, decisions concerning the admissibility of both instruments generally involve similar issues. Pope et al. observed that the admissibility of the MMPI-2 has tended to focus on whether there was adequate evidence that the MMPI-2 could serve as a sufficiently reliable basis for addressing the specific type of assessment issue before the court. The court's acceptance of the MMPI-2 for general personality assessment does not, for example, imply acceptance of this instrument for more specific assessment issues (e.g., the prediction of violence or the evaluation of sexual predators). Further, when testimony relies on a computerized scoring and/or interpretation system, the methodology for this scoring and interpretation may also be required to meet the test for adequate reliability and validity. Pope and his colleagues also noted that MMPI-2–based testimony will be admissible only to the extent that it helps the trier of fact (a judge or a jury) understand the legal issues at hand. Further, the testimony based on an MMPI-2 or MMPI-A typically should not preempt the judge's or jury's role in deciding guilt or innocence. Courts have blocked MMPI-2–based testimony, for example, when it was irrelevant to the decision at hand or when the admission of such testimony might tend to preempt the court's responsibility to decide the "ultimate issue" of guilt or innocence in a criminal trial.

Pope and his colleagues suggested several points useful in presenting the results of the MMPI-2 in court, and these points are also directly relevant for the presentation of MMPI-A findings. These suggestions have been adapted for the MMPI-A and can be summarized as follows:

1. Describe the MMPI-A as a widely researched and validated objective paper-and-pencil measure of psychopathology.
2. Note that the MMPI-A is the objective personality assessment instrument most widely used for evaluating adolescents (e.g., Archer & Newsom, 2000) and that it is also the most widely researched objective personality assessment instrument for this age group (e.g., Forbey, 2003).
3. Provide a brief overview of the development of the original version of the MMPI, and be prepared to summarize, if necessary, the adaptation of the MMPI specifically for adolescents (MMPI-A).
4. Explain the empirical scale construction method used to develop the MMPI and MMPI-A basic scales, and note the actuarial or probabilistic nature of the descriptors associated with elevated scores.
5. Describe and illustrate how the MMPI-A is used in personality assessment, and explain the use of the research literature in developing the correlate base for the clinical scales.
6. Illustrate how the MMPI-A is standardly used in personality description and clinical assessment (e.g., include a Power Point or slide presentation of a basic scale profile form).
7. If pertinent to the case, describe and illustrate how the clinical scales of the original version of the MMPI and the MMPI-A are composed of essentially the

same items and possess similar psychometric properties. This is most relevant if generalizing research findings from the original instrument to the MMPI-A.

8. Describe how the validity of a particular MMPI-A profile can be determined through the use of the validity scales. Be prepared to explain the validity scales related to random responding (*VRIN*), defensive responding (*L* and *K*), and overreporting of symptoms (*F*, F_1, and F_2).

9. Describe how MMPI-A findings for a particular adolescent are relevant to the forensic issue(s) before the court (e.g., competency to stand trial).

10. Limit the inferences based on MMPI-A data to those that may be supported by the empirical research and acknowledge any limitations in the data.

11. Present the information about the MMPI-A in a manner that is readily understandable to the judge or jury. Avoid technical jargon and excessive statistical references.

SUMMARY

The use of the MMPI-A in forensic settings does not represent a simple extension of standard clinical skills to a new environment. Instead, forensic assessment requires the development of a new knowledge base, an expanded data-gathering approach, and a specific set of presentational skills applied within a unique context. In order to provide useful forensic assessments and expert testimony, the psychologist must become familiar with the relevant legal concepts and standards (e.g., competency, insanity, waiver of jurisdiction, reverse transfer, status offense, and "best interests of the child") as well as the specific statutes that apply in his or her state. Forensic assessments are also typically more comprehensive than therapeutic assessments and involve the gathering of much more collateral data. This comprehensive approach is inherently related to the forensic psychologist's role, which is to provide objective information to address a specific legal standard or issue rather than assist in the development or evaluation of a therapeutic intervention. Because of the unique features and demands of the forensic environment, forensic psychology will continue to develop as a specialty area within the more general field of psychology and will have its own advanced training recommendations and code of ethics (Committee on Ethical Guidelines for Forensic Psychologists, 1991). For those psychologists willing to invest the necessary time in acquiring this new knowledge and skill base, forensic assessment will provide an exciting, challenging, and rewarding professional pursuit.

Interpretive Issues and Strategies

The MMPI-A, used in conjunction with data from other psychometric tests, psychosocial assessment results, and clinical interview findings, provides a rich source of information about a variety of respondent characteristics. MMPI-A findings include data on profile validity and the adolescent's test-taking attitude. They also include data on the degree to which the adolescent's responses were consistent and accurate, which serves to establish the technical validity of the responses. In addition, the MMPI-A profile provides information on the presence or absence of psychiatric symptoms along a number of dimensions of psychopathology as well as indicates the type, nature, and extent of symptomatology. Further, inspection of the adolescent's MMPI-A results should allow for an overall estimate of the adolescent's adjustment level and maturation. The MMPI-A will typically provide information on the adolescent's characteristic defense mechanisms and the relative effectiveness of these mechanisms in protecting the adolescent from consciously perceived affective distress and ego threat. The test interpreter should be able to form an impression of the adolescent's typical interpersonal relationships, including such issues as the need for dominance versus submissiveness and the tendency to be involved with others versus socially withdrawn and isolated.

The use of the MMPI-A will often yield valuable diagnostic impressions and hypotheses for the treatment team of an adolescent patient. It is important to stress, however, that test instruments such as the MMPI-A are most productively used to generate a variety of diagnostic possibilities rather than an exclusive and single diagnosis. Substantial research has shown that MMPI-derived diagnoses and clinician-derived diagnoses differ substantially in clinical studies of adult psychiatric patients (Graham, 2000) and adolescent patients (Archer & Gordon, 1988). Research (Pancoast et al., 1988) has also indicated that simple diagnostic systems for the MMPI appear to perform as well as more complex diagnostic classification systems developed for the MMPI by Goldberg (1965, 1972) and Meehl and Dahlstrom (1960). Finally and perhaps most importantly, the MMPI-A provides the clinician with information that can assist in the consideration of treatment options. Such information may include the adolescent's level of motivation to engage in psychotherapy and openness to the therapeutic process. The clinician may also be able to derive information that will help determine the type of therapy, or combination of therapies, most likely to be effective with the adolescent (e.g., supportive psychotherapies, insight-oriented psychotherapies, behavioral psychotherapies, or psychopharmacological interventions). The MMPI-A results may also allow inferences concerning the modalities of treatment that appear to be indicated, including individual, family, and group psychotherapies.

STEPS IN MMPI-A PROFILE INTERPRETATION

The ability to derive meaningful and useful information from the MMPI-A is a function of the overall interpretive process utilized with this instrument. Table 8.1 summarizes an effective approach for interpreting the MMPI-A.

The first two steps in this model emphasize the importance of considering the setting in which the MMPI-A is administered and evaluating the history and background information available for the adolescent. Interpretive hypotheses generated from MMPI-A findings should be carefully coordinated with what is known about the adolescent from extratest sources. It is possible to usefully interpret an MMPI-A profile in a "blind" fashion without consideration of the patient's background and history or features of the administration setting. Indeed, these latter sources of information are typically not utilized in computerized interpretations of the MMPI-2. Nevertheless, demographic, psychosocial history, and psychiatric history information generally increases the accuracy and utility of the inferences derived from the MMPI-A.

The third step concerns the evaluation of the technical validity of the MMPI-A profile. This step includes a review of the number of item omissions that occurred in the response process and an evaluation of response consistency and response accuracy. Validity assessment approaches are presented in detail in Chapter 4 of this text, based on the model proposed by Greene (2000). As previously noted, response consistency is primarily evaluated using the MMPI-A Variable Response Inconsistency ($VRIN$) scale, and scores from the True Response Inconsistency ($TRIN$) scale may be used for assessing the presence of an acquiescent or "nay-saying" response style. Inferences concerning response consistency can also be derived by examining the T-score elevation difference between the MMPI-A F_1 and F_2 subscales and the overall elevation of F. As noted, consistency is a necessary but not sufficient condition for technical validity. The accuracy of the adolescent's response patterns may be evaluated using the traditional validity scales F, L, and K, with particular attention to the overall configuration of these three validity measures. In addition to issues of technical validity, however, the MMPI-A validity measures can provide valuable information about the adolescent's willingness to engage in the psychotherapeutic process. For example, an MMPI-A validity configuration may indicate a technically valid profile and also demonstrate a level of K scale elevation indicative of a teenager who is likely to underreport psychiatric symptoms and to be guarded and defensive in the psychotherapy process. Thus, MMPI-A validity scales provide information concerning technical validity *and* extratest characteristics or correlates of the teenager that should be included in the overall interpretation of the adolescent's profile.

The fourth step in the interpretation of the MMPI-A profile involves an examination of the basic or standard scales, including an evaluation of the adolescent's codetype assignment based on his or her most elevated basic clinical scales. The process of evaluating the adolescent's MMPI-A codetype includes consideration of the degree of elevation manifested in the profile. The higher the adolescent's basic scale elevations, the more likely the adolescent is to display more of the symptoms or characteristics associated with a codetype classification. Additionally, the greater the

TABLE 8.1
Steps in MMPI-A Profile Interpretation

1. Setting in which the MMPI-A is administered
   a. Clinical/psychological/psychiatric
   b. School/academic evaluation
   c. Medical
   d. Neuropsychological
   e. Forensic
   f. Alcohol/drug treatment
2. History and background of patient
   a. Cooperativeness/motivation for treatment or evaluation
   b. Cognitive ability
   c. History of psychological adjustment
   d. History of stress factors
   e. History of academic performance
   f. History of interpersonal relationships
   g. Family history and characteristics
3. Validity
   a. Omissions
   b. Consistency
   c. Accuracy
4. Codetype (provides main features of interpretation)
   a. Degree of match with prototype
      (1) Degree of elevation
      (2) Degree of definition
      (3) Caldwell A-B-C-D Paradigm for multiple high points
   b. Low-point scales
   c. Note elevation of scales 2 (*D*) and 7 (*Pt*)
5. Supplementary and PSY-5 scales (supplement and confirm interpretation)
   a. Supplementary scale dimensions
      (1) Welsh *A* and *R* scales and the *IMM* scale
   b. Substance abuse scales
      (1) *MAC–R* and *PRO*
      (2) *ACK*
   c. Personality Psychopathology Five (PSY-5) scales
      (1) Aggressiveness and Disconstraint
6. Content scales
   a. Supplement, refine, and confirm basic scale data
   b. Interpersonal functioning (*A-fam*, *A-cyn*, and *A-aln*), treatment recommendations (*A-trt*), and academic difficulties (*A-sch* and *A-las*).
   c. Review scores on content component scales
   d. Consider effects of overreporting/underreporting
7. Review of Harris-Lingoes and *Si* subscales and critical item content
   a. Items endorsed can assist in understanding reasons for elevation of basic scales
   b. Review of Forbey and Ben-Porath MMPI-A critical items
8. Structural Summary (factor approach)
   a. Identify factors most relevant in describing an adolescent's psychopathology
   b. Use to confirm, simplify, and refine traditional interpretation

Note: Adapted from Archer (1997b). Copyright © 1997 by Lawrence Erlbaum Associate, Inc. Reprinted by permission.

degree to which the adolescent's specific MMPI-A profile corresponds to the prototypic profiles used in research investigations for that codetype, the more confidence can be placed in the accuracy of the codetype correlates attributed to the obtained profile. The degree of correspondence between a particular MMPI-A codetype and the prototypic profile characteristics for a given codetype may be ascertained, for example, by visual inspection of the Marks et al. (1974) modal profiles. In contrast, the MMPI-A Interpretive System software (version 3) distributed by Psychological Assessment Resources and written by Archer (1992a, 1995, 2003) uses a statistical approach to this issue. Specifically, this program provides a correlation coefficient that expresses the degree of association between an adolescent's MMPI-A profile and the mean MMPI-A profile characteristics for adolescents classified in that codetype grouping. Further, the program calculates the definition of the codetype, expressed in T-scores. The greater the degree to which the adolescent's codetype is clearly defined (i.e., the greater the T-score elevation difference between the two most elevated scales and the third highest scale), the more likely that the particular codetype descriptors will be found to be accurate. As noted in chapter 5, Caldwell's A-B-C-D Paradigm may prove useful in interpreting profiles with clinical-range elevations on several scales. In addition to high-point descriptors, it may also be useful to examine the low-point characteristics of the adolescent's MMPI-A profile for selected scales. Chapter 5 provides information on the correlates of scale values substantially below T = 50 for the basic MMPI-A scales. Finally, a specific review of MMPI-A basic scales 2 and 7 will provide information on the degree of affective distress currently experienced by the adolescent, permitting important inferences concerning the adolescent's motivation to engage in psychotherapy.

A review of the MMPI-A supplementary scales (step 5 in Table 8.1) should provide substantial information to support and refine basic scale interpretation. Welsh's *A* and *R* scales indicate the overall level of maladjustment and the use of repression as a primary defense mechanism, respectively, and the adolescent's level of psychological maturity may be assessed through use of the Immaturity (*IMM*) scale. Substance abuse screening information can be obtained by using the MMPI-A revision of the MacAndrew (1965) Alcoholism Scale (the *MAC–R*) as well as two new scales created for the MMPI-A (*ACK* and *PRO*) to evaluate alcohol and drug abuse problem areas (Weed, Butcher, & Williams, 1994). The Personality Psychopathology Five (PSY-5), recently extended to the MMPI-A by McNulty et al. (1997) and reviewed in chapter 6, provides important data on personality dimensions (e.g., Aggressiveness and Disconstraint) of substantial usefulness in evaluating adolescents.

In addition to supplementary scales, there are 15 content scales on the MMPI-A that may be used to improve profile interpretation (see step 6 in Table 8.1). Many of the MMPI-A content scales may be used to refine the interpretation of basic scales. For example, scale *A-anx* may be helpful in relation to scale *Pt*, scale *A-biz* in relation to scale *Sc*, and scales *A-con* and *A-fam* in relation to MMPI scale *Pd*. Further, content scales such as *A-trt* may provide very important information on the adolescent's probable initial approach to therapy, and *A-sch* and *A-las* may signal the presence of academic difficulties. Content scales including *A-fam*, *A-cyn*, and *A-aln* are also relevant to descriptions of the adolescent's interpersonal functioning. The content component scales developed by Sherwood et al. (1997) for 13 of the 15 MMPI-A content scales should prove quite valuable in refining the interpretation of the adolescent's protocol. For example, the *A-ang* component scales should provide important information for discriminating the potential for explosive and aggressive behaviors from more benign irritability, and the *A-trt* components hold promise in providing a more detailed understanding of the reasons why initial obstacles to treatment may be present in the psychological functioning of the adolescent. In evaluating content scale data, however, it is important to consider the effects of overreporting or underreporting (i.e., response accuracy) on content scale findings. Because content scales are constructed based on obvious items, adolescents may easily suppress content scale values when underreporting symptomatology and may grossly elevate content scale values when consciously or unconsciously overreporting symptomatology.

In the next stage (step 7) of profile analysis, the MMPI-A interpreter may wish to selectively examine the content of the adolescent's MMPI-A responses as manifested in the Harris-Lingoes subscales for the standard MMPI-A scales 2, 3, 4, 6, 8, and 9 and the *Si* subscales for 0 and as exhibited in responses to "critical" or "follow-up" items. A content review may refine interpretive hypotheses generated from examination of the MMPI-A basic, supplementary, and content scales. This content-based information, however, should be used only as a means of refining or clarifying hypotheses generated using the results of the standard MMPI-A scales. For example, it has been previously noted that Harris-Lingoes subscales should not be interpreted unless a clinical-range elevation has occurred on the corresponding MMPI-A basic scale and that findings for the Hy_1 (Denial of Social Anxiety) and Pd_3 (Social Imperturbability) subscales may not provide useful clinical information due to the psychometric limitations of these two subscales (Krishnamurthy et al., 1995). The recently developed MMPI-A critical item set by Forbey and Ben-Porath (1998) appears useful as a means of identifying content themes calling for clarification in posttest feedback with the adolescent. However, because responses to any single MMPI-A item are highly unreliable, substantial caution should be employed in interpreting individual item responses.

In the final stage (step 8) of profile analysis, the interpreter may wish to review the MMPI-A Structural Summary form as a means of organizing MMPI-A scale data in order to identify the most salient dimensions of the adolescent's current functioning. The first seven steps in the interpretive approach provide correlates and inferences concerning the adolescent's behaviors based on an organization of scales into traditional categories such as validity scales, basic clinical scales, content and supplementary scales, and Harris-Lingoes and *Si* subscales. The Structural Summary approach promotes a comprehensive assessment of the adolescent's functioning, deemphasizing the largely arbitrary distinction between categories of scales. The use of this approach serves to remind the clinician that data derived from the MMPI-A scales are highly intercorrelated and reflective of broad underlying dimensions of psychological functioning. As noted in Archer and Krishnamurthy (2002), interpretive guidelines for the Structural Summary form include the following two propositions:

- A majority of the scales or subscales associated with a particular factor must reach critical values ($T \geq 60$ or $T \leq 40$, depending on the scale or subscale) before the interpreter should emphasize that factor as salient in describing the adolescent's personality characteristics.
- The higher the percentage of scales and subscales within a factor that produce critical values (assuming the first proposition is met), the greater the role that factor should play in the description of the adolescent.

CLINICAL CASE EXAMPLES

The *MMPI-A Casebook* by Archer, Krishnamurthy, and Jacobson (1994) provides an in-depth review of 16 MMPI-A clinical case examples that illustrate important principles involved in the interpretation of MMPI-A profiles. These cases range from relatively straightforward profiles with single scale elevations to complex cases involving multiple scale high points. This text also provides an MMPI-A Interpretation

Practice Exercise Form for those readers who wish to take the opportunity to formulate their own thoughts and observations concerning these MMPI-A case materials prior to reviewing the interpretations provided in the text. The recent text by Archer and Krishnamurthy (2002) also presents several illustrative clinical cases as well as a suggested format for organizing test reports.

The purpose of this section of the current text is to provide a concise review of interpretations for five MMPI-A protocols produced by adolescents in a psychiatric setting, a forensic setting, a substance abuse treatment setting, a school evaluation setting, and a medical setting. These protocols were selected from assessment records to illustrate a variety of interpretive issues found in various adolescent populations. Specifically, they illustrate major principles related to determining profile validity, dealing with multiple high point codetypes, interpreting supplementary scale and content scale data, and using the MMPI-A Structural Summary. The MMPI-A interpretations provided for these protocols are not exhaustive, and it is likely that the reader may observe additional characteristics or features highly relevant to the description or treatment of these adolescents. The clinical correlate statements in this chapter are based on a combination of sources, including both adolescent and adult correlate studies with the original MMPI, MMPI-A findings presented in the test manual (Butcher et al., 1992), and Structural Summary correlates presented in detail in Archer, Krishnamurthy, et al. (1994) and Archer and Krishnamurthy (2002). Psychometric findings from other test instruments are occasionally included in the discussion of these clinical examples to provide additional relevant data and to offer a limited illustration of the ways in which results from other test instruments may enrich the interpretation of MMPI-A profiles. In these case examples, data from other test instruments are typically presented in a very abbreviated form, and the reader is referred to the basic source documents for these instruments to obtain more comprehensive information on their use. The clinical case examples in this chapter include discussions of the standard or basic MMPI-A scales, the supplementary scales, the content scales, and the Structural Summary findings. Data from additional MMPI-A sources (e.g., Harris-Lingoes subscales) are selectively integrated into test findings to illustrate specific points of interpretation.

Clinical Case Example I: 18-Year-Old Male Psychiatric Outpatient

> Mark S. was an 18-year-old African-American male from a middle-class background who was evaluated following referral for outpatient treatment. His presenting problems included the following: (a) increased depression and suicidal ideation, (b) decreased appetite and hypersomnia, (c) increased communication problems with family members, and (d) declining academic performance. Mark lived with his mother, stepfather, and younger half brother. He had displayed a marked decline in his academic performance during his senior year in a public high school but prior to this had been achieving at average levels of academic functioning. Mark was at risk for being required to repeat his senior year, and he was also beginning to display problems in school attendance at the time of the evaluation. In addition to the MMPI-A, Mark was administered the Wechsler Adult Intelligence Scale–III, which produced a Full Scale IQ score of 108, a Performance IQ score of 110, and a Verbal IQ score of 106. Additionally, Mark's mother completed the Child Behavior Checklist (CBCL) developed by Achenbach and Edelbrock (1983). Results of the CBCL indicated substantial elevations on internalizing symptoms, including depressed and anxious affect and an elevated score on the hostile withdrawn dimension of the CBCL. The patient's *DSM–IV–TR* admission diagnosis was Dysthymic Disorder (300.40).

Mark presented as a quiet and guarded young man. He arrived for the testing sessions on time and casually dressed. Rapport was difficult to establish with this adolescent. He tended to give brief responses to interview questions and maintain minimal eye contact with the examiner, often gazing down at the table or through the window. When the examiner questioned Mark about the cause of his current academic problems, he indicated that he was "having difficulty concentrating in class." Throughout testing, Mark's psychomotor functioning appeared to be somewhat slow, he often slouched in the chair, and he kept his arms at his side except when testing required physical participation.

Figure 8.1 presents Mark's admission MMPI-A basic scale profile on standard MMPI-A norms. Evaluating these findings using the validity assessment model proposed by Greene (2000), we can note that the item omission frequency ($? = 0$) and scores on measures of response consistency ($VRIN = 3$, $T = 45$; $TRIN = 11$, $T = 60$) are well within acceptable limits for this adolescent. Further, there is strong evidence that the accuracy of Mark's responses is acceptable, with his transitional and marginal-range elevation on L ($T = 63$) suggesting some tendency on Mark's part to emphasize conformity and conventional behaviors and to utilize denial as a primary defense mechanism. Additionally, Mark's T-score elevation on F ($T = 60$) occurs within a range typically found for adolescents exhibiting some evidence of significant psychopathology. Overall, however, Mark's validity scale data suggest that he responded to the MMPI-A in a consistent and accurate manner and that his test findings are amenable to valid and meaningful interpretation.

Mark's MMPI-A clinical scale profile presents a complex picture involving multiply elevated scales. Mark's extraordinary elevation on scale 2 ($T = 113$), combined with his relatively low score on scale 9 ($T = 43$), suggests that Mark might be described as profoundly depressed, with strong feelings of despondency, pessimism, inadequacy, and despair. Further, these thoughts and feelings may well be accompanied by psychomotor retardation and/or other biological correlates of depression. Moderate-range elevations on scales 1 and 6 suggest, respectively, that Mark may use somatization as a defense mechanism and might be described as hypersensitive and suspicious in his relationships with others. Marks et al. (1974) noted that the 1-6/6-1 codetype tended to occur more frequently among adolescents whose fathers were absent from the home environment. Additional moderate-range elevations on scale 3 reflect Mark's feelings of lassitude and malaise and the intensity of his somatic complaints (Harris-Lingoes subscales *Hy3* and *Hy4*). Inspection of the Harris-Lingoes subscales reveals that his moderate elevation on the *Pd* scale was a product of his endorsement of items related to familial discord (*Pd1*), social alienation (*Pd4*), and self-alienation (*Pd5*). Mark's T-score value of 72 on the *Mf* scale suggests several hypotheses, including that Mark has a low likelihood of antisocial or delinquent behaviors, a preference for a passive or submissive interpersonal style, and possible insecurity or conflict regarding sexual identity. Mark's elevation on the *Si* scale ($T = 70$) is consistent with his overall profile in suggesting significant social introversion or social discomfort. A review of the Social Introversion subscales indicates an elevation on Social Avoidance (*Si2*), which is associated with an avoidance of contact or involvement with others and a dislike or avoidance of social involvement. Finally, Mark's clinical-range elevation on scale 8 is accompanied by clinical-range elevations on the Harris-Lingoes subscales Social Alienation (*Sc1*), Emotional Alienation (*Sc2*), and Lack of Ego Mastery, Conative (*Sc4*). This latter Harris-Lingoes subscale has been associated with feelings of psychological weakness and vulnerability, problems in concentration and attention, and lack of energy. Elevations on *Sc4* have also been associated with guilt, depression and despondency, and the possibility of suicidal ideation.

Figure 8.2 provides data on the MMPI-A content and supplementary scales. Mark's profile displays a marked elevation on the *A-dep* scale, reflective of a substantial sense of depression and despondency. Archer and Gordon (1991b) also found elevations on this scale to be related to suicidal thoughts for girls and suicide attempts for boys. In addition, Mark's profile showed more moderate elevations on *A-anx* and *A-sod*, reflective of his anxiety, tension, and rumination about possible problems with concentration and his

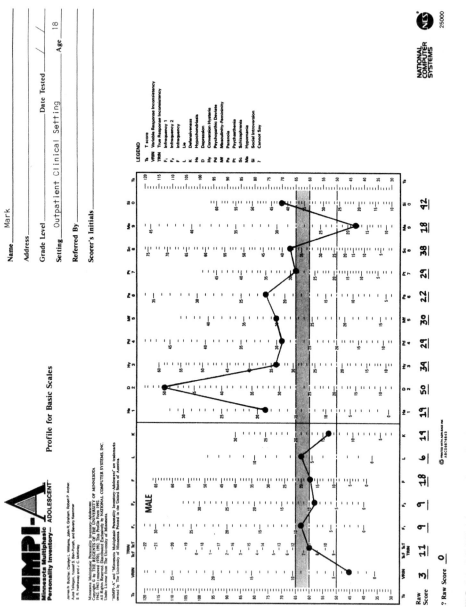

FIG. 8.1. MMPI-A basic scale profile for Clinical Case Example I (Mark). MMPI-A profile sheet reprinted by permission. Copyright © 1992 by the Regents of the University of Minnesota.

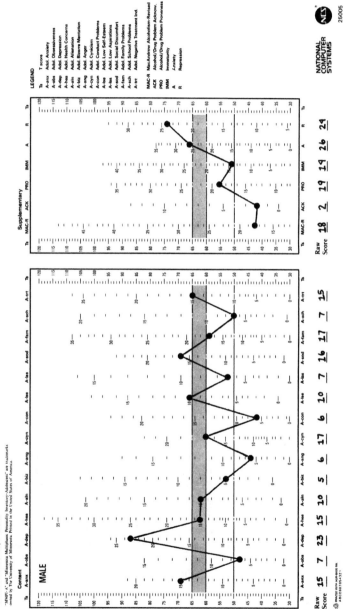

FIG. 8.2. MMPI-A content and supplementary scale profile for Clinical Case Example I (Mark). MMPI-A profile sheet reprinted by permission. Copyright © 1992 by the Regents of the University of Minnesota.

279

social discomfort, respectively. Finally, Mark produced borderline clinical elevations on the *A-lse* scale, reflecting deficits in self-esteem and feelings of adequacy, and on the *A-trt* scale. Interpretation of the *A-trt* scale was refined by reviewing Mark's content component scores for this scale, with results indicating that this borderline elevation resulted from Mark's apathy or despondency concerning his ability to change. Among the supplementary scales, Mark produced normal-range elevations on all measures of alcohol or substance abuse (*MAC–R, ACK,* and *PRO*) as well as on the Immaturity scale. Mark did produce a clinical-range elevation on Welsh's Anxiety (*A*) scale as well as a more pronounced elevation on Welsh's Repression (*R*) scale. Welsh (1956) suggested that a combination of elevated scores on both *A* and *R* was commonly associated with depressive diagnoses. On a descriptive level, this coelevation pattern would be consistent with the presence of substantial repressive defenses that were failing to protect the individual from substantial distress and ego threat.

Finally, information based on Mark's MMPI-A scale findings was used to create Fig. 8.3. On six of the eight Structural Summary dimensions, Mark produced scale or subscale values within normal ranges on the majority of scales. In contrast, Mark produced values within critical ranges on the majority of scales and subscales associated with the General Maladjustment dimension and with the Health Concerns dimension. Adolescents who produce elevations on a majority of the scales and subscales related to General Maladjustment have significant problems in adjustment in both their home and school environment and feel different and alienated from other teenagers. They are likely to be seen as withdrawn, ruminative, sad, and depressed and to feel less competent in social activities than their peers. These adolescents often report symptoms of tiredness and fatigue, sleep difficulties, and suicidal ideation. Further, adolescents with elevations on the scales involved in the dimension of Health Concerns are likely to be seen by others as dependent, socially isolated, shy, and unhappy. They are prone to tire quickly and are easily fatigued. Boys who score high on the Health Concerns factor may be viewed as exhibiting schizoid withdrawal, and these adolescents typically display lower levels of social competence in school.

Overall, the MMPI-A characteristics produced by Mark indicate a severely depressed adolescent with substantial feelings of social isolation, alienation, and inadequacy. Additionally, review of the Forbey–Ben-Porath MMPI-A critical items shows that Mark endorsed items 177, 283, and 399 as true, indicating a hopelessness about the future and the presence of suicidal ideation.

Archer and Slesinger (1999) found that adolescents who endorse these three MMPI-A items were likely to produce their highest elevations on scales 2 and 8. Friedman, Archer, and Handel (2004) recently reviewed the literature on the association between MMPI-2 and MMPI-A features and suicide. These authors concluded that there is little evidence that MMPI-2 or MMPI-A items, scales, or profile configurations are of practical use in determining an adolescent's or adult's likelihood of engaging in suicidal behavior. They cautioned that the actual probability of suicidal behavior in individual cases is mediated by numerous factors, including the individual's history of prior suicidal behavior, family history, and access to lethal methods and the presence or absence of a variety of symptoms, patterns, or psychiatric features, including such variables as depression, impulsivity, rage and anger, and/or alienation. Although the MMPI-2 or MMPI-A may not be able to accurately predict the occurrence of suicidal behavior, Friedman and his colleagues did stress the potential usefulness of test findings in uncovering the presence of suicidal ideation, which can serve as an important component of an overall assessment of suicidal risk or potential. Mark certainly had a sufficient number of features associated with heightened risk for suicide to alert the therapist to closely monitor this adolescent for the presence of ongoing suicide risk factors.

Mark participated in outpatient counseling for a period of 18 months, during which time a major focus of treatment was to resolve conflicts concerning sexual identity and sexuality. Mark's crisis during his senior year in high school was the result of a homosexual

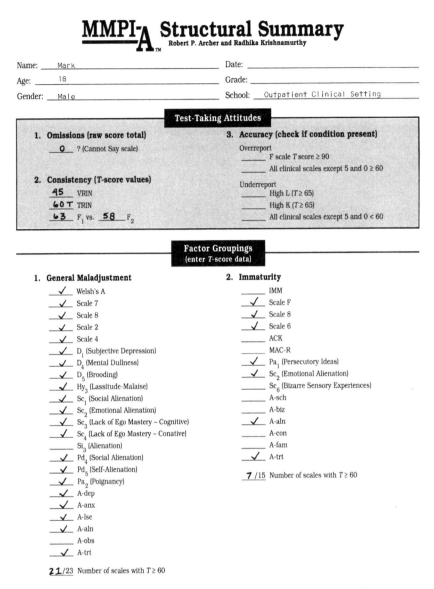

FIG. 8.3. MMPI-A Structural Summary for Clinical Case Example I (Mark). MMPI-A Structural Summary Form reprinted by permission. Copyright © 1994 by Psychological Assessment Resources, Inc.

encounter that underscored for this adolescent the growing awareness that he was gay. Mark was able to integrate this sense of sexual identity successfully across the 18-month period of counseling and is currently enrolled and successfully completing his education at a community college.

Clinical Case Example II: 14-Year-Old Male Adolescent in a Forensic Setting

Jared was a 14-year-old African-American adolescent evaluated at the request of the juvenile court following charges of burglary and auto theft. This case was recently briefly discussed by Archer and Baker (in press) and is presented in more detail in the current

3. Disinhibition/Excitatory Potential

_____ Scale 9

_____ Ma$_2$ (Psychomotor Acceleration)

_____ Ma$_4$ (Ego Inflation)

_____ Sc$_5$ (Lack of Ego Mastery, Defective Inhibition)

_____ D$_2$ (Psychomotor Retardation) (low score)*

_____ Welsh's R (low score)*

_____ Scale K (low score)*

_____ Scale L (low score)*

_____ A-ang

__✓__ A-cyn

_____ A-con

_____ MAC-R

__1__/12 Number of scales with $T \geq 60$ or ≤ 40 for scales with asterisk

4. Social Discomfort

__✓__ Scale 0

_____ Si$_1$ (Shyness/Self-Consciousness)

_____ Hy$_1$ (Denial of Social Anxiety) (low score)*

_____ Pd$_3$ (Social Imperturbability) (low score)*

_____ Ma$_3$ (Imperturbability) (low scores)*

__✓__ A-sod

__✓__ A-lse

__✓__ Scale 7

__4__/8 Number of scales with $T \geq 60$ or $T \leq 40$ for scales with asterisk

5. Health Concerns

__✓__ Scale 1

__✓__ Scale 3

__✓__ A-hea

__✓__ Hy$_4$ (Somatic Complaints)

__✓__ Hy$_3$ (Lassitude-Malaise)

__✓__ D$_3$ (Physical Malfunctioning)

__6__/6 Number of scales with $T \geq 60$

6. Naivete

_____ A-cyn (low score)*

_____ Pa$_3$ (Naivete)

_____ Hy$_2$ (Need for Affection)

_____ Si$_3$ (Alienation–Self and Others) (low score)*

_____ Scale K

__0__/5 Number of scales with $T \geq 60$ or $T \leq 40$ for scales with asterisk

7. Familial Alienation

__✓__ Pd$_1$ (Familial Discord)

_____ A-fam

__✓__ Scale 4

_____ PRO

__2__/4 Number of scales with $T \geq 60$

8. Psychoticism

__✓__ Pa$_1$ (Persecutory Ideas)

__✓__ Scale 6

_____ A-biz

_____ Sc$_6$ (Bizarre Sensory Experiences)

__2__/4 Number of scales with $T \geq 60$

Note. The presentation of scales under each factor label is generally organized in a descending order from the best to the least effective marker. Within this overall approach, scales are grouped logically in terms of basic clinical scales, Harris-Lingoes and Si subscales, and content scales. The majority of scales included in this summary sheet were correlated $\geq .60$ or $\leq -.60$ with the relevant factor for the MMPI-A normative sample.

FIG. 8.3. (Continued)

discussion. The purpose of this evaluation was to provide the court with information related to Jared's psychological functioning while awaiting adjudication, along with a recommendation concerning appropriate postadjudication placement. Jared's prior court history included charges of assault, disorderly conduct, and possession of marijuana. He had been on probation for the past 8 months and had spent 25 days in juvenile detention during the prior year. Throughout the evaluation, Jared might be described as rebellious and defiant, and he responded to questions in a haphazard and impulsive manner. Jared was the youngest of two children, and his older sibling did not reside at home (his oldest brother was incarcerated as an adult following a felony conviction). Jared's mother provided inconsistent living arrangements and substandard food and clothing for this child throughout much of his development. Jared lived with his father for a short period but was subsequently removed from his father's care following the occurrence of several physical altercations between them. Following his removal from his father's home, Jared was placed in a group home for delinquent boys. During his time in the group home, Jared was arrested for physically assaulting a female staff member. When Jared eventually returned to his biological mother's home, their relationship continued to have a strongly conflictual and tumultuous nature.

Jared's grades suffered because of frequent school suspensions for disruptive behaviors. His peer group included a number of other adolescents who had been involved extensively in the court system for delinquent behaviors. Since age 12, Jared had smoked marijuana and drunk beer with his friends whenever these substances were available to them. Jared was not addicted to any substances, however, nor had he ever undergone substance abuse treatment. Jared was administered the MMPI-A and other test instruments in order to provide a comprehensive evaluation that focused on his emotional and behavioral functioning. Results of the administration of the Wechsler Intelligence Scale for Children–Revised produced a Verbal IQ score of 86, a Performance IQ score of 95, and a Full Scale IQ score of 89. Jared's mother completed the CBCL and produced marked elevations on scales related to delinquent and hyperactive behaviors.

Jared's MMPI-A basic scale profile is shown in Fig. 8.4. We might begin the evaluation of the technical validity of Jared's profile by noting that he omitted six items on the Cannot Say (?) scale, clearly withing acceptable limits for profile interpretation. His scores on the response consistency measures *VRIN* (raw score = 7, T = 57) and *TRIN* (raw score = 9, T = 51) are also within acceptable standards based on guidelines provided in the MMPI-A manual (Butcher et al., 1992). Further, there was relatively limited difference (i.e., less than 20 T-score points) between Jared's elevations on scales F_1 (T = 73) and F_2 (T = 58), providing additional support for the assumption that Jared had not responded randomly to questions in the later part of the test booklet. Finally, the validity scale configuration of scales F, L, and K is well within acceptable limits and consistent with the meaningful interpretation of the MMPI-A clinical scale findings for this adolescent. In summary, his MMPI-A validity scales suggest that Jared responded to the test instrument in a consistent and accurate manner.

The basic scale profile produced by Jared is a well-defined 4/6 codetype, with the term definition referring to the T-score difference between the second and third most elevated clinical scales (6 and 9, respectively). In this regard, it is also possible to view the current profile as a well-defined single-scale elevation on scale 4, since the difference between scale 4 (T = 78) and scale 6 (T = 69) is 9 T-score points. However, since both of these scales are clearly clinically elevated, most interpreters would probably approach this as a 4/6 codetype but place particular emphasis on scale 4 characteristics. The 4-6/6-4 codetype is fairly common among adolescents and occurs in more than 5% of adolescent assessments in clinical settings. These teenagers are typically described as argumentative, resentful, and angry. They typically have presenting problems involving defiance, disobedience, and delinquent behaviors. Adolescents who produce this codetype are often referred for evaluation by court agencies for the types of conduct disorder behaviors found in Jared's history. These adolescents tend to place excessive demands on others but are resentful of any demands or limits placed on their own behavior. They are generally suspicious and distrustful and characteristically avoid deep emotional attachments. They use externalization, projection, and acting out as primary defense mechanisms. The 4-6/6-4 adolescent typically has problems with impulsivity and anger management and often acts without deliberation or forethought. Problems with authority figures are prevalent for these teenagers, and they are often seen by others as provocative and defiant. The 4-6/6-4 codetype is also frequently associated with adolescent drug use and abuse. These teenagers are difficult to motivate in psychotherapy and are reluctant to accept responsibility for their behavior. Within forensic settings, their tendency to become angry and

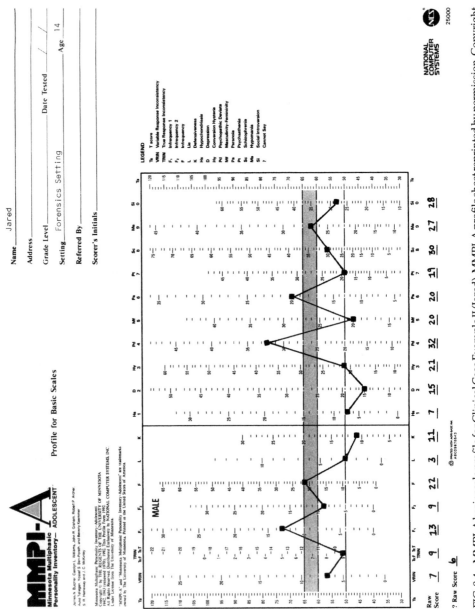

FIG. 8.4. MMPI-A basic scale profile for Clinical Case Example II (Jared). MMPI-A profile sheet reprinted by permission. Copyright © 1992 by the Regents of the University of Minnesota.

284

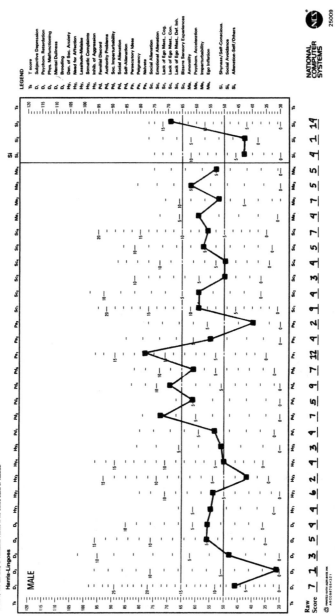

FIG. 8.5. MMPI-A Harris-Lingoes and *Si* subscales profile for Clinical Case Example II (Jared). MMPI-A profile sheet reprinted by permission. Copyright © 1992 by the Regents of the University of Minnesota.

argumentative may result in violent altercations or infractions, and acting-out and anti-social behavior is likely to be an initial primary treatment focus.

A review of the MMPI-A Harris-Lingoes and *Si* subscales provides a further refinement of the content areas endorsed in the formation of Jared's elevations on scales *4* and *6*. Jared's Harris-Lingoes and *Si* subscales profile is presented in Fig. 8.5. Among the Harris-Lingoes scale *4* subscales, for example, Jared produced elevations on *Pd2* (Authority Problems) and *Pd4* (Social Alienation), reflecting this adolescent's marked problems with dealing with others. Additionally, Jared's Harris-Lingoes scale *6* elevation on *Pa1* (Persecutory Ideas) reflects his strong feeling that he is being punished and treated unfairly by others as well as his tendency to externalize blame for problems and frustrations. Since none of the other basic clinical scales reach clinical-range elevations, further inspection of the Harris-Lingoes subscales would not be appropriate in this case.

Jared's content and supplementary scale profile is presented in Fig. 8.6. As shown in this figure, Jared produced marked clinical-range elevations on MMPI-A content scales *A-ang*, *A-sch*, and *A-trt*. His elevation on *A-ang* is similar to those produced by adolescents who are described as impatient, angry, and hostile, and his accompanying elevation on the *A-ang1* component scale underscores the potential for explosive and aggressive behaviors. His elevated score on *A-sch* indicates significant behavioral and/or academic problems within the school setting, and his significant elevations on both of the component scales associated with this content scale suggest the presence of conduct problems and negative attitudes concerning academic achievement and activities. Finally, Jared's T-score of 85 on the *A-trt* suggests the presence of initial attitudes that may complicate the adolescent's response to rehabilitation efforts. The content component scales for *A-trt* indicate that these problems include pessimism concerning the ability to change (Low Motivation, *A-trt1*) as well as reluctance to discuss feelings of discomfort or vulnerability with others (Inability to Disclose, *A-trt2*). Moving to the Supplementary Scale section of the profile, we see that Jared produced a significant elevation on the *ACK* scale (T = 70) and transitional or borderline elevations on the *MAC–R* and *PRO* scales. This pattern suggests that Jared is relatively candid in acknowledging his alcohol and marijuana use and that further detailed evaluation is probably indicated in the area of alcohol and substance abuse. Jared's score on the *IMM* scale (T = 71) suggests that Jared might be described as frustrated, impatient, and exploitive in interpersonal relationships. Adolescents who produce elevations in the same range typically have difficulty in academic and social environments and tend to be egocentric, simplistic, or concrete in their cognitive processes and to externalize blame. These adolescents are often resistant to or defy rehabilitative efforts and may come into conflict with staff in criminal justice facilities. Their immaturity may also strain relationships with other residents within detention or correctional facilities, since their interpersonal exploitiveness may trigger aggressive behaviors on the part of peers.

Jared's Structural Summary profile is presented in Fig. 8.7. Jared produced significant T-score values on 3 of the 4 scales and subscales associated with the Familial Alienation factor. This pattern is typically found among adolescents who encounter frequent conflicts and disciplinary problems both at home and at school. These adolescents are often seen as delinquent, aggressive, and hostile. Jared also produced elevations on 10 of the 15 scales and subscales related to the Immaturity factor. Adolescents who produce similar patterns on this factor have been described as impulsive, self-centered, egocentric, and displaying little psychological insight or self-awareness. They are likely to manifest behavioral problems at school and at home and to have a long history of disciplinary problems. Finally, Jared produced elevations on 7 of the scales and subscales related to the Disinhibition/Excitatory Potential factor. Adolescents who produce similar patterns have been described as impulsive and as dominant and aggressive in interpersonal relationships. In general, these adolescents use externalization as a primary defense mechanism and may have histories involving dishonesty, theft, and problems with physical aggression. These adolescents also frequently have histories involving alcohol or drug

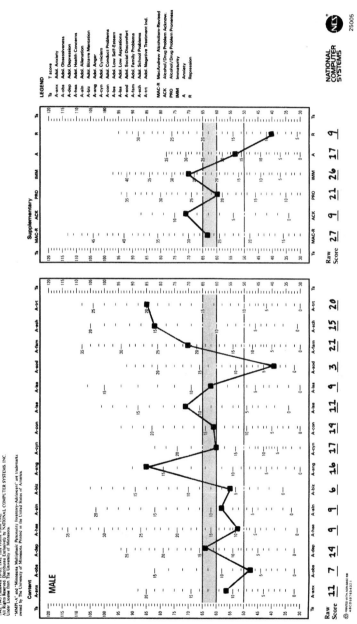

FIG. 8.6. MMPI-A content and supplementary scale profile for Clinical Case Example II (Jared). MMPI-A profile sheet reprinted by permission. Copyright © 1992 by the Regents of the University of Minnesota.

287

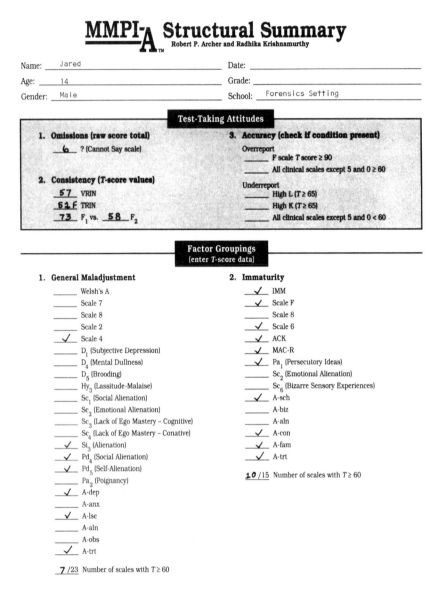

MMPI-A Structural Summary
Robert P. Archer and Radhika Krishnamurthy

Name: ___Jared___   Date: _____

Age: ___14___   Grade: _____

Gender: ___Male___   School: ___Forensics Setting___

Test-Taking Attitudes

1. Omissions (raw score total)

___6___ ? (Cannot Say scale)

2. Consistency (T-score values)

___57___ VRIN

___61 F___ TRIN

___73___ F$_1$ vs. ___58___ F$_2$

3. Accuracy (check if condition present)

Overreport

_____ F scale T score ≥ 90

_____ All clinical scales except 5 and 0 ≥ 60

Underreport

_____ High L (T ≥ 65)

_____ High K (T ≥ 65)

_____ All clinical scales except 5 and 0 < 60

Factor Groupings
(enter T-score data)

1. General Maladjustment

_____ Welsh's A

_____ Scale 7

_____ Scale 8

_____ Scale 2

___✓___ Scale 4

_____ D$_1$ (Subjective Depression)

_____ D$_4$ (Mental Dullness)

_____ D$_5$ (Brooding)

_____ Hy$_3$ (Lassitude-Malaise)

_____ Sc$_1$ (Social Alienation)

_____ Sc$_2$ (Emotional Alienation)

_____ Sc$_3$ (Lack of Ego Mastery – Cognitive)

_____ Sc$_4$ (Lack of Ego Mastery – Conative)

___✓___ Si$_3$ (Alienation)

___✓___ Pd$_4$ (Social Alienation)

___✓___ Pd$_5$ (Self-Alienation)

_____ Pa$_2$ (Poignancy)

___✓___ A-dep

_____ A-anx

___✓___ A-lse

_____ A-aln

_____ A-obs

___✓___ A-trt

___7___/23 Number of scales with T ≥ 60

2. Immaturity

___✓___ IMM

___✓___ Scale F

_____ Scale 8

___✓___ Scale 6

___✓___ ACK

___✓___ MAC-R

___✓___ Pa$_1$ (Persecutory Ideas)

_____ Sc$_2$ (Emotional Alienation)

_____ Sc$_6$ (Bizarre Sensory Experiences)

___✓___ A-sch

_____ A-biz

_____ A-aln

___✓___ A-con

___✓___ A-fam

___✓___ A-trt

___10___/15 Number of scales with T ≥ 60

FIG. 8.7. MMPI-A Structural Summary for Clinical Case Example II (Jared). MMPI-A Structural Summary Form reprinted by permission. Copyright © 1994 by Psychological Assessment Resources, Inc.

abuse. Their interpersonal relationships tend to be superficial, and they often end up in significant conflict with others. Their tendency toward conflict places these adolescents at risk for infractions when detained in juvenile justice settings. Their impulsivity often results in chronic rule breaking, and they are difficult to motivate to actively participate in rehabilitation programs.

Based on interpretation of the MMPI-A findings, combined with a comprehensive evaluation of this adolescent's educational, familial, and juvenile justice records, the forensic psychologist concluded that Jared's recidivism risk was moderate to high. Further, this psychologist noted that intense rehabilitative efforts would be needed with this adolescent, best pursued in a structured and secure setting. It was, therefore, recommended to the court that Jared be retained in the detention facility following adjudication

3. **Disinhibition/Excitatory Potential**

___✓___ Scale 9

_____ Ma_2 (Psychomotor Acceleration)

_____ Ma_4 (Ego Inflation)

_____ Sc_5 (Lack of Ego Mastery, Defective Inhibition)

___✓___ D_2 (Psychomotor Retardation) (low score)*

___✓___ Welsh's R (low score)*

_____ Scale K (low score)*

_____ Scale L (low score)*

___✓___ A-ang

___✓___ A-cyn

___✓___ A-con

___✓___ MAC-R

__7__/12 Number of scales with $T \geq 60$ or ≤ 40 for scales with asterisk

4. **Social Discomfort**

_____ Scale 0

_____ Si_1 (Shyness/Self-Consciousness)

_____ Hy_1 (Denial of Social Anxiety) (low score)*

_____ Pd_3 (Social Imperturbability) (low score)*

_____ Ma_3 (Imperturbability) (low scores)*

_____ A-sod

___✓___ A-lse

_____ Scale 7

__1__/8 Number of scales with $T \geq 60$ or $T \leq 40$ for scales with asterisk

5. **Health Concerns**

_____ Scale 1

_____ Scale 3

_____ A-hea

_____ Hy_4 (Somatic Complaints)

_____ Hy_3 (Lassitude-Malaise)

_____ D_3 (Physical Malfunctioning)

__0__/6 Number of scales with $T \geq 60$

6. **Naivete**

_____ A-cyn (low score)*

_____ Pa_3 (Naivete)

_____ Hy_2 (Need for Affection)

_____ Si_3 (Alienation-Self and Others) (low score)*

_____ Scale K

__0__/5 Number of scales with $T \geq 60$ or $T \leq 40$ for scales with asterisk

7. **Familial Alienation**

_____ Pd_1 (Familial Discord)

___✓___ A-fam

___✓___ Scale 4

___✓___ PRO

__3__/4 Number of scales with $T \geq 60$

8. **Psychoticism**

___✓___ Pa_1 (Persecutory Ideas)

___✓___ Scale 6

_____ A-biz

_____ Sc_6 (Bizarre Sensory Experiences)

__2__/4 Number of scales with $T \geq 60$

Note. The presentation of scales under each factor label is generally organized in a descending order from the best to the least effective marker. Within this overall approach, scales are grouped logically in terms of basic clinical scales, Harris-Lingoes and Si subscales, and content scales. The majority of scales included in this summary sheet were correlated $\geq .60$ or $\leq -.60$ with the relevant factor for the MMPI-A normative sample.

FIG. 8.7. (Continued)

to provide for rehabilitation in a secure environment. Jared's mother had not displayed a history of being able to place adequate behavioral controls on him in a manner that suggested he would be able to avoid future delinquent behaviors if returned to the home environment. A rehabilitation plan was developed from the MMPI-A and other data sources that included the recommendation that Jared participate in a group substance abuse program that employed relapse prevention concepts. Further, it was recommended that family therapy be utilized with Jared to increase the communication between Jared and his mother as well as to support and facilitate his mother's capacity to manage behavioral problems in the home environment. Individual and group counseling was also recommended to address Jared's anger management problems and his tendency to seek out delinquent peers. Finally, therapy was recommended to improve Jared's impulse control as well as his ability to relate in a nonconflictual and nonrebellious manner to authority figures. As noted earlier, Jared's MMPI-A responses are used to illustrate the ouput for adolescents in correctional or juvenile justice settings from the MMPI-A Interpretive System (Version 3) developed by PAR. This output is presented at the conclusion of this chapter (Appendix 8.1).

Clinical Case Example III: 16-Year-Old Adolescent Female in Substance Abuse Treatment

Carolyn is a 16-year-old Caucasian adolescent female with presenting problems that include drug abuse, decreased appetite and weight loss, temper control problems, lethargy, and marked family conflict. This patient was part of a family from a lower middle class background, and she had two younger siblings. Her mother and father had a long history of marked and occasionally violent arguments and conflicts, resulting in a decision by her parents to seek a divorce approximately 6 months prior to this evaluation. Carolyn was in the 11th grade at the time of this assessment, and most of her grades were in the average to above average range. She had a history of increasing disciplinary problems in the school and was described by her current teachers as rebellious, uncooperative, and defiant. At the time of her admission to drug and alcohol abuse residential treatment, her primary drug problems included daily use of marijuana and extensive use of cocaine over the past 12 months. Her mother felt that she had little or no control over Carolyn's drug-taking behaviors and that Carolyn's peer group consisted exclusively of other adolescents involved in drug abuse activities.

Administration of the Wechsler Adult Intelligence Scale–III resulted in a Verbal IQ score of 84, a Performance IQ score of 91, and a Full Scale IQ score of 86. Achievement test findings indicated a reading ability at the 8.5-grade level, math skills at the 10.6-grade level, and written language skills at the 8th-grade level.

Carolyn's MMPI-A basic scale profile is shown in Fig. 8.8. This adolescent did not omit any items on the MMPI-A ($? = 0$), and her $VRIN$ score (raw score = 3, T = 47) and $TRIN$ score (raw score = 8, T = 59) are both well within acceptable limits for adequate response consistency. Further, her validity scale configuration for scales F, L and K suggests that Carolyn was reasonably candid in her self-report and endorsed a substantial number of psychiatric symptoms ($F = 88$), within the range typically found among adolescents in clinical settings. Thus, she appeared relatively open and nondefensive in discussing psychiatric issues, and her MMPI-A validity scales suggest that she was consistent and accurate and that her clinical profiles are amenable to valid and meaningful interpretation.

The basic scale profile for Carolyn shows primary clinical-range elevations in a pattern that might be classified as a 4-2 codetype. This codetype is relatively common among adolescents and adults and is found in roughly 5% of adolescents evaluated in clinical settings. Adolescents who obtain this codetype often have difficulties with impulse control and act without sufficient deliberation. They show a marked disregard for and have repeated difficulties with authority figures. They often have a history of legal violations, including arrests, legal convictions, or court actions. Additionally, substance abuse and alcohol abuse are frequent problems associated with this codetype in both adolescents and adults. Further, the impulse control problems exhibited by adolescents with the 2-4/4-2 codetype may take several forms, including promiscuous sexual behavior for females and school truancy and running away from home for both males and females. Adolescents with this codetype frequently perceive their parents as unaffectionate and inconsistent and feel alienated and distant from their families. Primary defense mechanisms for these adolescents typically involve acting out and externalization. Their rebelliousness and impulsivity often contribute to the development of substance abuse disorders that occur comorbidly with their psychiatric symptomatology. Further, their problems with impulsivity are likely to be further exacerbated by substance abuse and

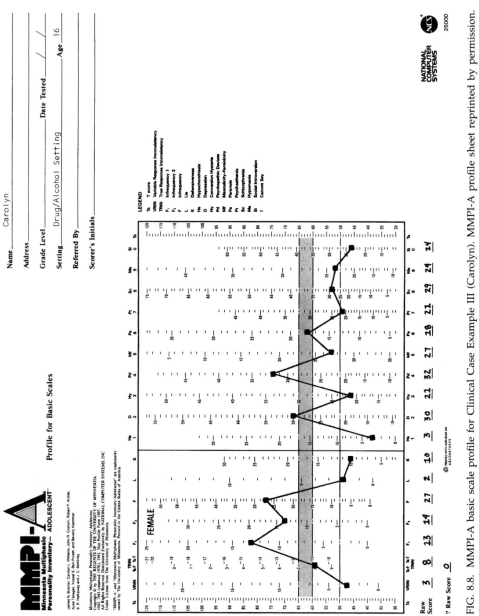

FIG. 8.8. MMPI-A basic scale profile for Clinical Case Example III (Carolyn). MMPI-A profile sheet reprinted by permission. Copyright © 1992 by the Regents of the University of Minnesota.

291

may increase the likelihood that these adolescents engage in other high-risk behaviors such as driving while intoxicated or engaging in high-risk sexual activity. The secondary marginal-range elevation on scale 6 (T = 62) of Carolyn's profile also suggests that she is relatively suspicious and distrustful in interpersonal relationships and may be perceived by others as hostile, resentful, and argumentative. These latter characteristics are also likely to render the establishment of a therapeutic relationship more difficult for this adolescent.

Carolyn's MMPI-A content and supplementary scale profile is presented in Fig. 8.9. This adolescent demonstrates marked elevations (T ≥ 90) on *A-fam* and *A-sch*, more moderate elevations on *A-las* and *A-ang*, and low clinical-range elevations on *A-con* and *A-dep*. Carolyn's extreme elevation on *A-fam* suggests that she is subject to frequent quarrels with family members and feels unsupported and misunderstood by her parents. She is likely to feel angry at, hostile toward, and frustrated with family members and may be at risk for running away from home. Her elevation on *A-sch* indicates that Carolyn is also encountering significant attitudinal and behavioral problems in the school setting, and her elevation on *A-ang* (as well as the content components for this scale) suggests that Carolyn might be described as angry, irritable, and hostile, with substantially less marked potential for explosive or physically aggressive behavior. Carolyn's *A-las* scores indicate that she may have learned to respond to educational academic frustrations by setting few or no educational objectives or goals. She is likely to become frustrated quickly and to give up in challenging situations. Adolescents with similar elevations typically have a history of underachievement and often have substance abuse problems. Her score on the *A-con* scale indicates her increasingly serious problems with conduct disorder and externalizing defenses and also reflects personality features that are likely to complicate any substance abuse treatment efforts. Finally, her low clinical-range elevation on the *A-dep* scale may be among the more optimistic signs for this adolescent, in that her relative depression and despair may motivate her to engage in a rehabilitation effort. As for supplementary scale findings, Carolyn produced clinical-range elevations on the *MAC–R* and *PRO* scales and a transitional or marginal-range elevation (60 ≤ T ≤ 64) on the *ACK* scale. This pattern is often found among adolescents who abuse drugs or alcohol or are at increased risk for these activities, and the elevation on the *ACK* scale relative to the elevations on the *MAC-R* and *PRO* scales suggest that Carolyn may be attempting to underreport or deny important aspects or features of her substance use. Therefore, her drug and alcohol use history should be carefully reviewed as part of a full evaluation of potential substance abuse problems.

Carolyn's Structural Summary is presented in Fig. 8.10. A review of the information provided for each of the factor scores indicates that Carolyn produced significant elevation patterns on two of the eight factors of the Structural Summary. Specifically, Carolyn produced significant scores on all 4 of the scales and subscales associated with Familial Alienation. Adolescents who produce significant elevations on this factor are more likely to experience family conflicts and to encounter disciplinary problems at school. They are frequently seen as aggressive, delinquent, or hostile, and they may be threatening, verbally abusive, or disobedient at home. Among adolescents with a substance abuse history, the origins of depressive symptomatology may be partly related to mood changes induced by substance use. Carolyn also manifested significant elevations on 11 of the 15 scales and subscales related to the Immaturity factor. Adolescents producing similar patterns are often seen as impulsive, self-centered, egocentric, and manifesting behavioral problems in the school setting and generating interpersonal conflicts in all settings.

Carolyn was discharged from residential substance abuse treatment following her participation in a 30-day program, and treatment was continued on a group and individual psychotherapy basis for an additional 12 months. In her therapy, an emphasis was placed on Carolyn's continuing to maintain sobriety, and on exploring her feelings regarding her alienation and anger concerning her parents and their divorce. Family therapy was also

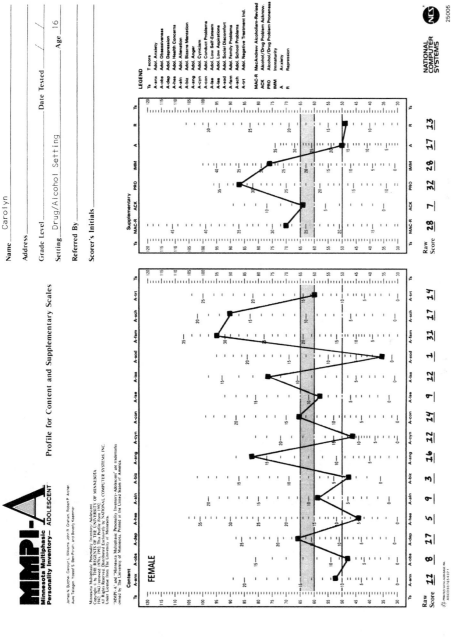

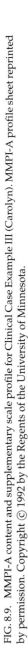

FIG. 8.9. MMPI-A content and supplementary scale profile for Clinical Case Example III (Carolyn). MMPI-A profile sheet reprinted by permission. Copyright © 1992 by the Regents of the University of Minnesota.

293

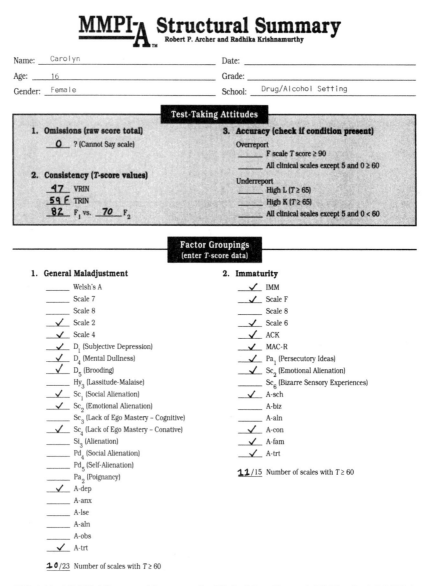

MMPI-A Structural Summary
Robert P. Archer and Radhika Krishnamurthy

Name: ____Carolyn_____   Date: _____

Age: ____16_____   Grade: _____

Gender: __Female_____   School: ___Drug/Alcohol Setting_____

Test-Taking Attitudes

1. Omissions (raw score total)

__0__ ? (Cannot Say scale)

2. Consistency (T-score values)

__47__ VRIN

__59 F__ TRIN

__82__ F₁ vs. __70__ F₂

3. Accuracy (check if condition present)

Overreport

_____ F scale T score ≥ 90

_____ All clinical scales except 5 and 0 ≥ 60

Underreport

_____ High L (T ≥ 65)

_____ High K (T ≥ 65)

_____ All clinical scales except 5 and 0 < 60

Factor Groupings
(enter T-score data)

1. General Maladjustment

_____ Welsh's A

_____ Scale 7

_____ Scale 8

__✓__ Scale 2

__✓__ Scale 4

__✓__ D₁ (Subjective Depression)

__✓__ D₄ (Mental Dullness)

__✓__ D₅ (Brooding)

_____ Hy₃ (Lassitude-Malaise)

__✓__ Sc₁ (Social Alienation)

__✓__ Sc₂ (Emotional Alienation)

_____ Sc₃ (Lack of Ego Mastery – Cognitive)

__✓__ Sc₄ (Lack of Ego Mastery – Conative)

_____ Si₃ (Alienation)

_____ Pd₄ (Social Alienation)

_____ Pd₅ (Self-Alienation)

_____ Pa₂ (Poignancy)

__✓__ A-dep

_____ A-anx

_____ A-lse

_____ A-aln

_____ A-obs

__✓__ A-trt

10/23 Number of scales with T ≥ 60

2. Immaturity

__✓__ IMM

__✓__ Scale F

_____ Scale 8

__✓__ Scale 6

__✓__ ACK

__✓__ MAC-R

__✓__ Pa₁ (Persecutory Ideas)

__✓__ Sc₂ (Emotional Alienation)

_____ Sc₆ (Bizarre Sensory Experiences)

__✓__ A-sch

_____ A-biz

_____ A-aln

__✓__ A-con

__✓__ A-fam

__✓__ A-trt

11/15 Number of scales with T ≥ 60

FIG. 8.10. MMPI-A Structural Summary for Clinical Case Example III (Carolyn). MMPI-A Structural Summary Form reprinted by permission. Copyright © 1994 by Psychological Assessment Resources, Inc.

used to assist Carolyn in developing a more open and nonconflictual relationship with her mother and to assist Carolyn's mother in setting appropriate limits on her behavior. Carolyn subsequently successfully graduated from high school and is currently enrolled in a technical training program.

Clinical Case Example IV: 14-Year-Old Male Adolescent Academic Referral

David was a 14-year-old Caucasian male adolescent who was administered the MMPI-A as part of an evaluation resulting from increasing school difficulties. David was failing the eighth grade and was scheduled to attend summer school in an effort to correct academic

3. Disinhibition/Excitatory Potential

_____ Scale 9

_____ Ma_2 (Psychomotor Acceleration)

_____ Ma_4 (Ego Inflation)

_____ Sc_5 (Lack of Ego Mastery, Defective Inhibition)

_____ D_2 (Psychomotor Retardation) (low score)*

_____ Welsh's R (low score)*

_____ Scale K (low score)*

_____ Scale L (low score)*

___✓___ A-ang

_____ A-cyn

___✓___ A-con

___✓___ MAC-R

___3__/12 Number of scales with $T \geq 60$ or ≤ 40 for scales with asterisk

4. Social Discomfort

_____ Scale 0

_____ Si_1 (Shyness/Self-Consciousness)

_____ Hy_1 (Denial of Social Anxiety) (low score)*

_____ Pd_3 (Social Imperturbability) (low score)*

_____ Ma_3 (Imperturbability) (low scores)*

_____ A-sod

_____ A-lse

_____ Scale 7

___0__/8 Number of scales with $T \geq 60$ or $T \leq 40$ for scales with asterisk

5. Health Concerns

_____ Scale 1

_____ Scale 3

_____ A-hea

_____ Hy_4 (Somatic Complaints)

_____ Hy_3 (Lassitude-Malaise)

_____ D_3 (Physical Malfunctioning)

___0__/6 Number of scales with $T \geq 60$

6. Naivete

_____ A-cyn (low score)*

_____ Pa_3 (Naivete)

_____ Hy_2 (Need for Affection)

_____ Si_3 (Alienation–Self and Others) (low score)*

_____ Scale K

___0__/5 Number of scales with $T \geq 60$ or $T \leq 40$ for scales with asterisk

7. Familial Alienation

___✓___ Pd_1 (Familial Discord)

___✓___ A-fam

___✓___ Scale 4

___✓___ PRO

___4__/4 Number of scales with $T \geq 60$

8. Psychoticism

___✓___ Pa_1 (Persecutory Ideas)

___✓___ Scale 6

_____ A-biz

_____ Sc_6 (Bizarre Sensory Experiences)

___2__/4 Number of scales with $T \geq 60$

Note. The presentation of scales under each factor label is generally organized in a descending order from the best to the least effective marker. Within this overall approach, scales are grouped logically in terms of basic clinical scales, Harris-Lingoes and Si subscales, and content scales. The majority of scales included in this summary sheet were correlated $\geq .60$ or $\leq -.60$ with the relevant factor for the MMPI-A normative sample.

PAR **Psychological Assessment Resources, Inc.**
P.O. Box 998/Odessa, Florida 33556/Toll-Free 1-800-331-TEST

FIG. 8.10. (Continued)

deficits in core courses. Previous records indicated increasing behavior and academic difficulties since his placement in middle school. David had been referred for disciplinary interventions approximately eight times in the past year for disrupting class, attendance problems, and conflicts with teachers. When asked how he felt about being referred for psychological evaluation, David responded, "I don't care, it's okay with me if you want to waste your time." David indicated that he had difficulty concentrating in his classes because he was bored and because the teaching staff and his peers tended to pick on him unfairly. In addition to the MMPI-A, this patient was administered the Wechsler Intelligence Scale for Children–Revised; he obtained a Verbal IQ score of 108, a Performance IQ score of 110, and a Full Scale IQ score of 108. On standardized achievement tests,

David exhibited reading skills at the 8th-grade second-month level, math skills were at the 7th-year fourth-month level, and written language skills at the 7th-grade level.

David's MMPI-A basic scale profile is shown in Fig. 8.11. David's Cannot Say (?) raw score of 7 was within acceptable limits, and his *VRIN* score (raw score = 9, T = 63) and *TRIN* score (raw score = 6, T = 68) were both within acceptable limits. It should be noted, however, that the scores on all three of these indices or scales are somewhat elevated, suggesting that David may have been careless or inattentive in responding to some MMPI-A questions. Nevertheless, his overall score suggests sufficient consistency to allow meaningful interpretation of the test findings. David's response pattern on validity scales *F*, *L*, and *K* indicate that he may use denial as a primary defense mechanism (*L*), and the moderate elevation on scale *F* (T = 65) indicates he may have significant psychological or emotional problems. Overall, his MMPI-A validity scale pattern suggests that David's responses are sufficiently consistent and accurate to allow for meaningful interpretation.

David's MMPI-A basic scale profile corresponds to a well-defined 2-6/6-2 codetype, with the difference between his second highest (scale 2) and third highest (scale 8) elevations being 5 T-score points. This codetype is relatively infrequent in samples of adolescents in clinical settings, and no research-based empirical correlates have been derived for this codetype with adolescents. Therefore, it is necessary to interpret this profile on an individual-scale basis. Adolescents who produce a moderate elevation on scale 6 (such as David's T-score of 73) are often described as resentful, hostile, and angry. They feel they have been mistreated or taken advantage of by others and are overly sensitive and suspicious in interpersonal exchanges. Primary defense mechanisms typically involve externalization or projection. Further, adolescents who produce a moderate elevation on scale 2 (similiar to David's T-score of 71) are often depressed, dissatisfied, and self-depreciatory and lack self-confidence. They have feelings of inadequacy and pessimism as well as feelings of guilt, worthlessness, and self-criticism. Adolescents referred for evaluation from school settings with this pattern often show levels of depressive symptomatology that interfere with classroom concentration and attention. The academic performance of these adolescents often improves following the initiation of effective treatment for their depression. Additionally, David has elevations in the transitional range (60 ≤ T ≤ 64) to the low clinical range (65 ≤ T ≤ 69) on several additional MMPI-A basic clinical scales. Taking the interpretation of these scales in the order of their relative elevation, David produced secondary elevations on MMPI-A scales *8, 1, 7, 0, 3*, and *4*. David's elevation on scale 8 is accounted for by feelings of social alienation, and his elevation on scale 1 (T = 65) is associated with a history of vague physical complaints, although adolescents with documented chronic physical illnesses also may score in this range. His elevation on Scale 7 reflects a marginal level of anxiety and self-criticalness and tension, and his elevation on the *Si* scale reflects social introversion and social discomfort. Finally, his transitional elevation on scale 3 is accounted for by the Harris-Lingoes Lassitude-Malaise (*Hy3*) component, and his T-score of 60 on scale 4 is associated with elevations on the Harris-Lingoes subscales of Self-Alienation (*Pd5*) and Familial Discord (*Pd1*).

David's content and supplementary scale profile is shown in Fig. 8.12. His primary content scale clinical-range elevations occur on the right side of the profile and involve scales *A-sch, A-fam, A-sod,* and *A-las*. This pattern underscores David's attitudinal behavioral problems in the academic setting, his perception of his family as uncaring or unsupportive, his degree of social discomfort and introversion, and his tendency to set few or no educational objectives or goals as a mechanism for avoiding frustration and guilt in the educational setting, respectively. Additionally, David produced a low clinical-range elevation on the *A-dep* scale, reflective of depressive and despondent symptomatology, and transitional range elevations on the *A-obs* and *A-biz* scales. Content component scales are not available for the *A-obs* scale, but evaluations on the *A-biz* component scales indicate that the *A-biz* elevation results from strong feelings of suspiciousness and interpersonal distrust (*A-biz2*). As for the supplementary scale scores, David's only elevation (transitional

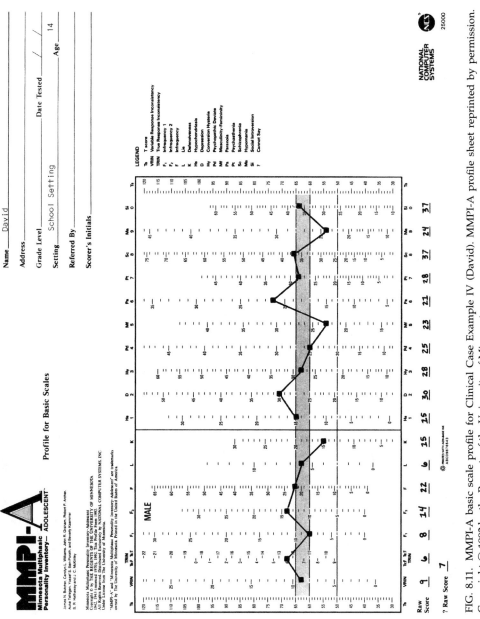

FIG. 8.11. MMPI-A basic scale profile for Clinical Case Example IV (David). MMPI-A profile sheet reprinted by permission. Copyright © 1992 by the Regents of the University of Minnesota.

297

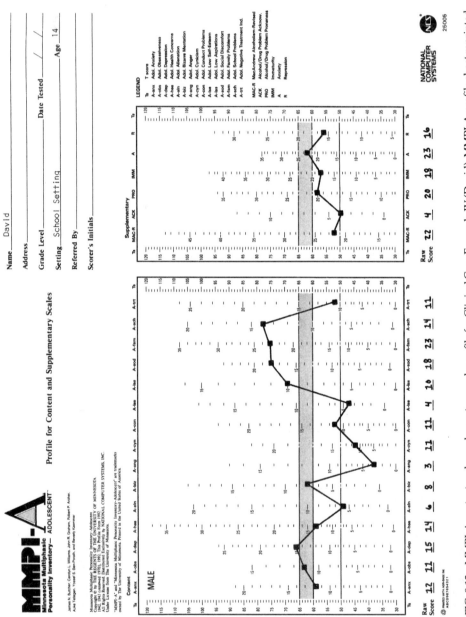

FIG. 8.12. MMPI-A content and supplementary scale profile for Clinical Case Example IV (David). MMPI-A profile sheet reprinted by permission. Copyright © 1992 by the Regents of the University of Minnesota.

298

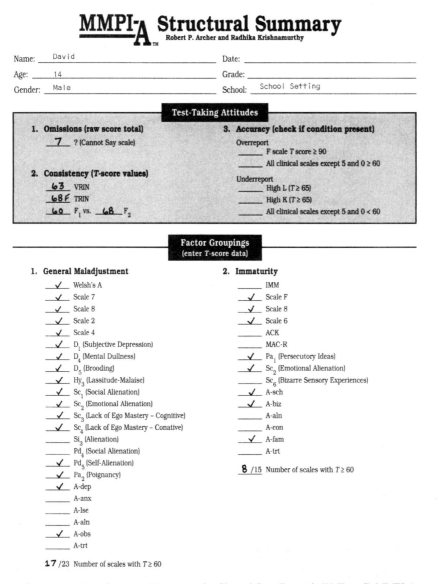

FIG. 8.13. MMPI-A Structural Summary for Clinical Case Example IV (David). MMPI-A Structural Summary Form reprinted by permission. Copyright © 1994 by Psychological Assessment Resources, Inc.

range, T = 62) was on the Welsh's Anxiety scale, reflective of feelings of tension, apprehension, and anxiety. Finally, review of the PSY-5 scales indicates a significant elevation on the Psychoticism dimension, accounted for by strong feelings of alienation and estrangement from others.

Figure 8.13 presents the Structural Summary findings for this adolescent. David produced significant scores on 5 of the 6 scales and subscales associated with the Health Concerns dimension. This pattern underscores David's perception of himself as physically ill, tired, or fatigued. Additionally, David produced significant values on 3 of the 4 subscales related to Familial Alienation. Thus, David is likely to have frequent family conflicts and experience disciplinary problems in school, including school suspensions or probationary actions. This suggests the internal conflicts or hostility found within his

3. **Disinhibition/Excitatory Potential**

_____ Scale 9

_____ Ma$_2$ (Psychomotor Acceleration)

_____ Ma$_4$ (Ego Inflation)

___✓___ Sc$_5$ (Lack of Ego Mastery, Defective Inhibition)

_____ D$_2$ (Psychomotor Retardation) (low score)*

_____ Welsh's R (low score)*

_____ Scale K (low score)*

_____ Scale L (low score)*

_____ A-ang

_____ A-cyn

_____ A-con

_____ MAC-R

1 /12 Number of scales with $T \geq 60$ or ≤ 40 for scales with asterisk

4. **Social Discomfort**

___✓___ Scale 0

___✓___ Si$_1$ (Shyness/Self-Consciousness)

___✓___ Hy$_1$ (Denial of Social Anxiety) (low score)*

___✓___ Pd$_3$ (Social Imperturbability) (low score)*

_____ Ma$_3$ (Imperturbability) (low scores)*

___✓___ A-sod

_____ A-lse

___✓___ Scale 7

_____ /8 Number of scales with $T \geq 60$ or $T \leq 40$ for scales with asterisk

5. **Health Concerns**

___✓___ Scale 1

___✓___ Scale 3

_____ A-hea

___✓___ Hy$_4$ (Somatic Complaints)

___✓___ Hy$_3$ (Lassitude-Malaise)

___✓___ D$_3$ (Physical Malfunctioning)

5 /6 Number of scales with $T \geq 60$

6. **Naivete**

_____ A-cyn (low score)*

___✓___ Pa$_3$ (Naivete)

_____ Hy$_2$ (Need for Affection)

_____ Si$_3$ (Alienation-Self and Others) (low score)*

_____ Scale K

1 /5 Number of scales with $T \geq 60$ or $T \leq 40$ for scales with asterisk

7. **Familial Alienation**

___✓___ Pd$_1$ (Familial Discord)

___✓___ A-fam

___✓___ Scale 4

_____ PRO

3 /4 Number of scales with $T \geq 60$

8. **Psychoticism**

___✓___ Pa$_1$ (Persecutory Ideas)

___✓___ Scale 6

___✓___ A-biz

_____ Sc$_6$ (Bizarre Sensory Experiences)

3 /4 Number of scales with $T \geq 60$

Note. The presentation of scales under each factor label is generally organized in a descending order from the best to the least effective marker. Within this overall approach, scales are grouped logically in terms of basic clinical scales, Harris-Lingoes and Si subscales, and content scales. The majority of scales included in this summary sheet were correlated $\geq .60$ or $\leq -.60$ with the relevant factor for the MMPI-A normative sample.

PAR **Psychological Assessment Resources, Inc.**
P.O. Box 998/Odessa, Florida 33556/Toll-Free 1-800-331-TEST

FIG. 8.13. (Continued)

family may often "spill over" into the academic setting. David also produced significant elevations on 3 of the scales and subscales associated with the Psychoticism factor. Adolescents who produce elevations on this factor are more likely to be teased and rejected by their peer group and to have a history of poor academic achievement. They are often seen as socially disengaged or schizoid, and they report anger control problems. David also produced significant elevations on 17 of the 23 scales and subscales associated with the General Maladjustment factor. Adolescents producing similar patterns have significant problems in adjustment and are seen as socially withdrawn, timid, dependent, ruminative, and depressed. Their overall level of emotional distress, including feelings of anxiety and depression, rumination, and dysphoria, is likely to impair their ability to perform in the academic environment. Finally, David produced significant elevations on 8 of the 15 scales and subscales associated with the Immaturity factor. Adolescents producing similar patterns are often described as self-centered, impulsive, and egocentric and display little awareness or insight into their psychological problems. They are likely to manifest behavioral problems in the school setting and are seen by others as argumentative.

In summary, David is an alienated, depressed, and ruminative adolescent who is interpersonally guarded and suspicious. He experiences a strong sense of alienation and perceives little support from teachers, peers, and his family. These psychological problems and features are likely a significant etiological factor in David's deteriorating academic performance. It was recommended that David participate in an intensive outpatient treatment program and that his response to this intervention be evaluated prior to this possible placement in classes for emotionally disturbed adolescents. At the time of this writing, the eventual outcome of this case is unknown.

Clinical Case Example V: 16-Year-Old Female Adolescent Evaluated in a Medical Setting

Rebecca was a 16-year-old Hispanic female adolescent from a low-income family that included two older sisters and one younger brother. Rebecca was fluent in English, and it was the primary language spoken in her home and educational settings. Rebecca was referred for psychological evaluation with presenting problems of depression, including anhedonia, feelings of hopelessness, marked lassitude, and psychomotor retardation. The referral was made from a diabetes clinic where Rebecca was receiving ongoing treatment following a diagnosis of diabetes that occurred approximately 2 years prior to the evaluation. Rebecca was an insulin-dependent diabetic with a poor history of treatment compliance, and she had a particular problem maintaining a dietary regimen consistent with diabetes care. Rebecca was referred for evaluation by her internist, with a request to provide clarification concerning the extent to which psychological issues might be contributing to Rebecca's compliance problems. Rebecca's mother completed the CBCL, which produced clinical-range elevations for this adolescent on internalizing behavioral problems, including the dimensions of uncommunicativeness and somatic complaints.

Rebecca's MMPI-A basic scale profile is shown in Fig. 8.14. This adolescent's total item omission score ($?= 0$) is well within acceptable limits, and her *VRIN* score (raw score $= 0$, T $= 36$) and *TRIN* score (raw score $= 8$, T $= 59$) are indicative of a consistent response pattern. Further, the difference between this adolescent's T-scores on F_1 (T $= 53$) and F_2 (T $= 44$) is relatively small and supports the conclusion of adequate consistency for this adolescent's MMPI-A responses. Rebecca's validity scale configuration on scales F, L, and K indicates a valid profile produced by an adolescent who might be described as fairly rigid and inflexible, with a tendency toward conformity and conventionality (L, T $= 64$). Further, her L scale elevation also reflects a tendency to use denial as a primary defense mechanism. Overall, this adolescent's MMPI-A profile appears consistent and accurate and subject to valid interpretation.

Rebecca's basic scale clinical profile is not adequately described by a 2- or 3-point code because of the substantial difference (20 T-score points) between her highest (scale 2) and second highest (scale 7) elevations and because only one of her basic scale scores falls clearly in the clinical range. Therefore, this profile should be primarily interpreted as a spike 2 code, with a secondary transitional-range elevation on scale 7. Approached in this manner, Rebecca's score on scale 2 reflects strong feelings of depression, dissatisfaction, and self-depreciation, which might be accompanied by loss of interest in daily activities and a loss of self-confidence. Adolescents who produce similar profiles often experience substantial feelings of guilt, worthlessness, and self-criticism. Unsurprisingly, given the magnitude of her scale 2 elevation (T $= 83$), all five of the scale 2 Harris-Lingoes subscales are also clinically elevated (T ≥ 65). Additionally, Rebecca's marginal elevation on scale 7 indicates that she might be described as anxious, tense, indecisive, and perfectionistic.

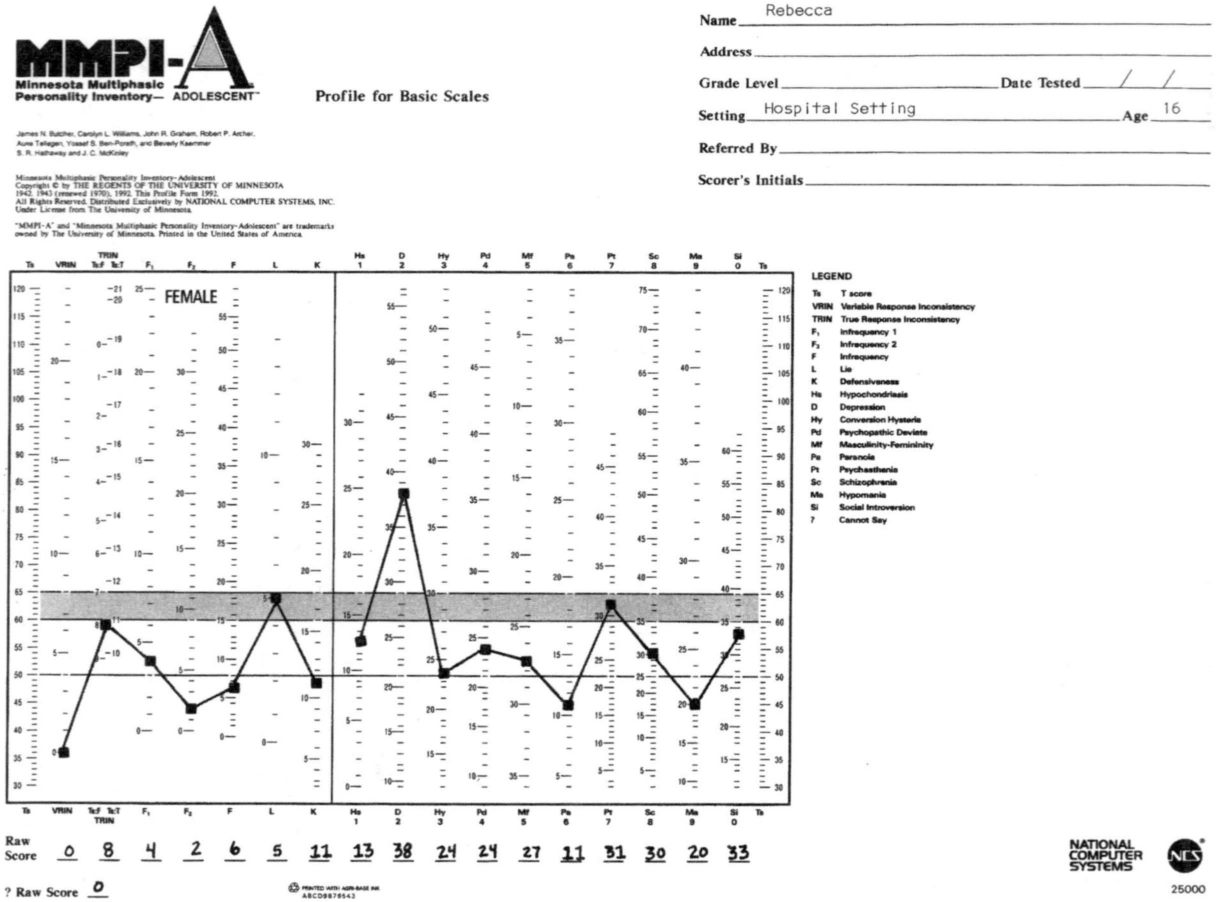

FIG. 8.14. MMPI-A basic scale profile for Clinical Case Example V (Rebecca). MMPI-A profile sheet reprinted by permission. Copyright © 1992 by the Regents of the University of Minnesota.

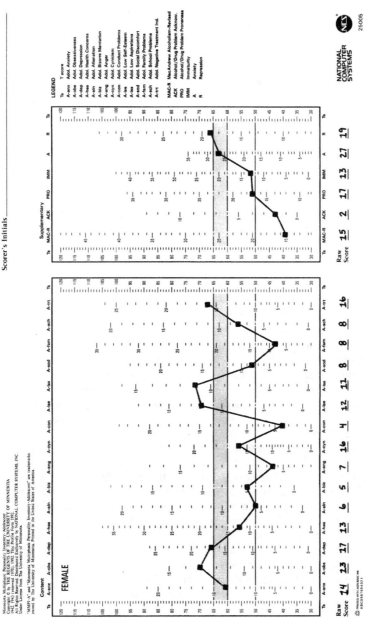

FIG. 8.15. MMPI-A content and supplementary scale profile for Clinical Case Example V (Rebecca). MMPI-A profile sheet reprinted by permission. Copyright © 1992 by the Regents of the University of Minnesota.

303

However, it is also notable that this level of emotional distress may serve as a positive motivator for engagement in psychotherapy efforts.

Rebecca's content and supplementary scale profile is shown in Fig. 8.15. Rebecca displays clinical-range elevations (T $\geq$ 65) on 5 of the 15 content scales, along with a transitional-range elevation on the *A-anx* scale (T = 61). Rebecca's elevation on the *A-las* scale indicates that she has set few educational or life goals or objectives, and her elevation on the *A-obs* scale reflects a pattern of ambivalence and difficulty making decisions and a tendency to ruminate and worry excessively. Further, her elevation on the *A-lse* scale reflects significant problems with self-esteem and self-confidence, and her elevation on the *A-trt* scale is typically found among adolescents who have initial barriers to treatment efforts. Breaking the *A-trt* scale out based on content component scores, we can see that her *A-trt* elevation is a result of her elevation on *A-trt2* (Inability to Disclose), often found among adolescents who are uncomfortable discussing personal information and who believe others are unable to understand them. Further, these adolescents may harbor substantial feelings of guilt or shame. Finally, Rebecca's clinical-range elevation on *A-dep* suggests the presence of significant feelings of depression, despondency, and hopelessness. In this regard, note that Rebecca endorsed the abbreviated item "The future seems hopeless" as true but did not critically endorse any of the other items related to suicidal ideation in the Forbey and Ben-Porath MMPI-A critical item set. Finally, Rebecca produced a transitional-range elevation on the *A-anx* scale, reflective of tension, apprehensiveness, worry, and anxiety. As for the MMPI-A supplementary scales, Rebecca produced a transitional-range elevation (T = 63) on the Welsh's Anxiety scale, reflective of general emotional distress, and a clinical-range elevation (T = 66) on the Repression scale, reflective of her use of the defense mechanisms of denial and repression as a way of dealing with unacceptable or discomforting feelings and experiences.

Figure 8.16 presents the MMPI-A Structural Summary findings for Rebecca. The factor that appears most relevant for the description of Rebecca's psychopathology is General Maladjustment. Rebecca's elevations on 16 of the 23 scales and subscales associated with General Maladjustment indicate the extent of her overall emotional distress. As noted by Archer, Krishnamurthy, et al. (1994) and Archer and Krishnamurthy (1994b, 2002), adolescents who produce elevations on a majority of the scales and subscales associated with this factor are likely to be experiencing significant problems in adjustment and are often self-conscious, timid, and socially withdrawn. They tend to be ruminative, are subject to sudden mood changes, and are especially likely to experience problems related to depression, fatigue, despondency, and distress. No other Structural Summary factor met the criteria used to define a factor as salient.

The evaluation report sent to Rebecca's diabetes clinic emphasized that she was experiencing clinical levels of depression and had a tendency to use denial and repression as primary defense mechanisms in dealing with threatening topics or unacceptable feelings. The MMPI-A findings resulted in her referral for psychological counseling, which rapidly evolved into an exploration of the extent to which the presence of diabetes both threatened and frightened this adolescent. It quickly became apparent that the dietary and medical regimen required by this chronic disease process caused Rebecca to feel isolated, different, and alone in relation to her peer group. Further, psychotherapy very profitably explored Rebecca's largely unconscious assumption that she was "in some way" responsible for her development of diabetes. The active and conscious exploration of these issues rapidly resulted in a dramatic improvement in her diabetes treatment compliance.

COMPUTER-BASED TEST INTERPRETATION (CBTI) SYSTEMS

The use of computer technology to assist in the administration, scoring, or interpretation of psychological tests is rapidly evolving. Butcher (1987b) edited a text that presents an overview of CBTI technology in relationship to a broad variety of

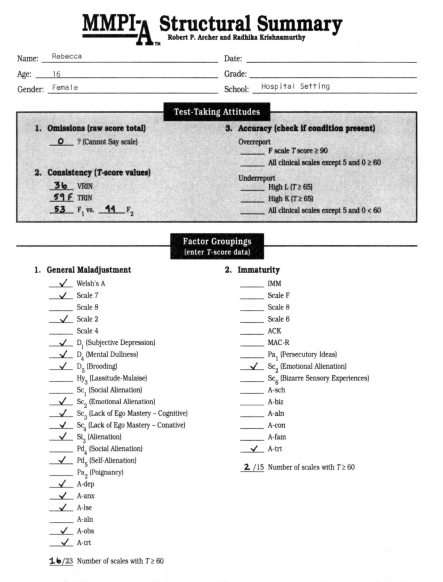

MMPI-A Structural Summary
Robert P. Archer and Radhika Krishnamurthy

Name: Rebecca   Date:

Age: 16   Grade:

Gender: Female   School: Hospital Setting

Test-Taking Attitudes

1. Omissions (raw score total)

____0____ ? (Cannot Say scale)

2. Consistency (T-score values)

__36__ VRIN

__59 F__ TRIN

__53__ F₁ vs. __44__ F₂

3. Accuracy (check if condition present)

Overreport

_____ F scale T score ≥ 90

_____ All clinical scales except 5 and 0 ≥ 60

Underreport

_____ High L (T ≥ 65)

_____ High K (T ≥ 65)

_____ All clinical scales except 5 and 0 < 60

Factor Groupings
(enter T-score data)

1. General Maladjustment

✓ Welsh's A

✓ Scale 7

_____ Scale 8

✓ Scale 2

_____ Scale 4

✓ D₁ (Subjective Depression)

✓ D₄ (Mental Dullness)

✓ D₅ (Brooding)

_____ Hy₃ (Lassitude-Malaise)

_____ Sc₁ (Social Alienation)

✓ Sc₂ (Emotional Alienation)

✓ Sc₃ (Lack of Ego Mastery – Cognitive)

✓ Sc₄ (Lack of Ego Mastery – Conative)

✓ Si₃ (Alienation)

_____ Pd₄ (Social Alienation)

✓ Pd₅ (Self-Alienation)

_____ Pa₂ (Poignancy)

✓ A-dep

✓ A-anx

✓ A-lse

_____ A-aln

✓ A-obs

✓ A-trt

16/23 Number of scales with T ≥ 60

2. Immaturity

_____ IMM

_____ Scale F

_____ Scale 8

_____ Scale 6

_____ ACK

_____ MAC-R

_____ Pa₁ (Persecutory Ideas)

✓ Sc₂ (Emotional Alienation)

_____ Sc₆ (Bizarre Sensory Experiences)

_____ A-sch

_____ A-biz

_____ A-aln

_____ A-con

_____ A-fam

✓ A-trt

2/15 Number of scales with T ≥ 60

FIG. 8.16. MMPI-A Structural Summary for Clinical Case Example V (Rebecca). MMPI-A Structural Summary Form reprinted by permission. Copyright © 1994 by Psychological Assessment Resources, Inc.

assessment measures and tasks, and Moreland (1990) examined the use of computer technology for adolescent and child personality assessment.

Butcher (1987a) noted that the MMPI was the first psychological test instrument for which a computer scoring and interpretation system was developed because of the extensive empirical literature available on the MMPI and the strong conceptual basis for actuarial interpretation of MMPI test findings provided by Meehl (1954, 1956, 1986) and others. Further, the MMPI was the most widely used objective measure of personality for adults (Lubin et al., 1984) and adolescents (Archer, Maruish, et al., 1991). As a consequence, the MMPI provided sufficient commercial incentive to motivate individuals to develop CBTI packages for this instrument. The use of CBTI technology

3. Disinhibition/Excitatory Potential

_____ Scale 9

_____ Ma_2 (Psychomotor Acceleration)

_____ Ma_4 (Ego Inflation)

_____ Sc_5 (Lack of Ego Mastery, Defective Inhibition)

_____ D_2 (Psychomotor Retardation) (low score)*

_____ Welsh's R (low score)*

_____ Scale K (low score)*

_____ Scale L (low score)*

_____ A-ang

_____ A-cyn

_____ A-con

_____ MAC-R

0 /12 Number of scales with $T \geq 60$ or ≤ 40 for scales with asterisk

4. Social Discomfort

_____ Scale 0

_____ Si_1 (Shyness/Self-Consciousness)

_____ Hy_1 (Denial of Social Anxiety) (low score)*

_____ Pd_3 (Social Imperturbability) (low score)*

_____ Ma_3 (Imperturbability) (low scores)*

_____ A-sod

✓ A-lse

✓ Scale 7

2 /8 Number of scales with $T \geq 60$ or $T \leq 40$ for scales with asterisk

5. Health Concerns

_____ Scale 1

_____ Scale 3

_____ A-hea

_____ Hy_4 (Somatic Complaints)

_____ Hy_3 (Lassitude-Malaise)

✓ D_3 (Physical Malfunctioning)

1 /6 Number of scales with $T \geq 60$

6. Naivete

_____ A-cyn (low score)*

_____ Pa_3 (Naivete)

_____ Hy_2 (Need for Affection)

_____ Si_3 (Alienation–Self and Others) (low score)*

_____ Scale K

0 /5 Number of scales with $T \geq 60$ or $T \leq 40$ for scales with asterisk

7. Familial Alienation

_____ Pd_1 (Familial Discord)

_____ A-fam

_____ Scale 4

_____ PRO

0 /4 Number of scales with $T \geq 60$

8. Psychoticism

_____ Pa_1 (Persecutory Ideas)

_____ Scale 6

_____ A-biz

_____ Sc_6 (Bizarre Sensory Experiences)

0 /4 Number of scales with $T \geq 60$

Note. The presentation of scales under each factor label is generally organized in a descending order from the best to the least effective marker. Within this overall approach, scales are grouped logically in terms of basic clinical scales, Harris-Lingoes and *Si* subscales, and content scales. The majority of scales included in this summary sheet were correlated $\geq .60$ or $\leq -.60$ with the relevant factor for the MMPI-A normative sample.

FIG. 8.16.   (Continued)

has spread far beyond the MMPI to include many diverse assessment instruments. Groth-Marnat and Schumaker (1989) reported that the Veterans Administration had computerized 62 psychological tests for general clinical use. These authors also noted that in a single 1987 issue of *Monitor on Psychology*, published by the American Psychological Association, there were 18 advertisements for psychological test software involving a total of 71 instruments. Krug (1987a, 1987b, 1993) provided a sourcebook describing over 300 CBTI products involving various aspects of psychological assessment. As noted by Groth-Marnat (2003), however, the domain of CBTI products is subject to such rapid change that the best source for accurate product information consists of the current catalogues of the major distributors of these products

The first application of CBTI to the MMPI was developed at the Mayo Clinic in Rochester, Minnesota (Rome et al., 1962; Swenson & Pearson, 1964). This computer-based system was designed to handle the large volume of patients seen at the Mayo Clinic. The first CBTI system to receive widespread professional use, however, was developed by Fowler (1964, 1985) and became operational in 1963. In 1965, the Roche Psychiatric Service Institute, a subdivision of Roche Laboratories, made the Fowler system commercially available on a national basis. Fowler (1985) reported that over the 17-year period during which the system was nationally marketed, one fourth of all clinical psychologists in the United States used this service, and approximately 1.5 million MMPI computer-based reports were produced. Another widely used and popular MMPI interpretation system was developed by Alex Caldwell (1971); it was revised for the MMPI-2 and is marketed as the Caldwell Report. In addition, James Butcher developed an interpretive system in the late 1970s that was licensed by the University of Minnesota to (what is currently) Pearson Assessments as the Minnesota Report (Fowler, 1985). Both the Caldwell Report and the Minnesota Report are examples of narrative report services using CBTI software that is not sold directly to the consumer. In contrast, Roger Greene (1989b), in collaboration with Psychological Assessment Resources (PAR), developed an unlimited-use software system for interpretation of the MMPI; it was revised in 1998 for the MMPI-2 and marketed as the MMPI-2 Adult Interpretive System. Examples of each of these three reports (i.e., Caldwell's, Butcher's, and Greene's) may be found in Friedman et al.'s (2001) text. Each of these reports has been periodically revised and updated to include new MMPI-2 output following the release of major modifications to the instrument.

Available CBTI interpretive systems for adolescents' MMPI profiles include the MMPI Adolescent Interpretive System, developed by Archer (1987a) and marketed through PAR, and the *Marks Adolescent Clinical Report*, developed by Philip Marks and Richard Lewak (1991) and distributed by Western Psychological Services. In addition, an MMPI-A interpretive report developed by Archer and distributed by PAR (the MMPI-A Interpretive System) was originally released in 1992 and revised twice, the third version released in 2003. MMPI-A reports have also been developed by James Butcher and Carolyn Williams (1992), distributed by Pearson Assessments, and by Philip Marks and Richard Lewak, distributed by Western Psychological Services. The third version of the PAR MMPI-A Adolescent Interpretive System, as applied to the second clinical case example presented in this chapter (i.e., Jared), is presented in Appendix 8.1. The output from this third version has several unique features, including information derived from the MMPI-A Structural Summary and the ability to graph on the same profile form both the client's basic scale profile and an overlay of the modal or prototype 4-6/6-4 profile obtained by adolescents producing this 2-point code type. The third version also delivers specific interpretive output for adolescents in six assessment settings, including outpatient psychiatric, inpatient psychiatric, medical/hospital, drug/alcohol treatment, school/academic, and correctional/juvenile justice.

The development of CBTI systems for the MMPI and other psychometric instruments has been accompanied by considerable controversy and debate. Automated CBTI reports are based on various combinations of clinical experience and research findings, resulting in what has been described as an actuarial-clinical approach to test interpretation (Graham, 2000). For certain instruments, particularly the MMPI-2, a wide variety of CBTI reports are available that differ greatly in quality and accuracy.

Several MMPI-2 CBTI systems have been written by individuals who are very knowledgeable in the use of this instrument and have augmented the available research
literature with their expert judgment concerning test interpretation procedures. Unfortunately, other commercially available CBTI reports have been written by individuals less skilled in MMPI-2 interpretation procedures and less knowledgeable about
the existing MMPI and MMPI-2 research. Graham (2000) noted that the quality of
interpretive programs varies widely, making it imperative that clinicians carefully
evaluate their adequacy. Matarazzo (1983, 1986) and Lanyon (1987) expressed concerns regarding the absence of validation studies of automated interpretations of the
MMPI. Matarazzo further noted that CBTI programs may give the appearance of
accuracy and that inexperienced clinicians may be unaware of their limitations and
potential for misuse. The American Psychological Association (1986) published a set
of guidelines for the development and use of CBTI products. These guidelines advise
professionals to limit their use of CBTI products to those instruments with which they
are familiar and have competency and to use such reports only in conjunction with
professional judgment. Butcher (1987b) noted that the advantages of CBTI reports
include the following:

1. *Objectivity.* CBTI products are not subject to interpreter bias, and test rules are
   automatically and consistently applied to the interpretation of cases.
2. *Use as a Source of Outside Opinion.* CBTI products may serve to provide a second
   opinion in forensic or legal cases. CBTI products are useful in this regard because
   test interpretation is not biased by any subjective preconceptions the interpreter
   may hold concerning a specific client.
3. *Rapid Turnaround.* CBTI reports can typically be generated within a few minutes
   after data are entered in the system.
4. *Cost-Effectiveness.* The cost of CBTI products varies widely depending on the test
   distributor, test authors, and nature of the service (e.g., software vs. test report
   service). Nevertheless, almost all types of CBTI reports are less expensive than
   clinician-generated reports.
5. *Reliability.* The reliability of a CBTI product is invariant over repeated uses,
   unaffected by the errors and lapses in memory manifested by human beings.

In addition to these advantages, Butcher (1987a) also listed several disadvantages
connected with CBTI products:

1. *The Question of Excessive Generality.* Computer-based reports are typically based
on prototypic profiles, which may differ in many specifics from the individual profile being interpreted. As noted by Butcher (1987a), "The most valid computerized
reports are those that most closely match the researched prototype" (p. 5). In the
worst cases, CBTI reports may include numerous statements that are highly generalizable and could apply to anyone. These types of reports, although appearing accurate to the novice test user, are of little help in identifying the unique features of the
individual.

2. *Potential for Misuse.* Because computerized reports are widely available and may
be mass produced, the potential for abuse of this type of product may be greater than
that of clinically derived personality interpretation reports. This issue is related to
the need to establish that a computer-assisted test administration is equivalent to a
standard paper-and-pencil test administration in terms of the test results. Honaker

(1988) noted that insufficient research attention has been directed to this equivalency issue, and it remains unresolved at this time.

3. *Clinician Startup Time.* Computerized psychological testing requires a clinician to become familiar with various aspects of computer use. Depending on the degree of "user-friendliness" of the CBTI product, gaining the necessary knowledge may be accomplished quickly or may be very time consuming and frustrating.

4. *Confusing Abundance of Packages.* Literally hundreds of CBTI products are currently available for clinician use, and it is becoming increasingly difficult for clinicians to determine the optimal CBTI products for their applications and setting. Not only must clinicians determine the quality of CBTI products, but they must consider the "fit" between their particular testing needs and these products, all of which are designed for particular settings and use volumes, and have their own methods of scoring or data transfer.

Added to these cautions is the recommendation that clinicians become aware of the limitations of CBTI reports. Moreland (1985a, 1985b) noted that CBTI programs should be used as only one element in the assessment process and should never be employed as a substitute for professional judgment. Even the best CBTI programs for the MMPI produce descriptive statements that are only moderately consistent with clinician descriptions of the patient (Graham, 2000). Butcher, Perry, and Atlis (2000) recently concluded that only 60% of the interpretations in the narratives of CBTI reports typically were appropriate, with shorter narratives containing higher percentages of valid/accurate interpretations. In choosing a CBTI product, the following five guidelines are offered to clinicians:

1. All CBTI products represent a combination or blending of the author's clinical judgment with research findings that have been established for a particular instrument. The potential test user, therefore, should be aware of the identity and expertise of the individual or individuals who developed the CBTI package. In a very real sense, a clinician acquiring a CBTI product is purchasing/leasing the clinical and scientific judgment of the test developers.

2. The clinician should know how the CBTI report was written. Specifically, to what extent was the CBTI based on empirical findings, and how broad was the empirical base used for the development of the test instrument? The clinician should review the CBTI manual for this information prior to purchasing the product and using computerized reports.

3. The clinician should determine the degree to which the company that markets the CBTI product supports its use and application. Before purchasing a CBTI product, it is reasonable for the clinician to request samples of interpretive output and to check the history of the company in terms of customer satisfaction. Does the company have an 800 number available for product use support? Does the company provide a detailed and "user-friendly" manual that contains sufficient detail to meaningfully assist the clinician in using the technical and clinical features of the product?

4. The clinician should determine whether the CBTI product is periodically revised to reflect changes in interpretive practice based on new research findings. This is particularly important for CBTI products related to the use of the MMPI-2 or the MMPI-A, for which empirical support is rapidly evolving.

5. The clinician should consider the extent to which the CBTI product has been subjected to empirical validation. Moreland (1985b) noted that CBTI products have generated two basic types of research studies: consumer satisfaction studies, in which

CBTI product users rate the degree of accuracy and usefulness of the product, and external criterion studies, in which comparisons are made between CBTI-based descriptors and patient ratings/descriptions made on the basis of external sources, including psychiatric diagnoses, medical records, and clinician judgments. Based on findings for the original version of the MMPI, it would be anticipated that the accuracy of MMPI-2 and MMPI-A interpretive statements will vary considerably from product to product. Further, Graham (2000) suggested that the accuracy of interpretive statements generated by a particular CBTI product may vary from codetype to codetype. Finally, Moreland (1984) noted that the codetype descriptors for rare codetypes are likely to be less accurate than descriptors for commonly occurring codetypes that have received extensive research attention.

APPENDIX 8.1

MMPI-A Interpretive System

developed by
Robert P. Archer, PhD
and
PAR Staff

Client Information

Name:	Jared
Client ID:	
Gender:	Male
Date Of Birth:	(not specified)
Age:	14
Grade Level:	0
Setting:	Correctional/Juvenile Justice
Test Date:	08/01/2003

The following MMPI-A interpretive information should be viewed as only one source of hypotheses about the adolescent being evaluated. No diagnostic or treatment decision should be based solely on these data. Instead, statements generated by this report should be integrated with other sources of information concerning this client, including additional psychometric test findings, mental status results, psychosocial history data, and individual and family interviews, to reach clinical decisions. The information contained in this report represents combinations of actuarial data derived from major works in the MMPI and MMPI-A literatures. This report is confidential and intended for use by qualified professionals only. It is recommended that clinicians do not release reports generated with this software to adolescents or their family members or guardians. This report should be released only if it is edited to incorporate information obtained from a comprehensive psychological evaluation about the adolescent. Clinicians should adhere to applicable ethical guidelines as well as state and federal regulations in handling computer-generated reports.

Note. MMPI-A Interpretive System (Version 3) developed by Robert P. Archer and distributed by Psychological Assessment Resources, Inc. Reprinted with permission of Psychological Assessment Resources, Inc. Copyright © 1992, 1995, 2003.

Client: Jared
ID#:

Test Date: 08/01/2003
Page 2

Profile Matches and Scores

	Client Profile	Highest Scale Codetype	Best Fit Codetype
Codetype match:		4-6/6-4	4-6/6-4
Coefficient of Fit:		0.866	0.866
Scores			
F (Infrequency)	65	59	59
L (Lie)	50	49	49
K (Correction)	46	48	48
Hs (Scale 1)	49	52	52
D (Scale 2)	43	55	55
Hy (Scale 3)	50	53	53
Pd (Scale 4)	78	73	73
Mf (Scale 5)	47	45	45
Pa (Scale 6)	69	68	68
Pt (Scale 7)	50	55	55
Sc (Scale 8)	56	57	57
Ma (Scale 9)	62	55	55
Si (Scale 0)	53	48	48
Codetype Definition in T Score Points:	7	11	11
Mean Clinical Scale Elevation:	57.0	58.6	58.6
Mean Excitatory Scale Elevation:	65.0	61.8	61.8
Mean Age - Females:		15.7	15.7
Mean Age - Males:		16.4	16.4
Percent of Cases:		6.2	6.2
Configural clinical scale interpretation is provided in the report for the following codetype(s): 4-6/6-4			
Unanswered (?) Items:	6		
Welsh Code:	4'6+9-80<u>37</u>/152: F+-L/K:		

Client: Jared   Test Date: 08/01/2003
ID#:   Page 3

Validity and Clinical Scales

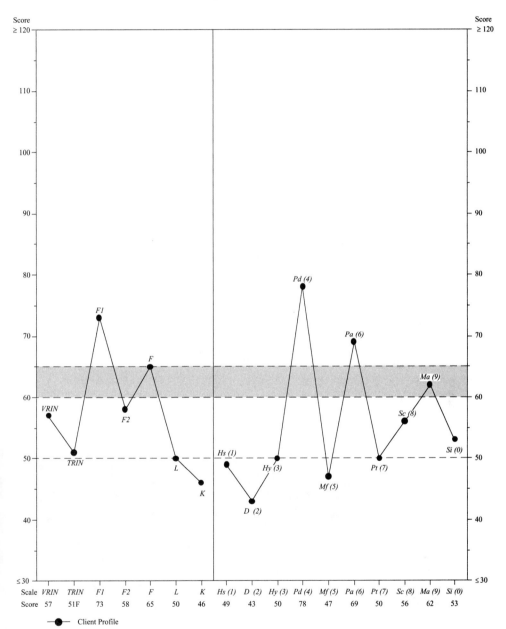

Scale	VRIN	TRIN	F1	F2	F	L	K	Hs (1)	D (2)	Hy (3)	Pd (4)	Mf (5)	Pa (6)	Pt (7)	Sc (8)	Ma (9)	Si (0)
Score	57	51F	73	58	65	50	46	49	43	50	78	47	69	50	56	62	53

● Client Profile

Content and Supplementary Scales

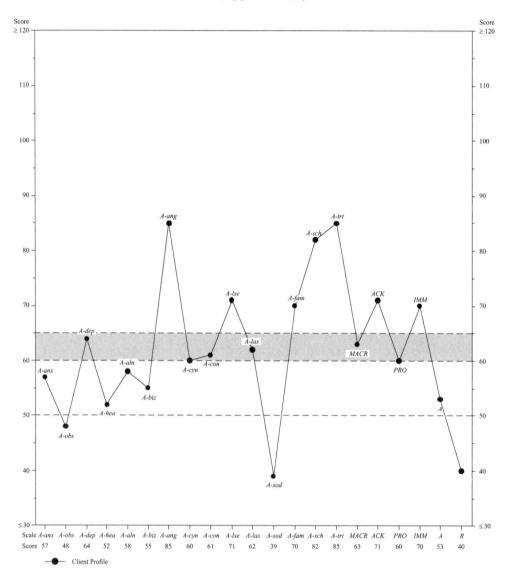

Scale	A-anx	A-obs	A-dep	A-hea	A-aln	A-biz	A-ang	A-cyn	A-con	A-lse	A-las	A-sod	A-fam	A-sch	A-trt	MACR	ACK	PRO	IMM	A	R
Score	57	48	64	52	58	55	85	60	61	71	62	39	70	82	85	63	71	60	70	53	40

●— Client Profile

Client: Jared   Test Date: 08/01/2003
ID#:   Page 5

Harris–Lingoes and Si Subscales

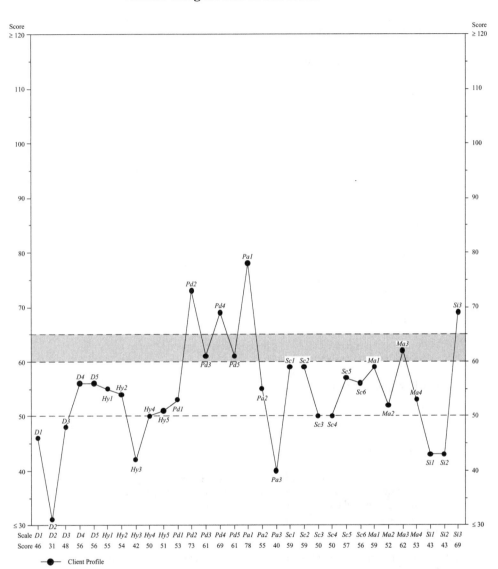

Scale	D1	D2	D3	D4	D5	Hy1	Hy2	Hy3	Hy4	Hy5	Pd1	Pd2	Pd3	Pd4	Pd5	Pa1	Pa2	Pa3	Sc1	Sc2	Sc3	Sc4	Sc5	Sc6	Ma1	Ma2	Ma3	Ma4	Si1	Si2	Si3
Score	46	31	48	56	56	55	54	42	50	51	53	73	61	69	61	78	55	40	59	59	50	50	57	56	59	52	62	53	43	43	69

●— Client Profile

Specified Setting

This adolescent was reported to have been in a correctional facility at the time the MMPI-A was administered.

Configural Validity Scale Interpretation

This adolescent has produced a consistent MMPI-A response pattern reflected in acceptable values on validity scales *VRIN* and *TRIN*.

No configural hypotheses are available for this *F-L-K* scale pattern of scores.

Both *F1* and *F2* are below *T*-score values of 90. *T*-score values of 90 or greater on either *F1* or *F2* are likely to indicate problems with profile validity.

Validity Scales

Raw (?) = 6

There were a few items omitted in completing this MMPI-A. These omissions may represent areas of limitation in the adolescent's life experience which rendered certain items unanswerable, or limitations in the adolescent's reading ability. There is little probability of profile distortion as a result of these few item omissions.

Variable Response Inconsistency (*VRIN*) = 57

VRIN scores in this range suggest that the adolescent responded to test items with an acceptable level of consistency.

True Response Inconsistency (*TRIN*) = 51F

TRIN scores in this range suggest that the adolescent responded to test items with an acceptable level of consistency.

Infrequency 1 (*F1*) = 73

This is an elevated range for the F1 score and it is often exhibited by adolescents in clinical settings. This range of elevation is likely to reflect an adolescent with significant psychopathology and substantial problems in adjustment.

Infrequency 2 (*F2*) = 58

Scores in this range suggest that the adolescent has responded in a valid manner to items which appear in the latter stage of the MMPI-A test booklet.

Infrequency (*F*) = 65

Scores in this range are considered to be moderately elevated and indicate the possibility of significant psychological and emotional problems. This adolescent appears to be acknowledging unusual or infrequently endorsed symptomatology to a degree characteristically reported by teenagers receiving psychiatric treatment.

Lie $(L) = 50$

Scores in this range suggest an appropriate balance between the admission and denial of common social faults. These adolescents are often viewed as flexible and psychologically sophisticated.

Correction $(K) = 46$

The majority of adolescents score in this range, which represents an appropriate balance between self-disclosure and guardedness. Prognosis for psychotherapy is often good in that such adolescents are open to discussion of life problems and symptoms.

Configural Clinical Scale Interpretation

4-6/6-4 Codetype

This MMPI-A codetype is classified as a 4-6/6-4 codetype. This codetype is fairly frequent among adolescents and occurs in more than 5% of adolescent assessments in clinical settings.

These teenagers are often described as angry, resentful, and argumentative. Additionally, an elevation on the *A-ang* content scale underscores the possibility that this adolescent experiences significant problems in anger control. They are usually referred for presenting symptoms involving defiance, disobedience, and negativism. Their treatment referrals are often initiated by court agencies. Adolescents with a 4-6/6-4 codetype typically place excessive demands on others for attention, affection, and sympathy, but are resentful of minor demands that may be placed on them in interpersonal relationships. They are generally suspicious and distrustful of the motives of others and characteristically avoid deep emotional attachments. They display little insight into their psychological problems, and their behaviors often result in rejection and anger by others. Additionally, *IMM* scores indicate this adolescent might be described as immature, easily frustrated, impatient, defiant, egocentric, and concrete. Adolescents with the 4-6/6-4 codetype often have large discrepancies between the way they perceive themselves (which is often very positive) and the way they are described by others. These adolescents are often referred for psychotherapy as a result of repeated conflicts with parents, which may take the form of chronic intense struggles. This adolescent's elevation on the *A-fam* content scale underscores the probability of significant frustration and anger in terms of family functioning. The 4-6/6-4 adolescent typically undercontrols his or her impulses and acts without sufficient thought or deliberation. Problems with authority figures are also prevalent for these teenagers, and they are described as provocative by others. Histories of drug abuse are frequently found for these adolescents.

Personality Disorder diagnoses (301.XX) have been associated with the 4-6/6-4 codetype, including features of Paranoid (301.0), Antisocial (301.7), and Narcissistic (301.81). Other diagnoses associated with this codetype include Oppositional Defiant Disorder (313.81) and Conduct Disorder (312.8). Primary defense mechanisms typically involve denial, projection, rationalization, and acting-out. These teenagers tend to avoid responsibility for their behavior. They are difficult to motivate in psychotherapy and are slow to develop a therapeutic relationship. These characteristics may greatly complicate his adjustment to life in the facility and he may be more likely than others to have conflicts with staff and other residents. At times, his tendency to be angry and argumentative may result in violent altercations. Additionally, *A-trt* content scale findings indicate this adolescent is likely to have problems in "opening up" to his therapist during the initial stages of psychotherapy. The provision of comprehensive intervention modalities including individual, family, and group psychotherapies appears indicated for these adolescents. The control of acting-out and the development of interpersonal trust are likely to be initial treatment issues.

Client: Jared
ID#:

Test Date: 08/01/2003
Page 9

Clinical Scales

Scale 1 (*Hs*) = 49

The obtained score is within normal or expected ranges. This adolescent has not expressed a pattern of unusual concerns or preoccupations regarding physical health or functioning.

Scale 2 (*D*) = 43

The obtained score is within normal or expected ranges and depressive symptomatology was not reported as a problem area for this adolescent.

Scale 3 (*Hy*) = 50

The obtained score is within normal or expected ranges and this adolescent probably has the capacity to acknowledge unpleasant issues or negative feelings.

Scale 4 (*Pd*) = 78

Scale 4 high points are very common among adolescents, particularly in psychiatric or criminal justice settings. Scores in this range are typical for adolescents who are characterized as rebellious, hostile toward authority figures, and defiant. These adolescents often have histories of poor school adjustment and problems in school conduct. Higher scores on this scale present an increased probability of overtly delinquent behavior. These adolescents often show an inability to delay gratification and are described as being impulsive and having little tolerance for frustration and boredom.

Primary defense mechanisms typically involve acting-out, and such behaviors may be unaccompanied by feelings of guilt or remorse. Although these adolescents typically create a good first impression and maintain an extroverted and outgoing interpersonal style, their interpersonal relationships tend to be shallow and superficial. They are eventually viewed by others as selfish, self-centered, and egocentric. These characteristics may increase the likelihood that this adolescent commits institutional infractions and that he becomes involved in conflicts and altercations with other residents. Elevations on Scale 4 are commonly found in individuals with involvement in pervasive criminal or antisocial criminal histories, so it is unlikely that the offense he recently committed was an isolated event. This adolescent would benefit from interventions that help him to reduce his impulsivity and to increase his ability to appreciate the consequences of his actions. This individual is likely to initially respond well to incarceration and his outgoing and extroverted style may allow him to quickly develop a new social network with other residents. However, he may resist rehabilitative opportunities and use his peers to further engage in institutional misbehavior.

Scale 5 (*Mf*) = 47

The obtained score is within normal or expected ranges and indicates standard interest patterns in the traditional masculine activities.

Scale 6 (*Pa*) = 69

Adolescents who obtain scores in this range tend to display marked interpersonal sensitivity and may be suspicious and distrustful in interpersonal relationships. They tend to be perceived by others as hostile, resentful, and argumentative. They often have difficulty in establishing therapeutic relationships due to marked interpersonal guardedness, and they may have problems in school adjustment.

Scale 7 (*Pt*) = 50

The obtained score is within normal or expected ranges and this adolescent appears to be capable of meeting current life experiences without excessive worry or apprehension.

Scale 8 (*Sc*) = 56

The obtained score is within normal or expected ranges and suggests intact reality testing and coherent thought processes.

Scale 9 (*Ma*) = 62

The *T*-score value obtained for this basic MMPI-A scale is within a marginal or transitional level of elevation. Some of the following descriptors, therefore, may not be applicable for this adolescent.

Scores in this range are typically obtained by adolescents who are described as overactive, impulsive, distractible, and restless. They frequently prefer action to thought and reflection. They are often unrealistic and grandiose in terms of goal-setting. These adolescents have a greater likelihood of school conduct problems and delinquent behaviors. They are perceived by others as self-centered, egocentric, talkative, and energetic. At marked elevations, scores in this range may reflect a presence of symptoms related to mania such as flight of ideas, grandiose self-perceptions, and euphoric mood.

Scale 0 (*Si*) = 53

The obtained score is within normal or expected ranges and reflects a balance between social introversion and extroversion in terms of attitude and behavior patterns.

Additional Scales

Content and Supplementary Scales

Content Scales

Anxiety (*A-anx*) = 57

The obtained score on this content scale is within normal or expected ranges.

Obsessiveness (*A-obs*) = 48

The obtained score on this content scale is within normal or expected ranges.

Depression (*A-dep*) = 64

Scores in this range represent marginal elevations on the Depression scale which may reflect mild or limited problems related to depression. These problems may include poor morale, apathy, or a tendency to experience depressive responses.

Health Concerns (*A-hea*) = 52

The obtained score on this content scale is within normal or expected ranges.

Alienation (*A-aln*) = 58

The obtained score on this content scale is within normal or expected ranges.

Bizarre Mentation (*A-biz*) = 55

The obtained score on this content scale is within normal or expected ranges.

Anger (*A-ang*) = 85

Scores in this range are produced by adolescents who may be described as irritable, grouchy, impatient, angry, and hostile. The range of problems with anger may include potential physical aggressiveness. Endorsement of individual items comprising the *A-ang* scale should be reviewed to aid in evaluating this issue.

Cynicism (*A-cyn*) = 60

Scores in this range represent a marginal elevation on the Cynicism scale, which may reflect a tendency to be guarded in relationships and suspicious of the motives of others.

Conduct Problems (*A-con*) = 61

Scores in this range represent marginal elevations on the Conduct Problems scale. This score may reflect an adolescent who has rebellious tendencies and problems with authority figures. These adolescents may have histories of disciplinary action in their school settings.

Low Self-Esteem (*A-lse*) = 71

Scores in this range may be produced by adolescents who feel inadequate, incompetent, or useless. They lack self-confidence and believe they have many faults and flaws. These teenagers may be interpersonally passive and socially uncomfortable.

Low Aspirations (*A-las*) = 62

Scores in this range represent marginal range elevations on the Low Aspirations scale. These adolescents may set low standards or goals for their performance and may become easily frustrated or procrastinate on tasks.

Social Discomfort (*A-sod*) = 39

The obtained score on this content scale is within normal or expected ranges.

Family Problems (*A-fam*) = 70

Scores in this range are produced by adolescents who have frequent quarrels with family members and report little love or understanding within their families. They feel misunderstood or unjustly punished by their families. They may report being physically or emotionally abused. These adolescents are often angry, hostile, or frustrated with family members and may wish to leave their homes.

School Problems (*A-sch*) = 82

Scores in this range are produced by adolescents who are encountering significant behavioral and/or academic problems within the school setting. These adolescents often have developed a negative attitude toward academic achievement and activities. The possibility of learning disabilities or developmental delays should be evaluated.

Negative Treatment Indicators *(A-trt)* = 85

Scores in this range are produced by adolescents who may present barriers to treatment stemming from apathy or despondency concerning their ability to change, or as a result of suspiciousness and distrust of help offered by others. These adolescents may believe they are incapable of changing, or that talking with others is not helpful. These characteristics may complicate the adolescent's response to rehabilitative efforts. Interventions should address his apathy, pessimism, and suspiciousness in order to increase his chances of benefiting from treatment.

Supplementary Scales

MacAndrew Alcoholism (MAC–R) = 63

Adolescents who score in this range tend to fall in the "gray" area regarding positive histories for drug or alcohol abuse. Therefore, it is recommended that this adolescent be carefully evaluated in terms of alcohol and substance abuse to establish whether there is a need for intervention in these areas.

Alcohol-Drug Problem Acknowledgement (ACK) = 71

Scores in this range are produced by adolescents who are acknowledging alcohol or drug use–related symptoms, attitudes, or beliefs. Staff working in the facility should be aware of this adolescent's substance use and attempts should be made to understand the association between his substance use and his behavior problems.

Alcohol-Drug Problem Proneness (PRO) = 60

Scores in this range are within acceptable or normal ranges on the PRO scale.

Immaturity (IMM) = 70

Scores in this range are produced by immature adolescents. These adolescents are easily frustrated, impatient, defiant, and exploitative in interpersonal relationships. They are likely to have histories of academic and social difficulties. They are egocentric, tend to externalize blame, and are simplistic and concrete in cognitive processes. Adolescents who produce elevations on the IMM scale often have lower intelligence and language abilities. They may be defiant and resistant to rehabilitative interventions and they are likely to have conflicts with staff within the facility. Their immaturity may also strain relationships with other residents within the facility and, depending on the physical maturity of the adolescent, may result in physical altercations and possibly victimization.

Anxiety (A) = 53

The obtained score is within normal or expected ranges and indicates unremarkable levels of anxiety and discomfort.

Repression (R) = 40

Adolescents with scores in this range have been described as spontaneous, excitable, enthusiastic, impulsive, talkative, and argumentative. In interpersonal relationships they are often perceived as self-seeking and self-indulgent. They tend to employ defense mechanisms which emphasize acting-out.

Harris-Lingoes and *Si* SubScales

The interpretation of Harris-Lingoes and *Si* subscales is provided in this program because of the potential relevance of these data to adolescent profiles. The correlates of these research scales have not been examined in adolescent populations, however, and the user is cautioned that the following interpretive statements are based on findings in adult populations.

Subjective Depression (*D1*) = 46

The obtained score is within normal or expected ranges.

Psychomotor Retardation (*D2*) = 31

Low *D2* scorers describe themselves as active and involved. They do not have problems in getting started on activities, and they find their everyday lives interesting and rewarding. They admit to having hostile and aggressive impulses at times.

Physical Malfunctioning (*D3*) = 48

The obtained score is within normal or expected ranges.

Mental Dullness (*D4*) = 56

The obtained score is within normal or expected ranges.

Brooding (*D5*) = 56

The obtained score is within normal or expected ranges.

Denial of Social Anxiety (*Hy1*) = 55

The obtained score is within normal or expected ranges.

Need for Affection (*Hy2*) = 54

The obtained score is within normal or expected ranges.

Lassitude-Malaise (*Hy3*) = 42

The obtained score is within normal or expected ranges.

Somatic Complaints (*Hy4*) = 50

The obtained score is within normal or expected ranges.

Inhibition of Aggression (*Hy5*) = 51

The obtained score is within normal or expected ranges.

Familial Discord (*Pd1*) = 53

The obtained score is within normal or expected ranges.

Authority Problems (*Pd2*) = 73

High *Pd2* scorers resent authority and societal demands, and they often have histories of academic and legal difficulties. They have definite opinions about what is right and wrong, and they stand up for their beliefs. These tendencies may make it difficult for this adolescent to adjust to incarceration and he may be more likely than others to have conflicts with staff members and other residents. He may also be more willing than others to engage in misconduct during incarceration.

Social Imperturbability (*Pd3*) = 61

The obtained score is within normal or expected ranges.

Social Alienation (*Pd4*) = 69

High *Pd4* scorers feel misunderstood, alienated, isolated, and estranged from others. They are lonely, unhappy, and uninvolved people who blame others for their own problems and shortcomings. They are often insensitive and inconsiderate in relationships and will later verbalize regret and remorse for their actions.

Self-Alienation (*Pd5*) = 61

The obtained score is within normal or expected ranges.

Persecutory Ideas (*Pa1*) = 78

High *Pa1* scorers view the world as very threatening. They feel misunderstood and unfairly blamed or punished. They are suspicious and untrusting, and they may have delusions of persecution. They externalize blame for their problems. These characteristics may make it difficult for this adolescent to develop supportive relationships during incarceration and his tendency to externalize blame may hinder the rehabilitative process.

Poignancy (*Pa2*) = 55

The obtained score is within normal or expected ranges.

Naiveté (*Pa3*) = 40

The obtained score is within normal or expected ranges.

Social Alienation ($Sc1$) = 59

The obtained score is within normal or expected ranges.

Emotional Alienation ($Sc2$) = 59

The obtained score is within normal or expected ranges.

Lack of Ego Mastery–Cognitive ($Sc3$) = 50

The obtained score is within normal or expected ranges.

Lack of Ego Mastery–Conative ($Sc4$) = 50

The obtained score is within normal or expected ranges.

Lack of Ego Mastery–Defective Inhibition ($Sc5$) = 57

The obtained score is within normal or expected ranges.

Bizarre Sensory Experiences ($Sc6$) = 56

The obtained score is within normal or expected ranges.

Amorality ($Ma1$) = 59

The obtained score is within normal or expected ranges.

Psychomotor Acceleration ($Ma2$) = 52

The obtained score is within normal or expected ranges.

Imperturbability ($Ma3$) = 62

The obtained score is within normal or expected ranges.

Ego Inflation ($Ma4$) = 53

The obtained score is within normal or expected ranges.

Shyness/Self-Consciousness ($Si1$) = 43

The obtained score on the $Si1$ subscale is within expected or normal ranges.

Social Avoidance ($Si2$) = 43

The obtained score on the *Si2* subscale is within expected or normal ranges.

Alienation—Self and Others (*Si3*) = 69

Adolescents who produce elevated scores on the *Si3* subscale may have symptomatology that serves to interfere in their relationships with others. They may be anxious and indecisive, fearful and suspicious, or maintain low self-concepts or self-esteem. This adolescent's tendency to be timid, fearful, and isolated places him at risk for victimization during incarceration by aggressive and dominant peers.

Client: Jared   Test Date: 08/01/2003
ID#:   Page 18

MMPI-A Structural Summary

Factor Grouping				
1. General Maladjustment		**2. Immaturity**		
Welsh's A (Anxiety)		IMM (Immaturity)		X
Pt (7) (Psychasthenia)		F (Infrequency)		X
Sc (8) (Schizophrenia)		Sc (8) (Schizophrenia)		
D (2) (Depression)		Pa (6) (Paranoia)		X
Pd (4) (Psychopathic Deviate)	X	ACK (Alcohol/Drug Problem Acknowledgement)		X
D1 (Subjective Depression)		MAC−R (MacAndrew Alcoholism Revised)		X
D4 (Mental Dullness)		Pa1 (Persecutory Ideas)		X
D5 (Brooding)		Sc2 (Emotional Alienation)		
Hy3 (Lassitude-Malaise)		Sc6 (Bizarre Sensory Experiences)		
Sc1 (Social Alienation)		A-sch (School Problems)		X
Sc2 (Emotional Alienation)		A-biz (Bizarre Mentation)		
Sc3 (Lack of Ego Mastery−Cognitive)		A-aln (Alienation)		
Sc4 (Lack of Ego Mastery−Conative)		A-con (Conduct Problems)		X
Si3 (Alienation−Self and Others)	X	A-fam (Family Problems)		X
Pd4 (Social Alienation)	X	A-trt (Negative Treatment Indicators)		X
Pd5 (Self-Alienation)	X			
Pa2 (Poignancy)				
A-dep (Depression)	X			
A-anx (Anxiety)				
A-lse (Low Self-Esteem)	X			
A-aln (Alienation)				
A-obs (Obsessiveness)				
A-trt (Negative Treatment Indicators)	X			
Number of Scales with *T*-Score >= 60	7/23	**Number of Scales with *T*-Score >= 60**		10/15
Mean *T*-Score Elevation	58.04	**Mean *T*-Score Elevation**		66.53

Factor Grouping			
3. Disinhibition/Excitatory Potential		**4. Social Discomfort**	
Ma (9) (Hypomania)	X	Si (0) (Social Introversion)	
Ma2 (Psychomotor Acceleration)		Si1 (Shyness/Self-Consciousness)	
Ma4 (Ego Inflation)		Hy1 (Denial of Social Anxiety) **Low**	
Sc5 (Lack of Ego Mastery–Defective Inhibition)		Pd3 (Social Imperturbability) **Low**	
D2 (Psychomotor Retardation) **Low**	X	Ma3 (Imperturbability) **Low**	
Welsh's R (Repression) **Low**	X	A-sod (Social Discomfort)	
K (Correction) **Low**		A-lse (Low Self-Esteem)	X
L (Lie) **Low**		Pt (7) (Psychasthenia)	
A-ang (Anger)	X		
A-cyn (Cynicism)	X		
A-con (Conduct Problems)	X		
MAC-R (MacAndrew Alcoholism Revised)	X		
Number of Scales with T Score >= 60 or Low Scales with T Score <= 40	7/12	**Number of Scales with T Score => 60 or Low Scales with T Score <= 40**	1/8
Mean T-Score Elevation (high)	61.63	**Mean T-Score Elevation (high)**	51.20
Mean T-Score Elevation (low)	41.75	**Mean T-Score Elevation (low)**	59.33
5. Health Concerns		**6. Naiveté**	
Hs (1) (Hypochondriasis)		A-cyn (Cynicism) **Low**	
Hy (3) (Hysteria)		Pa3 (Naiveté)	
A-hea (Health Concerns)		Hy2 (Need for Affection)	
Hy4 (Somatic Complaints)		Si3 (Alienation–Self and Others)**Low**	
Hy3 (Lassitude-Malaise)		K (Correction)	
D3 (Physical Malfunctioning)			
Number of Scales with T Score >= 60	0/6	**Number of Scales with T Score >= 60 or Low Scales with T Score <= 40**	0/5
Mean T-Score Elevation	48.50	**Mean T-Score Elevation (high)**	46.67
		Mean T-Score Elevation (low)	64.50
7. Familial Alienation		**8. Psychoticism**	
Pd1 (Familial Discord)		Pa1 (Persecutory Ideas)	X
A-fam (Family Problems)	X	Pa (6) (Paranoia)	X
Pd (4) (Psychopathic Deviate)	X	A-biz (Bizarre Mentation)	
PRO (Alcohol/Drug Problem Proneness)	X	Sc6 (Bizarre Sensory Experiences)	
Number of Scales with T Score >= 60	3/4	**Number of Scales with T Score >= 60**	2/4
Mean T-Score Elevation	65.25	**Mean T-Score Elevation**	64.50

Structural Summary Interpretation

The following Structural Summary information provides an assessment of the adolescent's functioning along the eight basic factor dimensions found for the 69 scales and subscales of the MMPI-A. Information is provided for those factors which appear to be most salient in describing this adolescent's psychopathology based on the criterion that a majority (i.e., greater than 50%) of the scales or subscales within a particular factor are at a critical level (either critically elevated or critically lowered) for each factor interpreted below. The software determines if a majority of the scale or subscale scores are at the critical level based on all of the scales and subscales within a particular factor, regardless of whether or not a score was entered into the software. Missing scale and/or subscale scores may make it more difficult for a respondent to have a majority of scores in the elevated range and, therefore, may reduce the usefulness of the Structural Summary. Missing scores are denoted with a "?" and scores at the critical level are denoted with an "X".

For factors meeting the criterion of having a majority of scores at the critical level, interpretations are organized from the factor showing the highest percentage of significant scale and subscale scores to those factors showing the lowest percentage of significant scale and subscale scores. Based on the assumption that the higher the percentage of scale or subscale scores are within a factor that produces critical values, it is more likely that the particular factor or dimension provides a more salient or important description of the adolescent. Examination of the specific pattern of scale elevations within a dimension can provide the clinician with additional and useful information in refining the description of the adolescent for that factor. Mean T-Score elevations are also provided in the Structural Summary. These means are based on the scale and subscale scores of the various factors and they do not include missing scores.

This adolescent has produced significant elevations on 3 scales and subscales associated with the Familial Alienation dimension. Adolescents who produce significant elevationst on this factor are more likely to experience significant family conflicts and to encounter disciplinary problems at school. They are frequently seen as hostile, delinquent, or aggressive, and they may be verbally abusive, threatening, or disobedient at home. Efforts should be made to determine the extent to which this adolescent's behavior problems have contributed to his family difficulties.

This adolescent is manifesting significant elevations on 10 scales and subscales associated with the Immaturity factor. Adolescents who obtain high scores on this factor are often described as egocentric, self-centered, impulsive, and limited in terms of self-awareness or psychological insight. They are likely to manifest behavioral problems in the school setting and to have interpersonal difficulties or are argumentative.

This adolescent has produced significant values on 7 scales and subscales associated with the Disinhibition/Excitatory Potential dimension. Adolescents who score high on this factor often display impulsivity, disciplinary problems, and conflicts with parents and peers. They tend to be dominant and aggressive in peer relationships. In general,

Client: Jared   Test Date: 08/01/2003
ID#:   Page 21

these adolescents tend to use externalization as a primary defense mechanism and to manifest behavioral problems including alcohol or drug abuse, theft, dishonesty, and problems in physical aggressiveness. These characteristics are likely to interfere with this adolescent's ability to adjust to incarceration. Although he might be able to make friends in the facility more easily than others, these relationships are likely to be superficial and will end up in conflict. His impulsivity and willingness to break rules increases the probability that he will commit infractions while incarcerated and he is more likely than other residents to have conflicts with staff because of this. His impulsivity, possible dishonesty, and use of externalization may complicate any rehabilitative efforts.

Adolescent Norms for the Original MMPI for Males and Females for Ages 14 and Below, 15, 16, and 17

Philip A. Marks
Peter F. Briggs

Note. Published in Marks, P. S., Seeman, W., and Haller, D. L. (1974). *The actuarial use of the MMPI with adolescents and adults* (pp. 155–162). Baltimore, MD: William and Wilkins. Also in Archer, R. P. (1987). *Using the MMPI with adolescents* (pp. 197–213). Hillsdale, NJ: Lawrence Erlbaum Associates. Originally published in Dahlstrom, W. G., Welsh, G. S., and Dahlstrom, L. E. (1972). *An MMPI handbook: Vol. 1. Clinical interpretation* (pp. 388–398). Minneapolis: University of Minnesota Press. Reprinted by permission.

TABLE A.1
T-Score Conversions for Basic Scales Without K-Corrections for Adolescents Age 14 and Below

Raw Score	Males ?	L	F	K	1 (Hs)	2 (D)	3 (Hy)	4 (Pd)	5 (Mf)	6 (Pa)	7 (Pt)	8 (Sc)	9 (Ma)	0 (Si)	Females ?	L	F	K	1 (Hs)	2 (D)	3 (Hy)	4 (Pd)	5 (Mf)	6 (Pa)	7 (Pt)	8 (Sc)	9 (Ma)	0 (Si)	Raw Score
0	41	32	36	23	34	9	10	10	0	23	30	32	15	11	41	31	36	19	36	11	7	14	126	28	29	32	16	13	0
1		37	38	25	37	12	13	12	3	25	32	33	17	12		36	39	22	39	13	9	16	124	30	30	34	18	15	1
2		42	40	27	40	15	16	14	5	27	33	35	19	14		41	41	24	41	15	11	19	122	32	32	35	20	16	2
3		46	42	29	43	17	18	16	8	30	34	36	21	15		46	44	27	44	17	13	21	120	34	33	36	22	18	3
4		51	44	31	46	19	20	18	10	33	36	37	23	16		50	46	29	46	20	15	23	118	36	34	37	24	19	4
5		56	46	33	49	21	22	21	12	35	37	38	25	18		55	49	31	49	22	18	25	115	38	36	38	26	20	5
6		61	48	35	52	23	25	23	15	38	38	39	27	19		59	51	33	51	24	20	27	113	40	37	40	28	21	6
7		66	50	37	55	26	27	25	17	41	40	40	29	20		64	54	35	54	26	22	29	111	43	39	41	30	23	7
8		71	52	39	58	28	29	28	20	44	41	41	31	22		69	56	38	56	28	24	31	109	45	40	42	32	24	8
9		76	54	41	61	30	31	30	22	46	43	42	33	23		73	59	40	59	30	27	34	107	47	42	43	35	25	9
10	44	80	56	43	64	32	33	32	24	49	44	43	35	24	44	78	61	42	61	32	29	36	104	49	43	45	37	26	10
11		85	58	45	67	35	36	35	27	52	45	44	37	26		83	64	44	64	34	31	38	102	51	44	46	39	28	11
12		90	60	48	70	37	38	37	29	55	47	45	39	27		87	66	47	66	36	33	40	100	54	46	47	41	29	12
13		95	62	50	73	39	40	39	31	57	48	46	41	28		92	69	49	69	38	35	42	99	56	47	48	43	30	13
14		100	64	52	76	41	42	42	34	60	49	47	43	30		97	71	51	71	41	38	44	97	58	49	49	45	32	14
15		105	66	54	79	43	44	44	36	63	51	48	45	31		101	74	53	74	43	40	46	95	60	50	51	47	33	15
16			68	56	82	46	47	46	38	65	52	50	47	33			76	56	76	45	42	49	92	62	52	52	49	34	16
17			70	58	84	48	49	49	41	68	54	51	49	34			79	58	79	47	44	51	90	65	53	53	51	35	17
18			71	60	87	50	51	51	43	71	55	52	50	35			81	60	81	49	46	53	88	67	54	54	54	37	18
19			73	62	90	52	53	53	46	74	56	53	52	37			84	62	84	51	49	55	86	69	56	56	56	38	19
20	47		75	64	93	55	56	56	48	76	58	54	54	38	47		86	65	86	53	51	57	84	71	57	57	58	39	20
21			77	66	96	57	58	58	50	79	59	55	56	39			89	67	89	55	53	59	81	73	59	58	60	40	21
22			79	68	99	59	60	60	53	82	60	56	58	41			91	69	91	57	55	61	79	75	60	59	62	42	22
23			81	70	102	61	62	62	55	84	62	57	60	42			94	71	94	59	58	64	77	78	62	60	64	43	23
24			83	72	105	63	64	65	57	87	63	58	62	43			96	73	96	62	60	66	75	80	63	62	66	44	24
25			85	74	108	66	67	67	60	90	65	59	64	45			99	76	99	64	62	68	73	82	64	63	68	45	25
26			87	76	111	68	69	69	62	93	66	60	66	46			101	78	101	66	64	70	70	84	66	64	70	47	26

334

	Males															Females													
Raw Score	?	L	F	K	1 (Hs)	2 (D)	3 (Hy)	4 (Pd)	5 (Mf)	6 (Pa)	7 (Pt)	8 (Sc)	9 (Ma)	0 (Si)	?	L	F	K	1 (Hs)	2 (D)	3 (Hy)	4 (Pd)	5 (Mf)	6 (Pa)	7 (Pt)	8 (Sc)	9 (Ma)	0 (Si)	Raw Score
27			89	79	114	70	71	72	65	95	67	61	68	47			104	80	104	68	66	72	68	86	67	65	72	48	27
28			91	81	117	72	73	74	67	98	69	62	70	49			106	82	106	70	69	74	66	89	69	67	75	49	28
29			93	83	120	75	75	76	69	101	70	63	72	50			109	85	109	72	71	76	64	91	70	68	77	51	29
30	50		95	85	123	77	78	79	72	104	71	65	74	51	50		111	87	111	74	73	79	62	93	72	69	79	52	30
31			97		126	79	80	81	74	106	73	66	76	53			114		113	76	75	81	59	95	73	70	81	53	31
32			99		129	81	82	83	76	109	74	67	78	54			116		116	78	78	83	57	97	74	71	83	54	32
33			101		132	83	84	86	79	112	75	68	80	56			119		118	80	80	85	55	99	76	73	85	56	33
34			103			86	87	88	81	114	77	69	82	57			121			83	82	87	53	102	77	74	87	57	34
35			105			88	89	90	83	117	78	70	84	58			124			85	84	89	51	104	79	75	89	58	35
36			107			90	91	93	86	120	80	71	86	60			126			87	86	92	48	106	80	76	91	59	36
37			109			92	93	95	88	123	81	72	88	61			129			89	89	94	46	108	82	77	94	61	37
38			111			95	95	97	91	125	82	73	90	62			131			91	91	96	44	110	83	79	96	62	38
39			113			97	98	100	93	128	84	74	92	64			134			93	93	98	42	113	84	80	98	63	39
40	53		115			99	100	102	95	131	85	75	94	65	53		136			95	95	100	40	115	86	81	100	64	40
41			117			101	102	104	98		86	76	96	66			139			97	98	102	37		87	82	102	66	41
42			119			103	104	106	100		88	77	98	68			141			99	100	104	35		89	84	104	67	42
43			121			106	107	109	102		89	78	100	69			144			102	102	107	33		90	85	106	68	43
44			123			108	109	111	105		91	80	101	70			146			104	104	109	31		92	86	108	69	44
45			125			110	111	113	107		92	81	103	72			149			106	106	111	29		93	87	110	71	45
46			127			112	113	116	109		93	82	105	73			152			108	109	113	26		94	88	113	72	46
47			129			115	115	118	112		95	83		75			154			110	111	115	24		96	90		73	47
48			131			117	118	120	114		96	84		76			156			112	113	117	22		97	91		75	48
49			133			119	120	123	117			85		77			159			114	115	119	20			92		76	49
50	56		135			121	122	125	119			86		79	56		161			116	118	122	18			93		77	50
51			137			123	124		121			87		80			164			118	120		15			95		78	51
52			139			126	126		124			88		81			166			120	122		13			96		80	52
53			141			128	129		126			89		83			169			123	124		11			97		81	53

(Continued)

TABLE A.1
(Continued)

Males

Raw Score	?	L	F	K	1 (Hs)	2 (D)	3 (Hy)	4 (Pd)	5 (Mf)	6 (Pa)	7 (Pt)	8 (Sc)	9 (Ma)	0 (Si)
54			143			130	131		128			90		84
55			145			132	133		131			91		85
56			147			135	135		133			92		87
57			149			137	138		135			93		88
58			151			139	140		138			95		89
59	58		153			141	142		140			96		91
60			155			143	144		143			97		92
61			157									98		93
62			159									99		95
63			161									100		96
64			163									101		98
65												102		99
66												103		100
67												104		102
68												105		103
69												106		104
70	62											107		106
71												108		
72												110		
73												111		
74												112		
75												113		
76												114		
77												115		
78												116		

Females

Raw Score	?	L	F	K	1 (Hs)	2 (D)	3 (Hy)	4 (Pd)	5 (Mf)	6 (Pa)	7 (Pt)	8 (Sc)	9 (Ma)	0 (Si)
54			172			125	126		9			98		82
55			174			127	129		7			99		83
56			177			129	131		4			101		85
57			179			131	133		2			102		86
58			182			133	135					103		87
59	58		184			135	138					104		88
60			187			137	140					106		90
61			189									107		91
62			192									108		92
63			194									109		94
64			197									110		95
65												112		96
66												113		97
67												114		99
68												115		100
69	62											117		101
70												118		102
71												119		
72												120		
73												121		
74												123		
75												124		
76												125		
77												126		
78												128		

TABLE A.2
T-Score Conversions for Basic Scales Without K-Corrections for Adolescents Age 15

Males

Raw Score	?	L	F	K	1 (Hs)	2 (D)	3 (Hy)	4 (Pd)	5 (Mf)	6 (Pa)	7 (Pt)	8 (Sc)	9 (Ma)	0 (Si)
0	41	32	37	22	36	9	12	10	6	27	29	33	15	10
1		37	38	24	39	11	15	13	8	29	31	34	17	12
2		42	40	26	41	13	17	15	10	31	32	35	19	13
3		46	41	28	44	15	20	17	12	33	34	36	21	15
4		50	43	30	46	18	22	19	14	35	35	37	22	16
5		55	45	32	48	20	24	22	16	37	37	38	24	17
6		59	46	34	51	22	26	24	18	40	38	39	26	19
7		63	48	37	53	24	28	26	20	42	39	40	28	20
8		67	50	39	55	27	30	28	22	44	41	41	30	21
9		72	52	41	58	29	32	30	24	46	42	42	32	23
10	44	76	53	43	60	31	34	32	26	48	44	43	34	24
11		80	55	45	62	33	36	34	28	50	45	44	36	25
12		85	57	47	65	36	38	37	31	52	46	45	38	27
13		89	58	49	67	38	40	39	33	54	48	46	40	28
14		93	60	51	69	40	42	41	35	56	49	47	42	30
15		98	62	53	72	43	44	43	37	58	51	48	43	31
16			63	55	74	45	46	45	39	60	52	49	45	32
17			65	58	76	47	48	47	41	63	54	50	47	34
18			67	60	79	49	50	49	43	65	55	51	49	35
19			68	62	81	52	52	52	45	67	56	52	51	36
20	47		70	64	84	54	54	54	47	69	58	53	53	38
21			72	66	86	56	57	56	49	71	59	54	55	39
22			73	68	88	58	59	58	51	73	61	55	57	40
23			75	70	91	61	61	60	53	75	62	56	59	42
24			77	72	93	63	63	62	56	77	64	57	61	43
25			78	74	95	65	65	64	58	79	65	58	63	44

Females

Raw Score	?	L	F	K	1 (Hs)	2 (D)	3 (Hy)	4 (Pd)	5 (Mf)	6 (Pa)	7 (Pt)	8 (Sc)	9 (Ma)	0 (Si)
0	41	31	36	21	37	9	9	13	120	26	29	32	19	13
1		36	38	23	39	11	11	15	118	29	31	34	20	14
2		40	41	25	41	13	13	17	115	31	32	35	22	15
3		45	43	27	43	15	15	19	113	33	33	36	24	17
4		49	45	29	46	17	17	21	111	36	35	37	26	18
5		53	47	32	48	19	19	23	109	38	36	39	28	19
6		58	50	34	50	21	21	25	107	40	37	40	29	21
7		62	52	36	52	24	23	27	105	42	39	41	31	22
8		66	54	38	55	26	25	30	103	44	40	42	33	23
9		70	57	40	57	28	27	32	101	47	41	43	35	24
10	44	75	59	42	59	30	29	34	100	49	43	44	37	26
11		79	61	45	61	32	31	36	98	51	44	45	39	27
12		83	63	47	64	34	33	38	96	53	45	46	41	28
13		88	66	49	66	37	35	40	94	55	47	47	42	30
14		92	68	51	68	39	37	42	92	58	48	48	44	31
15		96	70	53	70	41	39	44	90	60	49	49	46	32
16			72	56	72	43	42	46	88	62	51	50	48	33
17			75	58	75	45	44	48	86	64	52	51	50	35
18	47		77	60	77	47	46	51	84	66	53	53	52	36
19			79	62	79	49	48	53	82	68	55	54	54	37
20			82	64	81	52	50	55	79	71	56	55	56	39
21			84	67	84	54	52	57	77	73	58	56	57	40
22			86	69	86	56	54	59	75	75	59	57	59	41
23			89	71	88	58	56	61	73	77	60	58	61	42
24			91	73	90	60	58	63	71	79	62	59	63	44
25			93	75	93	62	60	65	69	82	63	60	65	45

(Continued)

337

TABLE A.2
(Continued)

Males

Raw Score	?	L	F	K	1 (Hs)	2 (D)	3 (Hy)	4 (Pd)	5 (Mf)	6 (Pa)	7 (Pt)	8 (Sc)	9 (Ma)	0 (Si)
26			80	76	98	67	67	66	60	81	66	59	65	46
27			82	78	100	70	69	69	62	83	68	60	66	47
28			83	81	102	72	71	71	64	86	69	61	68	48
29			85	83	105	74	73	73	66	88	71	62	70	50
30	50		87	85	107	77	75	75	68	90	72	63	72	51
31			88		109	79	77	77	70	92	73	64	74	52
32			90		112	81	79	79	72	94	75	65	76	54
33			92		114	83	81	81	74	96	76	66	78	55
34			93			86	83	84	76	98	78	67	80	56
35			95			88	85	86	79	100	79	68	82	58
36			97			90	87	88	81	102	81	69	84	59
37			98			92	89	90	83	104	82	70	86	60
38			100			95	91	92	85	106	83	71	87	62
39			102			97	94	94	87	109	85	72	89	63
40	53		103			99	96	96	89	111	86	73	91	64
41			105			101	98	99	91		88	74	93	66
42			107			104	100	101	93		89	75	95	67
43			108			106	102	103	95		90	76	97	69
44			110			108	104	105	97		92	77	99	70
45			112			111	106	107	99		93	78	101	71
46			114			113	108	109	101		95	79	103	73
47			115			115	110	111	104		96	80		74
48			117			117	112	114	106		98	81		75
49			119			120	114	116	108			82		77
50	56		120			122	116	118	110			83		78
51			122			124	118		112			84		79
52			124			126	120		114			85		81

Females

0 (Si)	9 (Ma)	8 (Sc)	7 (Pt)	6 (Pa)	5 (Mf)	4 (Pd)	3 (Hy)	2 (D)	1 (Hs)	K	F	L	?	Raw Score
46	67	61	64	84	67	67	62	65	95	77	95			26
48	69	62	66	86	65	69	64	67	97	80	98			27
49	70	63	67	88	63	71	66	69	99	82	100			28
50	72	64	68	90	61	74	68	71	102	84	102			29
52	74	65	70	93	59	76	70	73	104	86	104		50	30
53	76	66	71	95	57	78	72	75	106		107			31
54	78	68	72	97	55	80	74	78	108		109			32
55	80	69	74	99	53	82	76	80	110		111			33
57	82	70	75	101	51	84	79	82			114			34
58	83	71	76	103	49	86	81	84			116			35
59	85	72	78	106	47	88	83	86			118			36
61	87	73	79	108	45	90	85	88			120			37
62	89	74	80	110	42	92	87	90			123			38
63	91	75	82	112	40	95	89	93			125			39
64	93	76	83	114	38	97	91	95			127		53	40
66	95	77	85		36	99	93	97			130			41
67	96	78	86		34	101	95	99			132			42
68	98	79	87		32	103	97	101			134			43
70	100	80	89		30	105	99	103			136			44
71	102	82	90		28	107	101	106			139			45
72	104	83	91		26	109	103	108			141			46
73		84	93		24	111	105	110			143			47
75		85	94		22	113	107	112			146			48
76		86			20	115	109	114			148			49
77		87			18	118	111	116			150		56	50
79		88			16		113	119			152			51
80		89			14		115	121			155			52

338

Males

Raw Score	?	L	F	K	1 (Hs)	2 (D)	3 (Hy)	4 (Pd)	5 (Mf)	6 (Pa)	7 (Pt)	8 (Sc)	9 (Ma)	0 (Si)
53			125			129	122		116			86		82
54	58		127			131	124		118			87		83
55			129			133	126		120			88		85
56			130			135	128		122			89		86
57			132			138	131		124			90		87
58			134			140	133		127			91		89
59			135			142	135		129			92		90
60			137			145	137		131			93		91
61			139									94		93
62			140									95		94
63			142									96		95
64			144									97		97
65												98		98
66												99		99
67												100		101
68												101		102
69												102		103
70	62											103		105
71												104		
72												105		
73												106		
74												107		
75												108		
76												109		
77												110		
78												111		

Females

Raw Score	?	L	F	K	1 (Hs)	2 (D)	3 (Hy)	4 (Pd)	5 (Mf)	6 (Pa)	7 (Pt)	8 (Sc)	9 (Ma)	0 (Si)
53			157			123	118		12			90		81
54			159			125	120		10			91		82
55			162			127	122		8			92		84
56			164			129	124		6			93		85
57			166			131	126		3			94		86
58			168			134	128		1			95		88
59			171			136	130					97		89
60	58		173			138	132					98		90
61			175									99		92
62			178									100		93
63			180									101		94
64			182									102		95
65												103		97
66												104		98
67												105		99
68												106		101
69												107		102
70	62											108		103
71												109		
72												110		
73												112		
74												113		
75												114		
76												115		
77												116		
78												117		

TABLE A.3
T-Score Conversions for Basic Scales Without K-Corrections for Adolescents Age 16

Raw Score	Males ?	L	F	K	1 (Hs)	2 (D)	3 (Hy)	4 (Pd)	5 (Mf)	6 (Pa)	7 (Pt)	8 (Sc)	9 (Ma)	0 (Si)	Females ?	L	F	K	1 (Hs)	2 (D)	3 (Hy)	4 (Pd)	5 (Mf)	6 (Pa)	7 (Pt)	8 (Sc)	9 (Ma)	0 (Si)	Raw Score
0	41	31	35	20	33	8	10	10	0	34	28	30	11	8	41	29	35	22	35	8	10	11	127	21	27	32	12	10	0
1		35	37	22	36	11	12	12	3	35	30	32	13	10		34	37	24	37	10	12	14	125	24	29	33	14	12	1
2		40	39	24	39	13	15	15	5	36	31	33	15	11		38	39	26	40	12	14	16	122	27	30	34	17	13	2
3		44	40	27	42	15	17	17	8	37	33	35	17	12		42	41	28	42	14	16	18	120	29	32	35	19	15	3
4		49	42	29	45	18	19	19	10	39	34	36	19	14		47	44	30	44	16	18	20	118	32	33	36	21	16	4
5		53	44	31	47	20	21	21	12	40	36	37	21	15		51	46	33	47	18	20	23	116	35	34	38	23	17	5
6		58	46	33	50	22	23	23	15	42	37	38	23	17		56	48	35	49	20	22	25	113	37	36	39	26	18	6
7		62	47	36	53	24	26	25	17	43	39	39	25	18		60	50	37	51	22	24	27	111	40	37	40	28	20	7
8		67	49	38	56	27	28	28	20	45	40	40	28	20		64	53	39	54	24	26	29	109	42	38	41	30	21	8
9		71	51	40	59	29	30	30	22	46	42	41	30	21		69	55	41	56	26	28	31	106	45	40	42	32	22	9
10	44	76	53	42	62	31	32	32	24	48	43	42	32	22	44	73	57	44	58	28	30	33	104	48	41	43	35	23	10
11		80	54	45	64	33	34	34	27	49	45	43	34	24		78	59	46	61	30	32	36	102	50	42	44	37	24	11
12		85	56	47	67	36	37	36	29	51	46	44	36	25		82	62	48	63	32	34	38	100	53	44	45	39	26	12
13		89	58	49	70	38	39	38	31	52	48	45	38	27		86	64	50	65	34	36	40	98	55	45	46	41	27	13
14		94	60	51	73	40	41	41	34	54	49	46	40	28		91	66	52	67	36	38	42	96	58	46	47	44	28	14
15		99	61	54	76	42	43	43	36	55	51	48	43	29		95	68	55	70	38	40	44	94	61	48	48	46	29	15
16			63	56	78	45	45	45	39	57	52	49	45	31			71	57	72	40	42	47	91	63	49	49	48	31	16
17			65	58	81	47	47	47	41	58	54	50	47	32			73	59	74	43	44	49	89	66	50	50	50	32	17
18			66	60	84	49	50	49	43	60	55	51	49	34			75	61	77	45	46	51	87	68	52	51	53	33	18
19			68	63	87	51	52	51	46	61	56	52	51	35			77	63	79	47	48	53	84	71	53	52	55	34	19
20	47		70	65	90	54	54	53	48	63	58	53	53	37	47		80	66	81	49	50	55	82	74	54	53	57	36	20
21			72	67	93	56	56	56	50	64	59	54	55	38			82	68	84	51	52	57	80	76	56	54	59	37	21
22			73	70	95	58	58	58	53	66	61	55	58	39			84	70	86	53	54	60	77	79	57	55	62	38	22
23			75	72	98	60	61	60	55	67	62	56	60	41			86	72	88	55	56	62	75	81	58	56	64	39	23
24			77	74	101	63	63	62	57	68	64	57	62	42			89	74	91	57	57	64	73	84	60	58	66	41	24
25			79	76	104	65	65	64	60	70	65	58	64	44			91	77	93	59	59	66	70	87	61	59	68	42	25
26			80	79	107	67	67	66	62	71	67	59	66	45			93	79	95	61	61	68	68	89	62	60	71	43	26

Males

Raw Score	?	L	F	K	1 (Hs)	2 (D)	3 (Hy)	4 (Pd)	5 (Mf)	6 (Pa)	7 (Pt)	8 (Sc)	9 (Ma)	0 (Si)
27			82	81	109	69	69	69	65	73	68	61	68	46
28			84	83	112	71	71	71	67	74	70	62	70	48
29			86	85	115	74	74	73	69	76	71	63	73	49
30	50		87	88	118	76	76	75	72	77	73	64	75	51
31			89		121	78	78	77	74	79	74	65	77	52
32			91		124	80	80	79	76	80	76	66	79	54
33			92		126	83	82	82	79	82	77	67	81	55
34			94			85	85	84	81	83	79	68	83	56
35			96			87	87	86	84	85	80	69	85	58
36			98			89	89	88	86	86	82	70	88	59
37			99			92	91	90	88	88	83	71	90	61
38	53		101			94	93	92	91	89	85	72	92	62
39			103			96	96	95	93	91	86	74	94	63
40			105			98	98	97	95	92	87	75	96	65
41			106			101	100	99	98		89	76	98	66
42			108			103	102	101	100		90	77	100	68
43			110			105	104	103	103		92	78	103	69
44			112			107	106	105	105		93	79	105	71
45			113			110	109	107	107		95	80	107	72
46			115			112	111	110	110		96	81	109	73
47			117			114	113	112	112		98	82		75
48			118			116	115	114	114		99	83		76
49			120			119	117	116	117			84		78
50	56		122			121	120	118	119			85		79
51			124			123	122		121			86		81
52			125			125	124		124			88		82
53			127			128	126		126			89		83

Females

Raw Score	?	L	F	K	1 (Hs)	2 (D)	3 (Hy)	4 (Pd)	5 (Mf)	6 (Pa)	7 (Pt)	8 (Sc)	9 (Ma)	0 (Si)
27			95	81	98	63	63	71	66	92	64	61	73	44
28			98	83	100	65	65	73	64	94	65	62	75	46
29			100	85	102	67	67	75	61	97	66	63	77	47
30	50		102	88	105	69	69	77	59	99	67	64	80	48
31			104		107	71	71	79	57	102	69	65	82	49
32			107		109	73	73	82	54	105	70	66	84	51
33			109		112	75	75	84	52	107	71	67	86	52
34			111			77	77	86	50	110	73	68	89	53
35			113			79	79	88	47	112	74	69	91	54
36			116			81	81	90	45	115	75	70	93	55
37			118			83	83	92	43	118	77	71	95	57
38	53		120			85	85	95	40	120	78	72	98	58
39			122			87	87	97	38	123	79	73	100	59
40			125			89	89	99	36	125	81	74	102	60
41			127			92	91	101	34		82	75	104	62
42			129			94	93	103	31		83	77	106	63
43			131			96	95	106	29		85	78	109	64
44			134			98	97	108	27		86	79	111	65
45			136			100	99	110	24		87	80	113	67
46			138			102	101	112	22		89	81	115	68
47			140			104	103	114	20		90	82		69
48	56		143			106	105	116	17		91	83		70
49			145			108	107	119	15			84		72
50			147			110	109	121	13			85		73
51			149			112	111		10			86		74
52			152			114	113		8			87		75
53			154			116	115		6			88		77

(Continued)

TABLE A.3
(Continued)

Males

Raw Score	?	L	F	K	1 (Hs)	2 (D)	3 (Hy)	4 (Pd)	5 (Mf)	6 (Pa)	7 (Pt)	8 (Sc)	9 (Ma)	0 (Si)
54			129			130	128		129			90		85
55			131			132	130		131			91		86
56			132			134	133		133			92		88
57			134			137	135		136			93		89
58			136			139	137		138			94		90
59			138			141	139		140			95		92
60	58		139			143	141		143			96		93
61			141									97		95
62			143									98		96
63			144									99		98
64			146									101		99
65												102		100
66												103		102
67												104		103
68												105		105
69												106		106
70	62											107		107
71												108		
72												109		
73												110		
74												111		
75												112		
76												114		
77												115		
78												116		

Females

Raw Score	?	L	F	K	1 (Hs)	2 (D)	3 (Hy)	4 (Pd)	5 (Mf)	6 (Pa)	7 (Pt)	8 (Sc)	9 (Ma)	0 (Si)
54			156			118	117		4			89		78
55			158			120	119		1			90		79
56			161			122	121					91		80
57			163			124	123					92		82
58			165			126	124					93		83
59	58		167			128	126					94		84
60			170			130	128					95		85
61			172									97		86
62			174									98		88
63			176									99		89
64			179									100		90
65												101		91
66												102		93
67												103		94
68												104		95
69												105		96
70	62											106		98
71												107		
72												108		
73												109		
74												110		
75												111		
76												112		
77												113		
78												114		

TABLE A.4

T-Score Conversions for Basic Scales Without K-Corrections for Adolescents Age 17[a]

	Males														Females															
Raw Score	?	L	F	K	1 (Hs)	2 (D)	3 (Hy)	4 (Pd)	5 (Mf)	6 (Pa)	7 (Pt)	8 (Sc)	9 (Ma)	0 (Si)	?	L	F	K	1 (Hs)	2 (D)	3 (Hy)	4 (Pd)	5 (Mf)	6 (Pa)	7 (Pt)	8 (Sc)	9 (Ma)	0 (Si)	Raw Score
0	41	30	32	20	35	16	13	6	5	19	27	31	12	6	41	28	32	18	31	5	7	7	125	21	25	29	15	7	0
1		34	34	23	38	17	15	9	7	22	28	32	14	8		33	35	21	34	7	9	10	122	24	27	31	17	9	1
2		38	36	25	40	19	17	11	9	25	30	33	16	9		37	37	23	36	9	11	12	120	27	28	32	19	10	2
3		43	39	27	43	21	19	13	11	28	32	34	18	11		41	40	26	38	11	13	14	117	30	30	33	22	11	3
4		47	41	29	45	23	21	16	13	31	33	35	20	12		45	42	28	41	13	15	17	115	33	31	35	24	13	4
5		51	43	31	48	24	23	18	16	34	35	36	22	14		49	45	31	43	15	17	19	113	35	33	36	26	14	5
6		55	45	34	50	26	25	20	18	37	36	37	24	15		54	47	33	45	17	19	21	111	38	34	37	28	15	6
7		59	47	36	53	28	27	23	20	40	38	38	26	17		58	49	36	48	20	21	24	108	41	36	38	30	17	7
8		63	50	38	55	30	29	25	22	43	39	39	28	18		62	52	38	50	22	23	26	106	44	37	39	32	18	8
9		68	52	40	58	32	30	27	24	46	41	40	31	20		66	54	41	52	24	25	28	104	47	39	40	34	19	9
10	44	72	54	42	60	34	32	29	26	49	42	41	33	21	44	70	57	44	55	26	27	31	102	50	40	41	37	21	10
11		76	56	45	63	35	34	32	29	52	44	43	35	23		74	59	46	57	28	29	33	100	53	42	43	39	22	11
12		80	58	47	65	37	36	34	31	55	45	44	37	24		79	62	49	59	30	31	35	98	56	43	44	41	23	12
13		84	60	49	68	39	38	36	33	58	47	45	39	26		83	64	51	61	32	33	37	96	59	44	45	43	25	13
14		88	63	51	70	41	40	39	35	61	48	46	41	27		87	67	54	64	35	35	40	94	61	46	46	45	26	14
15		93	65	53	73	43	42	41	37	64	50	47	43	29		91	69	56	66	37	37	42	92	64	47	47	47	27	15
16			67	56	75	44	44	43	40	67	52	48	45	30			72	59	68	39	39	44	89	67	49	48	50	29	16
17			69	58	78	46	46	46	42	70	53	49	48	32			74	61	71	41	41	47	87	70	50	49	52	30	17
18			71	60	80	48	48	48	44	72	55	50	50	33			77	64	73	43	43	49	85	73	52	50	54	31	18
19			73	62	83	50	49	50	46	75	56	51	52	35			79	66	75	45	45	51	83	76	53	52	56	33	19
20	47		76	64	85	52	51	52	48	78	58	52	54	36	47		81	69	77	47	47	54	80	79	55	53	58	34	20
21			78	67	88	54	53	55	50	81	59	53	56	38			84	71	80	50	49	56	78	82	56	54	60	35	21
22			80	69	90	55	55	57	53	84	61	55	58	39			86	74	82	52	51	58	76	84	58	55	63	37	22
23			82	71	93	57	57	59	55	87	62	56	60	41			89	76	84	54	53	61	74	87	59	56	65	38	23
24			84	73	95	59	59	62	57	90	64	57	62	42			91	79	87	56	55	63	71	90	60	57	67	39	24
25			87	75	98	61	61	64	59	93	65	58	65	44			94	81	89	58	57	65	69	93	62	58	69	41	25

(Continued)

343

TABLE A.4
(Continued)

Males

Raw Score	?	L	F	K	1 (Hs)	2 (D)	3 (Hy)	4 (Pd)	5 (Mf)	6 (Pa)	7 (Pt)	8 (Sc)	9 (Ma)	0 (Si)
26			89	78	100	63	63	66	61	96	67	59	67	45
27			91	80	103	64	65	69	63	99	69	60	69	47
28			93	82	105	66	67	71	66	102	70	61	71	49
29			95	84	108	68	68	73	68	105	72	62	73	50
30	50		97	86	110	70	70	75	70	108	73	63	75	52
31			100		113	72	72	78	72	111	75	64	77	53
32			102		115	73	74	80	74	114	76	66	79	55
33			104		118	75	76	82	77	117	78	67	82	56
34			106			77	78	85	79	120	79	68	84	58
35			108			79	80	87	81	123	81	69	86	59
36			110			81	82	89	83	126	82	70	88	61
37			113			83	84	91	85	128	84	71	90	62
38			115			84	86	94	87	131	86	72	92	64
39			117			86	87	96	90	134	87	73	94	65
40	53		119			88	89	98	92	137	89	74	96	67
41			121			90	91	101	94		90	75	99	68
42			124			92	93	103	96		92	77	101	70
43			126			93	95	105	98		93	78	103	71
44			128			95	97	108	100		95	79	105	73
45			130			97	99	110	103		96	80	107	74
46			132			99	101	112	105		98	81	109	76
47			134			101	103	114	107		99	82		77
48			137			102	105	117	109		101	83		79
49			139			104	107	119	111			84		80
50	56		141			106	108	121	114			85		82
51			143			108	110		116			86		83
52			145			110	112		118			88		85

Females

Raw Score	?	L	F	K	1 (Hs)	2 (D)	3 (Hy)	4 (Pd)	5 (Mf)	6 (Pa)	7 (Pt)	8 (Sc)	9 (Ma)	0 (Si)
26			96	84	91	60	59	67	67	96	63	60	71	42
27			99	86	93	62	61	70	65	99	65	61	73	43
28			101	89	96	65	63	72	62	102	66	62	76	45
29			104	91	98	67	65	74	60	105	68	63	78	46
30	50		106	94	100	69	67	77	58	108	69	64	80	47
31			109		103	71	69	79	56	110	71	65	82	49
32			111		105	73	71	81	53	113	72	66	84	50
33			113		107	75	73	84	51	116	74	68	86	51
34			116			78	75	86	49	119	75	69	89	53
35			118			80	77	88	47	122	77	70	91	54
36			121			82	79	91	44	125	78	71	93	55
37			123			84	81	93	42	128	79	72	95	57
38			126			86	83	95	40	131	81	73	97	58
39			128			88	85	98	38	134	82	74	99	59
40	53		131			90	87	100	36	136	84	76	101	61
41			133			93	89	102	33		85	77	104	62
42			136			95	91	104	31		87	78	106	63
43			138			97	93	107	29		88	79	108	65
44			141			99	95	109	27		90	80	110	66
45			143			101	97	111	24		91	81	112	67
46			145			103	99	114	22		93	82	114	69
47			148			105	101	116	20		94	84		70
48			150			108	103	118	18		95	85		71
49			153			110	105	121	15			86		73
50	56		155			112	107	123	13			87		74
51			158			114	109		11			88		75
52			160			116	111		9			89		77

344

Males

Raw Score	?	L	F	K	Hs (1)	D (2)	Hy (3)	Pd (4)	Mf (5)	Pa (6)	Pt (7)	Sc (8)	Ma (9)	Si (0)
53			147			112	114		120			89		86
54			150			113	116		122			90		88
55	58		152			115	118		124			91		89
56			154			117	120		127			92		91
57			156			119	122		129			93		92
58			158			121	124		131			94		94
59			161			122	126		133			95		95
60			163			124	127		135			96		97
61			165									97		98
62			167									99		100
63			169									100		101
64			171									101		103
65												102		104
66												103		106
67												104		107
68												105		109
69												106		110
70	62											107		112
71												108		
72												109		
73												111		
74												112		
75												113		
76												114		
77												115		
78												116		

Females

Raw Score	?	L	F	K	Hs (1)	D (2)	Hy (3)	Pd (4)	Mf (5)	Pa (6)	Pt (7)	Sc (8)	Ma (9)	Si (0)
53			163			113	118		6			90		78
54			165			115	120		4			92		79
55			168			117	123		2			93		81
56			170			119	125					94		82
57			173			121	127					95		83
58			175			123	129					96		85
59			177			125	131					97		86
60	58		180			127	133					98		87
61			182									100		89
62			185									101		90
63			187									102		91
64			190									103		93
65												104		94
66												105		95
67												106		97
68												108		98
69												109		99
70	62											110		101
71												111		
72												112		
73												113		
74												114		
75												116		
76												117		
77												118		
78												119		

[a] Approximately 10% of the 17-year-old sample were 18-year-olds. This sample was reported by Marks, Seeman, and Haller (1974) in their norm tables as "Ages 17 and 18."

B

*Item Composition of MMPI-A Basic Scales,
Harris-Lingoes and Si Subscales,
Supplementary Scales, and Content Scales*

Note. Reprinted from Butcher, James N., Williams, Carolyn L., Graham, John R., Archer, Robert P., Tellegen, Auke, Ben-Porath, Yossef S., and Kaemmer, Beverly. *MMPI-A (Minnesota Multiphasic Personality Inventory–Adolescent): Manual for Administration, Scoring, and Interpretation.* Copyright © 1992 by the Regents of the University of Minnesota. Reproduced by permission. Means and standard deviations for each scale are based on the contemporary adolescent normative sample of 805 boys and 815 girls.

TABLE B.1
Basic Scales

VRIN—Variable Response Inconsistency (50 item-response pairs)
  For each of the following response pairs add one point.

6T - 86F	77F - 107T	188T - 403F
6F - 86T	78F - 90T	188F - 403T
20T - 211F	79T - 119F	212T - 298F
25T - 106F	80T - 101F	215T - 405F
25F - 106T	94F - 469T	215F - 405T
34F - 81T	95F - 132T	253T - 266F
43T - 248F	99T - 323F	286F - 314T
46F - 475F	124F - 379T	292F - 331T
53F - 62T	128F - 465F	304F - 355F
57T - 191F	144T - 247F	309T - 402F
60T - 121T	146T - 167T	318F - 370T
63T - 120T	154T - 178F	332T - 337F
63F - 120F	160F - 227T	355T - 375F
69T - 452F	177T - 283T	463T - 476T
70T - 223T	182T - 258F	477T - 478F
71F - 91T	182F - 258T	477F - 478T
77T - 107F	185F - 383T	

Males: Mean 4.64; S.D. 3.40.   Females: Mean 3.86; S.D. 2.84

TRIN—True Response Inconsistency (24 item-response pairs)

1) For each of the following response pairs *add* one point:

14T - 424T	70T - 223T	242T - 260T
37T - 168T	71T - 283T	264T - 331T
60T - 121T	95T - 294T	304T - 335T
62T - 360T	119T - 184T	355T - 367T
63T - 120T	146T - 167T	463T - 476T

2) For each of the following response pairs *substract* one point:

46F - 475F	71F - 282F	158F - 288F
53F - 91F	82F - 316F	245F - 257F
63F - 120F	128F - 465F	304F - 355F

3) Then add 9 points to the total raw score.

Males: Mean 9.21; S.D. 1.79.   Females: Mean 9.40; S.D. 1.56.

F_1—*Infrequency 1 (33 items)*

True

12	17	22	30	33	39	51	57	63	69	80	92	108
132	136	144	155	173	187	215	219	224	230	236		

False

6	74	86	98	104	120	182	193	198

Males: Mean 4.06; S.D. 3.95.   Females: Mean 3.13; S.D. 3.07.

F_2—*Infrequency 2 (33 items)*

True

242	250	264	273	283	297	303	309	315	321	328	332	337
342	350	358	366	384	392	399	405	415	422	428	433	439
458	463	470										

False

258	289	374	447

Males: Mean 5.09; S.D. 4.98.   Females: Mean 4.57; S.D. 4.61.

F—*Infrequency (66 items)*

True

12	17	22	30	33	39	51	57	63	69	80	92	108
132	136	144	155	173	187	215	219	224	230	236	242	250
264	273	283	297	303	309	315	321	328	332	337	342	350
358	366	384	392	399	405	415	422	428	433	439	458	463
470												

False

6	74	86	98	104	120	182	193	198	258	289	374	447

Males: Mean 9.15; S.D. 8.44.   Females: Mean 7.70; S.D. 7.22.

L—*Lie (14 items)*

True

None.

False

15	26	38	48	73	89	98	103	117	133	147	176	192
243												

Males: Mean 2.94; S.D. 2.34.   Females: Mean 2.26; S.D. 1.92.

K—Defensiveness (30 items)

True
79
False

26	34	55	72	107	111	116	121	124	130	142	150	151
160	164	185	201	227	265	271	289	298	317	318	320	325
327	333	341										

Males: Mean 12.70; S.D. 4.73.   Females: Mean 11.54; S.D. 4.39.

1 Hs—Hypochondriasis (32 items)

True

17	25	36	50	56	93	97	106	143	167	231	

False

2	3	8	10	18	42	44	54	87	113	135	140	146
157	166	168	172	196	210	233	239					

Males: Mean 7.68; S.D. 4.66.   Females: Mean 9.28; S.D. 5.04.

2 D—Depression (57 items)

True

5	14	17	28	35	36	43	53	70	88	113	121	124
139	141	163	167	174	203	218						

False

2	4	9	10	18	26	34	40	42	46	52	65	71
72	91	105	112	128	134	135	138	140	142	158	171	179
180	200	208	209	212	222	229	232	243	289	298		

Males: Mean 18.95; S.D. 5.51.   Females: Mean 20.81; S.D. 5.45.

3 Hy—Hysteria (60 items)

True

11	17	28	36	37	41	62	97	159	165	167	205	216

False

2	3	7	8	9	10	13	23	26	42	44	55	72
77	87	91	94	107	110	111	118	119	123	129	135	142
145	146	150	152	154	157	160	166	168	172	178	183	196
201	210	225	227	233	237	246	248					

Males: Mean 20.94; S.D. 5.66.   Females: Mean 22.85; S.D. 5.12.

---

4 Pd—Psychopathic Deviate (49 items)

True

16	19	20	28	29	32	39	49	51	53	68	78	85
90	95	101	109	184	191	206	211	247	269	286		

False

9	31	67	75	79	91	116	119	123	140	150	151	153
160	164	178	197	202	204	212	227	244	246	249	298	

Males: Mean 19.48; S.D. 5.28.   Females: Mean 20.33; S.D. 5.50.

---

5 Mf-m—Masculinity-Femininity (Masculine) (44 items)

True

59	61	64	76	114	116	122	131	159	169	185	194	197
206	235	240	251	253								

False

1	23	24	60	65	66	72	82	99	100	103	115	126
127	156	183	186	188	190	217	220	221	223	238	241	254

Males: Mean 21.28; S.D. 3.98.

---

5 Mf-f—Masculinity-Femininity (Feminine) (44 items)

True

59	61	64	76	114	116	122	131	169	185	194	206	235
240	253											

False

1	23	24	60	65	66	72	82	99	100	103	115	126
127	156	159	183	186	188	190	197	217	220	221	223	238
241	251	254										

Females: Mean 28.24; S.D. 3.73.

---

6 Pa—Paranoia (40 items)

True

15	16	20	21	22	39	95	109	132	136	137	139	155
219	253	259	266	285	286	287	314	315	332	337	350	

False

77	91	94	96	100	107	228	239	249	263	265	267	277
294	295											

Males: Mean 12.60; S.D. 4.12.   Females: Mean 12.99; S.D. 4.15.

---

7 Pt—Psychasthenia (48 items)

True

11	15	21	28	35	53	62	70	78	85	90	124	141
163	167	185	205	226	255	257	259	266	270	281	282	284
288	290	293	296	297	300	305	306	307	308	309	310	311

False

3	4	9	105	134	158	170	274	301

Males: Mean 17.97; S.D. 7.60.   Females: Mean 20.79; S.D. 8.07.

---

8 Sc—Schizophrenia (77 items)

True

15	16	19	20	21	28	29	32	35	39	41	43	45
62	81	88	132	137	141	159	161	163	173	175	181	205
208	214	218	219	226	231	236	240	251	255	256	259	261
264	268	272	273	276	278	279	283	287	291	296	299	300
302	303	305	309	314	321	332						

False

6	9	31	86	87	102	158	169	172	182	198	239	258
260	262	271	275	322								

Males: Mean 21.98; S.D. 10.23.   Females: Mean 23.26; S.D. 10.62.

---

9 Ma—Hypomania (46 items)

True

14	19	21	47	52	58	81	83	94	109	116	125	137
149	161	162	175	181	189	194	195	199	200	205	207	213
214	222	226	228	232	234	237	252	313				

False

84	89	96	102	103	130	148	151	160	227	246

Males: Mean 21.14; S.D. 5.01.   Females: Mean 21.81; S.D. 4.81.

---

0 Si—Social Introversion (62 items)

True

27	28	53	67	96	100	107	121	129	151	154	160	178
203	227	235	248	257	265	270	276	280	282	288	304	306
308	316	317	326	327	330	334	340					

False

29	46	75	82	102	125	174	180	197	217	221	239	245
262	292	298	301	312	319	323	324	329	331	335	336	338
339	343											

Males: Mean 25.99; S.D. 7.84.   Females: Mean 26.97; S.D. 8.01.

TABLE B.2
Harris-Lingoes Subscales

D_1—*Subjective Depression (29 items)*

True

28	35	36	43	53	70	88	121	124	139	141	163	167
203	218											

False

2	9	40	46	71	91	105	112	134	142	171	179	180
209	243	289	298									

Males: Mean 8.58; S.D. 4.25.   Females: Mean 9.87; S.D. 4.64.

D_2—*Psychomotor Retardation (14 items)*

True

35	43	163	218

False

9	26	34	46	52	72	128	179	180	200

Males: Mean 4.80; S.D. 2.01.   Females: Mean 4.79; S.D. 1.84.

D_3—*Physical Malfunctioning (11 items)*

True

17	113	167	174

False

2	18	42	135	138	140	142

Males: Mean 3.26; S.D. 1.49.   Females: Mean 3.70; S.D. 1.60.

D_4—*Mental Dullness (15 items)*

True

14	28	35	70	88	141	163	218

False

9	10	40	71	105	158	179

Males: Mean 3.62; S.D. 2.48.   Females: Mean 3.90; S.D. 2.61.

D_5—*Brooding (10 items)*

True

35	53	88	121	124	139	163	203

False

71	91

Males: Mean 2.78; S.D. 2.04.   Females: Mean 3.77; S.D. 2.15.

Hy₁—Denial of Social Anxiety (6 items)

True
None.
False
| 123 | 154 | 160 | 178 | 227 | 248 |

Males: Mean 3.13; S.D. 1.77.   Females: Mean 3.31; S.D. 1.77.

Hy₂—Need for Affection (12 items)

True
216
False
| 23 | 55 | 72 | 77 | 94 | 107 | 118 | 145 | 201 | 225 | 246 |

Males: Mean 5.04; S.D. 2.33.   Females: Mean 4.88; S.D. 2.40.

Hy₃—Lassitude–Malaise (15 items)

True
| 28 | 36 | 62 | 167 | 205 |

False
| 2 | 3 | 9 | 10 | 42 | 91 | 119 | 135 | 142 | 146 |

Males: Mean 4.00; S.D. 2.54.   Females: Mean 4.74; S.D. 2.79.

Hy₄—Somatic Complaints (17 items)

True
| 11 | 17 | 37 | 41 | 97 | 165 |

False
| 8 | 44 | 87 | 152 | 157 | 166 | 168 | 172 | 196 | 210 | 233 |

Males: Mean 4.02; S.D. 2.85.   Females: Mean 4.95; S.D. 3.07.

Hy₅—Inhibition of Aggression (7 items)

True
None.
False
| 7 | 13 | 26 | 110 | 111 | 129 | 150 |

Males: Mean 2.86; S.D. 1.33.   Females: Mean 2.92; S.D. 1.30.

Pd_1—*Familial Discord (9 items)*

True
| 19 | 51 | 184 | 191 | 269 |

False
| 79 | 119 | 202 | 204 |

Males: Mean 3.41; S.D. 1.86.   Females: Mean 3.87; S.D. 1.93.

Pd_2—*Authority Problems (8 items)*

True
| 32 | 101 |

False
| 31 | 67 | 123 | 153 | 246 | 249 |

Males: Mean 3.37; S.D. 1.58.   Females: Mean 2.75; S.D. 1.47.

Pd_3—*Social Imperturbability (6 items)*

True
None.

False
| 67 | 123 | 151 | 160 | 178 | 227 |

Males: Mean 3.33; S.D. 1.58.   Females: Mean 3.20; S.D. 1.63.

Pd_4—*Social Alienation (12 items)*

True
| 16 | 20 | 39 | 53 | 78 | 95 | 109 | 206 | 211 | 286 |

False
| 123 | 150 |

Males: Mean 4.83; S.D. 2.18.   Females: Mean 5.36; S.D. 2.25.

Pd_5—*Self-Alienation (12 items)*

True
| 28 | 29 | 49 | 53 | 68 | 78 | 85 | 90 | 109 | 247 |

False
| 9 | 91 |

Males: Mean 4.29; S.D. 2.43.   Females: Mean 4.74; S.D. 2.54.

Pa₁—Persecutory Ideas (17 items)

True

16	20	39	95	109	132	136	137	155	219	285	286	314
315	332	337										

False

294

Males: Mean 4.10; S.D. 2.78.   Females: Mean 4.09; S.D. 2.71.

Pa₂—Poignancy (9 items)

True

20	139	253	259	266	287	350

False

96	228

Males: Mean 3.22; S.D. 1.63.   Females: Mean 3.74; S.D. 1.89.

Pa₃—Naïveté (9 items)

True

15

False

77	94	100	107	263	265	267	295

Males: Mean 3.93; S.D. 1.89.   Females: Mean 3.75; S.D. 1.97.

Sc₁—Social Alienation (21 items)

True

16	19	20	39	43	132	137	181	208	240	259	264	272
300	302	314										

False

86	258	260	262	322

Males: Mean 6.17; S.D. 3.29.   Females: Mean 6.46; S.D. 3.24.

Sc₂—Emotional Alienation (11 items)

True

62	88	219	255	283	303	309	321

False

9	198	271

Males: Mean 2.29; S.D. 1.81.   Females: Mean 2.29; S.D. 1.81.

Sc₃—Lack of Ego Mastery, Cognitive (10 items)

True
28   29   141   163   173   279   291   296   305
False
158
Males: Mean 2.94; S.D. 2.20.   Females: Mean 3.10; S.D. 2.29.

Sc₄—Lack of Ego Mastery, Conative (14 items)

True
28   35   45   62   88   218   219   255   279   283   305
False
9   198   271
Males: Mean 4.10; S.D. 2.57.   Females: Mean 4.35; S.D. 2.71.

Sc₅—Lack of Ego Mastery, Defective Inhibition (11 items)

True
21   81   161   175   205   226   256   273   300   309   332
False
None
Males: Mean 3.47; S.D. 2.07.   Females: Mean 4.20; S.D. 2.16.

Sc₆—Bizarre Sensory Experiences (20 items)

True
21   29   41   161   175   214   231   236   276   278   287   291   299
332
False
87   102   169   172   239   275
Males: Mean 5.01; S.D. 3.33.   Females: Mean 5.46; S.D. 3.45.

Ma₁—Amorality (6 items)

True
125   213   232   234   252
False
246
Males: Mean 2.71; S.D. 1.40.   Females: Mean 2.37; S.D. 1.30.

Ma₂—Psychomotor Acceleration (11 items)

True
14   81   83   116   162   195   205   226   228
False
96   102
Males: Mean 6.52; S.D. 2.13.   Females: Mean 7.13; S.D. 1.97.

Ma₃—Imperturbability (8 items)

True
149   189   207
False
 89   130   151   160   227
Males: Mean 3.16; S.D. 1.59.   Females: Mean 2.94; S.D. 1.52.

Ma₄—Ego Inflation (9 items)

True
47   52   58   94   137   181   199   200   313
False
None
Males: Mean 4.45; S.D. 1.83.   Females: Mean 4.61; S.D. 1.74.

TABLE B.3
Si Subscales

Si₁—Shyness/Self-Consciousness (14 items)

True

| 151 | 154 | 160 | 178 | 227 | 248 | 257 | 270 |

False

| 46 | 245 | 262 | 301 | 312 | 336 |

Males: Mean 6.21; S.D. 3.12.   Females: Mean 6.23; S.D. 3.28.

Si₂—Social Avoidance (8 items)

True

| 304 | 316 |

False

| 82 | 292 | 319 | 331 | 335 | 339 |

Males: Mean 2.52; S.D. 2.03.   Females: Mean 1.90; S.D. 1.85.

Si₃—Alienation—Self and Others (17 items)

True

| 27 | 28 | 53 | 100 | 107 | 129 | 265 | 280 | 282 | 288 | 306 | 308 | 317 |
| 326 | 327 | 334 | 340 |

False

None

Males: Mean 7.58; S.D. 3.43.   Females: Mean 8.22; S.D. 3.68.

TABLE B.4
Supplementary Scales

MAC-R—MacAndrew Alcoholism Scale—Revised (49 items)

True

7	22	46	49	66	78	80	99	101	109	110	122	161
165	177	191	202	210	214	222	241	250	262	269	312	323
342	348	376	380	382	386	392	393	395	407	429	470

False

| 70 | 103 | 113 | 131 | 153 | 159 | 235 | 249 | 268 | 279 | 305 |

Males: Mean 21.07; S.D. 4.44.   Females: Mean 19.73; S.D. 4.14.

ACK—Alcohol/Drug Problems Acknowledgment (13 items)

True

81	144	161	247	269	338	342	429	458	467	474

False

249	431

Males: Mean 3.90; S.D. 2.45.   Females: Mean 3.68; S.D. 2.38.

PRO—Alcohol/Drug Problems Proneness (36 items)

True

32	38	57	82	101	117	191	336	345	376	381	389	435
438	440	452	455	462	476							

False

40	142	143	153	188	272	304	403	410	418	424	436	451
457	459	460	463									

Males: Mean 16.55; S.D. 4.42.   Females: Mean 16.74; S.D. 4.17.

IMM—Immaturity (43 items)

True

16	20	24	45	63	72	94	101	128	218	224	269	307
351	354	358	362	371	389	400	405	418	423	425	426	441
444	452	453	466									

False

64	71	105	120	153	170	322	336	419	431	436	448	476

Males: Mean 13.47; S.D. 6.29.   Females: Mean 11.75; S.D. 6.31.

A—Anxiety (35 items)

True

28	35	53	62	78	121	129	203	218	227	235	255	259
270	281	290	291	305	308	310	317	318	320	326	368	369
370	372	377	379	383	385	394	404					

False

360

Males: Mean 14.59; S.D. 7.17.   Females: Mean 16.90; S.D. 7.67.

R—Repression (33 items)

True

None.

False

1	7	10	13	34	42	66	112	115	122	128	138	161
171	180	186	188	232	239	240	277	289	325	329	331	335
339	341	348	386	388	390	396						

Males: Mean 13.41; S.D. 4.37.   Females: Mean 13.33; S.D. 3.50.

TABLE B.5
Content Scales

A-anx — Adolescent-anxiety (21 items)

True

14	28	36	163	185	255	279	281	285	318	353	377	383
402	404	468										

False

134	196	209	375	424

Males: Mean 7.84; S.D. 4.09.   Females: Mean 9.03; S.D. 4.40.

A-obs—Adolescent-obsessiveness (15 items)

True

52	78	83	129	185	293	307	308	310	368	370	394	412
421	444											

False
None

Males: Mean 6.91; S.D. 3.32.   Females: Mean 7.88; S.D. 3.23.

A-dep—Adolescent-depression (26 items)

True

35	49	53	62	68	88	124	139	177	203	219	230	242
259	283	311	347	371	372	379	399					

False

3	9	71	91	360

Males: Mean 7.59; S.D. 4.57.   Females: Mean 9.17; S.D. 5.08.

A-hea—Adolescent-health concerns (37 items)

True

11	17	25	37	41	50	56	93	97	106	143	167	187
231	422	443	470									

False

18	42	44	54	87	112	113	135	138	152	157	168	172
174	193	210	233	239	275	374						

Males: Mean 7.88; S.D. 5.31.   Females: Mean 9.03; S.D. 5.53.

A-aln—Adolescent-alienation (20 items)

True

16	20	39	211	227	242	317	362	369	413	438	446	463
471	473											

False

74	104	260	448	450

Males: Mean 5.95; S.D. 3.36.   Females: Mean 5.62; S.D. 3.49.

A-biz—Adolescent-bizarre mentation (19 items)

True

22	29	92	132	155	173	250	278	291	296	299	314	315
332	417	428	433	439								

False
387

Males: Mean 4.00; S.D. 3.13.   Females: Mean 4.05; S.D. 3.09.

A-ang—Adolescent-anger (17 items)

True

26	34	111	128	201	282	367	378	382	388	401	416	445
453	458	461										

False
355

Males: Mean 7.94; S.D. 3.23.   Females: Mean 8.51; S.D. 3.09.

A-cyn—Adolescent-cynicism (22 items)

True

47	55	72	77	100	107	118	211	213	225	238	263	265
267	295	325	330	334	371	373	395	406				

False
None

Males: Mean 12.36; S.D. 4.51.   Females: Mean 12.34; S.D. 4.72.

A-con—Adolescent-conduct problems (23 items)

True

32	99	117	224	232	234	252	345	354	356	361	391	442
445	455	456	462	469	477	478						

False

96	249	465

Males: Mean 9.62; S.D. 4.03.   Females: Mean 8.15; S.D. 3.85.

A-Ise—Adolescent-low self-esteem (18 items)

True

67	70	124	280	306	358	379	384	385	400	415	430	432
441	468											

False

58	74	105

Males: Mean 5.00; S.D. 3.21.   Females: Mean 5.83; S.D. 3.46.

A-las—Adolescent-low aspirations (16 items)

True

27	39	218	340	351	430	464		

False

170	188	324	397	403	409	411	436	447

Males: Mean 5.85; S.D. 2.63.   Females: Mean 6.00; S.D. 2.72.

A-sod—Adolescent-social discomfort (24 items)

True

43	151	160	178	248	264	290	304	316	328	408	410	475

False

46	82	245	262	292	319	331	335	336	339	450

Males: Mean 8.33; S.D. 4.36.   Females: Mean 7.19; S.D. 4.31.

A-fam—Adolescent-family problems (35 items)

True

19	57	137	181	184	191	194	215	240	269	277	302	303
344	352	359	363	366	381	396	405	438	440	454		

False

6	79	86	119	182	258	365	398	451	457	460

Males: Mean 11.37; S.D. 5.62.   Females: Mean 12.53; S.D. 5.67.

A-sch—Adolescent-school problems (20 items)

True

12	33	69	80	101	220	257	338	364	380	389	425	435
443	452	464	466									

False

153	166	459

Males: Mean 6.32; S.D. 3.37.   Females: Mean 5.83; S.D. 3.15.

A-trt—Adolescent-negative treatment indicators (26 items)

True

20	27	88	242	256	340	356	357	358	369	371	414	418
420	421	423	426	427	432	434	444	449	472			

False

419	431	437

Males: Mean 9.11; S.D. 4.21.   Females: Mean 9.30; S.D. 4.41.

C

T-Score Conversions for MMPI-A Basic Validity and Clinical Scales, Content and Supplementary Scales, and the Harris-Lingoes and Si Subscales

TABLE C.1
Uniform and Linear T-Score Conversions for Validity and Clinical Scales (Boys)

									Basic Profile Scales										
Raw	*VRIN*	*TRIN*	F_1	F_2	*F*	*L*	*K*	*Hs*	*D*	*Hy*	*Pd*	*Mf*	*Pa*	*Pt*	*Sc*	*Ma*	*Si*	*Raw*
0	36	101F	40	40	39	37	30	31	30	30	30	30	30	30	30	30	30	0
1	39	96F	42	42	40	42	30	35	30	30	30	30	30	30	30	30	30	1
2	42	90F	45	44	42	46	30	38	30	30	30	30	30	30	30	30	30	2
3	45	85F	47	46	43	50	30	41	30	30	30	30	30	32	31	30	30	3
4	48	79F	50	48	44	55	32	43	30	30	30	30	30	33	33	30	30	4
5	51	73F	52	50	45	59	34	45	30	30	30	30	32	35	34	30	30	5
6	54	68F	55	52	46	63	36	47	30	30	30	30	35	36	35	30	30	6
7	57	62F	57	54	47	67	38	49	30	30	30	30	38	37	36	30	30	7
8	60	57F	60	56	49	72	40	50	30	31	30	30	40	38	38	30	30	8
9	63	51F	63	58	50	76	42	52	32	32	31	30	42	39	39	30	30	9
10	66	54T	65	60	51	80	44	54	34	32	33	30	44	41	40	32	30	10
11	69	60T	68	62	52	84	46	55	36	34	35	30	46	42	41	34	31	11
12	72	66T	70	64	53	89	49	58	38	35	37	30	48	43	41	35	32	12
13	75	71T	73	66	55	93	51	60	40	36	39	30	50	44	42	37	33	13
14	78	77T	75	68	56	97	53	63	41	38	41	32	52	45	43	38	35	14
15	81	82T	78	70	57		55	65	43	39	42	34	54	46	44	39	36	15
16	83	88T	80	72	58		57	68	45	41	44	37	57	47	45	41	37	16
17	86	93T	83	74	59		59	71	46	43	45	39	60	48	45	42	38	17
18	89	99T	85	76	60		61	74	48	45	47	42	63	49	46	43	40	18
19	92	105T	88	78	62		63	76	50	46	48	44	66	50	47	45	41	19
20	95	110T	90	80	63		65	79	51	48	50	47	69	51	47	46	42	20
21	98	116T	93	82	64		68	82	53	50	51	49	73	53	48	48	44	21
22	101	120T	95	84	65		70	84	55	52	53	52	76	54	49	50	45	22
23	104	120T	98	86	66		72	87	56	54	55	54	79	55	50	52	46	23
24	107	120T	101	88	68		74	90	58	56	57	57	82	57	50	54	47	24
25	110		103	90	69		76	92	60	58	60	59	85	58	51	56	49	25
26	113		106	92	70		78	95	62	59	62	62	88	60	52	59	50	26
27	116		108	94	71		80	98	65	61	65	64	92	62	53	62	51	27
28	119		111	96	72		82	100	67	63	67	67	95	64	54	65	53	28
29	120		113	98	74		84	103	69	64	70	69	98	65	55	68	54	29
30	120		116	100	75		87	106	71	66	72	72	101	67	56	72	55	30
31	120		118	102	76			108	73	68	75	74	104	69	57	75	56	31
32	120		120	104	77			111	75	69	78	77	107	71	59	78	58	32
33	120		120	106	78				77	71	80	79	111	72	60	81	59	33
34	120				79				79	72	83	82	114	74	61	84	60	34
35	120				81				81	74	85	84	117	76	63	87	62	35
36	120				82				83	76	88	87	120	78	64	90	63	36
37	120				83				85	77	90	89	120	79	66	93	64	37
38	120				84				88	79	93	92	120	81	67	96	65	38
39	120				85				90	81	95	95	120	83	68	100	67	39
40	120				87				92	82	98	97	120	85	70	103	68	40

(Continued)

TABLE C.1
(Continued)

						Basic Profile Scales											
Raw	VRIN	TRIN	F_1	F_2	F	L	K	Hs	D	Hy	Pd	Mf	Pa	Pt	Sc	Ma	Si	Raw
41	120				88				94	84	101	100		86	71	106	69	41
42	120				89				96	86	103	102		88	73	109	70	42
43	120				90				98	87	106	105		90	74	112	72	43
44	120				91				100	89	108	107		92	75	115	73	44
45	120				92				102	90	111			94	77	118	74	45
46	120				94				104	92	113			95	78	120	76	46
47	120				95				106	94	116			97	80		77	47
48	120				96				108	95	118			99	81		78	48
49	120				97				111	97	120				82		79	49
50	120				98				113	99					84		81	50
51					100				115	100					85		82	51
52					101				117	102					87		83	52
53					102				119	104					88		85	53
54					103				120	105					89		86	54
55					104				120	107					91		87	55
56					106				120	108					92		88	56
57					107				120	110					94		90	57
58					108					112					95		91	58
59					109					113					97		92	59
60					110					115					98		94	60
61					111										99		95	61
62					113										101		96	62
63					114										102			63
64					115										104			64
65					116										105			65
66					117										106			66
67															108			67
68															109			68
69															111			69
70															112			70
71															113			71
72															115			72
73															116			73
74															118			74
75															119			75
76															120			76
77															120			77

Uniform and Linear T-Score Conversions for Validity and Clinical Scales (Girls)

						Basic Profile Scales													
Raw	VRIN	TRIN	F_1	F_2	F	L	K	Hs	D	Hy	Pd	Mf	Pa	Pt	Sc	Ma	Si	Raw
0	36	110F	40	40	39	38	30	30	30	30	30	120	30	30	30	30	30	0
1	40	104F	43	42	41	43	30	32	30	30	30	120	30	30	30	30	30	1
2	43	97F	46	44	42	49	30	35	30	30	30	120	30	30	30	30	30	2
3	47	91F	50	47	43	54	31	38	30	30	30	118	30	30	30	30	30	3
4	50	85F	53	49	45	59	33	40	30	30	30	115	30	31	32	30	30	4
5	54	78F	56	51	46	64	35	42	30	30	30	112	32	33	33	30	30	5
6	58	72F	59	53	48	70	37	44	30	30	30	110	34	34	35	30	30	6
7	61	65F	63	55	49	75	40	46	30	30	30	107	37	35	36	30	30	7
8	65	59F	66	57	50	80	42	48	30	30	30	104	39	36	37	30	30	8
9	68	53F	69	60	52	85	44	49	30	30	30	102	41	37	38	30	30	9
10	72	54T	72	62	53	90	46	51	31	30	32	99	43	38	39	31	30	10
11	75	60T	76	64	55	96	49	53	33	30	34	96	45	39	40	33	30	11
12	79	67T	79	66	56	101	51	54	34	32	36	94	47	40	41	34	31	12
13	82	73T	82	68	57	106	53	56	36	33	38	91	49	41	42	36	33	13
14	86	79T	85	70	59	111	56	58	38	35	40	88	52	42	43	37	34	14
15	89	86T	89	73	60		58	61	40	36	41	86	54	43	43	38	35	15
16	93	92T	92	75	61		60	63	41	38	43	83	56	44	44	39	36	16
17	96	99T	95	77	63		62	65	43	39	44	80	59	45	45	41	38	17
18	100	105T	98	79	64		65	68	45	41	46	77	62	46	45	42	39	18
19	103	111T	102	81	66		67	70	46	42	47	75	65	47	46	43	40	19
20	107	118T	105	83	67		69	72	48	44	48	72	68	48	47	45	41	20
21	110	120T	108	86	68		72	75	50	46	50	69	71	49	47	46	43	21
22	114	120T	112	88	70		74	77	52	48	51	67	73	50	48	48	44	22
23	117	120T	115	90	71		76	79	53	49	53	64	76	51	48	50	45	23
24	120	120T	118	92	73		78	82	55	51	55	61	79	52	49	52	46	24
25	120		120	94	74		81	84	57	53	57	59	82	53	50	55	48	25
26	120		120	96	75		83	86	59	55	59	56	85	55	51	58	49	26
27	120		120	99	77		85	89	61	58	62	53	88	56	51	61	50	27
28	120		120	101	78		88	91	63	60	64	51	91	58	52	64	51	28
29	120		120	103	79		90	93	65	62	67	48	93	59	53	68	53	29
30	120		120	105	81		92	96	67	65	69	45	96	61	54	71	54	30
31	120		120	107	82			98	69	67	72	43	99	63	55	75	55	31
32	120		120	109	84			101	71	70	74	40	102	65	56	78	56	32
33	120		120	112	85				73	72	77	37	105	67	58	82	58	33
34	120				86				75	74	79	35	108	68	59	85	59	34
35	120				88				77	77	82	32	111	70	60	89	60	35
36	120				89				79	79	84	30	113	72	62	92	61	36
37	120				91				81	82	86	30	116	74	63	96	63	37
38	120				92				83	84	89	30	119	76	65	99	64	38
39	120				93				85	86	91	30	120	78	66	103	65	39
40	120				95				87	89	94	30	120	79	68	106	66	40

(Continued)

TABLE C.1
(Continued)

	Basic Profile Scales																
Raw	VRIN	TRIN	F_1	F_2	F	L	K	Hs	D	Hy	Pd	Mf	Pa	Pt	Sc	Ma	Si	Raw
41	120				96				89	91	96	30		81	69	109	68	41
42	120				97				91	94	99	30		83	71	113	69	42
43	120				99				93	96	101	30		85	72	116	70	43
44	120				100				95	98	104	30		87	74	120	71	44
45	120				102				97	101	106			88	75	120	73	45
46	120				103				99	103	109			90	77	120	74	46
47	120				104				101	106	111			92	78		75	47
48	120				106				103	108	114			94	80		76	48
49	120				107				105	111	116				81		78	49
50	120				109				107	113					83		79	50
51					110				109	115					84		80	51
52					111				111	118					86		81	52
53					113				113	120					87		82	53
54					114				115	120					89		84	54
55					115				117	120					90		85	55
56					117				119	120					92		86	56
57					118				120	120					93		87	57
58					120					120					95		89	58
59					120					120					96		90	59
60					120					120					98		91	60
61					120										99		92	61
62					120										101		94	62
63					120										102			63
64					120										104			64
65					120										105			65
66					120										107			66
67															108			67
68															110			68
69															111			69
70															113			70
71															114			71
72															116			72
73															117			73
74															119			74
75															120			75
76															120			76
77															120			77

TABLE C.2
Uniform T-Score Conversions for Content Scales (Boys)

Content Scales

Raw	A-anx	A-obs	A-dep	A-hea	A-aln	A-biz	A-ang	A-cyn	A-con	A-lse	A-las	A-sod	A-fam	A-sch	A-trt	Raw
0	32	32	32	31	33	36	30	30	30	34	30	32	30	31	30	0
1	35	35	35	35	36	41	32	30	31	39	34	35	32	36	32	1
2	37	38	38	39	40	45	35	33	34	42	38	37	35	39	35	2
3	39	40	41	42	42	48	38	35	36	45	41	39	37	42	38	3
4	41	42	43	44	45	50	40	36	38	47	43	41	39	44	40	4
5	43	44	45	46	47	53	42	38	40	49	46	43	40	46	42	5
6	45	46	47	48	49	55	44	39	42	52	49	45	42	48	43	6
7	47	48	49	49	52	58	46	40	43	54	52	47	43	50	45	7
8	49	51	51	50	54	62	48	41	45	58	56	49	44	53	46	8
9	52	54	52	52	58	66	51	42	47	62	62	51	46	56	48	9
10	54	58	54	53	62	70	54	43	49	66	69	53	47	60	50	10
11	57	63	57	54	66	74	58	45	52	71	75	55	48	65	52	11
12	59	67	59	55	70	77	64	46	54	75	81	58	50	69	55	12
13	63	72	61	57	74	81	69	48	57	79	88	60	51	74	58	13
14	66	77	64	59	78	85	74	50	61	84	94	63	53	78	61	14
15	69	82	66	62	82	89	79	53	64	88	100	66	54	82	65	15
16	72		69	64	87	93	85	57	68	92	106	69	57	87	69	16
17	75		71	67	91	97	90	60	72	97		72	59	91	73	17
18	79		74	69	95	101		65	75	101		75	62	96	77	18
19	82		77	72	99	105		69	79			78	64	100	81	19
20	85		79	74	103			74	83			81	67	105	85	20
21	88		82	77				78	86			83	70		88	21
22			84	80				82	90			86	72		92	22
23			87	82					94			89	75		96	23
24			89	85								92	78		100	24
25			92	87									81		104	25
26			94	90									83		108	26
27				92									86			27
28				95									89			28
29				97									91			29
30				100									94			30
31				102									97			31
32				105									100			32
33				108									102			33
34				110									105			34
35				113									108			35
36				115												36
37				118												37

TABLE C.2
Uniform T-Score Conversions for Content Scales (Girls)

	Content Scales															
Raw	A-anx	A-obs	A-dep	A-hea	A-aln	A-biz	A-ang	A-cyn	A-con	A-lse	A-las	A-sod	A-fam	A-sch	A-trt	Raw
0	30	30	31	30	33	36	30	30	30	33	31	32	30	31	30	0
1	33	33	34	34	37	41	30	31	32	37	35	36	30	35	33	1
2	36	36	36	37	41	45	33	33	35	40	38	39	33	39	36	2
3	39	38	39	39	43	48	36	35	38	43	40	41	35	42	38	3
4	41	40	41	42	46	50	38	37	40	45	43	43	37	45	40	4
5	43	42	43	44	48	53	40	38	43	47	45	45	39	47	42	5
6	44	43	44	45	50	55	42	40	45	50	48	47	40	50	43	6
7	45	45	46	47	53	58	44	41	47	52	52	49	42	53	45	7
8	47	48	48	49	55	62	46	42	49	55	56	51	43	56	46	8
9	48	51	49	50	59	65	49	43	51	58	61	53	44	59	48	9
10	50	54	51	52	62	69	52	44	53	62	66	55	45	63	50	10
11	52	59	52	53	66	73	57	45	56	65	72	58	46	67	52	11
12	54	64	54	55	69	76	62	46	59	69	77	60	48	71	54	12
13	57	70	56	56	73	80	67	48	63	73	82	63	49	75	57	13
14	61	75	58	58	77	84	72	50	66	77	87	66	50	79	60	14
15	65	81	61	60	80	87	77	53	70	81	93	69	52	83	64	15
16	69		63	62	84	91	83	56	74	84	98	72	54	87	67	16
17	73		66	64	87	95	88	60	77	88		75	56	90	71	17
18	77		68	66	91	98		64	81	92		78	58	94	75	18
19	81		71	68	94	102		68	85			81	61	98	78	19
20	85		73	70	98			72	88			84	64	102	82	20
21	89		76	72				77	92			86	67		85	21
22			78	74				81	96			89	70		89	22
23			81	76					99			92	73		93	23
24			83	78								95	75		96	24
25			86	80									78		100	25
26			88	82									81		104	26
27				84									84			27
28				86									87			28
29				88									90			29
30				90									92			30
31				92									95			31
32				95									98			32
33				97									101			33
34				99									104			34
35				101									107			35
36				103												36
37				105												37

TABLE C.3
Linear T-Score Conversions for Supplementary Scales (Boys and Girls)

	Supplementary Scales												
	Boys							Girls					
Raw	MAC-R	ACK	PRO	IMM	A	R	Raw	MAC-R	ACK	PRO	IMM	A	R	Raw
0	30	34	30	30	30	30	0	30	35	30	31	30	30	0
1	30	38	30	30	31	30	1	30	39	30	33	30	30	1
2	30	42	30	32	32	30	2	30	43	30	35	31	30	2
3	30	46	30	33	34	30	3	30	47	30	36	32	30	3
4	30	50	30	35	35	30	4	30	51	30	38	33	30	4
5	30	54	30	37	37	31	5	30	56	30	39	34	30	5
6	30	59	30	38	38	33	6	30	60	30	41	36	30	6
7	30	63	30	40	39	35	7	30	64	30	42	37	32	7
8	30	67	31	41	41	38	8	30	68	30	44	38	35	8
9	30	71	33	43	42	40	9	30	72	31	46	40	38	9
10	30	75	35	44	44	42	10	30	77	34	47	41	40	10
11	30	79	37	46	45	44	11	30	81	36	49	42	43	11
12	30	83	40	48	46	47	12	31	85	39	50	44	46	12
13	32	87	42	49	48	49	13	34	89	41	52	45	49	13
14	34		44	51	49	51	14	36		43	54	46	52	14
15	36		46	52	51	54	15	39		46	55	48	55	15
16	39		49	54	52	56	16	41		48	57	49	58	16
17	41		51	56	53	58	17	43		51	58	50	60	17
18	43		53	57	55	60	18	46		53	60	51	63	18
19	45		56	59	56	63	19	48		55	61	53	66	19
20	48		58	60	58	65	20	51		58	63	54	69	20
21	50		60	62	59	67	21	53		60	65	55	72	21
22	52		62	64	60	70	22	55		63	66	57	75	22
23	54		65	65	62	72	23	58		65	68	58	78	23
24	57		67	67	63	74	24	60		67	69	59	80	24
25	59		69	68	65	76	25	63		70	71	61	83	25
26	61		71	70	66	79	26	65		72	73	62	86	26
27	63		74	72	67	81	27	68		75	74	63	89	27
28	66		76	73	69	83	28	70		77	76	64	92	28
29	68		78	75	70	86	29	72		79	77	66	95	29
30	70		80	76	71	88	30	75		82	79	67	98	30
31	72		83	78	73	90	31	77		84	81	68	100	31
32	75		85	79	74	92	32	80		87	82	70	103	32
33	77		87	81	76	95	33	82		89	84	71	106	33
34	79		89	83	77		34	84		91	85	72		34
35	81		92	84	78		35	87		94	87	74		35
36	84		94	86			36	89		96	88			36
37	86			87			37	92			90			37
38	88			89			38	94			92			38
39	90			91			39	97			93			39
40	93			92			40	99			95			40
41	95			94			41	101			96			41
42	97			95			42	104			98			42
43	99			97			43	106			100			43
44	102						44	109						44
45	104						45	111						45
46	106						46	113						46
47	108						47	116						47
48	111						48	118						48
49	113						49	120						49

TABLE C.4
Linear T-Score Conversions for Harris-Lingoes and SI Subscales (Boys)

Raw	D_1	D_2	D_3	D_4	D_5	Hy_1	Hy_2	Hy_3	Hy_4	Hy_5	Pd_1	Pd_2	Pd_3	Pd_4	Pd_5	Raw
0	30	30	30	35	36	32	30	34	36	30	32	30	30	30	32	0
1	32	31	35	39	41	38	33	38	39	36	37	35	35	32	36	1
2	35	36	42	43	46	44	37	42	43	44	42	41	42	37	41	2
3	37	41	48	47	51	49	41	46	46	51	48	48	48	42	45	3
4	39	46	55	52	56	55	46	50	50	59	53	54	54	46	49	4
5	42	51	62	56	61	61	50	54	53	66	59	60	61	51	53	5
6	44	56	68	60	66	66	54	58	57	74	64	67	67	55	57	6
7	46	61	75	64	71		58	62	60	81	69	73		60	61	7
8	49	66	82	68	76		63	66	64		75	79		65	65	8
9	51	71	89	72	81		67	70	67		80			69	69	9
10	53	76	95	76	85		71	74	71					74	73	10
11	56	81	102	80			76	77	74					78	78	11
12	58	86		84			80	81	78					83	82	12
13	60	91		88				85	82							13
14	63	96		92				89	85							14
15	65			96				93	89							15
16	67								92							16
17	70								96							17
18	72															18
19	75															19
20	77															20
21	79															21
22	82															22
23	84															23
24	86															24
25	89															25
26	91															26
27	93															27
28	96															28
29	98															29
30	100															30
31	103															31
32	105															32

	Subscales (Pa, Sc, Ma, & Si)																
Raw	Pa_1	Pa_2	Pa_3	Sc_1	Sc_2	Sc_3	Sc_4	Sc_5	Sc_6	Ma_1	Ma_2	Ma_3	Ma_4	Si_1	Si_2	Si_3	Raw
0	35	30	30	31	37	37	34	33	35	31	30	30	30	30	38	30	0
1	39	36	34	34	43	41	38	38	38	38	30	36	31	33	43	31	1
2	42	42	40	37	48	46	42	43	41	45	30	43	37	36	47	34	2
3	46	49	45	40	54	50	46	48	44	52	33	49	42	40	52	37	3
4	50	55	50	43	59	55	50	53	47	59	38	55	48	43	57	40	4
5	53	61	56	46	65	59	53	57	50	66	43	62	53	46	62	42	5
6	57	67	61	49	71	64	57	62	53	73	48	68	58	49	67	45	6
7	60	73	66	53	76	68	61	67	56		52	74	64	53	72	48	7
8	64	79	72	56	82	73	65	72	59		57	81	69	56	77	51	8
9	68	85	77	59	87	77	69	77	62		62		75	59		54	9
10	71			62	93	82	73	82	65		66			62		57	10
11	75			65	98		77	86	68		71			65		60	11
12	78			68			81		71					69		63	12
13	82			71			85		74					72		66	13
14	86			74			88		77					75		69	14
15	89			77					80							72	15
16	93			80					83							75	16
17	96			83					86							77	17
18				86					89								18
19				89					92								19
20				92					95								20
21				95													21

TABLE C.4
Linear T-Score Conversions for Harris-Lingoes and Si Subscales (Girls)

	Subscales (D, Hy, & Pd)														
Raw	D_1	D_2	D_3	D_4	D_5	Hy_1	Hy_2	Hy_3	Hy_4	Hy_5	Pd_1	Pd_2	Pd_3	Pd_4	Pd_5	Raw
0	30	30	30	35	33	31	30	33	34	30	30	31	30	30	31	0
1	31	30	33	39	37	37	34	37	37	35	35	38	36	31	35	1
2	33	35	39	43	42	43	38	40	40	43	40	45	43	35	39	2
3	35	40	46	47	46	48	42	44	44	51	45	52	49	39	43	3
4	37	46	52	50	51	54	46	47	47	58	51	59	55	44	47	4
5	40	51	58	54	56	60	50	51	50	66	56	65	61	48	51	5
6	42	57	64	58	60	65	55	55	53	74	61	72	67	53	55	6
7	44	62	71	62	65		59	58	57	81	66	79		57	59	7
8	46	67	77	66	70		63	62	60		71	86		62	63	8
9	48	73	83	70	74		67	65	63		77			66	67	9
10	50	78	89	73	79		71	69	66					71	71	10
11	52	84	96	77			75	72	70					75	75	11
12	55	89		81			80	76	73					80	79	12
13	57	95		85				80	76							13
14	59	100		89				83	79							14
15	61			92				87	83							15
16	63								86							16
17	65								89							17
18	68															18
19	70															19
20	72															20
21	74															21
22	76															22
23	78															23
24	80															24
25	83															25
26	85															26
27	87															27
28	89															28
29	91															29
30	93															30
31	96															31
32	98															32

							Subscales (Pa, Sc, Ma, & Si)										
Raw	Pa_1	Pa_2	Pa_3	Sc_1	Sc_2	Sc_3	Sc_4	Sc_5	Sc_6	Ma_1	Ma_2	Ma_3	Ma_4	Si_1	Si_2	Si_3	Raw
0	35	30	31	30	37	36	34	31	34	32	30	31	30	31	40	30	0
1	39	36	36	33	43	41	38	35	37	39	30	37	30	34	45	30	1
2	42	41	41	36	48	45	41	40	40	47	30	44	35	37	51	33	2
3	46	46	46	39	54	50	45	44	43	55	30	50	41	40	56	36	3
4	50	51	51	42	59	54	49	49	46	63	34	57	47	43	61	39	4
5	53	57	56	46	65	58	52	54	49	70	39	64	52	46	67	41	5
6	57	62	61	49	70	63	56	58	52	78	44	70	58	49	72	44	6
7	61	67	66	52	76	67	60	63	54		49	77	64	52	78	47	7
8	64	73	72	55	81	71	63	68	57		54	83	70	55	83	49	8
9	68	78	77	58	87	76	67	72	60		59		75	58		52	9
10	72			61	93	80	71	77	63		65			62		55	10
11	76			64	98		75	82	66		70			65		58	11
12	79			67			78		69					68		60	12
13	83			70			82		72					71		63	13
14	87			73			86		75					74		66	14
15	90			76					78							68	15
16	94			79					81							71	16
17	98			83					83							74	17
18				86					86								18
19				89					89								19
20				92					92								20
21				95													21

*T-Score Conversions for Basic MMPI-A
Scales Permitting Estimates of the Marks
and Briggs Adolescent T-Score Values
Provided in Dahlstrom, Welsh, and
Dahlstrom (1972)*

Note. Adapted from Butcher, James N., Williams, Carolyn L., Graham, John R., Archer, Robert P., Tellegen, Auke, Ben-Porath, Yossef S., and Kaemmer, Beverly. *MMPI-A (Minnesota Multiphasic Personality Inventory–Adolescent): Manual for Administration, Scoring, and Interpretation*. Copyright © 1992 by the Regents of the University of Minnesota.

TABLE D.1

T-Score Values for MMPI-A Basic Scales for Adolescent Males Ages 14 and Below Based on Marks and Briggs Norms (Dahlstrom, Welsh, and Dahlstrom, 1972)

Raw	L	F	K	Hs	D	Hy	Pd	Mf	Pa	Pt	Sc	Ma	Si	Raw
0	32	42	30	34	30	30	30	30	30	30	32	30	30	0
1	39	44	30	37	30	30	30	30	30	32	33	30	30	1
2	46	46	30	40	30	30	30	30	30	33	35	30	30	2
3	51	47	30	43	30	30	30	30	30	34	36	30	30	3
4	56	48	31	46	30	30	30	30	33	36	37	30	30	4
5	61	50	33	49	30	30	30	30	35	37	38	30	30	5
6	66	52	35	52	30	30	30	30	38	38	39	30	30	6
7	71	53	37	55	30	30	30	30	41	40	40	30	30	7
8	76	54	39	58	30	30	30	30	44	41	41	31	30	8
9	80	56	41	61	32	31	30	30	46	43	42	33	30	9
10	85	58	43	64	35	33	32	30	49	44	43	35	30	10
11	90	59	45	67	37	36	35	31	52	45	44	37	30	11
12	95	60	48	70	39	38	37	35	55	47	45	39	31	12
13	100	62	50	73	41	40	39	38	57	48	46	41	33	13
14	105	64	52	76	43	42	42	41	60	49	47	43	34	14
15		65	54	79	46	44	44	43	63	51	48	45	35	15
16		66	56	82	48	47	46	47	65	52	50	47	37	16
17		68	58	84	50	49	49	50	68	54	51	49	38	17
18		69	60	87	54	51	51	53	71	55	52	50	40	18
19		70	62	90	57	53	53	55	74	56	53	52	41	19
20		71	64	95	59	56	56	59	76	58	54	54	42	20
21		73	66	99	61	58	58	62	79	59	55	56	44	21
22		75	68	102	63	60	60	65	82	60	56	58	46	22
23		77	70	105	66	62	62	67	84	62	57	60	47	23
24		78	72	108	68	64	65	71	87	63	58	62	49	24
25		79	74	111	70	67	67	74	90	65	59	64	50	25
26		81	76	114	72	69	69	76	93	66	60	66	51	26
27		83	79	117	75	71	72	79	95	67	61	68	53	27
28		84	81	120	77	73	74	83	98	69	62	70	54	28
29		85	83	120	79	75	76	86	101	70	63	72	56	29
30		87	85	120	81	78	79	88	104	71	65	74	57	30
31		89		120	83	80	81	91	106	73	66	76	58	31
32		90		120	86	82	83	95	109	74	67	78	60	32
33		91			88	84	86	98	112	75	68	80	61	33
34		93			90	87	88	100	114	77	69	82	62	34
35		95			92	89	90	102	117	78	70	84	64	35
36		96			95	91	93	106	120	80	71	86	65	36
37		97			97	93	95	109	120	81	72	88	66	37
38		99			99	95	97	112	120	82	73	90	68	38
39		101			101	98	100	114	120	84	74	92	69	39
40		102			103	100	102	117	120	85	75	94	70	40
41		103			106	102	104	120		86	76	96	72	41
42		105			108	104	106	120		88	77	98	73	42
43		107			110	107	109	120		89	78	100	75	43
44		108			112	109	111	120		91	80	101	76	44
45		109			115	111	113			92	81	103	77	45
46		111			117	113	116			93	82	105	79	46
47		113			119	115	118			95	83		80	47
48		114			120	118	120			96	84		81	48
49		115			120	120	120				85		83	49
50		117			120	120					86		84	50
51		119			120	120					87		85	51
52		120			120	120					88		87	52

(Continued)

TABLE D.1
(Continued)

Raw	L	F	K	Hs	D	Hy	Pd	Mf	Pa	Pt	Sc	Ma	Si	Raw
53		120			120	120					89		89	53
54		120			120	120					90		91	54
55		120			120	120					91		92	55
56		120			120	120					92		93	56
57		120			120	120					93		95	57
58		120				120					95		96	58
59		120				120					96		98	59
60		120				120					97		99	60
61		120									98		100	61
62		120									99		102	62
63		120									100			63
64		120									101			64
65		120									102			65
66		120									103			66
67											104			67
68											105			68
69											106			69
70											107			70
71											108			71
72											110			72
73											111			73
74											112			74
75											113			75
76											114			76
77											115			77

T-Score Values for MMPI-A Basic Scales for Adolescent Females Ages 14 and Below Based on Marks and Briggs Norms (Dahlstrom, Welsh, and Dahlstrom, 1972)

Raw	L	F	K	Hs	D	Hy	Pd	Mf	Pa	Pt	Sc	Ma	Si	Raw
0	31	44	30	36	30	30	30	120	30	30	32	30	30	0
1	39	46	30	39	30	30	30	120	30	30	34	30	30	1
2	46	47	30	41	30	30	30	120	32	32	35	30	30	2
3	50	49	30	44	30	30	30	118	34	33	36	30	30	3
4	55	51	30	46	30	30	30	115	36	34	37	30	30	4
5	59	54	31	49	30	30	30	112	38	36	38	30	30	5
6	64	56	33	51	30	30	30	109	40	37	40	30	30	6
7	69	57	35	54	30	30	30	107	43	39	41	30	30	7
8	73	59	38	56	30	30	31	104	45	40	42	32	30	8
9	78	61	40	59	32	30	34	101	47	42	43	35	30	9
10	83	64	42	61	34	30	36	99	49	43	45	37	30	10
11	87	65	44	64	36	31	38	97	51	44	46	39	30	11
12	92	66	47	66	38	33	40	95	54	46	47	41	32	12
13	97	69	49	69	41	35	42	91	56	47	48	43	33	13
14	101	71	51	71	43	38	44	88	58	49	49	45	34	14
15		72	53	74	45	40	46	86	60	50	51	47	35	15
16		74	56	76	47	42	49	84	62	52	52	49	37	16
17		76	58	79	49	44	51	80	65	53	53	51	39	17
18		79	60	81	52	46	53	77	67	54	54	54	40	18
19		81	62	84	55	49	55	75	69	56	56	56	42	19
20		82	65	86	57	51	57	73	71	57	57	58	43	20

(Continued)

TABLE D.1
(Continued)

Raw	L	F	K	Hs	D	Hy	Pd	Mf	Pa	Pt	Sc	Ma	Si	Raw
21		84	67	89	59	53	59	69	73	59	58	60	44	21
22		86	69	91	62	55	61	66	75	60	59	62	45	22
23		89	71	94	64	58	64	64	78	62	60	64	47	23
24		90	73	96	66	60	66	62	80	63	62	66	48	24
25		91	76	99	68	62	68	58	82	64	63	68	49	25
26		94	78	101	70	64	70	55	84	66	64	70	51	26
27		96	80	104	72	66	72	53	86	67	65	72	52	27
28		99	82	106	74	69	74	51	89	69	67	75	53	28
29		100	85	109	76	71	76	47	91	70	68	77	54	29
30		101	87	111	78	73	79	44	93	72	69	79	56	30
31		104		113	80	75	81	42	95	73	70	81	57	31
32		106		116	83	78	83	40	97	74	71	83	58	32
33		107			85	80	85	36	99	76	73	85	59	33
34		109			87	82	87	33	102	77	74	87	61	34
35		111			89	84	89	31	104	79	75	89	62	35
36		114			91	86	92	30	106	80	76	91	63	36
37		116			93	89	94	30	108	82	77	94	65	37
38		117			95	91	96	30	110	83	79	96	67	38
39		119			97	93	98	30	113	84	80	98	68	39
40		120			99	95	100	30	115	86	81	100	69	40
41		120			102	98	102	30		87	82	102	71	41
42		120			104	100	104	30		89	84	104	72	42
43		120			106	102	107	30		90	85	106	73	43
44		120			108	104	109	30		92	86	108	75	44
45		120			110	106	111			93	87	110	76	45
46		120			112	109	113			94	88	113	77	46
47		120			114	111	115			96	90		78	47
48		120			116	113	117			97	91		80	48
49		120			118	115	119				92		81	49
50		120			120	118					93		82	50
51		120			120	120					95		83	51
52		120			120	120					96		85	52
53		120			120	120					97		86	53
54		120			120	120					98		87	54
55		120			120	120					99		88	55
56		120			120	120					101		90	56
57		120			120	120					102		92	57
58		120				120					103		94	58
59		120				120					104		95	59
60		120				120					106		96	60
61		120									108		97	61
62		120									109		99	62
63		120									110			63
64		120									112			64
65		120									113			65
66		120									114			66
67											115			67
68											117			68
69											118			69
70											119			70
71											120			71
72											120			72
73											120			73
74											120			74
75											120			75
76											120			76
77											120			77

TABLE D.2

T-Score Values for MMPI-A Basic Scales for Adolescent Males Age 15 Based on Marks and Briggs Norms
(Dahlstrom, Welsh, and Dahlstrom, 1972)

Raw	L	F	K	Hs	D	Hy	Pd	Mf	Pa	Pt	Sc	Ma	Si	Raw
0	32	41	30	36	30	30	30	30	30	30	33	30	30	0
1	39	43	30	39	30	30	30	30	30	31	34	30	30	1
2	46	44	30	41	30	30	30	30	31	32	35	30	30	2
3	50	45	30	44	30	30	30	30	33	34	36	30	30	3
4	55	46	30	46	30	30	30	30	35	35	37	30	30	4
5	59	48	32	48	30	30	30	30	37	37	38	30	30	5
6	63	50	34	51	30	30	30	30	40	38	39	30	30	6
7	67	51	37	53	30	30	30	30	42	39	40	30	30	7
8	72	52	39	55	30	30	30	30	44	41	41	30	30	8
9	76	53	41	58	30	32	30	30	46	42	42	32	30	9
10	80	55	43	60	31	34	32	31	48	44	43	34	30	10
11	85	56	45	62	33	36	34	33	50	45	44	36	30	11
12	89	57	47	65	36	38	37	36	52	46	45	38	31	12
13	93	58	49	67	38	40	39	39	54	48	46	40	32	13
14	98	60	51	69	40	42	41	41	56	49	47	42	34	14
15		61	53	72	43	44	43	43	58	51	48	43	35	15
16		62	55	74	45	46	45	46	60	52	49	45	36	16
17		63	58	76	47	48	47	49	63	54	50	47	38	17
18		65	60	79	49	50	49	51	65	55	51	49	39	18
19		66	62	81	53	52	52	53	67	56	52	51	40	19
20		67	64	85	56	54	54	57	69	58	53	53	42	20
21		68	66	88	58	57	56	60	71	59	54	55	44	21
22		70	68	91	61	59	58	62	73	61	55	57	46	22
23		71	70	93	63	61	60	64	75	62	56	59	47	23
24		72	72	95	65	63	62	67	77	64	57	61	48	24
25		73	74	98	67	65	64	70	79	65	58	63	50	25
26		75	76	100	70	67	66	72	81	66	59	65	51	26
27		76	78	102	72	69	69	74	83	68	60	66	52	27
28		77	81	105	74	71	71	78	86	69	61	68	54	28
29		78	83	107	77	73	73	81	88	71	62	70	55	29
30		80	85	109	79	75	75	83	90	72	63	72	56	30
31		81		112	81	77	77	85	92	73	64	74	58	31
32		82		114	83	79	79	88	94	75	65	76	59	32
33		83			86	81	81	91	96	76	66	78	60	33
34		85			88	83	84	93	98	78	67	80	62	34
35		86			90	85	86	95	100	79	68	82	63	35
36		87			92	87	88	98	102	81	69	84	64	36
37		88			95	89	90	101	104	82	70	86	66	37
38		90			97	91	92	104	106	83	71	87	67	38
39		91			99	94	94	106	109	85	72	89	69	39
40		92			101	96	96	109	111	86	73	91	70	40
41		93			104	98	99	112		88	74	93	71	41
42		95			106	100	101	114		89	75	95	73	42
43		96			108	102	103	116		90	76	97	74	43
44		97			111	104	105	119		92	77	99	75	44
45		98			113	106	107			93	78	101	77	45
46		100			115	108	109			95	79	103	78	46
47		101			117	110	111			96	80		79	47
48		102			120	112	114			98	81		81	48
49		103			120	114	116				82		82	49
50		105			120	116					83		83	50

(Continued)

TABLE D.2
(Continued)

Raw	L	F	K	Hs	D	Hy	Pd	Mf	Pa	Pt	Sc	Ma	Si	Raw
51		106			120	118					84		85	51
52		107			120	120					85		87	52
53		108			120	120					86		89	53
54		110			120	120					87		90	54
55		112			120	120					88		91	55
56		113			120	120					89		93	56
57		114			120	120					90		94	57
58		115				120					91		95	58
59		117				120					92		97	59
60		118				120					93		98	60
61		119									94		99	61
62		120									95		101	62
63		120									96			63
64		120									97			64
65		120									98			65
66		120									99			66
67											100			67
68											101			68
69											102			69
70											103			70
71											104			71
72											105			72
73											106			73
74											107			74
75											108			75
76											109			76
77											110			77

T-Score Values for MMPI-A Basic Scales for Adolescent Females Age 15 Based on Marks and Briggs Norms (Dahlstrom, Welsh, and Dahlstrom, 1972)

Raw	L	F	K	Hs	D	Hy	Pd	Mf	Pa	Pt	Sc	Ma	Si	Raw
0	31	43	30	37	30	30	30	120	30	30	32	30	30	0
1	38	45	30	39	30	30	30	116	30	31	34	30	30	1
2	45	46	30	41	30	30	30	113	31	32	35	30	30	2
3	49	47	30	43	30	30	30	111	33	33	36	30	30	3
4	53	50	30	46	30	30	30	109	36	35	37	30	30	4
5	58	52	32	48	30	30	30	106	38	36	39	30	30	5
6	62	54	34	50	30	30	30	103	40	37	40	30	30	6
7	66	55	36	52	30	30	30	101	42	39	41	31	30	7
8	70	57	38	55	30	30	30	100	44	40	42	33	30	8
9	75	59	40	57	30	30	32	97	47	41	43	35	30	9
10	79	61	42	59	32	30	34	94	49	43	44	37	30	10
11	83	62	45	61	34	31	36	92	51	44	45	39	30	11
12	88	63	47	64	37	33	38	90	53	45	46	41	31	12
13	92	66	49	66	39	35	40	87	55	47	47	42	32	13
14	96	68	51	68	41	37	42	84	58	48	48	44	33	14
15		69	53	70	43	39	44	82	60	49	49	46	35	15
16		70	56	72	45	42	46	79	62	51	50	48	36	16
17		73	58	75	47	44	48	76	64	52	51	50	38	17
18		75	60	77	52	46	51	73	66	53	53	52	40	18
19		77	62	79	54	48	53	71	68	55	54	54	41	19
20		78	64	81	56	50	55	69	71	56	55	56	42	20

(Continued)

TABLE D.2
(Continued)

Raw	L	F	K	Hs	D	Hy	Pd	Mf	Pa	Pt	Sc	Ma	Si	Raw
21		79	67	84	58	52	57	66	73	58	56	57	44	21
22		82	69	86	60	54	59	63	75	59	57	59	45	22
23		84	71	88	62	56	61	61	77	60	58	61	46	23
24		85	73	90	65	58	63	59	79	62	59	63	48	24
25		86	75	93	67	60	65	56	82	63	60	65	49	25
26		89	77	95	69	62	67	53	84	64	61	67	50	26
27		91	80	97	71	64	69	51	86	66	62	69	52	27
28		93	82	99	73	66	71	49	88	67	63	70	53	28
29		94	84	102	75	68	74	45	90	68	64	72	54	29
30		95	86	104	78	70	76	42	93	70	65	74	55	30
31		98		106	80	72	78	40	95	71	66	76	57	31
32		100		108	82	74	80	38	97	72	68	78	58	32
33		101			84	76	82	35	99	74	69	80	59	33
34		102			86	79	84	32	101	75	70	82	61	34
35		104			88	81	86	30	103	76	71	83	62	35
36		107			90	83	88	30	106	78	72	85	64	36
37		109			93	85	90	30	108	79	73	87	66	37
38		110			95	87	92	30	110	80	74	89	67	38
39		111			97	89	95	30	112	82	75	91	68	39
40		114			99	91	97	30	114	83	76	93	70	40
41		116			101	93	99	30		85	77	95	71	41
42		117			103	95	101	30		86	78	96	72	42
43		118			106	97	103	30		87	79	98	73	43
44		120			108	99	105	30		89	80	100	75	44
45		120			110	101	107			90	82	102	76	45
46		120			112	103	109			91	83	104	77	46
47		120			114	105	111			93	84		79	47
48		120			116	107	113			94	85		80	48
49		120			119	109	116				86		81	49
50		120			120	111					87		82	50
51		120			120	113					88		84	51
52		120			120	115					89		85	52
53		120			120	118					90		86	53
54		120			120	120					91		88	54
55		120			120	120					92		89	55
56		120			120	120					93		91	56
57		120			120	120					94		93	57
58		120				120					95		94	58
59		120				120					97		95	59
60		120				120					98		97	60
61		120									100		98	61
62		120									101		99	62
63		120									102			63
64		120									103			64
65		120									104			65
66		120									105			66
67											106			67
68											107			68
69											108			69
70											109			70
71											110			71
72											112			72
73											113			73
74											114			74
75											115			75
76											116			76
77											117			77

TABLE D.3
T-Score Values for MMPI-A Basic Scales for Adolescent Males Age 16 Based on Marks and Briggs Norms
(Dahlstrom, Welsh, and Dahlstrom, 1972)

Raw	L	F	K	Hs	D	Hy	Pd	Mf	Pa	Pt	Sc	Ma	Si	Raw
0	31	40	30	33	30	30	30	30	34	30	30	30	30	0
1	38	42	30	36	30	30	30	30	35	30	32	30	30	1
2	44	44	30	39	30	30	30	30	36	31	33	30	30	2
3	49	45	30	42	30	30	30	30	37	33	35	30	30	3
4	53	46	30	45	30	30	30	30	39	34	36	30	30	4
5	58	47	31	47	30	30	30	30	40	36	37	30	30	5
6	62	49	33	50	30	30	30	30	42	37	38	30	30	6
7	67	50	36	53	30	30	30	30	43	39	39	30	30	7
8	71	51	38	56	30	30	30	30	45	40	40	30	30	8
9	76	53	40	59	31	30	30	30	46	42	41	30	30	9
10	80	54	42	62	33	32	32	30	48	43	42	32	30	10
11	85	55	45	64	36	34	34	31	49	45	43	34	30	11
12	89	56	47	67	38	37	36	35	51	46	44	36	30	12
13	94	58	49	70	40	39	38	39	52	48	45	38	31	13
14	99	59	51	73	42	41	41	41	54	49	46	40	32	14
15		60	54	76	45	43	43	43	55	51	48	43	34	15
16		61	56	78	47	45	45	47	57	52	49	45	35	16
17		63	58	81	49	47	47	50	58	54	50	47	37	17
18		64	60	84	53	50	49	53	60	55	51	49	38	18
19		65	63	87	56	52	51	55	61	56	52	51	39	19
20		66	65	91	58	54	53	59	63	58	53	53	41	20
21		68	67	95	60	56	56	62	64	59	54	55	43	21
22		70	70	98	63	58	58	65	66	61	55	58	45	22
23		71	72	101	65	61	60	67	67	62	56	60	46	23
24		72	74	104	67	63	62	71	68	64	57	62	48	24
25		73	76	107	69	65	64	74	70	65	58	64	49	25
26		75	79	109	71	67	66	76	71	67	59	66	51	26
27		77	81	112	74	69	69	79	73	68	61	68	52	27
28		78	83	115	76	71	71	83	74	70	62	70	54	28
29		79	85	118	78	73	73	86	76	71	63	73	55	29
30		80	88	120	80	76	75	88	77	73	64	75	56	30
31		82		120	83	78	77	91	79	74	65	77	58	31
32		83		120	85	80	79	95	80	76	66	79	59	32
33		84			87	82	82	98	82	77	67	81	61	33
34		86			89	85	84	100	83	79	68	83	62	34
35		87			92	87	86	103	85	80	69	85	63	35
36		88			94	89	88	107	86	82	70	88	65	36
37		89			96	91	90	110	88	83	71	90	66	37
38		91			98	93	92	112	89	85	72	92	68	38
39		92			101	96	95	114	91	86	74	94	69	39
40		93			103	98	97	117	92	87	75	96	71	40
41		94			105	100	99	120		89	76	98	72	41
42		96			107	102	101	120		90	77	100	73	42
43		97			110	104	103	120		92	78	103	75	43
44		98			112	106	105	120		93	79	105	76	44
45		99			114	109	107			95	80	107	78	45
46		101			116	111	110			96	81	109	79	46
47		103			119	113	112			98	82		81	47
48		104			120	115	114			99	83		82	48
49		105			120	117	116				84		83	49
50		106			120	120					85		85	50

(Continued)

TABLE D.3
(Continued)

Raw	L	F	K	Hs	D	Hy	Pd	Mf	Pa	Pt	Sc	Ma	Si	Raw
51		108			120	120					86		86	51
52		109			120	120					88		88	52
53		110			120	120					89		90	53
54		112			120	120					90		92	54
55		113			120	120					91		93	55
56		114			120	120					92		95	56
57		115			120	120					93		96	57
58		117				120					94		98	58
59		118				120					95		99	59
60		119				120					96		100	60
61		120									97		102	61
62		120									98		103	62
63		120									99			63
64		120									101			64
65		120									102			65
66		120									103			66
67											104			67
68											105			68
69											106			69
70											107			70
71											108			71
72											109			72
73											110			73
74											111			74
75											112			75
76											114			76
77											115			77

T-Score Values for MMPI-A Basic Scales for Adolescent Females Age 16 Based on Marks
and Briggs Norms (Dahlstrom, Welsh, and Dahlstrom, 1972)

Raw	L	F	K	Hs	D	Hy	Pd	Mf	Pa	Pt	Sc	Ma	Si	Raw
0	30	41	30	35	30	30	30	120	30	30	32	30	30	0
1	36	43	30	37	30	30	30	120	30	30	33	30	30	1
2	42	44	30	40	30	30	30	120	30	30	34	30	30	2
3	47	46	30	42	30	30	30	118	30	32	35	30	30	3
4	51	48	30	44	30	30	30	116	32	33	36	30	30	4
5	56	50	33	47	30	30	30	112	35	34	38	30	30	5
6	60	52	35	49	30	30	30	109	37	36	39	30	30	6
7	64	53	37	51	30	30	30	106	40	37	40	30	30	7
8	69	55	39	54	30	30	30	104	42	38	41	30	30	8
9	73	57	41	56	30	30	31	101	45	40	42	32	30	9
10	78	59	44	58	30	30	33	98	48	41	43	35	30	10
11	82	60	46	61	30	32	36	96	50	42	44	37	30	11
12	86	62	48	63	32	34	38	94	53	44	45	39	30	12
13	91	64	50	65	34	36	40	90	55	45	46	41	30	13
14	95	66	52	67	36	38	42	87	58	46	47	44	31	14
15		67	55	70	38	40	44	84	61	48	48	46	32	15
16		68	57	72	40	42	47	82	63	49	49	48	33	16
17		71	59	74	43	44	49	78	66	50	50	50	35	17
18		73	61	77	45	46	51	75	68	52	51	53	37	18
19		75	63	79	48	48	53	73	71	53	52	55	38	19
20		76	66	81	51	50	55	70	74	54	53	57	39	20

(Continued)

TABLE D.3
(Continued)

Raw	L	F	K	Hs	D	Hy	Pd	Mf	Pa	Pt	Sc	Ma	Si	Raw
21		77	68	84	53	52	57	67	76	56	54	59	41	21
22		80	70	86	55	54	60	64	79	57	55	62	42	22
23		82	72	88	57	56	62	61	81	58	56	64	43	23
24		83	74	91	59	57	64	59	84	60	58	66	44	24
25		84	77	93	61	59	66	55	87	61	59	68	46	25
26		86	79	95	63	61	68	52	89	62	60	71	47	26
27		89	81	98	65	63	71	50	92	64	61	73	48	27
28		91	83	100	67	65	73	47	94	65	62	75	49	28
29		92	85	102	69	67	75	43	97	66	63	77	51	29
30		93	88	105	71	69	77	40	99	67	64	80	52	30
31		95		107	73	71	79	38	102	69	65	82	53	31
32		97		109	75	73	82	36	105	70	66	84	54	32
33		98			77	75	84	32	107	71	67	86	55	33
34		100			79	77	86	30	110	73	68	89	57	34
35		102			81	79	88	30	112	74	69	91	58	35
36		104			83	81	90	30	115	75	70	93	60	36
37		106			85	83	92	30	118	77	71	95	62	37
38		107			87	85	95	30	120	78	72	98	63	38
39		109			89	87	97	30	120	79	73	100	64	39
40		111			92	89	99	30	120	81	74	102	65	40
41		113			94	91	101	30		82	75	104	67	41
42		114			96	93	103	30		83	77	106	68	42
43		116			98	95	106	30		85	78	109	69	43
44		118			100	97	108	30		86	79	111	70	44
45		120			102	99	110			87	80	113	72	45
46		120			104	101	112			89	81	115	73	46
47		120			106	103	114			90	82		74	47
48		120			108	105	116			91	83		75	48
49		120			110	107	119				84		77	49
50		120			112	109					85		78	50
51		120			114	111					86		79	51
52		120			116	113					87		80	52
53		120			118	115					88		82	53
54		120			120	117					89		83	54
55		120			120	119					90		84	55
56		120			120	120					91		86	56
57		120			120	120					92		88	57
58		120				120					93		89	58
59		120				120					94		90	59
60		120				120					95		91	60
61		120									97		93	61
62		120									99		94	62
63		120									100			63
64		120									101			64
65		120									102			65
66		120									103			66
67											104			67
68											105			68
69											106			69
70											107			70
71											108			71
72											109			72
73											110			73
74											111			74
75											112			75
76											113			76
77											114			77

TABLE D.4

T-Score Values for MMPI-A Basic Scales for Adolescent Males Age 17 Based on Marks and Briggs Norms (Dahlstrom, Welsh, and Dahlstrom, 1972)

Raw	L	F	K	Hs	D	Hy	Pd	Mf	Pa	Pt	Sc	Ma	Si	Raw
0	30	39	30	35	30	30	30	30	30	30	31	30	30	0
1	37	41	30	38	30	30	30	30	30	30	32	30	30	1
2	43	43	30	40	30	30	30	30	30	30	33	30	30	2
3	47	44	30	43	30	30	30	30	30	32	34	30	30	3
4	51	45	30	45	30	30	30	30	31	33	35	30	30	4
5	55	47	31	48	30	30	30	30	34	35	36	30	30	5
6	59	49	34	50	30	30	30	30	37	36	37	30	30	6
7	63	50	36	53	30	30	30	30	40	38	38	30	30	7
8	68	52	38	55	32	30	30	30	43	39	39	30	30	8
9	72	54	40	58	34	30	30	30	46	41	40	31	30	9
10	76	56	42	60	35	32	30	31	49	42	41	33	30	10
11	80	57	45	63	37	34	32	33	52	44	43	35	30	11
12	81	58	47	65	39	36	34	37	55	45	44	37	30	12
13	84	60	49	68	41	38	36	40	58	47	45	39	30	13
14	93	62	51	70	43	40	39	42	61	48	46	41	32	14
15		63	53	73	44	42	41	44	64	50	47	43	33	15
16		65	56	75	46	44	43	47	67	52	48	45	35	16
17		67	58	78	48	46	46	50	70	53	49	48	36	17
18		68	60	80	51	48	48	53	72	55	50	50	38	18
19		69	62	83	54	49	50	55	75	56	51	52	39	19
20		71	64	87	55	51	52	58	78	58	52	54	41	20
21		73	67	90	57	53	55	61	81	59	53	56	43	21
22		76	69	93	59	55	57	63	84	61	55	58	45	22
23		78	71	95	61	57	59	66	87	62	56	60	47	23
24		79	73	98	63	59	62	69	90	64	57	62	49	24
25		80	75	100	64	61	64	72	93	65	58	65	50	25
26		82	78	103	66	63	66	74	96	67	59	67	52	26
27		84	80	105	68	65	69	77	99	69	60	69	53	27
28		85	82	108	70	67	71	80	102	70	61	71	55	28
29		87	84	110	72	68	73	83	105	72	62	73	56	29
30		89	86	113	73	70	75	85	108	73	63	75	58	30
31		91		115	75	72	78	87	111	75	64	77	59	31
32		92		118	77	74	80	91	114	76	66	79	61	32
33		93			79	76	82	94	117	78	67	82	62	33
34		95			81	78	85	96	120	79	68	84	64	34
35		97			83	80	87	98	120	81	69	86	65	35
36		98			84	82	89	102	120	82	70	88	67	36
37		100			86	84	91	105	120	84	71	90	68	37
38		102			88	86	94	107	120	86	72	92	70	38
39		104			90	87	96	109	120	87	73	94	71	39
40		105			92	89	98	113	120	89	74	96	73	40
41		106			93	91	101	116		90	75	99	74	41
42		108			95	93	103	118		92	77	101	76	42
43		110			97	95	105	120		93	78	103	77	43
44		111			99	97	108	120		95	79	105	79	44
45		113			101	99	110			96	80	107	80	45
46		115			102	101	112			98	81	109	82	46
47		117			104	103	114			99	82		83	47
48		118			106	105	117			101	83		85	48
49		119			108	107	119				84		86	49
50		120			110	108					85		88	50

(Continued)

TABLE D.4
(Continued)

Raw	L	F	K	Hs	D	Hy	Pd	Mf	Pa	Pt	Sc	Ma	Si	Raw
51		120			112	110					86		89	51
52		120			113	112					88		91	52
53		120			115	114					89		93	53
54		120			117	116					90		95	54
55		120			118	118					91		97	55
56		120			120	120					92		98	56
57		120			120	120					93		100	57
58		120				120					94		101	58
59		120				120					95		103	59
60		120				120					96		104	60
61		120									97		106	61
62		120									99		107	62
63		120									100			63
64		120									101			64
65		120									102			65
66		120									103			66
67											104			67
68											105			68
69											106			69
70											107			70
71											108			71
72											109			72
73											111			73
74											112			74
75											113			75
76											114			76
77											115			77

T-Score Values for MMPI-A Basic Scales for Adolescent Females Age 17 Based on Marks and Briggs Norms (Dahlstrom, Welsh, and Dahlstrom, 1972)

Raw	L	F	K	Hs	D	Hy	Pd	Mf	Pa	Pt	Sc	Ma	Si	Raw
0	30	40	30	31	30	30	30	120	30	30	30	30	30	0
1	35	42	30	34	30	30	30	120	30	30	31	30	30	1
2	41	43	30	36	30	30	30	117	30	30	32	30	30	2
3	45	45	30	38	30	30	30	115	30	30	33	30	30	3
4	49	47	30	41	30	30	30	113	33	31	35	30	30	4
5	54	49	31	43	30	30	30	109	35	33	36	30	30	5
6	58	51	33	45	30	30	30	106	38	34	37	30	30	6
7	62	52	36	48	30	30	30	104	41	36	38	30	30	7
8	66	54	38	50	30	30	30	102	44	37	39	32	30	8
9	70	57	41	52	30	30	30	99	47	39	40	34	30	9
10	74	59	44	55	30	30	31	96	50	40	41	37	30	10
11	79	60	46	57	30	30	33	94	53	42	43	39	30	11
12	83	62	49	59	32	31	35	92	56	43	44	41	30	12
13	87	64	51	61	35	33	37	88	59	44	45	43	30	13
14	91	66	54	64	37	35	40	85	61	46	46	45	30	14
15		67	56	66	39	37	42	83	64	47	47	47	30	15
16		69	59	68	41	39	44	80	67	49	48	50	31	16
17		72	61	71	43	41	47	77	70	50	49	52	33	17
18		74	64	73	47	43	49	74	73	52	50	54	35	18
19		76	66	75	50	45	51	71	76	53	52	56	37	19
20		77	69	77	52	47	54	69	79	55	53	58	38	20

(Continued)

TABLE D.4
(Continued)

Raw	L	F	K	Hs	D	Hy	Pd	Mf	Pa	Pt	Sc	Ma	Si	Raw
21		79	71	80	54	49	56	65	82	56	54	60	39	21
22		81	74	82	56	51	58	62	84	58	55	63	41	22
23		83	76	84	58	53	61	60	87	59	56	65	42	23
24		84	79	87	60	55	63	58	90	60	57	67	43	24
25		86	81	89	62	57	65	54	93	62	58	69	45	25
26		89	84	91	65	59	67	51	96	63	60	71	46	26
27		91	86	93	67	61	70	49	99	65	61	73	47	27
28		93	89	96	69	63	72	47	102	66	62	76	49	28
29		94	91	98	71	65	74	43	105	68	63	78	50	29
30		96	94	100	73	67	77	40	108	69	64	80	51	30
31		99		103	75	69	79	38	110	71	65	82	53	31
32		101		105	78	71	81	36	113	72	66	84	54	32
33		102			80	73	84	32	116	74	68	86	55	33
34		104			82	75	86	30	119	75	69	89	57	34
35		106			84	77	88	30	120	77	70	91	58	35
36		109			86	79	91	30	120	78	71	93	60	36
37		111			88	81	93	30	120	79	72	95	62	37
38		112			90	83	95	30	120	81	73	97	63	38
39		113			93	85	98	30	120	82	74	99	65	39
40		116			95	87	100	30	120	84	76	101	66	40
41		118			97	89	102	30		85	77	104	67	41
42		119			99	91	104	30		87	78	106	69	42
43		120			101	93	107	30		88	79	108	70	43
44		120			103	95	109	30		90	80	110	71	44
45		120			105	97	111			91	81	112	73	45
46		120			108	99	114			93	82	114	74	46
47		120			110	101	116			94	84		75	47
48		120			112	103	118			95	85		77	48
49		120			114	105	118				86		78	49
50		120			116	107					87		79	50
51		120			118	109					88		81	51
52		120			120	111					89		82	52
53		120			120	113					90		83	53
54		120			120	115					92		85	54
55		120			120	117					93		86	55
56		120			120	119					94		88	56
57		120			120	120					95		90	57
58		120				120					96		91	58
59		120				120					97		93	59
60		120				120					98		94	60
61		120									101		95	61
62		120									102		97	62
63		120									103			63
64		120									104			64
65		120									105			65
66		120									106			66
67											108			67
68											109			68
69											110			69
70											111			70
71											112			71
72											113			72
73											114			73
74											116			74
75											117			75
76											118			76
77											119			77

E

Forbey and Ben-Porath MMPI-A Critical Items

Note. Table reproduced from J. D. Forbey and Y. S. Ben-Porath (1998). *A Critical Item Set for the MMPI-A* (MMPI-2/MMPI-A Test Report No. 4), pp. 10–14. Minneapolis: University of Minnesota Press. Reproduced by permission of the University of Minnesota Press.

TABLE E.1
MMPI-A Critical Item Set

Item	Keyed Direction	Scale Membership	Content Group
22.	True	F1, 6, A-biz, MAC–R	Unusual Thinking
30.	True	F1	Eating Problems
31.	False	4, 8	Sexual Concerns
33.	True	F1, A-sch	School Problems
36.	True	1, 2, 3, A-anx	Anxiety
59.	True (M)		
	False (F)	5	Sexual Concerns
62.	True	3, 7, 8, A-dep, A	Depression/Suicidal Ideation
71.	False	2, A-dep, IMM	Depression/Suicidal Ideation
80.	True	F1, A-sch, MAC–R	School Problems
88.	True	2, 8, A-dep, A-trt	Depression/Suicidal Ideation
90.	True	4, 7	Self-Denigration
92.	True	F1, A-biz	Hallucinatory Experiences
95.	True	4, 6	Paranoid Ideation
101.	True	4, A-sch, MAC–R, IMM	School Problems
108.	True	F1	Eating Problems
113.	False	1, A-hea, MAC–R	Somatic Complaints
132.	True	F1, 6, 8, A-biz	Paranoid Ideation
136.	True	F1, 6	Paranoid Ideation
138.	False	2, A-hea, R	Somatic Complaints
141.	True	2, 7, 8	Cognitive Problems
144.	True	F1, ACK	Substance Use/Abuse
155.	True	F1, 6, A-biz	Paranoid Ideation
158.	False	2, 7, 8	Cognitive Problems
159.	True	3, 5-m, 8	Sexual Concerns
161.	True	8, 9, ACK, MAC–R	Substance Use/Abuse
163.	True	2, 7, 8, A-anx	Anxiety
165.	True	3, MAC–R	Somatic Complaints
169.	False	8	Somatic Complaints
172.	False	1, 3, 8, A-hea	Somatic Complaints
173.	True	F1, 8, A-biz	Anxiety
175.	True	8, 9	Somatic Complaints
177.	True	A-dep, MAC–R	Depression/Suicidal Ideation
214.	True	8, 9, MAC–R	Somatic Complaints
219.	True	F1, 6, 8, A-dep	Self-Denigration
224.	True	F1, A-con, IMM	Conduct Problems
230.	True	F1, A-dep	Self-Denigration
231.	True	1, 8, A-hea	Somatic Complaints
242.	True	F2, A-dep, A-trt, A-aln	Depression/Suicidal Ideation
247.	True	4, A-ack	Substance Use/Abuse
249.	False	4, 6, A-con, MAC–R, ACK	Conduct Problems
250.	True	F2, A-biz, MAC–R	Unusual Thinking
251.	True	5-m, 8	Sexual Concerns
275.	False	8, A-hea	Somatic Complaints
278.	True	8, A-biz	Hallucinatory Experiences
283.	True	F2, 8, A-dep	Depression/Suicidal Ideation
288.	True	7, 0	Cognitive Problems
291.	True	8, A-biz, A	Unusual Thinking
294.	False	6	Paranoid Ideation
296.	True	7, 8, A-biz	Unusual Thinking
297.	True	F2, 7	Anxiety
299.	True	8, A-biz	Hallucinatory Experiences

(Continued)

TABLE E.1
(Continued)

Item	Keyed Direction	Scale Membership	Content Group
303.	True	F2, 8, A-fam	Aggression
309.	True	F2, 7, 8	Anxiety
315.	True	F2, 6, A-biz	Paranoid Ideation
321.	True	F2, 8	Self-Denigration
332.	True	F2, 6, 8, A-biz	Paranoid Ideation
337.	True	F2, 6	Paranoid Ideation
342.	True	F2, MAC-R, ACK	Substance Use/Abuse
345.	True	A-con, PRO	Conduct Problems
353.	True	A-anx	Anxiety
354.	True	A-con, IMM	Conduct Problems
365.	False	A-fam	Family Problems
366.	True	F2, A-fam	Family Problems
380.	True	A-sch, MAC-R	School Problems
389.	True	A-sch, PRO, IMM	School Problems
392.	True	F2, MAC-R	Self-Denigration
399.	True	F2, A-dep	Depression/Suicidal Ideation
405.	True	F2, A-fam, IMM	Family Problems
417.	True	A-biz	Unusual Thinking
428.	True	F2, A-biz	Paranoid Ideation
429.	True	MAC–R, ACK	Substance Use/Abuse
431.	False	A-trt, ACK, IMM	Substance Use/Abuse
433.	True	F2, A-biz	Hallucinatory Experiences
439.	True	F2, A-biz	Hallucinatory Experiences
440.	True	A-fam, PRO	Conduct Problems
445.	True	A-ang, A-con	Conduct Problems
453.	True	A-ang, IMM	Aggression
458.	True	F2, A-ang, ACK	Substance Use/Abuse
460.	False	A-fam, PRO	Conduct Problems
465.	False	A-con	Aggression
467.	True	ACK	Substance Use/Abuse
474.	True	ACK	Substance Use/Abuse

Item Composition of the MMPI-A Content Component Scales

Note. Table reproduced from N. E. Sherwood, Y. S. Ben-Porath, and C. L. Williams (1997). *3: The MMPI-A Content Component Scales: Development, Psychometric Characteristics, and Clinical Application* (MMPI-2/MMPI-A Test Reports), pp. 42–48. Minneapolis: University of Minnesota Press. Reproduced by permission of the University of Minnesota Press.

TABLE F.1
Item Composition of the MMPI-A
Content Component Scales

Adolescent Depression

A-dep1: Dysphoria
53.	(T)
62.	(T)
91.	(F)
139.	(T)
360.	(F)

A-dep2: Self-Depreciation
49.	(T)
124.	(T)
311.	(T)
347.	(T)
379.	(T)

A-dep3: Lack of Drive
3.	(F)
9.	(F)
35.	(T)
71.	(F)
88.	(T)
371.	(T)
372.	(T)

A-dep4: Suicidal Ideation
177.	(T)
242.	(T)
283.	(T)
399.	(T)

Adolescent Health Concerns

A-hea1: Gastrointestinal Complaints
17.	(T)
25.	(T)
56.	(T)
106.	(T)

A-hea2: Neurological Symptoms
37.	(T)
41.	(T)
50.	(T)
54.	(F)
87.	(F)
93.	(T)
97.	(T)
113.	(F)
138.	(F)
143.	(T)
152.	(F)
157.	(F)
168.	(F)
172.	(F)
231.	(T)
239.	(F)
275.	(F)
374.	(F)

(Continued)

TABLE F.1
(Continued)

A-hea3: General Health Concerns

42.	(F)
112.	(F)
135.	(F)
167.	(T)
187.	(T)
210.	(F)
422.	(T)
443.	(T)

Adolescent Alienation

A-aln1: Misunderstood

20.	(T)
211.	(T)
369.	(T)
438.	(T)
260.	(F)

A-aln2: Social Isolation

227.	(T)
450.	(F)
463.	(T)
471.	(T)
473.	(T)

A-aln3: Interpersonal Skepticism

16.	(T)
39.	(T)
317.	(T)
362.	(T)
446.	(T)

Adolescent Bizarre Mentation

A-biz1: Psychotic Symptomatology

22.	(T)
29.	(T)
92.	(T)
173.	(T)
250.	(T)
278.	(T)
291.	(T)
296.	(T)
299.	(T)
433.	(T)
439.	(T)

A-biz2: Paranoid Ideation

132.	(T)
155.	(T)
314.	(T)
315.	(T)
428.	(T)

(Continued)

TABLE F.1
(Continued)

Adolescent Anger

A-ang1: Explosive Behavior
      34.   (T)
    128.   (T)
    367.   (T)
    382.   (T)
    445.   (T)
    453.   (T)
    458.   (T)
    461.   (T)

A-ang2: Irritability
     26.   (T)
    111.   (T)
    201.   (T)
    282.   (T)
    355.   (T)
    388.   (T)
    401.   (T)
    416.   (T)

Adolescent Cynicism

A-cyn1: Misanthropic Beliefs
     55.   (T)
     72.   (T)
     77.   (T)
    100.   (T)
    107.   (T)
    213.   (T)
    238.   (T)
    263.   (T)
    265.   (T)
    267.   (T)
    330.   (T)
    371.   (T)
    406.   (T)

A-cyn2: Interpersonal Suspiciousness
     47.   (T)
    118.   (T)
    211.   (T)
    225.   (T)
    295.   (T)
    325.   (T)
    334.   (T)
    373.   (T)
    395.   (T)

(Continued)

TABLE F.1
(Continued)

Adolescent Conduct Problems

A-con1: Acting-out Behaviors
32.	(T)
224.	(T)
249.	(F)
354.	(T)
356.	(T)
391.	(T)
445.	(T)
456.	(T)
462.	(T)
469.	(T)

A-con2: Antisocial Attitudes
117.	(T)
232.	(T)
234.	(T)
252.	(T)
361.	(T)
442.	(T)
455.	(T)
465.	(F)

A-con3: Negative Peer Group Influences
345.	(T)
477.	(T)
478.	(T)

Adolescent Low Self-Esteem

A-lse1: Self-Doubt
58.	(F)
70.	(T)
74.	(F)
105.	(F)
124.	(T)
306.	(T)
358.	(T)
379.	(T)
384.	(T)
415.	(T)
432.	(T)
441.	(T)
468.	(T)

A-lse2: Interpersonal Submissiveness
67.	(T)
280.	(T)
385.	(T)
400.	(T)
430.	(T)

(Continued)

TABLE F.1
(Continued)

Adolescent Low Aspirations

A-las1: Low Achievement Orientation

170.	(F)
188.	(F)
324.	(F)
397.	(F)
403.	(F)
409.	(F)
411.	(F)
436.	(F)

A-las2: Lack of Initiative

27.	(T)
218.	(T)
340.	(T)
351.	(T)
430.	(T)
447.	(F)
464.	(T)

Adolescent Social Discomfort

A-sod1: Introversion

46.	(F)
82.	(F)
262.	(F)
264.	(T)
292.	(F)
304.	(T)
316.	(T)
319.	(F)
328.	(T)
331.	(F)
335.	(F)
339.	(F)
410.	(T)
450.	(F)

A-sod2: Shyness

43.	(T)
151.	(T)
160.	(T)
178.	(T)
245.	(F)
248.	(T)
290.	(T)
336.	(F)
408.	(T)
475.	(T)

(Continued)

TABLE F.1
(Continued)

Adolescent Family Problems

A-fam1: Familial Discord

19.	(T)
57.	(T)
79.	(F)
119.	(F)
137.	(T)
181.	(T)
191.	(T)
240.	(T)
269.	(T)
277.	(T)
344.	(T)
352.	(T)
359.	(T)
363.	(T)
366.	(T)
381.	(T)
396.	(T)
398.	(F)
440.	(T)
457.	(F)
460.	(F)

A-fam2: Familial Alienation

6.	(F)
86.	(F)
182.	(F)
184.	(T)
215.	(T)
258.	(F)
365.	(F)
405.	(T)
438.	(T)
451.	(F)
454.	(T)

Adolescent School Problems

A-schl: School Conduct Problems

80.	(T)
101.	(T)
380.	(T)
389.	(T)

A-sch2: Negative Attitudes

12.	(T)
69.	(T)
153.	(F)
425.	(T)
435.	(T)
452.	(T)
464.	(T)
466.	(T)

(Continued)

TABLE F.1
(Continued)

Adolescent Negative Treatment Indicators

A-trtl: Low Motivation

27.	(T)
88.	(T)
340.	(T)
358.	(T)
414.	(T)
418.	(T)
419.	(F)
421.	(T)
426.	(T)
432.	(T)
444.	(T)

A-trt2: Inability to Disclose

256.	(T)
356.	(T)
357.	(T)
369.	(T)
423.	(T)
431.	(F)
437.	(F)
472.	(T)

Scale-Level Factor Structure for the MMPI-A Normative Sample

TABLE G.1
Scale-Level Factor Structure for the MMPI-A Normative Sample

MMPI-A Sacle	Factors							
	1	2	3	4	5	6	7	8
Basic Scales								
VRIN	.22	.71*	−.12	−.05	.31	−.07	.21	.18
TRIN	.22	.34	.42	−.17	−.02	−.26	.08	.21
F_1	.46	.88*	.06	−.12	.41	−.16	.41	.25
F_2	.50*	.90*	.10	−.23	.40	−.22	.29	.36
F	.51*	.95*	.09	−.19	.43	−.21	.37	.34
L	−.13	.22	−.55*	.17	.15	.17	−.07	.14
K	−.52*	−.15	−.67*	.57*	−.10	.63*	−.24	−.21
Hs	.65*	.43	.12	−.24	.92*	−.15	.34	.21
D	.75*	.27	−.25	.34	.58*	−.10	.26	.12
Hy	.38	.16	−.26	.20	.74*	.35	.27	.02
Pd	.71*	.52*	.25	−.07	.43	−.20	.77*	.18
Mf	.21	−.30	.01	−.13	.20	.14	.07	.12
Pa	.66*	.62*	.21	−.20	.49	.06	.44	.54*
Pt	.89*	.44	.51*	−.56*	.49	−.42	.34	.28
Sc	.86*	.73*	.45	−.42	.56*	−.38	.48	.39
Ma	.36	.43	.77*	.06	.19	−.30	.38	.19
Si	.65*	.36	.01	−.85*	.31	−.53*	.18	.27
Content Scales								
ANX	.84*	.40	.42	−.46	.50*	−.39	.37	.29
OBS	.65*	.31	.63*	−.49	.27	−.48	.24	.27
DEP	.91*	.51*	.31	−.46	.43	−.35	.44	.28
HEA	.58*	.57*	.12	−.21	.90*	−.14	.33	.27
ALN	.69*	.64*	.22	−.50*	.33	−.48	.49	.37
BIZ	.60*	.71*	.40	−.23	.44	−.31	.29	.47
ANG	.45	.34	.63*	−.29	.20	−.44	.34	.10
CYN	.44	.33	.60*	−.36	.07	−.84*	.26	.19
CON	.39	.60*	.54*	−.13	.11	−.37	.41	−.10
LSE	.74*	.52*	.25	−.56*	.38	−.39	.27	.22
LAS	.47	.45	.01	−.32	.27	−.22	.26	−.16
SOD	.44	.43	−.22	−.72*	.21	−.40	.12	.32
FAM	.60*	.59*	.37	−.27	.34	−.34	.78*	.19
SCH	.50*	.71*	.29	−.27	.30	−.31	.44	−.06
TRT	.68*	.64*	.35	−.52*	.29	−.55*	.35	.25
Supplementary Scales								
A	.86*	.38	.53*	−.61*	.35	−.50*	.31	.28
R	.00	.11	−.69*	−.02	.23	.19	−.04	.01
MAC-R	.18	.54*	.48	.12	.07	−.18	.35	.06
ACK	.44	.67*	.41	−.08	.27	−.17	.50*	.02
PRO	.39	.49	.35	.00	.25	−.11	.61*	−.23
IMM	.61*	.82*	.27	−.36	.33	−.47	.47	.10
Harris-Lingoes Subscales								
D_1	.91*	.37	.09	−.48	.53*	−.30	.37	.15
D_2	.29	.05	−.50*	−.23	.15	.03	−.07	−.06
D_3	.46	.23	−.06	−.16	.56*	−.09	.23	.10
D_4	.85*	.41	.12	−.34	.48	−.23	.35	.04
D_5	.86*	.33	.29	−.43	.42	−.27	.35	.23
Hy_1	−.39	−.16	−.18	.87*	−.02	.39	−.01	−.11
Hy_2	−.39	−.25	−.49	.43	−.05	.79*	−.20	−.20
Hy_3	.81*	.33	.11	−.31	.62*	−.21	.44	.10
Hy_4	.56*	.42	.12	−.22	.89*	−.14	.30	.22
Hy_5	−.13	−.14	−.45	.09	.06	.26	−.09	−.06

(Continued)

TABLE G.1
(Continued)

MMPI-A Sacle	Factors							
	1	2	3	4	5	6	7	8
Pd_1	.46	.32	.21	−.15	.28	−.19	.80*	.11
Pd_2	.06	.38	−.01	.27	.17	.10	.35	−.16
Pd_3	−.38	−.08	−.13	.88*	−.05	.35	.02	−.15
Pd_4	.71*	.38	.41	−.35	.28	−.38	.49	.42
Pd_5	.80*	.43	.40	−.33	.32	−.33	.44	.22
Pa_1	.66*	.69*	.39	−.29	.34	−.39	.48	.55*
Pa_2	.62*	.39	.31	−.31	.37	−.19	.38	.40
Pa_3	−.27	−.22	−.40	.28	−.01	.84*	−.16	−.06
Sc_1	.74*	.58*	.38	−.43	.35	−.43	.62*	.44
Sc_2	.66*	.65*	.05	−.26	.38	−.19	.31	.24
Sc_3	.77*	.53*	.42	−.29	.42	−.33	.30	.23
Sc_4	.83*	.47	.30	−.39	.37	−.34	.31	.08
Sc_5	.56*	.48	.61*	−.28	.42	−.24	.26	.31
Sc_6	.58*	.68*	.39	−.23	.64*	−.22	.30	.40
Ma_1	.15	.30	.39	.01	−.01	−.26	.16	−.14
Ma_2	.29	.09	.72*	−.10	.13	−.18	.17	.11
Ma_3	−.28	.09	−.09	.71*	−.06	.27	.03	−.10
Ma_4	.32	.28	.61*	−.21	.09	−.44	.33	.28
Si Subscales								
Si_1	.41	.15	−.05	−.88*	.13	−.33	.03	.16
Si_2	.18	.33	−.41	−.36	.17	−.21	.07	.29
Si_3	.72*	.42	.53*	−.56*	.26	−.67*	.28	.15

Note: Asterisk indicates factor loading ≥ .50 or ≤ −.50.

References

Achenbach, T. M. (1978). Psychopathology of childhood: Research problems and issues. *Journal of Consulting and Clinical Psychology, 46*, 759–776.

Achenbach, T. (1991a). *Manual for the Child Behavior Checklist/4-18 and 1991 profile.* Burlington: University of Vermont, Department of Psychiatry.

Achenbach, T. (1991b). *Manual for the teacher's report form and 1991 profile.* Burlington: University of Vermont, Department of Psychiatry.

Achenbach, T. (1991c). *Manual for the youth self-report and 1991 profile.* Burlington: University of Vermont, Department of Psychiatry.

Achenbach, T. M., & Edelbrock, C. S. (1983). *Manual for the Child Behavior Checklist and revised child behavior profile.* Burlington: University of Vermont.

Ackerman, M. J., & Ackerman, M. C. (1997). Custody evaluation practices: A survey of experienced professionals (revised). *Professional Psychology Research and Practice, 28*, 137–145.

Acklin, M. W. (1993). Integrating the Rorschach and the MMPI in clinical assessment: Conceptual and methodological issues. *Journal of Personality Assessment, 60*, 125–131.

Alperin, J. J., Archer, R. P., & Coates, G. D. (1996). Development and effects of an MMPI-A K-correction procedure. *Journal of Personality Assessment, 67*, 155–168.

Ambrosini, P. J., Metz, C., Prabucki, K., & Lee, J. C. (1989). Video tape reliability of the third revised edition of the K–SADS–III–R. *Journal of the American Academy of Child and Adolescent Psychiatry, 28*, 723–728.

American Psychiatric Association. (1994). *Diagnostic and statistical manual of mental disorders* (4th ed.). Washington, DC: Author.

American Psychiatric Association (2000). *Diagnostic and Statistical Manual of Mental Disorders (4th ed., text revision).* Washington, DC: Author.

American Psychological Association, Committee on Psychological Tests and Assessment (CPTA). (1986). *Guidelines for computer-based tests and interpretations.* Washington, DC: Author.

American Psychological Association (2002). *Developing adolescents: A reference for professionals.* Washington: DC: Author.

Anastasi, A. (1982). *Psychological testing* (5th ed.). New York: Macmillan.

Andrucci, G. L., Archer, R. P., Pancoast, D. L., & Gordon, R. A. (1989). The relationship of MMPI and sensation seeking scales to adolescent drug use. *Journal of Personality Assessment, 53*, 253–266.

Anthony, N. (1976). Malingering as role taking. *Journal of Clinical Psychology, 32*, 32–41.

Arbisi, P. A., & Ben-Porath, Y. S. (1995). An MMPI-2 infrequent response scale for use with psychopathological populations: The Infrequency Psychopathology scale F(p). *Psychological Assessment, 7*, 424–431.

Archer, R. P. (1984). Use of the MMPI with adolescents: A review of salient issues. *Clinical Psychology Review, 4*, 241–251.

Archer, R. P. (1987a). MMPI Adolescent Interpretive System [Computer software]. Odessa, FL: Psychological Assessment Resources.

Archer, R. P. (1987b). *Using the MMPI with adolescents.* Hillsdale, NJ: Lawrence Erlbaum Associates.

Archer, R. P. (1989). *MMPI assessment of adolescent clients* (Clinical Notes on the MMPI, No. 12). Minneapolis: National Computer Systems.

Archer, R. P. (1990). Responses of adolescents on the MMPI-2: Comparisons with MMPI findings. In R. C. Colligan (Chair), *The MMPI and adolescents: Historical perspective, current research, and future developments.* Symposium conducted at the annual convention of the American Psychological Association, Boston.

Archer, R. P. (1992a). *MMPI-A: Assessing Adolescent Psychopathology.* Hillsdale, NJ: Lawrence Erlbaum Associates.

Archer, R. P. (1992b). MMPI-A Interpretive System [Computer software]. Odessa, FL: Psychological Assessment Resources.

Archer, R. P. (1992c). Review of the Minnesota Multiphasic Personality Inventory-2 (MMPI-2). In *The Eleventh Mental Measurements Yearbook* (pp. 558–562). Lincoln: University of Nebraska, Buros Institute of Mental Measurements.

Archer, R. P. (1995). MMPI-A Interpretive System (Version 2) [Computer software]. Odessa, FL: Psychological Assessment Resources.

Archer, R. P. (1997a). Future directions for the MMPI-A: Research and clinical issues. *Journal of Personality Assessment, 68,* 95–109.

Archer, R. P. (1997b). *MMPI-A: Assessing Adolescent Psychopathology (2nd Edition).* Mahwah, NJ: Lawrence Erlbaum Associates.

Archer, R. P. (2003). MMPI-A Interpretive System (Version 3) [Computer software]. Odessa: FL: Psychological Assessment Resources.

Archer, R. P., Aiduk, R., Griffin, R., & Elkins, D. E. (1996). Incremental validity of the MMPI-2 content scales in a psychiatric sample. *Assessment, 3,* 79–90.

Archer, R. P., & Baker, E. M. (in press). Use of the Minnesota Multiphasic Personality Inventory-Adolescent (MMPI-A) in juvenile justice settings. In D. Seagraves and T. Grisso, *Handbook of screening and assessment tools for juvenile justice.* New York: Guilford Press.

Archer, R. P., Ball, J. D., & Hunter, J. A. (1985). MMPI characteristics of borderline psychopathology in adolescent inpatients. *Journal of Personality Assessment, 49,* 47–55.

Archer, R. P., Belevich, J. K. S., & Elkins, D. E. (1994). Item-level and scale-level factor structures of the MMPI-A. *Journal of Personality Assessment, 62,* 332–345.

Archer, R. P., Bolinskey, P. K., Morton, T. L., & Farris, K. L. (2003). MMPI-A characteristics of male adolescents in juvenile justice and clinical treatment settings. *Assessment, 10,* 400–410.

Archer, R. P., & Elkins, D. E. (1999). Identification of random responding on the MMPI-A. *Journal of Personality Assessment, 73,* 407–421.

Archer, R. P., Elkins, D. E., Aiduk, R., & Griffin, R. (1997). The incremental validity of MMPI-2 supplementary scales. *Assessment, 4,* 193–205.

Archer, R. P., Fontaine, J., & McCrae, R. R. (1998). Effects of two MMPI-2 validity scales on basic scale relations to external criteria. *Journal of Personality Assessment, 70,* 87–102.

Archer, R. P., & Gordon, R. A. (1988). MMPI and Rorschach indices of schizophrenic and depressive diagnoses among adolescent inpatients. *Journal of Personality Assessment, 52,* 276–287.

Archer, R. P., & Gordon, R. A. (1991a). [Correlational analysis of the MMPI-A normative data set]. Unpublished raw data.

Archer, R. P., & Gordon, R. A. (1991b, August). Use of content scales with adolescents: Past and future practices. In R. C. Colligan (Chair), *MMPI and MMPI-2 supplementary scales and profile interpretation—content scales revisited.* Symposium conducted at the annual convention of the American Psychological Association, San Francisco.

Archer, R. P., & Gordon, R. A. (1994). Psychometric stability of MMPI-A item modifications. *Journal of Personality Assessment, 62,* 416–426.

Archer, R. P., Gordon, R. A., Anderson, G. L., & Giannetti, R. A. (1989). MMPI special scale clinical correlates for adolescent inpatients. *Journal of Personality Assessment, 53,* 654–664.

Archer, R. P., Gordon, R. A., Giannetti, R. A., & Singles, J. M. (1988). MMPI scale clinical correlates for adolescent inpatients. *Journal of Personality Assessment, 52,* 707–721.

Archer, R. P., Gordon, R. A., & Kirchner, F. H. (1987). MMPI response-set characteristics among adolescents. *Journal of Personality Assessment, 51,* 506–516.

Archer, R. P., Gordon, R. A., & Klinefelter, D. (1991). [Analyses of the frequency of MMPI and MMPI-A profile assignments for 1762 adolescent patients]. Unpublished raw data.

Archer, R. P., Griffin, R., & Aiduk, R. (1995). MMPI-2 clinical correlates for ten common codes. *Journal of Personality Assessment, 65,* 391–407.

Archer, R. P., Handel, R. W., & Lynch, K. D. (2001). The effectiveness of MMPI-A items in discriminating between normative and clinical samples. *Journal of Personality Assessment, 77,* 420–435.

Archer, R. P., Handel, R. W., Lynch, K. D., & Elkins, D. E. (2002). MMPI-A validity scale uses and limitations in detecting varying levels of random responding. *Journal of Personality Assessment, 78,* 417–431.

Archer, R. P., & Jacobson, J. M. (1993). Are critical items "critical" for the MMPI-A? *Journal of Personality Assessment, 61,* 547–556.

Archer, R. P., & Klinefelter, D. (1991). MMPI factor analytic findings for adolescents: Item- and scale-level factor structures. *Journal of Personality Assessment, 57,* 356–367.

Archer, R. P., & Klinefelter, D. (1992). Relationships between MMPI codetypes and *MAC* scale elevations in adolescent psychiatric samples. *Journal of Personality Assessment, 58,* 149–159.

Archer, R. P., & Krishnamurthy, R. (1993a). Combining the Rorschach and MMPI in the assessment of adolescents. *Journal of Personality Assessment, 60,* 132–140.

Archer, R. P., & Krishnamurthy, R. (1993b). A review of MMPI and Rorschach interrelationships in adult samples. *Journal of Personality Assessment, 61,* 277–293.

Archer, R. P., & Krishnamurthy, R. (1994a). *MMPI-A Structural Summary* [Summary form]. Odessa, FL: Psychological Assessment Resources.

Archer, R. P., & Krishnamurthy, R. (1994b). A structural summary approach for the MMPI-A: Development and empirical correlates. *Journal of Personality Assessment, 63,* 554–573.

Archer, R. P., & Krishnamurthy, R. (1997). MMPI-A scale-level factor structure: Replication in a clinical sample. *Assessment, 4,* 337–349.

Archer, R. P., & Krishnamurthy, R. (2002). *Essentials of MMPI-A assessment.* New York: Wiley.

Archer, R. P., Krishnamurthy, R., & Jacobson, J. M. (1994). *MMPI-A casebook.* Tampa, FL: Psychological Assessment Resources.

Archer, R. P., Maruish, M., Imhof, E. A., & Piotrowski, C. (1991). Psychological test usage with adolescent clients: 1990 survey findings. *Professional Psychology, 22,* 247–252.

Archer, R. P., & Newsom, C. R. (2000). Psychological test usage with adolescent clients: Survey update. *Assessment, 7,* 227–235.

Archer, R. P., Pancoast, D. L., & Gordon, R. A. (1994). The development of the MMPI-A Immaturity (IMM) scale: Findings for normal and clinical samples. *Journal of Personality Assessment, 62,* 145–156.

Archer, R. P., Pancoast, D. L., & Klinefelter, D. (1989). A comparison of MMPI code types produced by traditional and recent adolescent norms. *Psychological Assessment, 1,* 23–29.

Archer, R. P., & Slesinger, D. (1999). MMPI-A patterns related to the endorsement of suicidal ideation. *Assessment, 6,* 51–59.

Archer, R. P., Stolberg, A. L., Gordon, R. A., & Goldman, W. R. (1986). Parent and child MMPI responses: Characteristics among families with adolescents in inpatient and outpatient settings. *Journal of Abnormal Child Psychology, 14,* 181–190.

Archer, R. P., Stredny, R. V., Mason, J. A., & Arnau, R. C. (2004). An examination and replication of the psychometric properties of the Massachusetts Youth Screening Instrument–2nd edition (MAYSI–2) among adolescents in detention settings. *Assessment, 11*(4), 1–13.

Archer, R. P., Tirrell, C. A., & Elkins, D. E. (2001). Evaluation of an MMPI-A Short Form: Implications for adaptive testing. *Journal of Personality Assessment, 76*(1), 76–89.

Archer, R. P., White, J. L., & Orvin, G. H. (1979). MMPI characteristics and correlates among adolescent psychiatric inpatients. *Journal of Clinical Psychology, 35,* 498–504.

Arita, A. A., & Baer, R. (1998). Validity of selected MMPI-A content scales. *Psychological Assessment, 10,* 59–63.

Baer, R. A., Ballenger, J., Berry, D. T. R., & Wetter, M. W. (1997). Detection of random responding on the MMPI-A. *Journal of Personality Assessment, 68,* 139–151.

Baer, R. A., Ballenger, J., & Kroll, L. S. (1998). Detection of underreporting on the MMPI-A in clinical and community samples. *Journal of Personality Assessment, 71,* 98–113.

Baer, R. A., Wetter, M. W., & Berry, D. T. R. (1992). Detection of underreporting of psychopathology on the MMPI: A meta-analysis. *Clinical Psychology Review, 12,* 509–525.

Baer, R. A., Wetter, M. W., & Berry, D. T. R. (1995). Effects of information about validity scales on underreporting of symptoms on the MMPI-2: An analogue investigation. *Assessment, 2,* 189–200.

Bagby, R. M., Buis, T., & Nicholson, R. A. (1995). Relative effectiveness of the standard validity scales in detecting fake-bad and fake-good responding: Replication and extension. *Psychological Assessment, 7,* 84–92.

Bagby, R. M., Rogers, R., & Buis, T. (1994). Detecting malingering and defensive responding in the MMPI-2 in a forensic inpatient sample. *Journal of Personality Assessment, 62,* 191–203.

Bagby, R. M., Rogers, R., Buis, T., & Kalemba, V. (1994). Malingered and defensive response styles on the MMPI-2: An examination of the validity scales. *Assessment, 1,* 31–38.

Bagby, R. M., Rogers, R., Buis, T., Nicholson, R. A., Cameron, S. L., Rector, N. A., et al. (1997). Detecting feigned depression and schizophrenia on the MMPI-2. *Journal of Personality Assessment, 68,* 650–664.

Ball, J. C. (1960). Comparison of MMPI profile differences among Negro-White adolescents. *Journal of Clinical Psychology, 16,* 304–307.

Ball, J. C. (1962). *Social deviancy and adolescent personality: An analytical study with the MMPI.* Lexington: University of Kentucky Press.

Ball, J. C., & Carroll, D. (1960). Analysis of MMPI Cannot Say scores in an adolescent population. *Journal of Clinical Psychology, 16,* 30–31.

Ball, J. D., Archer, R. P., & Imhof, E. A. (1994). Time requirements of psychological testing: A survey of practitioners. *Journal of Personality Assessment, 63,* 239–249.

Ball, J. D., Archer, R. P., Struve, F. A., Hunter, J. A., & Gordon, R. A. (1987). MMPI correlates of a controversial EEG pattern among adolescent psychiatric patients. *Journal of Clinical Psychology, 43,* 708–714.

Bandura, A. (1964). The stormy decade: Fact or fiction? *Psychology in the School, 1,* 224–231.

Barron, F. (1953). An ego-strength scale which predicts response to psychotherapy. *Journal of Consulting Psychology, 17,* 327–333.

Basham, R. B. (1992). Clinical utility of the MMPI research scales in the assessment of adolescent acting out behaviors. *Psychological Assessment, 4,* 483–492.

Bell, H. M. (1934). *Adjustment inventory.* Stanford, CA: Stanford University Press.

Bence, V. M., Sabourin, C., Luty, D. T., & Thackrey, M. (1995). Differential sensitivity of the MMPI-2 depression scales and subscales. *Journal of Clinical Psychology, 51,* 375–377.

Ben-Porath, Y. S. (1990). MMPI-2 items. In *MMPI-2 News and Profiles, 1*(1), 8–9.

Ben-Porath, Y. S. (1994). The ethical dilemma of coached malingering research. *Psychological Assessment, 6,* 14–15.

Ben-Porath, Y. S., Butcher, J. N., & Graham, J. R. (1991). Contribution of the MMPI-2 content scales to the differential diagnosis of schizophrenia and major depression. *Psychological Assessment, 3,* 634–640.

Ben-Porath, Y. S., Hostetler, K., Butcher, J. N., & Graham, J. R. (1989). New subscales for the MMPI-2 Social Introversion (Si) scale. *Psychological Assessment, 1,* 169–174.

Ben-Porath, Y. S., McCully, E., & Almagor, M. (1993). Incremental validity of the MMPI-2 content scales in the assessment of personality and psychopathology by self-report. *Journal of Personality Assessment, 61,* 557–575.

Ben-Porath, Y. S., & Sherwood, N. E. (1993). *The MMPI-2 content component scales* (MMPI-2/MMPI-A Test Report No. 1). Minneapolis: University of Minnesota Press.

Ben-Porath, Y. S., Slutske, W. S., & Butcher, J. N. (1989). A real-data simulation of computerized adaptive administration of the MMPI. *Psychological Assessment, 1,* 18–22.

Ben-Porath, Y. S., & Tellegen, A. (1995). How (not) to evaluate the comparability of MMPI and MMPI-2 profile configurations: A reply to Humphrey and Dahlstrom. *Journal of Personality Assessment, 65,* 52–58.

Bernreuter, R. G. (1933). The theory and construction of the Personality Inventory. *Journal of Social Psychology, 4,* 387–405.

Berry, D. T. R., Wetter, M. W., Baer, R. A., Larsen, L., Clark, C., & Monroe, K. (1992). MMPI-2 random responding indices: Validation using a self-report methodology. *Psychological Assessment, 4,* 340–345.

Berry, D. T. R., Wetter, M. W., Baer, R. A., Widiger, T. A., Sumpter, J. C., Reynolds, S. K., et al. (1991). Detection of random responding on the MMPI-2: Utility of F, back F and VRIN scales. *Psychological Assessment, 3,* 418–423.

Bertelson, A. D., Marks, P. A., & May, G. D. (1982). MMPI and race: A controlled study. *Journal of Consulting and Clinical Psychology, 50,* 316–318.

Black, K. (1994). A critical review of the MMPI-A. *Child Assessment News, 4,* 9–12.

Blais, M. A. (1995). MCMI-II personality traits associated with the MMPI-2 masculinity-femininity scale. *Assessment, 2,* 131–136.

Blanchard, J. S. (1981). Readability of the MMPI. *Perceptual and Motor Skills, 52,* 985–986.

Blos, P. (1962). *On adolescence: A psychoanalytic interpretation.* New York: The Free Press.

Blos, P. (1967). The second individuation process of adolescence. *Psychoanalytic Study of the Child, 22,* 162–186.

Boccaccini, M. T., & Brodsky, S. L. (1999). Diagnostic test use by forensic psychologists in emotional injury cases. *Professional Psychology, 30,* 253–259.

Bolinskey, P. K., Arnau, R. C., Archer, R. P., & Handel, R. W. (2004). A replication of the MMPI-A PSY-5 scales and development of facet subscales. *Assessment, 11,* 40–48.

Bond, J. A. (1986). Inconsistent responding to repeated MMPI items: Is its major cause really carelessness? *Journal of Personality Assessment, 50,* 50–64.

Bonfilio, S. A., & Lyman, R. D. (1981). Ability to simulate normalcy as a function of differential psychopathology. *Psychological Reports, 49,* 15–21.

Boone, D. (1994). Reliability of the MMPI-2 subtle and obvious scales with psychiatric inpatients. *Journal of Personality Assessment, 62,* 346–351.

Boone, D. (1995). Differential validity of the MMPI-2 subtle and obvious scales with psychiatric inpatients: Scale 2. *Journal of Clinical Psychology, 51,* 526–531.

Brandenburg, N. A., Friedman, R. M., & Silver, S. E. (1989). The epidemiology of childhood psychiatric disorders: Prevalence findings from recent studies. *Journal of the American Academy of Child and Adolescent Psychiatry, 29,* 76–83.

Brauer, B. A. (1992). The signer effect on MMPI performance of deaf respondents. *Journal of Personality Assessment, 58,* 380–388.

Brems, C., & Johnson, M. E. (1991). Subtle-obvious scales of the MMPI: Indicators of profile validity in a psychiatric population. *Journal of Personality Assessment, 56,* 536–544.

Breton, J. J., Bergeron, L., Valla, J. P., Berthiaume, C., Gaudet, N., Lambert, J., et al. (1999). Quebec child mental health survey: Prevalence of *DSM–III–R* mental health disorders. *Journal of Child Psychology and Psychiatryand Allied Disciplines, 40,* 375–384.

Briggs, P. F., Wirt, R. D., & Johnson, R. (1961). An application of prediction tables to the study of delinquency. *Journal of Consulting Psychology, 25,* 46–50.

Buechley, R., & Ball, H. (1952). A new test of "validity" for the group MMPI. *Journal of Consulting Psychology, 16,* 299–301.

Burke, K. C., Burke, J. D., Regier, D. A., & Rae, D. S. (1990). Age at onset of selected mental disorders in five community populations. *Archives of General Psychiatry, 47,* 511–518.

Butcher, J. N. (1985). Why MMPI short forms should not be used for clinical predictions. In J. N. Butcher & J. R. Graham (Eds.), *Clinical applications of the MMPI* (pp. 10–11). Minneapolis: University of Minnesota Department of Conferences.

Butcher, J. N. (1987a). Computerized clinical and personality assessment using the MMPI. In J. N. Butcher (Ed.), *Computerized psychological assessment: A practitioner's guide* (pp. 161–197). New York: Basic Books.

Butcher, J. N. (Ed.). (1987b). *Computerized psychological assessment: A practitioner's guide.* New York: Basic Books.

Butcher, J. N. (1990). *MMPI-2 in psychological treatment.* New York: Oxford University Press.

Butcher, J. N. (Ed.). (1996). *International adaptations of the MMPI-2: A handbook of research and clinical applications.* Minneapolis: University of Minnesota Press.

Butcher, J. N., Dahlstrom, W. G., Graham, J. R., Tellegen, A., & Kaemmer, B. (1989). *Minnesota Multiphasic Personality Inventory-2 (MMPI-2): Manual for administration and scoring.* Minneapolis: University of Minnesota Press.

Butcher, J. N., Graham, J. R., & Ben-Porath, Y. S. (1995). Methodological problems and issues in MMPI, MMPI-2, and MMPI-A research. *Psychological Assessment, 7,* 320–329.

Butcher, J. N., Graham, J. R., Ben-Porath, Y. S., Tellegen, A., Dahlstrom, W. G., & Kaemmer, B. (2001). *Minnesota Multiphasic Personality Inventory-2 (MMPI-2): Manual for administration, scoring, and interpretation* (rev. ed.). Minneapolis: University of Minnesota Press.

Butcher, J. N., Graham, J. R., Williams, C. L., & Ben-Porath, Y. S. (1990). *Development and use of the MMPI-2 content scales.* Minneapolis: University of Minnesota Press.

Butcher, J. N., & Hostetler, K. (1990). Abbreviating MMPI item administration: What can be learned from the MMPI for the MMPI-2? *Psychological Assessment, 2,* 12–21.

Butcher, J. N., & Owen, P. L. (1978). Objective personality inventories: Recent research and some contemporary issues. In B. B. Wolman (Ed.), *Clinical diagnosis of mental disorders: A handbook* (pp. 475–545). New York: Plenum.

Butcher, J. N., Perry, J. N., & Atlis, M. M. (2000). Validity and utility of computer-based test interpretation. *Psychological Assessment, 12,* 6–18.

Butcher, J. N., & Tellegen, A. (1978). Common methodological problems in MMPI research. *Journal of Consulting and Clinical Psychology, 46,* 620–628.

Butcher, J. N., & Williams, C. L. (1992). The Minnesota Report: Adolescent Interpretive System [Computer software]. Minneapolis: National Computer Systems.

Butcher, J. N., & Williams, C. L. (2000). *Essentials of MMPI-2 and MMPI-A interpretation* (2nd ed.). Minneapolis: University of Minnesota Press.

Butcher, J. N., Williams, C. L., Graham, J. R., Archer, R. P., Tellegen, A., Ben-Porath, Y. S., et al. (1992). *MMPI-A (Minnesota Multiphasic Personality Inventory-Adolescent): Manual for administration, scoring, and interpretation.* Minneapolis: University of Minnesota Press.

Caldwell, A. B. (1969). *MMPI critical items.* Unpublished mimeograph. (Available from Caldwell Report, 1545 Sawtelle Boulevard, Ste. 14, Los Angeles, CA 90025.)

Caldwell, A. B. (1971, April). *Recent advances in automated interpretation of the MMPI.* Paper presented at the sixth annual MMPI Symposium, Minneapolis.

Caldwell, A. B. (1976, January). *MMPI profile types.* Paper presented at the eleventh annual MMPI Workshop and Symposium, Minneapolis.

Caldwell, A. B. (1977a). *Questions people ask when taking the MMPI.* (Special Bulletin No. 3, available from Caldwell Report, 1545 Sawtelle Blvd., Ste. 14, Los Angeles, CA 90025.)

Caldwell, A. B. (1977b, February). *Treatment recommendations for patients with different MMPI types.* Paper presented at the twelfth annual MMPI Workshop and Symposium, St. Petersburg Beach, FL.

Caldwell, A. B. (1988). *MMPI supplemental scale manual:* Caldwell Report. Los Angeles.

Caldwell, A. B. (2001). What do the MMPI scales fundamentally measure? Some hypotheses. *Journal of Personality Assessment, 76,* 1–17.

Calvin, J. (1975). *A replicated study of the concurrent validity of the Harris subscales for the MMPI.* Unpublished doctoral dissertation, Kent State University, Kent, OH.

Cantwell, D. P., Lewinsohn, P. M., Rohde, P., & Seeley, J. R. (1997). Correspondence between adolescent report and parent report of psychiatric diagnostic data. *Journal of the American Academy of Child and Adolescent Psychiatry, 36*, 610–619.

Capwell, D. F. (1945a). Personality patterns of adolescent girls: I. Girls who show improvement in IQ. *Journal of Applied Psychology, 29*, 212–228.

Capwell, D. F. (1945b). Personality patterns of adolescent girls: II. Delinquents and nondelinquents. *Journal of Applied Psychology, 29*, 284–297.

Cashel, M. L., Ovaert, L., & Holliman, N. G. (2000). Evaluating PTSD in incarcerated male juveniles with the MMPI-A: An exploratory analysis. *Journal of Clinical Psychology, 56*, 1535–1549.

Cashel, M. L., Rogers, R., Sewell, K. W., & Holliman, N. G. (1998). Preliminary validation of the MMPI-A for a male delinquent sample: An investigation of clinical correlates and discriminant validity. *Journal of Personality Assessment, 71*, 46–69.

Center for Disease Control and Prevention. (1999). *Suicide deaths and rates per 100,000.* Available: http://www.cdc.gov/ncipc/data/us9794/suic.htm.

Cheung, F. M., & Ho, R. M. (1997). Standardization of the Chinese MMPI-A in Hong Kong: A preliminary study. *Psychological Assessment, 9*, 499–502.

Cheung, F. M., Song, W., & Butcher, J. N. (1991). An infrequency scale for the Chinese MMPI. *Psychological Assessment, 3*, 648–653.

Clark, M. E. (1994). Interpretive limitations of the MMPI-2 anger and cynicism content scales. *Journal of Personality Assessment, 63*, 89–96.

Clavelle, P. R. (1992). Clinicians' perceptions of the comparability of the MMPI and MMPI-2. *Psychological Assessment, 4*, 466–472.

Clopton, J. R. (1978). MMPI scale development methodology. *Journal of Personality Assessment, 42*, 148–151.

Clopton, J. R. (1979). Development of special MMPI scales. In C. S. Newmark (Ed.), *MMPI: Clinical and research trends* (pp. 354–372). New York: Praeger.

Clopton, J. R. (1982). MMPI scale development methodology reconsidered. *Journal of Personality Assessment, 46*, 143–146.

Clopton, J. R., & Neuringer, C. (1977). MMPI Cannot Say scores: Normative data and degree of profile distortion. *Journal of Personality Assessment, 41*, 511–513.

Cohn, L. D. (1991). Sex differences in the course of personality development: A meta-analysis. *Psychological Bulletin, 109*, 252–266.

Colligan, R. C. (Chair). (1988, August). *MMPI subscales and profile interpretation: Harris and Lingoes revisited.* Symposium conducted at the annual convention of the American Psychological Association, Atlanta.

Colligan, R. C., & Offord, K. P. (1989). The aging MMPI: Contemporary norms for contemporary teenagers. *Mayo Clinic Proceedings, 64*, 3–27.

Colligan, R. C., & Offord, K. P. (1991). Adolescents, the MMPI, and the issue of K-correction: A contemporary normative study. *Journal of Clinical Psychology, 47*, 607–631.

Colligan, R. C., & Offord, K. P. (1992). Age, stage, and the MMPI: Changes in response patterns over an 85-year age span. *Journal of Clinical Psychology, 48*, 476–493.

Colligan, R. C., & Osborne, D. (1977). MMPI profiles from adolescent medical patients. *Journal of Clinical Psychology, 33*, 186–189.

Colligan, R. C., Osborne, D., & Offord, K. P. (1980). Linear transformation and the interpretation of MMPI T-scores. *Journal of Clinical Psychology, 36*, 162–165.

Colligan, R. C., Osborne, D., & Offord, K. P. (1984). Normalized transformations and the interpretation of MMPI T-scores: A reply to Hsu. *Journal of Consulting and Clinical Psychology, 52*, 824–826.

Colligan, R. C., Osborne, D., Swenson, W. M., & Offord, K. P. (1983). *The MMPI: A contemporary normative study.* New York: Praeger.

Committee on Ethical Guidelines for Forensic Psychologists. (1991). Specialty guidelines for forensic psychologists. *Law and Human Behavior, 15*, 655–665.

Corrales, M. L., Cabiya, J. J., Gomes, F., Ayala, G. X., Mendoza, S., & Velasquez, R. J. (1998). MMPI-2 and MMPI-A research with U.S. Latinos: A bibliography. *Psychological Reports, 83*, 1027–1033.

Costello, E. J., Angold, A., Borns, B. J., Stangl, D. K., Tweed, D. L., Erkanli, A., et al. (1996). The Great Smokey Mountain Study of Youth: Goals, design, methods, and the prevalence of DSM–III–R disorders. *Archives of General Psychiatry, 53*, 1129–1137.

Cumella, E. J., Wall, A. D., & Kerr-Almeida, N. (1999). MMPI-A in the inpatient assessment of adolescents with eating disorders. *Journal of Personality Assessment, 73*, 31–44.

Dahlstrom, W. G. (1992). Comparability of two-point high-point code patterns from original MMPI norms to MMPI-2 norms for the restandardization sample. *Journal of Personality Assessment, 59*, 153–164.

Dahlstrom, W. G., Archer, R. P., Hopkins, D. G., Jackson, E., & Dahlstrom, L. E. (1994). *Assessing the readability of the Minnesota Multiphasic Personality Inventory instruments—the MMPI, MMPI-2, MMPI-A* (MMPI-2/MMPI-A Test Report No. 2). Minneapolis: University of Minnesota Press.

Dahlstrom, W. G., & Dahlstrom, L. E. (Eds.). (1980). *Basic readings on the MMPI: A new selection on personality measurement.* Minneapolis: University of Minnesota Press.

Dahlstrom, W. G., Lachar, D., & Dahlstrom, L. E. (1986). *MMPI patterns of American minorities.* Minneapolis: University of Minnesota Press.

Dahlstrom, W. G., & Welsh, G. S. (1960). *An MMPI handbook: A guide to use in clinical practice and research.* Minneapolis: University of Minnesota Press.

Dahlstrom, W. G., Welsh, G. S., & Dahlstrom, L. E. (1972). *An MMPI handbook: Vol. I. Clinical interpretation* (rev. ed.). Minneapolis: University of Minnesota Press.

Dahlstrom, W. G., Welsh, G. S., & Dahlstrom, L. E. (1975). *An MMPI handbook: Vol. II. Research applications* (rev. ed.). Minneapolis: University of Minnesota Press.

Dannenbaum, S. E., & Lanyon, R. I. (1993). The use of subtle items in detecting deception. *Journal of Personality Assessment, 61,* 501–510.

Dawson, R. (2000). Judicial waiver in theory and practice. In J. Fagan & F. Zimring (Eds.), *The changing borders of juvenile justice: Transfer of adolescents to the criminal court* (pp. 45–82). Chicago: University of Chicago Press.

Dodrill, C. B., & Clemmons, D. (1984). Use of neuropsychological tests to identify high school students with epilepsy who later demonstrate inadequate performances in life. *Journal of Consulting and Clinical Psychology, 52,* 520–527.

Drake, L. E. (1946). A social I-E scale for the MMPI. *Journal of Applied Psychology, 30,* 51–54.

Drowns, R., & Hess, K. (2000). *Juvenile justice* (3rd. ed.). Stamford, CT: Wadsworth.

Dusky v. U.S., 362 U.S. 402 (1960).

Edens, J. F., Skeem, J. L., Cruise, K. R., & Cauffman, E. (2001). Assessment of juvenile psychopathy and its association with violence: A critical review. *Behavioral Sciences and the Law, 19,* 53–80.

Edwards, D. W., Morrison, T. L., & Weissman, H. N. (1993a). The MMPI and MMPI-2 in an outpatient sample: Comparisons of code types, validity scales, and clinical scales. *Journal of Personality Assessment, 61,* 1–18.

Edwards, D. W., Morrison, T. L., & Weissman, H. N. (1993b). Uniform versus linear T-scores on the MMPI-2/MMPI in an outpatient psychiatric sample: Differential contributions. *Psychological Assessment, 5,* 499–500.

Ehrenworth, N. V. (1984). *A comparison of the utility of interpretive approaches with adolescent MMPI profiles.* Unpublished doctoral dissertation, Virginia Consortium for Professional Psychology, Norfolk, VA.

Ehrenworth, N. V., & Archer, R. P. (1985). A comparison of clinical accuracy ratings of interpretive approaches for adolescent MMPI responses. *Journal of Personality Assessment, 49,* 413–421.

Elkind, D. (1978). Understanding the young adolescent. *Adolescence, 13,* 127–134.

Elkind, D. (1980). Egocentrism in adolescence. In R. E. Muuss (Ed.), *Adolescent behavior and society: A book of readings* (3rd ed., pp. 79–88). New York: Random House.

Elkind, D., & Bowen, R. (1979). Imaginary audience behavior in children and adolescents. *Developmental Psychology, 15,* 38–44.

Erikson, E. H. (1956). The concept of ego identity. *Journal of the American Psychoanalytic Association, 4,* 56–121.

Espelage, D. L., Cauffman, E., Broidy, L., Piquero, A. R., Mazzerolle, P., & Steiner, H. (2003). A cluster-analytic investigation of MMPI profiles of serious male and female juvenile offenders. *Journal of the American Adacemy of Child and Adolescent Psychiatry, 42,* 770–777.

Exner, J. E., Jr. (1993). *The Rorschach: A comprehensive system: Vol. 1. Basic foundations* (3rd ed.). New York: Wiley.

Exner, J. E., Jr., McDowell, E., Pabst, J., Stackman, W., & Kirk, L. (1963). On the detection of willful falsifications in the MMPI. *Journal of Consulting Psychology, 27,* 91–94.

Exner, J. E., Jr., & Weiner, I. B. (1982). *The Rorschach: A comprehensive system: Vol. 3. Assessment of children and adolescents.* New York: Wiley.

Finlay, S. W., & Kapes, J. T. (2000). Scale 5 of the MMPI and MMPI-2: Evidence of disparity. *Assessment, 7,* 97–101.

Finn, S. E. (1996). *Manual for using the MMPI-2 as a therapeutic intervention.* Minneapolis: University of Minnesota Press.

Finn, S. E., & Tonsager, M. E. (1992). Therapeutic effects of providing MMPI-2 test feedback to college students awaiting therapy. *Psychological Assessment, 4,* 278–287.

Flesch, R. (1948). A new readability yardstick. *Journal of Applied Psychology, 32,* 221–233.

Foerstner, S. B. (1986). *The factor structure and factor stability of selected Minnesota Multiphasic Personality Inventory (MMPI) subscales: Harris and Lingoes subscales, Wiggins content scales, Wiener subscales, and Serkownek subscales.* Unpublished doctoral dissertation, University of Akron, Akron, OH.

Fontaine, J. L., Archer, R. P., Elkins, D. E., & Johansen, J. (2001). The effects of MMPI-A T-score elevation on classification accuracy for normal and clinical adolescent samples. *Journal of Personality Assessment, 76,* 264–281.

Forbey, J. D. (2003, June). *A review of the MMPI-A research literature.* Paper presented at the 38th Annual Symposium on Recent Developments in the Use of the MMPI-2 and MMPI-A, Minneapolis.

Forbey, J. D., & Ben-Porath, Y. S. (1998). *A critical item set for the MMPI-A* (MMPI-2/MMPI-A Test Report No. 4). Minneapolis: University of Minnesota Press.

Forbey, J. D., & Ben-Porath, Y. S. (2000). A comparison of sexually abused and non-sexually abused adolescents in a clinical treatment facility using the MMPI-A. *Child Abuse and Neglect, 24,* 557–568.

Forbey, J. D., & Ben-Porath, Y. S. (2003). Incremental validity of the MMPI-A content scales in a residential treatment facility. *Assessment, 10,* 191–202.

Forbey, J. D., Handel, R. W., & Ben-Porath, Y. S. (2000). Real data simulation of computerized adaptive administration of the MMPI-A. *Computers in Human Behavior, 16,* 83–96.

Forth, A. E., & Burke, H. C. (1998). Psychopathology and adolescence: Assessment, violence, and developmental precursors. In D. H. Cooke, A. E. Forth, & R. D. Hare (Eds.), *Psychopathy: Theory, research, and implications for society* (pp. 205–229). Boston: Kluwer Academic.

Forth, A. E., & Kosson, D. S., & Hare, R. D. (1996). Psychopathy Checklist: Youth Version. Toronto: Multihealth Systems.

Fowler, R. D. (1964, September). *Computer processing and reporting of personality test data.* Paper presented at the annual meeting of the American Psychological Association, Los Angeles.

Fowler, R. D. (1985). Landmarks in computer-assisted psychological assessment. *Journal of Consulting and Clinical Psychology, 53,* 748–759.

Frederick, C. (1985). Selected foci in the spectrum of posttraumatic stress disorders. In J. Lauve & S. Murphy (Eds.), *Perspectives on disaster recovery* (pp. 110–130). East Norwalk, CT: Appleton-Century-Crofts.

Freud, A. (1958). Adolescence. *Psychoanalytic Study of the Child, 13,* 255–278.

Frick, P., O'Brien, H., Wootton, J., & McBurnett, K. (1994). Psychopathy and conduct problems in children. *Journal of Abnormal Psychology, 103,* 700–707.

Friedman, A., Archer, R. P., & Handel, R. W. (2004). The MMPI/MMPI-2, MMPI-A and suicide. In R. Yufit & D. Lester (Eds.), *Assessment, treatment, and prevention of suicidal behavior.* New York: Wiley.

Friedman, A. F., Lewak, R., Nichols, D. S., & Webb, J. T. (2001). *Psychological assessment with the MMPI-2.* Mahwah, NJ: Lawrence Erlbaum Associates.

Friedman, A. F., Webb, J. T., & Lewak, R. (1989). *Psychological assessment with the MMPI.* Hillsdale, NJ: Lawrence Erlbaum Associates.

Friedman, J. M. H., Asnis, G. M., Boeck, M., & DiFiore, J. (1987). Prevalence of specific suicidal behaviors in a high school sample. *American Journal of Psychiatry, 144,* 1203–1206.

Gallucci, N. T. (1994). Criteria associated with clinical scales and Harris-Lingoes subscales of the Minnesota Multiphasic Personality Inventory with adolescent inpatients. *Psychological Assessment, 6,* 179–187.

Gallucci, N. T. (1997a). Correlates of MMPI-A substance abuse scales. *Assessment, 4,* 87–94.

Gallucci, N. T. (1997b). On the identification of patterns of substance abuse with the MMPI-A. *Psychological Assessment, 3,* 224–232.

Ganellen, R. J. (1994). Attempting to conceal psychological disturbance: MMPI defensive response sets and the Rorschach. *Journal of Personality Assessment, 63,* 423–437.

Gantner, A., Graham, J., & Archer, R. P. (1992). Usefulness of the *MAC* scale in differentiating adolescents in normal, psychiatric, and substance abuse settings. *Psychological Assessment, 4,* 133–137.

Gilberstadt, H., & Duker, J. (1965). *A handbook for clinical and actuarial MMPI interpretation.* Philadelphia: Saunders.

Glaser, B. A., Calhoun, G. B., & Petrocelli, J. V. (2002). Personality characteristics of male juvenile offenders by adjudicated offenses as indicated by the MMPI-A. *Criminal Justice and Behavior, 29,* 183–201.

Gocka, E. F., & Holloway, H. (1963). *Normative and predictive data on the Harris and Lingoes subscales for a neuropsychiatric population* (Rep. No. 7). American Lake, WA: Veterans Administration Hospital.

Godwin, C. D., & Helms, J. L. (2002). Statistics and trends in juvenile justice and forensic psychology. In N. G. Ribner (Ed.), *The California School of Professional Psychology handbook of juvenile forensic psychology* (pp. 3–28). San Francisco: Jossey-Bass.

Goldberg, L. R. (1965). Diagnosticians vs. diagnostic signs: The diagnosis of psychosis vs. neurosis from the MMPI. *Psychological Monographs, 79* (9, Whole No. 602).

Goldberg, L. R. (1972). Man vs. mean: The exploitation of group profiles for the construction of diagnostic classification systems. *Journal of Abnormal Psychology, 79,* 121–131.

Goldman, V. J., Cooke, A., & Dahlstrom, W. G. (1995). Black-White differences among college students: A comparison of MMPI and MMPI-2 norms. *Assessment, 2,* 293–299.

Gomez, F. C., Johnson, R., Davis, Q., & Velasquez, R. J. (2000). MMPI-A performance of African and Mexican American adolescent first-time offenders. *Psychological Reports, 87,* 309–314.

Gottesman, I. I., & Hanson, D. R. (1990, August). Can the MMPI at age 15 predict schizophrenics-to-be? In R. C. Colligan (Chair), *The MMPI and adolescents: Historical perspective, current research, future developments.* Symposium conducted at the annual convention of the American Psychological Association, Boston.

Gottesman, I. I., Hanson, D. R., Kroeker, T. A., & Briggs, P. F. (1987). New MMPI normative data and power-transformed T-score tables for the Hathaway-Monachesi Minnesota cohort of 14,019 fifteen-year-olds and 3,674 eighteen-year-olds. In R. P. Archer, *Using the MMPI with adolescents* (pp. 241–297). Hillsdale, NJ: Lawrence Erlbaum Associates.

Gottesman, I. I., & Prescott, C. A. (1989). Abuses of the MacAndrew Alcoholism scale: A critical review. *Clinical Psychology Review, 9,* 223–242.

Gough, H. G. (1947). Simulated patterns on the MMPI. *Journal of Abnormal and Social Psychology, 42,* 215–225.

Gough, H. G. (1954). Some common misconceptions about neuroticism. *Journal of Consulting Psychology, 18,* 287–292.

Gould, M. S., Wunsch-Hitzig, R., & Dohrenwend, B. (1981). Estimating the prevalence of child psychopathology: A critical review. *Journal of the American Academy of Child Psychiatry, 20,* 462–476.

Graham, J. R. (1987). *The MMPI: A practical guide* (2nd ed.). New York: Oxford University Press.

Graham, J. R. (2000). *MMPI-2: Assessing personality and psychopathology* (3rd ed.). New York: Oxford University Press.

Graham, J. R., Ben-Porath, Y. S., & McNulty, J. L. (1999). *MMPI-2 correlates for outpatient community mental health settings.* Minneapolis: University of Minnesota Press.

Graham, J. R., Schroeder, H. E., & Lilly, R. S. (1971). Factor analysis of items on the Social Introversion and Masculinity-Femininity scales of the MMPI. *Journal of Clinical Psychology, 27,* 367–370.

Graham, J. R., Timbrook, R. E., Ben-Porath, Y. S., & Butcher, J. N. (1991). Code-type congruence between MMPI and MMPI-2: Separating fact from artifact. *Journal of Personality Assessment, 57,* 205–215.

Graham, J. R., Watts, D., & Timbrook, R. E. (1991). Detecting fake-good and fake-bad MMPI-2 profiles. *Journal of Personality Assessment, 57,* 264–277.

Graham, P., & Rutter, M. (1985). Adolescent disorders. In M. Rutter & L. Hovsov (Eds.), *Child and adolescent psychiatry: Modern approaches* (pp. 351–367). Oxford: Blackwell.

Gray, W. S., & Robinson, H. M. (1963). *Gray Oral Reading Test.* Indianapolis, IN: Bobbs-Merrill.

Grayson, H. M. (1951). *A psychological admissions testing program and manual.* Los Angeles: Veterans Administration Center, Neuropsychiatric Hospital.

Grayson, H. M., & Olinger, L. B. (1957). Simulation of "normalcy" by psychiatric patients on the MMPI. *Journal of Consulting Psychology, 21,* 73–77.

Green, S. B., & Kelley, C. K. (1988). Racial bias in prediction with the MMPI for a juvenile delinquent population. *Journal of Personality Assessment, 52,* 263–275.

Greenberg, S. A., Otto, R. K., & Long, A. C. (2003). The utility of psychological testing in assessing emotional damages in personal injury litigation. *Assessment, 10,* 411–419.

Greene, R. L. (1978). An empirically derived MMPI carelessness scale. *Journal of Clinical Psychology, 34,* 407–410.

Greene, R. L. (1979). Response consistency on the MMPI: The *TR* Index. *Journal of Personality Assessment, 43,* 69–71.

Greene, R. L. (1980). *The MMPI: An interpretive manual.* Boston: Allyn & Bacon.

Greene, R. L. (1982). Some reflections on "MMPI short forms: A literature review." *Journal of Personality Assessment, 46,* 486–487.

Greene, R. L. (1987). Ethnicity and MMPI performance: A review. *Journal of Consulting and Clinical Psychology, 55,* 497–512.

Greene, R. L. (1988). Introduction. In R. L. Greene (Ed.), *The MMPI: Use with specific populations* (pp. 1–21). San Antonio, TX: Grune & Stratton.

Greene, R. L. (1989a). *Assessing the validity of MMPI profiles in clinical settings* (Clinical Notes on the MMPI, No. 11). Minneapolis: National Computer Systems.

Greene, R. L. (1989b). MMPI Adult Interpretive System [Computer software]. Odessa, FL: Psychological Assessment Resources.

Greene, R. L. (1991). *The MMPI-2/MMPI: An interpretive manual.* Boston: Allyn & Bacon.

Greene, R. L. (1994). Relationships among MMPI codetype, gender, and setting in the MacAndrew Alcoholism Scale. *Assessment, 1,* 39–46.

Greene, R. L. (1998). MMPI-2 Adult Interpretive System (Version 2) [Computer software] Odessa, FL: Psychological Assessment Resources.

Greene, R. L. (2000). *MMPI-2: An interpretive manual* (2nd ed.). Boston: Allyn & Bacon.

Greene, R. L., Arredondo, R., & Davis, H. G. (1990, August). *The comparability between the MacAndrew Alcoholism Scale–Revised (MMPI-2) and the MacAndrew Alcoholism Scale (MMPI).* Paper presented at the annual meeting of the American Psychological Association, Boston.

Greene, R. L., & Garvin, R. D. (1988). Substance abuse/dependence. In R. L. Greene (Ed.), *The MMPI: Use in specific populations* (pp. 157–197). San Antonio, TX: Grune & Stratton.

Grisso, T. (1988). *Competency to stand trial evaluations: A manual for practice.* Sarasota, FL: Professional Resources Press.

Grisso, T. (1997). The competence of adolescents as trial defendants. *Psychology, Public Policy, and the Law, 3,* 3–32.

Grisso, T. (1998). *Forensic evaluation of juveniles.* Sarasota, FL: Professional Resources Press.

Grisso, T. (2003). *Evaluating competencies, forensic assessments and instruments* (2nd. ed.). New York: Kluwer/Plenum.

Grisso, T., & Barnum, R. (1998). *Massachusetts Youth Screening Instrument: User's manual and technical report.* Sarasota, FL: Professional Resources Press.

Grisso, T., & Barnum, R. (2003). *Massachusetts Youth Screening Instrument: Version 2: User's manual and technical report.* Sarasota, FL: Professional Resources Press.

Grisso, T., Barnum, R., Fletcher, K. E., Cauffman, E., & Peuschold, D. (2001). Massachusetts Youth Screening Instrument for mental health needs for juvenile justice youths. *Journal of the American Academy of Child and Adolescent Psychiatry, 40,* 541–548.

Grossman, H. Y., Mostofsky, D. I., & Harrison, R. H. (1986). Psychological aspects of Gilles de la Tourette Syndrome. *Journal of Clinical Psychology, 42,* 228–235.

Groth-Marnat, G. (2003). *Handbook of psychological assessment* (4th ed.). New York: Wiley.

Groth-Marnat, G., & Schumaker, J. (1989). Computer-based psychological testing: Issues and guidelines. *American Journal of Orthopsychiatry, 59,* 257–263.

Gumbiner, J. (1997). Comparison of scores on the MMPI-A and the MMPI-2 for young adults. *Psychological Reports, 81,* 787–794.

Gumbiner, J. (1998). MMPI-A profiles of Hispanic adolescents. *Psychological Reports, 82,* 659–672.

Gumbiner, J. (2000). Limitations in ethnic research on the MMPI-A. *Psychological Reports, 87,* 1229–1230.

Gynther, M. D. (1972). White norms and Black MMPIs: A prescription for discrimination? *Psychological Bulletin, 78,* 386–402.

Gynther, M. D. (1989). MMPI comparisons of Blacks and Whites: A review and commentary. *Journal of Clinical Psychology, 45,* 878–883.

Hafner, A. J., Butcher, J. N., Hall, M. D., & Quast, W. (1969). Parent personality and childhood disorders: A review of MMPI findings. In J. N. Butcher (Ed.), *MMPI: Research developments and clinical applications* (pp. 181–189). New York: McGraw-Hill.

Hall, G. S. (1904). *Adolescence: Its psychology and its relationship to physiology, anthropology, sociology, sex, crime, religion, and education.* New York: Appleton.

Hanson, D. R., Gottesman, I. I., & Heston, L. L. (1990). Long-range schizophrenia forecasting: Many a slip twixt cup and lip. In J. E. Rolf, A. Masten, D. Cicchetti, K. Neuchterlein, & S. Weintraub (Eds.), *Risk and protective factors in the development of psychopathology* (pp. 424–444). New York: Cambridge University Press.

Hare, R. D. (1991). *The Hare Psychopathy Checklist–Revised.* Toronto: Multi-Health Systems.

Hare, R., Forth, A., & Kosson, D. (1994). *The Psychopathy Checklist: Youth Version* (Research version). Toronto: Multihealth Systems.

Harkness, A. R., & McNulty, J. L. (1994). The Personality Psychopathology Five (PSY-5): Issues from the pages of a diagnostic manual instead of a dictionary. In S. Strack & M. Lorr (Eds.), *Differentiating normal and abnormal personality* (pp. 291–315). New York: Springer.

Harkness, A. R., McNulty., J. L., & Ben-Porath, Y. S. (1995). The Personality Psychopathology Five (PSY-5): Constructs and MMPI-2 scales. *Psychological Assessment, 7,* 104–114.

Harkness, A. R., McNulty, J. L., Ben-Porath, Y. S., & Graham, J. S. (2002). *5: MMPI-2 Personality Psychopathology Five (PSY-5) scales: Gaining an overview for case conceptualization and treatment planning* (MMPI-2/MMPI-A Test Report). Minneapolis: University of Minnesota Press.

Harms, P. (2003, September). *Detention in delinquency cases, 1990–1999* (Fact sheet). Washington, DC: U.S. Department of Justice, Office of Juvenile Justice and Delinquency Prevention.

Harper, D. C. (1983). Personality correlates and degree of impairment in male adolescents with progressive and nonprogressive physical disorders. *Journal of Clinical Psychology, 39,* 859–867.

Harper, D. C., & Richman, L. C. (1978). Personality profiles of physically impaired adolescents. *Journal of Clinical Psychology, 34,* 636–642.

Harrell, T. H., Honaker, L. M., & Parnell, T. (1992). Equivalence of the MMPI-2 with the MMPI in psychiatric patients. *Psychological Assessment, 4,* 460–465.

Harris, R. E., & Christiansen, C. (1946). Prediction of response to brief psychotherapy. *Journal of Psychology, 21,* 269–284.

Harris, R. E., & Lingoes, J. C. (1955). *Subscales for the MMPI: An aid to profile interpretation.* Department of Psychiatry, University of California School of Medicine and the Langley Porter Clinic. Mimeographed materials.

Hart, S. D., Watt, K. A., & Vincent, G. M. (2002). Commentary on Seagrave and Grisso: Impressions on the state of the art. *Law and Behavior, 26*, 241–245.

Hathaway, S. R. (1939). The personality inventory as an aid in the diagnosis of psychopathic inferiors. *Journal of Consulting Psychology, 3*, 112–117.

Hathaway, S. R. (1947). A coding system for MMPI profiles. *Journal of Consulting Psychology, 11*, 334–337.

Hathaway, S. R. (1956). Scales 5 (Masculinity-Femininity), 6 (Paranoia), and 8 (Schizophrenia). In G. S. Welsh & W. G. Dahlstrom (Eds.), *Basic readings on the MMPI in psychology and medicine* (pp. 104–111). Minneapolis: University of Minnesota Press.

Hathaway, S. R. (1964). MMPI: Professional use by professional people. *American Psychologist, 19*, 204–210.

Hathaway, S. R. (1965). Personality inventories. In B. B. Wolman (Ed.), *Handbook of clinical psychology* (pp. 451–476). New York: McGraw-Hill.

Hathaway, S. R., & Briggs, P. F. (1957). Some normative data on new MMPI scales. *Journal of Clinical Psychology, 13*, 364–368.

Hathaway, S. R., & McKinley, J. C. (1940). A multiphasic personality schedule (Minnesota): I. Construction of the schedule. *Journal of Psychology, 10*, 249–254.

Hathaway, S. R., & McKinley, J. C. (1942). A multiphasic personality schedule (Minnesota): III. The measurement of symptomatic depression. *Journal of Psychology, 14*, 73–84.

Hathaway, S. R., & McKinley, J. C. (1943). *The Minnesota Multiphasic Personality Inventory* (rev. ed.). Minneapolis: University of Minnesota Press.

Hathaway, S. R., & McKinley, J. C. (1967). *Minnesota Multiphasic Personality Inventory manual* (rev. ed.). New York: Psychological Corporation.

Hathaway, S. R., & Monachesi, E. D. (1951). The prediction of juvenile delinquency using the Minnesota Multiphasic Personality Inventory. *American Journal of Psychiatry, 108*, 469–473.

Hathaway, S. R., & Monachesi, E. D. (1952). The Minnesota Multiphasic Personality Inventory in the study of juvenile delinquents. *American Sociological Review, 17*, 704–710.

Hathaway, S. R., & Monachesi, E. D. (Eds.). (1953). *Analyzing and predicting juvenile delinquency with the MMPI.* Minneapolis: University of Minnesota Press.

Hathaway, S. R., & Monachesi, E. D. (1961). *An atlas of juvenile MMPI profiles.* Minneapolis: University of Minnesota Press.

Hathaway, S. R., & Monachesi, E. D. (1963). *Adolescent personality and behavior: MMPI patterns of normal, delinquent, dropout, and other outcomes.* Minneapolis: University of Minnesota Press.

Hathaway, S. R., Monachesi, E. D., & Salasin, S. (1970). A follow-up study of MMPI high 8, schizoid children. In M. Roff & D. F. Ricks (Eds.), *Life history research in psychopathology* (pp. 171–188). Minneapolis: University of Minnesota Press.

Hathaway, S. R., Reynolds, P. C., & Monachesi, E. D. (1969). Follow-up of the later careers and lives of 1,000 boys who dropped out of high school. *Journal of Consulting and Clinical Psychology, 33*, 370–380.

Hedlund, J. L., & Won Cho, D. (1979). [MMPI data research tape for Missouri Department of Mental Health patients]. Unpublished raw data.

Heilbrun, K., Marczyk, G. R., DeMatteo, D., Zillmer, E. A., Harris, J., & Jennings, T. (2003). Principles of forensic mental health assessment: Implications for neuropsychological assessment in forensic contexts. *Assessment, 10*, 329–343.

Herkov, M. J., Archer, R. P., & Gordon, R. A. (1991). MMPI response sets among adolescents: An evaluation of the limitations of the subtle-obvious subscales. *Psychological Assessment, 3*, 424–426.

Herkov, M. J., Gordon, R. A., Gynther, M. D., & Greer, R. A. (1994). Perceptions of MMPI item subtlety: Influences of age and ethnicity. *Journal of Personality Assessment, 62*, 9–16.

Herman-Giddens, M. E., Slora, E. J., Wasserman, R. C., Bourdony, C. J., Bhapkar, M. B., Koch, G. G., et al. (1997). Secondary sexual characteristics and menses in young girls seen in office practice: A study from the Pediatric Research in Office Settings Network. *Pediatrics, 99*, 505–512.

Hicks, M. M., Rogers, R., & Cashel, M. L. (2000). Prediction of violent and total infractions among institutionalized male juvenile offenders. *Journal of the American Academy of Psychiatry and Law, 28*, 183–190.

Hillard, J. R., Slomowitz, M., & Levi, L. S. (1987). A retrospective study of adolescents' visits to a general hospital psychiatric emergency service. *American Journal of Psychiatry, 144*, 432–436.

Hillary, B. E., & Schare, M. L. (1993). Sexually and physically abused adolescents: An empirical search for PTSD. *Journal of Clinical Psychology, 49*, 161–165.

Hilts, D., & Moore, J. M. (2003). Normal range MMPI profiles among psychiatric inpatients. *Assessment, 10*, 266–272.

Hoffmann, A. D., & Greydanus, D. E. (1997). *Adolescent medicine.* Stamford, CT: Appleton & Lange.

Hoffmann, N. G., & Butcher, J. N. (1975). Clinical limitations of three MMPI short forms. *Journal of Consulting and Clinical Psychology, 43*, 32–39.

Hofstra, M. B., Van Der Ende, J., & Verhulst, F. C. (2002). Child and adolescent problems predict DSM-IV disorders in adulthood: A 14-year follow-up of a Dutch epidemiological sample. *Journal of the American Academy of Child & Adolescent Psychiatry, 41*(2), 182–189.

Hollrah, J. L., Schlottmann, R. S., Scott, A. B., & Brunetti, D. G. (1995). Validity of the MMPI subtle scales. *Journal of Personality Assessment, 65*, 278–299.

Holmbeck, G. N., & Updegrove, A. L. (1995). Clinical-development interface: Implications of developmental research for adolescent psychotherapy. *Psychotherapy, 32*, 16–33.

Holt, R. R. (1980). Loevinger's measure of ego development: Reliability and national norms for male and female short forms. *Journal of Personality and Social Psychology, 39*, 909–920.

Honaker, L. M. (1988). The equivalency of computerized and conventional MMPI administration: A critical review. *Clinical Psychology Review, 8*, 561–577.

Honaker, L. M. (1990). MMPI and MMPI-2: Alternate forms or different tests? In M. E. Maruish (Chair), *The MMPI and MMPI-2: Comparability examined from different perspectives.* Symposium conducted at the annual convention of the American Psychological Association, Boston.

Huesmann, L. R., Lefkowitz, M. M., & Eron, L. D. (1978). Sum of MMPI scales *F, 4*, and *9* as a measure of aggression. *Journal of Consulting and Clinical Psychology, 46*, 1071–1078.

Hume, M. P., Kennedy, W. A., Patrick, C. J., & Partyka, D. J. (1996). Examination of the MMPI-A for the assessment of psychopathy in incarcerated adolescent male offenders. *International Journal of Offender Therapy and Comparative Criminology, 40*, 224–233.

Humm, D. G., & Wadsworth, G. W. (1935). The Humm-Wadsworth Temperament Scale. *American Journal of Psychiatry, 92*, 163–200.

Humphrey, D. H., & Dahlstrom, W. G. (1995). The impact of changing from the MMPI to the MMPI-2 on profile configurations. *Journal of Personality Assessment, 64*, 428–439.

Husband, S. D., & Iguchi, M. Y. (1995). Comparison of MMPI-2 and MMPI clinical scales and high-point scores among methadone maintenance patients. *Journal of Personality Assessment, 64*, 371–375.

Imhof, E. A., & Archer, R. P. (1997). Correlates of the MMPI-A Immaturity (IMM) scale in an adolescent psychiatric sample. *Assessment, 5*, 169–179.

In re Gault, 387 U.S. 1 (1967).

Janus, M. D., de Grott, C., & Toepfer, S. M. (1998). The MMPI-A and 13-year-old inpatients: How young is too young? *Assessment, 5*, 321–332.

Janus, M. D., Toepfer, S., Calestro, K., & Tolbert, H. (1996). *Within normal limits profiles and the MMPI-A.* Unpublished manuscript.

Janus, M. D., Tolbert, H., Calestro, K., & Toepfer, S. (1996). Clinical accuracy ratings of MMPI approaches for adolescents: Adding ten years and the MMPI-A. *Journal of Personality Assessment, 67*, 364–383.

Jastak, S., & Wilkinson, G. S. (1984). *Wide Range Achievement Test–Revised.* Wilmington, DE: Jastak Associates.

Johnson, R. H., & Bond, G. L. (1950). Reading ease of commonly used tests. *Journal of Applied Psychology, 34*, 319–324.

Kaplowitz, P. B., & Oberfield, S. E. (1999). Reexamination of the age limit for defining when puberty is precocious in girls in the United States: Implications for evaluation and treatment. *Pediatrics, 104*, 936–941.

Kaser-Boyd, N. (2002). Children who kill. In N. G. Ribner (Ed.), *The California School of Professional Psychology Handbook of Juvenile Forensic Psychology.* (pp. 195–229). San Francisco: Jossey-Bass.

Kashani, J. H., Beck, N., Hoeper, E. W., Fallahi, C., Corcoran, C. M., McAllister, J. A., et al. (1987). Psychiatric disorders in a community sample of adolescents. *American Journal of Psychiatry, 144*, 584–589.

Kashani, J. H., & Orvaschel, H. (1988). Anxiety disorders in mid-adolescence: A community sample. *American Journal of Psychiatry, 145*, 960–964.

Katz, R. C., & Marquette, J. (1996). Psychosocial characteristics of young violent offenders: A comparative study. *Criminal Behaviour and Mental Health, 6*, 339–348.

Kazdin, A. E. (2000). Adolescent development, mental disorders, and decision making of delinquent youths. In P. Grisso & R. G. Schwartz (Eds.), *Youth on trial: A developmental perspective on juvenile justice* (pp. 33–65). Chicago: University of Chicago Press.

Keilin, W. G., & Bloom, L. J. (1986). Child custody evaluation practices: A survey of experienced professionals. *Professional Psychology, 17*, 338–346.

Kelley, C. K., & King, G. D. (1979). Cross-validation of the 2-8/8-2 MMPI codetype for young adult psychiatric outpatients. *Journal of Personality Assessment, 43*, 143–149.

Kent v. U.S., 383 U.S. 541 (1966).

Kimmel, D. C., & Weiner, I. B. (1985). *Adolescence: A developmental transition.* Hillsdale, NJ: Lawrence Erlbaum Associates.

Kincannon, J. C. (1968). Prediction of the standard MMPI scale scores from 71 items: The Mini-Mult. *Journal of Consulting and Clinical Psychology, 32*, 319–325.

King, G. D., & Kelley, C. K. (1977). MMPI behavioral correlates of spike-5 and two-point codetypes with scale 5 as one elevation. *Journal of Clinical Psychology, 33*, 180–185.

Klinefelter, D., Pancoast, D. L., Archer, R. P., & Pruitt, D. L. (1990). Recent adolescent MMPI norms: T-score elevation comparisons to Marks and Briggs. *Journal of Personality Assessment, 54*, 379–389.

Klinge, V., Lachar, D., Grissell, J., & Berman, W. (1978). Effects of scoring norms on adolescent psychiatric drug users' and nonusers' MMPI profiles. *Adolescence, 13*, 1–11.

Klinge, V., & Strauss, M. E. (1976). Effects of scoring norms on adolescent psychiatric patients' MMPI profiles. *Journal of Personality Assessment, 40*, 13–17.

Kohutek, K. J. (1992a). The location of items of the Wiggins content scales on the MMPI-2. *Journal of Clinical Psychology, 48*, 617–620.

Kohutek, K. J. (1992b). Wiggins content scales and the MMPI-2. *Journal of Clinical Psychology, 48*, 215–218.

Kopper, B. A., Osman, A., Osman, J. R., & Hoffman, J. (1998). Clinical utility of the MMPI-A content scales and Harris-Lingoes subscales in the assessment of suicidal risk factors in psychiatric adolescents. *Journal of Clinical Psychology, 54*, 191–200.

Koss, M. P., & Butcher, J. N. (1973). A comparison of psychiatric patients' self-report with other sources of clinical information. *Journal of Research in Personality, 7*, 225–236.

Kosson, D. S., Cyterski, T. D., Steuerwald, B. L., Neumann, C. S., & Walker-Matthews, S. (2002). The reliability and validity of the psychopathy checklist youth version in nonincarcerated adolescent males. *Psychological Assessment, 14*, 97–109.

Krakauer, S. (1991). *Assessing reading-deficit patterns among adolescents' MMPI profiles.* Unpublished doctoral dissertation, Virginia Consortium for Professional Psychology, Norfolk.

Krakauer, S. Y., Archer, R. P., & Gordon, R. A. (1993). The development of the Items-Easy (Ie) and Items-Difficult (Id) subscales for the MMPI-A. *Journal of Personality Assessment, 60*, 561–571.

Krishnamurthy, R., & Archer, R. P. (1999). A comparison of two interpretive approaches for the MMPI-A Structural Summary. *Journal of Personality Assessment, 73*, 245–259.

Krishnamurthy, R., Archer, R. P., & House, J. J. (1996). The MMPI-A and Rorschach: A failure to establish convergent validity. *Assessment, 3*, 179–191.

Krishnamurthy, R., Archer, R. P., & Huddleston, E. N. (1995). Clinical research note on psychometric limitations of two Harris-Lingoes subscales for the MMPI-2. *Assessment, 2*, 301–304.

Krug, S. E. (1987a). *Psychware sourcebook: 1987–88* (2nd ed.). Kansas City, MO: Test Corporation of America.

Krug, S. E. (1987b). *Psychware sourcebook* (3rd ed.). Kansas City, MO: Test Corporation of America.

Krug, S. E. (1993). *Psychware sourcebook* (4th ed.). Kansas City, MO: Test Corporation of America.

Lachar, D. (1974). *The MMPI: Clinical assessment and automated interpretation.* Los Angeles: Western Psychological Services.

Lachar, D., Klinge, V., & Grissell, J. L. (1976). Relative accuracy of automated MMPI narratives generated from adult norm and adolescent norm profiles. *Journal of Consulting and Clinical Psychology, 44*, 20–24.

Lachar, D., & Sharp, J. R. (1979). Use of parents' MMPIs in the research and evaluation of children: A review of the literature and some new data. In J. N. Butcher (Ed.), *New developments in the use of the MMPI* (pp. 203–240). Minneapolis: University of Minnesota Press.

Lachar, D., & Wrobel, T. A. (1979). Validating clinicians' hunches: Construction of a new MMPI critical item set. *Journal of Consulting and Clinical Psychology, 47*, 277–284.

Lachar, D., & Wrobel, N. H. (1990, August). Predicting adolescent MMPI correlates: Comparative efficacy of self-report and other-informant assessment. In R. C. Colligan (Chair), *The MMPI and adolescents: Historical perspectives, current research, and future developments.* A symposium presented to the annual convention of the American Psychological Association, Boston.

Lamb, D. G., Berry, D. T. R., Wetter, M. W., & Baer, R. A. (1994). Effects of two types of information on malingering of closed head injury on the MMPI-2: Analogue investigation. *Psychological Assessment, 6*, 8–13.

Landis, C., & Katz, S. E. (1934). The validity of certain questions which purport to measure neurotic tendencies. *Journal of Applied Psychology, 18*, 343–356.

Lanyon, R. I. (1967). Simulation of normal and psychopathic MMPI personality patterns. *Journal of Consulting Psychology, 31*, 94–97.

Lanyon, R. I. (1987). The validity of computer-based personality assessment products: Recommendations for the future. *Computers in Human Behavior, 3*, 225–238.

Lees-Haley, P. R., Smith, H. H., Williams, C. W., & Dunn, J. T. (1996). Forensic neuropsychological test usage: An empirical survey. *Archives of Clinical Neuropsychology, 11*, 41–51.

Levitt, E. E. (1989). *The clinical application of MMPI special scales.* Hillsdale, NJ: Lawrence Erlbaum Associates.

Levitt, E. E., Browning, J. M., & Freeland, L. J. (1992). The effect of MMPI-2 on the scoring of special scales derived from MMPI-1. *Journal of Personality Assessment, 59*, 22–31.

Levitt, E. E., & Gotts, E. E. (1995). *The clinical applications of MMPI special scales* (2nd ed.). Hillsdale, NJ: Lawrence Erlbaum Associates.

Lewak, R. W., Marks, P. A., & Nelson, G. E. (1990). *Therapist guide to the MMPI & MMPI-2: Providing feedback and treatment.* Muncie, IN: Accelerated Development, Inc.

Lewandowski, D., & Graham, J. R. (1972). Empirical correlates of frequently occurring two-point code types: A replicated study. *Journal of Consulting and Clinical Psychology, 39,* 467–472.

Lewinsohn, P. M., Hops, H., Roberts, R. E., Seeley, J. R., & Andrews, J. A. (1993). Adolescent psychopathology: I. Prevalence and incidence of depression in other *DSM–III–R* disorders in high school students. *Journal of Abnormal Psychology, 102,* 133–144.

Lewinsohn, P. M., Klein, D. N., & Seeley, J. R. (1995). Bipolar disorders in a community sample of older adolescents: Prevalence, phenomenology, comorbidity, and course. *Journal of the American Academy of Child and Adolescent Psychiatry, 34,* 454–463.

Lindsay, K. A., & Widiger, T. A. (1995). Sex and gender bias in self-report personality disorder inventories: Item analyses of the MCMI-II, MMPI, and PDQ-R. *Journal of Personality Assessment, 65,* 1–20.

Loevinger, J. (1976). *Ego development: Conceptions and theories.* San Francisco: Jossey-Bass.

Loevinger, J., & Wessler, R. (1970). *Measuring ego development: Vol. I. Construction and use of a sentence completion test.* San Francisco: Jossey-Bass.

Long, K. A., & Graham, J. R. (1991). The Masculinity-Feminity scale of MMPI-2: Is it useful with normal men in an investigation conducted with the MMPI-2? *Journal of Personality Assessment, 57,* 46–51.

Losada-Paisey, G. (1998). Use of the MMPI-A to assess personality of juvenile male delinquents who are sex offenders and non-sex offenders. *Psychological Reports, 83,* 115–122.

Lovitt, R. (1993). A strategy for integrating a normal MMPI-2 and dysfunctional Rorschach in a severely compromised patient. *Journal of Personality Assessment, 60,* 141–147.

Lowman, J., Galinsky, M. D., & Gray-Little, B. (1980). *Predicting achievement: A ten-year follow-up of Black and White adolescents* (IRSS Research Report). Chapel Hill: University of North Carolina at Chapel Hill, Institute for Research in Social Science.

Lubin, B., Larsen, R. M., & Matarazzo, J. D. (1984). Patterns of psychological test usage in the United States: 1935–1982. *American Psychologist, 39,* 451–454.

Lubin, B., Larsen, R. M., Matarazzo, J. D., & Seever, M. F. (1985). Psychological test usage patterns in five professional settings. *American Psychologist, 40,* 857–861.

Lubin, B., Wallis, R. R., & Paine, C. (1971). Patterns of psychological test usage in the United States: 1935–1969. *Professional Psychology, 2,* 70–74.

Lueger, R. J. (1983). The use of the MMPI-168 with delinquent adolescents. *Journal of Clinical Psychology, 39,* 139–141.

Lumry, A. E., Gottesman, I. I., & Tuason, V. B. (1982). MMPI state dependency during the course of bipolar psychosis. *Psychiatric Research, 7,* 59–67.

Luty, D., & Thackrey, M. (1993). Graphomotor interpretation of the MMPI-2? *Journal of Personality Assessment, 60,* 604.

Lynch, K. D., Archer, R. P., & Handel, R. W. (2004). *The relationship of MMPI-A item effectiveness to item content, diagnostic category, and classification accuracy.* Unpublished manuscript.

MacAndrew, C. (1965). The differentiation of male alcoholic out-patients from nonalcoholic psychiatric patients by means of the MMPI. *Quarterly Journal of Studies on Alcohol, 26,* 238–246.

MacAndrew, C. (1979). On the possibility of psychometric detection of persons prone to the abuse of alcohol and other substances. *Addictive Behaviors, 4,* 11–20.

MacAndrew, C. (1981). What the MAC scale tells us about men alcoholics: An interpretive review. *Journal of Studies on Alcohol, 42,* 604–625.

MacBeth, L., & Cadow, B. (1984). Utility of the MMPI-168 with adolescents. *Journal of Clinical Psychology, 40,* 142–148.

Mailloux, D. L., Forth, A. E., & Kroner, D. G. (1997). Psychopathy and substance abuse in male adolescent offenders. *Psychological Reports, 81,* 529–530.

Marcia, J. E. (1966). Development and validation of ego identity status. *Journal of Personality and Social Psychology, 3,* 551–558.

Marijke, M. D., Van der Ende, J., & Verhulst, F. C. (2002). Child and adolescent problems predict *DSM–IV* disorders in adulthood: A fourteen-year follow up of a Dutch epidemiological sample. *Journal of the American Academy of Child and Adolescent Psychiatry, 41,* 182–189.

Marks, P. A. (1961). An assessment of the diagnostic process in a child guidance setting. *Psychology Monographs, 75* (3, Whole No. 507).

Marks, P. A., & Briggs, P. F. (1972). Adolescent norm tables for the MMPI. In W. G. Dahlstrom, G. S. Welsh, & L. E. Dahlstrom, *An MMPI handbook: Vol. 1. Clinical interpretation* (rev. ed., pp. 388–399). Minneapolis: University of Minnesota Press.

Marks, P. A., & Haller, D. L. (1977). Now I lay me down for keeps: A study of adolescent suicide attempts. *Journal of Clinical Psychology, 33,* 390–400.

Marks, P. A., & Lewak, R. W. (1991). The Marks MMPI Adolescent Feedback and Treatment Report [Computer software]. Los Angeles: Western Psychological Services.

Marks, P. A., & Seeman, W. (1963). *The actuarial description of personality: An atlas for use with the MMPI.* Baltimore: Williams & Wilkins.

Marks, P. A., Seeman, W., & Haller, D. L. (1974). *The actuarial use of the MMPI with adolescents and adults.* Baltimore: Williams & Wilkins.

Markwardt, F. C. (1989). *Peabody Individual Achievement Test–Revised.* Circle Pines, MN: American Guidance Service.

Matarazzo, J. D. (1983). Computerized psychological testing. *Science, 221,* 323.

Matarazzo, J. D. (1986). Computerized clinical psychological test interpretations: Unvalidated plus all mean and no sigma. *American Psychologist, 41,* 14–24.

McCarthy, L., & Archer, R. P. (1998). Factor structure of the MMPI-A content scales: Item-level and scale-level findings. *Journal of Personality Assessment, 7,* 84–97.

McDonald, R. L., & Gynther, M. D. (1962). MMPI norms for southern adolescent Negroes. *Journal of Social Psychology, 58,* 277–282.

McFarland, S. G., & Sparks, C. M. (1985). Age, education, and the internal consistency of personality scales. *Journal of Personality and Social Psychology, 49,* 1692–1702.

McGrath, R. E., Pogge, D. L., Stein, L. A. R., Graham, J. R., Zaccario, M., & Piacentini, T. (2000). Development of the Infrequency-Psychopathology scale for the MMPI-A: The Fp-A scale. *Journal of Personality Assessment, 74,* 282–295.

McGrath, R. E., Pogge, D. L., & Stokes, J. M. (2002). Incremental validity of selected MMPI-A content scales in an inpatient setting. *Psychological Assessment, 14,* 401–409.

McKinley, J. C., & Hathaway, S. R. (1943). The identification and measurement of the psychoneuroses in medical practice. *Journal of the American Medical Association, 122,* 161–167.

McNulty, J. L., Harkness, A. R., Ben-Porath, Y. S., & Williams, C. L. (1997). Assessing the Personality Psychopathology Five (PSY-5) in adolescents: New MMPI-A scales. *Psychological Assessment, 9,* 250–259.

Meehl, P. E. (1951). *Research results for counselors.* St. Paul, MN: State Department of Education.

Meehl, P. E. (1954). *Clinical versus statistical prediction: A theoretical analysis and a review of the evidence.* Minneapolis: University of Minnesota Press.

Meehl, P. E. (1956). Wanted: A good cookbook. *American Psychologist, 11,* 263–272.

Meehl, P. E. (1986). Causes and effects of my disturbing little book. *Journal of Personality Assessment, 50,* 370–375.

Meehl, P. E., & Dahlstrom, W. G. (1960). Objective configural rules for discriminating psychotic from neurotic MMPI profiles. *Journal of Consulting Psychology, 24,* 375–387.

Meehl, P. E., & Hathaway, S. R. (1946). The K factor as a suppressor variable in the MMPI. *Journal of Applied Psychology, 30,* 525–564.

Megargee, E. I. (1979). Development and validation of an MMPI-based system for classifying criminal offenders. In J. N. Butcher (Ed.), *New developments in the use of the MMPI* (pp. 303–324). Minneapolis: University of Minnesota Press.

Megargee, E. I. (1994). Using the Megargee MMPI-based classification system with MMPI-2's of male prison inmates. *Psychological Assessment, 6,* 337–344.

Megargee, E. I. (1997). Using the Megargee MMPI-based classification system with the MMPI-2's of female prison inmates. *Psychological Assessment, 9,* 75–82.

Meyer, G. J. (1993). The impact of response frequency on the Rorschach constellation indices and on their validity with diagnostic and MMPI-2 criteria. *Journal of Personality Assessment, 60,* 153–180.

Micucci, J. A. (2002). Accuracy of MMPI-A scales ACK, MAC-R and PRO in detecting comorbid substance abuse among psychiatric inpatients. *Assessment, 9,* 111–122.

Miller, H. R., & Streiner, D. L. (1985). The Harris-Lingoes subscales: Fact or fiction? *Journal of Clinical Psychology, 41,* 45–51.

Millon, T. (1993). *Millon Adolescent Clinical Inventory.* Minneapolis: Pearson Assessments.

Millon, T., Green, C. J., & Meagher, R. B. (1977). *Millon Adolescent Personality Inventory.* Minneapolis: National Computer Systems.

Milne, L. C., & Greenway, P. (1999). Do high scores on the Adolescent–School Problems and Immaturity scales of the MMPI-A have implications for cognitive performance as measured by the WISC-III? *Psychology in the Schools, 36,* 199–203.

Miranda v. Arizona, 384 U.S. 436 (1966).

Mlott, S. R. (1973). The Mini-Mult and its use with adolescents. *Journal of Clinical Psychology, 29,* 376–377.

Monachesi, E. D. (1948). Some personality characteristics of delinquents and non-delinquents. *Journal of Criminal Law and Criminology, 38,* 487–500.

Monachesi, E. D. (1950). Personality characteristics of institutionalized and non-institutionalized male delinquents. *Journal of Criminal Law and Criminology, 41*, 167–179.

Monachesi, E. D., & Hathaway, S. R. (1969). The personality of delinquents. In J. N. Butcher (Ed.), *MMPI: Research developments and clinical applications* (pp. 207–219). Minneapolis: University of Minnesota Press.

Monroe, L. J., & Marks, P. A. (1977). MMPI differences between adolescent poor and good sleepers. *Journal of Consulting and Clinical Psychology, 45*, 151–152.

Moore, C. D., & Handal, P. J. (1980). Adolescents' MMPI performance, cynicism, estrangement, and personal adjustment as a function of race and sex. *Journal of Clinical Psychology, 36*, 932–936.

Moreland, K. L. (1984, Fall). Intelligent use of automated psychological reports. *Critical Items: A Newsletter for the MMPI Community, 1*, 4–6.

Moreland, K. L. (1985a). Computer-assisted psychological assessment in 1986: A practical guide. *Computers in Human Behavior, 1*, 221–233.

Moreland, K. L. (1985b). Validation of computer-based test interpretations: Problems and prospects. *Journal of Consulting and Clinical Psychology, 53*, 816–825.

Moreland, K. L. (1990). Computer-assisted assessment of adolescent and child personality: What's available. In C. R. Reynolds & R. W. Kamphaus (Eds.), *Handbook of psychological and educational assessment of children: Personality, behavior, and context* (pp. 395–420). New York: Guilford.

Morrison, T. L., Edwards, D. W., Weissman, H. N., Allen, R., & DeLaCruz, A. (1995). Comparing MMPI and MMPI-2 profiles: Replication and integration. *Assessment, 2*, 39–46.

Morton, T. L., & Farris, K. L. (2002). MMPI-A Structural Summary characteristics of male juvenile delinquents. *Assessment, 9*, 327–333.

Morton, T. L., Farris, K. L., & Brenowitz, L. H. (2002). MMPI-A scores and high points of male juvenile delinquents: Scales 4, 5, and 6 as markers of juvenile delinquency. *Psychological Assessment, 14*, 311–319.

National Center for Health Statistics. (1998a). *Leading causes of death by race and sex for selected age groups: United States 1979–96.* Rockville, MD: Author.

National Center for Health Statistics. (1998b). *United States mortality statistics 1989–1996.* Rockville, MD: Author.

National Institute of Mental Health. (1990). *National plan for research on child and adolescent mental disorders* (DHHS Publication No. ADM 90–1683). Washington, DC: U.S. Government Printing Office.

Negy, C., Leal-Puente, L., Trainor, D. J., & Carlson, R. (1997). Mexican-American adolescents' performance on the MMPI-A. *Journal of Personality Assessment, 69*, 205–214.

Nelson, L. D. (1987). Measuring depression in a clinical population using the MMPI. *Journal of Consulting and Clinical Psychology, 55*, 788–790.

Nelson, L. D., & Cicchetti, D. (1991). Validity of the MMPI depression scale for outpatients. *Psychological Assessmenty, 3*, 55–59.

Newmark, C. S. (1971). MMPI: Comparison of the oral form presented by a live examiner to the booklet form. *Psychological Reports, 29*, 797–798.

Newmark, C. S., Gentry, L., Whitt, J. K., McKee, D. C., & Wicker, C. (1983). Simulating normal MMPI profiles as a favorable prognostic sign in schizophrenia. *Australian Journal of Psychology, 35*, 433–444.

Newmark, C. S., & Thibodeau, J. R. (1979). Interpretive accuracy and empirical validity of abbreviated forms of the MMPI with hospitalized adolescents. In C. S. Newmark (Ed.), *MMPI: Clinical and research trends* (pp. 248–275). New York: Praeger.

Newsom, C. R., Archer, R. P., Trumbetta, S., & Gottesman, I. I. (2003). Changes in adolescent response patterns on the MMPI/MMPI-A across four decades. *Journal of Personality Assessment, 81*, 74–84.

Nichols, D. S. (1987). *Interpreting the Wiggins MMPI content scales* (Clinical Notes on the MMPI No. 10). Minneapolis: National Computer Systems.

Nichols, D. S. (1992). Review of the Minnesota Multiphasic Personality Inventory-2 (MMPI-2). In *The eleventh mental measurements yearbook* (pp. 562–565). Lincoln: University of Nebraska, Buros Institute of Mental Measurements.

Nichols, D. S. (2001). *Essentials of MMPI-2 assessment.* New York: Wiley.

Nichols, D. S., & Greene, R. L. (1995). *MMPI-2 Structural Summary interpretive manual.* Odessa, FL: Psychological Assessment Resources.

Offer, D., & Offer, J. B. (1975). *From teenager to young manhood.* New York: Basic Books.

Ogloff, J. R. P. (1995). The legal basis of forensic applications of the MMPI-2. In Y. S. Ben-Porath, J. R. Graham, G. C. N. Hall, R. D. Hirschman, & M. S. Zaragoza (Eds.), *Forensic applications of the MMPI-2* (pp. 18–47). Thousand Oaks, CA: Sage.

Orr, D. P., Eccles, T., Lawlor, R., & Golden, M. (1986). Surreptitious insulin administration in adolescents with insulin-dependent diabetes mellitus. *Journal of the American Medical Association, 256*, 3227–3230.

Osberg, T. M., & Poland, D. L. (2002). Comparative accuracy of the MMPI-2 and MMPI-A in the diagnosis of psychopathology in 18-year-olds. *Psychological Assessment, 14*, 164–169.

Otto, R. K., & Collins, R. P. (1995). Use of the MMPI-2/MMPI-A in child custody evaluations. In Y. S. Ben-Porath, J. R. Graham, G. C. N. Hall, R. D. Hirschman, & M. S. Zaragoza (Eds.), *Forensic applications of the MMPI-2* (pp. 222–252). Thousand Oaks, CA: Sage.

Overall, J. E., & Gomez-Mont, F. (1974). The MMPI-168 for psychiatric screening. *Educational and Psychological Measurement, 34*, 315–319.

Paikoff, R. L., & Brooks-Gunn, J. (1991). Do parent-child relationships change during puberty? *Psychological Bulletin, 110*, 47–66.

Pancoast, D. L., & Archer, R. P. (1988). MMPI adolescent norms: Patterns and trends across 4 decades. *Journal of Personality Assessment, 52*, 691–706.

Pancoast, D. L., & Archer, R. P. (1992). MMPI response patterns of college students: Comparisons to adolescents and adults. *Journal of Clinical Psychology, 48*, 47–53.

Pancoast, D. L., Archer, R. P., & Gordon, R. A. (1988). The MMPI and clinical diagnosis: A comparison of classification system outcomes with discharge diagnoses. *Journal of Personality Assessment, 52*, 81–90.

Paolo, A. M., Ryan, J. J., & Smith, A. J. (1991). Reading difficulty of MMPI-2 subscales. *Journal of Clinical Psychology, 47*, 529–532.

Pena, L. M., Megargee, E. I., & Brody, P. (1996). MMPI-A patterns of male juvenile delinquents. *Psychological Assessment, 8*, 388–397.

Petersen, A. C. (1985). Pubertal development as a cause of disturbance: Myths, realities, and unanswered questions. *Genetic, Social, and General Psychology Monographs, 111*, 205–232.

Petersen, A. C., & Hamburg, B. A. (1986). Adolescence: A developmental approach to problems and psychopathology. *Behavior Therapy, 17*, 480–499.

Piaget, J. (1975). The intellectual development of the adolescent. In A. H. Esman (Ed.), *The psychology of adolescence: Essential readings* (pp. 104–108). New York: International Universities Press.

Pinsoneault, T. B. (1997). A combined rationally-empirically developed variable response scale for detecting the random response set in the Jesness Inventory. *Journal of Clinical Psychology, 53*, 471–484.

Pinsoneault, T. B. (1999). Efficacy of the three randomness validity scales for the Jesness Inventory. *Journal of Personality Assessment, 73*, 395–406.

Piotrowski, C., & Keller, J. W. (1989). Psychological testing in outpatient mental health facilities: A national study. *Professional Psychology, 20*, 423–425.

Piotrowski, C., & Keller, J. W. (1992). Psychological testing in applied settings: A literature review from 1982–1992. *Journal of Training and Practice in Professional Psychology, 6*, 74–82.

Pogge, D. L., Stokes, J. M., Frank, J., Wong, H., & Harvey, P. D. (1997). Association of MMPI validity scales and therapist ratings of psychopathology in adolescent psychiatric inpatients. *Assessment, 4*, 17–27.

Pogge, D. L., Stokes, J. M., McGrath, R. E., Bilginer, L., & DeLuca, V. A. (2002). MMPI-A Structural Summary Variables: Prevalence and correlates in an adolescent inpatient psychiatric sample. *Assessment, 9*, 334–342.

Pope, K. S., Butcher, J. N., & Seelen, J. (2000). *The MMPI, MMIP-2, and MMPI-A in court: A practical guide for expert witnesses and attorneys* (2nd. ed.). Washington, DC: American Psychological Association.

Powers, S. I., Hauser, S. T., & Kilner, L. A. (1989). Adolescent mental health. *American Psychologist, 44*, 200–208.

Pritchard, D. A., & Rosenblatt, A. (1980). Racial bias in the MMPI: A methodological review. *Journal of Consulting and Clinical Psychology, 48*, 263–267.

Puzzanchera, C., Stahl, A. L., Finnegan, T. A., Tierney, N., & Snyder, H. N. (2003, July). *Juvenile court statistics 1999.* Pittsburgh, PA: National Center for Juvenile Justice.

Rathus, S. A. (1978). Factor structure of the MMPI-168 with and without regression weights. *Psychological Reports, 42*, 643–646.

Rathus, S. A., Fox, J. A., & Ortins, J. B. (1980). The MacAndrew scale as a measure of substance abuse in delinquency among adolescents. *Journal of Clinical Psychology, 36*, 579–583.

Regoli, R., & Hewitt, J. (2000). *Delinquency in society* (4th ed.) New York: McGraw-Hill.

Reich, W., & Earls, F. (1987). Rules for making psychiatric diagnoses in children on the basis of multiple sources of information: Preliminary strategies. *Journal of Abnormal Child Psychology, 15*, 601–616.

Rempel, P. P. (1958). The use of multivariate statistical analysis of Minnesota Multiphasic Personality Inventory scores in the classification of delinquent and nondelinquent high school boys. *Journal of Consulting Psychology, 22*, 17–23.

Rinaldo, J. C. B., & Baer, R. A. (2003). Incremental validity of the MMPI-A content scales in the prediction of self-reported symptoms. *Journal of Personality Assessment, 80*, 309–318.

Roberts, R. E., Attkisson, C. C., & Rosenblatt, A. (1998). Prevalence of psychopathology among children and adolescents. *American Journal of Psychiatry, 155*, 715–725.

Rogers, R., Bagby, R. M., & Chakraborty, D. (1993). Feigning schizophrenic disorders on the MMPI-2: Detection of coached simulators. *Journal of Personality Assessment, 60*, 215–226.

Rogers, R., Hinds, J. D., & Sewell, K. W. (1996). Feigning psychopathology among adolescent offenders: Validation of the SIRS, MMPI-A, and SIMS. *Journal of Personality Assessment, 67*, 244–257.

Rogers, R., Sewell, K. W., & Salekin, R. T. (1994). A meta-analysis of malingering on the MMPI-2. *Assessment, 1*, 227–237.

Rogers, R., Sewell, K. W., & Ustad, K. L. (1995). Feigning among chronic outpatients on the MMPI-2: A systematic examination of fake-bad indicators. *Assessment, 2*, 81–89.

Romano, B., Tremblay, R. E., Vitaro, F., Zoccolillo, M., & Pagani, L. (2001). Prevalence of psychiatric disorders and the role of perceived impairment: Findings from an adolescent community sample. *Journal of Child Psychology and Psychiatry, 42*, 451–461.

Rome, H. P., Swenson, W. M., Mataya, P., McCarthy, C. E., Pearson, J. S., Keating, F. R., et al. (1962). Symposium on automation techniques in personality assessment. *Proceedings of the Staff Meetings of the Mayo Clinic, 37*, 61–82.

Roper, B. L., Ben-Porath, Y. S., & Butcher, J. N. (1991). Comparability of computerized adaptive and conventional testing with the MMPI-2. *Journal of Personality Assessment, 57*, 278–290.

Roper, B. L., Ben-Porath, Y. S., & Butcher, J. N. (1995). Comparability and validity of computerized adaptive testing with the MMPI-2. *Journal of Personality Assessment, 65*, 358–371.

Rosen, A. (1962). Development of MMPI scales based on a reference group of psychiatric patients. *Psychological Monographs, 76* (8, Whole No. 527).

Rosenberg, L. A., & Joshi, P. (1986). Effect of marital discord on parental reports on the Child Behavior Checklist. *Psychological Reports, 59*, 1255–1259.

Rothke, S. E., Friedman, A. F., Dahlstrom, W. G., Greene, R. L., Arredondo, R., & Mann, A. W. (1994). MMPI-2 normative data for the F-K Index: Implications for clinical, neuropsychological, and forensic practice. *Assessment, 1*, 1–15.

Rutter, M., Graham, P., Chadwick, O. F. D., & Yule, W. (1976). Adolescent turmoil: Fact or fiction? *Journal of Child Psychology and Psychiatry, 17*, 35–56.

Sageman, M. (2003). Three types of skills for effective forensic psychological assessments. *Assessment, 10*, 321–328.

Schinka, J. A., Elkins, D. E., & Archer, R. P. (1998). Effects of psychopathology and demographic characteristics on MMPI-A scale scores. *Journal of Personality Assessment, 71*, 295–305.

Schuerger, J. M., Foerstner, S. B., Serkownek, K., & Ritz, G. (1987). History and validities of the Serkownek subscales for MMPI scales 5 and 0. *Psychological Reports, 61*, 227–235.

Scott, R. L., Butcher, J. N., Young, T. L., & Gomez, N. (2002). The Hispanic MMPI-A across five countries. *Journal of Clinical Psychology, 58*, 407–417.

Scott, R. L., Knoth, R. L., Beltran-Quiones, M., & Gomez, N. (2003). Assessment of psychological functioning in adolescent earthquake victims in Columbia using the MMPI-A. *Journal of Traumatic Stress, 16*, 49–57.

Scott, R., & Stone, D. (1986). MMPI measures of psychological disturbance in adolescent and adult victims of father-daughter incest. *Journal of Clinical Psychology, 42*, 251–259.

Seagrave, D., & Grisso, T. (2002). Adolescent development and the measurement of juvenile psychopathy. *Law and Human Behavior, 26*, 219–239.

Serkownek, K. (1975). *Subscales for scales 5 and 0 of the MMPI.* Unpublished manuscript.

Shaevel, B., & Archer, R. P. (1996). Effects of MMPI-2 and MMPI-A norms on T-score elevations for 18-year-olds. *Journal of Personality Assessment, 67*, 72–78.

Sherwood, N. E., Ben-Porath, Y. S., & Williams, C. L. (1997). *The MMPI-A content component scales: Development, psychometric characteristics and clinical application* (MMPI-2/MMPI-A Test Report No. 3). Minneapolis: University of Minnesota Press.

Sieber, K. O., & Meyer, L. S. (1992). Validation of the MMPI-2 social introversion subscales. *Psychological Assessment, 4*, 185–189.

Sivec, H. J., Lynn, S. J., & Garske, J. P. (1994). The effect of somatoform disorder and paranoid psychotic role-related dissimulations as a response set on the MMPI-2. *Assessment, 1*, 69–81.

Snyder, H. N. (2000, December). Juvenile arrests 1999. *Juvenile Justice Bulletin* (U.S. Department of Justice, Office of Juvenile Justice and Delinquency Prevention), pp. 1–12.

Snyder, H. N. (2003, December). Juvenile arrests 2001. *Juvenile Justice Bulletin* (U.S. Department of Justice, Office of Juvenile Justice and Delinquency Prevention), p. 12.

Snyder, H. N., & Sickmund, M. (1999). *Juvenile offenders and victims: 1999 national report.* Washington, DC: U. S. Department of Justice, Office of Juvenile Justice and Delinquency Prevention.

Spielberger, C. D. (1988). *State–Trait Anger Expression Inventory–Research Edition.* Odessa, FL: Psychological Assessment Resources.

Spirito, A., Faust, D., Myers, B., & Bechtel, D. (1988). Clinical utility of the MMPI in the evaluation of adolescent suicide attempters. *Journal of Personality Assessment, 52*, 204–211.

Spivack, G., Haimes, P. E., & Spotts, J. (1967). *Devereux Adolescent Behavior (DAB) Rating Scale manual*. Devon, PA: The Devereux Foundation.

Stehbens, J. A., Ehmke, D. A., & Wilson, B. K. (1982). MMPI profiles of rheumatic fever adolescents and adults. *Journal of Clinical Psychology, 38*, 592–596.

Stein, L. A. R., & Graham, J. R. (1999). Detecting fake-good MMPI-A profiles in a correctional facility. *Psychological Assessment, 11*, 386–395.

Stein, L. A. R., & Graham, J. R. (2001). Use of the MMPI-A to detect substance abuse in a juvenile correctional setting. *Journal of Personality Assessment, 77*, 508–523.

Stein, L. A. R., Graham, J. R., & Williams, C. L. (1995). Detecting fake-bad MMPI-A profiles. *Journal of Personality Assessment, 65*, 415–427.

Stein, L. A. R., McClinton, B. K., & Graham, J. R. (1998). Long-term stability of MMPI-A scales. *Journal of Personality Assessment, 70*, 103–108.

Stone, L. J., & Church, J. (1957). Pubescence, puberty, and physical development. In A. H. Esman (Ed.), *The psychology of adolescence: Essential readings* (pp. 75–85). New York: International Universities Press.

Storm, J., & Graham, J. R. (1998, March). *The effects of validity scale coaching on the ability to malinger psychopathology*. Paper presented at the 33rd Annual Symposium on Research Developments in the Use of the MMPI-2 and MMPI-A, Clearwater Beach, FL.

Strong, E. K., Jr. (1927). Differentiation of certified public accountants from other occupational groups. *Journal of Educational Psychology, 18*, 227–238.

Strong, E. K., Jr. (1943). *Vocational interests of men and women*. Stanford, CA: Stanford University Press.

Super, D. E. (1942). The Bernreuter Personality Inventory: A review of research. *Psychological Bulletin, 39*, 94–125.

Sutker, P. B., Allain, A. N., & Geyer, S. (1980). Female criminal violence and differential MMPI characteristics. *Journal of Consulting and Clinical Psychology, 46*, 1141–1143.

Sutker, P. B., & Archer, R. P. (1979). MMPI characteristics of opiate addicts, alcoholics, and other drug abusers. In C. S. Newmark (Ed.), *MMPI clinical and research trends* (pp. 105–148). New York: Praeger.

Sutker, P. B., Archer, R. P., & Kilpatrick, D. G. (1981). Sociopathy and antisocial behavior: Theory and treatment. In S. M. Turner, K. S. Calhoun, & H. E. Adams (Eds.), *Handbook of clinical behavior therapy* (pp. 665–712). New York: Wiley.

Svanum, S., & Ehrmann, L. C. (1992). Alcoholic subtypes and the MacAndrew alcoholism scale. *Journal of Personality Assessment, 58*, 411–422.

Svanum, S., McGrew, J., & Ehrmann, L. C. (1994). Validity of the substance abuse scales of the MMPI-2 in a college student sample. *Journal of Personality Assessment, 62*, 427–439.

Swenson, W. M., & Pearson, J. S. (1964). Automation techniques in personality assessment: A frontier in behavioral science and medicine. *Methods of Information in Medicine, 3*, 34–36.

Tanner, J. M. (1969). Growth and endocrinology of the adolescent. In L. Gardner (Ed.), *Endocrine and genetic diseases of childhood* (pp. 19–60). Philadelphia: Saunders.

Tanner, J. M., Whitehouse, R. H., & Takaishi, M. (1966). Standards from birth to maturity for height, weight, height velocity, and weight velocity: British children, 1965, Part I. *Archives of Disease in Childhood, 41*, 454–471.

Tellegen, A., & Ben-Porath, Y. S. (1992). The new uniform T-scores for the MMPI-2: Rationale, derivation, and appraisal. *Psychological Assessment, 4*, 145–155.

Tellegen, A., & Ben-Porath, Y. S. (1993). Code-type comparability of the MMPI and MMPI-2: Analysis of recent findings and criticisms. *Journal of Personality Assessment, 61*, 489–500.

Teplin, L. A., Abram, K. M., McClelland, G. M., Dulcan, M. K., & Mericle, A. A. (2002). Psychiatric disorders in youth in juvenile detention. *Archives of General Psychiatry, 59*, 1133–1143.

Timbrook, R. E., & Graham, J. R. (1994). Ethnic differences on the MMPI-2? *Psychological Assessment, 6*, 212–217.

Timbrook, R. E., Graham, J. R., Keiller, S. W., & Watts, D. (1993). Comparison of the Wiener-Harmon subtle-obvious scales and the standard validity scales in detecting valid and invalid MMPI-2 profiles. *Psychological Assessment, 5*, 53–61.

Tirrell, C. A., Archer, R. P., & Mason, J. (2004). *Concurrent validity of the MMPI-A substance abuse scales: MAC-R, ACK, and PRO*. Manuscript in preparation.

Todd, A. L., & Gynther, M. D. (1988). Have MMPI Mf scale correlates changed in the past 30 years? *Journal of Clinical Psychology, 44*, 505–510.

Torbet, P., Gable, R., Hurst, H., Montgomery, I., Szymanski, L., & Thomas, D. (1996). *State responses to serious and violent juvenile crime*. Washington, DC: U.S Department of Justice, Office of Juvenile Justice and Delinquency Prevention.

Toyer, E. A., & Weed, N. C. (1998). Concurrent validity of the MMPI-A in a counseling program for juvenile offenders. *Journal of Clinical Psychology, 54*, 395–399.

Truscott, D. (1990). Assessment of overcontrolled hostility in adolescence. *Psychological Assessment, 2*, 145–148.

Tyler, F. T. (1951). A factorial analysis of 15 MMPI scales. *Journal of Consulting Psychology, 15*, 451–456.

U. S. Department of Justice, Office of Juvenile Justice and Delinquency Prevention. (2000, May). *Office of Juvenile Justice and Delinquency Prevention research 2000.* Washington, DC: Author.

Vondell, N. J., & Cyr, J. J. (1991). MMPI short forms with adolescents: Gender differences and accuracy. *Journal of Personality Assessment, 56,* 254–265.

Wallace, J. B., Calhoun, A. D., Powell, K. E., O'Neil, J., & James, S. P. (1996). *Homicide and suicide among Native Americans, 1979–1992.* (Violence Surveillance Series, No. 2). Atlanta: Centers for Disease Control and Prevention, National Center for Injury Prevention and Control.

Walters, G. D. (1983). The MMPI and schizophrenia: A review. *Schizophrenia Bulletin, 9,* 226–246.

Walters, G. D. (1988). Schizophrenia. In R. L. Greene (Ed.), *The MMPI: Use in specific populations* (pp. 50–73). San Antonio, TX: Grune & Stratton.

Ward, L. C., & Ward, J. W. (1980). MMPI readability reconsidered. *Journal of Personality Assessment, 44,* 387–389.

Wasyliw, O. E., Haywood, T. W., Grossman, L. S., & Cavanaugh, J. L. (1993). The psychometric assessment of alcoholism in forensic groups: The MacAndrew scale and response bias. *Journal of Personality Assessment, 60,* 252–266.

Watson, C. G., Thomas, D., & Anderson, P. E. D. (1992). Do computer-administered Minnesota Multiphasic Personality Inventories underestimate booklet-based scores? *Journal of Clinical Psychology, 48,* 744–748.

Wechsler, D. (1992). *Wechsler Individual Achievement Test manual.* San Antonio, TX: The Psychological Corporation.

Weed, N. C., Ben-Porath, Y. S., & Butcher, J. N. (1990). Failure of the Wiener and Harmon Minnesota Multiphasic Personality Inventory (MMPI) subtle scales as personality descriptors and as validity indicators. *Psychological Assessment, 2,* 281–285.

Weed, N. C., Butcher, J. N., McKenna, T., & Ben-Porath, Y. S. (1992). New measures for assessing alcohol and drug dependence with the MMPI-2: The *APS* and *AAS. Journal of Personality Assessment, 58,* 389–404.

Weed, N. C., Butcher, J. N., & Williams, C. L. (1994). Development of MMPI-A alcohol/drug problem scales. *Journal of Studies on Alcohol, 55,* 296–302.

Weiner, I. B. (1993). Clinical considerations in the conjoint use of the Rorschach and MMPI. *Journal of Personality Assessment, 60,* 148–152.

Weiner, I. B., & Del Gaudio, A. C. (1976). Psychopathology in adolescence: An epidemiological study. *Archives of General Psychiatry, 33,* 187–193.

Weissman, M. M., Wickramaratne, P., Warner, V., John, K., Prusoff, B. A., Merikangas, K. R., et al. (1987). Assessing psychiatric disorders in children: Discrepancies between mothers' and children's reports. *Archives of General Psychiatry, 44,* 747–753.

Welsh, G. S. (1948). An extension of Hathaway's MMPI profile coding system. *Journal of Consulting Psychology, 12,* 343–344.

Welsh, G. S. (1956). Factor dimensions A and R. In G. S. Welsh & W. G. Dahlstrom (Eds.), *Basic reading on the MMPI in psychology and medicine* (pp. 264–281). Minneapolis: University of Minnesota Press.

Wetter, M. W., Baer, R. A., Berry, D. T. R., & Reynolds, S. K. (1994). The effect of symptom information on faking on the MMPI-2. *Assessment, 1,* 199–207.

Wetter, M. W., Baer, R. A., Berry, D. T. R., Robison, L. H., & Sumpter, J. (1993). MMPI-2 profiles of motivated fakers given specific symptom information: A comparison to matched patients. *Psychological Assessment, 3,* 317–323.

Wetter, M. W., Baer, R. A., Berry, D. T. R., Smith, G. T., & Larsen, L. H. (1992). Sensitivity of MMPI-2 validity scales to random responding and malingering. *Psychological Assessment, 4,* 369–374.

Wetter, M. W., & Corrigan, S. K. (1995). Providing information to clients about psychological tests: A survey of attorneys' and law students' attitudes. *Professional Psychology, 26,* 1–4.

Wiederholt, J. L., & Bryant, B. R. (1986). *Gray Oral Reading Tests, Revised.* Austin, TX: PRO-ED.

Wiener, D. N. (1948). Subtle and obvious keys for the MMPI. *Journal of Consulting Psychology, 12,* 164–170.

Wiggins, J. S. (1966). Substantive dimensions of self-report in the MMPI item pool. *Psychological Monographs, 80* (22, Whole No. 630).

Wiggins, J. S. (1969). Content dimensions in the MMPI. In J. N. Butcher (Ed.), *MMPI: Research developments and clinical applications* (pp. 127–180). New York: McGraw-Hill.

Wilkinson, G. S. (1993). *The Wide Range Achievement Test administration manual: 1993 edition.* Wilmington, DE: Wide Range, Inc.

Williams, C. L. (1986). MMPI profiles from adolescents: Interpretive strategies and treatment considerations. *Journal of Child and Adolescent Psychotherapy, 3,* 179–193.

Williams, C. L., Ben-Porath, Y. S., & Hevern, B. W. (1994). Item level improvements for use of the MMPI with adolescents. *Journal of Personality Assessment, 63,* 284–293.

Williams, C. L., & Butcher, J. N. (1989a). An MMPI study of adolescents: I. Empirical validity of standard scales. *Psychological Assessment, 1,* 251–259.

Williams, C. L., & Butcher, J. N. (1989b). An MMPI study of adolescents: II. Verification and limitations of code type classifications. *Psychological Assessment, 1*, 260–265.

Williams, C. L., Butcher, J. N., Ben-Porath, Y. S., & Graham, J. R. (1992). *MMPI-A content scales: Assessing psychopathology in adolescents.* Minneapolis: University of Minnesota Press.

Williams, C. L., Graham, J. R., & Butcher, J. N. (1986, March). *Appropriate MMPI norms for adolescents: An old problem revisited.* Paper presented at the 21st Annual Symposium on Recent Developments in the Use of the MMPI, Clearwater, FL.

Williams, C. L., Hearn, M. D., Hostetler, K., & Ben-Porath, Y. S. (1990). *A comparison of several epidemiological measures for adolescents: MMPI, DISC, and YSR.* Unpublished manuscript, University of Minnesota, Minneapolis.

Wimbish, L. G. (1984). *The importance of appropriate norms for the computerized interpretations of adolescent MMPI profiles.* Unpublished doctoral dissertation, Ohio State University, Columbus.

Wirt, R. D., & Briggs, P. F. (1959). Personality and environmental factors in the development of delinquency. *Psychological Monographs: General and Applied*, Whole No. 485, 1–47.

Wisniewski, N. M., Glenwick, D. S., & Graham, J. R. (1985). MacAndrew scale and sociodemographic correlates of alcohol and drug use. *Addictive Behaviors, 10*, 55–67.

Wolfson, K. P., & Erbaugh, S. E. (1984). Adolescent responses to the MacAndrew Alcoholism scale. *Journal of Consulting and Clinical Psychology, 52*, 625–630.

Woodworth, R. S. (1920). *Personal data sheet.* Chicago: Stoelting.

Wrobel, N. H. (1991, August). Utility of the Wiggins content scales with an adolescent sample. In R. C. Colligan (Chair), *MMPI and MMPI-2 supplementary scales and profile interpretation—content scales revisited.* Symposium conducted at the annual conference of the American Psychological Association, San Francisco.

Wrobel, N. H., & Gdowski, C. L. (1989, August). *Validation of Wiggins content scales with an adolescent sample.* Paper presented at the annual convention of the American Psychological Association, New Orleans.

Wrobel, N. H., & Lachar, D. (1992). Refining adolescent MMPI interpretations: Moderating effects of gender in prediction of descriptions from parents. *Psychological Assessment, 4*, 375–381.

Wrobel, N. H., & Lachar, D. (1995). Racial differences in adolescent self-report: A comparative validity study using homogeneous MMPI content scales. *Psychological Assessment, 7*, 140–147.

Wrobel, T. A. (1992). Validity of Harris and Lingoes MMPI subscale descriptors in an outpatient sample. *Journal of Personality Assessment, 59*, 14–21.

Zager, L. (1988). The MMPI-based criminal classification system: A review, current status, and future directions. *Criminal Justice and Behavior, 15*, 39–57.

Zinn, S., McCumber, S., & Dahlstrom, W. G. (1999). Cross-validation and extension of the MMPI-A IMM scale. *Assessment, 6*, 1–6.

Author Index

Subject Index